Company Archives

The Survey of the Records of 1000 of the First Registered Companies in England and Wales

This book summarises the results of the Company Archive Survey undertaken by the Business Archives Council between 1980 and 1984. The Survey was made possible by the generous support of the Economic and Social Research Council.

Company Archives

The Survey of the Records of 1000 of the First Registered Companies in England and Wales

Lesley Richmond
and
Bridget Stockford

Gower

Published by

Gower Publishing Company Limited,
Gower House,
Croft Road,
Aldershot,
Hants GU11 3HR,
England

Gower Publishing Company,
Old Post Road,
Brookfield,
Vermont 05036,
U.S.A.

British Library Cataloguing in Publication Data

Richmond, Lesley
Company Archives. The Survey of the Records of 1000 of the First Registered Companies in England and Wales

1. Business records—Great Britain
1. Title 11. Stockford, Bridget

ISBN O 566 03547 2

Printed in Great Britain by
Blackmore Press, Shaftesbury

Contents

Introduction

1. The Company Archive Survey

Encouraged by the reception of its surveys of the records of several major British industries[1] and cognisant of the growing volume of research based upon business records[2], the Business Archives Council planned in the late 1970s to undertake a survey of the records of the oldest surviving companies on the Register of Companies. Its purpose was threefold. Such a project would go some way to redeeming the promise implicit in many of the Council's general pronouncements on its objectives since its creation in 1934—the compilation of a *general* register of business archives held by existing firms. Secondly, and of more pressing importance, a systematic national search, conducted by professionally trained archivists, might ensure the preservation of records which would otherwise be destroyed. The third objective was to encourage research into such archives.

More than any other body, the Council was able to appreciate the serious threat to the survival of Britain's earliest business records. The danger came from mounting storage costs, the reorganisation invariably associated with mergers, the liquidations attendant upon economic slumps and stagnation, and the increasing trend towards the computer processing of business information. If the records of Britain's joint stock limited companies could be listed, it was believed that their chances of survival would be enhanced. It has been demonstrated repeatedly that mere knowledge of the existence of archives in private hands makes for their continued survival. The majority of companies are flattered, rather than irritated and apprehensive, by an outsider's interest in their past. When adverse economic conditions or intolerable pressure on available space makes it impossible for firms to continue to look after their records, the existence of a proper list—often the simple fact that someone has thought it worthwhile to compile one—frequently results in the transfer of a collection to a suitable repository. Listing is usually followed by the establishment of a procedure whereby a researcher may gain access to the records.

In establishing its Company Archives Survey, the Business Archives Council sought help from the Registrar of Companies of the Department of Trade and Industry, who kindly made available lists of the 1200 oldest English and Welsh companies on the 1979 and, later, the 1980 Register of Companies. Although the complete lists span the period 1856-1889, the majority of these companies were registered in the 1870s and 1880s (see Table 1). The 1200 companies are the survivors of an original population some twenty-five times larger in size: overall, 4 per cent of the 30,334 companies registered in London between August 1856 and May 1889 were extant in 1980, a figure that is broadly consistent with the findings of a study of the earliest Scottish companies[3]. The Business Archives Council recognised that these companies were not necessarily representative of those formed at the same time. Indeed, the mere fact of their survival made them unusual. Users of this book therefore should not treat information about the companies covered by the Survey as in any way a statistically representative sample of typical 19th century business. A more influential factor in undertaking the survey was the likelihood that records of these companies (rather than companies which failed or firms which did not register) would have survived, irrespective of the nature of their activities and their size. The fact that such companies have a statutory duty to retain their principal corporate and accounting records[4] promised to make such a survey fruitful, and so it proved. It was believed that these companies were a priority for survey work on the grounds that most were unlikely to have been the subject of recent local or national surveys and unlikely to have made formal arrangements for the preservation of their records.

Beginning work on the Company Archives Survey in 1980, the Council envisaged that the list of 1200 companies supplied by the Registrar of Companies would enable the Survey to cover at least 1000 companies. It was recognised that the original list of 1200 companies would include errors and discrepancies in the names, registered numbers, addresses or formation dates of companies listed on the registers; there would also be cases where there would be no effective starting point in attempts to trace a company and its records. The precaution of using 1200 names in the basic list rather than 1000 names proved to be effective. It was not necessary either to reduce the number of companies to be sought out or to request a list of more recent names from the Register. The result of this strategy was that the Survey sought after the records of 1006 registered companies. This total included all 710 companies registered before June 1884; the remaining 296 companies covered by the Survey comprised 60 per cent of the 490 surviving companies registered between June 1884 and May 1889.

Surveys were generated for 674 of these companies and form the basis of this book. The remaining 332 of the 1006 companies investigated by the project either replied but could not assist or did not reply despite repeated efforts to contact them. In addition to these 674 'core' surveys, the project has also produced approximately 1000 surveys of companies, institutions and partnerships associated with or subsidiary to the registered companies[5]. The combined total of companies whose records have been surveyed by the project is over 1600, which makes it by far the largest single survey of business records yet undertaken in the United Kingdom. It is estimated that the archive resources surveyed by the Survey have been located in 900 different locations, and that these resources occupy over 27000 feet (8000 metres) of shelf space.

Some measure of the range of business activities covered by the Survey can be obtained from an analysis of the original activities of the 674 'core' companies (see Table 2). In 1980 these same companies varied remarkably in size and business, covering the entire spectrum from small, independent private companies to holding companies or groups with complex structures. They were mainly engaged in domestic and international enterprise but a significant number represent the institutionalization of local services, professional activities and the Englishman's beliefs and hobbies.

The origin and age of these companies is rarely as straightforward as it may seem. Many companies or their subsidiaries and associates were founded as partnerships well before their date of registration, most obviously in companies with 17th and 18th century origins (for example Firmin & Sons, Berger Jenson & Nicholson, and a number of breweries). Others were formed in the early 19th century following legislation permitting the formation of joint stock companies (without limited liability) in certain areas of business, for example banking. In contrast, the Survey also covered large numbers of subsidiary or associate companies founded in the 20th century. These companies, including companies founded as recently as the 1970s, are not normally reached by archival surveys or even by business history research. A wide variation in location is also obvious. Although approximately one-third of the companies have a London address, their archives reflect the capital's international and national activities. Outside London, subject companies were dispersed throughout the British Isles; they included companies which, although registered in England and Wales, were or are in practice based in Scotland, Northern Ireland or Eire.

2. Historical Framework

The statutes under which the majority of the joint stock companies whose records are surveyed in this book came into being were the Companies Acts of 1856 and 1862[6]. Henceforth, all that was required for a company to limit its liability was the filing of a Memorandum of Association, signed by at least seven subscribers, giving the company's name, objects, nominal capital and the number of shares into which it was to be divided. Upon the grant of a Certificate of Incorporation by the Registrar of Joint Stock Companies, a company was permitted to begin business as soon as its directors thought fit, however small its subscribed capital. It was required to attach the 'limited' to its name. Thereafter, the company had merely to submit to the Registrar an annual Summary of Capital and Shares and to inform him of any changes that had taken place among the directorate, the first directors having been named in the original Articles of Association[7].

The 1856 Act specified no minimum nominal or paid-up capital, nothing was said about the denomination of shares and there were none of the distasteful publicity requirements of earlier legislation. "English company law [had] become the most permissive in Europe"[8]. The Board of Trade—to whom the registration and regulation of joint stock companies had been entrusted by the Act of 1844—never anticipated nor intended that the limited company form would (or should) be used by private partnerships or by sole traders. Yet such proved to be the case. Initially, few took advantage of the Act of 1856. Indeed, informed contemporary opinion regarded the Act as a dead letter[9]; even the obligation that companies originally registered under the Act of 1844 (the first Public and General Act providing for the registration, incorporation and regulation of Joint Stock Companies) re-register under the Act of 1856, failed significantly to swell the number of incorporations. Not until the early 1870s did annual registrations exceed 1000, and it is perhaps significant that it was from this decade that the formation of private companies (not legally recognised until the Companies Act of 1907) regularly began to outnumber the public companies that were the intended beneficiaries of the Acts of 1856 and 1862[10]. A fuller examination of the records listed in this book in conjunction with further research into the files of their dissolved contemporaries in the public record offices in the British Isles will doubtless elucidate this phenomenon.

TABLE 1

The Date of Registration and Status of the 1200 Oldest English and Welsh Companies on the 1980 Register of Companies

No. of surviving companies, by status in 1979

	Year of Registration	Public Ltd	Public[1] Unlimited	Private Ltd
	1856	3	0	8
	1857	2	0	2
	1858	0	0	0
	1859	2	0	1
	1860	2	1	1
	1861	1	0	4
	1862	9	0	7
	1863	8	0	7
	1864	14	0	13
	1865	10	0	9
	1866	5	0	4
	1867	2	0	4
	1868	1	0	7
	1869	6	0	8
	1870	5	1	2
	1871	9	2	13
	1872	12	0	13
	1873	20	1	21
	1874	8	1	24
	1875	19	3	14
	1876	5	3	8
	1877	5	5	17
	1878	9	2	15
	1879	8	1	13
	1880	25	3	36
	1881	19	1	33
	1882	15	4	27
	1883	8	3	31
	1884	21	4	24
	1885	23	2	40
	1886	20	4	46
	1887	13	17	43
	1888	30	22	57
To May	1889[3]	24	0	49
1856-May	1889	363	80	598

Proportion of Public Companies : 36.9 **Proportion of Private Companies : 63.1**

Notes:

1. The choice of the unlimited form of company - which in virtually every other respect is identical to the limited company - was very unusual until 1967. The Companies Act of that year encouraged the conversion of hitherto limited public and private companies to unlimited companies by exempting such companies from certain provisions of the Companies Act of 1948 relating to disclosure requirements. Thus, an unlimited company was relieved of the obligation to submit a certified copy of the balance sheet (and the relevant annexation to the balance sheet) demanded of limited companies. Within four to five years of the passage of the Companies Act of 1967, the number of unlimited companies had increased fourfold (from 1000 to 4000). See Ranking & Spier's *Company Law*, Eleventh edition (London : H F L (Publishers) Ltd, 1972 pp 11-15; Tom Hadden, *Company Law and Capitalism* (London: Weidenfield & Nicolson, 1972), pp 150, 153. It is safe to assume that a list of the oldest English and Welsh companies on the 1966 Register of Companies would have contained very few unlimited companies, whether public or private.
2. Excludes companies registered in the Stannaries, 1863-1888

Private[1] Unlimited	TOTAL	No. of English/Welsh[2] Companies registered in each year	Percentage survival
0	11	222	5.0
0	4	370	1.1
0	0	292	0.0
0	3	325	0.9
0	4	401	1.0
0	5	4 59	1.1
0	16	478	3.3
0	15	724	2.1
0	27	914	3.0
0	19	935	2.0
0	9	676	1.3
0	6	435	1.4
0	8	411	1.9
2	16	431	3.7
2	10	539	1.9
4	28	698	4.0
1	26	941	2.8
0	42	1 089	3.9
5	38	1 124	3.4
11	47	1 078	4.4
5	21	939	2.2
7	34	846	4.0
3	29	778	3.7
10	32	923	3.5
2	66	1 160	5.7
3	56	1 446	3.9
6	52	1 476	3.5
8	50	1 533	3.3
14	60	1 370	4.4
6	71	1 344	5.3
11	81	1 738	4.7
28	101	1 893	5.3
28	137	2 346	5.8
3	76	-	-
159	1 200	30 334	c. 4.0[4]

3. Because the Statistics for 1889 do not constitute a full year, the final two columns are omitted.

4. Percentage derived from expressing 1200 companies, the last of which was registeredin May, 1889, as a proportion of the total number of English and Welsh companies registered up to 31 December, 1888.

Sources: Columns (1)-(5), Registrar of Companies, Department of Trade.

Column 6 : 1856-1862, H A Shannon's United Kingdom figures (The First Five Thousand Limited Companies and their Duration, Economic History, II (1932), p421) *minus* the number of companies registered in Scotland (P L Payne, *The Early Scottish Limited Companies* (Edinburgh: Scottish Academic Press, 1980), p19); 1886-1888, *The Stock Exchange Official Intelligence*, XL (1922), p1790, figures for companies registered in England (excluding the Stannaries).

Table 2

Analysis of Original Activities of the 674 'Core' Companies

Activity	Number of companies	% of total
Utilities and services	96	14.2
Insurance and investment	69	10.2
Professional associations	63	9.3
Food & drink	60	8.9
Property	55	8.2
Banking	52	7.7
Engineering	42	6.2
Clubs and club premises	34	5.0
Paper and products	31	4.6
Textiles and products	28	4.2
Iron, steel and products	26	3.9
Political, charitable religious, educational	26	3.9
Wholesale and warehousing	21	3.2
Mining and quarrying	17	2.5
Agriculture, forestry and fishing	14	2.1
Chemicals and products	11	1.6
Others	29	4.3
Total	674	100.0

More importantly, systematic investigation of the records in the lists which follow may permit a fuller understanding of the factors making for longevity. Previous inquiries have indicated that mere size at birth seems to have had a negligible influence upon life expectancy, and that more significant were the nature of the firm's activities, the quality of its direction and management and the character of the economic environment in which it operated[11]. Did the firms whose records are listed here constantly adapt to change by, say, diversification, structural reorganisation, and a flexibility in entrepreneurial/managerial recruitment? How big a role did sheer chance play? Can survival among limited companies be rationally explained or is extreme longevity a matter of luck, comparable to a favourable distribution of playing cards in a game of patience?

There is a further problem. How often does the continued existence of a company name conceal fundamental changes in the firm's activities and the composition of its internal structure, ownership and management? To take a hypothetical example: suppose the Paragon Manufacturing Co Ltd of Newcastle-upon-Tyne came into existence in 1871 as a result of the conversion of what had hitherto been a partnership engaged in the manufacture of cast metal components for railway locomotives and rolling stock. Within fifteen years the firm had integrated backwards into iron smelting and colliery ownership, the major products had become steamships, and the original directors and sometime partners had given way to an entirely new group of thrusting entrepreneurs who had established themselves in steel manufacture. By 1901 the Paragon Manufacturing Co Ltd represented only a unit in a semi-integrated heavy manufacturing group managed by a number of salaried officials responsible to a board of directors whose chairman was a member of the board of a London-based holding company. The parent company managed to survive the acute difficulties of inter-war years by the adoption of the multi-divisional form of organisation and a complete transformation of its activities. The Paragon Manufacturing Co Ltd remained in being but by 1955 its activities were confined to making certain pressed steel components for military vehicles, its senior executive being responsible to the chairman of the weapons division of the group. The reason for this extended example is to ask whether the Paragon Manufacturing Co Ltd on the 1980 Register is in any real sense the lineal descendent of the original firm of the same name? I suspect that in *manufacturing* activities *true* longevity is rare; very old firms are largely confined to service industries and professional associations. Or is it that manufacturing firms can *only* survive by radical transformation? Careful examination of the records may help to resolve this issue.

If potential users of this book are indifferent to the solution of such questions, there is a wealth of evidence for comparative research on company formation, owwnership and management, the evolution of accountancy practices, and the efficiency (or otherwise) of the capital market. Social historians and sociologists will doubtless welcome knowledge of the existence of substantial bodies of material on educational institutions. Professional bodies and architectural historians will find a rich quarry in the archives of the large number of property and building companies that have been surveyed. There is, within these pages, something for almost everyone: regional, local, urban, agricultural and business historians, biographers and industrial archaeologists. Not least the lists of records offer new material for non-specialists and enthusiasts: sources for genealogy, the study of railways, shipping, and brewing history, the fine arts, sports and leisure. This book is, in effect, a guide to a veritable cornucopia of records of British enterprise, all the more valuable because the vast majority of them have never been available for research because of ignorance of their very existence. I, for one, knew nothing of the marine insurance mutual clubs.

Most of the records listed remain in the custody of the companies that created them. That is as it should be, so long as they are well looked after, but one of the anticipated results of the Survey has been the discovery of many records which would otherwise undoubtedly have been lost or destroyed. When the Survey staff came across historically valuable material in danger of dispersal or destruction, advice was offered on its preservation or transfer to a suitable repository. There were many such cases. For example, the records of the Lawes Chemical Co Ltd, covering the period 1872-1969 were deposited on permanent loan with the Librarians Department of the London Borough of Barking. The company was founded by Sir John Bennett Lawes in 1843 to manufacture superphosphate in Deptford from where it moved to Barking. It was incorporated in 1872 and went into liquidation in 1969. The records of the Grand Junction Canal Company Ltd, one of the successors of the Company of the Proprietors of the Grand Junction Canal, were deposited with the Public Record Office. Other records—such as those of the Wallsend Slipway Engineers Ltd, J Chadwicks & Co Ltd, dyers and bleachers of Oldham, and several overseas investment companies—went to various county and municipal records offices and university libraries. For example, the records of three South American investment companies were placed with University College London, and now form part of the Latin American business collection.

The Survey has been instrumental in saving irreplaceable archives of outstanding historical value. If nothing else had been achieved, this work of preservation more than justifies the tireless dedication of the surveying officers and the grant from the Economic & Social Research Council (formerly the Social Science Reasearch Council) which made the Survey possible.

3. Acknowledgements

Let there be no doubt concerning the prodigious effort involved in the conduct of a national survey on this scale. The Survey was launched on 1 September 1980, following the Social Science Research Council's agreement to make a grant to the Business Archives Council for a period of three years and four months (later extended for a further twelve months). It was directed by a management committee consisting of Dr David Avery (Director of the Survey), Edwin Green, Michael Moss, Dr John Orbell and Professor P L Payne (representing the SSRC), all experienced archivists and business historians, long associated with the manifold activities of the Business Archives Council. The management committee's major functions were to recruit and thereafter advise the Survey staff, edit the surveys, manage the finances, and prepare annual reports to the SSRC. Overall control was vested in a supervisory board comprising Sam Twining, Chairman of the Business Archives Council, Major Tom Ingram, the Council's Deputy Chairman, David Carr and Merrick Kidd, Honorary Treasurers to the Business Archives Council, Alison Turton, Secretary-General of the Business Archives Council, Alfred Knightbridge (representing the Public Record Office), John Bates (Scottish Record Office) and Trevor Parkhill (Public Record Office of Northern Ireland).

The members of the management committee met regularly, conducted a vast amount of correspondence, and were always ready to tender advice and help in the sometimes delicate negotiations involved in gaining access to what are, in many cases, very private archives. They also determined the nature, content and layout of the summary lists and, after careful proof-reading, made arrangements for their publication and dissemination. However invidious it may be to single out the work of specific individuals, the contributions of Edwin Green, chairman of the management committee, Michael Moss and John Orbell must be emphasised. The task of the management committee was facilitated by the unswerving support of the officers of the Business Archives Council, even when the conduct of the Survey threatened to overwhelm the Council's other activities. A great debt is due to Sam Twining and Tom Ingram and it should be recorded that the Council's President, the Right Hon Lord Denning, former Master of the Rolls, always displayed great interest in the Survey[12]. It has to be confessed the use of Lord Denning's name opened several doors which might otherwise have remained obstinately closed!

The sheer hard graft was performed by the Survey manager, Lesley Richmond (nee Millar) (formerly Director of the Council's Records Advisory Service); the Survey officers, Clair Sharp (October 1980-July 1982), Bridget Stockford (July 1982-September 1984, when she succeeded Lesley Richmond as manager of the project), and Claire Findlay; and the Administrative Assistants, successively Elaine McDowall, Audrey Simpson, Judith Hanna, and Patience Olurankinse. Preparation of the text for publication would not have been possible without the assistance of Hazel Shepherd, Rita Hemphill, Helen Maher, Noreen McCarron, Elizabeth Cowie, David McLeish, Moira McCulloch, Peter Markus and Karen Thomson.

Only those who have themselves donned a boilersuit, worn a face mask and worked for hours (sometimes with the aid of a torch) listing the hundredweights of dust-laden records that frequently comprise a large collection of business records can fully appreciate the magnitude of their achievement. Simply to list the places that they have visited is reminiscent of the stories of old time music hall performers. Although a majority of the surveys were accomplished in a day or two, a substantial number took from four or five days to two to three weeks or more. For example, huge collections were unearthed at Bass, Courage, Chubb, Extel, Express Dairies, the British Medical Association and the Girls Public Day School Trust. The lists in this book represent summaries of these surveys, which were sometimes over 100 pages in length.

As a university teacher long enough in the profession to be conscious of a growing vulnerability to the pressures of 'voluntary' premature retirement (or even redundancy), I am aware that there are students who welcome lengthy preliminaries because they represent those parts of a book that do not need to be read, but there can be little excuse to extend this introduction. Nevertheless, it cannot be concluded without thanking all those who gave of their time and knowledge to make this Survey possible: the warmth of the response by company directors and officials has been quite overwhelming. The grateful thanks of the Business Archives Council to the Economic and Social Research Council (successor to the SSRC) must also be recorded. To fund this project represented a considerable act of faith by the Research Council; only rarely have recipients of such grants not been institutions of higher education. The Council is also indebted to the Registrar of Companies and his staff for their co-operation, and to those archivists, librarians and curators throughout the country who have given help and encouragement. Finally I must express the thanks and admiration of the management committee to the Survey staff, Lesley Richmond, Clair Sharp, Bridget Stockford and Claire Findlay.

It has been a privilege and a pleasure to have been associated with this project and it is my sincere hope that this remarkable guide to the records of the earliest surviving English joint stock companies will be useful to students of business history, business and management studies and many areas of economic and social history, that the archives themselves will be intensively studied, and that future publications in many fields will thereby be greatly enriched.

Peter L Payne
Professor of Economic History
University of Aberdeen.

Notes

1. For example, P Mathias and AWH Pearsall (eds), *Shipping: A Survey of Historical Records* (Newton Abbot: David & Charles, 1971), the result of collaboration between the Business Archives Council and the National Maritime Museum; HAL Cockerell and E Green, *The British Insurance Business, 1547-1970* (London: Heinemann Educational, 1976) in the compilation of which the Council provided advice; LA Ritchie, *Modern British Shipbuilding. A Guide to Historical Records* (London: National Maritime Museum, 1980); LS Pressnell and John Orbell, *A Guide to the Historical Records of British Banking* (Aldershot: Gower Publishing, 1985). The Council's journal *Business Archives* contains lists of archives, scheduled by subject, reported to the National Register of Archives.

2. The Council was receiving approximately 100 research enquiries a year in the latter half of the 1970s.

3. See PL Payne, *The Early Scottish Limited Companies, 1856-1895* (Edinburgh: Scottish Academic Press, 1980), pp 180-5.

4. The legal position is somewhat ambiguous. Although there would appear to be no statutory obligation *as such* under the Companies Act for the permanent retention of any documents, a company *is* required by statute to make certain records available for inspection by its members and/or the public. See the Memorandum by the Chartered Institute of Secretaries, 'Disposal and Retention of Documents', March 1970. A list of the books, registers and documents which must be available for inspection and of which copies or extracts may be requisitioned is given in Appendix III of *Secretarial Administration* (London: Jordan & Sons, 1984), while the *Accountants Digest*, No.42, (1976/7) provides details of those records which companies *should* keep 'indefinitely'. They include the following categories: nominal and private ledgers, numerous types of records relating to superannuation schemes, the main cash books, all wages and registers concerned with the company's investments, the majority of the documents relating to share registration, the accounts of individual debtors and the major corporate documents (balance sheets, profit and loss accounts, minutes, and company registers). I am indebted to Lesley Richmond for information and advice on this subject.

5. For example, the Express Dairy Co Ltd comprises no less than 145 companies and the Eastern Telegraph Co Ltd, 64.

6. A recent exceptionally clear paper on the evolution and impact of the 19th century legislation on the joint stock company is that by PW Ireland, 'The Rise of the Limited Liability Company', *International Journal of the Sociology of Law*, Vol 12, No 3 (October, 1984). I am greatly indebted to Mr Ireland for a proof copy of this article and a mimeographed copy of its unpublished predecessor, 'The Triumph of the Company Legal Form, 1856-1914. There is also much of interest in the collection of papers edited by Tony Orhnial, *Limited Liability and the Corporation* (London: Croom Helm, 1982).

7. See Payne, op cit, pp 5, 17.

8. PL Cottrell, *Industrial Finance, 1830-1914. The Finance and Organisation of English Manufacturing Industry* (London: Methuen, 1980) p 52

9. JB Jefferys, *Business Organisation in Great Britain, 1856-1914* (New York: Arno Press, 1977), p 54. (This is the published version of Jeffreys' doctoral dissertation, University of London, 1938).

10. On this subject, see the perceptive comments by Ireland in *International Journal of the Sociology of Law*.

11. Payne, op cit, pp 96-104.

12. In July 1984 Lord Denning was succeeded as President of the Business Archives Council by Professor Peter Mathias.

Users' Guide to Company Archives

This guide is designed to help the user to exploit the information contained in the entries in this book and to suggest ways in which it can be supplemented. Users should also consult the conventions appearing at the beginning of the index section.

Format of entries

The entries on the 674 'core' companies surveyed appear in chronological order by date of registration. Each entry has been numbered in sequence from 1 to 674, and these numbers have been used as the sole means of cross-reference in the text and in the indexes. The layout of each entry is as follows:

Entry number Company name
Date of registration
Registration number
Registered office address
Principal activity
History (summary)
Records (location of records and summary lists)
Reference (relevant publications)

The **Company name** is the full title that was shown in the Register of Companies in September 1980. Previous names and any known changes in title after September 1980 are given in the History section of each entry; an exception to this rule is the alterations of titles to include 'PLC' as a result of the Companies Act 1980. In the titles initial definite articles have been omitted, 'Company' and 'Limited' have been abbreviated to 'Co' and 'Ltd', and ampersands have been substituted where 'and' appears in a title. Those limited companies without 'Limited' after their names have official permission to omit the usual suffix. In this book the simplest way of locating any company name is to consult *the Name index*.

The **Registration date** gives the date of a company's first registration as a limited liability concern. Later registrations are mentioned in the History section where possible.

The **Registration number** was allotted to each company on registration. It appears on all official documents relating to the company and is the number under which all returns to the Register of Companies are filed. Under the 1856 Act, companies were numbered from 1 onwards. Following the passage of the 1862 Act, which repealed and consolidated previous legislation, companies were again numbered from 1. As companies registered under the Act of 1856 were not required to re-register, this meant that individual numbers were no longer unique. Thus, there are two series of numbers 1-2920, the first of which applies to companies registered from 1856 to November 1862, and the second, for the period October 1862—March 1866, which carry the suffix 'C'. From number 2921 onwards the 'C' is omitted.

The **Registered office** is the address given on the official return to the Registrar of Companies in September 1980. *Modern county and local names have been used throughout.* This address is not necessarily the head office, the main centre of business, or the location of a company's records. For the purpose of contacting companies, preference should be given to addresses of companies given in the Records section of each entry. Later changes of registered address can be discovered from the Register of Companies (see page xx). Users will notice that some addresses are in Scotland, Northern Ireland, Eire, and the Commonwealth, which are sometimes covered by separate legislation or maintain separate registers under the same legislation. This arises because companies based in these countries have elected to register in England and Wales instead of or in addition to registering under the legislation or with the registrar of a second country.

The **Principal activity** of each company is the original main business and has been used in the compilation of the *Subject index.* Changes in activity, the activities of subsidiary or associated companies, are described in the 'History section' of each entry as far as possible.

The **History section** of each entry outlines the origins, locations, activities, changes in name, linkages and present status of the company. These sections are not intended to be definitive and it has not been possible to standardise the detail provided in each. Outline histories have been compiled from the published or privately published sources given in the Reference section, from the surviving records and from official returns to the Registrar of Companies for England and Wales, although in some instances very little information could be discovered.

The **Records section** of each entry is headed by the location of the records in 1985, whether they were held with the parent company or its agents, or in a record repository. As far as possible the Business Archives Council will keep a record of subsequent changes in the location of record collections. Changes in address of many publicly funded record offices can be discovered through reference to the Royal Commission on Historical Manuscripts' *Record Repositories in Great Britain* (London HMSO). In many entries there is more than one location as a result of the division of collections. These locations are numbered as **Records (1), Records (2)**, and so on.

Each Records section begins with a summary list of the records of the core company, followed by lists of records of the subsidiaries, associated companies, and related concerns of the core company which were discovered during the course of the survey of its records. For example, the entry for Pyrotenax Overseas Ltd (number 52) also includes a 'Records entry' for its subsidiary, The Atlantic Telegraph Co Ltd. The main series of records for all types of companies and other bodies are arranged in the following order: minute books and other corporate records, accounting records, production and sales records, staff records, property records, and miscellaneous records. Each series is dated as accurately as possible. Where no records have survived this is stated in the 'Records section'. *In a small number of cases where only the location is given, it proved impossible to obtain a full listing of records.*

The **Reference section** lists any publications or manuscript histories used in the compilation of the History section of an entry. Many of these were privately published or distributed and may not be found in the copyright libraries or public libraries. This section does not offer an exhaustive bibliography. Other printed sources which should be explored include the catalogue of the British Library, the copyright libraries and the Guildhall Library, London. Specialist trade and professional journals (many of them indexed) have been published since the late 18th century and should be considered when researching a particular company or business. Since the late 1960s the Business Archives Council's journal *Business Archives*, has carried an annual list of business histories published in the previous year.

Access to records

The records listed in this book are summaries of detailed lists or catalogues prepared by the Company Archive Survey. These are available for consultation at the National Register of Archives (Royal Commission on Historical Manuscripts, Quality House, 8 Quality Court, Chancery Lane, London WC2A 1HP). The Commission in turn will distribute copies of the larger or more important lists to the Scottish Record Office, Edinburgh; the National Library of Wales, Aberystwyth; the Public Record Office of Northern Ireland, Belfast; the Bodleian Library, Oxford; Cambridge University Library; John Rylands University Library of Manchester; and the Institute of Historical Research, University of London. The lists can also be consulted by appointment at the Business Archives Council (185 Tower Bridge Road, London SE1 2UF). The full lists are particularly useful for users interested in major studies of individual companies or in the exact specification of individual archival items.

The inclusion of the records of any company or other concern in this book does not mean that access to those records will be given. Access to records which are held by companies or other private owners is at their discretion. Users should write seeking permission to the Secretary of the company at the address given in the relevant Records section unless otherwise stated. The Business Archives Council recommends that users should give as full an explanation of their research interests as possible and that they should respect any special conditions of access. Where records have been deposited elsewhere, users should write to the Archivist or Librarian at the repository named in the relevant Records section. Some records in public repositories are governed by conditions of access, and for this reason users should not expect instant access to records listed in this book. The Business Archives Council recommends that users should contact the appropriate repository well before making a research expedition. If, for any reason, a user cannot contact a company, other concern or repository mentioned in this book, he or she should write for advice to the Business Archives Council.

Supplementary sources of information

Users should not neglect alternative sources of information, both on the 674 'core' companies and on the many hundreds of other concerns covered in this book. Under the terms of legislation for companies, all concerns featured in this book were required to make annual returns to the Registrar of Companies[1]. These contain memoranda and articles of association, schedules of directors and shareholders and annual balance sheets for public companies (after 1907). For companies still registered in England and Wales these returns are held at Companies House, Crown Way,

Maindy, Cardiff CF4 3UZ. Since the mid 1960s the returns have been microfilmed and microfiche copies are available in the London Search Room, Companies Registration Office, 55-71 City Road, London EC1 1BB. The microfiched documents are arranged under six headings:

G: General Documents—comprising the memorandum and articles of association (which include names of promoters) at the company's registration and documents relating to any subsequent changes, minutes of agreement, circulars to shareholders concerning increase in capital, notifications of changes in registered address and changes of title, and lists of directors.

A: Annual Returns and Accounts, comprising the returns for the first few years of the company's life and then from the mid-1970s.

M: Mortgages—papers relating to mortgages from the mid-1970s

MD: Mortgage Documents—the legal documents only without supporting papers from the mid-1970s.

MR: Mortgage Register—from the mid-1970s

S: Shareholders Lists—from the mid-1970s.

Fees are payable for the production of the microfiche which then become the researcher's property. Initially only fiche G, A and M are produced but the other fiche can be purchased separately. The company registration number is needed to call up both the actual and microfiche documents in Cardiff and London, and can be checked against alphabetical indexes available in both places. Finding aids at Companies House include an invaluable index of changes in name.

When a company is removed from the Register for any reason, its files are retained for legally-specified periods at Companies House in Cardiff. The names of such companies are transferred to separate registers available in Cardiff and London. After twenty years the files are transferred to the Public Record Office at Kew, Richmond, Surrey TW9 4DU, where they are held in class BT31. These files for companies removed from the Register before 1948 were weeded, leaving annual returns for the first and last years and intermediate tenth years in a company's life, along with memoranda and articles of association and other miscellaneous corporate records. After 1948 the files are preserved in their entirity. Reference is by means of company numbers, which in practice are most easily located via the Companies House finding aids. Returns for all defunct public companies are preserved at the Public Record Office, whilst only a 1 per cent sample of those for private limited companies is retained. Since private companies were not recognised until the Companies Act of 1907, this procedure only applies to private companies registered from 1908 and not to companies registered previously which chose to adopt private status. Where microfilm files exist for defunct companies, these files will be retained in their entirety and transferred to the Public Record Office from 1988 onwards[2]. For those users who do not have ready access to Companies House, information about companies quoted on the London Stock Exchange can be found in *Burdett's Official Intelligence* (1882-98), *The Stock Exchange Official Intelligence* (1899-1933), *The Stock Exchange Year Book* (1875-1933) and *The Stock Exchange Official Year Book* (1934 to date). A *Register of Defunct and Other Companies* was published separately every year until 1979/80. This provides a cumulative list of public companies referred to in these publications which have ceased trading. The information is now incorporated in *The Stock Exchange Official Year Book*.

Anyone interested in the history of individual companies and their activities should also consider a wide range of alternative sources. These include trade and post office directories, patent records held by the Science Reference Division of the British Library, and the annual indexes to the *London Gazette* at the British Library. Other sources at the Public Record Office which may be particularly relevant are probate records, Treasury files, records of customs and excise, and the files of the special wartime government departments. Any business will also leave its mark on the records of local or national trade associations, trade unions, banks and insurance companies. For these related sources, complementary guides are available[3].

Notes

1. Similar arrangements exist for companies registered in Scotland, Northern Ireland, Eire and the Channel Islands. TM Alridge, *Directory of Registrars and Records* (London: Oyez Longman, 4th ed 1984), p 74 ff

2. A valuable case study of the usefulness of this source is CT Watts and MJ Watts, 'Company Records as a Source for the Family Historian', *Genealogists' Magazine*, vol 21 (1938), pp 44-54. Files of defunct companies on the Scottish register are held at the Scottish Record Office, HM General Register House, Edinburgh EH1 3YY. Those on the Northern Ireland register are held at the Public Record Office of Northern Ireland, 66 Balmoral Avenue, Belfast BT9 6NY

3. For example, M Wilcox (ed RA Storey), *The Confederation of British Industry Predecessor Archive* (Coventry: University of Warwick Library Occasional Publications No 12, 1984); J Bennett (ed RA Storey, *Trade Union and Related Records* (Coventry: University of Warwick Library Occasional Publications No 5, 3rd ed 1983); LS Pressnell and John Orbell, *A Guide to the Historical Records of British Banking* (Aldershot: Gower Publishing, 1985); and HAL Cockerell and E Green, *The British Insurance Business, 1547-1970* (London: Heinemann Educational, 1976)

Company Archives: Lists of Records

Abbreviations

agm	annual general meeting
c	circa
cent	century
Co	company
E	East
est	established
inc	incorporated, ie registered
incl	inclusive, including
Ltd	Limited
memo	memorandum
misc	miscellaneous
N	North
nd	no date
PLC	public limited company
S	South
W	West
WW	World War

1 ASHFORD CATTLE MARKET CO LTD
25 Sep 1856
00118
11 Bank Street, Ashford, Kent PN23 1DE
Cattle market

History: provisionally registered in 1855 as Ashford Stock Market Co but incorporated under present title in 1856, to provide suitable premises for the show and sale of cattle in Ashford, Kent, on market days on first, third and fifth Tuesdays of the month. In 1984 continued to provide market facilities.

Records: at Ashford Cattle Market, 11 Bank Street, Ashford, Kent PN23 1DE
directors and general meeting minutes 1856-date; shareholders register 1890,1935-62; share transfer register 1935-63; list of directors and trustees 1856-99; directors register 1935-43; deaths register 1870s-1930s; mortgage and charge register 1881-1930; corporate documents 1855-1922; memo and articles of association 1856-1930s; annual returns 1935-54; annual report and balance sheet 1938-9,1963; balance sheets 1935-41; audited statement of accounts 1963; account book 1947-70; tolls summary book 1948-68; toll schedules c1856-1910; manager service agreements 1949; title deeds, leases and other documents re Ashford property 1856-1978; market plans 1856-1978; misc correspondence 1930s-1970s

2 ORIENTAL GAS CO LTD
26 Sep 1856
00121
Sardinia House, Sardinia Street, Lincoln's Inn Fields, London WC2 3LZ
Gas

History: founded in 1853 by British inventors seeking to supply gas in Calcutta, India. Incorporated in 1856, built gas works and has supplied gas in Calcutta ever since. After Independence in 1947 it became an Indian owned company although it has remained registered in UK.

Records: at Ferguson Maidment, Sardinia House, Sardinia Street, Lincoln's Inn Fields, London WC2 3LZ
general meeting minutes 1854-1968; shareholders list 1853; members registers c1939 on; directors registers 1944-1968; stock transfers register 1946-1979; stock transfer certificates 1946-7; settlement deed 1853

3 BRITISH INDIA STEAM NAVIGATION CO LTD
29 Sep 1856
00133
Beaufort House, St Botolph Street, London EC3A 7DX
Shipping

History: founded and incorporated in 1856 by William Mackinnon (1823-93) general merchant near Calcutta, India as Calcutta & Burmah Steam Navigation Co Ltd to operate a mail service between Calcutta and Rangoon, Burma. Mackinnon, Mackenzie & Co, Calcutta became managing agents. Changed name to above in 1862. Indian establishments were at Garden Reach workshops, Calcutta and Mazagon Dock, Bombay. Secretaryship was based in

Glasgow until 1892 when it moved to London. In 1865 formed Netherlands India Steam Navigation Co and entered the Dutch East Indies internal trade. From 1872 carried P&O mail, passengers and cargo from Aden to Zanzibar. Following the opening of the Suez Canal, a UK service was started in 1874. Arranged mail contract with Queensland government from 1881 to 1895. Purchased Apcar Line in 1912. Sir William Mackinnon was succeeded by James M Hall in 1893 and Duncan Mackinnon. In 1913 James L Mackay (later 1st Earl of Inchcape was appointed chairman. Amalgamated with P&O (Peninsular & Oriental Steam Navigation Co est 1835) in 1914 and Lord Inchcape became chairman of the combination. Both companies continued to be run as separate concerns. Acquired Hain Line and Nourse Line in 1917. In 1922 was largest single merchant fleet in the world with 158 vessels. Services continued after WW2 when the independence of India and Pakistan led to the withdrawal of coasting trades in the sub-continent and other lines gradually declined. Services between UK and Africa, Australia, India, Pakistan and Sri Lanka continued. Educational cruises were introduced in 1962. Routes and services were gradually shared with P&O and a fleet of tankers built. Rationalization within the P&O Group was completed in Oct 1971.

Records (1): at British India Steam Navigation, Beaufort House, St Botolph Street, London EC3A 7DX
directors and general meeting minutes 1961-date; accounting records 1950s-date; current records 1970s on

Records (2): at National Maritime Museum, Romney Road, Greenwich, London SE10 9NF
directors and general meeting minutes 1856-1961; annual reports and accounts 1865-1970; general ledgers and journals 1935-59; ships accounts 1927-58; supplies, repairs and stevedoring, pay and pensions accounts 1938-69; Calcutta office general accounts 1935-55; passage books 1951-69; properties register and files 1889-1965; landing craft log books and files 1966-70; correspondence: secretarys 1865-1900, re mail contracts, trooping, relief expeditions 1863-1962, confidential 1885-93,1912-32; staff: records 1868-1957, pension fund registers nd; maintenance, repair and new building files 1958-67; *Handbook* 1866-1939,1949-69; house magazine and newsletters nd; centenary press cuttings 1956

Records (3): at Inchcape, 40 St Mary Axe, London EC3A 8EU
accounts, agreements, shipping and traffic correspondence 1925-52; agency papers 1951-7

Records (4): at School of Oriental & African Studies Library, University of London, Malet Street, London WC1 7HP
Sir William Mackinnon papers 1856-93

George Blake, *B I Centenary 1856-1956* (1956)

4 THAMES & GENERAL LIGHTERAGE LTD
23 Oct 1856
00258
India Buildings, Liverpool, Merseyside L2 0RR
Lighterage

History: incorporated as Thames Steam Tug & Lighterage Co Ltd in 1856 to carry goods and tow other vessels on the River Thames. Within few years towage was dropped as it proved unprofitable. By 1860 possessed 12 iron barges and 1 steam tug, rising to 124 barges, 3 steam tugs, steam lighter and a sea going steam vessel in 1865. Goods lightered rose from 180,427 tons in 1861/2 to 251,926 tons by 1873. First offices were at 148 Fenchurch Street, London, moving to 1 Fenchurch Buildings by 1894 and to 24-25 Great Tower Street by 1919. Around 1900 owned warehouse, wharf and other premises at Brentford, London, and by 1920s had acquired Heathwall Wharf at Nine Elms Lane, Battersea. By late 1920s had biggest fleet of barges on Thames, specialising in large heavy loads eg coal and cement. Merged in 1960 with General Lighterage Co Ltd to form Thames & General Lighterage Ltd, which was acquired, along with its subsidiary C Albany & Sons Ltd by Transport Development Group Ltd in Oct 1961. Sold by latter to Ocean Cory Ltd, a subsidiary of Ocean Transport & Trading Ltd in 1979. In 1979 was still largest lighterage company operating on Thames with 250 lighters and 17 tugs, handling 500,000 tons of freight, mainly consisting of import and export traffic, interport movements, refuse disposal services and certain civil engineering works. Operated throughout Port of London from Brentford to Sheerness on Thames, from Bow Creek to Enfield on the Lee Navigation and into Brent Meadow Wharf on the Grand Union Canal. Also owned New Caledonian Wharf and Brentford Barge Works.

Records (1): at Ocean Transport & Trading, Archives Department, India Buildings, Liverpool, Merseyside L2 0RR
shareholders meeting minutes 1857-74; shareholders list 1856-60; memo and articles of association 1856-1948; corporate documents 1880-1963

Records (2): at Ocean Cory, Windsor House, 1270 London Road, Norbury, London SW16 4XH
papers and correspondence re takeover by Ocean Cory, 1975-80; tonnage record 1978-9

Records (3): at Transport Development Group, Kingsgate House, Victoria Street, London SW1
freight rates list 1912; fares list 1920; technical booklet nd

5 BORNEO CO LTD

31 Oct 1856
00398
40 St Mary Axe, London EC3A 8EU
Far Eastern traders

History: incorporated in 1855 under Limited Liability Act and re-registered as above in 1856 under Joint Stock Companies Act. Formed from Far East trading firm, MacEwan & Co, (est 1842) in partnership with Robert Henderson, Glasgow merchant and company's first chairman. Company headquarters were in Singapore although they traded in general commodities all over the Far East - in Calcutta, Hong Kong, Java, Thailand, Sarawak, Sabah and Brunei. Were involved in building of Singapore's new harbour in 1860s and in founding the Alexandra Brickworks at the turn of the century. Hong Kong branch which closed in 1890, traded mainly in silk and rice with Thailand. In Calcutta a jute mill and sugar factory were established in 1859. In Sarawak the company mined antimony, cinnabar, gold and coal and was also involved in pepper and rubber cultivation and banking. In Thailand, rice exporting, banking, and pepper, teak and rubber cultivation were the company's main activities. In 1925 Borneo Motors Ltd was incorporated in Singapore to operate the motor vehicle distribution business established there. After WW2, during which most of the European staff were interned, further expansion was made in the Far East and elsewhere, into brick and concrete manufacture in Canada in the 1950s, timber and saw milling in Australia and motor distribution in the Caribbean in the 1960s. In Nov 1966 the company merged to become wholly owned subsidiary of Inchcape & Co Ltd, the international trading company. Their Far Eastern concerns remained unaltered while the rest were absorbed by other Inchcape companies.

Records: at Inchcape, 40 St Mary Axe, London EC3A 8EU
board minutes 1856-1965; directors committee minutes 1931-3; general meeting minutes 1857-1967; list of shareholders 1856; shareholders ledger 1856-8; share certificates 1856; register of directors 1900-63; register of directors shareholdings 1948-61; papers re directors 1954-67; corporate documents 1856-90; secretarys notes re legal documents and letters 1921-62; annual report and accounts 1968; audited accounts 1956-65; Fai Paritt mine, Bau: reports 1919-21, managers letters to Kuching manager 1919-22, history and photographs 1898-1921; outfit and stores inventory 1920; teak extraction and delivery costs 1931-46; reports on up country working, cinnabar deposits and teak 1922-40; engineering and motor vehicle department catalogues 1923-30; company brochure 1960; salary books 1879-1943; copy Sarawak land grants 1857-71; Bangkok property ledger 1929-54; property valuations in Malaya, Singapore, Borneo, Brunei and Sabah 1964,1967; sketch Kuala Lumpur offices 1960; correspondence between JC Temple and R Henderson 1857-9, re business 1857-67, Ludwig V Helmes partnership 1876-7, Krakatoa eruption 1883, centenary booklet 1943-55; photographs of premises, plantations, mining operations, ships, launches, staff, workers, countryside in various Far East countries 1869-1968; photographs and press cuttings re Rajahs of Sarawak 1880-1940s; copy letters of appointment by King of Siam to Mrs Anna Leonowens 1862; Chungmai jungle diaries 1904-09; war diary 1939-45; histories, press cuttings and historical notes on company activities, directors, general managers, managers and centenary 1928-64; photographs of centenary celebrations 1956
Alexandra Brickworks Ltd: minutes 1962-4
Borneo Motors Ltd: photographs of staff, premises and plant openings 1920s-68

Henry Longhurst, *The Borneo Story* (1956)
Sir Percival Griffiths, *A History of the Inchcape Group* (1977)

6 BERWICK SALMON FISHERIES CO LTD

1 Nov 1856
00425
1 Main Street, Spittal, Berwick upon Tweed, Northumberland TD15 1QY
Fisheries

History: origins lay in Old Shipping Co (est prior to 1766) by a group of local men, mainly coopers in Berwick upon Tweed who held shares in a small sailing fleet (numbering 11 in 1800) engaged in London, coastal and foreign trade. As commodities carried included salmon, the company leased fishing rights on the River Tweed. Berwick Shipping Co was formed in 1820 by members of Old Shipping Co and Commercial Shipping Co (est 1798) of Berwick, both companies ceasing to trade in that year. The new company worked the fisheries and continued the shipping trade. In 1837 steam vessels were introduced on the Hull, Leith and Newcastle runs. In 1850 the company merged with General Shipping Co of Berwick (est 1825) and was incorporated in 1856 as Berwick Shipping Co Ltd. The shipping vessels were sold off in 1869 as business had become unprofitable and the company's name changed to above in 1872. Company's main premises from 1901 to 1979 were at the old lifeboat station at Quayside, Berwick. New premises with facilities for deep freezing salmon were built at Spittal on the south bank of the Tweed in 1964. In 1965 acquired the share capital of Border Fare Ltd (inc 1962), frozen food company. In 1966 employed 90 fishermen. First company to be issued with certificate of re-registration as a Public Limited Company in Dec 1980.

Records: at Berwick Salmon Fisheries, 1 Main Street, Spittal, Berwick upon Tweed, Northumberland TD15 1QY
committee, directors and general meeting minutes 1820-date; shareholders: registers 1856-1916, ledgers 1875-1958; share and share transfer certificates, documents and correspondence 1821-1968; share transfer register 1857-1943; dividends paid book 1931-58; articles of agreement 1820; memo and articles of association 1820-date; corporate papers 1842-1925; mortgage register 1884-c98; annual reports and accounts 1851-date; balance sheets 1821,1829-47 and profit and loss accounts 1857-64,1921-54; shareholders profits 1821-45; London trade accounts 1839-64; ledgers: 1919-61, boatyard 1919-74, retail 1920-40, fish 1925-64, fish sales 1928-71, fisheries 1932-66, fishmongers 1943-72, ice 1952-63, shellfish 1960-3, sales 1964-73, purchases 1963-73; sales books 1937-71; day books: retail sales 1937-55, boatyard 1919-64, ice 1952-63, shellfish 1960-3, purchases 1962-3, sales 1962-4; cash paid books 1940-4; cash books: 1934-63, fishmongers 1934-44, petty 1938-72; fisheries: profit book 1916-61, expenses analysis 1945-76; Edinburgh agents account book 1848-58; ice accounts 1821-46; customers references 1869-c1940; memo, report and correspondence re French trade 1896-7,1909; shipped salmon totals 1796-1848; fish seasons comparisons 1810-98; fisheries produce sheets 1840-date; fishings 7 year averages 1901-34; Tweed catches statistics and diagrams 1808-94,1957-71; fish log book 1852-61; fisheries summaries 1900-20; coarse fishing catches 1917-20; fish weight books 1937-71; fish consignment books 1937-73; seal damage reports 1971-5; fishing equipment stock sheets 1939-60; notes on fish re prices returns, exports, infections etc 1845-1949; twine costs nd; carriage book 1900-29; arrangements and sections of cobles c1926; fisheries: leases and title deeds 1645-1936, tithe papers 1828-79, valuations c1592-1941, damage and dispute papers 1817-58, rents and expenses 1854-1929, dividends 1821-74, profit and loss details 1903-30, plans and sketches 1806-1960s; River Tweed Commission assessment: rolls 1908-38, intimations 1913-59, cash book 1904-61; fishermen engagement: book 1835-50, conditions 1850-1,1890,1928-61; fisheries workers book 1870-1; apprenticeship indenture 1835; fisheries: memos and arrangements 1903-61, allowances nd, fish money distribution papers 1928-70, paysheets 1938-71; fishing books 1957-64; boatyard book 1957-60; employee record sheets 1970-1; leather supply agreements 1904-06; workmens insurance papers 1910-45; pension scheme papers 1953-60; batt and shiel specifications, plans, cost papers etc 1911-21; Quayside and Spittal premises plans and rebuilding papers 1922-63; fire insurance papers 1833-1947; out letter book 1927-9; correspondence re financial arrangements, twine knitting, poaching, cormorants, seals, fish, French trade, research etc 1842-1974; photographs of staff, directors, fishermen, fish, royal visits 1900s-80s; legal opinions, newscuttings, evidence, reports and correspondence re Salmon Fisheries Bills 1856-1933 and New Scotch Water Rights 1871-1907; articles, books and newscuttings on salmon fishing 1871-1965; River Tweed Commission, police, pollution and other committee minutes and reports 1872-1965; Berwick Harbour Commission minutes 1958-65

River Tweed Salmon Net Fishing Association: minutes, cash books and papers 1956-69
Old Shipping Co: stock in trade valuations and transfer statements 1808-28
General Shipping Co of Berwick: articles of agreement 1825,1840-1; annual reports 1830-47; share transfer agreements 1829-38; balance sheet 1828; profit and loss account 1846; ship bill of sale 1837; dividend account 1842

A Salmon Saga: The Story of the Berwick Salmon Fisheries Company Ltd 1856-1956 (priv pub 1956)

7 BL HOLDINGS LTD

4 Nov 1856
00529
10 Cornwall House, Regent's Park, London NW1 4QP
Property

History: incorporated by deed of settlement in 1856 as British Land Co Ltd by the National Freehold Land Society to avoid contravening building society regulations by carrying out all land transactions for the society. Both shared the same staff and premises at 14 Moorgate Street, London until 1878 when owing to a dispute the business connection was cut. The company repaid all its outstanding loans but continued to operate from same premises with a separate staff until 1917, the society being a tenant of the company. In 1944 the National Building Society, previously the National Freehold Land Society, amalgamated with the Abbey Road Building Society to form the Abbey National Building Society. Began from the late 1890s to acquire income producing property investments and after WW1 re-invested income in yielding securities. In early 1930s large holdings of government stocks were sold and shop premises purchased. WW2 bombing caused great damage to company's property and rental income. It totally destroyed its headquarters based from 1917 at 67 Basinghall Street, London. Offices were established in Reigate, Surrey and 36-38 Copthall Avenue, London for the rest of the war, moving to 25 Abchurch Lane, London in 1945. A new board in 1954 reorganised company's finances and acquired substantial properties and Selected Land & Property Co Ltd (inc 1928). Messrs Goddard & Smith became managing agents. Acquired 2 other property companies Adamant Investment Corporation Ltd (inc 1927) and Dyott Properties Ltd. Properties owned by company and its subsidiaries increased from 329 in 1954 to 1864 in 1956. In 1959 BL Holdings Ltd was incorporated to effect the merger of Adamant Investment Corporation Ltd, British Land Co Ltd and Selected Land & Properties Co Ltd. Its name was changed in 1959 to British Land Co Ltd and simultaneously company's name was changed to above.

Records: at British Land, 10 Cornwall House, Regent's Park, London NW1 4QP settlement deed 1856; balance sheets 1907 on; property plans nd

1856-1956 The Centenary of The British Land Company Limited (priv pub 1956)

8 GRESHAM HOUSE ESTATE CO LTD

14 May 1857
00871
24 Austin Friars, London EC2N 2EN
Property and investment

History: formed when government sold HM Excise Office in Old Broad Street to founders of the company in 1853 and incorporated as above in 1857. The site was sold in 1959. The company also owned property in Bishopsgate and in 1921 acquired Broad Street Estates Ltd (inc 1913), which owned property opposite Gresham House which was sold in 1953. Formed a subsidiary, Great Winchester Street Estates Ltd, in 1928 to hold land in that street (liquidated in 1958 and land sold in 1960). The company also acquired H Bucknell & Sons Ltd (inc 1890) cork merchants of Glasgow, London and Portugal which was subsequently sold to Bremar Ltd; RE Thomson & Co (Sunbury) Ltd, instrument makers and engineers; and Robert Noblett Ltd, leather merchants and manufacturers.

Records (1): at Gresham House Estate, 24 Austin Friars, London EC2N 2EN
directors minutes 1901-date; share: ledger c1950-60, dividends 1961-4, transfers register 1934-50; debenture register 1927-41; annual reports and accounts 1953-61; trial balance 1931-7,1961-6; profit and loss accounts and balance sheets 1966; house accounts cash books 1922-68, and statements 1955-60; nominal ledger 1927-36; account book 1929-38; cash book 1955-62; petty cash book 1956-69; quarterly rent roll 1890-1928,1950-9; correspondence and plans re South Bank development 1961-2; salary books 1949-60; photographs and drawings of directors 1827-1922, and staff 1949-50; plan of office nd; secretary out letter books 1950-9
Broad Street Estates Ltd: board and general minutes 1947-63; reports and accounts 1961-6; draft accounts 1931-9; balance and audited accounts 1961-6; accounts book 1962-7; salary books 1949-60
Great Winchester Street Estates Ltd: annual reports and accounts 1961-6; draft balances 1929-34; audited accounts 1961-6; salaries book 1949-60
H Bucknell & Sons Ltd: board and general meeting agendas and attendance book 1943-69; general meeting minutes 1932; shareholders registers c1895-1960; share: certificate book 1967-8, documents and correspondence 1890-1960; directors register 1948-62; probate register 1939-67; annual reports and accounts 1891-1968; annual returns 1942-51; ledger sheets 1955-63; exchange control accounts 1964-6; journal 1964-8; cash book 1964-9; bills: payable 1941-61, receivable 1953-66; general correspondence 1964
RE Thomson & Co (Sunbury) Ltd: corporate papers and audited accounts 1948-66
Robert Noblett Ltd: corporate papers, profit and loss accounts and balance sheets 1954-67

Records (2): at Guildhall Library, Aldermanbury, London EC2P 2EJ
management committee meeting and board minutes 1853-1901; annual reports and accounts 1931-7; annual returns 1885-1904; account statements 1871-1914; nominal ledger 1927-36; investment ledger 1930-48; quarterly rent rolls 1859-79,1914-50; tenancies register 1860-1936; excess rates book 1948-56; secretarys out letter books 1860-1949
Broad Street Estates Ltd: directors and general meeting minutes 1913-47; share certificate book 1913-66; account statements 1931-9; draft accounts 1922-30; ledgers 1920-45; journals 1915-58; cash books 1915-56; payments register 1926-59; quarterly rent rolls 1914-53; excess rates book 1948-56; plans of Old Broad Street 1934-55
Great Winchester Street Estates Ltd: share certificate book 1929-66; annual reports and accounts 1929-34; ledger 1929-38; tenancy agreements 1943-59; plans of 128 Great Winchester Street 1946-56

Gresham House Estate Company Ltd 1857-1957 - Centenary Review by the Chairman (priv pub 1957)

9 BRITISH CONGOLEUM LTD

22 May 1857
00883
Lune Mills, Lancaster, Lancashire LA1 5QN
Leather cloth

History: incorporated in 1857 as Leather Cloth Co Ltd to manufacture leather cloths etc, with sole rights to manufacturing patent of JR&CP Crockett of Newark, New Jersey, USA. Factory built in Abbey Road, West Ham, London, with registered offices situated in Cannon Street, London, offices at 94 Boulevard de Sebastopol, Paris, and a warehouse in Salford, Greater Manchester from 1949. The company was run from Paris by Belgian and French directors with an English manager except during WW2 when an English committee ran operations. Main business was in perambulator coverings but by 1936 with 500 factory workers, rubber cloth production was added to oil and cellulose cloth coverings. The workforce had fallen to 185 by 1948, and the 1950s world textile crisis together with competition from plastic coverings continued company's decline. Acquired by Jas Williamson & Son Ltd, linoleum manufacturers of Lancaster (est 1844) in 1955 and ceased to trade in 1956, becoming a private company in 1979. Williamsons sold the works in 1961 and in 1963 merged with Michael Nairn & Co Ltd, linoleum manufacturers of Kirkcaldy, Fife, name changed to Nairn-Williamson Ltd, and to Nairn Floors Ltd in 1973. Nairn-Williamson group of companies was acquired by Unilever Ltd in 1975.

Records: at British Congoleum, the Registered Office, Lune Mills, Lancaster, Lancashire LA1 5QN, or c/o Head Office, Nairn Floors, Victoria Road, Kirkcaldy, Fife, KY1 2SB
directors meeting minutes 1939-date; general meeting minutes 1929-date; share warrant registers 1906-40; share ledger 1950-date; share transfer: register 1952-date, forms 1952-80; directors and secretarys register 1940s-date; seal book 1909-70; memo and articles of association 1948, 1979

10 BIRMINGHAM TEMPERANCE HALL CO LTD

6 Jun 1857
00899
47 Newhall Street, Birmingham, W Midlands B3 3QH
Temperance hall

History: founded and incorporated in 1857 as above by members of Birmingham Temperance Society (est 1830) to acquire land on which to build a hall for the society which was holding its meetings in Ann Street. Land was acquired in Upper Temple Street on which the new hall was built to the designs of Yeoville Thomason. Hall was completely reconstructed between 1898 and 1901 after which it housed trade exhibitions, concerts etc until new safety regulation proved too costly to implement and it was sold to Birmingham Law Society in 1931. The company continued to collect ground rents from property in the vicinity of Birmingham Temperance Hall.

Records (1): Birmingham Temperance Hall, 47 Newhall Street, Birmingham, W Midlands B3 3QH
members register 1894-date; share transfer registers 1932-date; directors register c1927-date;

registration papers and documents 1857-date; annual summaries 1894-1908; historical booklet 1969

Records (2): at Birmingham Reference Library, Central Libraries, Chamberlain Square, Birmingham, W Midlands B3 3HQ
articles of association 1858; rebuilding fund appeal 1899; meeting, lecture, concert programmes 1859-1919

Ewart Faulkner, *The Birmingham Temperance Society 1830-1969* (priv pub 1969)

11 RYE CATTLE MARKET CO LTD

17 Feb 1859
01452
Estates Office, Cinque Ports Street, Rye, E Sussex TN31 7AL
Cattle market

History: original livestock market of Rye, E Sussex was held at junction of Market Road and Cinque Ports Street, the tolls being collected by the Pomfret family, local landowners and bankers. By mid 19 cent farmers and dealers desired a more convenient and effective market and incorporated the above in 1859 to provide a new cattle market. Richard C Pomfret was its first chairman. Purchased 2 acres of ground adjoining railway station on which a central market hall was erected, stock pens built and railway sidings laid. A further hall was built in 1873 called Agricultural Hall, and it was sold in 1912. Prior to WW2 handled large numbers of fat and store sheep and cattle, calves, pigs and horses. During WW2 it became a centre for collection, grading and distribution by the Ministry of Food. By mid 1970s was principally a fatstock auction market for sheep and lambs with an average annual throughput of 37,000 head. Auctioneers for the market in 1982 were Vidler & Co with Finn-Kelcey, Collier & Ashenden.

Records (1): at Rye Cattle Market, Estates Office, Cinque Ports Street, Rye, E Sussex TN31 7AL
directors meeting minutes 1930-date; general meeting minutes 1860-date; members register current; directors registers 1904-date; debenture: register 1912-67, certificates and transfers 1912-51; share and stock transfer documents 1859-1967; dividend lists and documents 1968-74; annual returns 1941-68; annual reports and accounts 1941-70; balance sheets and accounts 1927-31,1957-69; private ledgers 1910-37; Vidler & Co accounts 1965-7; income tax papers 1967-8; cleaners wage books 1961-4; corn market notice 1817; *Official Handbook* 1937

Records (2): at E Sussex Record Office, Pelham House, St Andrew's Lane, Lewes, E Sussex BN7 1YT
directors: meeting minutes 1859-1924, report 1925; general meeting minutes 1860-95; share: ledger 1859-1902, transfers 1893-1921; shareholders correspondence and share documents 1859-c1964; dividend account and receipt book 1885-1908; probate register 1883-1903; memo and articles of association 1859; annual report and accounts 1922,1966-70; account book 1920-9; sales books 1893-1931; receipts and correspondence 1920s-31; Vidler & Co auction books: Rye market 1913-54, Rye fat stock market 1920-1, ram sales 1950-5, Rye market and Northiam sales 1924-32; animal sales note book 1929; pay sheets 1924; market hall extension notes nd; letter books 1881-1903; correspondence: re foot and mouth 1922-4, with Wm Dawes & Co 1900-20,1950s

12 CONSOLIDATED BANK LTD

11 Jul 1859
01583
52 Threadneedle Street, London EC2R 8AL
Banking

History: formed in 1863 on amalgamation of Bank of Manchester Ltd and Heywood, Kennards & Co, 4 Lombard Street, London EC3, banking firm (est 1800). Former was established in 1829, collapsing in 1842 and only resuming business in Apr 1852 with a new deed of settlement and board of directors. Registered with limited liability in Jul 1859. Absorbed Hankey & Co (est prior to 1685), banking firm of Fenchurch Street, London EC3 in 1863 and moved to Fenchurch Street in 1864. Took over business and accounts of the failed Bank of Threadneedle Street (est 1855) in May 1866 which caused its own downfall. Petition for its winding up presented on 28 May and the official liquidator was provisionally appointed. The bank reopened, and had recovered by the early 1870s. Opened branches in Manchester at Patricroft and Longsight in 1887, and Deansgate in 1893; at Pendleton, Lancashire in 1887; and in Greater Manchester at Leigh and Tyldesley in 1888, Radcliffe in 1892, and at the Cattle Market, Salford in 1894. Amalgamated in 1896 with Parr's Banking Co & the Alliance Bank Ltd which became Parr's Bank Ltd in 1896 and merged in 1918 with London County & Westminster Bank Ltd to form London County Westminster & Parr's Bank Ltd.

Records: at National Westminster Bank, 41 Lothbury, London EC2P 2BP
board: minutes 1863-96, agenda 1873-96; daily minutes 1863-96; shareholders list 1880; circulars and notices 1863-99; amalgamation papers 1866-96; directors reports 1874-93; half-yearly balance sheets and accounts 1863-96; comparative statistics 1885,1890,1893; salary books 1864-93; staff lists 1896; London branch correspondence 1863-95; branch accounts 1863-96; managers letters 1867-97

TE Gregory, *The Westminster Bank Through a Century* Vol 1&2 (1936)

13 EAST LANCASHIRE PAPER GROUP LTD

29 Mar 1860
01815
Church Street East, Radcliffe, Greater Manchester M26 9PR
Paper manufacturing

History: incorporated in 1860 as East Lancashire Paper Mill Co Ltd, mill being built in Church Street, Radcliffe, Greater Manchester, near River Irwell, by James Hill, contractor, to designs by Joseph Chatwood. Paper produced by summer of 1862. London agents from late 1860s were Frank Green & Co, paper merchants, Upper Thames Street, and Scottish agents from mid 1880s were Robt Bruce & Sons of West Nile Street, Glasgow. Successful until the 1890s when business began to decline. In 1897 the management was reorganised, Charles R Seddon, previously engineer to Yates, Duxbury & Sons at Hall-i-th' Wood and Heap Bridge Mills, appointed manager. He enlarged and modernised the plant and switched production from newsprint and cheaper papers to quality papers. Became managing director in 1913 and was first president of the Employers' Federation of Paper Makers and president of the Paper Makers' Association. Policy continued by son John Seddon and grandson Charles G Seddon. During WW2 produced armaments as well as paper, using straw as substitute for esparto grass. Formed with Wallpaper Manufacturers Ltd at end of war, Straw Pulp Manufacturing Co Ltd which operated from Mount Sion Works, 2 miles downstream from East Lancashire Mills and produced initially unbleached straw pulp and after 1957 when became subsidiary of East Lancashire Paper Mills Co Ltd, bleached straw pulp and top quality esparto pulp. By 1960 had 3 other subsidiaries, AH James & Co Ltd, Arnold Belford Ltd, Newton Mill Ltd, and employed over 700 people. Name changed by 1974 to above and was the parent company of group of 9 subsidiaries engaged as paper manufacturers, convertors and merchants employing 1750 people with London offices at 18 Blackfriars Lane, London. In 1981 had 21 subsidiaries.

Records: at East Lancashire Paper Group, Church Street East, Radcliffe, Greater Manchester M26 9PR
directors and shareholders meeting minutes 1868-date; shareholders: registers pre 1929, ledgers 1876-1954, transfers 1931-57; directors register 1942; corporate loan receipts 1896-1910; annual returns 1943-50; annual directors reports 1898-1940; account statements 1880-1964; cash book 1949-75; petty cash books 1948-57; production: book 1959-63, costings 1949-64, totals 1967; customer order books 1896-7,1926-59; sales book 1955-63; stock summaries 1955; purchase: analysis book 1956-7, ledger sheets 1923-59; rent ledger 1929-59; wages books 1897-1960

14 SOUTHSEA CLARENCE ESPLANADE PIER CO LTD

14 Aug 1860
01955
Clarence Esplanade, Southsea, Hampshire
Pier

History: formed in 1858 to construct and manage a pier at Southsea, Hampshire. Incorporated as above in 1860. Pier was operated as a place of entertainment as well as for embarkation and disembarkation of passengers. Pier was extended in c1873.

Records: at Portsmouth City Records Office, 3 Museum Road, Portsmouth, Hampshire PO1 2LE
directors meeting minutes 1858-1955; account books 1938-54; cash book 1941-57; account statements 1943-4; pier, refreshment rooms and shop leases, agreements, licences and correspondence 1881,1900-59; general manager application correspondence 1909; pier: reconstruction specification 1951, account 1955, plans 1951-7, photograph c1880

15 TRUST & AGENCY CO OF AUSTRALASIA LTD

18 Nov 1860
02037
St Alphage House, 2 Fore Street, London EC2Y 5DH
Finance

History: founded and incorporated in 1860 as above by James Hora, who became its first manager, to give loans secured by mortgages in Australia. First London offices were at St Swithin's Lane, moving to 147 Cannon Street in 1881 and to Winchester House, Old Broad Street in 1938. By 1887 had established branches in New Zealand and in Argentina after 1908. The last Argentinian branch was closed in 1966. In about 1960 all the company's properties were disposed of and it began operating as a financial trust. Set up a subsidiary, Tragen Investment Co Ltd, in 1962. Since 1929 had been managed by Touche Ross & Co, accountants, and in 1974 became a subsidiary of Touche Remnant & Co, the management company of the former. Acquired by Reardon Smith Line Ltd in 1978.

Records: at Australian National University, PO Box 4, Canberra, ACT 2600, Australia
directors meeting minutes 1861-1967; general meeting: minutes 1861-1976, proceedings 1883-1941; members registers 1872-1913; share registers 1863-71; debenture: registers 1866-1918, trust deed 1904, and share holders address book c1880; misc corporate papers 1887-1961; annual reports and accounts 1861-1976; seal registers 1936-68; balance sheets and profit and loss accounts 1860-1961; ledgers 1866-1951; journals 1860-1904; London: journals 1904-51, cash books 1912-51; bank book 1860-1; investment book 1883-1920; office insurance policies 1955-63; misc correspondence 1922-66

16 BRIGHTON GRAND HOTEL CO LTD

13 Dec 1860
02073
Grand Metropolitan House, 7-8 Stratford Place, London W1N 0AJ
Hotel

History: incorporated as Brighton Hotel Co Ltd in 1860 and bought Battery House, Battery Place, Brighton, E Sussex in 1861. Built the 8 storied Grand Hotel in Kings Road to design of JH Whichord (1823-85). Name changed to above in 1884. During 1920s was acquired by Spiers & Pond Ltd, hoteliers and caterers, who were taken over in 1960 by Express Dairy Co Ltd which was acquired by Grand Metropolitan Ltd in 1969. Subsequently owned by De Vere Hotel & Restaurants PLC, which was acquired by Greenall Whitley & Co Ltd in 1984.

Records (1): at Express Dairy, 430 Victoria Road, South Ruislip, Greater London HA4 0HF
share ledgers 1942-60; directors registers 1948-70; seals register 1947-71; annual reports and accounts 1965-71; annual accounts 1964-7; staff discount and management papers 1967-8

Records (2): at Brighton Library, Church Street, Brighton, E Sussex BN1
Mr Quiddingtons testimonial with related correspondence 1874-1940

17 BURY BREWERY CO LTD

23 Jan 1861
02119
Star Brewery, Blackburn, Lancashire BB1 5BU
Brewing

History: incorporated as above in 1861 to purchase business of Edward and Robert Edmundson, brewers of George Street, Bury, Greater Manchester. Acquired in 1949 by Daniel Thwaites & Co Ltd, brewers of Blackburn, Lancashire. Ceased to brew prior to 1960.

Records: at Daniel Thwaites, Star Brewery, Blackburn, Lancashire BB1 5BU
correspondence 1928

18 WHITBREAD INTERNATIONAL LTD

23 Jan 1861
02120
Chiswell Street, London EC1Y 4SD
Brewing

History: incorporated in 1861 as Bury Co-operative Brewing & Distilling Co Ltd. Changed name to Crown Brewing Co Ltd in 1866. Brewery was situated in Rochdale Road, Bury, Greater Manchester. Acquired brewing business of Richard Rushton based at Nelson Brewery, Bolton Street, Bury in 1895. Company controlled 127 tied public houses by 1959 when it was acquired by Dutton's Blackburn Brewery Ltd which was itself acquired by Whitbread & Co Ltd in 1964. Subsequently changed name to above.

Records: at Whitbread, High Street, Blackburn, Lancashire BB1 1HG
directors meeting: minutes 1921-65, agenda 1936-64; members register 1950-9; memo and articles of association 1959

19 SOUTHAMPTON, ISLE OF WIGHT & SOUTH OF ENGLAND ROYAL MAIL STEAM PACKET CO LTD

10 Sep 1861
02404
12 Bugle Street, Southampton, Hampshire SO9 4LJ
Shipping

History: incorporated in 1861 as above by the amalgamation of the Isle of Wight Steam Packet Co and the Isle of Wight Royal Mail Steam Co. In 1865 acquired the Southampton, Isle of Wight & Portsmouth Steam Boat Co Ltd, in 1884 the Southampton New Steam Towing Co Ltd, and in 1908 the Bournemouth & South Coast Steam Packet Co Ltd. In 1947 the company took over Cosens & Co Ltd, marine and general engineers and operators of the Buff Funnel pleasure steamers. Excursions, especially between Southampton and the Isle of Wight, have formed the mainstay of the company's passenger services. Has also provided towing services in the port of Southampton.

Records: at Southampton, Isle of Wight & South of England Royal Mail Steam Packet, 12 Bugle Street, Southampton, Hampshire SO9 4LJ
directors minutes 1861-1980; general meeting minutes 1862-1980; shareholders meeting agendas 1864-1962; attendance registers 1952-60s; share allotment 1940s; share transfer ledger c1930s; register of transfers 1915-date; dividend register 1929-70s; ordinary, debentures and preference share certificates 1915-date; memo and articles of association 1861-date; annual reports and accounts 1862-1980; abstracts, statistics etc c1867-90; bought ledger 1949-50s; sales day books 1960s-80s; cash books 1970s; plant ledger 1886-1940; shipping register c1910-date; ship working sheets and managers wage bills 1898-date; ship and tug day books 1939-45; photographs, transparencies, postcards and newscuttings of ships, tugs, launchings, crew, passengers, directors etc c1880s-1970s; printed timetables, fare lists, posters, bills etc 1898-1950s; newscuttings re excursions, fares, services and the company 1900s-80s; illustrated brochure and handbooks, 1928-52; 35mm film of paddle steamer excursions c1930s
Southampton Steam Towing Co Ltd: deed of settlement 1853; registration certificates 1853-6

GW O'Connor, *The First Hundred Years, 1861-1961* (priv pub 1961)

20 HONG KONG & CHINA GAS CO LTD

3 Jun 1862
02714
90 Calverley Road, Tunbridge Wells, Kent TN1 2UN
Gas

History: incorporated as above in 1862 to manufacture and sell gas in Victoria, Hong Kong and in cities in China. First gas works was built at West Point, Hong Kong Island, with British plant. Streets first lit on 3 Dec 1864 by 500 public lamps supplied with gas by 15 miles of pipe. Second gas works opened in Jordan Road, Kowloon, to serve mainland Hong Kong in 1887 and third in Ma Tau Kok district, Kowloon in 1933. New works built on latter site from 1953-6, causing closure of former. Control passed to local interests in 1955 although retained UK registration. New plant was installed at Ma Tau Kok and West Point Works closed in 1960, submarine gas mains having supplied Hong Kong Island from Dec 1958. Additional oil gas plant erected in 1963. In 1865 sold 9 million cubic feet of gas; in 1884 32 million; 1920 154 million; 1939 177 million; 1961 845 million; and 1976 4 billion cubic feet. In 1981 the staff of over 800 operated distribution network of over 400 miles covering Hong Kong Island and Kowloon, and reaching Tsuen Wan and Shatin in New Territories. Gas no longer used to light streets, homes and offices, but for heating, hot water and cooking.

Records (1): at Hong Kong & China Gas, 24th Floor, Leighton Centre, 77 Leighton Road, GPO Box 134, Hong Kong
directors minutes 1862-date; local Hong Kong committee meeting: minutes 1929-38, agendas 1938-41; signed memo and articles of association 1862; agreements and correspondence re supply of gas, flat purchase, business regulations, labour relations, provident scheme 1861-1975; annual reports and accounts and newscuttings re agm proceedings 1920-42

Records (2): at CBJ Securities, 90 Calverley Road, Tunbridge Wells, Kent TN1 2UN
memo and articles of association 1862; corporate documents 1862,1898

21 UNION BANK OF MANCHESTER LTD

9 Jul 1862
02755
54 Lombard Street, London EC3P 3AH
Banking

History: founded as a joint stock bank in 1836, business starting at 65 King Street, Manchester, moving to Brown Street on 1 Aug, and to York Street in 1846. Opened branches at Knutsford, Cheshire, in 1856 and Northwich, Cheshire, and Salford, Greater Manchester, in 1862, total reaching 15 by 1873 and 160 by 1926. Registered with limited liability in 1862. Acquired business of J Sewell & Nephew (est 1841) of Manchester in 1888; EW Yates & Co, Liverpool, in 1904; Blackburn Bank Ltd in 1906; Downes & Co of Nantwich and Audlem, Cheshire, in 1907; Halifax & District Permanent Banking Co Ltd (est 1829) with branches at Halifax, Bradford, Huddersfield and Sheffield, W&S Yorkshire, in 1917; and East Morley & Bradford Deposit Bank Ltd (est 1870) in 1918. Share capital was acquired by Barclays Bank Ltd (est prior to 1694) in 1919 and bank was completely merged with same in 1940.

Records: at Barclays Bank, 54 Lombard Street, London EC3P 3AH
board meeting minutes 1836-1935; committee meeting minutes: directors 1914-21, consultative 1908-14; agm minutes 1837-1907; shareholders: register 1918-19, journal 1835-56; dividend register 1837-59; corporate papers and correspondence re formation 1836, and Barclays Bank 1919-39; annual reports and accounts 1864-1939; profit and loss accounts and balance sheets 1913-39; premises ledgers 1908-44; bad debt memoranda 1840s; bad and doubtful debts ledgers 1830s; bill drawers register 1850s; signature book 1917-25; clerkship applications 1836-41; secrecy declarations 1936 on; premises papers 1846; misc correspondence 1864-7; circulars 1897-1904; branch profit and loss account book nd; branches - Accrington: balance sheet and memoranda book 1884 on, signature books 1873-1935, probate register 1897-1916, diary note book 1902 on; Southport: head office circulars nd

George Chandler, *Four Centuries of Banking* Vol 2 (1968)

22 LOWER NORWOOD CO-OPERATIVE BUILDING CO LTD

8 Aug 1862
02793
46 Knights Hill, West Norwood, London SE27
Property

History: incorporated in 1862 to purchase land and buildings in and near Lower Norwood, London and to erect or adapt buildings for the working classes, to be let or sold to shareholders or others. Directors set up South London Co-operative Building Co Ltd in 1866 and both companies were run together from registered offices in the Lower Norwood Institute. Montague Long was secretary and manager of both companies from about 1890 until his death in 1940.

Records: at Lambeth Archives Department, Minet Library, 52 Knatchbull Road, London SE5 9QY
rent books 1889-1910; Montague Long: repairs book 1904-20, letter books 1910-26, land valuation returns notebook 1909, obituary 1909

23 BATH THEATRE ROYAL CO LTD

27 Aug 1862
02814
5 Queen's Street, London EC4N 1SU
Theatre

History: John Palmer, a wealthy brewer and tallow chandler of Bath, Avon, took over the project of building a theatre in Orchard Street on the death of John Hippisley who also ran Bristol Theatre. The theatre opened in 1750. In 1786 became first provincial 'Theatre Royal' but due to its small size a new building was designed by George Dance the younger and John Palmer, and financed by subscriptions headed by the Prince of Wales and Duke of York. Built on a site adjoining Beaufort Square, the theatre opened in 1805 and was destroyed by fire in 1862. A new theatre was built within a year, designed by CJ Phipps. Bath Theatre Royal Co Ltd was incorporated in order to raise the capital. The theatre was then leased to various individuals until in 1979 it was purchased from Triumph Theatre Productions by a trust headed by Jeremy Fry. In 1981 the theatre was registered as a charity and run as a non-profit making concern, 423 public performances being seen by more than 200,000 patrons in the 1980-1 season. The company was a subsidiary of Triumph Theatre Productions in 1981.

Records (1): at Theatre Royal Bath, Theatre Royal, Sawclose, Bath, Avon BA1 1ET
minutes 1904-73; directors holdings register 1948-54; tontine scheme: proposals 1804, trustees minutes 1838-43, subscribers lists, circulars and correspondence 1807-47, legal documents and correspondence 1833-58; legal documents and correspondence re trustee disputes 1833-63; theatre trustees: correspondence 1834,1861, solicitors accounts 1833-63, vouchers 1832-66; balance sheets and accounts 1940-67; ledgers 1862-3,1971-2; cash books 1895-1973; seasonal accounts 1842-62; day book 1940-67; weekly receipts and expenses books 1969-73; tontine annuitants account statements 1833-60; cancelled payments list 1833-53; financial correspondence 1839-42; correspondence and documents re royal patent and licence 1804-1902; legal documents re rates appeal 1833,1845; leasing documents, papers, accounts and correspondence 1831-62; theatre valuation 1843; maintenance papers, repair estimates, receipts and accounts 1830-62; correspondence and accounts re fire 1862-3; papers, documents and correspondence re Palmer family and Bath Theatre 1804-49, inventories of new wardrobe, scenery, stage props and manuscripts 1837-9; music index nd; wages books 1838-9; pantomime artistes salary book 1967-73; theatre acts 1843,1860
Bristol Theatre Royal: legal charges 1831-2; rates receipts 1832-5; accounts 1831-5; rent correspondence 1833
Theatre Royal, Drury Lane, London: letting conditions c1840; copy lease 1819
Manchester Theatre Royal: letting conditions 1833

Records (2): with Charles Clarke, Gatcombe Court, Nr Flax Bourton, Bristol, Avon BS19 1PX
directors minutes 1973-6; correspondence, legal and administrative documents, financial papers and accounts, press cuttings etc re buying and selling of theatre 1973-5; correspondence re and plans, cost and photographs of renovation of same 1973-5; financial papers and profit and loss figures 1973-5; correspondence and papers re bookings, programmes, critics reaction etc 1973-5; correspondence and papers re staff 1974-5; correspondence, papers and press cutting re opening of theatre by Duke of Gloucester 1974

Records (3): at Bath Reference Library, 18 Queen Square, Bath, Avon
enabling act to licence playhouse in Bath 1768; Orchard Street theatre log book 1770-7; boxkeepers book 1774-5; playbills, posters, broadsides, programmes and newscuttings 1815-date; papers of William Abbott, Bath actor 1843; inventory of stage props 1828; articles on theatre and theatrical performances 1865-1971; programmes and papers re presentation to theatre manager 1887

24 PEN-YR-ORSEDD SLATE QUARRY CO LTD

19 Sep 1862
02843
Richmond House, 1 Rumford Place, Liverpool, Merseyside L3 9QS
Slate quarry proprietors and operators

History: incorporated as above in 1862 to operate the Pen-yr-orsedd quarries, Nantlle, Caernarfon, Gwynedd which were opened c1816. The quarry was acquired by WA Darbishire & Co in 1863, with an authorised capital of £20,000, and was one of the 5 largest slate quarries in Caernarfonshire. Company went into voluntary liquidation in 1978, the quarry being sold to the Gloddfa Ganol Slate Quarry Co of Blaenau Ffestiniog, Gwynedd. Still operated in 1983 but at a much reduced level.

Records: at Gwynedd Archives Service, Caernarfon Area Record Office, County Offices, Shire Hall Street, Caernarfon, Gwynedd LL55 1SH
minute books 1862-1976; reports 1867,1912-62; share register 1862-1977; share: capital and summaries 1877-1978, certificates 1863-1977, transfer register 1863-1975; dividend warrants 1901-63; articles of association and association papers 1862-1937; medal certificates 1875-89; leases, tenancy agreements, etc 1862-1968; account statements 1907-70; account book 1952-6; farms and cottages rent books 1936-79; valuation 1907; insurance policies 1920-63; ledgers 1903-59; journals 1924-56; cash books 1889-1965; balance sheets 1868-1961; production records 1921-67; stock books 1927-61; cost books 1924-59; sales records 1924-78; cargo books 1929-68; time and wages books 1926-71; pay sheets analysis 1912-13,1931-64; accident books 1897-1964; compensation books 1930-58; rainfall charts 1931-66; quarry medical club records 1931-48; quarry union: works committee minutes 1945-62, collection books 1937-65; letter books 1880-1910; correspondence 1862-1971; plans 1862-1973; photographs 1905-34

25 BANK OF LONDON & SOUTH AMERICA LTD

27 Sep 1862
02854
40-66 Queen Victoria Street, London EC4P 4EL
Banking

History: founded and registered in 1862 as London, Buenos Aires & River Plate Bank Ltd to provide banking facilities in River Plate region of South America. Opened for business in Jan 1863, name changed to London & River Plate Bank Ltd in 1865, by 1866 had opened 3 branches in Argentina and Uruguay, and by 1907 had branches in Brazil, Chile, Paris and New York. Acquired London & Brazilian Bank Ltd (est 1862) and changed name to above in 1923, by which time it also had branches in Colombia and Paraguay. Acquired business, except nitrate assets, of Anglo-South American Bank Ltd (est 1888) in 1936. By 1951 had 66 branches and in 1970 acquired Bank of London & Montreal Ltd (est 1958). Acquired by Lloyds Bank International Ltd in May 1971.

Records (1): at Lloyds Bank International, 40-66 Queen Victoria Street, London EC4P 4EL
board: minutes 1862-date, agendas and papers 1926-71; daily committee minutes 1890-9; agm: minutes 1882-date, reports 1882-1925; directors shareholdings register 1890s; annual reports 1863-date; balance sheets: detailed 1863-1907, amalgamated 1923-31; profit and loss accounts: detailed 1863-1907, analysis 1921-36; profit and loss ledgers: head office 1923-31, amalgamated 1923-53; general ledgers 1860s,1938-58; private ledger 1924-53; journal 1862; head office statistics 1926-48; correspondence 1865-7,1870-3; head office circulars 1936-65; branch: profit and loss statements 1896-1925, summary profit and loss accounts 1921-36, comparative statements 1930-60, capital and loan ledgers 1923-59, inspection reports 1886-1920, results letters 1934-54, control letters 1935-45

Records (2): at Lloyds Bank, 71 Lombard Street, London EC3P 3BS
amalgamation papers 1908-23

Records (3): at University College Library, Gower Street, London WC1E 6BT
ledgers and journals 1888-1945; secretarys letters 1863-1923; branch letter books 1863-1950

David Joslin, *A Century of Banking in Latin America* (1963)

26 STANDARD BANK LTD

15 Oct 1862
02877
10 Clements Lane, London EC4N 7AB
Banking

History: registered as Standard Bank of British South Africa Ltd in 1862 in London by group of businessmen to promote trade and development in Africa. First branch opened in Port Elizabeth in 1863 and by end of 1864 had 15 offices and had absorbed 5 other South African banks: Commercial Bank of Port Elizabeth (est 1853), Colesberg Bank (est 1861), British Kaffrarian Bank (est 1857), Fauresmith Bank (est 1863) and Beaufort West Bank (est 1854). Also absorbed Fort Beaufort & Victoria Bank (est 1860) in 1873; Albert Bank, Burgersdorp (est 1861) in 1874; Swellendam Bank (est 1852) and London & South African Bank (est 1860) in 1877; Caledon Agricultural Bank (est 1861) and Malmesbury Agricultural & Commercial Bank (est 1862) in 1878; and Wellington Bank (est 1850) in 1890. As operated outside British jurisdiction, in 1883 'British' was removed from title. Expanded into Zimbabwe in 1892, Malawi in 1901, Zambia in 1906, Kenya in 1911, and Uganda in 1912, and opened branches in Hamburg, West Germany in 1904 and New York, USA in 1905. In 1920 acquired African Banking Corporation Ltd (est 1891) which had absorbed in 1891-2 Western Province Bank (est 1847), Kaffrarian Colonial Bank (est 1862) and Worcester Commercial Bank (est 1850). Between the WWs strove to maintain and consolidate positions especially during depression of 1930s but after 1945 expanded rapidly. Name shortened to above in 1962 and its business in the Republic of South Africa and in South West Africa was transferred to a subsidiary, Standard Bank of South Africa Ltd. In 1965 acquired Bank of West Africa Ltd, founded in London in 1894, bringing over 60 branches in Nigeria, nearly 30 in Ghana and others in Sierra Leone and The Gambia. Negotiations for a merger with Chartered Bank, incorporated by Royal Charter in 1853 as Chartered Bank of India, Australia & China, led in 1969 to the incorporation of Standard & Chartered Banking Group Ltd (renamed Standard Chartered Bank Ltd in Oct 1975) which acquired the two banks in Feb 1970. In 1975 all branches of both banks in the UK became branches of parent company. Outside Europe and North America they operate under own separate name. In 1979 had 35 branches, sub-branches and agencies in Kenya, 16 in Lesotho and 1 in Seychelles, and in the rest of Africa most offices were branches of subsidiary or associated banks incorporated in country of operation.

Records: at Standard Chartered Bank, 10 Clements Lane, London EC4N 7AB include:
board: and committee minutes and papers 1862-1959; annual reports 1863-date; current account ledgers 1875-1927; abstracts of weekly balances 1893-1960; general managers' correspondence 1898-1959; branch inspection reports 1897

JA Henry, *The First Hundred Years of the Standard Bank* (1963)

27 GAS METER CO LTD

24 Oct 1862
02902
Thorn House, Upper St Martin's Lane, London WC2H 9ED
Gas engineers

History: incorporated as above in 1862 to purchase the gas meter manufactory, plant, business and contracts of Croll, Rait & Co of Kingsland, London, and to manufacture gas meters etc. Offices remained in Kingsland Road, London. Purchased in 1920 by Parkinson & WB Cowan Ltd, gas engineers and meter manufacturers of Birmingham (est 1816). Parkinson Cowan Ltd was purchased by Thorn Electrical Industries Ltd in 1972, Gas Meter Co Ltd having ceased to trade many years previously.

Records: at Thorn EMI, Thorn House, Upper St Martin's Lane, London WC2H 9ED
share ledgers 1880-1963; shareholders lists 1926-32; memo and articles of association 1866; private ledger 1867-71

28 MARINE & GENERAL MUTUAL LIFE ASSURANCE SOCIETY

25 Oct 1862
00006C
MGM House, Heene Road, Worthing, W Sussex BN11 2DY
Life assurance

History: established in London in 1852 as Marine Life & Casualty Mutual Assurance Society to offer life assurance to mariners and marine passengers. The first directors included Samuel Cunard, founder of the Cunard shipping line, 3 directors of the P&O shipping line and other prominent shipowners. Until the 1880s most of its policy holders were employees of the P&O or Royal Mail Steam Packet Co. Changed name to above in 1862 and under chairmanship of Sir Thomas Sutherland (also chairman of P&O) between 1886-1912 entered the general life assurance market. Acquired Briton Life Association Ltd (est 1875) in 1886. Premium income rose from £40,000 in mid 1880s to nearly £150,000 by 1900 and to over £500,000 by 1919 when assurance fund totalled £2.2 million. Between the WWs the shipping industry connection declined in importance. By 1952 most shipping companies operated their own pension and insurance schemes and the society's assurance fund of nearly £5 million was developed for general life assurance. By 1981 the society's funds had reached £138 million and the society operated through 20 branches. Original head offices were at 137 Leadenhall Street moving to 60 Fenchurch Street in 1854, to 14 Leadenhall Street in 1863, to 48 Fenchurch Street (all London EC3) in 1924 and to Worthing, W Sussex in 1974.

Records: at Marine & General Mutual Life Assurance Society, MGM House, Heene Road, Worthing, W Sussex BN11 2DY
board meeting: minutes 1852-date, agendas 1852-4; finance committee minutes 1857-60; general meeting minutes 1852-date; settlement deeds 1852,1887; takeover correspondence 1948-57; secretarys letter book 1852-5; scaling books 1875-1959; general ledgers 1852-69,1941 on; journals 1852-67,1941 on; district returns 1938-57; bonus account 1859,1864; new policies account: 1870-1950, ledger 1926-36, journals 1937 on; annuities reassurance journals 1895-1955; bonus surrenders journal 1870 on; death claims journals 1895-1955; office expenses cash book 1856-65; petty cash book 1852-8; premium receipts 1955-62; policies: registers 1852 on,

assignment, endorsement and probate registers 1852-1951, superannuation 1852 on, death claims 1853-94, maturity 1910-55, lapsed and surrendered 1905-48, reassurance 1926-c57, proposal schedules 1947 on; annuities surrender values 1905 on; bonus surrenders 1885-1952; annuity and mortality experience working papers c1924-48; actuarial rate memoranda 1950; investments and loan ledger 1865-70; loan and mortgage register 1854-1946; staff pensions and overtime books 1924-52; salaries: branch offices 1930-52, head office 1911-55
Briton Life Association Ltd: board minutes 1882-7; policies: registers 1875 on, prospectus 1881; actuarial valuations 1899-1904

LH Humpherson, *The First Hundred Years of the Marine & General Life Assurance Society* (priv pub 1952)

29 AERATED BREAD CO LTD

28 Oct 1862
02907
17 Camden Road, London NW1 9LJ
Bakers and tea rooms

History: incorporated as above in 1862 as bakers, confectioners and light refreshment contractors. First bakery was situated in Islington, London until the turn of the century when it moved to Brewer Street, Soho, London. The Camden Road factory was built in 1930. By 1923 had 150 branch shops in London and at their zenith, 250 tearooms, which have all been sold. Allied Bakeries Ltd took over the company in 1955, becoming a subsidiary itself of Associated British Foods Ltd. Rationalization of the bakery shops was undertaken in 1976 leaving 50 'Bakers' Oven' hot bread shops in operation. The Camden factory in 1981 made savoury goods.

Records (1): at Aerated Bread, 17 Camden Road, London NW1 9LJ
directors reports and balance sheets 1863-1911; photographs of tea rooms and staff with notes on staff wages 1950s; *ABC Blue Pocket Guide to London* c1920s

Records (2): at Bedfordshire Record Office, County Hall, Bedford, Bedfordshire MK42 9AP
bread making machinery agreement 1894; plan of machinery 1886; letter re rent 1874; misc papers of Hayward Tyler re Aerated Bread companies 1865-1910

30 LONDON & SOUTH WESTERN BANK LTD

1 Nov 1862
02919
170 Fenchurch Street, London EC3P 3AT
Banking

History: founded and incorporated as above in 1862, business beginning in 1863. Head office was established at 27 Regent Street, London and by Dec 1863 had 12 provincial branches and agencies mainly in south west England. The rural branches at Bath, Avon; Chard and Crewkerne, Somerset; Helston, Penzance and Redruth, Cornwall; Plymouth, Devon; and Southampton, Hampshire were closed by 1873, 4 rural branches remaining at Bristol, Avon; and Honiton, Ottery St Mary and Sidmouth, Devon. To compensate, branches were established in the immediate suburbs of London. Head office in London was transferred to 29 Lombard Street in 1865, to 7 Fenchurch Street in 1871 and 170 Fenchurch Street in 1888, being rebuilt and extended into Gracechurch Street in 1912. Branches numbered 25 in 1873, 48 in 1883, 98 in 1893, 144 in 1903, 199 in 1913, and 204 in 1917. Amalgamated with old rivals London & Provincial Bank Ltd (est 1864) in 1917 to form London Provincial & South Western Bank Ltd, which itself amalgamated with Barclays Bank Ltd (est prior to 1694) in 1918.

Records: at Barclays Bank, 54 Lombard Street, London EC3P 3AH
board minutes 1862-1918; share registers 1862 on; dividend book 1864; issues registers 1897-1912; seal registers 1863-1903; articles of association 1862-1912; annual reports 1897,1899; staff: rules, regulations and agreements 1898-1901, report book 1899-1933; clerks instructions 1909; salaries graduation regulations 1911; head office circulars 1890-1918; inspectors branch report book 1892-1912; branches - Barnes: bills register 1890-1912; Bow: minutes 1872-1908; Brentford: authorities 1888-1907; Camberwell: impersonal ledger 1873 on; Charlton: profit and loss statements 1911-17; Chelsea: minutes 1887-1920, loan ledger 1894-1932; Crofton Park: head office instruction book 1909, property valuation book 1914-36; Dulwich: minutes 1891-1937; Ealing Broadway: general order books 1879-93; East Finchley: minutes 1892 on; East Sheen: staff book 1899 on; Finchley: order book 1885-1900; Forest Hill: quarterly returns 1883; Highgate: staff report book 1899 on; Holland Park: bad debts written off book 1884 on, staff record book 1899 on; Ilford: general order book 1898 on; Lavender Hill: minutes 1895 on; Lewisham Way: staff report book 1898-1949; Merton: staff report book 1898 on; Mile End: inspection reports 1894-1910; New Southgate: confidential letters 1890; Poplar: authorities book 1883-1920; South Ealing: managers private letter book 1912; Southend on Sea: loan increases 1910-14, correspondence 1909; Streatham Common: staff book 1899 on; Tooting Broadway: managers minutes 1879 on; Tulse Hill: minutes 1892 on; Upper Norwood: minutes 1865-1910s; Vauxhall: fittings inventory 1896; Wandsworth: minutes 1865 on; West Norwood: general order books 1882-97; West Streatham: minutes 1908-50; Willesden Green: general order books 1891-1902

PW Matthews and AW Tuke *History of Barclays Bank Ltd* (1926)
A Short History of London & South Western Bank Ltd (priv pub 1913)

31 RAILWAY PASSENGERS ASSURANCE CO LTD

6 Nov 1862
00058C
1 St Helen's, Undershaft, London EC3P 3DQ
Insurance

History: promoted by HF Holt, solicitor, in order to insure rail travellers against accidents in response to alarm created by railway disasters in 1840s. Registered in 1849, and re-registered as above as a limited company in 1862. Obtained an act of parliament which exempted insurance payments from the assessment of damages against railway companies. Railway booking clerks sold insurance tickets: 1d for third class, 2d for second class and 3d for first class passengers, which gave accident benefits of £200, £500 and £1000 respectively. In 1852 and 1855 took powers to transact general accident business and in 1880 was amongst the first companies to offer employers' liability insurance. Premium income rose from £22,435 in 1858 to £243,000 in 1891. Offered guarantee insurance from 1897, burglary insurance from 1900, and sickness and accident cover from 1905. Remained a small and highly centralised office based at 64 Cornhill, London, with branches in W London from 1863-80 and appointing agents in Amsterdam, Netherlands in about 1890; Bombay, India in 1901; and South Africa and Canada in 1902. Acquired in 1910 by Edinburgh based North British & Mercantile Insurance Co Ltd which was taken over in 1959 by Commercial Union Assurance Co Ltd, but continued to operate under its own name and have its own management.

Records (1): at Commercial Union, 1 St Helen's, Undershaft, London EC3P 3DQ
board meeting minutes 1936-65; committee meeting minutes 1962-5; general meeting minutes 1849-1969; shareholders register 1907 on; members register 1962 on; share transfers 1906-53; monthly balances 1849-69; journal 1855-65; eastern counties agents diary and expenses 1849; chronological notes 1925; pensioners correspondence c1948; legal proceedings 1854; newscuttings 1850-62

Records (2): at Guildhall Library, Aldermanbury, London EC2P 2EJ
board minutes 1848-1935; general purposes and finance committee minutes 1909-31; settlement deed 1849

Records (3): at National Library of Scotland, Department of Manuscripts, George IV Bridge, Edinburgh, Lothian EH1 1EW
microfilm: board minutes 1936-56, general meeting minutes 1849-1956

Records (4): at Mitchell Library, Rare Books & Manuscripts Department, North Street, Glasgow, Strathclyde G3 7DN
share: ledger 1857, registers 1875-97; shareholding agreements 1886-1924; monthly balances 1869-80; general ledger 1944; financial working papers 1911-60

Edward Liveing, *A Century of Insurance: The Commercial Union Assurance Group 1861-1961* (1961)

32 KENTSTONE PROPERTIES LTD

27 Nov 1862
00086C
72 King Street, Maidstone, Kent
Property

History: incorporated as Maidstone Cottage Improvement Co Ltd to purchase and improve cottages for reletting to labourers. In 1875 owned 152 cottages, total increased to maximum of 575 in 1946. 170 cottages, including 3 original lots, were owned in 1980. Since 1955 the company has also owned commercial property in Kent and Surrey. Name was changed in 1973 to above. The company in 1980 had 3 subsidiaries, Hebros Holdings Ltd, Kentstone Finance Ltd, and Baynecrest Ltd, all investment companies.

Records (1): at Kentstone Properties, 72 King Street, Maidstone, Kent
minutes 1944-80; share correspondence and documents 1944-80

Records (2): with Company Chairman, 2 Bridge Street, Loose, Maidstone, Kent
memo and articles of association 1955; annual reports and balance sheets 1874-1980; property list 1956-80; photographs of properties 1969-78; typed history 1973; lead plaque nd

33 UNION MARINE & GENERAL INSURANCE CO LTD

15 Jan 1863
00182C
Phoenix House, 18 King William Street, London EC4P 4HR
Insurance

History: incorporated in 1863 as Union Marine Insurance Co Ltd on amalgamation of 2 Liverpool underwriting firms Charles Langton & Co and Rawson, Aitkin & Co. Opened London office in 1864 and made an agency agreement in 1865 with Ocean Marine Insurance Co Ltd of London (est 1859). Premium income by mid 1860s was over £200,000. Agencies were opened in Bombay and Calcutta, India and Hangzhou and Shanghai, China in 1868; Singapore; Java; Madras, India; and Colombo, Sri Lanka in 1871; Manila, Phillipines in 1872; San Francisco, USA in 1873; Montreal, Canada; and Bordeaux, France in 1875; Belfast in 1893; New York, USA (converted into a branch in 1904) in 1880; and Glasgow and Manchester in 1893. Acquired Rathbone, Martin & Co, a Liverpool underwriting firm in 1883 and International Marine Insurance Co Ltd (est 1879 in London) in 1893. Moved into 11 Dale Street, Liverpool in 1905. Acquired by Phoenix Assurance Co Ltd in 1911 but continued underwriting in its own name. Premium income exceeded £1 million by 1920 but dropped drastically in mid 1920s. Entered the fire and casualty insurance market in North America in 1931 and changed name to above. Premium income recovered to nearly £2 million by 1942 and in 1981 had reached £11 million.

Records (1): at Phoenix Assurance, Phoenix House, 18 King William Street, London EC4P 4HR
board meeting minutes: 1963-6, London 1864-84,1894-1903, Manchester 1898 on; committee meeting minutes: finance 1863-1958, joint 1893, special purposes 1864-1915, with agenda 1903-15, transfer 1863-93, underwriting 1863-1958; directors register 1901-22; seal books nd; general meeting: minutes 1893-1950, agenda 1893-1937, reports 1864-1908; share: agreements and certificates 1873-93, allotment books 1863,1911, ledgers 1863-93,1911-41; shareholders lists 1867-75,1912; members registers 1863-93; annual reports and accounts 1864-1920,1931-7; annual accounts 1918-65; agents instructions c1921; claims: journal 1894-1904, foreign register 1903-05; underwriting: managers reports 1911-16, journal 1865-79, note book 1872-5, risk books 1845-6,1863,1901; staff: applications 1895-1905, register 1864-1919

Records (2): at Merseyside County Archives, 64-66 Islington, Liverpool, Merseyside L3 8LG
correspondence, reports, accounts c1863-1940; claims correspondence c1940-68

Records (3): at National Maritime Museum, Romney Road, Greenwich, London SE10 9NF
account journals 1884-1917

George Hurren, *Phoenix Renascent, A History of the Phoenix Assurance Co Ltd 1782-1968* (1973)

34 METHODIST NEWSPAPER CO LTD

13 Mar 1863
00295C
122 Golden Lane, London EC1Y 0UL
Newspaper

History: incorporated as Wesleyan Methodist Newspaper Co Ltd in order to run the *Methodist Recorder*, a weekly penny Christian newspaper, first published on 4 Apr 1861. It also had a joint directorate with *The Watchman and Wesleyan Advertiser* from 1863-83 when the latter ceased publication. The shareholding is maintained at 50 per cent clerical and 50 per cent lay.

Records (1): at Methodist Newspaper, 176 Fleet Street, London EC4A 2EP
directors, general and sub-committee meeting minutes 1863-date; directors attendance book 1971-date; share ledger c1935-date; memo and articles of association 1910-70; annual reports and accounts 1967-73; profit and loss accounts 1953-6; publishing accounts 1950s-73; advertising accounts 1965-6; cash books 1950s-80; cash analysis 1965-8; petty cash books 1923-73; register of contributors c1954-65; printers contracts 1930s; *Methodist Recorder* 1861-date; *The Watchman and Wesleyan Advertiser* c1835-81; employment contracts 1970s-80; photographs of editors 1880s-1970s; list of itinerant Methodist preachers 1756-1857

Records (2): at British Library, Newspaper Library, Colindale Avenue, London NW9 5HE
Methodist Recorder 1861-date

35 LONDON & SUBURBAN LAND & BUILDING CO LTD

1 May 1863
00371C
11 Buckingham Street, London WC2N 6DF
Property

History: established as London & Suburban Freehold Land & Building Society in 1852 in order to enable its founders to obtain freehold votes. Incorporated as above in 1863 with its registered offices in the City of London. Has owned small amounts of property in London and its suburbs which have been rented out on long leases. Acquired in 1973 by Clarebrooke Holdings Ltd.

Records: at London & Suburban Land & Building, 11 Buckingham Street, London WC2N 6DF
directors minutes 1863-date; general minutes 1864-date; dividend book 1965-73; share documents 1927-61; probate register 1943-72; seals register 1925-51; general ledger 1951-date; nominal ledger 1954-date; journal 1940-73; cash book 1955-73; title deeds, tenancy agreements and correspondence re property in London and suburbs 1763-1961; property photographs 1960s-70s

36 PLYMOUTH HOTEL CO LTD

19 May 1863
00402C
Duke of Cornwall Hotel, Millbay Road, Plymouth, Devon PL1 3LG
Hotel

History: incorporated as above in 1863 by a group of local businessmen and the local railway company to build a hotel named the Duke of Cornwall Hotel, opposite Millbay railway station, Plymouth, Devon, to accommodate railway and steam liner travellers. Main part of building built in 1860s with extension added in 1930s. Remained open throughout WW2 and bought the Continental Hotel, Plymouth, in 1977.

Records: at Duke of Cornwall Hotel, Millbay Road, Plymouth, Devon PL1 3LG
board and committee meeting minutes 1863-1932; general meeting minutes 1863-97; share ledger c1920-50; share dividend book 1868-1947; share transfer register 1864-1940; bonds and mortgages register c1915-33; memo and articles of association 1863; revenue accounts 1885-95; trial balances 1901; grocers account book 1907-09; Duke of Cornwall Hotel catalogues 19 cent-c1930; correspondence re rebuilding bar, shareholders and directors dinner 1882-95

37 TORQUAY HOTEL CO LTD

3 Jul 1863
00512C
7 Hanover Square, London W1R 0PS
Hotel

History: incorporated as above in 1863 to supply Torquay, Devon with 'a first class modern hotel'. While this hotel, The Imperial in Parkhill Road, was being built (1864-6) the company ran the already established Royal Hotel, terminating the lease when the new hotel was completed. The freehold of The Imperial was purchased in 1887 and additional buildings were erected. In 1898 the adjoining Marina Hotel was acquired and a connecting wing built in 1922. The Imperial had 177 rooms plus conference, exhibition and sports facilities in 1982, when the company was a dormant subsidiary of Trusthouse Forte PLC.

Records: at Trusthouse Forte Hotels, St Martins House, 20 Queensmere, Slough, Berkshire SL1 1XY
directors and general meeting minutes with annual reports and accounts 1863-date; finance committee minutes 1863-97; share ledger 1863-1937; shares summary with report and accounts 1909-38; allotment book 1925

38 REIGATE INVESTMENT CO LTD

16 Jul 1863
00537C
43 Church Street, Reigate, Surrey
Property and investment

History: incorporated as above to complement work of Holmesdale Benefit Building Society by investing in stocks and shares in order to raise money to purchase land for property development in conjunction with the Reigate Stock, Share & Estates Co Ltd. Whole estates were developed in this way until 1910, after which only individual plots and property were laid out and sold. By 1980 the company acted only as a holding company for its remaining property investments.

Records: at Holmesdale Benefit Building Society, 43 Church Street, Reigate, Surrey
minutes 1863-date; shareholders register 1863-date; annual reports and accounts 1863-date; account ledgers 1863-date; list of properties 1920s on; estate plans 1860s-1910s

39 GREENCOAT PROPERTIES LTD

17 Jul 1863
00543C
7 Wolsey Road, East Molesey, Surrey KT8 9EL
Property

History: founded and incorporated in 1863 as Improved Industrial Dwellings Ltd to create dwellings for industrial workers in London. Name changed in 1958 to above. In 1975 had 18 wholly owned subsidiary property development and investment companies. In 1981 wholly involved in commercial property investment and development in UK with commercial and residential property in France.

Records: at Greencoat Properties, 7 Wolsey Road, East Molesey, Surrey KT8 9EL
directors register 1873-date; corporate documents 1863,1958; annual reports and accounts 1970s-date; private ledger 1880-1967; estates register incl dwelling plans etc 1870-95; land valuation register 1909; title deeds and mortgage agreements 1868-78

40 NORTHERN MARITIME INSURANCE CO LTD

17 Aug 1863
00599C
Phoenix House, 18 King William Street, London EC4P 4HR
Insurance

History: incorporated in 1863 as above by a group of Newcastle upon Tyne merchants, shipowners and bankers to undertake marine insurance. Acquired in 1887 the business of Newcastle Commercial Marine Insurance Co Ltd (est 1863). Offices were at Customs House Chambers, Quayside, Newcastle, Tyne & Wear, moving to King Street in 1877 and to Phoenix House, Queen Street in 1908. Acquired in 1917 by Union Marine & General Insurance Co Ltd (est 1863) which had been acquired by Phoenix Assurance Co Ltd in 1911. Company in 1936 had branch offices in London, Cardiff, Liverpool and Sydney, Australia.

Records: at Phoenix Assurance, Phoenix House, 18 King William Street, London EC4P 4HR
board meeting minutes 1863-1965; Union Marine shareholding agreement 1912; share: ledgers 1863-1918, certificate receipts 1887-1951; annual reports and accounts 1931-7; balance sheets 1864-79

George Hurren, *Phoenix Renascent, A History of the Phoenix Assurance Co Ltd 1782-1968* (1973)

41 SLALOM LAGER LTD

10 Sep 1863
00633C
Lion Brewery, Blackburn, Lancashire BBI 5NH
Hotel

History: incorporated in 1863 as Victoria Pier & Promenade Hotel Co (Southport) Ltd to purchase the Victoria Hotel, Southport, Merseyside and carry on the business of hotel and boarding house. The original subscribers all came from Manchester. By 1947 when it was purchased by Matthew Brown & Co Ltd, brewers of Blackburn, Lancashire, its name had changed to Victoria Hotel (Southport) Ltd. It was altered again in 1980 to above, Slalom Lager being produced by Matthew Brown at its Lion Brewery, Blackburn.

Records (1): at Matthew Brown, Lion Brewery, Blackburn, Lancashire BBI 5NH
directors meeting minutes 1916-30; memo and articles of association 1919

Records (2): at Merseyside County Archives, 64-66 Islington, Liverpool, Merseyside L3 8LG
annual reports and accounts 1869-1919

42 LONDON METROPOLE HOTEL LTD

20 Nov 1863
00785C
Edgware Road, London W2 1JU
Hotel

History: incorporated as Bedford Hotel Co Ltd in 1863 to run the Bedford Hotel, Kings Road, Brighton. The 110 bedroomed hotel, designed by Thomas Cooper, a Brighton architect, was opened in 1829 and rapidly became the most fashionable hotel in Brighton. Members of the British and foreign royal families and eminent British citizens, including Charles Dickens were frequent visitors. A fire destroyed the building in 1964, although a new 17 storey hotel and conference centre designed by Seifert & Partners has been built in its place. In 1961 the company's name was changed to South Coast Hotels Ltd and it was bought by AVP Industries Ltd. In 1972 the name was changed to Harbet Hotels Ltd and again in 1974 to above. The company is a subsidiary of Lonrho Ltd and manages the Birmingham Metropole and the Warwick Hotel at the National Exhibition Centre, Birmingham, and the London Metropole at Marble Arch, London. The Bedford Hotel is managed by Hotel Metropole (Brighton) Ltd which also runs the Brighton Metropole.

Records (1): at London Metropole Hotel, Company Secretary's Offices, Birmingham Metropole, National Exhibition Centre, Birmingham, W Midlands B40 1PP
directors and share registers 1948-80; annual returns 1930-80; share transfers 1949-80; corporate documents 1930-80

Records (2): at Hotel Metropole (Brighton), Financial Controllers Office, Brighton Metropole, Kings Road, Brighton, E Sussex BN1 2FU
fire plans for Bedford Hotel 1973

Records (3): at Brighton Library, Church Street, Brighton, E Sussex BN1
photographs of exterior of Bedford Hotel 1853-1970s

Records (4): at Bedford Hotel, Kings Road, Brighton, E Sussex BN1 2JF
letters from Charles Dickens to Joseph Ellis, proprietor of the hotel, 1852-7

43 ENGLISH REAL ESTATES LTD

29 Dec 1863
00865C
Cavenham House, Millington Road, Hayes, London UB3 4AY
Property

History: established in 1861 and incorporated in 1863 as London Labourers' Dwellings Society Ltd to improve dwellings for labouring classes in London. Built new properties from time to time but more frequently purchased existing buildings needing improvement. In 1931 owned 1538 tenements mainly in E&SE London. In 1956 had 2500 tenements in Stepney, Lambeth, Tottenham, East Ham, Willesden, Bermondsey, Finsbury, Walthamstow, Acton, Hackney, Deptford, Crayford and Mitcham. Acquired in 1957 by Alliance Property Co Ltd which was acquired in 1973 by Argyle Securities Holdings Ltd which in 1982 was a subsidiary of Generale Occidentale SA, France.

Records: none survive

44 STAVELEY INDUSTRIES LTD

29 Dec 1863
00866C
Portland House, Stag Place, London SW1 5BU
Holding (formerly iron and steel)

History: traces origins to Walter Mather who took a lease on a forge, furnace and iron works at Staveley, Derbyshire in 1783. He rebuilt the plant and output grew from an annual average of 418 tons of pig iron in 1785-8 to 776 tons in 1790s. Also produced castings such as hammers, anvils, mill parts, etc. Mather died in 1796 by which time the business was run by his two sons, but in early 1800s it was controlled by GH Barrow, the second husband of one of Mather's daughters-in-law. The business quickly diversified into coal mining, supplying much coal to the London market. In 1840 the business was transferred to Barrow's younger brother, Richard. The iron works were rebuilt in the 1840s and output rose from 5000 tons of castings in 1840 to 20,000 tons in 1864 while coal output increased from 50,000 tons to 700,000 tons. Pig iron output stabilised, advancing from 12,500 tons in 1845 to just 13,000 tons in 1865. In 1863 the business was converted into a joint stock company with a capital of £600,000 under the title of the Staveley Coal & Iron Co Ltd. HD Pochin, the Salford chemical manufacturer, and David Chadwick, the financial agent, were major shareholders, but Barrow retained 1250 of the 6000 shares. He died in 1865 and was succeeded as chairman by Pochin while Charles Markham, a railway manager, was recruited as managing director. In his years of management coal output rose from 800,000 tons in 1870 to 1 million in 1890 while in the same years castings increased from 30,000 to 60,000 tons. By 1876 Pochin could claim the castings business was probably the largest in the world. Markham was succeeded by his son, CP Markham, who was acting chairman from the early 1890s. Under his management coal output grew from 1 million tons in 1890 to 2 million tons in 1930, while castings output increased from 60,000 to 100,000 tons. The business had become specialists in the output of pipes and benefited from the surge in demand from the gas and water supply industries. In early 1900s heavy investment was made in coking and chemical plant to produce chemicals such as sulphuric acid, benzol, sulphate of ammonia, carbolic acid, etc. By 1918 profit contributions were coal and coke 59 per cent, chemicals 21 per cent, pig iron 12 per cent and foundries 8 per cent. The company stagnated in the 1920s and 1930s, suffering from the depression in the coal industry and the loss of a technological lead in pipe manufacture. The company's coal interests were nationalised in 1946 and the iron works were drawn into the public sector in 1951. Much of the compensation paid by the state was distributed to shareholders as a capital dividend while the remainder was used to acquire machine tool, general engineering and electrical products companies. The company was converted into a holding company and in 1961 renamed as above. In 1980 the group carried on the business of manufacturers of machine tools; producers of salt, lime, refined pig iron and foundry products; electrical contractors; and producers of industrial and commercial weighing equipment.

Records (1): at Staveley Industries, Portland House, Stag Place, London SW1 5BU
directors meeting minutes 1930-date; private minutes 1930-67; members register 1953-70; seal book 1949-71; annual returns 1948-58; annual report and accounts 1891-date; balance sheets 1924-39; consolidated accounts 1948-59

Records (2): at Derbyshire Record Office, County Offices, Matlock, Derbyshire DE4 3AG
trade catalogues nd

SD Chapman, *Stanton and Staveley. A Business History* (1981)

45 MARITIME INSURANCE CO LTD

8 Feb 1864
00950C
Surrey Street, Norwich, Norfolk NR1 3NG
Insurance

History: incorporated as above in 1864 to adopt the insurance underwriting business of Price & Case, Liverpool into a new marine insurance company. By 1890s was one of the leading hull underwriters in the UK. A controlling interest was acquired in 1914 by Scottish Union & National Insurance Co which was itself acquired in 1959 by Norwich Union Fire Insurance Society, a subsidiary of Norwich Union Life Insurance Society. Principal activity of the company in 1968 was the transaction of marine, aviation and transit insurance business.

Records: at Norwich Union Insurance Group, PO Box 4, Surrey Street, Norwich, Norfolk NR1 3NG
board, committee and general meeting minutes 1928-date; shareholders attendance register 1949-68; annual reports and accounts 1891-date

46 CITY OFFICES CO LTD

17 Mar 1864
01069C
Palmerston House, 51 Bishopsgate, London EC2N 3AS
Property

History: incorporated in 1864 to acquire property in the City of London in Cornhill, Clement's Lane, Leadenhall Street, Great Tower Street and Bishopsgate, and elsewhere in England and Wales. Company's main property holdings are still in the City of London although property is also owned throughout the UK. Palmerston Restaurant Ltd was purchased in 1949 and sold in 1966. Lombard Restaurant Ltd was purchased in 1960 and ceased trading in 1969.

Records (1): at City Offices, Baltic House, Leadenhall Street, London EC3
directors meeting minutes 1864-1947; agm reports: 1951-6; debenture minutes and agendas 1894-1947; members register 1925-7; director holdings register 1951-6; shares and stock register 1895-1929; shares and stock transfer register 1864-1947; share ledgers 1864-1920; share, share transfer and dividend certificates 1933-60; share record cards 1922-64; share

circulars 1955-63; register of probates 1925-40; annual returns 1940,1945; annual reports and accounts 1950-7; ledgers 1864-1958; journal 1902-52; cash book 1929-52; mortgage agreements, bonds and other legal property documents 1702-20 cent; rental charges 1926-31

Records (2): at City Offices, Palmerston House, 51 Bishopsgate, London EC2N 3AS
general meeting minutes 1864-1913; directors attendance register 1919-57; unclaimed dividends book 1898-1979; mortgage and bonds register 1891-1949; memo and articles of association 1864-1925; annual reports and accounts 1864-1925,1957-date; photographs of directors and chairmen 1889-1964

47 NORTH WESTERN BANK LTD

24 Mar 1864
01102C
Poultry, London EC2P 2BX
Banking

History: founded by John Moss, Liverpool merchant and shipowner, as private bank of Moss, Dales & Rogers, opening at end of 1807 in Exchange Buildings, Liverpool, and moving to newly built premises in Dale Street in 1811. By 1860s was known as Moss & Co and became a joint stock bank incorporated with limited liability in 1864 as above to obtain additional finances. From 1885-93 opened 8 branches, all within Liverpool. Amalgamated in 1897 with London & Midland Bank Ltd, renamed London City & Midland Bank Ltd in 1898, London Joint City & Midland Bank Ltd in 1918, and Midland Bank Ltd in 1923.

Records: at Midland Bank, Poultry, London EC2P 2BX
board meeting minutes 1866-97; shareholders meeting minutes 1866-97; share registers 1864-97; amalgamation papers 1897; prospectus and annual reports 1864-90; general ledger 1882-5; customer current account ledgers 1838-64; bad debt books 1865-94

WF Crick and JE Wadsworth, *A Hundred Years of Joint Stock Banking* (1936)

48 FORE STREET INVESTMENTS LTD

24 Mar 1864
01106C
31 Hammersmith Grove, London W6 7EN
Property (formerly warehousing)

History: incorporated in 1864 as Fore Street Warehouse Co Ltd to acquire the wholesale warehousing business of Morrison, Dillon & Co at Fore Street in the City of London. Its first directors were warehousemen, merchants and bankers. Gradually assumed the character of a property company and in the 1960s changed its name to above. In 1984 was a subsidiary of George Wimpey PLC, the construction and civil engineering company.

Records: at Wimpey Property Holdings, 31 Hammersmith Grove, London W6 7EN
board meeting: minutes 1937, agendas 1958-64, attendance book 1910-60; register: directors and managers 1920-72, mortgages 1964, shareholders 1925-58

49 BTR PROPERTY HOLDINGS LTD

31 Mar 1864
01122C
Silvertown House, Vincent Square, London SW1P 2PL
Property (formerly rubber and gutta percha product manufacturers)

History: established in Cornhill, London by 1798 as Arrowsmith & Silver, colonial merchants, army agents, clothiers and outfitters. During 1800s became Silver & Co and by 1823 was under the control of Stephen W Silver who expanded firm and set up a rubber waterproof clothing factory at Greenwich which transferred in 1852 to West Hane, later known as Silvertown. By 1862 firm manufactured misc India rubber and ebonite articles including insulated telegraph wire. Incorporated in 1864 as Silver's India Rubber Works & Telegraph Cable Co Ltd, name changing to India Rubber, Gutta Percha & Telegraph Works Co Ltd in 1864. Walter Hancock, founder of Gutta Percha Co and West Ham Gutta Percha Co became manager of the gutta percha department and his companies were purchased by the company in Dec 1864. A new gutta percha factory was subsequently built at Silvertown. Purchased Franco-American Co's factory at Persan-Beaumont for manufacture of India rubber and ebonite goods in 1864 (sold in 1934). From 1868 to 1918 submarine cable manufacture expanded, obtaining world wide contracts for cable and acquiring cable laying ships. Promoted Direct Spanish Telegraph Co Ltd in 1872, West Coast of America Telegraph Co Ltd in 1876 and South American Cable Co Ltd in 1891. By 1892 had branches in Liverpool; Glasgow; Bradford, W Yorkshire; Sheffield, S Yorkshire; Portsmouth, Hampshire; North Shields and Newcastle upon Tyne, Tyne & Wear; Belfast; Dublin; Newport and Cardiff, S Glamorgan; Birmingham; Coventry; and Manchester. Manufactured gutta percha golfballs from 1888 to 1953 and between 1889 and 1920 produced electrical plant for various UK towns. By 1890s was involved in pneumatic tyre production becoming manager of Palmer Tyre Ltd in 1895 and acquiring same in 1901. Began to manufacture motor and bicycle cord tyres at Persan in 1909. Promoted Jointless Rim Ltd in 1906 to manufacture jointless cycle rims from steel at Arrol Works, Birmingham (closed after WW1). By 1923 Silvertown works covered 16.5 acres and the company had branches in Australia, New Zealand, India, South Africa and Argentina, and offices in principal UK towns. In 1934 acquired by British Goodrich Rubber Co Ltd which was later acquired by BTR Ltd industrial rubber producers. Electric cable and wire manufacture ceased in 1937. Silvertown factory was severely damaged by enemy action in 1940 and a factory in Penfold Street, London was acquired to manufacture Palmer aircraft products. In 1941 acquired a controlling interest in Morgan Ebonite Co Ltd with a factory at Failsworth, Manchester and in 1945 acquired a factory at Chadwell Heath, Essex (sold 1952) for manufacture of ebonite pipe-stems and rubber gloves. In 1954 products included Silvertown PVC fire resistant belting for coal mines; escalator handrails; anti-static and decorative flooring; tobacco pipe-stems; gutta percha and ebonite; and Palmer aircraft brakes and controls, tyres and wheels. Name changed to Silvertown Rubber Co Ltd in 1955. Silvertown factory was sold in 1965 and the company became a holding company for BTR Property, changing its name to above in 1972.

Records: at Greater London Record Office, 40 Northampton Road, London EC1R 0HB
meeting minutes: board 1864-1937, directors private 1868-71, general 1864-1918, shareholders committee 1875, debenture trustee 1887-97,1901-02, finance and executive committee 1864-6; share ledgers c1917-38; balance sheets and accounts 1920-36; ledgers: 1931-4, private 1934-61;

journals: 1939-42, private 1934-60; cash book: private 1926-62, petty 1933-8; cheque account books 1933-8; bills receivable books 1935-64; nominal accounts: Calcutta 1889-1954, Christchurch 1920-44; Durban private ledger 1900-22
Jointless Rim Ltd: private ledger 1906-61; cash book 1906-60
Palmer Tyre Ltd: private ledgers 1899-1960; journal 1909-61; cash books: 1958-65, private 1899-1957

50 JOHN BROWN & CO LTD

1 Apr 1864
01125C
8 The Sanctuary, London SW1P 3JU
Steel, coal, shipbuilding and machine tool manufacturers

History: John Brown trained as a merchant in Sheffield and in 1836 took over the factoring side of Earle Horton, merchants there. In the late 1830s he opened a steel works in Orchard Street and in the early 1840s moved to larger premises in Furnival Street, named the Atlas Steel Works. In 1848 he invented the conical spring buffer which rapidly came to dominate the railway market. In 1854 he purchased the Queen's Works in Salville Street and built a new Atlas works on the site, which opened in 1856. During 1859 Brown and his partner JD Ellis abandoned the manufacture of puddled steel in favour of the newly developed Bessemer steel. This decision yielded enormous orders for rails from all over the world. At the same time Brown experimented with the production of armour plate and by 1867 it was reputed that three quarters of the iron clads of the British Navy were armoured by the firm. The concern was incorporated as John Brown & Co Ltd in 1864 with a capital of £1 million. Amongst the promoters, were ELS Benzon, also associated with Vickers, and HD Pochin of Manchester, a company promoter who had interests in Palmers Shipbuilding & Iron Co, Sheepbridge Coal & Iron Co, Tredegar Iron & Coal Co, Bolckow Vaughan & Co, and Staveley Coal & Iron Co. The first years of the company were uncertain, but revived during the 1870s. The company purchased Aldwark Main and Car House Collieries at Rotherham and took a joint share with Bolckow Vaughan in Spain. In 1886 a large forging press was installed for manufacturing armour plate, guns and marine shafting and in 1890 they sunk the Rotherham Main pit. In 1899 the company acquired the shipyard and marine engine works of J&G Thomson Ltd of Clydebank, Strathclyde, renamed John Brown Shipbuilding & Engineering Co Ltd, to provide an outlet for heavy forgings. In 1902 the company amalgamated with Thomas Firth & Sons Ltd, also steel makers in Sheffield, and in 1907 reached a similar understanding with the Belfast Shipbuilders, Harland & Wolff. During 1905-06 the company joined with Cammell Laird of Liverpool and Fairfield Shipbuilding & Engineering Co to form the Coventry Ordnance Works to share Admiralty contracts and to manufacture naval gun mountings with works in Coventry and Scotstoun, Glasgow. During WW1 the company expanded rapidly to meet demand for munitions and acquired the control of Canforth Iron Co in 1917, jointly with Darlington Forge Co. Control of Harland & Wolff was lost to the Royal Mail Group. In 1919 took over Cravens Railway Carriage & Wagon Co and merged Coventry Ordnance Works with Dick Kerr & Co of Preston, Willans & Robinson of Rugby, and Siemens Brothers & Co to form English Electric Co. The company suffered badly in the post war depression and in the 1925-26 coal strike. The company's capital was reconstructed in 1930 and its steel interest transferred to Thomas Firth & Sons Ltd which was renamed Thomas Firth & John Brown Ltd after WW2. In 1934 the company joined with the newly formed English Steel Corporation to establish Firth - Vickers Stainless Steels Ltd, and in 1937 with Associated Electrical Industries Ltd took a large interest in Westland Aircraft Ltd of Yeovil, Somerset. In 1937 the company purchased Markham & Co Ltd, general engineeers of Chesterfield from Staveley Coal & Iron Co. During WW2 the company again expanded rapidly to meet demand for munitions. Its coal and steel interest were nationalized after the war. When the steel industry was denationalized the company decided not to buy back Thomas Firth & John Brown Ltd, which continued as a separate concern. In 1966 its shipyard at Clydebank was sold to Upper Clyde Shipbuilders Ltd; but the company retained control of the engine works, renamed John Brown Engineering Ltd. The company diversified into oil installations, precision and chemical engineering, and the manufacture of gas turbines.

Records (1): at John Brown, 8 the Sanctuary, London SW1P 3JU
directors meeting minutes 1864-1962; debenture holders meeting minutes 1924-51; general ledgers 1891-1950; loan and mortgage ledger 1921-c44; Clydebank property ledger nd; private journal 1947-50; cash book 1947-51; bank balance books 1922-41; Atlas Works and Swinton deed book nd; staff pension premiums book 1931-40
Tredegar Iron & Coal Co Ltd: directors meeting minutes 1873-84

Records (2): at Thos Firth & John Brown, Smithfield House, Sheffield, S Yorkshire S1 2AS
annual reports and accounts 1898-1902; nominal ledger 1894-c1923; property ledger 1902-25; Clydebank: summary ledgers 1899-1937, journal 1899-1937; journals 1890-1935; production figures 1885-92; works committee meeting minutes 1919-23; Atlas Works: title deeds 1950s on, plans 1864-9; Sheffield and Swinton premises agreements and documents 1867-90s; Nunnery Colliery plans reports, legal opinions and correspondence 1924-44; chairman and managing director letter books 1892-9; ship damage claim correspondence 1921; ships, Clydebank, Atlas and Southampton Works and royal visit photographs 1890s-1940s; visitors books 1861-96; history brochure 1924

Records (3): at Glasgow University Archives, The University, Glasgow, Strathclyde G12 8QQ
list of ships built 1852-1970; minutes 1890-1952; board papers: J&G Thomson Ltd 1863-1900, Clydebank Engineering & Shipbuilding Co Ltd 1896-1966, John Brown & Co (Clydebank) Ltd 1902-68; agms, balance sheets, directors reports John Brown & Co (Clydebank) 1954-68, parent company 1930-67; annual accounts (Clydebank) 1933-56; financial files 1901-69; administrative files 1903-69; shipyard diaries 1871-1968; directors letter books 1857-1956; secretarys letter books 1929-64; official letter books 1909-52; shipyard general letter books, 1956-64; Admiralty letter books 1942-66; Cunard letter books 1930-61; Swedish-American Line letter books 1963-6; London office letter books 1949-62; Sheffield office letter books 1951-7; register of correspondence 1945-65; enquiries, tenders and contract files 1886-1967; shipyard and plant files 1884-1967; Clydebank property and workers houses files 1882-1952; rating and valuation files 1901-62; shipyard valuation books 1884-1938; plant and property registers 1899-1963; engine and boiler works valuation books 1884-1938; plant and property registers 1899-1963; fixed charges and overhead records 1897-1959; general charges, additions to capital accounts, tools and utensils and stock-in-trade books 1920-62; insurance records 1872-1965; ledgers 1847-1961; journals 1847-1953; cash books 1847-1959; cash sheets 1888-1941; financial statements copy books 1868-1914; misc account books 1872-1965; Dalmuir yard Admiralty operations accounting records 1943-7; sundry debtors personal account ledgers 1899-1936; sales and sundry debtors books 1899-1963; sundry debtors sales etc journals 1899-37; sales and sundry debtors claim books 1904-64; amounts received from

sundry debtors books 1906-63; private pay and salary books 1853-1955; wages books 1872-1967; wages books (second series) 1945-59; pay bill books 1905-63; wages analyses 1910-57; weekly abstracts of wages 1930-58; wage rates 1889-1970; labour conditions and training files 1902-61; employment returns 1914-71; contract acceptance copy letter books (engine department) 1920-62; Admiralty payments: instalments on vessels 1900-45; instalments on contracts 1919-57; profit and loss contract registers 1899-1931; contract extras and rebates 1913-56; draft quotations books 1939-66; estimating books 1883-1967; tender books 1888-1963; abstract cost books 1871-1945; contract cost registers 1899-1946; managers progressive books 1887-1966; engine and water turbine cost books 1928-61; boiler cost books 1881-1959; hull cost books 1912-61; managers wages progressive cost books 1896-1938; wages cost books (by department) c1906-65; finished cost books c1896-1959; comparison of costs and estimates book c1901-62; accounts abstract books 1946-62; general calculation and data books for proposed ships 1877-1951; scroll specification books 1901-51; specification books 1895-1966; engine particulars books c1881-1945; vessel particulars 1872-1970; iron and steel order books c1918-58; steel contract books 1929-57; abstracts of sectional weights 1906-41; record of weights worked into hulls 1868-1938, into engines and boilers 1935-67, into plant and machinery 1952-67; sundry order books 1923-63; turbines and generators folders 1945-61; record of turbines and stabilisers manufactured 1903-61; particular vessels files 241-740, 1890-1970; technical data folders 1887-1958; engine drawings nos 540-625, c1934-45; ship plans no 4-728, 1862-1965; small boat plans 1900-50; ordinary standard tracings 1900-50; launch invitations no 367-731, 1906-66; newscuttings books 1880-1964; brochures 1913-64; photo albums ships nos 184-744 and UCS no 102-120, c1881-1972; photo albums engines for ships no 195-274 and misc subjects c1882-1965

Records (4): at Scottish Record Office, PO Box 36, HM General Register House, Edinburgh, Lothian EH1 3YY
negatives (38,000 items)

Records (5): at Scottish Film Archives, 74 Victoria Crescent Road, Glasgow, Strathclyde G12
cinematic film of shipbuilding, launches, trials and tank tests c1926-71 (list available)

Sir A Grant, *Steel and Ships. The History of John Brown's (1950)*

51 BRITISH STEEL CORPORATION (CHEMICALS) LTD

4 Apr 1864
01140C
9 Albert Embankment, London SE1 7SN
Iron, steel, coal and bricks

History: incorporated in 1864 as Consett Iron Co Ltd, iron and steel manufacturers and coal owners based at Consett Ironworks, Consett, Durham. By 1923 had offices in Newcastle upon Tyne, Glasgow, Birmingham, Manchester and London. Products in 1931 consisted of ship, boiler and chequer plates, sections, joists and bars, slabs, blooms and billets; haematite and foundry pig iron; beehive and patent foundry coke and coke nuts; gas, bunkering, coking and smithy coals; silica and fireclay bricks and shapes; refined tars and bitumen mixtures, pitch, creosote etc; and other chemical by-products. Coal properties were vested in National Coal Board from 1947. Acquired undertaking of New Jarrow Steel Co Ltd in 1949. Subsequently became part of British Steel Corporation and changed name to above.

Records: at British Steel Corporation, Northern Regional Records Centre, Unit F2, Commerce Way, Skippers Lane Industrial Estate, South Bank, Middlesbrough, Cleveland TS6 6UT

52 PYROTENAX OVERSEAS LTD

7 Apr 1864
01147C
21 Bloomsbury Street, London WC1B 3QN
Cable manufacturers

History: founded as Gutta Percha Co in Feb 1845 by Charles Hancock, artist, and Henry Bewley, Dutch chemist, to manufacture various gutta percha products. Moved into factory premises in Stratford, E London, and offices in Leadenhall Street, City of London, in 1846 and opened factory at 18 Wharf Road, City Road, in 1847. Provided cable in 1850 for laying first submarine telegraph cable across English Channel and in 1856-7 across the Atlantic. By 1864 had provided 14,000 nautical miles of cable in most seas and oceans of the world. Amalgamated with Glass Eliott & Co of Greenwich, wire rope manufacturers, in 1864 to form Telegraph Construction & Maintenance Co Ltd. Laid successful Atlantic cable in 1866 and by 1950 had made 82 per cent - 385,000 nauts - of submarine cables laid in world, majority after 1880 laid and repaired by own cable ships. In 1869 London offices moved from 54 to 38 and in 1936 to 22 Old Broad Street. Main factories were at Morden Wharf (closed 1895) and Enderby Wharf, Greenwich, and at Wharf Road (closed 1935). From 1920s produced metallurgical alloys and from 1930s high frequency, power and telephone cables. Formed jointly with Siemens Brothers & Co Ltd, cable manufacturers, new company Submarine Cables Ltd in Oct 1935 to manufacture submarine cables at Greenwich. By 1950 owned 6 other subsidiary companies: Selbourne Plantation Co Ltd, formed 1915 to develop and work gutta percha estate in Malaya; Transformer Sheets Ltd, grain-oriented silicon iron producers; Telcon-Magnetic Cores Ltd, promoters of manufacture and distribution of grain-oriented silicon iron cores; Temco Ltd, high electrical resistance wire producers; AWA Telcon Pty Ltd, promoters of products in Australasia; and Telcon Cables (SA) Ltd, promoters of products in South Africa. Acquired in 1959 by British Insulated Callender's Cables Ltd (BICC Ltd from 1975) and name changed to above in 1967. In early 1980s was a dormant company.

Records (1): at BICC, PO Box 1, Prescot, Merseyside L34 5SZ
minute books 1864-1950
Atlantic Telegraph Co Ltd: minute book 1856-8

Records (2): at Cable & Wireless, Mercury House, 110-124 Theobalds Road, London WC1X 8RX
cable: agreements 1868-1912, section sheets c1915-37; cableship specification nd; technical publication nd; illustrated programme of visit to works 1903

Records (3): at Science Museum Library, South Kensington, London SW7 5NH
cable contracts 1869-1929; cable lay reports 1914-18; cable ship log books 1901-30; papers and files of CAO Berner, cable engineer early 20 cent; glass negatives, slides and photographs of cableships and cable laying; house magazines early 20 cent; newscuttings 20 cent

GL Lawford and LR Nicholson, *The Telcon Story 1850-1950* (1950)

53 SWINDON CENTRAL MARKET CO LTD

11 Apr 1864
01157C
16 Marlborough Road, Swindon, Wiltshire SN3 IQY
Cattle market

History: market had existed in Swindon, Wiltshire since reign of Henry III and in 1627 Charles I granted a charter to Thomas Goddard to hold a market every Monday. It was held in the High Street, extending occasionally into Wood Street and Cricklade Street, and the corn market in the Square. In 1852 Swindon Market Co was formed to erect in the Square, a market house, now known as the town hall. Was built by Mr Major to designs of Sampson Sage, architect, but was mainly used for public meetings. Swindon Central Market Co Ltd was incorporated in 1864 to erect a corn exchange which was built by John Philips to designs of Wilson & Wilcox of Bath, Avon, architects. It was opened in 1866 and provided a site for corn, cattle, wool, cheese, and provision markets. Took over interests of Swindon Market Co in 1874. Remained street market until 1887 when Ambrose L Goddard transferred it to present site west of Marlborough Road, Lower Town, adjoining Dores Yard, a sale yard where cattle sales were conducted by Messrs Dore, Smith & Radway. Purchased reversion of its lease from Goddard Estate in 1930 and Dores Yard in 1949, following sale in 1948 of corn exchange which had been let as a skating rink from 1909 and a cinema from 1919-39. Carried out improvements to market in 1950s to accommodate the cattle, poultry, sheep and pigs sold there. In early 1980s market covered a 2 acre site and was well attended.

Records: at Swindon Central Market, 16 Marlborough Road, Swindon, Wiltshire SN3 IQY
directors minutes 1917-date; general meeting minutes 1864-date; newscuttings re annual meetings 1866,1885-1903,1926-30; members etc register 1937-date; shares transfers registration certificate book 1923-date; memo of association 1902; corporate documents and correspondence, 1915,1938; retiring directors list 1911-16; notice re market removal 1887; translation of grant to Thomas Goddard nd; annual reports and accounts 1888,1907-09,1914; deeds register 1913-49; Even Swindon Cinema Co Ltd rent accounts 1939-40; illustrated handbook 1960s

Swindon Official Markets Guide (1960s)

54 CITY OF LONDON REAL PROPERTY CO LTD

11 Apr 1864
01160C
35 St Thomas Street, London SE1 9SN
Property and investment

History: established by James and John Innes, partners in a firm of rum importers and Jamaican sugar plantation owners and incorporated as above in 1864. Early investments comprised office buildings in Mincing Lane, Mark Lane and Gracechurch Street, London. The company established the London Offices Co and City & Westminster Properties Ltd in 1920 (both companies were subsequently merged with the parent company) and East India Avenue Co Ltd, formed jointly with the Royal Mail Steam Packet Co in 1914. Wool Exchange & General Investments Ltd (now Dunsmark Investments Ltd) were acquired in 1959 and Corinthian Investments Ltd in 1961. Acquired in 1969 by Land Securities Investment Trust

Ltd and the management of its business transferred to Land Securities (Management) Ltd.

Records: at Land Securities (Management), Landsec House, 21 New Fetter Lane, London EC4P 4PY
directors minutes 1864-c1929; members registers 1864-1900; share: ledgers c1891-1958, register 1927-32; stock register 1927-52; stockholders registers c1890-1930; probates registers 1865-1964; debenture: registers 1888-96, transfers 1864-92; closed share accounts 1922-58; share transfer: registers 1922-65, documents 1864-7,1920-70; dividend sheets 1958-63; shareholders notices etc 1864-1913; memo and articles of association 1864; annual reports and accounts 1865-1909; ledgers: c1864-1931, general 1910-67, working account 1885-1906, advances c1960, bought c1971-4; cash books 1955-67; property ledger 1880-1933; histories of offices to let 1920s-30s; service charges cards 1967-70; leases 1960s-70s; tenants: account ledgers 1864-70,c1960, rent books c1864-1907; house magazines 1934-5; general letter books 1876-9; correspondence 1950 on; historical publications 1914-1964

The City of London Real Property Company Limited Centenary 1864-1964 (priv pub 1964)

55 CONTINENTAL UNION TRUST CO LTD

18 Apr 1864
01189C
Mermaid House, 2 Puddle Dock, London EC4V 3AT
Investment (formerly gas supply)

History: incorporated in 1864 as Continental Union Gas Co Ltd in order to rescue Société en Commandite Union des Gaz from its financial problems, taking control of the 13 French and Italian gas stations of the latter which supplied gas to Albi, Beaucaire, Nîmes, Roanne, Rueil and Nanterre, Sète, Strasbourg and Vienne in France, and Alessandria, Genoa, Milan and Modena in Italy. In 1865 the gas stations at Montargis, France and Messina, Sicily, were purchased and worked separately. Obtained 80 per cent shareholding of Union des Gaz after its reconstruction as a Société Anonyme, ceasing to directly manage its affairs. Montargis works were transferred to Union des Gaz and the Messina works were destroyed by an earthquake in 1908. By 1910, 87 per cent of capital was invested in Union des Gaz shares and 13 per cent in English gas companies shares. Between 1920 and 1928 its French assets were valorised and in 1929 sold Union des Gaz shares to a group of French gas and electrical undertakings. Name changed to above and it became a trust company. In 1982 resolved to concentrate its investment in North America and changed its name to TR North America Investment Trust PLC. Managed in 1982 by Touche, Remnant & Co.

Records (1): at TR North America Investment Trust, Mermaid House, 2 Puddle Dock, London EC4V 3AT
directors meeting minutes 1943-date; general meeting: minutes 1900-date, proceeding reports 1864-1929
Records (2): at Touche Remnant, Belfast House, Abbots Lane, London SE1
directors meeting minutes 1865-1943; stock holders registers c1906-c29; share holders accounts ledgers 1929-59; stock and share transfer forms 1920s-60s; directors register 1917-48; directors fee lists 1924,1928; prospectus 1864; memo and articles of association 1864-1956; underwriting book 1935-60; trust deeds 1936-60; share documents and correspondence 1928-61; shareholders and stockholders letters 1864-77,1915-60; capital reorganisation papers

1928-9; annual reports and accounts 1905-69; balance sheet and profit and loss accounts 1863/4-1958; ledgers 1902-60; journals 1918-59; cash books 1933-68; income and profits tax papers c1922-53; Messina station pensions: payments register 1909-20, papers and correspondence 1918-46; pension fund trust deeds, accounts, securities valuation and correspondence 1930-67; London offices leases, plans and papers 1877-1940; office furniture inventory 1879

56 FARNHAM MARKET HOUSE & TOWN HALL CO LTD

26 May 1864
01305C
Bethune House, 88 West Street, Farnham, Surrey GU9 7EN
Property

History: incorporated as above in 1864 to build a new market house and town hall and to secure the market tolls of Farnham, Surrey. Purchased Goats Head Inn in the Borough/Castle Street on which site FC Birch built the corn exchange and town hall to the Gothic design of Edward Wyndham Tarn of London. Buildings were opened in March 1866 and rebuilt to Georgian designs of WT Benslyn, H Falkner and GM Alywin, architects, with lock up shops on ground floor and a dance hall incorporated on first floor, in 1930. Continued to manage this property in 1982.

Records: at Farnham Market House & Town Hall, Bethune House, 88 West Street, Farnham, Surrey GU9 7EN
directors and general meeting minutes 1864-date; chairmans agenda book 1941-54; shareholders: register 1864-1954, lists 1864-85, correspondence and notes 1864-97; share: ledgers 1864-1954, application and allotment books 1864,1932-48, register 1864, transfer register 1864-1954 and documents 1867-80, records 1950s on; directors register 1904-31; debenture registers 1934-61; mortgage register 1929-44; annual returns 1864-78,1904-18; annual reports and accounts 1864-1935; ledgers 1864-date; cash books 1864-1919; room hire book 1892-1931; exchange gallery fund account nd; donations promised list 1864; press cuttings and notices re Farnham fair tolls c1864-1979; town hall plans and photographs 1933; new exchange opening programme 1866; furnishings inventory 1888

Nigel Temple, *Farnham Buildings and People* (1963)

57 NPK HOLDINGS LTD

14 Jun 1864
01346C
31 Market Hill, Royston, Hertfordshire SG8 9JS
Investment (formerly fertilizer manufacturers)

History: incorporated as Farmers Manure Co Ltd to manufacture manure under the best scientific principles, discount being given to shareholders. In 1866 capital was increased by £20,000 and factory erected. From 1872 to 1912 increased cost of raw materials, agricultural depression and unfavourable weather depressed business. In 1919 factory was extended and share capital increased by £5000 followed by £10,000 a year later. Record tonnage in 1934 coincided with extensive alterations, and installation of modern plant including granulating equipment in 1943. Acquired WT Nash & Co in 1933 and SM Fordham & Co Ltd in 1950.

Name of company changed to Farmers Fertilizer Co Ltd in 1955 and capital reorganisation took place in 1960. In 1962 record turnover was achieved and scope of activities widened in 1969 by acquisition of three local businesses. In 1973 reached agreement with Fisons Ltd to set up a jointly owned company to which the fertilizer business was sold. In 1975 fuel business was sold to Charrington Fuels Ltd and name changed to above. In early 1980s was a property holding and investment company.

Records (1): at NPK Holdings, 31 Market Hill, Royston, Hertfordshire SG8 9JS
directors and general meeting minutes 1864-1978

Records (2): at Hertfordshire Record Office, County Hall, Hertford, Hertfordshire SG13 8DE
members and share registers 1864-1970; share: applications and allotments 1919, new issue 1921, transfer registers 1865-1972, counterfoils 1936-72; annual reports and accounts 1870-1976; impersonal ledgers 1870-1971; bought ledger 1931-72; nominal and credit summary books 1934-72; cash books 1935-73; manure ledger 1933-38; sales ledger 1936-8; stock book 1902-69; salary book 1934-6

58 SOUTHERN NEWSPAPERS LTD

14 Jun 1864
01350C
45 Above Bar, Southampton, Hampshire SO9 7BA
Newspapers

History: first issue of *Southampton Herald & Isle of Wight Gazette*, 4 page Tory county weekly, was published in 1823 by E Skelton & Son, booksellers and commercial printers of 22 High Street, Southampton, Hampshire. It was sold in 1826 to John Coupland, journalist, who changed its name to *Hampshire Advertiser*, built new offices, installed new machinery and increased its circulation to the highest in Hampshire. In 1864 Hampshire Advertiser County Newspaper & Printing & Publishing Co Ltd was incorporated to run the newspaper with Robert B King, Coupland's successor, as general manager. Opened new printing office at 29 High Street in 1884. In 1891 bought Hampshire Independent Newspaper & Printing & Publishing Co Ltd with its premises at 52 Above Bar, Southampton, which became the company's headquarters in early 1900s. Its newspapers, the evening *Southern Echo* and the *Hampshire Independent* continued to be published until 1923 when it amalgamated with the *Advertiser*. Began publishing the *Football Echo*, a sports weekly in 1898, the *Southampton Pictorial* in 1912, and the *Dorset Daily Echo* in 1921. Purchased the *Bournemouth Daily Echo* in 1900 and the *Southampton Times* in 1925. Name changed to Hampshire Advertiser & Echos Ltd in 1922 and to above in 1927. By 1939 had branch offices at Winchester, Hampshire; Bournemouth, Weymouth and Dorchester, Dorset; and Salisbury, Wiltshire. Southampton and Weymouth offices were destroyed during WW2 and production was transferred to Bournemouth. New offices were opened at Newport, Isle of Wight in 1949; Andover, Hampshire in 1955; Hythe, Southampton Water and Alton, Hampshire in 1958; Bridport, Dorset; and Basingstoke, Hampshire in 1961; and Fareham, Hampshire in 1964. In 1953 acquired Bournemouth Times Ltd with its 3 weeklies, the *Bournemouth Times*, the *Poole & Dorset Herald* and *Swanage Times*, and subsidiary Hardy Press Ltd, printers. Acquired *Christchurch Times* in 1960 and WH Hallett Ltd, jobbing printers of Poole, Dorset in 1964. In 1958 company's newspaper titles changed from 'Daily' to 'Evening'. In 1980 published the daily *Southern Evening Echo*, *Bournemouth Evening Echo* and *Dorset Evening Echo*. WH

Hallett Ltd published the weeklies acquired in 1953 and 1960, and another subsidiary published the bi-weekly *Basingstoke Gazette*. Other subsidiaries included Southernprint Ltd, magazine and periodical printers, and Southern Motor Utilities Ltd, operating a private hire service and selling petrol and new and used cars from Bournemouth.

Records (1): at Southern Newspapers, 45 Above Bar, Southampton, Hampshire SO9 7BA
directors meeting minutes 1864-1960; general managers reports 1950-62; general meeting: minutes 1909-60, notices 1941-53; agenda book 1941-60; members registers 1886-94,1941-60; directors register 1941-60; share transfer registers 1876-1908,1944-56; dividend sheets 1948-71; articles of association 1922; annual reports and accounts 1909-80; journals 1940-59; cash book 1921-9; *Bournemouth Daily Echo* cash book 1918-32; paper supply contracts and correspondence 1939-58; wage rates 1946-61; employment agreement 1954; house journal *Echograms/Echoing Times* 1925-82; circular letters 1941-6; letter book 1959; property agreements, leases, plans, correspondence etc 1898-1961; legal opinions 1913-20; *Southampton Herald & Isle of Wight Gazette* 1823-6; *Hampshire Advertiser* 1827-1940; *Southern Echo* 1888-date
Hampshire Independent Newspaper & Printing & Publishing Co Ltd: directors meeting minutes and papers 1859-85; general meeting minutes and papers 1860-86; shareholders register 1859-66; misc articles of association 1859; accounts statements 1860-2; ledger 1894-1906
Dorset Daily Press Ltd: report 1921; members, directors, share transfer register and share ledger 1921-4

Records (2): at British Library, Newspaper Library, Colindale Avenue, London NW9 5HE
Hampshire Advertiser 1829-1940; *Southern Echo* 1888-date; *Hampshire Independent* 1836-1923 (except 1896-7,1911); *Football Echo* 1898,1900-14,1919-39,1946-date; *Bournemouth (Daily/Evening) Echo* 1900-date (except 1911); *Dorset (Daily/Evening) Echo* 1921-date; *Bournemouth Times* 1868-date (except 1898); *Poole & Dorset Herald* 1846-date (except 1872,1896-8,1907,1911); *Swanage Times* 1958-date; *Christchurch Times* 1858-1918,1925-date; *Basingstoke Gazette* 1878-date (except 1896-7,1913)

Gordon Sewell, *Echoes of a Century 1864-1964 The Centenary History of Southern Newspapers Ltd* (1964)

59 ELDONWALL INDUSTRIAL LTD

17 Jun 1864
01359C
4 Carlton Gardens, Pall Mall, London SW1Y 5AR
Property (formerly iron and coal)

History: incorporated in 1864 as Ashton Vale Iron Co Ltd to purchase lease of colliery and ironworks known as Ashton Vale Coal & Iron Works at Long Ashton, Avon and plant, lands, houses and lease of ironstone trail at Kingswood, Gloucester, known as Hopewell Iron Stone Pits. Carried on trade as iron, steel and tinplate manufacturers and coalowners and dealers. Name changed to Ashton Vale Estates Ltd in 1963 and to above in 1965. Acquired by

Town & City Properties Ltd in c1975.

Records: none survive

60 REFUGE ASSURANCE CO LTD

20 Jun 1864
01364C
103 Oxford Street, Manchester, Greater Manchester M60 7HA
Insurance

History: established in Manchester as Refuge Friend-in-Deed Life Assurance & Sick Fund Friendly Society in 1858. Moved to Dukinfield, Cheshire in 1859. Renamed Refuge Friendly Society in 1864, as above in 1881 and Refuge Assurance PLC in 1981. Originally a local burial and sickness society for meeting subscribers' claims up to a maximum of £200. Acquired the business of the Working Man's Benefit Society of Macclesfield in 1862 and Manchester & Salford Independent Burial Society in 1863. Converted to industrial life assurance and registered as limited company in 1864. Headquarters returned to Manchester in 1866, Oxford Street head office being designed by A Waterhouse in 1891. Appointed agents and opened branches throughout north west England and Yorkshire and later remainder of UK; a London office being established c1872. Had separate industrial and ordinary life assurance branches from 1887. By 1913 total sums assured were over £18 million, rising to £29 million by 1947. Undertook general insurance business from 1953. Acquired Federated Employers Insurance Association in 1953 but sold it to Allstate Insurance, Illinois, USA in 1975. Total assurance funds exceeded £500 million by 1983.

Records: at Refuge Assurance, 103 Oxford Street, Manchester, Greater Manchester M60 7HA board: meeting minutes 1862-1947, general meeting minutes 1864-72, agendas, rough minutes and correspondence 1867-1900, notices and resolutions 1864-1900; share: allotment book c1870, ledger 1872, applications 1872, offer 1884, summary 1884-1904, certificates and transfer documents 1864-88,1922, personal transfers notes 1885-90, analysis 1949; register: members 1886-1901, directors 1901; annual list and summary 1901-30, friendly societies return 1867; memo and articles of association 1864-1961; rule books 1858-72; correspondence re change of name 1860; actuarys reports 1866,1871,1815,1884; annual report and accounts 1875-6,1884,1893-1903,1919-47; balance sheet valuation statements 1876-1926; collections and expenses analysis 1888; cash increases division 1914-23; loans, payments and arrears register 1877-92; cash book: 1858-70, treasurers 1859-66, policy 1863-7; prospectus, with broadsheet and leaflet 1863-1922; deaths register 1864-74; policy: duplicate register 1864-9,1869-73, premium values 1902-09, Blackburn office register cards 1915, sickness insurance and certificates 1862-72, tables 1864-76; life insurance: registers 1879, policies 1859-1906, certificates 1863-9; premium receipt cards 1862-97; proposal forms 1865-85; renewal notice 1898; surrender value tables 1899; members register 1856-66; collecting books 1864,c1874; instructions: superintendents and agents 1890-1915, staff 1932; papers re staff organisation remuneration, service, training, sports and social 1866-1966; canvassing pack 1895-1932; staff war service analysis 1914,1916; war book posters and passes 1939-40; picnics, social events, dinner and luncheon photographs, programmes and speeches, 1891-1980; portraits and photographs of directors and staff 1903-58,nd; house magazine 1957-80; leases, valuation report, correspondence, photograph and thesis on premises in Corporation Street,

Manchester 1866-1972; Blackburn premises papers 1868; correspondence 1859-1974; letter book 1889-1901; legal records 1865-1961; press cuttings 1849-1975; war memorial committee report, account book, dedication ceremony 1922,1953; company history drafts, sources and correspondence 1958

61 PEARL ASSURANCE CO LTD

11 Jul 1864
01419C
High Holborn, London WC1V 7EB
Insurance

History: registered in 1864 as Pearl Life Assurance Loan & Investment Co Ltd, the successor to the Pearl Loan Co (operating in Whitechapel, London in late 1850s) and Pearl Life Assurance Association & Sick Benefit Society, registered as a friendly society in 1862. Undertook industrial life assurance business, initially in E London, with headquarters in Commercial Road, and City Road from 1870, London Bridge for 1877, and High Holborn from 1913. Renamed Pearl Life Assurance Co in 1874 and undertook ordinary life assurance from 1875. Patrick J Foley, director and manager (later managing director) 1864 until 1908, was responsible for rapid growth in late 19 cent. Premium income reached £2.7 million by 1913, when Pearl was third-ranking life office in UK. Acquired Integrity Friendly Society (est 1858) in 1885, London Edinburgh & Glasgow Assurance Co Ltd in 1910 and South of England Mutual Benefit Friendly Society in 1901. Renamed above in 1914 and took powers to transact fire insurance in 1917. Total assurance funds exceeded £921 million by 1978.

Records: at Pearl Assurance, High Holborn, London WC1V 7EB
meeting minutes: board 1866 on, general 1893 on; ledgers 1864 on; cash books 1949 on; bill books 1929 on; valuations 1885 on; agency agreements 1887,1892,1910 on; registers: policy 1874 on, claims 1948 on; policy forms 1887 on; proposals 1903 on; prospectuses 1887 on; Holborn site deeds and contracts nd

DCS Pegg, 'Patrick James Foley', *Dictionary of Business Biography* Vol 2 (1984)

62 NATIONAL VULCAN ENGINEERING INSURANCE GROUP LTD

25 Jul 1864
01471C
St Mary's Parsonage, Manchester, Greater Manchester M60 9AP
Insurance

History: incorporated in 1864 as National Boiler Insurance Co Ltd to give insurance and inspection services for steam boilers. Originally based in London and controlled by local boards in London and Manchester but tensions between the two led to the closure of the London office and removal of headquarters to Manchester in 1865. By 1868 had only 2000 boilers under inspection but premium income advanced from £7588 in 1872-3 to £29,618 in 1897. Took powers to transact engine and accident insurance in 1892 and was renamed National Boiler & General Insurance Co Ltd. Insurance of gas and steam engines was undertaken in 1893, oil engines in 1895 and electrical engines in 1898. A Glasgow office operated from 1883 and a London branch was opened in 1893. New head offices were built between 1902 and 1911. Premium income was over £100,000 in 1912. Acquired by Alliance

Assurance Co Ltd in 1922 and by 1938 premium income had reached £500,000. In 1930s specialised in insurance of electricity generating stations and in 1950s and 1960s in nuclear power stations. From 1965 operated with Vulcan Boiler & General Insurance Co Ltd, incorporated in 1859 as Steam Boiler Assurance Co Ltd and acquired by London Assurance Corporation in 1920 as National & Vulcan Engineering Insurance Group. London Assurance Corporation merged with Sun Insurance Office Ltd in 1959 and Alliance Assurance Co Ltd in 1965 to form Sun Alliance & London Insurance Group. Company changed name to above in 1971 to streamline organisation of new combined company. In 1981 operated 28 branches in the UK.

Records: at Greater Manchester Record Office, 56 Marshall Street, New Cross, Ancoats, Manchester, Greater Manchester M4 5FU
directors, general and committee meeting minutes and papers 1864-1948; meeting agendas 1909-59; agm proceedings 1898-1907; shareholders circulars 1865-1923; share: certificates 1920-76, transfer register 1917-81; directors registers 1931-79; agreement registers 1865-70,c1915; securities registers 1915-60; seal registers 1931-73; Stationers Hall registration certificates 1898-1912; agreement with British Engine and Scottish insurance companies 1904; memo and articles of association 1864-92; annual returns 1928-30; balance sheets and accounts 1864-1923; audited accounts 1948-79; accounts statements 1908-48; advertisement c1900; insurance: policies and forms 1885-9,c1950, rate books 1920, proposals accepted 1958-65, agreements and correspondence 1884-1939; electrical plant accident registers 1905-51; constructions examined reports 1937-56; alteration registers 1960s-70s; special service books 1940-60s; posting registers 1950-60s; inspectors: circular books 1902-12, rough calculations 1930-60s; consulting: engineers technical notes 1905, department technical letters 1920-6; specifications 1938-46; consultative special reports 1938-56; plug patent papers and correspondence 1877-88; patent, inspection, service agreements c1890-1923; steam boiler technical booklet 1898; executive salaries 1947-65; engine department general office instructions 1911-31; assistant engineer duties 1928; employment conditions 1953; staff list 1955; staff photographs 1902-47; plans, drawings, reports, photographs, brochures and papers re St Mary's Parsonage building c1820-1922
Vulcan Boiler & General Insurance Co Ltd: committee meeting minutes 1858-9; directors meeting minutes 1859-1970; sub-committee meeting minutes 1910-38; general meeting minutes 1859-1966; directors and committee meeting agendas 1952-66; members register and share ledger 1935-46; directors registers 1910-66; settlement deed 1859; memo and articles of association 1896; annual shareholders reports 1859-1908; investment: ledgers 1890-1965, register c1945-68; profit and loss account ledger 1865-1936; revenue account ledger 1904-26; insurance: prospectuses 1864-1950, policies 1892-1918, proposal forms 1883-1917, notes, premium charts, brochures, instructions etc 1904-69, electrical policies register 1948-71, circulars, agreements etc 1880-1928; engineers reports 1859-1920; claims register 1892; inspectors information 1900-13; steam vessel and boiler examination schedule 1918; surveyors notebooks 1879,1930-40; house magazine 1904-09,1922-66; office procedure reports 1951-3; staff: commission account 1866-1909, news-sheet 1958-66, photographs c1900-61; premises: building committee meeting minutes 1964, photographs c1910,1954-60; correspondence re history and general 1906-48; newscuttings 1879-94

WH Chaloner, *National Boiler 1864-1964. A Century of Progress in Industrial Safety* (priv pub 1964)

WH Chaloner, *Vulcan. The History of One Hundred Years of Engineering and Insurance 1859-1959* (priv pub 1959)

63 VULCAN FOUNDRY LTD

27 Aug 1864
01556C
132 Long Acre, London WC2E 9AH
Steam and diesel locomotive manufacturers

History: established at Newton le Willows, Merseyside, in 1830 by Charles Tayleur, Liverpool engineer. He was joined by Robert Stephenson the railway engineer, in 1832 and the first locomotives were completed in 1833. In 1847 Tayleur and Stephenson took over the Bank Quay Foundry at Warrington. The partnership was incorporated as Vulcan Foundry Co Ltd in 1864 and 'company' was dropped from the title in 1898. Locomotives, despite temporary production of military equipment during both WWs, were built for the world market until 1970, when general diesel engine production became the main activity. In 1944 the company acquired Robert Stephenson & Hawthorns Ltd, locomotive builders and began to collaborate with English Electric Co Ltd. This led to their absorption by that company in 1955. Subsequently amalgamated with General Electric Co Ltd in 1968 to form General Electric & English Electric Cos Ltd which changed name to General Electric Co Ltd in 1970. Ruston Paxman Diesels Ltd became a management company of GEC Diesels Ltd in 1970 subsequently changing their name to Ruston Diesels Ltd in 1975.

Records (1): at Ruston Diesels, Vulcan Foundry, Newton le Willows, Merseyside
memo and articles of association 1909; advertisements, illustrated catalogues, booklets etc of products c1919-1970s; copy list of locomotives built 1833-1950s; boiler test and engine trials 1889-1905; photographs and illustrations of locomotives, other products, machinery etc c1898-1960s; index to glass negatives of locomotives nd; site plans 1832-1950s; photographs of site, workers, visitors etc 1940s-60s; copy apprentice indenture 1893; works posters 1909-37; roll of honour 1918; photographs of staff and directors 1910s-40s; misc copy documents, photographs, articles and booklets on history and locomotives 1829-1977

Records (2): at Newton le Willows Library, Crow Lane East, Newton le Willows, Merseyside
dividends nd; memo and articles of association 1909-46; annual reports and accounts 1901-02; balance sheet and revenue account 1867-82; tables of account 1896; customer accounts 1847-55; sales record 1890; illustrated booklet on foundry nd; list of locomotives built 1833-1950s; boiler test and engine trials 1874-1906; copy land titles 1833 on; photographs of site and works 1897-1960s; staff agreement 1930; appointment letters 1950; company rules and regulations 1897-1921; annual dinner menus 1930s-60s; photographs of staff and chairmen 1920s-64; letter books 1864-90s; correspondence re staff, history and general matters 1890s-1940; company secretary diaries 1950-63; misc notes and articles on history and locomotives 1844-1960, including sketch and thickness of *Lady Octavia*, Bank Quay Foundry ship

Records (3): at St Helens Central Library, Victoria Square, St Helens, Merseyside WA10 1DY
articles of association 1946; legal corporate documents including managers contract patents and agreements nd; balance sheets and accounts 1867-82; statement of accounts 1903-08; record of sales c1951; catalogue - India nd; copy list of locomotives built 1833-1950s; record engines and tenders built 1870-1930; boiler test records 1874-1906; photographs of

locomotives nd; engineering drawings nd; sketch map of Vulcan 1832; copy indenture for Vulcan cottages 1836; photographs of site, works, staff, machinery, visitors etc 1897-1960; apprentices indenture 1873; training booklets nd; works posters 1872-1937; letter books 1864-93; correspondence re production, Liverpool to Manchester Railway, Iron Trades Manufacturers Association, centenary trip and history of company 1824-1964: calendars and diaries 1927-63; articles and booklets and misc documents re railways and locomotives 1827-1960
Bank Quay Foundry: accounts 1847-55

Records (4): at Merseyside County Archives, 64-66 Islington, Liverpool L3 8LG
locomotive drawings photographs etc 1833-1956

Vulcan's Heritage: A Brief History of the Vulcan Site (priv pub 1975)

64 HULL & EAST RIDING LAND MORTGAGE & INVESTMENT CO LTD

22 Sept 1864
01615C
5 Parliament Street, Hull, Humberside HU1 2AZ
Property

History: incorporated as above in Hull, Humberside, in 1864 to deal in land, property and securities. Main area of operation was Hull and Humberside.

Records: at Hull & East Riding Land Mortgage & Investment, 5 Parliament Street, Hull, Humberside HU1 2AZ
directors minutes 1864-1938; memo and articles of association 1864; directors report and accounts 1931; audited accounts 1865-date; journal 1926-32

65 CENTRAL PIER BLACKPOOL LTD

10 Oct 1864
01636C
7 Hanover Square, London W1R 0PS
Pier proprietors

History: incorporated in 1864 as South Blackpool Jetty Co Ltd to build an iron and wooden jetty at Layton with Warbreck, South Blackpool, Lancashire for promenading, landing and embarking passengers and merchandise, and other purposes. Purchased by Trust Houses Forte Group in 1967, changing name in 1968 to above. Struck off Register of Companies in 1979 but was reinstated in 1980 in order to settle complications with freehold interest.

Records: at Trusthouse Forte Leisure, 17 Golden Square, London W1R 3AG
general meeting minutes 1969-date; registration papers c1967-date

66 JOHN CROSSLEY & SON LTD

19 Nov 1864
01706C
Dean Clough Mills, Halifax, W Yorkshire
Carpet manufacturing

History: established in 1830 by John Crossley and partners. Rapidly expanded business from 1837 to 1864 with his 3 sons, Francis, John and Joseph developing printed tapestries and velvets and concentrated the carpet manufactory at Dean Clough Mills, Halifax, W Yorkshire which eventually comprised 11 sheds. Workforce increased from 300 in 1837 to 5000 in 1884. Incorporated as above in 1864. By 1923 had offices at 59 Portland Street, Manchester and at 84-86 Newgate Street and 20-22 King Edward Street, London and manufactured the following specialities: Axminster, Brussels, Saxony, Wilton and tapestry carpets and rugs and chenille, tapestry and velvet squares. Merged in 1953 with Carpet Trades Ltd (est 1777, inc 1936) of Kidderminster, Hereford and Worcester to form John Crossley - Carpet Trades (Holdings) Ltd which became Carpets International Ltd in 1969. Company had 2 subsidiaries in the 1960s, W&RK Lee Ltd and Spur Doubling Mill Ltd. In 1977 had branches in Belfast; Birmingham; Bristol, Avon; Dublin; Glasgow; Leeds, W Yorkshire; Liverpool; London; Manchester; and Newcastle, Tyne & Wear and employed 2200 people. Dean Clough Mills ceased trading in 1982.

Records (1): at Carpets International, New Road, Kidderminster, Hereford & Worcester DY10 1AL
directors meeting minutes 1864-date

Records (2): at W Yorkshire Record Office, Registry of Deeds, Newstead Road, Wakefield, W Yorkshire WF1 2DE
directors meeting minutes (microfilm) 1864-1950; general meeting minutes 1865-1968; share transfer registers 1864-1945; debenture ledgers 1866-1905; memo and articles of association 1864-1953; annual reports and accounts 1865-1956; directors and secretarys: out books 1859-1942, in letters and receipts 1853-92; secretarys correspondence c1931-83; audited annual accounts 1865-92; profit and loss accounts c1865-1961; trial balances 1877-1910; departmental: profit and loss accounts 1922-39, ledger 1892-1944, journals 1864-1959; private ledger 1886-92; deposit ledgers 1874-1930; real accounts ledgers 1870-1937; sales and bought ledgers 1909-37; private cash books 1874-1925; foreign, Australian, Egyptian and Canadian bill books 1907-55; misc receipts and legal accounts 1866-1931; carpet dispatch books 1893-1975; order books 1912-31; home ledgers 1911-33; London ledgers 1881-1931; foreign ledgers 1911-31; American: day books 1915-31, stock sheets and ledger balances 1887-90; home and abroad (Dublin, France, Germany, New York, Roumania, Shanghai, Africa) travellers and agents correspondence and papers incl commission accounts 1900-47; sales offices and warehouses out letter books 1936-46; licence, patent, design agreements and papers 1895-1938; print: registers 1871-1927, order books 1896-1919; work order books 1878-1913; Braithwaite & Co Ltd yarn supply papers and accounts 1919-41; stock sheets 1867-1948; machinery stock valuations 1891-1926; mill leases and underleases with papers 1809-1957; sale rooms and warehouse leases and underleases 1890-1957; Manor Heath Estate, Halifax papers 1877-1913; wages books 1914-71; salaries book 1916-54; personnel cards 1911-60; young persons factory registers 1867-1921; Sir Francis Crossley: estate papers 1872-1904, executors meeting minutes 1872-5, cash book 1856-72; Joseph Crossley estate papers 1883-93; Crossley & Porter Orphan Home expenses account 1868-79; American non-carpet interest records 1871-1913, incl plantation accounts 1871-91; EC Palmer and Louisiana Savings Bank court case papers 1872-80; drainage warrants letters and reports 1875-1903; Halifax Light Opera Society records 1924-71

New Sharlston Colliery Co: records 1860-1943, incl directors meeting minutes 1865-83
Ovenden Worsted Co Ltd: records 1871-1944, incl directors and general meeting minutes 1871-1906
Russian Carpet Co: records, mainly accounts 1887-1933

67 HILLIER'S BACON CURING CO LTD

11 Mar 1865
01954C
Newmarket, Nailsworth, Stroud, Gloucestershire GL6 0RG
Bacon and pork products

History: established as a 'hanging shop' in Market Street, Nailsworth, Gloucestershire by Isaac Hillier in 1819. Business moved to premises at Newmarket, Nailsworth in 1830 where Irish pigs were slaughtered and bacon cured. Incorporated as above in 1865 by which time 300 pigs per week were slaughtered rising to 600 per week by 1926. Due to post war slump fell to 100 pigs per week in 1929 but rose to 600 again by 1936 and by 1954 to 1500. Factory was extensively modernised and mechanised in post war years and by 1970 could handle 2000 pigs per week. Acquired by Ranks Hovis McDougall Ltd in 1964. By late 1960s was selling pies, sausages, bacon and cooked meats within a 50 mile radius of Nailsworth and employed 250 people. New sausage and pre-pack bacon factory was built between 1969-77 on site of Newmarket Court, mansion house built by Isaac Hillier. Ranks Hovis McDougall Ltd sold company to Mr HM Newton-Clare in Aug 1980 and in Apr 1982 the slaughtering of pigs and curing of bacon ceased, pie production moving to new factory in Jun. Receiver appointed in 1982. Sovereign Foods Ltd, a subsidiary of Barretts & Baird (Wholesale) Ltd, purchased, from the receiver, Depthbrook Ltd which subsequently traded as Hilliers Cotswold Ltd.

Records (1): at Hilliers Cotswold, Newmarket, Nailsworth, Stroud, Gloucestershire GL6 0RG
board meeting minutes 1944-82; trading premises and J Hillier estate plans 1865

Records (2): at Gloucestershire Record Office, Worcester Street, Gloucester, Gloucestershire GL1 3DW
board meeting minutes 1865-1944; share: ledger 1865-1964, transfer register 1865-1955; shareholders mortgage and debenture register 1912-49; annual returns 1904-24; memo and articles of association 1865,1936,1964; photocopy plans 1865

Records (3): at Institute of Agricultural History & Museum of English Rural Life, University of Reading, Whiteknights, Reading, Berkshire RG6 2AG
Newmarket premises deeds 1682-1891

68 CHESTER GROSVENOR HOTEL CO LTD

20 Mar 1865
01978C
Eastern Estate Office, Eccleston, Chester, Cheshire
Hotel

History: incorporated in 1865 as Chester Hotel Co Ltd to acquire and run the Grosvenor Hotel, Chester, built by Richard Grosvenor, 2nd Marquis of Westminster between 1863 and 1865 on the site of the Royal Hotel, built after 1784 and acquired by the Grosvenor family in

1800. The hotel was situated in Eastgate Street, designed by architects Kyrke, Penson & Ritchie and opened on 1 Jan 1866. Acquired in 1961 by the trustees of 2nd Duke of Westminster's will who embarked upon £1 million plus refurbishment and redevelopment plan. Hotel and company changed name to above in 1980. In 1983 had about 100 bedrooms.

Records (1): at Chester Grosvenor Hotel, Eastgate Street, Chester, Cheshire CH1 1LT
directors: meeting minutes 1958-date, register c1900-date; share: certificates 1948-80, ledger 1873-1961, transfer ledger 1923-80; apartment bills 1874,1889; hotel guide entries 1911-13

Records (2): at Eaton Hall Muniment Room, Eaton Hall, Chester, Cheshire
directors meeting minutes 1865-1958; general meeting minutes 1871-95; memo and articles of association 1865-8; annual reports and accounts 1866-87

Ian Callister, *Chester Grosvenor. A History* (priv pub 1983)

69 EASTBOURNE PIER CO LTD

3 Apr 1865
02019C
7 Hanover Square, London W1R 0PS
Piers

History: promoted by Duke of Devonshire and incorporated as above in 1865 to construct a promenade pier in Eastbourne, E Sussex. Construction began in 1866 under direction of Eugenius Birch, railway and pier engineer, and pier opened in 1870. From 1888 stage shows were presented. A full-scale theatre building with tea rooms, licensed bars and offices being built on pier head in 1901. Music Pavilion built on shore end in 1925 which housed a family entertainment centre by 1960s. During WW2 pier was requisitioned and cut in two but it reopened in 1946. Purchased by Trusthouse Forte Leisure Ltd, subsidiary of Trusthouse Forte Ltd, in 1969 and in 1980s provided various popular entertainments and amenities.

Records (1): at E Sussex Record Office, Pelham House, St Andrew's Lane, Lewes, E Sussex BN7 1UN
directors meeting: minutes 1877-1965, agendas 1944-70, attendance book 1944-70; management committee minutes and agendas 1906-47; general meeting minutes 1869-1971; members register c1865-c1903; share: registers nd, ledgers 1908-58, transfer registers 1869-1967, certificates and transfer documents c1889-c1946; debenture transfer: register c1904-67; dividend: book 1949-67, account book 1909-47, warrants 1920-52; mortgages and charges: registers 1870-1933, interest account books 1905-52, agreements and transfer documents c1870-1930; memo and articles of association with resolutions 1865-1948; annual returns 1942-53; general meeting report 1931; chairmans agm speech 1960-7; annual report and accounts 1944-65; balance sheet and profit and loss account 1952; New Pavilion capital account 1899-1902; general ledgers 1913-36; private ledgers 1951-62; daily receipts ledger 1963-7; cash books 1865-82,1912-70; daily receipts book 1918-53; toll book 1910-35; turnstile register 1928-47; invoice book 1939-53; theatre production agreement 1914; correspondence re: theatre management 1918, entertainments 1932-5, and licences 1951-72; vending agreements 1958-73; Pier Theatre leaflets, handbills, programme posters, tickets, photographs, press cuttings etc 1913-c74; wages books 1911-58; staff register c1901-46; employment agreements 1952,1965-6; pension scheme rules 1960; staff training papers 1976; title deeds and property documents 1868-1954; correspondence and documents re kiosks, pier

repairs, war damage, equipment, theatre furnishings etc 1900-65; photographs of pier and theatre 1870-1954; plans of pier and kiosks 1868,1954-61

Records (2): at Trusthouse Forte Leisure, 17 Golden Square, London W1R 3AG
general meeting minutes 1971-date

70 LLOYDS BANK LTD

20 Apr 1865
02065C
71 Lombard Street, London EC3 2BS
Banking

History: established as Taylors & Lloyds in Birmingham in 1765. Original capital was £8000, subscribed by the Taylor family, button manufacturers, and the Lloyds family, ironmasters. Obtained London agency through Hanbury, Taylor, Lloyd & Bowman in 1770. The Taylor family withdrew from the partnership in 1852, and in 1865 it became a joint stock bank (renamed Lloyds Banking Co Ltd), with a nominal capital of £2 million and 13 branch offices. Rapid expansion followed under the general managership of Howard Lloyd from 1871 to 1902. The bank opened a London office and became a member of the London Clearing House in 1884, following the acquisition of the private banks of Barnetts, Hoares, Hanbury & Lloyd and Bosanquet, Salt & Co (est in 1770s). Renamed Lloyds Bank Ltd in 1889. By 1902 the bank had acquired over 50 other banks (mostly private country bankers) and it operated over 260 branches. The move of headquarters from Birmingham to London was completed in 1910. Major acquisitions included the Wilts & Dorset Banking Co Ltd (est 1835, acquired 1914) and the Capital & Counties Bank Ltd (est 1834, acquired 1918). By 1925 the number of branches had risen to 1655 and to over 2300 (UK total) in 1984. Acquired Armstrong & Co, Paris, in 1911 and formed Lloyds Bank (France) Ltd, which was reorganised as Lloyds & National Provincial Foreign Bank Ltd in 1917. Obtained shareholdings in Bank of British West Africa Ltd in 1918 (disposed of 1964-5) and National Bank of New Zealand Ltd in 1919 (later converted to full ownership). Acquired Cox & Co, army bank agents in 1923. Largest foreign interests were London & River Plate Bank Ltd, which had been founded in 1862 and was acquired by Lloyds in 1918, and London & Brazilian Bank Ltd (1862-1923), which were merged to form Bank of London & South America Ltd (BOLSA) in 1923. BOLSA acquired the Anglo-South American Bank Ltd (est 1888) in 1936 and was the largest element in the formation of Lloyds Bank International Ltd in 1971.

Records: at Lloyds Bank, 71 Lombard Street, London EC3 2BS
board meeting minutes 1865 on; chairmans agendas 1866-1902; private meeting minutes 1889-1923; memoranda: secretarys private 1868-71, bill committee 1878-84; committee meeting minutes: Birmingham and agenda 1884-92, building 1886-7, country and agenda 1867-1901, daily 1886-1901, investment 1891-1947, law and sealing 1908-51, London 1884-1901, premises 1890-1937, properties 1891-1902, special 1871-1900, staff 1909-64, W Yorkshire chairmans 1921-30, W Yorkshire 1920-30; agm minutes 1865 on; share: allotment book 1865, registers 1866 on; Lloyds family papers 19 cent; articles of association 1865 on; seal register 1883-95; secretarys department procedure book 1924-61; annual report and accounts 1865 on; balance sheets 1865-85; comparative statistics of banks subsequent to amalgamation 1902-14; profit and loss accounts 1866-1903; private ledgers 1765-1865; daily balance of receipts and payments 1835-64; bank note registers 1842-65; cash book: rough 1765-71, shareholders 1866;

customer ledger 1863-5; staff: senior salary book 1876-1918, rules and instructions 19 cent; widows fund: ledgers 1865-1916, subscription book 1900-16; ledger: premises 1865-71, properties and investments 1884-99; letter books: private 1865-77, and correspondence Howard Lloyd 1868-1902, joint general manager relating to staff 1919-22; branch managers rules 1889; South Wales inspector letter book 1902-15; letters to branch managers re treasureship bonds 1906-14; branches - Birkenhead: Charing Cross memoranda 1900s; Birmingham - Bull Ring: profit and loss book 1893-1922, security ledgers 1893-1922, Cherry Street: private memoranda 1866-75, Colmore Row: private memoranda 1890-1906, security registers 1870s on, standing order book 1870s on, staff attendance book 1883-4, Edgbaston: private memoranda 1870s on, High Street: private memoranda 1868-1905, profit and loss books 1871-1931, inspection reports 1882-1914, Ivy Bush: private memoranda 1894 on, New Street: profit and loss book 1889-1922, bill register 1887-1918, Small Heath: letter book 1914-31; Blackburn: salary book 1900-16; Bridport: profit and loss book 1914-30; Bristol - Bond Street: private memoranda 1890s on, St George: profit and loss book 1892-1926, St Philips: security registers 1885 on; Burton upon Trent: private memoranda 1876-98; Cardiff Docks: letter books 1896 on; Carmarthen: stock ledger 1892-1927; Chester le Street: profit and loss book 1903-18; Coventry: private memoranda 1874-1914; Deal: profit and loss book 1896-1925; Dudley: private memoranda 1879-1909, letter book 1898-1924; Ellesmere: private memoranda 1883 on, security register 1883 on; Gloucester: private memoranda 1889-1906, letter books 1891-1918; Halesowen: private memoranda 1870 on, profit and loss book 1903 on; Iron Bridge: private memoranda 1874-1906; Kidderminster: private memoranda 1889-1902; Lichfield: profit and loss book 1866 on, letter book 1895-1922; Enfield, London: private memoranda 1886 on; Maidenhead: minutes 1899 on; Manchester: minutes 1901-06, profit and loss books 1900-30, bills diary 1901-08; Margate: summary of balances 1891-1900, security registers 1891-1919; Oldbury: profit and loss books 1866 on, securities books 1867 on, signature books 1864 on, letter books 1886-1925; Pontypool: private memoranda 1890 on, profit and loss books 1890 on, security registers 1890 on; Port Talbot: private memoranda 1898 on, security registers 1898 on, standing order books 1898 on; Ramsgate: private memoranda 1898 on; Redditch: private memoranda 1892 on, profit and loss book 1892-1916; Rugby: private memoranda 1878 on; Shrewsbury: private memoranda 1877-8, correspondence 1883-4; Smethwick: security register 1880 on; Stanley: profit and loss book 1903-20, security registers 1901-11; Swadlincote: profit and loss book; Swansea: security registers 1893 on; letter books 1883-1917; Tamworth: private memoranda 1879 on, security registers 1870-1917; Taunton: profit and loss book 1906-15; Tenbury Wells: private memoranda 1889 on; Wednesbury: security memoranda 1865-81, security registers 1881 on; West Bromwich: security register 1883 on, standing order book 1882 on; Westgate on Sea: profit and loss book 1891 on, security register 1891 on; Wolverhampton: private memoranda 1876-98, security registers 1873 on, authorities books 1879-9, letter books 1886-1916

RS Sayers, *Lloyds Bank in the History of English Banking* (1957)
JR Winton, *Lloyds Bank 1918-1969* (1982)

71 MANCHESTER COMMERCIAL BUILDINGS CO LTD

21 Apr 1865
02069C
12 St Ann's Square, Manchester, Greater Manchester
Property

History: incorporated as above in 1865 to acquire property in Manchester or Salford, Greater Manchester. Acquired by MEPC Ltd, property investment and development company in 1957. In 1982 had a mixed portfolio of commercial and residential property in and around Manchester.

Records: at MEPC, Brook House, 113 Park Lane, London WIA 4AY
directors and general meeting minutes 1947-date, memo and articles of association 1865; registration papers incl annual returns 1957-date; debenture trust deed 1897

72 MARKENDALE LANCASHIRE LTD

25 May 1865
02163C
228 Briscoe Lane, Manchester, Greater Manchester M10 6XG
Hide and skins merchants

History: founded by Richard Markendale in Manchester in early 19 cent. Incorporated in 1865 as Richard Markendale & Co Ltd at which time operated from Wood Street, Deansgate, Manchester to carry on business of hide and skin brokers, tanners, fell-mongers and curers. Moved to Regent Road Bridge, Water Street, in 1884 and to Briscoe Lane in 1974. Ministry of Food controlled industry during WW2, amalgamating all local companies into the Manchester & District Hide, Skin & Fat Co Ltd which was administered by company until ceased in 1954. Merged with Lancashire Butchers Hide & Skin Co Ltd in 1969 to form above and took over the Co-operative Wholesale Society hide market in Manchester and Arthur Smith (Wigan) Ltd, fell-mongers, in 1970. In 1982 business consisted of servicing abbatoirs, cleaning hides and skins, and trading in same on a local, national and international basis. Also had branch at Welsh Row Head, Nantwich, Cheshire.

Records: at Markendale Lancashire, 228 Briscoe Lane, Manchester, Greater Manchester M10 6XG
directors and committee meeting minutes 1914-date; share transfer register 1865-date; memo and articles of association 1865-1933; purchase: ledger 1965-73, journal 1969-73; day book and ledger 1955-68; weekly balances 1930-44; cash books 1962-77; Manchester hide skin and fat market price sheets 1876-1934; Salford stock market receipts 1894-8; Hanley's Repository wool sale catalogue 1936; hide weight registers 1969-74; wages books 1901-40; photographs of directors and officials c1940-50 and Regents Road Bridge premises nd
Lancashire Butchers Hide & Skin Co Ltd: members register etc 1894-1944; annual reports and accounts 1937-64; private ledgers 1932-69; day books 1940-69; cash books: general 1937-68, butchers payments 1954-69
Manchester & District Hide Skin & Fat Co Ltd: private ledger 1941-51; Ministry of Food weekly account balances 1940-51

73 PARR'S BANK LTD

29 May 1865
02173C
Warrington Old Bank, 10 Winwick Street, Warrington, Cheshire
Banking

History: established at Warrington, Cheshire in about 1782 by Joseph Parr, sugar refiner, Thomas Lyon, and Walter Kerfoot, solicitor, as Parr, Lyon & Co. Opened offices at St Helens, Merseyside in 1839 and Runcorn, Cheshire in 1853. Known as Parr, Lyon & Greenall from 1825-51 and as Parr & Co by 1865. Parr's Banking Co Ltd formed in 1865 to acquire the business. Under leadership of John Dun, general manager, had acquired or opened 43 offices in the Cheshire, Lancashire, Greater Manchester and Merseyside areas by 1890. In 1891 acquired Fuller, Banbury & Co of Lombard Street, London which secured bank's entry to the London Clearing House. Amalgamated with Alliance Bank Ltd in 1892 to form Parr's Banking Co & the Alliance Bank Ltd. Style reverted to Parr's Bank Ltd in 1896. Subsequent amalgamations included the Consolidated Bank Ltd of London in 1896, the Derby & Derbyshire Banking Co Ltd in 1898, the Ashton, Stalybridge, Hyde & Glossop Bank Ltd in 1900, Pare's Leicestershire Banking Co Ltd in 1902, Stuckey's Banking Co Ltd which operated with over 60 branches in Somerset and Gloucestershire, in 1909 and Crompton & Evans' Union Bank Ltd, of Derby, in 1913. As a result of these amalgamations the bank operated 320 branches and 91 sub-branches by 1914. In 1918 merged with the London County & Westminster Bank Ltd to form the London County Westminster & Parr's Bank Ltd, whose name was changed to Westminster Bank Ltd in 1923.

Records (1): at National Westminster Bank, 41 Lothbury, London EC2P 2BP
board meeting minutes 1865-1918; general managers reports 1897-1901; committee meeting minutes: select 1865-6, weekly 1892-5, general purpose 1908-29, daily 1909-13, branch and premises 1898-1902, 'A' 'B' 'C' 1910-23; agm minutes 1866-1918; shareholders list 1897; share ledger 1865-90; directors register 1901-16; partnership agreements 1804-57; corporate papers re profits, formation, amalgamation etc 1860-1918; annual reports and accounts 1865-1917; debts owed 1851; customer correspondence re securities and bad debts 1823-1902; scheme of changes 1912; salary books 1856-1931; officer lists 1897-1922; instruction book 1903; papers re Parr family 19 cent; directors correspondence 1897; notebook of J Rae 1890-1905; branch and staff statistics 1904; branch results 1913; branches - Chester: salary book 1914-54; Clifton: bill ledger 1909 on; Leicester: list overdrawn accounts 1904; Loughborough: meeting minutes 1903-07; Charing Cross: comparative statements and profit analysis 1896-1903; Cavendish Square: meeting minutes 1901-06; Matlock: meeting minutes 1915; Northwich: meeting minutes 1888-1901; Runcorn: meeting minutes 1860 on, premises expenditure 1892 on; Sandbach: discount ledger 1883 on; Teddington: meeting minutes 1900-18, returns 1899-1918, general ledger 1899-1918, deposit ledger 1899-1917, loan ledger 1901-18

Records (2): at Warrington Central Library, Museum Street, Warrington, Cheshire WA1 1JB
deeds, accounts and papers re Lyon family estate 1566-1928; deeds, papers and correspondence re Parr family estates 1600-1900

74 SOUTHERN'S PROPERTIES LTD

28 Jul 1865
02313C
St Helen's, 1 Undershaft, London EC3P 3DQ
Property (formerly insurance)

History: incorporated in 1865 as Provident Clerks & General Guarantee Association Ltd, a fidelity guarantee insurance company. Provident Clerks & General Accident Insurance Co Ltd, an associate company, was established in 1876 and both shared the same management and premises at 61 Coleman Street, London. They amalgamated in 1907 to form Provident Clerks & General Guarantee & Accident Co Ltd. Name was shortened to Provident Accident & Guarantee Co Ltd in 1917 but business remained mainly general accident and fidelity guarantee insurance. Acquired in 1918 by Northern Assurance Co Ltd which merged it with White Cross Insurance Co Ltd, motor insurance specialists (est 1906 as Red Cross Insurance Association but changed name in 1912 in deference to Geneva Convention Act) in 1925 to form Provident Accident & White Cross Insurance Co Ltd. Name was shortened to White Cross Insurance Co Ltd in 1949. Operated under its own name until Northern was acquired by Commercial Union Assurance Co Ltd in 1968. Name changed to above during 1970s and became a property company. Placed in liquidation in 1978.

Records: at Commercial Union Assurance, St Helen's, 1 Undershaft, London EC3P 3DQ
directors meeting minutes 1925-9; general meeting minutes 1911-68

75 LANTERN LODGES (NORTHERN) LTD

31 Jul 1865
02319C
66 Hammersmith Road, London W14 OPA
Property

History: incorporated in 1865 as Keswick Hotel Co Ltd to acquire the Keswick Hotel, Keswick, Cumbria together with the lease of the refreshment rooms of Keswick railway station. The initial share capital was 3000 shares of £10. In 1973 was acquired by J Lyons & Co Ltd. Name subsequently changed to Falcon Squash Clubs Ltd and the company's objects were changed to squash club proprietors. Name changed to above in 1973 and subsequently became a subsidiary of Allied-Lyons PLC on the acquisition of J Lyons & Co Ltd by Allied Breweries Ltd. Placed in liquidation in 1983

Records: no records known to survive

76 KEIGHLEY FLEECE MILLS CO LTD

14 Aug 1865
02364C
PO Box 58, Midland Mills, Valley Road, Bradford, W Yorkshire BDI 4RL
Room and power

History: William Sugden, woolstapler and stuff piece manufacturer, commenced building of Fleece Mills, Keighley, W Yorkshire in 1819. After death, in about 1835 when succeeded by son William, power looms were introduced but as more yarn was sold weaving was abandoned by 1850. As business declined parts of the mills were let to tenants who were supplied with power. William Sugden junior died in 1852 and business passed on to his brother John G Sugden, an agriculturalist and by his death in 1864 the business of the mills was in decline. His widow sold the propery to the founders of Keighley Fleece Mills Co Ltd, incorporated in 1865 to generate and sell motive power and heat. In 1959 Charles Hanson & Co Ltd (est 1898), worsted spinners specialising in mohair and alpaca yarns, and tenants since 1904, installed a new boiler plant. Thereafter company only leased out the property and did not provide any services to its remaining tenants. In 1960 became wholly owned subsidiary of Hansons who were themselves acquired by Jeremiah Ambler & Sons Ltd, mohair spinners of Midland Mills,

Bradford, W Yorkshire (est 1789) in 1967. Amblers merged with Robert Clough Keighley Ltd, worsted spinners and manufacturers of Grove Mill, Keighley (est 1800) and CF Taylor & Co Ltd of Shipley, W Yorkshire (inc 1916) in 1970 to form British Mohair Spinners Ltd. Production ceased at Fleece Mills in 1980 and by 1982 part of the site had been demolished and the land sold for development.

Records: at Keighley Fleece Mills, PO Box 58, Midland Mills, Valley Road, Bradford, W Yorkshire BDI 4RL
directors and general meeting minutes 1872-date; members registers etc 1904-date; share certificate book 1936-date; balance sheets and accounts 1980-2; sundries ledger 1892-1930 with balances to 1917; plans of Fleece Mills property, 1865,1963; correspondence and papers re leasing and selling of property 1963-80; centenary publication 1965

The Keighley Fleece Mills Co Ltd ... 1865-1965 (priv pub 1965)

77 THRELFALLS (LIVERPOOL & BIRKENHEAD) LTD

29 Aug 1865
02400C
PO Box 38, High Street, Blackburn, Lancashire BB1 1HG
Brewing

History: incorporated in 1865 as Birkenhead Amalgamated Brewing Co Ltd to take over the brewing concerns of Aspinall's Brewery of Cleveland Street and Cook's Brewery, Oxton Road, Birkenhead, Merseyside. Name changed to Birkenhead Brewery Co Ltd in 1872. Company controlled 120 tied houses by 1962 when it was acquired by Threlfalls Chesters Ltd, of Liverpool which was itself acquired by Whitbread & Co Ltd in 1967. Subsequently changed name to above.

Records: at Whitbread, Chiswell Street, London EC1Y 4SD
directors meeting minutes 1865-1968; agms minutes 1866-1946; probate register 1865-1948; register of directors 1917-55; shares (rough) transfer books 1907-62; pension fund trust deed & rules 1947; press cuttings book 1924-50; memo of association (amended) 1872; correspondence binders for 37 tied houses c1930-69, reports and accounts 1968-70; finance committee minutes book 1969-70; managed houses trading accounts 1970-1; executive committee minutes book 1968-70

78 BRABY GROUP LTD

24 Oct 1865
02537C
Cowley Mill Road, Uxbridge, London UB8 2QG
Metal storage container and plant manufacturers, (formerly zinc manufacturers)

History: established by Charles Jack, zinc manufacturer, in Tottenham Court New Road, St Pancras, London, in 1839. Acquired by Frederick Braby in 1854, moving to Fitzroy Works, New Road, (now Euston Road) in 1855. Incorporated as Frederick Braby & Co Ltd in 1865. Original zinc manufacturing and importing was extended to include perforating and manufacture of wire netting and galvanized sheets. Ida and Victoria Works, Deptford, were opened in 1866 and 1870 and branches established in Liverpool in 1871, Glasgow 1875, Adelaide, Australia 1886-96, Borough High Street, London 1893, Bristol, Avon 1896, and

Falkirk, Central 1899. Also had offices in Dublin and Belfast and established rolling mills at Glasgow from 1908. After WW2 started to produce aluminium products and subsequently closed Glasgow factory. Factories in Euston and Deptford moved to Crayford, Kent, and then to Uxbridge, Greater London, in 1960s. Acquired Auto Diesels Ltd (est 1936) in 1959, changed name to above and acquired by Economic Group Ltd (est 1922), gas appliance manufacturers, in 1970. Latter changed name to Braby Leslie Ltd in 1974.

Records (1): at Braby Leslie, Cowley Mill Road, Uxbridge, London UB8 2QG
directors minutes 1865-date; general meetings reports 1870-88; agm notes 1870-88; dividend lists 1950s-60s; transfer register 1885-1972; corporate notices and annual reports and accounts 1864-1920; memo and articles of association 1865; chairmans papers with historical notes 20 cent; dividend cash book 1949-70; sales cash book 1964-71; illustrated catalogues 1873-98; staff superannuation fund ledger 1924-40; works pension fund journal 1949-59; photographs and engraving of chairmen and directors 19 cent; annual reports and accounts, programmes etc of works sporting and social clubs 1889-1911

Records (2): at Business Archives Council Library, 185 Tower Bridge Road, London SE1 2UF
illustrated catalogue, leaflets and discount lists 1928-32

JE Richardson, *Chronicle of Fitzroy Works and of Frederick Braby and Co Ltd* (priv pub 1925)

79 GATESHEAD BOWLING GREEN CO LTD
7 Nov 1865
02569C
Prince Consort Road, Gateshead, Tyne & Wear NE8 1LS
Bowling club

History: incorporated as above in 1865 to manage a bowling club at Gateshead, Tyne & Wear. Member of Durham County Bowling Association and Northern Counties Private Bowling Clubs Association.

Records: at Gateshead Bowling Green, Prince Consort Road, Gateshead, Tyne & Wear NE8 1LS

80 RADNORSHIRE CO LTD
27 Nov 1865
02630C
Wylcwm Place, Knighton, Powys
Agricultural merchants

History: incorporated in 1865 by local businessmen as Radnorshire Coal, Lime & General Supply Co Ltd to buy, sell and deal in coal, coke, lime, timber, manure, bricks, tiles, slates, building materials, feeding stuffs and artificial fertilizers. Offices were situated in Broad Street, Knighton, Powys. By 1885 were merchants, colliery agents, lime burners, cement manufacturers, brickmakers, stone quarry owners, millers, wheel-wrights and carriage and railway wagon builders. By 1909 had 16 depots in Salop and Powys, sawmills at Knighton and lime kilns at Dolyhir, Old Radnor. Acquired Montgomeryshire Coal & Lime Co Ltd, Llanidloes, Powys and Llandrindod Coal Co Ltd, Llandrindod Wells, Powys, by 1920. Head offices moved to Wylcwm Place in 1921 and name changed to above in 1946.

Acquired Bates & Hunt (Agricultural) Ltd (inc 1934) and its subsidiary Bates & Hunt (Crop Spraying) Ltd, agricultural merchants in 1952. Acquired in 1963 by Ranks Hovis McDougall Ltd and in 1975 was trading as manufacturers of animal feed stuffs, processors of cereal and herbage seeds and agricultural merchants. Ceased to trade in 1980 and acquired in 1983 by Dalgety PLC.

Records: at Dalgety, 19 Hanover Square, London W1R 9DA
current

81 LIEBIGS EXTRACT OF MEAT CO LTD

4 Dec 1865
02654C
Thames House, Queen Street Place, London EC4R 1DH
Food canning and cattle ranching

History: incorporated as above in 1865 to exploit a Liebig patent in River Plate, Argentina. Meat extract plant established at Fray Bentos in Uruguay. Pioneers in the manufacture of concentrated foods, awarded a gold medal at the Paris Exposition 1867, in recognition of their foundation of a new industry. Manufacturers of Oxo among other meat products. By 1958 owned directly or through its 32 subsidiaries, cattle ranches and factories for the preparation of canned meats, extracts etc in Argentina, Paraguay, Uruguay, Zimbabwe and Sudan, also packing factories and sales organisations in UK (through Oxo Ltd), France, Belgium, Italy, Netherlands, Switzerland, Canada, USA, South Africa, Central and East Africa. In 1968 amalgamated with Brooke, Bond & Co Ltd with latter changing name to Brooke Bond Liebig Ltd. In early 1980s was a principal operating subsidiary of latter.

Records (1): at Liebigs Extract of Meat, Thames House, Queen Street Place, London EC4R 1DH
board meeting minutes 1865 on; ledgers 1865 on; order books 1900s on; shipment books 1870s on; letter books 1890 on; legal documents, letters and reports, re law suits in connection with Liebig patent c1865 on; draft company history nd

Records (2): at Liebigs Extract of Meat, Paseo Colon 221, Buenos Aires, Argentina
managers reports, estancia reports etc for Fray Bentos and Colon establishments 1894-1910; journal, cash book 1864-6; contract book 1864-8; letter books 1897-1920

82 LAMPORT & HOLT LINE LTD

18 Dec 1865
02694C
Albion House, 30 St James Street, Liverpool, Merseyside L2 7SY
Shipping

History: founded in 1845 on partnership of William J Lamport (died 1874) and George Holt (died 1895). First offices at Fenwick Buildings, Fenwick Street, Liverpool, moving to Drury Buildings, Water Street, and then to Royal Liver Buildings in 1912. Fleet of wooden sailing vessels trading with east coast of North America, India, South Africa, River Plate and west coast of South America numbered 13 by 1850. Partners also had shares in steamships until in 1864 started own steamship line in Brazil and River Plate trade. Registered in 1865 as Liverpool, Brazil & River Plate Steam Navigation Co Ltd with partnership acting as managers. Services ran from London, Glasgow, Antwerp and USA east coast ports to River Plate and east and west coasts of South America. From 1845-71, 42 sailing ships and 5 steamers had passed through hands and in 1870s formed Société de Nav Royale Belge Sud-Americaine in Antwerp to deal with Belgian traffic. Fleet size in 1875 was 31 ships of 48,236 gross tonnage rising to 50 ships of 93,331 gross tonnage in 1888. Formed Argentine Steam Lighter Co Ltd in 1884 to operate passenger and cargo services on River Plate which continued to c1900. From 1900s purpose built passenger liners and refrigerated cargo ships were introduced, Liverpool to Brazil and River Plate passenger service opening in 1908. In 1911 Lamport & Holt partnership became public company, Lamport & Holt Ltd, and was taken over by Royal Mail Steam Packet Co Ltd (under chairmanship of Owen C Phillips, later Lord Kylsant). UK passenger trade was subsequently run by latter, leaving New York, Brazil and River Plate services with calls at Trinidad and Barbados to Lamport & Holt Ltd. On outbreak of WW1 owned 36 steamers of 198,992 gross tonnage, 11 being lost during war, but by 1924 had 50 ships of 322,857 gross tonnage. With collapse of Kylsant empire in 1929/30 was put into receivership and of 41 ships owned in 1930, 20 had been sold by 1935. In mid 1934 above was formed to acquire assets of Lamport & Holt Ltd and its subsidiary Liverpool, Brazil & River Plate Steam Navigation Co Ltd. Lost 13 vessels during WW2 and in 1944 became part of the Vestey Group when acquired by Frederick Leyland & Co Ltd, which was managed by Blue Star Line. At end of war, fleet numbered 9 ships of 65,396 gross tonnage, but rose to 16 ships of 105,970 gross tonnage by 1953. Inaugurated UK to Asunciøn, Paraguay, service in 1953 and discontinued New York to River Plate service in 1955, all tonnage being withdrawn from New York in 1967. Moved to new premises at 30 James Street in 1975 and at same time new company, Blue Star Ship Management Ltd, assumed responsibility of ship husbandry of all Lamport & Holt, Blue Star Line and Booth Steam Ship Co Ltd (acquired by Vestey in 1946) ships. From 1970s operated UK - River Plate service with Argentine National Line and Houlder Brothers. From 1976 operated Brazil and River Plate services jointly with Blue Star Line, Houlder Brothers and Royal Mail Lines as British Lines Service.

Records (1): at Lamport & Holt Line, Albion House, 30 St James Street, Liverpool, Merseyside L2 7SY

minutes 1912-34; board meeting report 1930; directors: attendance registers 1934-56, correspondence 1912-30; scaling committee minutes 1934-44; directors and shareholders register nd; shares registers 19-20 cent; share certificates, papers and correspondence 20 cent; associate members applications 1917-27; mortgages register 1934-54; deeds register 1907-23; memo and articles of association 1865; creditors arrangement scheme 1933; accounts statements 1910,1930-44; ledgers 1895-1922; steamers cash book 1963; master and mates certificates 1871-97; apprentice indentures 1912-18; stevedores licence 1934; officers general instructions nd; superannuation fund records nd; vessel certificates, bills of sale, damage accounts, mortgage papers etc 1867-1955; lumber steamers list 1895; Buenos Aires shipping register 1874-1906; tug lists nd; new ships planning and costs details nd; homeward freights register 1912; general fleet reports 1930; *TSS Vandyke* visitors book 1938; ships photographs, plans, brochures etc 20 cent; operations: schedule 1930, report on South American passenger service nd, misc papers 1920s-30s; voyage results 1911-12; New York commission papers 1912-13; press cuttings 20 cent; scrapbook 1895; misc papers 20 cent; history 1950

Lamport & Holt Ltd: minutes 1911-34; prospectus statement 1911; memo and articles of association 1911; agreements 1911-39; shareholders applications and correspondence 1944; preference share registers nd; debenture: trust deeds 1911, scheme 1933; ledgers 1911-34;

capital ledger 1920; nominal ledger nd; private ledgers c1911; private journals 1908-34; income and expenditure details 1930-3; receivership papers 1934; stevedores notebooks 1896,1903; hatch capacities 1907; general ship information 1899; fleet history 1945
Anglo-South American Airline Ltd: directors attendance book nd; ledger nd; cash book nd; misc papers 1944
Booth Steam Ship Co Ltd: standing instructions to captains nd
H&W Nelson: correspondence 1924-30

Records (2): at Liverpool Record Office, City Libraries, William Brown Street, Liverpool, Merseyside L3 8EW
steamers movement books 1934-60; coffee out turns 1907-32

PM Heaton 'The Lamport and Holt Fleet 1845-1977' in *Sea Breezes* Vol 51 (Jun - Dec 1977)

83 CUMBRIAN NEWSPAPERS GROUP LTD
1 Jan 1866
02729C
Newspaper House, Dalston Road, Carlisle, Cumbria CA2 5UA
Newspapers

History: first issue of *The Patriot* or *Carlisle & Cumberland Advertiser* was published in Carlisle, Cumbria on 3 Jun 1815 under editorship of Robert Perring. Perring left in 1829 to become editor and part-proprietor of *Leeds Intelligence* (later *Yorkshire Post*) but returned in 1847 as joint editor and proprietor. He retired in 1865 and sold the weekly *Carlisle Patriot* to the Carlisle Conservative Newspaper Co Ltd, incorporated in 1866. John Burgess was appointed editor in 1867, beginning 3 generations of editorial control which were to last for over 100 years. *East Cumberland News*, a more popular weekly newspaper, was published from 1883. In 1910 the 2 newspapers were amalgamated to form *Cumberland News* and an evening paper, *Cumberland Evening News* was published from 1910-18. The company's offices at 27 English Street were rebuilt in 1926. Company acquired ownership of *Penrith Observer* (est 1860) in 1947, transferring its printing to Carlisle, and control of *Workington Star* (est 1888) in 1951. Acquired new premises in Kings Arms Lane in early 1950s and changed name to Cumberland Newspapers Ltd in 1952. In 1962 bought controlling interest in Brash Bros Ltd, of Cockermouth, Cumbria, publishers of *West Cumberland Times* (est 1874), transferring its printing plant to Workington, Cumbria, and of Whitehaven News Ltd which published *The Whitehaven News* (est c1856) and *West Cumberland News* (est 1918). Amalgamated the *West Cumberland Times*, *West Cumberland News* and *Cumberland Star* to form *West Cumberland Times & Star*, and *Evening Star* and *Evening News* in 1967. All newspapers were subsequently printed in Carlisle except *Cumberland and Westmorland Herald* printed at Penrith, Cumbria, and *Carlisle Journal* (est 1798), printed at Cockermouth, Cumbria. Purchased *Cumberland Journal* in 1968 and merged it into *Cumberland News*. Company acquired control of Cumberland & Westmorland Printing Co Ltd and amalgamated *Penrith Observer* with *Cumberland & Westmorland Herald* in 1968. Moved from English Street to Dalston Road, Carlisle in 1973 and subsequently changed name to above. In 1982 company published 4 weekly newspapers: *Cumberland News*, *West Cumberland Times & Star*, *The Whitehaven News* and *Hexham Courant*, and 1 evening paper *Cumberland Evening News & Star*.

Records (1): at Cumbrian Newspapers Group, Newspaper House, Dalston Road, Carlisle, Cumbria CA2 5UA
board: and general meeting minutes 1957-67, reports 1923-7, agendas 1951-62; agm reports and agendas 1951-62; members register 1866-83; share: certificate books 1866-1910, transfer documents 1883-c1940, and register 1872-1907, correspondence and papers 1866-1952; dividend: payable book 1919-26, requests 1935-9; corporate documents and correspondence 1865-1950; memo and articles of association 1865-1936; annual reports and accounts 1928-38,1951-62; balance sheets and accounts 1867-1961; nominal ledgers 1907-25; cost sheets 1927,1932; bank book 1919-22; income tax papers 1920s; financial papers and correspondence 1908-30s; sales: certificates 1923,1928-33, statistics 1937-8,1952; circulation certificates 1919-20; readership survey 1952; newspaper reports 1906,1913; newsprint returns 1954-74; printing examples and instructions 1926-53; plant: inventories and valuations 1936-52; purchasing papers and correspondence 1906-28, plans 1910-20s; English Street factory register 1879-92; wages account 1868; printers agreement booklets 1924-51; pension scheme documents and correspondence c1945-60s; property: documents and correspondence 1889-1925, valuations and inventories 1904-24; rebuilding costs 1903,1926; Dr Wadely Concerts papers and correspondence 1951-2; correspondence: RN Burgess 1930-1, misc 1909-20s; newscuttings 1920s-50s; newspapers 1818 on
Penrith Observer Ltd: members register 1933-48; share: certificates, transfer documents 1933-48, correspondence and circulars 1933, holders list 1937; debenture: register 1937-41, interest book 1938-48, correspondence 1937, holders lists 1938-44; memo and articles of association 1933; managers reports 1939-44; annual reports and accounts 1938-43; annual returns 1941-8; balance sheet and accounts 1934-43; accounting papers 1937; plant inventory 1948; insurance policies 1935-49
R Scott Ltd: papers and correspondence re sale of *Penrith Observer* 1933; trading and profit and loss accounts 1929-31
Whitehaven News Ltd: employees profit sharing booklet 1927; title deeds and papers of Theatre Royal, Whitehaven 1769-1909

Records (2): JL Burgess, Carlisle, Cumbria (c/o Cumbrian Newspapers)
board: and general meeting minutes 1906-7, reports 1953,1963-9; executive board meeting minutes 1965-7

Records (3): at Cumbria Record Office, The Castle, Carlisle, Cumbria CA3 8UR
board reports, agendas and papers 1965-8; executive board minutes, reports and papers 1965-7; share: register 1866-1936, ledger 1945-66, certificate books 1899-1967, transfer register 1866-1936 and documents 1906-66; correspondence 1900-59; shareholders: register 1930-60, lists 1930-67; debenture: register 1900-20; certificates 1927-67; papers and correspondence 1900-20; dividend books 1926-66; corporate papers and correspondence 1900-20; directors correspondence 1918,1936-46; memo and articles of association 1865-6 with resolutions 1936-60; annual reports and accounts 1882,1906-14,1929-37; balance sheets and accounts 1915-67; private ledger 1925-55; trading account book 1959-66; cash books 1954-67; photography department day book 1919-55; cost: sheets 1911-47,1956, analyses 1890-1901; bank passbook 1922-30; misc financial papers 1944-56; sales advertisements and staff total accounts book 1929-36; agents and street sales book 1936-7; annual advertisement totals 1935-44; print totals analysis book 1949-55; machinery catalogues drawings, plans and photographs c1900-67; jobbing office stock taking book 1926-62; staff: agreements 1939-50, register 1906-44,

instructions 1920, correspondence 1950-7, list 1940-55; reporters: apprenticeship indenture 1950s; wages: list book 1917-67, books 1940-4,1959-64; memo 1951; salaries cost analyses 1949-56; sickness fund rules 1948; pension and life assurance scheme: booklet 1953, correspondence 1955-65; English Street premises: plans and photographs 1962; plant inventory and valuations 1959,1965, alteration papers 1924-6, lease negotiations 1955-64; Kings Arms Lane premises plan 1955; Editors correspondence and papers inc equipment, building, articles, staff, newsagents, advertising, circulation, contributors, supplies, readers, history, newsprint 1882-1977; JL Burgess 1945-77; promotion papers, correspondence, newscuttings, programmes, photographs etc incl Carlisle Pageants and Historical Exhibition 1928-77; companys anniversary celebration papers 1965; history 1965; engraving blocks 1960s: JL Burgess personal papers, correspondence with and re Press Association, Reuters, Border Television, local radio, Border Regiment, Newspaper Society, Cumbria and Carlisle development 1941-73

Brash Brothers Ltd: partnership deeds and papers 1887-99; directors and general meeting minutes 1899-1953; members register and share ledger 1899-1927; shareholders agreements and requests 1905-06; share: certificates 1899,1906-65, transfer register 1906-27, documents 1906,1913; debenture documents and papers 1899-1933; memo and articles of association 1899-1931; acquisition papers: proposed 1918-21, actual 1953-68; annual returns 1906-54; annual reports and accounts 1917-54; annual and half yearly accounts 1960-7; income tax papers 1921-9; bill heads 1870; employees: register 1909-65, application lists and papers 1925-65; insurance policies and papers 1913-34; sales shop: and works valuations 1921-7, fitting out papers 1900; libel correspondence 1890-3; correspondence and receipts re book publication 1879-80

Cumberland Star Ltd: annual and half yearly accounts 1951-67

Cumberland & Westmorland Herald Newspapers & Printing Co Ltd: annual reports and accounts 1935-57; annual returns 1937; printing photographs nd

Penrith Observer Ltd: directors meeting: minutes 1949, attendance book 1933-47; shareholders: lists 1940s, correspondence 1940-8; acquisition papers and correspondence 1933; liquidation papers 1949; annual and half yearly accounts 1933-47; bank book 1941-8; reporting correspondence 1936-8; plant and office valuation 1934; history nd

Steel Brothers Ltd: annual returns, reports and balance sheets 1915-53

Whitehaven News Ltd: shareholders circulars 1962; annual returns 1944; annual and half yearly accounts 1960-7; acquisition papers 1962-3; correspondence re editor, proprietors, advertising and news coverage 1952-66

Workington Star Ltd: directors meeting minutes, reports and papers 1952-8, annual returns 1945,1950; annual accounts 1951-8; acquisition papers 1951-2; premises: plans 1954, lease 1933; pension fund and life assurance scheme booklet 1957; correspondence re staff, premises, equipment and finance 1949-68

Records (4): at British Library, Newspaper Library, Colindale Avenue, London NW9 5HE
Carlisle Journal 1808,1813-15,1819,1851-1965; *Carlisle Patriot* 1821-1910 (except 1857); *Cumberland News* 1913-68; *Cumberland News & Carlisle & Cumberland Journal* 1968-date; *Cumberland Evening News (and Star)* 1910-date; *East Cumberland News* 1883-1910; *Penrith Observer* 1860-1968 (except 1897-8); *West Cumberland News* 1918-67

Cumberland Newspapers Group Ltd (priv pub 1972)

84 SOUTH LONDON CO-OPERATIVE BUILDING CO LTD

29 Mar 1866
02928
46 Knights Hill, West Norwood, London SE27
Property

History: incorporated as above in 1866 to purchase land and buildings within 3 miles of St Lukes Church, Lower Norwood, London and to erect, alter and adapt buildings for shops or dwelling houses, to be let or sold to shareholders or others. The first directors were involved with the running of Lower Norwood Co-operative Building Co Ltd and the two companies were run together from registered offices in the Lower Norwood Institute. In 1886 the objects were changed to include adapting buildings for working class dwellings, and in 1961 the 3 mile barrier was removed. Montague Long was secretary and manager of both companies from about 1890 until his death in 1940.

Records: at Lambeth Archives Department, Minet Library, 52 Knatchbull Road, London SE5 9QY
share ledger 1866-84; rent books 1889-1910; Montague Long: repairs book 1904-20, letter books 1910-26, land valuation returns notebook 1909, obituary 1940

85 GRINDLAYS BANK LTD

23 Mar 1866
02945
Minerva House, PO Box 7, Montague Close, London SE1 9DH
Banking

History: established in Calcutta in 1863 as Calcutta City Banking Corporation, changing name in 1864 to the National Bank of India. The bank was an Indian registered company, promoted by British and Indian businessmen. Its business included discounting bills and notes, dealing in exchange, and lending on security of real and personal property and securities. The bank did much to finance India's external trade in indigo, tea and coffee. In 1866 its head office was transferred to London (where it had established a branch in 1864) and a British registered company of the same name was incorporated to acquire the business. The Indo-Egyptian Bank, based in Bombay, was acquired in the early 1860s and its office became the bank's Bombay branch. Branches were established in Hong Kong 1869, Shanghai 1875, Madras 1877, Colombo 1881, Karachi 1884, Rangoon 1886, Zanzibar 1893, Mombasa 1896 and Nairobi 1904. By 1900 the bank had 19 branches and the balance sheet total had grown from £328,736 in 1864 to over £9.5 million. Capital and reserves stood at £850,000 and the staff numbered 800. In 1920 the projected acquisition by Lloyds Bank Ltd was disallowed. The entire share capital of Grindlays Bank Ltd (bankers and agents connected with India since 1826) was acquired from National Provincial Bank Ltd in 1948. The Eastern branches of Lloyds Bank Ltd were absorbed in 1961 and in 1965 the bank acquired a two third interest in Brandts Ltd (merchant bankers), the remaining third being acquired in 1972. This company was subsequently known as Grindlay Brandts Ltd. In 1958 Grindlays business was totally absorbed and name changed to National Overseas & Grindlays Bank Ltd, then to National & Grindlays Bank Ltd in 1959. In 1969 the London group business of the Ottoman Bank was acquired. Name changed to above in 1975. Acquired by Australia & New Zealand Banking Group Ltd in 1984.

Records: at Grindlays Bank, Minerva House, PO Box 7, Montague Close, London SE1 9DH directors meeting minutes 1866-date; accounts committee meeting minutes 1964-9; regional committee meeting minutes 1965-9; general meeting: minutes 1927-date, proceedings 1905-52; articles of association, branch memoranda etc 1890-1952; proposed merger papers 1918-19; annual reports and accounts 1890-1952; balance sheets and accounts 1935-62; profit and loss analysis 1955-68; bad and doubtful debts book 1868-1948; general ledgers India 1955-6; safe custody security ledgers c1933-57; adjustment ledger cash books 1899-1947; Indian branches furniture account books 1949-62; London office account book 1902-45; signature book 1862-83; pension fund trustee and management committee meeting minutes: native staff 1897-1937, officers 1913-46; Indian: staff provident fund ledgers 1946-65, newsletter 1847; staff circulars, newsletters and house magazine c1914-date; branch photographs 1920s-70s
Grindlays & Co Ltd: directors meeting minutes 1924-47; JH Matthews letter books, papers and correspondence 1877-1922
Grindlay Brandts Ltd: directors and general meeting minutes 1952-date; securities books c1896-1933; bond books 1913-c35
Cox Shipping Agency Ltd: directors meeting minutes 1922-68; annual returns 1930-45

Geoffrey Tyson, *100 years of Banking in Asia and Africa* (1963)

86 BRITANNIC ASSURANCE CO LTD
12 Apr 1866
03002
Moor Green, Moseley, Birmingham, W Midlands B13 8QS
Insurance

History: incorporated in Birmingham in 1866 as British Workman's Mutual Assurance Co Ltd specialising in industrial life assurance. Established branches in Lancashire and Yorkshire in late 1860s and subsequently throughout the UK. Undertook ordinary life assurance in 1875, accident insurance in 1881 and general insurance in 1925. Acquired United Family Life Assurance & Sick Society in 1876, Royal Albert Legal Friendly Benefit Society in 1879, Industrial Assurance Co of Great Britain (est 1883) based at Norwich, Norfolk in 1885, and British Legal Life Assurance & Loan Co Ltd (est 1863 in Glasgow) in 1927. Premium income, amounting to £700,000 in 1900, reached £1.4 million by 1916 and £5 million by 1936. Changed name to British Workman's & General Assurance Co Ltd in 1892 and to above in 1905. Moved its head office from Broad Street, Birmingham to Moor Green, Moseley in 1963.

Records: at Britannic Assurance, Moor Green, Moseley, Birmingham, W Midlands B13 8QS board meeting minutes 1866-date; agm extract 1867; share: ledgers 1866-80,1909-36, certificates 1891-1909; annual reports and accounts 1882-date; annual account working papers 1920 on; ledgers: 1872-1915, nominal 1898 on, journals 1944-9; expenses analysis 1910-20; business statistics 1866 on,1915-48; Stroud district managers accounts statement 1943; ordinary life policy registers: 1866-7,1875-1901,1923-66, Aston 1905 on, Birmingham 1907-29; industrial life policy registers: 1897-8,1907-22, rewritten 1867-1940, lapsed 1900 on; endowment policy registers 1946 on; proposal registers: Accrington 1865-75, Newry 1886-1929; policies 1872-1934; prospectuses 1883-1904; premium receipt books 1890-1979; claims registers: deaths 1919-47, surrenders 1926 on, war payments 1939-51; actuarial correspondence 1897-1910; agency appointment: registers nd, correspondence 1877-90; agents guide books nd, staff pension fund ledgers 1923 on; chief office staff association

magazine 1922-date; field staff association magazine 1957-74; divisional long service and company dinners, papers and correspondence 1902-74; sports days newscuttings and programmes 1915-50; staff: photographs 19 cent-1966, tributes 1926; investment: ledgers 1915 on, policy loans 1926 on; offices: photographs 1935, circulars and newscuttings 1963; centenary papers newscuttings and correspondence 1966
British Legal Life Assurance & Loan Co Ltd: finance and office committee meeting minutes 1907-18; shareholders meeting minutes 1896-1907; share ledger 1910; journals 1899-1927; policies: registers 1864-1908, free 1914-25, lost 1866 on, Scottish 1896-7; premium: registers 1865-73, receipt books 1926-9; proposal cards c1922 on

87 NALDER & NALDER LTD

16 Apr 1866
03006
Challow Works, Nr Wantage, Oxfordshire OX12 9SY
Agricultural engineering

History: founded in about 1858 by brothers, Thomas and William Nalder, at Challow Ironworks, East Challow, Oxfordshire. Built up a large business in threshing machines, grain separators and malt screens, exporting around the world. Incorporated as above in 1866 as agricultural engineers, iron founders and agricultural equipment and machine hirers. Acquired in 1975 by Barrett Engineers Ltd of East Challow. By 1977 were mechanical engineers specialising in design and manufacture of malting and brewing equipment, cocoa bean and nut processing machinery, horticultural sizers and graders, screw conveyors and bucket elevators.

Records: at Institute of Agricultural History & Museum of English Rural Life, University of Reading, Whiteknights, Reading, Berkshire RG6 2AG
shareholders list 1866-1940s; share and debenture transfers 1866-1945; memo and articles of association 1958; balance sheets and accounts 1876,1896,1906-59; financial analysis books 1870-1955; general ledger 1857-66; sales ledgers 1860s-1967; unpaid account lists 1876-1967; day book 1906-21; cash books: principal 1924-43, petty 1904-45; bank books 1899-1928; invoice books 1874-1951; reminder book 1911; advice books c1910-c49; agency book 1910-49; advertisements 1888-1902; cost books 1864-1938; estimate books 1901-49; cost/estimate register 1899-1906; patent specifications 1880-99; costing books 1889-1917,1957-9; production report books 1905-20; threshing machine: registers 1868-1909, specification books 1877-94; board registers 1914-40s; pattern registers nd; assembly work books 1920s; stock: books 1866-1955, register 1920s, taking book 1937-52; orders: 1871-1930, registers 1889-1968, analysis books 1919-26; detail books 1862-1914; consignment: rate books 1892-1924, registers 1929-64; cartage and haulage registers 1905-35; technical notebooks 1919-20; drawings register 1888-1916; sketch books 1915-40s; machinery glass negatives and photographs nd; wages book 1857-60; employee certificates nd; workmens voluntary sick fund cash books 1870-1926; employers insurance papers 1935-50; correspondence registers 1889-1900,1938-55; letter books 1865-1950; customer files 1910-38

88 METROPOLITAN BANK (OF ENGLAND & WALES) LTD

1 Aug 1866
03203
Poultry, London EC2P 2BX
Banking

History: established as a joint stock bank in 1829 as Birmingham Banking Co, on initiative of Joseph Gibbins, a former partner in a local private bank. First country bank to obtain a Bank of England discount account on condition that it would issue Bank of England notes. Established branches at Dudley and Walsall and accumulated deposits of over £1 million by 1866. Suspended in 1866 as a result of the Overend Gurney & Co crisis and heavy bad debts. Reconstructed as a limited company in 1866. Acquired Stourbridge & Kidderminster Banking Co (est 1834) in 1880, Staffordshire Joint Stock Bank Ltd (est 1864) in 1889, and Cooper Purton & Sons of Bridgnorth (est 1817) in 1889. Merged with Royal Exchange Bank Ltd (est 1861) in 1889 to become Metropolitan & Birmingham Bank Ltd and removed headquarters to London. Acquired South Wales Union Bank Ltd in 1892 and National Bank of Wales Ltd in 1893 and took present title. Progress hampered by bad debts inherited from National Bank of Wales Ltd but by 1910 it had gathered deposits of nearly £1 million, operated 150 branches, and had developed elaborate financial control systems. In 1914 acquired by London City & Midland Bank Ltd, renamed London Joint City & Midland Bank Ltd in 1918 and Midland Bank Ltd in 1923.

Records (1): at Midland Bank, Poultry, London EC2P 2BX
board meeting minutes 1866-1914, general meeting minutes 1900-14; share ledgers 1911-14; deed of settlement 1830; conveyance of assets 1871; amalgamation papers 1914; annual report and accounts 1885-1914; balance sheet: weekly returns 1878-1914, quarterly 1897-1914; analysis 1913-14; general ledgers 1829-1949; statement of affairs 1870; signature books 1889-1914; security books 1889-1914; insurance register c1900-14; private staff minutes 1876-1914; letter books 1892-7; Neath branch securities book 1895-1905; newscuttings 1894-1914

Records (2): at Birmingham Reference Library, Central Libraries, Chamberlain Square, Birmingham, W Midlands B3 3HQ
investigation committee report 1868; prospectus 1866-80; newscuttings 1866-9

WF Crick and JE Wadsworth, *A Hundred Years of Joint Stock Banking* (1936)

89 FENNY COMPTON WATER CO LTD

13 Oct 1866
03284
Hill House, Church Street, Fenny Compton, Warwickshire
Water supply

History: incorporated in 1866 to provide water for Fenny Compton, Warwickshire, brought down by gravity feed from a spring in the Burton Dassett hills. By 1883, 40 homes were supplied and in 1983 was still supplying water.

Records: at Fenny Compton Water, Hill House, Church Street, Fenny Compton, Warwickshire
directors and general meeting minutes 1866-date; members register 1866-date; share:

certificate books 1927-79, and transfer correspondence 1867-1959; annual returns 1867-1976; balance sheets 1922-66; petty cash books 1877-1980

90 ARTAGEN PROPERTIES LTD
8 Jan 1867
03413
160 Brompton Road, London SW3 1HS
Property

History: founded and incorporated in 1867 by William Austin, drain laying contractor, as Artizans, Labourers & General Dwellings Co Ltd, to build housing for the industrious poor in London. First houses were built in Rollo and Landseer Streets, Battersea, and resold to recoup working capital and buy land at Salford, Greater Manchester, on which 78 houses were built in 1879. In 1872 purchased 40 acres in Battersea on which Shaftesbury Park Estate of 1200 two-storey houses was built, which were either sold on 99 year leaseholds or let on weekly rates. By 1874 had purchased sites in Liverpool; Birmingham; Gosport, Hampshire; and Baildon, Leeds; and had offices mainly for raising money in Manchester; Oldham, Greater Manchester; Huddersfield, W Yorkshire; and Plymouth, Devon. In that year purchased 80 acres in Westminster for Queens Park Estate and 61 acres in Stratford for Cann Hall Estate in 1875. Company's chairman was arrested for fraud in 1877 but financial order was restored. In 1882, 100 acres were purchased in Hornsey for Noel Park Estate, wholly completed in 1929. Between 1885-92, 1467 block dwellings - 2 or 3 flats sharing common WC and sink - were built in Central and W London, which were occupied by labouring poor rather than artisans like the estates. Purchased 66 acres in Streatham for Leigham Court Park Estate, completed in 1928, consisting of maisonettes, flats, shops and houses. Sold off provincial estates in 1922, leaving 9200 lettings on portfolio in 1926. Purchased 324 acres at Pinnerwood Park Estate for middle class housing estate in 1931 while continuing pre WW1 modernisation programme which was resumed after more damaging WW2. Changed name to Artizans & General Properties Co Ltd in 1952 and from 1954 re-invested in commercial property. Head offices moved in 1961 from 1 Cromwell Road to 160 Brompton Road, London. Formed wholly owned subsidiary companies: Pinner Properties Ltd in 1955 to manage some of London and Pinner Estates; Vista Flats Ltd and Vista Developments for Birmingham developments; Artizans Housing Association in 1951 to build on war damaged sites at Shaftesbury and Queens Park Estates; Artagen Investments Proprietory Ltd in Australia in 1965; and Artagen BV in the Netherlands, Artagen Montoyer in Belgium, and Artagen Immobiliere SA in France. Acquired William Brown & Sons (Builders) Ltd in 1959 and consolidated it with Artagen Construction Ltd to carry out smaller building work. Participated in Calthrope Estate, Edgbaston, Birmingham redevelopment in 1958, and made property investments in Canada and USA and in office developments in London and its suburbs in the 1960s. Sold old residential estates in 1965-6 to local authorities, leaving 604 residential units: 377 houses at Pinner, 117 flats in Birmingham and 110 flats in London. Had changed name to above by 1976 when became wholly owned subsidiary of Sun Life Assurance Society Ltd. Changed name to Sun Life Properties Ltd in 1981.

Records (1): at Sun Life Properties, 160 Brompton Road, London SW3 1HS
board: minutes 1958-69, agenda 1967-8, attendance books 1957-69; sealing committee minutes 1957-9; Shaftesbury Park and Lavender Hill committee minutes 1881-5; reports of

agms 1878-1971; resolution notices and shareholders circulars 1872-1938; share allotment book 1881-3; shareholders list 1976; dividend warrants 1952-3; outstanding dividends book 1887 on; memo and articles of association 1884-1935; annual reports and accounts 1872-1965; balance sheets pre 1900-54; journals 1962-70; staff pension fund trustee minutes 1951 on; rent demands c1970; architects and surveyors report on property 1947; valuation papers 1957-75; tenancies register 1920-60; deeds register 1854-1965; correspondence and press cuttings re Royal Palace Hotel takeover bid 1958-9; photographs and prints of Shaftesbury Park Estate nd; photographs of chairman nd; correspondence and papers re centenary dinner 1967; corporate and accounting papers, including minutes and balance sheets of subsidiary companies c1950-60

Artagen Construction Ltd: directors holdings register 1948-53

Artizans Housing Association: directors holdings register 1951-4; balance sheets 1951-4

William Brown & Sons (Builders) Ltd: directors attendance register 1957-67; misc tenders 1965-7

Pinnerwood Construction/Pinner Properties Ltd: directors: holdings register 1948-53, attendance register 1957-67

Rowton Houses Ltd: prospectus for Rowton House, early 20 cent

Vista Developments Ltd: minutes and corporate documents 1962-71; photographs and press cuttings 1962; grading and drainage contract 1963

Records (2): at Lambeth Archives Department, Minet Library, 52 Knatchbull Road, London SE5 9QY

board minutes 1867-1953; committee minutes: block buildings 1885-92, deeds 1877-1956, finance 1877-90, general estates 1886-1949, Hornsey 1881-5, Leigham Court 1893-1906, managing 1914-c54, Noel Park 1885-1906, Queens Park 1881-6; committee agendas: general estates 1890-6, managing 1953-4, Noel Park 1883-5, Queens Park 1884-7; agm: reports 1933-52, attendance book 1909-58; prospectuses, dividend notes and resolutions 1870; share and stock registers 1867-1957; share allotment books 1882-92; share ledgers 1868-92; members ledgers 1887-1945; share transfer registers 1869-1959; share transfer journal 1878-9; share balances 1950-5; share capital receipts 1878-1910; forfeited shares book 1878-9; dividend payments books 1948-58; stockholders ledger 1945-54; unclaimed stock returns book 1879-1950s; stock balances 1953; investments register 1957; directors and managers register 1901-33; proprietors indexes 1877-1954; probate registers 1871-1958; annual returns 1942-57; monthly returns 1901-09; general ledgers 1873-1952; deposit ledgers 1867-1922; ledgers pre 1900-49; journals 1877-1957 on; cash books 1876-1961 on; deposit cash books 1875-1957; petty cash book 1900,1959-66; bank reconciliation books 1961-7; depositors interest and balances 1878-1922; deposit receipts 1878-83; salary books 1889-1947; estate rentals ledger 1872-83; shops rental ledger 1957-60; repairs analysis 1941-9; estate deeds schedule 1872-83; Leigham Court: rental ledgers 1891-1907, journal 1891-6; tenancies register c1900-64; Noel Park: general ledger 1899, rental ledgers 1883-1906, journals 1895-1900 tenancies register c1910-64; Pinnerwood Park: rental ledger 1957-60; Queens Park: tenancies registers 1889-1964, repayment ledger 1876, property record 1960s; Shaftesbury Park: property record 1960s

Artagen Construction Ltd: journals 1955-60; cash book 1956-7; cash statement book 1955-6

Artizans Housing Association: directors fees 1956-62; ledger 1951-5; cash books 1951-61

William Brown & Sons (Builders) Ltd: directors fees 1960-2; inventory and valuation of fixtures and fittings of 3 Keith Grove and Valetta Road, W12 1956

Pinnerwood Construction/Pinner Properties Ltd: directors fees 1955-62; journals 1932-62; cash books 1956-61; trade discount book 1955-7; works order book 1933-55
Vista Developments Ltd: cash book 1961
Vista Flats Ltd: cash book 1951-61

Artizans Centenary 1867-1967 (priv pub 1967)

91 SKIPTON MILL CO LTD

22 Mar 1867
03467
Union Mill, Newtown, Skipton, N Yorkshire
Room and power

History: incorporated in 1867 as above to acquire Union Mill, Newtown, Skipton, N Yorkshire and operate as a room and power company, letting loom space to textile manufacturers. Erected new 200 capacity loom shed in 1871, dyehouse and warehouses in 1874, 12 cottages in Union Street in 1878 and another 4 in 1885. By 1921, 630 looms were operating. In 1984 still rented out space in Union Mill.

Records: at Skipton Mill, Union Mill, Newtown, Skipton, N Yorkshire
directors and general meeting minutes 1871-92,1921-date; share certificate book 1888-1920; memo and articles of association 1921; premises documents 1869-1912; mill plans, elevations and sections 1867-c74

92 VICKERS LTD

03543
Vickers House, PO Box 177, Millbank Tower, London SW1P 4RA
Shipping

History: founded as Naylor Hutchinson, Vickers & Co of Sheffield in 1930 to forge and roll crucible steel rails. Rapidly built up a strong American export trade, appointing a German immigrant, ELS Benzon, as their agent and in 1840 taking him into the partnership. In 1867 incorporated as Vickers, Sons & Co Ltd with Benzon (also a director of John Brown), as chairman, and the new River Don Works was opened in Sheffield. Under the management of the brothers Colonel TE and Albert Vickers the business expanded quickly to become one of the leading and most technically successful iron and steel manufacturers by the end of the 1880s. In 1888 following the Naval Defence Act the firm began to manufacture armour plate and ordnance. The Maxim Gun Co, formed to make automatic hand weapons, was founded in 1883 with help from the Vickers Brothers. In 1888 the Maxim Gun Co amalgamated with the Nordenfeld Guns & Ammunition Co to form Maxim Guns & Ammunition Co Ltd in which Vickers continued to hold a large shareholding. At the same time links were forged with Barrow Shipbuilding Co of Barrow in Furness in Cumbria (founded in 1871) which changed its name to the Naval Construction & Armaments Co Ltd. In 1897 Vickers, Sons & Co Ltd acquired these two firms and changed its names to Vickers, Sons & Maxim Ltd and in 1901 formed the Wolseley Tool & Motor Car Co, as a subsidiary. At the same time it took a half share in the Glasgow armaments and shipbuilding firm William Beardmore & Co. In the decade before WW1 Vickers pioneered the construction of submarines, airships, aircraft, and military motor vehicles and opened satellite plants in several countries including Japan,

Russia and Italy. In 1907 Vickers joined with Armstrong Whitworth to acquire the Whitehead Torpedo Company. During WW1 Vickers turned out huge quantities and a bewildering variety of munitions. There were further acquisitions notably the optical instrument makers T Cooke & Sons of London in 1915. After the war the firm turned away from armaments towards peaceful products, merchant ships, locomotives, civil aircraft, motor vehicles and optical instruments. As part of this policy Vickers took over in 1919 the Metropolitan Amalgamated Railway Carriage & Wagon Co Ltd and formed a new subsidiary Metropolitan Vickers Electrical Co. Suffering badly in the depression of the early 1920s Vickers capital was reconstructed early in 1926 and the investments in Beardmore and Wolseley Tool & Motor Car Co were sold. The following year Vickers shipbuilding, armaments and steelmaking interests were merged with those of Armstrong to form Vickers-Armstrong. In 1928 Metropolitan-Vickers was sold to International General Electric Co. At the same time Vickers expanded its aircraft business through the acquisition of Supermarine and Metropolitan-Cammell, Wagon & Finance Co was formed to take over the rolling stock interests of Vickers and Cammell Laird and a controlling interest in Midland Railway Carriage & Wagon Co Ltd and the Leeds Forge Co Ltd. At the beginning of 1929 English Steel Corporation was formed to rationalize the steelmaking interests of Vickers Armstrong. Following rearmament in 1935 the company recovered rapidly, developing the Spitfire fighter aircraft, through Supermarine. During WW2 the firm dominated the armament industry, building large numbers of Spitfires and Wellington bombers, tanks, field artillery, manual guns and vessels. The company adjusted quickly to peacetime trading, pioneering new designs of civilian aircraft and high technology weapon systems. In 1960 Vickers aircraft interests were merged into the newly created British Aircraft Corporation. Its holding in English Steel Corporation was rationalized in 1912 and its aircraft and shipbuilding interests in 1977. Following the collapse of Rolls Royce, Vickers and Rolls Royce Motors merged in about 1983.

Records (1): at Vickers, Vickers House, PO Box 177, Millbank Tower, London SW1P 4RA during 1984 preparations were being made to transfer the records to Cambridge University Library, Department of Manuscripts, and it was not possible to carry out a thorough survey of the records. Previous surveys and information supplied by the company indicate that the archive is extensive, including: minutes 1867-date, minutes Vickers-Armstrong 1928-1955, notes on informal discussions following board meetings 1943-59; directors attendance books 1895-98,1928-51; general meeting minutes 1868-1943; Electric Boat Co letter book 1901-07; letter books 1904-12; report on Barrow yard 1931-2; Barrow contract book 1898-1905; correspondence re battleship contracts 1898-1919; Barrow launch books nos 1-672 1873-1932; Walkers ship particulars nos 1-193 1931-68; newscuttings 1878-1927; photo albums of ships and yards from c1909; Maxim Gun Co Ltd board minutes 1884-88; Nordenfeld Guns & Ammunition Co Ltd board minutes 1886-88; Maxim Guns & Ammunition Co Ltd board minutes 1888-98; microfilm file series c1900-date

Records (2): at Vickers Shipbuilding & Engineering, Barrow Shipbuilding Works, Barrow in Furness, Cumbria LA14
list of ships built (Barrow) 1-1099 from 1873, list of ships built (Walker) 1-193 1931-69; summary balance sheets 1889-1977; general ledgers 1928-50s; journals 1930s-50s; capital expenditure books 1906-22; inventory and valuation 1948; wages overtime book 1882; (Barrow Shipbuilding Co) daily average piecework rate books 1950-63; contract records of costs and charges 1932-3; contract book ships costs 1938-55; ships contracts (extras, credits,

insurance and work in progress) 1908-57; ship specifications and summarised costs nos 767-1075 (Barrow), nos 17-179 (Walker) nd; prime and wages cost books 1947-65; machinery and ship contracts nos 442-710 1917-46; ship and submarine contracts nos 436-791 1912-41; agreements, deeds, conveyances and related correspondence 1874-1973; Walker general particulars book (Walker) nos 1-193 nd; particulars book of trials results U class submarines; launch details nos 1-12; (Walker) hull and engine specifications (Barrow) 1-996; hull plans ship nos 184-1071 (incomplete), engine plans nos 7-8, 77-903 (incomplete); electrical arrangement plans from 701; plant and machinery plans from c1890; demarcation files from 1905, photos from c1873

JD Scott, *Vickers A History* (1962)
C Trebilcock, *The Vickers Brothers* (1977)
Sir Harold Evans, *Vickers Against the Odds* 1956-1977 (1978)

93 BRITISH & FOREIGN MARINE INSURANCE CO LTD

5 Aug 1867
03671
1 North John Street, Liverpool, Merseyside
Insurance

History: established at Exchange Buildings, Liverpool in 1863 to underwrite cargo and freight insurance only. Directors formed a sister company, Mercantile Marine Insurance Co Ltd, to underwrite hull insurance in 1863. The Mercantile Marine company was wound up in 1867 and the British & Foreign then took powers to underwrite hull insurance. Under the direction of RN Dale, the Liverpool underwriter, was one of the most successful marine insurance companies. Dale had built up a large overseas business with 50 agents by 1873. In 1891 acquired a larger London business by taking over the Universal Marine Insurance Co of Cornhill, London (est 1859) which had considered a merger with the British & Foreign as early as 1863. Acquired by Royal Insurance Co Ltd (est 1845) but continued to underwrite marine insurance in its own name.

Records: at Royal Insurance Archives, Liverpool Record Office, City Libraries, William Brown Street, Liverpool, Merseyside L3 8EW
board meeting: minutes 1863-1957, agenda 1905-09, seal book 1931-51, correspondence files 1863 on; general meeting minutes 1863-1908; committee meeting minutes: 1863-1900, general purposes 1863-6, underwriting 1901-08; amalgamation papers 1909; register 1909 on, transfer register 1902-21; annual report and accounts 1863-1929; agency powers of attorney 1901-67; investment: memoranda 1879-1908, loan ledger 1929 on; policies: claims casualty books 1919 on, daily casualty register 1913-20, salvage 1930-43, notes on marine business c1900 on; time risk books 1935-7

94 WITHY GROVE PRESS LTD

6 Aug 1867
03672
Thomson House, Withy Grove, Manchester, Greater Manchester M60 4RJ
Printers

History: incorporated in 1867 as Northern Counties Conservative Newspaper Co Ltd to purchase the copyright of *Newcastle Daily Journal* and the printing business of Andrew and John Minsforth Carr of Newcastle upon Tyne,then in liquidation. Original offices were at 108 Grey Street, Newcastle, moving to Clayton Street in 1874. Acquired in 1934 by Allied Newspapers Ltd (inc 1924) which became Kemsley Newspapers Ltd in 1943, Thomson Newspapers Ltd in 1943 and Thomson Organisation Ltd in 1961. Company changed name to Sunday Graphic Ltd in 1960 and to above in 1963. From 1960s carried on business as general printers in Manchester. Ceased to trade in 1983.

Records: at Thomson Withy Grove, Thomson House, Withy Grove, Manchester, Greater Manchester M60 4RJ
directors and general meeting: minutes 1896-1908, agendas 1877-83; share register 1867-1917; balance sheets and accounts 1869-1927; trading statement 1965; stock and work in progress 1965-6; unidentified 20 cent

95 EVANS' COTTAGE HOMES

6 Jan 1868
03846
41 Church St, Birmingham, W Midlands B3 2DY
Housing charity

History: founded in 1867 when Alfred Smith Evans (1802-70), Birmingham merchant and partner in Evans & Askin, nickel silver manufacturers, gave £5500 for a fund to provide homes and annuities for gentlewomen of reduced fortunes. Land was purchased at Selly Oak as a site for the homes, (with an area at the back, long used as Corporation allotments) and freehold ground rents were acquired at Winson Green Road, Victoria Street and Frederick Street, Birmingham as investments. Incorporated in 1868 as above as an unlimited company having no share capital. To qualify for a home ladies had to be over 50 and have a yearly income of over £25. Building began, with further Evans donations, on 9 homes in 3 blocks. Between 1868 and 1924 the cottage homes accommodated 41 ladies. From the end of WW1 the company's ground rents, largely derived from low income generating properties, have been sold. In 1973 the old houses were demolished and 25 flats and a warden's house were erected at Lodge Hill Road, Selly Oak, on the allotment land at the back of the homes. The site of the original homes was sold to the Girls' Friendly Society.

Records: at Evans' Cottage Homes, 41 Church Street, Birmingham, W Midlands B3 2DY
sub-committee meeting minutes 1928-48; memo and articles of association 1868; special resolution 1973; letter re foundation of homes 1867; ledger 1945-68; cash book 1927-66; by-laws and regulations 1869; home application register 1928-51; property documents 1860-1976; insurance policies 1977-81; photograph block: Evans Cottage Homes c1870, AS Evans c1870; historical pamphlet 1925

96 CARDIFF ARCADE CO LTD

20 Jan 1868
03857
Barry Lane, Cardiff, S Glamorgan CF1 1UR
Property

History: incorporated as above in 1868 to purchase freehold and leasehold premises between Saint Mary Street and The Hayes, Cardiff, S Glamorgan in order to build an arcade containing shops and offices. Purchased 5,6,7&8 Royal Arcade in 1927 and became a wholly owned subsidiary of Deymel Investments Ltd in 1959

Records: at Deymel Investments, 26 The Hayes, Cardiff, S Glamorgan CF1 IUR
minutes 1895-date; members registers 1867-date; journal 1928-54

97 KARDOMAH LTD

3 Jul 1868
04059
1-4 Connaught Place, London W2 2GX
Coffee house (previously tea and coffee suppliers)

History: in 1844 Samuel and Christopher Vey founded a grocery business in James Street, Liverpool, specialising in tea and coffee. The Liverpool China & India Tea Co Ltd was incorporated in 1868 to acquire the business, now operating at 32 London Road, Liverpool, valued at £2940. The grocery business was discontinued and company concentrated on selling tea and coffee. In 1881 the company moved to Buckley's Buildings, Dale Street, Liverpool, a central location. In 1883 a branch opened in Paris. By 1894 the company was marketing a proprietory brand of packet tea, 'Kardomah'; a depot was set up in Castle Street and an exhibition cafe opened in conjunction to advertise the tea. This pattern was repeated with later branches and by 1898 the memo of association was extended to cover the business of cafe and restaurant proprietors. By 1926 the company had 26 branches; including Paris, Cambridge, Cardiff, Chester, Liverpool, Manchester, Newport and Swansea; and a bakery established in Red Cross Street, Liverpool. In 1938 name was changed to above, by 1939 36 cafes were established serving 9 million people with an average check value of 8.27d. Business suffered during WW2, with premises at Cardiff, Liverpool and London destroyed by bombing. Self-service counters were introduced to cope with staff shortages, by 1944 36 cafes offered self-service, accounting for 61 per cent of cafe takings. After 1945 the cafe business expanded, company purchased similar concerns of JS Winn & Co Ltd in 1945, Sharpe Green & Son Ltd and Biscards Ltd in 1953 and Schofield & Co (Tea Merchants) Ltd in 1955. Branch, wholesale and packet tea and coffee trade continued to progress. In 1963 Kardomah Ltd was taken over by Fortes Holdings Ltd and in 1966 its name was changed to Fortes Popular Restaurants Ltd. It continued to operate as before and supplied tea and coffee to Fortes. In 1971 the company was purchased from Fortes by Cadbury Schweppes and by agreement its name was changed back to Kardomah Ltd. It was further agreed between the two major companies that Fortes could continue to operate the cafe business under the Kardomah name whilst Cadbury Schweppes used the Kardomah name in the continuation of the wholesale and packet tea and coffee business. The company has since remained a subsidiary of Cadbury Schweppes.

Records: at Cadbury Schweppes, Dollis Hill House, 105 Brook Road, London NW2
directors and general meeting minutes: 1868-1971, notes 1868; prospectus 1868; transfer certificates 1869-79; memo and articles of association 1900; ledger: creditors 1868-78, nominal 1880-93; private journal 1868-76; accounting working papers 1900-35

98 PRESS ASSOCIATION LTD

6 Nov 1868
04197
85 Fleet Street, London EC4P 4BE
News agency

History: founded by provincial newspaper proprietors as Press Association Co Ltd in 1865 to organise a system of news collecting and reporting in London with correspondents all over the UK to supply accurate, prompt and impartial news to provincial newspapers. Little was achieved until the 1868 Telegraph Act ensured a state run telegraph system. Company was wound up and above incorporated in 1868 to carry out the original scheme. An agreement was made with Reuters to transmit their foreign news in Dec 1868 and operations began in Feb 1870. Have operated a joint sports service with Exchange Telegraph Co Ltd (Extel, est 1872) since 1906 and they jointly bought Central News Ltd (est 1863) in 1937. Started London News Service in 1909 and bought London News Agency in 1919. Bought controlling shares in Reuters Ltd in 1925, buying up remainder in 1930, but later became joint partners with 3 other newspaper and agency associations. Also started a news photo service with Reuters in 1944 as PA Reuter Photos Ltd and bought Pardons Cricket Reporting Agency (est 1880) in 1965. Headquarters have always been near Fleet Street, first at 7 Wine Office Court, then 14 New Bridge Street and Red Lion Square before moving to Byron House in 1922. This latter site was redeveloped in the 1930s to form the present head offices of both the PA and Reuters and allied news agencies at 85 Fleet Street. The PA has editorial and telegraph offices in the Houses of Parliament and in the High Courts in London, and in Birmingham, Bristol, Glasgow, Leeds, Manchester and Newcastle upon Tyne, and editorial offices in Liverpool and Swansea. It transmits a complete service of home news to London newspapers, BBC, ITN, Reuters and the London offices of overseas newspapers and news agencies. Provincial newspapers receive a complete service of home news and pictures and the world news of Reuters and Associated Press of America and the Associated Press world picture service.

Records (1): at Press Association, 85 Fleet Street, London EC4P 4BE
board minutes nd-1976; board reports 1945-78; secretarys reports 1916,1940-57; directors attendance register 1868-1975; management committee: minutes 1868-post 1942, agenda 1868-1952; committee memoranda 1916-27; general managers reports 1941-63; managers memoranda 1909-16; finance committee: minutes 1949-63, attendance register 1966-76; centenary and image committee minutes 1965-9; general meeting: minutes 1869-1964, reports 1869-1963, notices 1911-63; extraordinary general meeting reports and notices 1920-78; agms: reports 1870-1978, attendance register 1904-73; correspondence and documents re members luncheons and agms 1938-63; reports of members luncheons 1951-65; register of members 1868-1947; share allotment register 1868-1903; register of shares c1868-c1920; share ledger 1868-88; register of share transfers 1869-1980; register of charges 1900-26; register of directors 1944-71; register of directors holdings 1937-67; register of notes issued 1926-51; debenture holders: minutes 1940-2, attendance register 1940-2; share and share transfer certificates 1904-70; correspondence and documents re allotment, shareholders and transfers 1868-1970; correspondence, minutes, reports and other documents re formation of company 1865-1900; memo and articles of association with papers re alterations 1868-1970; agreements 1873-1951; contracts and agreements register 1868-1909; circulars 1869-1944; seal register 1869-1921; chairmens statements 1955-71; annual returns 1870-1974; annual reports and accounts 1911-

77; balance sheets 1869-1926; audited accounts 1950-66; statements of accounts 1887-1939,1960; summaries of accounts 1913-22; joint provincial market accounts 1926-41; general election telegraphic accounts 1923-35; general ledgers 1936-60; members ledgers 1911-53; non-members ledger c1941-51; non-members and newsroom ledger c1912-44; nominal ledgers 1954-77; reporting ledgers 1937-42; special reporting ledgers 1975-7; purchase ledgers 1973-6; sales ledgers 1975-7; customers ledger 1943-7; correspondents ledgers 1970-7; linage ledgers 1938-40; private wire ledger 1922-3; telephone ledgers 1912-47; building revenue and expenses transfer ledgers 1940-53; property charges ledger 1954-60; building and trading ledger 1940-50; Byron House ledger 1919-23; new building ledger 1939; petty cash trading ledger 1952-4; journals 1895-1969; private journal 1924-39; telephone journal 1914-49; job account book 1946-8; telegraph charges account book 1938-48; telex transmission account book 1958-9; general and sundry day books 1909-53; subscription day books 1904-40; order day books 1901-40; telephone day books 1922-53; telephone subscription day books 1906-49; special reporting day books 1937-42; linage day books 1931-45; joint law service day books 1931-42; racing service day book 1937-41; sports day book 1927-40; copy supplied day book 1955; news telephoned direct day book 1940-1; reporting day book 1938-42; building day book 1953-67; cash books 1868-1972; petty cash books 1906-53; cash paid books 1940-50; correspondents cash payments books 1934-76; cash received books 1940-9; payments received books 1920-60; cash balance books 1938-53; tax records and reports 1949-62; financial papers of assistant secretary c1958-66; office salary books 1870-1968; branch salary books 1941-54; telegraph salary book 1943-4; salary summaries 1940-53; private wire wages book 1920-40; salary and wages balance book 1930-42; editorial and general overtime books 1937-40; salary lists 1912-44; notifications of staff and salary changes 1942-63; staff tax records 1940-67; insurance contributions 1916-41; reporting expense accounts 1908-76; correspondents expenses accounts 1940-76; staff register 1923-33; personnel files 1963-6; correspondence re appointment of manager 1868-79; details of directors 1948-73; photographs of directors nd; *Link*, house magazine 1959-78; PA annuity fund: minutes 1893-1956, board minutes 1939-63, committee minutes 1963-79, agm reports 1964-5, circulars and papers re general meetings 1951-78; agreements 1897-1978, register of seals 1948-76, nomination book 1922-38, annual returns 1940-75, reports and accounts 1893-1977, printed accounts 1921-56, general ledgers 1895-1955, members contribution ledger 1921-53, probationers contribution ledger 1921-53, summaries ledger 1895-1935, annuitants payment ledger 1954-61, annuitants payment book 1947-61, weekly payments book 1921-53, register of investments and interests c1950-70, cash books 1914-57, tax records 1939-58, valuation reports 1929-64, misc correspondence and papers re accounts and investments 1927-76, rules 1918-77, membership and annuitant records 1930-73, membership correspondence 1921-70; staff annuity fund: notices of meetings 1921-61, fund deeds 1896-1921, annual reports and accounts 1897-1938, audited accounts 1903-37, general ledger 1936-8, investment ledger 1935-54, journal 1895-1928, fund investigation reports 1900-36, misc correspondence 1918-29; officers annuity fund: audited accounts 1958-64, statements of accounts 1940-5, ledger 1921-58, agreement 1939, correspondence and documents re valuations 1940-59; officer superannuation fund: annual report and accounts 1910; annuity fund trust: corporate documents 1938-74, audited accounts 1939-49; general ledger 1963-73, contributions register 1950-2, cash book 1958-68; staff life insurance scheme: corporate documents 1955-64; employee records 1958-70; insurance and endowment fund: minutes 1883-1934, annual reports and accounts 1882,1899-1912, treasurer's account book 1887-1900, cash book 1882-1949, weekly repayment books 1883-

1903, list of payments 1951-61, policy register 1882-c1950, correspondence and documents with Scottish Provident Institution 1866-1903; PA Reuters staff restaurant committee: minutes 1953-71, cash book 1939-40, restaurant stock record 1940-3; catering account journal 1939-48, day book 1945-8, canteen account cash book 1939; PA sports club: minutes 1923-37; photograph of dinner 1933; printed tariff rates with circulars thereto 1868-1974; rates and costs for news 1879-1959; members, non-members and newsroom order books 1901-40; register of subscriptions 1944,1950; register of subscribers 1949-53; register of news services required 1925-9; cricket and football subscriptions 1911-40; lists of specials offered 1913-24; 'D' notices 1914-39; pictures broadcast logsheets 1960; unused copy register 1941-5; correspondents address book c1915; racing results telephone service contracts 1905-31; working agreements 1906-61; news service contracts 1940-58; news supplies agreements 1960-6; instructions for reporters and newspapers 1908-61; correspondence, reports, costs, copy etc re various services 1905-59; correspondence and papers re legal (mainly libel) cases involving PA 1892-1938; reports, correspondence and papers re telegraphy, telephones, broadcasting and press messages 1868-1938; memoranda re telegraphic facilities 1920-8; correspondence re wire loss 1914-18; private wire maintenance records 1948-53; teleprinter scheme purchase day and sales return book 1946-9; histories of PA and newscuttings and correspondence re same 1922-62; news photographs 1900-date; general newscuttings c1883-date; leases 1869-1961; register of leases 1948-69; insurance policies 1940s-60s; inventory of and correspondence re 14 New Bridge Street 1892,1912; correspondence, accounts, papers, plans etc re Byron House 1919-34; inventory of property nd; hire purchase agreements and accounts 1920-2; property managers' correspondence and papers 1930-48; correspondence re reorganisation of building 1958-65; photographs of premises c1930; plant depreciation register 1942-72; plant working papers 1941-70; directors letter book 1868; managers letter book 1869-70; correspondence with newspapers, Reuters, Newspaper Proprietors Association, Official Press Bureau and others re services, 'D' notices, Spanish Civil War, Edward VIII and Mrs Simpson, staff and general matters 1906-60; correspondence and papers of HC Robbins 1916-21; correspondence and menus re chairman's dinner 1936-64

Exchange Telegraph Co Ltd - PA Joint Service: agreements 1906-63; correspondence, notes and court proceedings of arbitration 1908-10; balance sheets with analysis 1915-36; balance book 1935-49; pool accounts 1922-63; revenue accounts 1927-64; schedules and accounts 1946-59; general ledger 1943-9; general day book 1914-53; cash book 1915-50; pool telephone accounts 1908; specials: copy accounts 1951, ledger sheets 1947-9, telephone day book 1931-53; tax records 1949-51; wages books 1906-40; salary books 1940-53; correspondents cash payments book 1935-40; agreement with National Union of Journalists 1922; order books 1923-42; letter book 1936-8; correspondence and papers 1923-49

PA Reuter Photos Ltd: minutes 1945-66; directors attendance book 1961-5; managers reports and correspondence 1961-5; register of members 1945-9; share certificates 1945-65; corporate documents 1944-65; memo and articles of association 1965; correspondence and papers re liquidation 1966; annual returns 1950-60; audited accounts 1945-66; private ledger 1953-63; first photographs passed on wire 1940s; stock and plant working papers 1961-9

PA Share Purchase Co Ltd: minutes 1911-52; secretary reports 1922-37; register of members and directors 1911-52; register of directors holdings 1942-50; share and share transfer certificates 1911-45; correspondence re shares and members 1932-44; memo and articles of association 1911; liquidation papers 1951-2; seal register 1911-52; annual returns 1911-46; annual report 1946; printed accounts 1942-51; audited accounts 1911-52; cash book 1911-51;

financial correspondence and tax papers 1929-52
PA Reuter Features Ltd: directors minutes 1942-65; directors attendance book 1961-4; committee minutes 1964; register of members 1943-8; register of directors holdings 1958-62; share and share transfer certificates 1942-60; corporate documents 1942-60; audited accounts 1947-65; contract job cards 1951-9
Reuters Ltd: joint board minutes (with PA) 1941; general manager memo 1925; agm proceedings 1957; agreements and correspondence with PA 1921-50; memo and articles of association 1865-1950; corporate documents and correspondence 1926-36; reporting charges account book 1899-1936; telegraph services account books 1901-15; specials account book 1936-40; job account books 1916-35; transmission costs 1905-06; service bulletins 1918-23; agreements for news service 1930; leaflets and booklets on history and organisation 1915-39; general correspondence and papers 1921-44
Reuters Telegram Co Ltd: annual report and account and chairmans speech and agm report 1908
Central News Limited: memo and articles of association 1880,1934; subscriptions journal 1936-47; parliamentary service general ledger 1936-53; journal 1947-53; cash book 1947-9; petty cash book 1947-53; day book c1940s-53; legal case report CNL v PA 1883
Central Press Photos Ltd: memo and articles of association 1934
Column Printing Co Ltd: memo and articles of association 1923
London News Agency Ltd: liquidation correspondence and accounts 1919-20

Records (2): at Cumbria Record Office, The Castle, Carlisle, Cumbria CA3 8UR
annual reports with balance sheets 1925-51; annual reports and accounts 1948,1950; general meeting notices 1938-9,1951; members luncheon speech 1951; memo and articles of association 1936; staff file 1952-5; correspondence: JL Burgess, Reuters and PA 1954-67

George Scott, *Reporter Anonymous. The Story of the Press Association* (1968)

99 INVESTMENT CO LTD

14 Nov 1868
04205
St Martin's House, 16 St Martins Le Grand, London EC1A 4EP
Property and investment

History: incorporated in 1868 as above as a company holding property in the City and West End of London. It was purchased by Alliance Property Co Ltd in 1958 and operates as an investment company in Dorking, Surrey, specialising in the holding of preference shares.

Records: at Investment, Woodlands Park, Blackbrook, Dorking, Surrey RH5 4DU
certificate of incorporation 1885; current records

100 INCORPORATED LAW SOCIETY OF LIVERPOOL

13 Feb 1869
04302
Castle Chambers, Cook Street, Liverpool, Merseyside L2 9SH
Law society

History: founded in 1827 as Liverpool Law Library Society at the instigation of attorney Joshua Lace to provide a law library for the general use of attorneys and solicitors in Liverpool. Lace became the society's first president. The library housed in the Clarendon Buildings was opened in 1828 and the society's membership stood at 52. In 1834 its name was changed to Liverpool Law Society to emphasise its wider and collective roll as voice of the local profession. In 1869 it was incorporated as above as a company limited by guarantee to protect the character, status and interests of attorneys and solicitors practising in Liverpool or within a 20 miles radius; to promote honourable practice and to settle disputed points of practice. From 1870 it contributed to the cost of lectures for articled clerks. The society's offices and library moved around offices in Liverpool as premises were outgrown. They were at Unity Buildings, Cable Street from 1859 to 1865, then the library moved to 14 Cook Street until 1877 when it moved to 13 Union Court moving to 10 Cook Street in 1897. In May 1941 the latter premises were blitzed by enemy bombs and the entire library of over 35,000 volumes was destroyed. A new library and offices were quickly procured. Membership in 1897 stood at 393 and in 1984 was about 600.

Records (1): at Incorporated Law Society of Liverpool, Castle Chambers, Cook Street, Liverpool, Merseyside L2 9SH
council and committee meeting minutes 1941-date; annual reports 1941-date; circulars 1941-date; accounts 1941-date; correspondence 1961-date; library catalogues 1958-date; annual dinner menus 1941-date.

Records (2): Liverpool University, Sydney Jones Library, PO Box 123, Liverpool, Merseyside L69 3DA
library catalogue and committee report 1829

Records (3): Liverpool Record Office & Local History Department, City Libraries, William Brown Street, Liverpool, Merseyside L3 8EW
annual report and accounts with proceedings of annual meetings 1918,1941-66,1972; library catalogue, articles of association, rules and members lists 1880,1892,1911

Records (4): Liverpool University Archives, PO Box 147, Senate House, Abercromby Square, Liverpool, Merseyside L69 3BX
annual reports and accounts with lists of members and officials 1859-1904

Peter H Williams, *A Gentleman's Calling. The Liverpool Attorney-at-law* (priv pub 1980)

101 LONDON & COUNTY SECURITIES LTD

1 Mar 1869
04321
St Mary Axe House, 56-60 St Mary Axe, London EC3A 8BJ
Finance

History: incorporated in 1869 as London & County Advance & Discount Co Ltd to trade as lenders and borrowers of money. Offices were at 57-58 Chancery Lane, London from at least 1890s to 1920s. Name changed to London & County (A&D) Ltd in 1962 and to above in 1973. Advances were secured on properties and equities. From 1972 its main business was banking and associated services. Company's shares were suspended early in the secondary banking crisis in 1973. Liquidator was appointed in 1975.

Records: at Spicer & Pegler, Liquidators, St Mary Axe House, 56-60 St Mary Axe, London EC3A 8BJ
minutes c1880s-1975; shareholding records 20 cent; annual reports and accounts 1963-75; statutory records 20 cent; balance sheet and accounts 1900-43; ledgers 20 cent; accounts list 1928-56; subsidiary companies: statutory and shareholding records, minutes and accounts 20 cent
Drakes Ltd: general meeting minutes 1951-69
Drakes Engineers Ltd: directors and general meeting minutes 1949-69
Drakes Halifax Ltd: directors and general meeting minutes 1922-70
Drakes Management Services Ltd: minutes 1942-70
Drakes Group: statutory records, accounts, cash books, correspondence, properties and working papers 20 cent
Franco British Electrical Ltd: minutes 1909-70
Franco Signs Ltd: directors and general meeting minutes 1936-70; shareholding records 1942-70
FB Elcom Ltd: minutes 1945-70
FB Sugdon Ltd: minutes 1945-60

Margaret Reid, *The Secondary Banking Crisis 1973-75* (1982)

102 BRISTOL & WESTERN COUNTIES BUTCHERS' HIDE, SKIN, FAT & WOOL CO LTD

17 Mar 1869
04333
6-8 Albert Road, Bristol, Avon BS2 0XA
Hide, skin and fat agents

History: incorporated as above in 1869 by group of Bristol butchers to establish a market for the selling of animal hides, skins, fat and offal. Original premises were at 88 Thomas Street, Bristol, Avon moving to 46 West Street in 1927. By 1920s had premises at Taunton, Somerset; Camborne, Cornwall; Chippenham, Wiltshire; and Exeter, Devon. In accordance with Ministry of Food regulations, Bristol & District Hide Market Ltd was incorporated in 1943 to manage the company's operations and those of Bowsher Brothers Ltd, Thomson's Hide Market Ltd and Bath Hide & Skin Market Ltd. A similar arrangement was made with the incorporation of Exeter Hide & Skin Co Ltd to manage its own business in Exeter as well as those of Tremletts Ltd and London Butchers' Hide Co Ltd. Ministry control ceased in 1954 but a similar management arrangement continued in that Bristol Butchers' Hide & Skin Co Ltd was incorporated to purchase the goodwill and trading interests of the above, Tremletts Hide Market Ltd and Bowsher Brothers Ltd. The Exeter and Camborne markets were excluded from the arrangement. In 1970 Tremletts Ltd sold its third share in Exeter hide market to the company and London Butchers' Hide Co Ltd who continued to run the market as co-partners. In early 1970s the Camborne market was closed. In 1972 Bristol Butchers' Hide & Skin Co Ltd moved from Marsh Burton, its premises since 1957, to 6-8 Albert Road, Bristol.

Records (1): at Bristol Butchers' Hide & Skin, 6-8 Albert Road, Bristol, Avon BS2 0XA
directors meeting minutes 1927-74; general meeting minutes 1973-7

Records (2): at Bristol Record Office, Council House, College Green, Bristol, Avon BS1 5TR
members registers etc 1869-1958; Thomas Street lease 1861

103 WILLIAM THOMPSON & CO LTD

24 Mar 1869
04345
McMullen Road, Darlington, Durham DL1 1YQ
Silk spinners and manufacturers

History: founded in 1792 when William Thompson, John Noble and John Armstrong bought the Ellel Corn Mill at Galgate near Lancaster and converted it into a mill for spinning waste silk. Armstrong family crest was adopted as trade-mark. Won gold Exhibition medals at Paris 1855 and 1878, and London 1862. Incorporated in 1869 as above with William Satterthwaite as chairman and mill manager until his death in 1879, when George William Maxsted succeeded him. James Robinson was mill manager from 1879-87, and in 1887 George and Samuel Marshall Satterthwaite became joint managers. Spun lace yarns for Nottingham and Calais markets until 1880s when fine short spun yarns were produced for Bradford market. Purchased Galgate Low Mill in 1891. GW Maxsted died in 1898 and his son CH Maxsted succeeded him as chairman until his death in 1915. In 1918 company was taken over by a group including William Armitage (inside mill manager from 1914) who became managing director. Specialities at this time were lace, plush and sewing threads, with exports going to Europe, Egypt and India. After depression of 1920s and 1930s, the business was reconstructed in 1937 and production started with rayon and other vegetable fibres in 1940. After WW2 business again fell off. By early 1950s was producing spun silk, rayon, blended yarns, silk and wool twists, and nylon staple. By 1957 demand for silk was no longer sufficient to utilise full capacity but introduction of other fibres was excessively expensive. Taken over in 1957 by Patons & Baldwins Ltd, Darlington, Durham, hand knitting and rug yarn manufacturers, who continued business under old name. Mill closed and company ceased to trade in 1971.

Records (1): at Patons & Baldwins, McMullen Road, Darlington, Durham DL1 1YQ
directors meeting minutes 1869-date; general meeting minutes 1869-1956; chairmans reports 1925-47; shareholders register 1869-98; share: register nd, transfer documents 1887-1957; directors register c1949 on; annual reports and accounts 1869-1928; balance sheets, profit and loss accounts and accounting papers 1869-1947,1963-71; private ledger 1909-53; cash books 1961-72; profits tax correspondence 1945-52; trade mark papers 1946; Pakistan sales correspondence 1970; stock summaries 1969-70; steam boiler certificate 1920; inventory and valuation of mill 1920; insurance schedule 1919; electrical specification 1950s; machinery notes nd; pension scheme trust deed, policies, papers and correspondence 1965-71; accident book 1967-71; factory registers 1951-70; fire protection reports and plans 1947-65

Records (2): at Lancaster District Library, Local Studies Department, Market Street, Lancaster, Lancashire LA1 1HY
ledgers 1877-1958; nominal ledger 1918-59; day books 1793-1803,1869-1947; cash books: 1874-1960, analysis 1937-58, petty 1956-8; bills books: receivable 1865-1924, payable 1907-41; gas account book 1860-1938; stock accounts books 1869-1959; accounts due and payable and orders book 1868-74; sundry invoice journal 1905-37; silk waste and invoice book 1910-58; financial papers nd; sales books 1858-92; old waste purchase and delivery books 1858-1959; stock books: 1865-70,1918-68, Paris 1858-1916; silk reports c1919; letters patent 1841; patent

yarn details 1884-6; silk production notebooks nd; yarn order books 1902-58; yield books 1904-37; production weekly weights 1923-50; samples book 1937-48; silk run books 1904-62; machinery: quotations, orders and papers 1880-1959, anthracite gasplant plans pre 1959; mill inventories 1904,1920; wages: note book 1861, books 1901-58; apprentices indentures nd; employment applications 1925-70; factory registers 1893-1951; building: note book 1851, extension correspondence nd; fire watchers book 1940-3; managers: note book 1869, correspondence 1940s; outletter book 1900; newscuttings 1896-1971; mill visit reports 1964; Ellel War Memorial Institute gift deed and correspondence nd; articles, booklets etc re company history and silk 20 cent

104 SHEFFIELD BUTCHERS' HIDE & SKIN CO LTD

3 Apr 1869
04357
Cricket Inn Road, Sheffield, S Yorkshire S2 5AU
Hide and skin agents

History: incorporated in 1869 as above by group of Sheffield butchers to protect the same, by means of mutual association, in the sale etc of hide, skins, fat and offal of beasts slaughtered by them and to establish a market to conduct the same. Only butchers could become shareholders. Original premises were at 11 The Wicket, Sheffield, S Yorkshire, moving to larger purpose built premises at Pond Hill in 1880. Opened branches in S Yorkshire at Rotherham and Barnsley by 1908, Mexborough and Hoyland in 1909 and Beighton by 1920. Purchased business of Woodman & Wilson in 1919. Due to re-development in central Sheffield, moved to Cricket Inn Road in 1956. Main activity in early 1980s was the collection and sale of hides, skins, fats and bones.

Records: at Sheffield Butchers' Hide & Skin, Cricket Inn Road, Sheffield, S Yorkshire S2 5AU directors and general meeting minutes 1890-date; members registers: and share ledgers 1869-1978, and share transfers 1869-1922; annual returns 1870,1909,1924-36; memo and articles of association 1869-1924; annual reports and accounts 1880-1960,1970; balance sheets 1958,1961-2; journal 1906-82; property document 1919; Pond Hill premises photographs c1956; fellmonger licences 1911-13; history article 1969

105 CGW HOLDINGS LTD

27 Apr 1869
04392
253A London Road, Hadleigh, Benfleet, Essex SS7 5UW
Gas

History: formed in 1868 and incorporated in 1869 as Colombo Gas & Water Co Ltd to supply Colombo, the capital of Sri Lanka, with gas. The contract to build the gas works was awarded to Laidlaw & Sons of Glasgow. The works were in operation by Aug 1872. The plant was renewed in 1899 and 1922-4. The company also supplied the town of Kandy with electricity between 1900 and 1922. Gas continued to be supplied to Colombo until the early 1970s when the Sri Lankan government nationalised the company whose name had been changed to above and it was subsequently placed in liquidation.

Records (1): with the Liquidator, CGW Holdings, 253A London Road, Hadleigh, Benfleet, Essex SS7 5UW
secretary and general managers reports 1960s; general managers, directors and local committee correspondence 1960s-70; shareholders minutes 1957-74; dividend lists 1961-5; chairmans statements 1961-5; annual report and accounts 1963-72; cash books and financial papers 1960s-70s; gas and coal tariffs 1960s-70s; agents correspondence 1972; coal shipment papers and correspondence 1964-73; development project reports, minutes, costings, correspondence etc 1969-70; general manager and engineer service agreements 1962-8; wages books 1965-70; general correspondence 1962-74

Records (2): at the Guildhall Library, Aldermanbury, London EC2P 2EJ
directors minutes 1870-80; shareholders register 1869-1957; share register 1957-65; share transfer register 1870-1953; share dividend register 1949-63; stock transfer forms 1948-65; corporate documents 1869-72; memo and articles of association 1925,1970; general ledger 1945-57; journal 1933-47; cash books 1942-53; photographs of equipment etc in Colombo 1905-21; provident fund membership register 1934-61

Fifty-two Years of Gas Supply 1872-1924 (priv pub 1925)

106 LONDON GUARANTEE & REINSURANCE CO LTD

1 May 1869
04403
Phoenix House, 18 King William Street, London EC4P 4HR
Insurance

History: incorporated in 1869 as London Guarantee & Accident Co Ltd to undertake accident and guarantee insurance. Original offices were in St Martin's Place, London moving to 20 Lincoln's Inn Fields in 1915. Acquired guarantee business of European Assurance (est 1853) in 1871, Railway Accident Mutual (est 1873) in 1877 and Guarantee Association of Scotland (est 1873) in 1884. By 1921 had 57 UK branches and 37 overseas branches in USA, Canada, Australia, Denmark, South Africa, China and India, and was undertaking guarantee, fire, accident and marine business. Premium income was over £2.9 million. Acquired in 1922 by Phoenix Assurance Co Ltd and moved in 1932 into Phoenix House, King William Street. Name changed to above after 1973.

Records: at Phoenix Assurance, Phoenix House, 18 King William Street, London EC4P 4HR
board: meeting agendas 1934-60, committee meeting minutes 1872 on; share: register 1872-1914, allotment book 1892, transfer allotment book 1922; annual reports and accounts 1888-1969

George Hurren, *Phoenix Renascent. A History of the Phoenix Assurance Co Ltd 1782-1968* (1973)

107 WINCHESTER COTTAGE IMPROVEMENT SOCIETY LTD

8 Sep 1869
04545
19 St Peter Street, Winchester, Hampshire SO23 8BU
Property

History: incorporated as above in 1869 to improve the dwellings of the labouring classes in Winchester, Hampshire. Re-registered as a public limited company in 1981.

Records: at Winchester Cottage Improvement Society, 19 St Peter Street, Winchester, Hampshire SO23 8BU
directors and general meeting minutes 1869-date; members register and share ledger 1928-date; share: register 1869, certificate books 1950-date; memo and articles of association 1952-62; annual reports and accounts 1878,1888-95,1927-date; revenue: and capital accounts 1870-87, loan and improvement accounts 1901-08, accounts and balance sheets 1942-date; general ledgers 1896-date; cash books 1940-date; wages book 1953-60; rent: arrears list 1871, increase lists 1902,1915; Christmas allowances lists 1946,1950-9

108 CARDIFF & PROVINCIAL PROPERTIES LTD

22 Oct 1869
04600
10 Museum Place, Cardiff, S Glamorgan CF1 3BG
Property

History: incorporated as Cardiff Workmen's Cottage Co Ltd in 1869 to purchase land on which to build dwellings and shops for the labouring classes. By 1943 it owned 335 houses in Cardiff in Cumnock Terrace, Kingarth Street, Cumrae Street, Inchmarnock Street, Kilcattan Street, Kerrycroy Street, Ascog Street, Gwendoline Street, Howard Street, Lady Margaret Terrace, Gwendoline Place, Cumnock Place and Sanquar Street. In 1950 another 25 houses adjoining these properties were bought. During 1960s some houses were sold and other properties were purchased in Cardiff and elsewhere in England and Wales, and to acknowledge the change, the company's name was altered to above in 1962. Re-registered as a public limited company in Feb 1982.

Records: at Cardiff & Provincial Properties, 10 Museum Place, Cardiff, S Glamorgan CF1 3BG
directors: and general meeting minutes 1943-date, attendance book 1903-date; share: transfer register 1872-date, records current; annual reports and accounts 1944-74; ledger c1917-71; photographs of properties 1960s-70s

109 LONDON BOAT HOUSE CO LTD

22 Jun 1870
04711
London Rowing Club Boat House, Embankment, Putney, London SW15
Sports club-houses

History: incorporated in 1870 as above to provide new club and boat-house for London Rowing Club, founded in 1856. The new building was erected on the site of the club's old boat-house on Putney Embankment, London to the designs of George Dunnage, architect, and opened in 1871. Extensions were made in 1875 and 1884 and renovations were carried out in 1970s under direction of Simon Crosse, architect.

Records: at London Boat House, London Rowing Club Boat House, Embankment, Putney, London SW15

memo and articles of association 1870, with resolutions to 1954; annual reports and accounts 1907-28
London Rowing Club: letter book 1856-62; annual reports 1856-1938; newscuttings, circulars, race reports, annual dinner menus, rules etc c1907-56; history 1981

110 LIVERPOOL SOCIETY OF CHARTERED ACCOUNTANTS

20 Apr 1870
04869
5 Fenwick Street, Liverpool, Merseyside L2 ONZ
Accountants' society

History: established as a company limited by guarantee as Incorporated Society of Liverpool Accountants, the first such body formed in England. Its objects were the protection of character, status and interests of Liverpool accountants; the promotion of honorable practice; the settlement of disputed points of practice; and the consideration of general questions affecting the interests of the profession or the alteration and administration of the law. Assisted in formation in 1880 of Institute of Chartered Accountants in England and Wales but retained its own identity. By 1880 had 29 members and in 1883 formed students' association. In 1984 membership totalled 2156 and society operated branches in its surrounding regions; organised sectional interest groups; promoted education through its library and lecture programmes; circulated members on changes in accounting practice; and organised social events.

Records: at Liverpool Society of Chartered Accountants, 5 Fenwick Street, Liverpool, Merseyside L2 ONZ
committee and general meeting: minutes 1870-date, papers 1870-1936; memo and articles of association 1870-1937; annual reports and accounts 1917-36,1968 on; balance sheets 1931-44; ledgers 1916-57; cash books 1905-58; members signature book 1870-1940; subscription registers 1914-49,1963; roll of honour 1918; presidents, members, officers etc photographs 1870s-1970s; meeting notices, addresses etc 1894-1904; library: committee meeting minutes 1930-54, ledger 1910-21, cash books 1910-64; student association: committee meeting minutes and papers 1907-51, general meeting minutes and papers 1914-50, balance sheets and accounts 1938-51, rules 1914, proceedings books, lectures, examination questions, annual meeting reports, annual accounts and officers lists 1887-91; branches - Chester and North Wales: papers and correspondence 1953-63; S Lancashire: papers and correspondence 1953-70s, cash book 1953-74, accounts 1956-71; press cuttings 1894-1904,1934

Ian Hargraves, *The Liverpool Society of Chartered Accountants Centenary 1870-1970* (priv pub 1970)

111 MIDLAND EDUCATIONAL CO LTD

23 May 1870
04923
583 Moseley Road, Birmingham, W Midlands B12
Stationers

History: incorporated as above in 1870 by local schoolmasters to supply books and stationery to schools. Board promoted meetings of teachers, encouraging them to become shareholders. In 1889 new premises were built in Corporation Street, Birmingham and a new branch was established in Leicester. In 1934 acquired Barnby's Ltd, 'all toy shops' in Birmingham, later opening shops in Coventry and Solihull, W Midlands and Bristol, Avon. Between 1946 and 1949 acquired stationery firms of W Mark & Co (1935) Ltd, Northampton; JC Bond Ltd, Kettering, Northamptonshire; AO Jones & Co Ltd, Worcester; GW Russell & Co Ltd, Hereford; and Bodycot & Brewin Ltd general printers of Leicester. Warehouse purchased in Hockley, Birmingham in 1951 and new printing works erected for subsidiary company, Midland Printing Co Ltd. By 1970 had branches at Bristol, Coventry, Leicester, Solihull, Stratford upon Avon, Warwickshire, and Wolverhampton, W Midlands. Became a wholly owned subsidiary of Alfred Preedy & Sons Ltd in 1978.

Records: at Midland Educational, Burnt Tree House, Tipton, W Midlands
directors report notebook c1878-1914; debenture ledger 1895-1950; annual returns 1941-7; memo and articles of association c1870; register of seals 1929-39; annual report and accounts 1902-13,1934; balance sheets 1952-60; private ledger: 1877-1906, Birmingham 1908-34, Leicester to 1934, binders c1950; stock book 1959-63

112 LEEDS LAW SOCIETY

13 Jul 1870
05017
1 Albion Place, Leeds, W Yorkshire LS1 6JL
Law society

History: founded in 1805 as law society for solicitors, barristers being excluded. Incorporated as company limited by guarantee as above in 1870 to protect and advance the status of solicitors and promote honourable practice. Established law library in 1875. Moved into the Law Institute building, 1 Albion Place, Leeds, W Yorkshire, in 1878. Helps in training of students, advises members of professional and legal matters and publishes monthly *Newsletter*

Records: at Leeds Law Society, 1 Albion Place, Leeds, W Yorkshire LS1 6JL
general meeting: minutes 1894 on, proceedings 1871-1900; committee meeting minutes 1827-48,1894 on; annual reports and accounts with lists of members and dignitaries 1919 on; library regulations and catalogue and memo and articles of association 1914

113 INCORPORATED COUNCIL OF LAW REPORTING FOR ENGLAND & WALES LTD

28 Jul 1870
05034
3 Stone Buildings, Lincoln's Inn, London WC2 3XN
Law report publishing

History: founded in 1865 as the Council of Law Reporting to establish a set of reports of judicial decisions in the Superior Courts for publication for the benefit of the profession and the public and not for commercial gain. The council is made up of representatives from the Incorporated Law Society and the Inns of Court. Incorporated in 1870 as above. Original headquarters were at 3 New Square moving to 10 Old Square, Lincoln's Inn, in 1866 then to 30 Montague Street in 1918, Serjeants Inn in 1938 and to present address after WW2. Publishing house is situated in Cursitor Street, London.

Records: at Incorporated Council of Law Reporting for England & Wales, 3 Stone Buildings, Lincoln's Inn, London WC2 3XN
council minutes 1941-80; annual reports and financial statements 1866-1980; *Law Reports* 1940-80

WTS Daniel, *History and Origin of the Law Reports. A Compilation of Various Documents* (1884)
William Latey, *A Short History of the Law Reports, 1865-1965* (1965)

114 RR WHITEHEAD & BROTHERS LTD

9 Aug 1870
05059
Royal George Mills, Greenfield, Nr Oldham, Greater Manchester OL3 7LS
Felt manufacturers

History: established by 1799 at Oak View Mill, a small carding and scribbling mill at Greenfield, near Oldham, Greater Manchester, under control of William Whitehead and his 4 sons Ralph R, James H, Francis F and John D. On William's death in 1832 firm became known as RR Whitehead & Brothers. In 1835 the firm bought Royal George Mills, fulling and scribbling mills at Greenfield, built in 1786 and originally known as Gibbs Mills. Oak View Mill was sold in 1837. During the 1840s the company manufactured flags. Purchased Charlotte or High Grove Mill, cotton spinning mill, and Throstle Nest Mill during the 1850s. FF Whitehead left the firm in 1847, followed by JD Whitehead in 1861. JH Whitehead died in 1870 and RR Whitehead in 1871. RR Whitehead junior, who founded the Arcady and Byrdcliffe communities in USA in 1890s, took control of the company which was incorporated as above in 1870. Purchased the Wandle Felt Co which had a factory at Mitcham, Surrey and offices at 14 Hanover Street, Long Acre, London. Felt manufacture was moved to Royal George Mills and Mitcham factory was closed. London offices remained, moving to 10&12 Endell Street and Castle Street, Long Acre in 1914. Acquired in 1932 by Porrits & Spencer Ltd, woollen manufacturers of Sunny Bank Mills, Helmshore, Lancashire which subsequently became part of the Scapa Group Ltd of Blackburn. In 1983 company manufactured pressed felts, cut felt parts for mechanical and industrial purposes and piano felts.

Records (1): at Bury Cooper Whitehead, Hudcar Mills, Bury, Lancashire BL9 6HD
directors: and general meeting minutes 1870-date, register 1932-date; share certificate book 1902-date

Records (2): at RR Whitehead & Brothers, Royal George Mills, Greenfield, Nr Oldham, Greater Manchester OL3 7LS
members register and share ledger c1900-35; share transfer: registers 1926-35, documents c1900-c63, notices 1900; annual lists and summaries 1908-48; memo and articles of association 1870s-1916; corporate agreements 1900s-70s; takeover papers and correspondence 1929-32; annual reports and accounts 1914-32; balance sheets and accounts 1901-69; Mitcham and Hanover: private ledgers 1854-1931, factory ledger 1858-1932; private ledgers 1870-1968; cash

book 1963-71; directors account bank books 1887-1942; agency agreements 1930s-60s; order book 1895-1907; production and sales analysis 1936-63; stock book: 1921, felt 1958-68; costing papers and books 1952-69; wool and blend prices 1961-9; expenses allocation tables 1945-69; carded weight book 1952-3; carding losses 1960s; manufacturing losses 1977-8; departmental machine book 1950-63; methods report c1972; patents, specifications, trade-marks and related documents 1846-1960s; salary and wage books 1932-74; pension scheme record sheets 1946-62; staff: notice 1864, letter 1926, newscutting 1974; Royal George Mills: photographs 1960s-80s, plans 1825-1950, inventories and valuations 1914-50, insurance policies, schedules and summaries 1914-60s; sewage and trade waste papers and correspondence 1925-30; Saddleworth property: title deeds, documents and papers 1639-1970s; London offices leases 1859-1959; other property papers and correspondence 1924-56; out letter books 1875-92, 1916-32; general files 1945-date; JD Whitehead diary 1827; road stopping books 1935-80; articles on company history 1949; solicitors costs and correspondence 1911-31; trade associations correspondence and papers 1918, 1931-2, 1955-66

Tanned Leather Co Ltd: directors and general meeting minutes 1871-9; memo and articles of association 1858, 1871; share certificates 1871-3; private ledger 1863-79; patents, licences and related documents 1851-71

115 REIGATE STOCK, SHARE & ESTATES CO LTD

6 Oct 1870
05116
43 Church Street, Reigate, Surrey
Property and investment

History: incorporated as above in 1870 to acquire the business of Reigate Investment Co Ltd, in purchasing land for development. Worked closely with Holmesdale Benefit Building Society. Invested in stock and shares in order to finance the purchase of land on which houses were built and then let or sold. Whole estates were developed in this way until 1910 after which only individual plots and property were developed and sold. By 1980 only acted as a holding company for its remaining property investments.

Records: at Holmesdale Benefit Building Society, 43 Church Street, Reigate, Surrey
minutes 1870-date; register of shareholders 1870-date; annual reports and accounts 1870-date; account ledgers 1870-date; list of properties c1920s; estate plans 1870s-1910s

116 BIRMINGHAM LAW SOCIETY

9 Dec 1870
05188
8 Temple Street, Birmingham, W Midlands B2 5BT
Law Society

History: founded in 1818 at meeting held at Royal Hotel, Temple Row, Birmingham, at which 19 'Attorneys or Solicitors resident in Birmingham or within 10 miles' were enrolled. Membership reached 40 by 1828, 257 by 1888, 453 by 1948 and 701 by 1968. Main aim is to promote fair and honourable practice within profession and to protect interests of members. Incorporated as company limited by guarantee as above in 1870. Established Law Library, finest outside London, in 1818 in Cannon Street, subsequently housed in Waterloo Street

1831-41, Waterloo Rooms 1841-76, Wellington Passage 1876-1933, Temperance Hall, Temple Street, 1934-date. Since 1866 and 1893 has awarded a gold and bronze medal to articled clerks for merit in examinations. In 1980s organises lectures on general legal practice and courses for articled clerks, legal secretaries etc, circularises members with new legal information and publishes its own *Bulletin*.

Records: at Birmingham Law Society, 8 Temple Street, Birmingham, W Midlands B2 5BT
meeting minutes 1818-1966; sub-committee minutes 1909-63; rules and memo and articles of association 1818-82; circulars 1890-1904; annual reports and accounts 1873-1966; cash books 1914-30; photographs of premises and dignitaries 19-20 cent; Library contents booklet 1972

GM Butts, *A Short History of the Birmingham Law Society 1818-1968* (priv pub 1968)

117 LONDON PROVINCIAL & SOUTH WESTERN BANK LTD
6 Jan 1871
05226
170 Fenchurch Street, London EC3P 3AH
Banking

History: formed in London in 1864 as Provincial Banking Corporation Ltd to take over the firm of Day, Nicholson & Stone (est 1782) of Rochester and Chatham, Kent, and the East of England Bank (est 1836). Acquired the Bank of Wales (est 1863) in 1865. By 1870 had 3 offices in London - head office recently moved from 25 Poultry to 7 Lothbury and branches in Edgware Road and Kingsland Road. Its country business was scattered through south east and east England and in Wales. Reconstructed in late 1870, title changing to London & Provincial Bank Ltd and incorporated in 1871. Several loss making Welsh branches were closed but new branches were established at Lewisham, London and Sutton, Surrey, and the business of Fincham & Simpson (est 1802) at Diss, Norfolk, and Eye, Suffolk, was acquired by the end of 1871. Branch opened at Twickenham, Middlesex, and business of J&JW Halters of Haverfordwest and Norbeth, Dyfed, was acquired in 1872. Branches were opened in 1873 at Woolwich and Stoke Newington, London; Eastbourne, E Sussex; Carmarthen, Dyfed; and Richmond, Surrey, bringing number of branches to 41. By 1878 after the North Kent Bank (est 1864) had been acquired, branch numbers rose to 58 and continued to rise to 76 by 1888, 126 by 1898, 186 by 1908 and 232 by 1917. Little business done in London until new larger premises were built at 3,4&5 Bank Buildings, Lothbury, in 1904. Amalgamated in 1917 with its old rivals London & South Western Bank Ltd (est 1862) to form above which amalgamated with Barclays Bank Ltd in 1918.

Records (1): at Barclays Bank, 54 Lombard Street, London EC3P 3AH
board minutes 1864-1918; committee meeting minutes 1870-1918; members register 1918; articles of association 1871-1904; amalgamation papers 1918; annual reports 1864-1918; half yearly accounts 1870-1917; regulations: for officers 1914, branch managers 1915; head office circulars 1876-1918; branches - Annesley: bond register 1900 on, interview book 1904-06; Beckenham: branch establishment requests 1874, weekly balances 1884-5; Bexleyheath: security register 1898 on; Brecon: probate register 1894-1926; Builth Wells: bills register 1882 on; Carshalton: draft books 1911-19; Catford: general authorities register 1890-1927; Fishguard: security register 1884 on; Forest Gate: inspection minutes and staff reports 1898 on; Hackney: security register 1898-1901, general order book 1892-1901; Haverfordwest:

security register 1885 on; Lee Green: minutes 1900 on; Llanelli: head office circulars 1876-98; Merthyr Tydfil: customer authorities 1889 on, appearance book 1878-85; Penarth: inspection minutes 1884-1925; Ponders Green: minutes 1892 on; St Clears: inspection minutes 1887-1940; Stoke Newington: security book 1878-90, customer ledger 1874-5; Swansea: deposit ledger 1863-9, customer ledger 1868-71, general managers letters 1888-94; Treherbert: head office circulars 1876-1907; Walthamstow: minutes 1880-1; Woolwich: character books 1906-35

Records (2): at University College of Swansea, Library, Singleton Park, Swansea, W Glamorgan SA2 8PP
amalgamation papers 1918-39

PW Matthews and AW Tuke, *History of Barclays Bank Ltd* (1926)

118 JOSEPH RODGERS & SONS LTD

11 Jan 1871
05235
65 Garden Street, Sheffield, S Yorkshire S1 4BJ
Cutlery manufacturers

History: the Rodgers family were cutlers in Sheffield from the second half of 17 cent being granted the trade-mark of a star and Maltese cross in 1682. Moved in 1724 to Norfolk Street factory which was extended in 1850 and 1860. From 1821 held a royal warrant. Partners Joseph Rodgers and Robert Newbold incorporated business as above in 1871. Works were extended in 1880s and 1890s and by 1907 covered over 5 acres. Originally pen knives were manufactured but razors, table cutlery and scissors were added from 1800 and steel in 1890s. Acquired steel works of William Jackson & Co in 1907. Acquired in 1970s by Richards of Sheffield (Holdings) Ltd, stainless steel table-ware and cutlery manufacturers, which were acquired by Meteor Industries Ltd in 1984.

Records: at Meteor Industries, 65 Garden Street, Sheffield, S Yorkshire S1 4BJ
minutes etc 1940s on

Under Five Sovereigns (priv pub c1907)

119 MANCHESTER LAW SOCIETY

19 Jan 1871
05254
1 Brazennose Street, Manchester, Greater Manchester M2 5FJ
Law society

History: founded as Manchester Law Association in 1838 to support the respectability of the profession, promote fair and liberal practice, decide questions of usage and prevent abusage; a Manchester Law Society, a benevolent institution, having existed from 1809-15. From 1845 shared premises with the Manchester Law Library Society (est 1845) at 4 Norfolk Street, 1845-65, Cross Street Chamber 1865-84, and Kennedy Street 1885-date. Incorporated as a company limited by guarantee in 1871 as Manchester Incorporated Law Association, changing name to above in 1910. Always favoured assisting legal education, giving prizes to articled clerks and contributing financially to Manchester University law classes. Gave practical support to the Provincial Law Society Association from 1844-50, based in Manchester and to the Poor Man's

Lawyer Movement, founded 1898 in connection with the Manchester University Settlement to give affordable legal advice to the 'deserving poor'. In 1980 membership, which it kept up to date with changes in law and practice, stood at c900.

Records: at Manchester Law Society, 1 Brazennose Street, Manchester, Greater Manchester M2 5FJ
committee and council minutes 1838-1954; sub-committee and committee minutes 1845-1964; conveyancing sub-committee minutes 1898-1912; finance sub-committee minutes 1884-1954; Law Association sub-committee minutes 1861-91; Law Society annual provincial meeting committee minutes 1893,1906,1923-4; library sub-committee minutes 1967-70; organising banquet and excursions committee minutes 1937-8; agm proceedings 1809-86; members register 1909-56; members notices, press cuttings etc 1903-30; decisions and opinions of society on professional practice and legal charges 1838-1913,1958-71; out letter books 1897-1935
Manchester and Salford Poor Man's Lawyer Association: committee minutes 1934-59
Provincial Law Society Association: meeting proceedings 1845-50

Kenneth H Atkinson, *A Short History of The Manchester Law Society 1838-1924* (priv pub 1924)

120 McCORQUODALE LEASING LTD

8 Feb 1871
05279
McCorquodale House, 15 Cavendish Square, London W1M 0HT
Paper

History: founded and incorporated in 1871 as North Wales Paper Co Ltd by George McCorquodale, founder of the McCorquodale printing group, to carry on paper making at Oakenholt, Clwyd. Initially used local straw in production but from 1879, except for WW years, mixture of esparto grass and chemical wood pulp was used. In 1927 production stood at 75-100 tons of paper per week. In 1960s due to overseas competition and outdated machinery, business ceased to be profitable and the mill closed in the 1970s, the plant and machinery being sold in 1979 to JJ Makin Ltd, paper manufacturers of Rochdale, to be used for producing wallpaper base. Name changed to above in 1979 and in 1981 acted as administrative section of the McCorquodale Group.

Records: at McCorquodale, McCorquodale House, 15 Cavendish Square, London W1M 0HT
board minutes 1916-date; general meeting minutes 1902-date; shareholders particulars and addresses 1930s-40s; share registers 1935-61; share ledger 1961; share transfer register 1921-69; share certificates 20 cent; dividend payments 1924-63; dividend warrants 20 cent; directors shareholdings registers 1930s-date; probate register 1902-61; memo and articles of association 1872-1979; misc corporate documents 20 cent; annual list and summary 1906-20; annual returns 1941-56; annual reports and accounts 1949-60; half yearly accounts 1900-67; balance book 1889-96; general ledger 1880-95; production run reports 1960s; valuations and inventory of property and machinery 1919-67; fire insurance policy 1939; plan of Oakenholt Water 1877; general correspondence files 1950s-70s

John D Ball, *McCorquodale & Company Ltd. The History of a Printing Firm* (1970)

121 VAL DE TRAVERS ASPHALTE LTD

15 Feb 1871
05292
Conyngham Hall, Knaresborough, N Yorkshire H95 9AY
Asphalt

History: incorporated in 1871 as Val de Travers Asphalte Paving Co Ltd to acquire the business of Val de Travers Asphalte Co Ltd, owners of asphalt mine at Linden, near Hanover, West Germany and carry on as asphalt paving manufacturers. During 1872 set up Manchester Val de Travers Asphalte Paving Co Ltd; Scottish Val de Travers Asphalte Paving Co Ltd, Glasgow; Irish Val de Travers Asphalte Paving Co Ltd, Dublin; Birmingham & Midland Counties Val de Travers Asphalte Paving Co Ltd; and North of England Val de Travers Asphalte Paving Co Ltd. Original registered offices were at 14-16 Palmerston Buildings, Old Broad Street, London, also held freehold of Sun Wharf, Alvar Street, Deptford, and leasehold of Baltic Wharf, Limehouse. Absorbed Compagnie Générale des Asphaltes des France in 1903 and by 1906 had mining properties and concessions at Seyssel, France; Ragusa, Italy; Travers, Switzerland; and Guanipa, Venezuela (sold in 1916). Also had offices in Alexandria, Egypt; New York; Paris; and at 73&75 Gee Street, London. Registered offices moved to Hamilton House, 155 Bishopsgate in about 1902 and to 106 Salisbury House, Finsbury Circus in 1923. In 1920 acquired controlling interest in United Limmer & Vorwohle Rock Asphalte Co Ltd (est prior to 1871), owners of asphalt mines at Hennings, Egestorffs and Vorwohle, Germany and an asphalt cement faced tiling factory. By 1923 had branches in Liverpool; Newcastle upon Tyne; Glasgow; Seyssel, France; Travers, Switzerland; Ragusa, Italy; and Alexandria and Cairo, Egypt. Specialities were compressed rock asphalt for roads and footways and mastic asphalt for roofs, floors, etc. Registered offices moved in 1938 to 21-22 Old Bailey, London. For duration of WW2 lost control of Italian and German mines. In 1947 had 10 subsidiary companies: Diamond Tread Co (1938) Ltd, Ditton Court Quarry, Larksfield, Maidstone, Kent; Thomas Faldo & Co (1929) Ltd; ACW Hobman & Co Ltd, Stockhold Road, Bermondsey, London; London Asphalte Co Ltd; Sicilian Rock Asphalte Co Ltd; Sigrist (Hauliers) Ltd; Taroads Ltd, Bell Bar, near Hatfield, Hertfordshire; United Limmer & Vorwohle Rock Asphalte Co Ltd; WG Walker (Glasgow) Ltd; and Compagnie des Mines d'Asphalte de Seyssel; 8 branch offices and depots at Birmingham; Canterbury, Kent; Exeter, Devon; Glasgow; Lincoln; Liverpool; Manchester and Newcastle upon Tyne; and the Sun Wharf at Deptford. Sold French mine and company in 1949, and Ragusa mine was acquired by Italian government in 1950. Name changed to above in 1954. Sold United Limmer & Vorwohle Rock Asphalte Co Ltd in 1956. Branches established at Plymouth, Devon in 1956 and Belfast in 1959. Acquired Matlock Asphalte & Bitumen Co Ltd, Cawdor Quarry, Matlock, Derbyshire in 1960; Norman W Dunn & Co Ltd, York, civil engineering contractors and tarsprayers in 1964; and Buttington Road Rolling Co Ltd, Trewen, Welshpool, Powys, civil engineering contractors in 1965. Road departments expanded rapidly from 1966 as motorway construction increased. By 1974 head offices had moved to Battlebridge House, 87-113 Tooley Street, London. Acquired in 1974 by Thomas Tilling Ltd, industrial holding company. Assets transferred in 1978 to Tilcon Ltd and company ceased to trade.

Records: at Tilcon, Conyngham Hall, Knaresborough, N Yorkshire H95 9AY
directors meeting minutes 1880-2; general meeting minutes 1871; agm proceedings 1927-36; share ledger 1958 on; seal books 1871-1960; annual reports and accounts 1872-4,1902-67

Birmingham & Midland Counties Val de Travers Asphalte Paving Co Ltd: directors meeting minutes 1871-1937; general meeting minutes 1872-1907; annual reports and accounts 1872-1937; banking correspondence 1927-34
United Limmer & Vorwohle Rock Asphalte Co Ltd: directors meeting minutes 1911-56; general meeting minutes and agm proceedings 1872-1921; Linden manager reports 1875-80; seal book 1934-52; annual reports and accounts 1872-1919

122 BRISTOL LAW SOCIETY

18 Feb 1871
05295
Law Library, Guildhall, Broad Street, Bristol, Avon BS1 2HL
Law society

History: a law society was founded in Bristol, Avon in 1770 by attorneys at law and solicitors in Chancery. Meetings were held every second Tuesday and the first and last days of every term in the Bush Tavern, Corn Street. Between 1770 and 1780 it had 20-22 members and its last recorded meeting was in 1789. Bristol Law Library Society was founded in 1819 to establish a law library which was set up in the Guildhall, Broad Street. In 1870 the law library was transferred to Bristol Incorporated Law Society, incorporated in 1871 as a company limited by guarantee. The objects of the new society included promoting honourable practice amongst attorneys and solicitors, protecting their interests as a profession, settling disputes, improving legal education, and maintaining a law library. 70 solicitors enrolled in the society. The law library was moved from Broad Street to the Assize Courts in Small Street where offices were also taken, but moved back to the Guildhall after WW2. Changed name to above in late 1960s. The society started a duty solicitor scheme in magistrates courts, and in 1984 oversaw the legal advice centres in the area and organised and ran programmes of continuing legal education.

Records: at Bristol Law Society, Law Library, Guildhall, Broad Street, Bristol, Avon BS1 2HL
council: and general meeting minutes, correspondence and papers 1871-1952, attendance book 1904-56; general purposes and finance committee: minutes 1937-43, 1959-73, report 1948; library committee: minutes 1937-55, reports 1951-5, agendas 1954-5, correspondence 1948-55; conveyancing costs committee minutes 1937-9,1953-68; subcommittees minutes 1946-7; committee: meeting attendance books 1916-17, 1936-7, members lists 1947-8,1959,1971-2; agenda books 1899-1912; annual reports and accounts 1871-1946; memo and articles of association 1871-1957; secretary out letter books 1871-1925; circulars, notices etc 1886-1949; members signatures 1871-86; library: by-laws 1887, suggestions book 1894-c1956, correspondence 1948-55; librarians duties nd; newscuttings re members 1903-c66; photographs 1900s; Law Society provincial meetings: event programmes, circulars, notices, newscuttings, menus etc 1894,1910,1931-2; publications, *Year Book* 1970s; Bristol & District Board of Legal Studies: reports and accounts 1913-35, attendance book 1905-23; lecture notices, syllabuses, particulars and attendances 1900s-36
Bristol Law Library Society: management committee and general meeting: minutes 1819-70, reports 1870; rules 1819-44; members signatures 1819-27; papers and correspondence 1849-70; audited accounts 1869-70
Bristol Law Society: minutes 1774-89; attendance and fines books 1770-80; fines incurred 1773-5,1777-8; rules 1774-5; accounts 1774-5,1777-8

123 MERCHANTS MARINE INSURANCE CO LTD

17 Mar 1871
05334
1 St Helen's, Undershaft, London EC3P 3DQ
Insurance

History: incorporated in 1871 as above for the underwriting of marine insurance. Based at 37 Cornhill, London it was acquired by Employers' Liability Assurance Corporation Ltd in 1919. Continued to operate under own name even after Employers' Liability was acquired by Northern Assurance Co Ltd which was taken over by Commercial Union Assurance Co Ltd in 1968.

Records: at Commercial Union Assurance, 1 St Helen's, Undershaft, London EC3P 3DQ
accounts and reports 1871-1944

124 PUBLIC PICTURE GALLERY FUND (BIRMINGHAM) UNLIMITED

5 May 1871
05409
41 Church Street, Birmingham, W Midlands B3 2DY
Fine arts

History: founded by Thomas Clarkson Osler and incorporated in 1871 as an unlimited company to promote the fine arts of painting, drawing, etching, engraving and sculpture. Since its inception has helped Birmingham Art Gallery to purchase many items.

Records: at Ryland Martineau, 41 Church Street, Birmingham, W Midlands B3 2DY
minutes 1871-date; memo and articles of association 1870; list of pictures purchased 1871-1971; PAG Osler working papers 1979-81; Holliday bequest papers 1979-81; misc papers 19-20 cent; letter book 1871-1926

125 FALLOWFIELD BOWLING & LAWN TENNIS CLUB LTD

10 May 1871
05418
81 Wellington Road, Fallowfield, Manchester, Greater Manchester
Sports club-houses

History: established as a bowling club prior to 1860, property at Fallowfield, Manchester being purchased in 1868. Fallowfield Bowling Club Ltd was incorporated in 1871 to buy same from HM Steinthal and Joseph Broome, leading Manchester cotton merchants who became president, and vice president and treasurer respectively, and to lay out and maintain a bowling green, quoiting ground, etc. The new ground was opened in 1872 with amenities including a croquet lawn, gymnasia, see-saw and swings. Permanent pavilion and billiards room opened in 1878, and lawn tennis was introduced in 1880. Name changed to above in 1891, and pavilion extension was opened in 1893. After financial difficulties, share capital was reorganised in 1909. Tennis courts were extended in 1912-13, ladies pavilion built in 1921 and 4 hard courts constructed between 1925 and 1928. Struggled to exist during 1930s and 1940s but recovered during late 1950s. Premises extended again in 1972. In 1974 a new club was constituted, distinct from the company, and new shares issued.

Records: at Fallowfield Bowling & Lawn Tennis Club, 81 Wellington Road, Fallowfield, Manchester, Greater Manchester
board and general meeting minutes 1870-date; tennis section committee minutes 1924-40; share certificate stubs 1925-74; shareholders list c1870; annual reports and accounts 1870-date; club rules 1880-1920; members nomination books 1881-1970; visitors books 1868-93; bowling club register 1879-81; suggestion book 1893-1979

Fallowfield Bowling and Lawn Tennis Club. A Hundred Years in Retrospect (1960)

126 LIMMER HOLDINGS LTD

12 May 1871
05428
PO Box 8, Ettingshall, Wolverhampton, Northamptonshire WV4 6JP
Asphalt

History: incorporated in 1871 as Limmer Asphalte Paving Co Ltd to manufacture asphalt and lay paving. Obtained offices in Lime Street, London and secured paving contracts for Dublin and London streets. By end of 1871 had formed agencies in Lancashire, Cheshire, Yorkshire, Staffordshire and Scotland. Received asphalt from United Limmer & Vorwohle Rock Asphalte Co Ltd (est prior to 1871) which owned mines in Germany at Hennings, Egestorffs and Vorwohle. During 1870s and 1880s paved streets in London and Paris. Amalgamated in 1916 with Trinidad Lake Asphalte Paving Co Ltd (inc 1897) and changed name to Limmer & Trinidad Lake Asphalte Paving Co Ltd. By 1957 had following subsidiaries: Bwlch Gwyn Quarry (Anglesey) Ltd; Claridges Patent Asphalte Co Ltd; Ham Hill (Sand Pits) Co Ltd; Hutchison Instrument Co Ltd; Industrial Concrete Products Ltd; Limmer & Trinidad (International) Asphalte Co Ltd; Pilkington's Asphalte Co Ltd; Raponi (Flooring) Ltd; Roadways Equipment (1938) Ltd; Safeway Products Ltd; Seyssel Asphalte Co Ltd; Trinidad Lake Asphalte Co (North Western) Ltd; Trinidad Mastic Supply Co Ltd; and Wm Eyers & Co Ltd. Name changed to above in 1968. Acquired by Tarmac Ltd in 1971.

Records: at Tarmac, PO Box 8, Ettingshall, Wolverhampton, Northamptonshire WV4 6JP
directors and general meeting: minutes 1871-89,1916-72, agenda book 1871-2; general meeting proceedings 1873-88; annual reports and accounts 1872-4,1881-7; quarrying and roofing photographs c1880

127 ALLIANCE BANK LTD

26 May 1871
05446
4 Bartholomew Lane, London EC2
Banking

History: founded in 1862 as Alliance Bank of London & Liverpool Ltd, business commencing in London in May and Liverpool in Jul. Established branches at Southwark, London and Birkenhead, Merseyside in 1863 and at Manchester in 1864. Name changed to above in 1865. Southwark branch was sold in 1870 to London Joint Stock Bank Ltd and whole bank was reconstructed in 1871, the Liverpool business being sold to National Bank of Liverpool Ltd and the London business being liquidated and reformed into a new registered company of the same name. In 1872 the Manchester business was transferred to form the basis of the

Lancashire & Yorkshire Bank Ltd. Amalgamated in 1892, by which time it had 12 London branches, with Parr's Banking Co Ltd (est 1865) to form Parr's Banking Co & the Alliance Bank Ltd, which was renamed Parr's Bank Ltd in 1896 and amalgamated in 1918 with London County & Westminster Bank Ltd (est 1836) to form London County Westminster & Parr's Bank Ltd. Title changed to Westminster Bank Ltd in 1923.

Records: at National Westminster Bank, 41 Lothbury, London EC4P 2BP
board minutes 1864-92; committee minutes: London 1869-78, Manchester 1871-2, branch 1886-92, sub 1865-86; general meeting minutes 1871-92; shareholders list 1863; prospectus 1862; articles of association 1862; papers re reconstruction 1868-71 and amalgamation 1892; instructions and notices 1866-92; annual reports 1863-92; security register 1862-5; customer correspondence 1859-65

TE Gregory, *The Westminster Bank Through a Century* Vol 1&2 (1936)

128 FOSTER PORTER & CO LTD

20 Jun 1871
05494
Temple House, Seacroft Ring Road, Leeds, W Yorkshire LS14 1NH
Wholesale drapery warehousemen

History: established in London in 1842 and incorporated as above in 1871 to carry on the wholesale drapery warehouse business after Mr Porter's death. Main premises were leased in London at 44-49 Wood Street (freehold purchased 1873-4) but also had premises at 55 Wood Street, 26&27 Addle Street, 23-25 Philip Lane, and 1-7 Back Court, Cheapside. New warehouse was built in 1874, destroyed by fire in 1882 and another opened in 1884. By 1923 was supplying goods to Lagos, Nigeria and South Africa, and had offices in Cardiff, S Glamorgan. Main premises completely destroyed in 1940 by enemy action and new head offices established at 200-203 Tottenham Court Road, with other leased premises in Oxford Street and Maddox Street. By 1943 was trading through 19 provincial stockrooms. Purchased 200-203 Tottenham Court Road in 1946 and 204-208 in 1951, Wood Street freehold being compulsorily purchased in 1950. Opened stockrooms in Aberdeen, Grampian in 1953, Bournemouth, Dorset and Carlisle, Cumbria in 1955, Liverpool and Plymouth, Devon in 1956, and Bristol, Avon in 1957. Owned 'Bulldog', 'Glendower', 'Stag' and 'Glentex' trademarks. Acquired in 1957 by Ansbacher & Co, merchant bankers, and by 1959 had become a property company. Taken over in 1961 by Great Universal Stores Ltd and in 1983 was controlled by GUS Property Management Ltd as part of the former's property division.

Records: at GUS Property Management, Temple House, Seacroft Ring Road, Leeds, W Yorkshire LS14 1NH
directors meeting minutes 1871-1959; general meeting minutes 1871-1982; agm newscuttings 1915-57; directors register 1901-77; annual reports and accounts 1872,1882

129 BIRKENHEAD SCHOOL LTD

13 Jul 1871
05549
11 Kingsmead Road South, Birkenhead, Merseyside L43 6TA
School

History: founded in 1860 by Sir W Jackson, B Darbyshire, Halsall Segar, and others to set up a school in Birkenhead, Merseyside to provide a religious, classical, mathematical and mercantile education. Incorporated Birkenhead Proprietary School Ltd to finance and manage new school which opened in large rented house in Park Road North, with 13 pupils under the headmastership of Rev JT Pearse. By 1865 numbers had risen to 85 consisting of 72 day boys and 13 boarders. In 1871 purchased 4 acres of land on west side of Shrewsbury Road on which to build a new school for 250 boys. New company was incorporated in 1871 as above to manage new school. Numbers rose to 157 by 1877, 200 by 1909, and 350 by 1921. Erected a boarding house in 1876-7 and a school chapel in 1882. Started a preparatory department in 1889.

Records: at Birkenhead School, 11 Kingsmead Road South, Birkenhead, Merseyside L43 6TA governors: meeting minutes 1923-date, attendance book 1942-5, correspondence 1942-58; committee meeting minutes: 1964-date, finance 1962-date; share: certificate book 1933-41, transfer documents 1920s-40s; mortgage register c1880-1900; debenture: register and ledger 1922-63, documents 1872-c1963, holders trustee correspondence 1896-1919; corporate documents 1921; annual returns 1940-62; annual report and accounts 1940-62; nominal ledgers 1951-65; personal ledgers 1951-64; fees receipt books 1875-8; masters meeting minutes 1886-97,1921; examination results 1864-77,1886-97; prize lists 1890-1905; scholarship and fund papers c1906-30s; school: masters and pupils lists 1925-62, prospectuses 1921-c60, calendars 1944-62, concert, speech day, sports, event programmes 1877,1927-63, plans 1954,1960, chapel service papers 1919-73; title deeds and documents 1860 on; war damage papers 1941-8; newscuttings 1871-1930s,1962-4; staff, pupils, sports, events, buildings etc photographs 1865-1970s; history articles and notes 1947-50s; athletic committee: meeting minutes and results lists 1879-1938, cash book 1881-1931, records books 1910-46; football and cricket clubs fixture lists 1919-23; natural history society journal 1945-61; preparatory school: bank book 1869-75, year books 1919-30; Old Birkonians Society: registers 1861-1930s, year books incl annual reports and accounts, members lists and rules 1924-60, war list 1946, honours lists 1927-50, accounts 1927-9, trust fund deeds and accounts 1923-35, magazine 1909-81, annual dinner programmes 1906-66, London branch papers 1947-57, football and rugby programmes and fixture lists 1923-60s
Birkenhead Proprietory School Ltd: memo and articles of association c1860; secretary report 1865; architects memoranda 1866

130 ALLIANCE ECONOMIC INVESTMENT CO LTD

18 Jul 1871
05560
4 Carlton Gardens, Pall Mall, London SW1Y 5AB
Property

History: incorporated in 1871 as above to acquire and improve property on which houses were to be built and then rented or sold. Also received money on deposit, which it invested, and administered loans. Registered offices were at 35 Lincoln's Inn Fields, London from 1871 to 1940. Purchased property throughout London, the majority of it in the western residential areas. By 1937 had a subsidiary company, Allicon Houses Ltd, which ran 3 large houses in Priory Road, West Hampstead. During late 1930s income from rents decreased due to competition from new blocks of flats being built in London, and company began to convert its houses into flats. Offices were destroyed by enemy bombs in 1940 and company moved to 45 Doughty Street. Had 382 houses in 1939: 17 were totally destroyed by 1945; 60 badly damaged; and 160 slightly damaged. Merged with Charlwood Properties Ltd (inc 1884 as East End Dwellings Co Ltd) to form Charlwood Alliance Properties Ltd which was acquired in 1974 by Town & City Properties Ltd.

Records: at Westminster City Libraries Archives Department, Victoria Library, 160 Buckingham Palace Road, London SW1W 9UD
directors and general meeting minutes 1871-87, 1932-51; annual reports and accounts 1932-51; general meeting proceedings 1932-51

131 WHITWORTH ELECTRIC (HOLDINGS) LTD

25 Jul 1871
05580
129 Elm Grove, Southsea, Hampshire
Holding (previously coal mining)

History: incorporated as Nantyglo & Blaina Ironworks Ltd in 1871, named after two mining locations near Newport, Gwent. Original capital of £750,000 was reduced to £468,750 in 1882. Manufactured rails and plates for shipment from company's Newport Wharf. Ironworks closed in late 1870s and company then concentrated on coal mining. The mines were leased by the Lancaster family and annual production of 2 million tons was attained in 1890s. Early exponent of regular weekly and fortnightly wage payments and owner-occupation of homes. Renamed Nantyglo & Blaina Estates Ltd in 1930, and after nationalization of coal industry in 1947 capital was reduced to £16,500. Acquired Whitworth Electric Co Ltd in 1959 and company became distributor of electrical components. Name changed to above in 1972.

Records (1): at National Museum of Wales, St Fagans, Cardiff, S Glamorgan CF5 6XB
committee meeting minutes 1875; particulars of properties 1872; surface estate reports 1880

Records (2): Gwent County Record Office, County Hall, Cwmbran, Gwent NP4 2XH
share papers 1874-1901; annual reports, balance sheets and correspondence 1872-81; iron sale particulars 1873-83; contracts 1873-5; sales catalogues 1881-2; works records 1872-1913; workings reports 1872-90; inventories 1874-7; papers re Nantyglo works 1871-5; title deeds, maps and plans 1538-c1900; leases: building 1827-82, general 1860-90; survey and report on iron works 1878

132 REDHILL MARKET HALL CO LTD

29 Jul 1871
05591
Market Hall, Redhill, Surrey RH1 1NT
Market hall

History: established in 1857 when the Redhill Market House Co Ltd was formed by residents of Redhill to build a market hall and public rooms and to make arrangements for a corn and general market. The building, designed by J&H Francis of London, consisted of a large assembly room on the first floor with a corn market underneath. In 1871 the Market House company was liquidated and the above formed to acquire the business. The indoor market was discontinued shortly after 1900 and an outside cattle market established, which operated until the 1970s. The market hall was purchased by the local authority in 1978, and demolished in early 1982.

Records: at Redhill Market Hall, Chancery House, 3 Hatchlands Road, Redhill, Surrey RH1 6AA
directors minutes, 1871-1980; general meeting minutes 1871-1980; agenda for directors and general meetings 1871-1962; register of members 1871-1980; share and debenture transfer certificates and correspondence 1873-1960; documents concerning mortgage 1872-83; printed annual reports and accounts 1872-1980; annual returns 1940-52; working accounting papers 1932-66; ledgers 1871-1967; journal 1917-47; account books 1957-71; cash book 1933-78; petty cash books 1943-77; title deeds and printed sales particulars of property around market hall 1897-1932; newscuttings 1891-1980; plans of market hall 1950s; photographs of market hall 1885-1970s; photograph of company secretary c1910; printed ticket to lecture 1893
Redhill Market House Co Ltd: directors and committee minutes 1856-70; general meeting minutes 1859-70; agenda of directors and general meetings 1860-6; register of shareholders 1860-70; list of shareholders 1860-70; printed prospectus 1857; printed report and accounts 1860,1867-70

133 THOMPSON INVESTMENTS LTD
18 Sep 1871
05699
9-10 Grafton Street, London W1X 4DA
Property (formerly department store)

History: incorporated in 1871 on the initiative of Major FB McCrea as Army & Navy Co-operative Society Ltd to supply members with goods for domestic consumption as cheaply as possible without profit. Membership was limited to army and navy officers and relatives, who held shares. As profits increased, a gentleman's club, restaurants, reading rooms, travel agencies and a range of other services were soon offered. The warehouse in Victoria Street, London became known as 'The Stores' and branches were opened in the provinces. The publication of an annual price list started a mail order business. Army & Navy Auxiliary Co-operative Supply Ltd was established in 1880 to deal in fresh provisions and the society began to manufacture certain goods in workshops at Victoria. First depot was opened in 1891 in Bombay, India to cater for members on overseas service, followed by branches at Karachi in 1891 and Calcutta in 1902. Stores continued to flourish until WW1 when taxation and rationing began to reduce members' incomes and membership began to be broadened. Victoria Street frontage was re-designed in 1920 to install display windows and the warehouse was opened to the general public. Name changed to Army & Navy Stores Ltd in 1934. Disposed of last branches in India in 1952 and embarked on a programme of expansion in provincial England. Army & Navy Stores were acquired in 1973 by House of Fraser Ltd although the property and company was sold to Amalgamated Caledonian Assets Ltd for redevelopment of the site, House of Fraser being granted a lease of the premises. Name then changed to Amcal (Victoria) Ltd and in 1975 to above.

Records: at Glasgow University Archives, The University, Glasgow, Strathclyde G12 8QQ
directors: meeting minutes 1872-1964, attendance book c1897-1943; general meeting: reports 1873-1965, chairmans speeches 1880-1941; articles of association 1871-1914; prospectus 1871; annual reports and accounts 1872-1909,1979; balance sheets: and accounts 1918-31,

departmental 1899-1915, manufacturing departments 1898-1912; journals 1920-71; manufacturing department reports 1878-87; statistics: departmental trading 1976, buildings, staff, premises and advertising 1872-1903; workshop diaries 1890-9; stock books: gun 1882-c90,nd, pistol 1880-93,1923-65, revolver 1893-1922, second-hand guns 1889-1960; catalogues, price lists, sales literature and papers 1872-1970s; Indian depots: balance sheets 1891-1916, sales charts 1923-8, papers 1896, advertisements c1920s,1937, price lists 1901,1933, opening papers 1891,1901-02, photographs 1890s-1930s, sales correspondence 1911-12; salary ledger 1919-38; menus 1893-1926; staff magazine 1935; membership: tickets, correspondence and papers c1890s-1933; staff, workshops, stores etc photographs 1890s-1970: finance management and history articles 1876-1971; centenary papers 1960s-71
Army & Navy Auxiliary Co-operative Supply Ltd: directors meeting minutes 1880-1919; general meeting minutes 1881-1919; agenda books 1880-1921; articles of association 1900; catalogues 1907; correspondence 1880-4
Artillery Mansions Ltd: directors meeting minutes 1899-1900

134 WALLSEND SLIPWAY ENGINEERS LTD

2 Oct 1871
05728
Benton House, 136 Sandyford Road, Newcastle upon Tyne, Tyne & Wear NE2 1QE
Marine engineers

History: incorporated in 1871 as Wallsend Slipway Co Ltd to establish works where the firms of C Mitchell & Co, Watts Milburn & Co, and Nelson, Donkin & Co could carry out repairs to their vessels. Between 1873 and 1897 dealt with 2804 vessels. From 1874 when ship repairs slackened off undertook marine engine manufacture to keep the workforce together. Opened dry dock in 1877 and changed name to Wallsend Slipway Engineering Co Ltd in 1878. Established repairing branch at Cardiff, S Glamorgan in 1886 which formed Wallsend Pontoon Co Ltd (inc 1887) which was sold in 1895 and became known as Mercantile Pontoon Co of Cardiff. Opened second dry dock in 1895. Dismantled both slipways in 1909. Initially manufactured only cylindrical and locomotive type boilers but later entered water tube type. Maximum yearly output was 346,310 indicated hp which placed it at the head of output of world's marine engineers. Changed name to above in 1978. In 1982 products included shell, water tube and waste heater boilers, pressure vessels and heavy fabrication, and main contracting and project management. Name changed to Sir James Laing & Son Ltd in 1983.

Records (1): at Wallsend Slipway Engineers, Point Pleasant, Wallsend, Tyne & Wear NE28 6QW
share papers and correspondence 1903-05; memo and articles of association c1918-77; foremen and staff mutual benefit society contributions book 1947-78; history booklets 1911-29; sites and products photographs

Records (2): at British Shipbuilders, Benton House, 136 Sandyford Road, Newcastle upon Tyne, Tyne & Wear NE2 1QE
directors and general meeting minutes 1952-date; memo and articles of association c1977

Records (3): at Tyne & Wear Archives Department, Blandford House, West Blandford Street, Newcastle upon Tyne, Tyne & Wear NE1 4JA
accounting and staff records; drawings etc 19-20 cent

135 SAMUEL FOX & CO LTD

1 Nov 1871
05799
9 Albert Embankment, London SE1 7SN
Iron and steel

History: incorporated as above in 1871 to acquire the business of the firm of same name established in 1842, manufacturing iron and steel at the Stocksbridge Works, near Sheffield, S Yorkshire. Acquired in 1918 by United Steel Companies Ltd which was nationalised in 1967.

Records: at British Steel Corporation, Northern Regional Records Centre, Unit F2, Commerce Way, Skippers Lane Industrial Estate, South Bank, Middlesbrough, Cleveland TS6 6UT

136 BOLTON HIDE SKIN & FAT CO LTD

15 Dec 1871
05894
48 Central Street, Bolton, Greater Manchester
Hide and skin market

History: incorporated to protect the butchers of Bolton by establishing a market for sale, purchase or exchange of hides, skins, fat and offal. Only butchers were eligible to be shareholders. Plant and goodwill bought for £350. Record profits in 1890 led to purchase of land in Idle Lane, Bolton, Greater Manchester for new warehouse. By 1923 company had premises in Bolton and Wigan, Greater Manchester and was in constant competition with hide markets of Manchester. In 1974 became subsidiary of WD Mark & Sons Ltd of York.

Records: at WD Mark & Sons, 30 Lawrence Street, York, N Yorkshire YO1 3BW
directors and general meetings: rough 1872-94,1923-44, agendas 1882-4; directors report and accounts 1872-1909

137 CHINA NAVIGATION CO LTD

31 Jan 1872
06005
Regis House, 43-46 King William Street, London EC4R 9BE
Shipping

History: incorporated as above in 1872 by John S and William H Swire, sons of the founder of John Swire & Sons, merchants and shipping agents of London and Liverpool (est 1832), to exploit opening for increased steam shipping on the Yangtze River. Ordered 3 ships to be built for Lower Yangtze trade and in 1873 purchased the Union Steam Navigation Co with its 2 ships and property leases in Shanghai and other river ports. By mid 1870s interests had spread to Canton River trade and by late 1870s to Shanghai-Ningpo and Shanghai-Tientsin routes despite intense competition and rate wars. In 1883 merged with Coast Boats Ownery established in 1874 by JS Swire to handle coastal trade. By 1894 fleet had expanded to 29 ships calling at ports along the Yangtze River, the North and South China coasts, in the Philippines, South East Asia, Australia, Japan and Russia. Requisitioned by British government in 1940 and property and shipping in Hong Kong and Shanghai was seized by Japanese. Butterfield &

Swire, Far Eastern trading company of John Swire & Sons, was appointed Eastern agent from inception.

Records (1): at John Swire & Sons, Regis House, 43-46 King William Street, London EC4R 9BE
minutes 1947 on; photograph album of company ships, Far Eastern scenes and commercial activities 1873-1966

Records (2): at School of Oriental & African Studies Library, University of London, Malet Street, London WC1E 7HP
minutes 1872-1946; share registers 1872 on; debentures 1897,1909; corporate agreements 1877-1914; annual accounts and working papers 1871-1918,1936-45; steamers accounts 1874-84; shore property accounts 1897-1924; ship: earnings 1906-41, operating statements 1965-6; pool: settlements 1906-41, statements 1966-7; voyage results 1959-65; journals 1919-46; accounts and financial correspondence 1900-47; taxation correspondence and papers 1922-39; wharf charges 1884; fuel oil contracts 1926-38; service agreements and correspondence with: Scott's Shipbuilding & Engineering Co 1913-21, and Taikoo Dockyard & Engineering Co 1952; tonnage wear and tear allowances 1921-41; war claim schedules and working papers 1944-5; staff agreements 1932-6,1945-50; staff book 1930-41; profit sharing scheme papers 1924; provident fund papers and correspondence 1929-30,1942-6; pension fund and staff war casualties correspondence 1941-8; lease particulars 1874-95; property registers 1885-1941; Hanzhou property deed and plan 1921; floating property book 1926-41; property correspondence 1900-47; legal case papers re ship collision 1895, and anti-piracy costs 1930; correspondence and reports re piracy 1925-49, and teaboy dispute 1933-8; local and departmental correspondence 1882-1902; correspondence between London managers, local agents and others re companys management and business, incl steamers, staff routes, pool agreements, and Chinese trade 1871-1948

Records (3): at Scottish Record Office, PO Box 36, HM General Register House, Edinburgh, Lothian EH1 3YY
Scott's Shipbuilding & Engineering Co: agreements, specifications and plans of various vessels 1905-48, contract files 1945-52, correspondence re tonnage and ships 1942-64, glass negatives and photographs of vessel construction, trials and launches c1930-c51

Records (4): at Essex Record Office, County Hall, Chelmsford, Essex CM1 1LX
log book of Captain HE Laver

Sheila Marriner and Francis E Hyde, *The Senior John Samuel Swire 1825-98. Management in Far Eastern Shipping Trades* (1967)

138 LIVERPOOL ESTATE CO LTD

2 Feb 1872
06008
30 Exchange Street East, Liverpool, Merseyside L2 3QA
Property

History: incorporated in 1872 as above to purchase land to develop in Birkenhead, Merseyside. Adjunct to business of Mason, Grierson & Bewley, solicitors of Church Street,

Liverpool and Smith & Sons, estate agents of Duncan Street, Birkenhead. Owned properties which were leased to tenants in Birkenhead and Widnes, Cheshire. By 1974 owned mainly domestic terraced and semi-detached houses and flats valued at £77,000. From 1976 acquired more commercial property in Liverpool. Acquired in 1983 by Merseyside Estates Ltd.

Records: at Merseyside Estates, 30 Exchange Street East, Liverpool, Merseyside L2 3QA
minutes 1980 on; members register etc 1946 on; memo and articles of association 1950; title deeds 19-20 cent

139 NORTH EASTERN BANKING CO LTD

7 Feb 1872
06016
54 Lombard Street, London EC3P 3AH
Banking

History: registered and opened for business in Newcastle upon Tyne, Tyne & Wear in 1872. By 1875 had branches at West Hartlepool, Middlesbrough, Loftus and Stockton on Tees, Cleveland; Consett, Chester le Street and Spennymoor, Durham; Jarrow, Gateshead and Houghton le Spring, Tyne & Wear; Barrow in Furness, Cumbria; and Amble and Hexham, Northumberland; agencies at the Cattle Market and Quayside, Newcastle upon Tyne; and sub-branches at Allendale Town, Northumberland and Brotton, Cleveland. Purchased in 1875 Alnwick & County Bank (est 1858) with its branches at Alnwick, Belford, Bellingham, Berwick on Tweed, Morpeth, Rothbury and Wooler, Northumberland. New head offices in Grey Street and Pilgrim Street, Newcastle were opened in 1877. Barrow branch was closed in 1878 but by 1892 new branches had been opened at South Shields, Sunderland and Byker, Tyne & Wear; Newbiggin by the Sea, Wark and Warkworth, Northumberland; Tow Law, Durham; and Helton le Hole, Cumbria. Amalgamated in 1892 with Dale Young & Co (est 1858) which had 5 offices in Newcastle, South Shields and Jarrow. Between 1893 and 1913 opened about 23 sub-branches and 24 branches at Ashington, Birtley and Prudhoe, Northumberland; Blackhill, Stanley, Sedgefield, Barnard Castle, Bishop Auckland, Darlington, Durham, Seaham Harbour, Wolsingham, Dipton, Blaydon and Wearhead, Durham; and Gosforth, Monkwearmouth, Millfield, Gallowgate, Southwick, Jesmond, Whitley Bay, Wallsend and North Shields, Tyne & Wear. Amalgamated in 1914 with Bank of Liverpool Ltd (est 1831) which amalgamated with Martin's Bank Ltd in 1918 to form Bank of Liverpool & Martins Ltd (shortened to Martin's Bank Ltd in 1928) and merged with Barclays Bank Ltd in 1969.

Records: at Barclays Bank, 54 Lombard Street, London EC3P 3AH
shareholders list 1873-93; share papers 1873-1910; prospectus 1872; articles of association 1872-1911; papers and correspondence re actual and proposed amalgamations 1875-1914; annual reports 1873-1914; deposit and interest rates 1903-12; securities book 1885-9; papers re industrial companies 1880-1920; daily instructions 1873-1915; misc staff correspondence 1912-19; special letter books 1874-1920; correspondence with Bank of England and agents 1872-1901; official circulars 1872-99; branch accounts and statistics schedule 1897-8; Ashington branch: deposit account ledgers 1879-1900s, issued drafts register 1892 on

George Chandler, *Four Centuries of Banking* Vol 1&2 (1964,1968)

140 GENERAL CONFERENCE OF THE NEW CHURCH CO LTD

16 Feb 1872
06039
20 Bloomsbury Way, London WC1A 2TH
Religious body

History: The New Church signified by the New Jerusalem in the Apocalypse or Revelation of St John was founded by followers of the works of Emanuel Swedenborg (1688-1772) a Swedish scientist, philosopher and theologian. A Swedenborg study group was started in London in 1782-3, while a society to print his works had been established in Manchester in 1780 by Rev John Clowes who was responsible for the spread and strength of the New Church in the north and midlands of England. The first General Conference of New Church members was held in 1789, and first periodical of the Church was published in 1790. Birmingham New Church Temple opened Jun 1791. Manchester Society started 1791; Liverpool 1793; Hatton Cross, London 1797; Accrington, Lancashire 1802. By 1842 the Church was made up of 40-50 societies and by 1851 had 50 places of worship. Incorporated as a company limited by guarantee in 1872. In 1935 had 68 churches and about 6000 members, and in 1980, 43 societies and 2161 members and adherents. The Church is to be found in most European countries, North America, Australia, New Zealand, South and West Africa, and India.

Records (1): General Conference of the New Church, 20 Bloomsbury Way, London WC1A 2TH
conference: minutes 1789-date, reports 1874-92, committee reports to same 1863-1961, president signatures 1789-1913, attendance register 1832-1927, correspondence and addresses 1816-74, secretarys correspondence and papers 1825-1939, committee minutes 1825-1953; Augmentation Fund Midland District committee minutes 1877-1920, Ministerial Advisory Council minutes and papers 1932-1953, tape recordings 1957-60, press cuttings 1874; South of Trent Trustee minutes 1823-43; North of Trent Trustee minutes 1850-1943; Overseas Missions Committee: minutes 1874-1971, reports, correspondence and papers of various missions 1919-71, South African Section minutes and papers 1917-47, South African native mission sub-committee minutes, reports, financial papers, correspondence, photographs and lantern slides 1916-70, West African Section minutes 1947-50, West African mission reports, papers and photographs 1934-60s, correspondence, reports and papers re Burma, India, China, Japan and other Asian missions 1916-73, photographs and slides of Indian Mission 1925-40s; Indian New Church magazine 1915-17; Australian New Church journal 1888-1961; South African New Church magazine 1926-60; New Church day school committee minutes 1832-45; education committee minutes 1893-1914; magazine index committee minutes and correspondence 1890-1924; library and documents committee: minutes 1894-1977, correspondence 1934-53; liturgy revision committee minutes 1913-20; New Testament translation committee minutes and correspondence 1913-44; New Church Version of the Word committee minutes and correspondence 1923-44; New Hymn Book committee minutes, papers and correspondence 1936-47; New Methods committee minutes 1938-46; monthly meeting minutes 1827-48; legal documents and agreements re Church rights 1791-1927; memo and articles of association and rules 1872,1948,1977; *Year Books* 19 cent-date; papers and correspondence re wills 20 cent; correspondence re publications, services, lectures, meetings, persons, ministers etc 18-20 cent; Conference fund ledger 1895-1937; general ledger 1932-56; investment ledger 1883-96; cash book 1966-7; investment valuations 1969-71; treasurers out

letter book 1914-16; deed register 1890; schedules and papers re local and non-conference properties 1950s-70; lantern slides of New Church ministers, places of worship and schools in USA c1890-1900; tracts, sermons, doctrinal writings and forms of worship c1788-1892; library catalogues c1887-date; New Church books, pamphlets and periodicals 18-20 cent; Accrington Society: baptismal register 1828-34, Sunday school report 1873, education committee minutes 1863-70 and reports 1859,1864; Alloa Society: baptismal register 1881-1901, members register 1855-1901; Ashton under Lyne Society: minutes 1857-1916, education committee minutes 1869-92, baptismal register 1848-1926, marriage register 1890-1938, members roll 1863-1912, trustees account book 1848-69; Bath Society: rules 1843, history with letters and photographs nd; Barnsley Society: church committee minutes 1911-45, Young People's Society minutes 1936, Sunday school minutes 1900-34, baptismal register 1910-73, marriage register 1914-68, burial register 1910-73, members roll 1927-61; Besses o' the Barn Society: education committee minutes 1878-91; Birmingham Society: education committee minutes 1863-74 and reports 1845-7,1851, published history 1916; Blackburn Society: church committee minutes 1892-1950, Sunday school minutes 1875-1900; baptismal register 1897-1935, children church register and junior members roll 1915-59; Bolton Society: church committee minutes 1865-1970, baptismal register 1914-65, members roll 1875-1959; Bournemouth Society: isolated receivers committee minutes 1919-24, baptismal register 1913-21, junior members roll 1918; Brightlingsea Society: church minutes 1827-1900, Junior Members and Mutual Improvement Societies minutes 1886-93, baptismal register 1813-68, marriage register 1880-98, Sunday school register and account books 1863-75, account books 1814-87, cash books 1827-67; Brighton Society: church committee minutes and documents 1860-70; Bristol Society: meeting minutes, accounts, reports and church inventory 1791-1835, church committee minutes 1845-1904, Sunday school minutes 1870-7, baptismal register 1795-1819, monthly publication 1899-1900, elocutionary association minutes 1878-9, theological class minutes 1890-1; Bury Society: baptismal registers 1844-96; Chatham Society: church committee minutes 1888-94, baptismal register 1845-90, reports and account books 1889-95; Clayton le Moors Society: education committee minutes 1874-92; Colchester Society: church minutes and members list 1888-91; Cross Hills Society: church minutes 1894-1951, baptismal registers 1900-43, marriage register 1932-9, cash books 1894-1951; Dalton Society: members list 1834-48, attendance register nd, copy correspondence 1869-70, journal 1847-80; Darwen Society: cash books 1892-4,1918, letters, papers, plan and insurance policies post 1850; Derby Society: church minutes 1836-1955, committee minutes 1818; Dundee Society: church minutes 1829-48, baptismal register 1822-8, members register 1825-56; Edinburgh Society: church minutes 1818-91, baptismal register 1826-1933, papers re history nd; Embsay Society: education committee minutes 1884-92; Failsworth Society: education committee minutes 1863, reports, programmes, order of special services etc 1907-17; Glasgow Societies - Brunswick Street: Theological Society minutes 1835-87, baptismal registers 1820-92, Cathedral Street: deaconess meeting minutes 1898-1901, young people's doctrinal class minutes 1898-1901, Queens Drive: church minutes 1897-1955, mutual improvement committee minutes and members roll 1877-1914, Young People's Society minutes 1947-52; Greenock Society: church minutes 1880-4, members roll 1879, cash books 1880-9; Hastings Society: Sunday services and study circle minutes 1859-67; Heywood Society: education committee minutes 1863-92; Hockley Society: members book 1867; Horncastle Society: church minutes 1911-22, account books 1875-1918, cash books 1869-1905, services record 1873-1900, misc papers 19 cent; Horsham Society: church minutes 1933-9; Hull Society: church minutes 1926-37, baptismal list 1914-43, marriage register 1878-

1939, burial list 1912-15, members roll 1913-43, junior members list 1914-39; Ipswich Society: church minutes 1844, baptismal register 1842-80, membership roll 1833-88, correspondence 1856; Keighley Society: rules 1845, cash book 1892-1900; Kidderminster Society: church minutes 1895-1953, committee minutes 1911-56, baptismal register 1898-1956, marriage register 1911-57, sacramental register 1935-45, members roll 1958, cash books 1925-61, ministers signatures 1909-58; Leicester Society: correspondence 1959-67; Leeds Society: meeting minutes 1828-46, baptismal register 1824-1945, marriage register 1906-28, members roll 1826-1944, junior members roll 1924-39; Liverpool Society: church minutes 1835-1970, sub-committee minutes 1946-7, Women's League minutes 1901-40, Young People's Society minutes 1901-50, Sunday school minutes 1902-41, missionary committee minutes 1888-92, baptismal register 1815-77, marriage registers 1858-1925, rules and list of members 1825, members register 1881-1970, junior members roll 1884-1946, pewholders register 1838-60, account books 1837-84, accounts and vouchers 1856-1963, misc correspondence nd, newscuttings 1904-15; London Societies - Anerley: church committee minutes 1880-1921, trustee minutes 1882-1909, reports, pamphlets, newsletter and historical notes nd, Battersea: subscribers and ministerial fund account book 1859-72, Bermondsey: church committee minutes 1885-94, baptismal register 1886-92, members roll late 19 cent, Brixton: church committee minutes, notes, cuttings, letters and accounts 1879-85, Bromley: church committee minutes 1885-1901, baptismal roll 1884-98, members roll 1892, cash book 1882-1902, Camberwell: committee and general meeting minutes 1878-1939, baptismal register 1864-1927, marriage registers 1872-1966, senior members roll 1864-1928, junior members roll 1854-1958, members signature book 1867-86, press cuttings 1867-1915, history of society 1934, Camden Road: church minutes 1946-9, Cramer Street: school reports 1874,1877, Deptford: church minutes 1877-91, baptismal register 1866-1939, marriage register 1917-43, membership books 1865-1925,1935, junior members roll 1890-1939, Friar Street: church committee minutes 1817-61, members list 1827, rules 1814,1840, Great Eastcheap: church minutes 1787-1853, members register 1788-1891, Great Queen Street: church minutes 1805-14, Sunday school accounts 1851, Hatton Garden: agm report 1830, Sunday school report 1844, Islington: church committee minutes 1852-1930, benevolent fund minutes 1853-84, Sunday school minutes 1850-4,1925-30, Sunday school teachers meeting minutes 1856-60, Dorcas Society minutes 1862, baptismal registers 1913-29, marriage register 1914 on, member rolls 1853-1930, junior members roll 1923-9, Sunday school registers 1850-60, account books 1850-80, Kensington: Palace Gardens committee minutes 1885-7, Palace Gardens Sunday school teachers minutes 1876-1919, committee minutes 1909-21, building fund minutes 1925-7, marriage register 1947-63, correspondence re Child and Bayley dispute 1895, Lambeth: trustees committee reports 1819-23, Longacre: agm report 1923, Peckham: church minutes and members roll 1885-91, Pentonville: preliminary association minutes 1829-34, Plaistow: church minutes 1893-1940, Young People's Society minutes 1924-39, baptismal register 1921-36, marriage register 1915-38, members roll 1901-39, attendances and offertories 1910, Sunday school cash book 1924-38, Willesden: minutes 1924-70, baptismal registers 1881-1963, marriage register 1917-67, burial register 1915-35, member rolls 1881-1962, junior members roll 1902-53, children church register 1916-22, collection journals 1912-23, vestry journals 1924-63, account books 1930s-56, misc papers nd: Longton Society: committee minutes 1886-1918, members roll 1843-1922, junior members roll 1911-13, attendance register 1903, Sunday school attendance book 1906, account book 1898; Lowestoft Society: church minutes 1867-1905, account books 1873-93, misc correspondence and papers 1889; Manchester Society:

education committee minutes 1863-71 and reports 1828-42; Melbourne Society: church minutes 1819-1938, trustee minutes 1854-1923; Middleton (North Yorkshire) Society: education committee minutes 1873-92 and report 1862, marriage registers 1932-58; Middleton (Manchester) Society: education committee minutes 1885-6; Moseley Society: baptismal register 1890-1972, marriage register 1910-67, burial register 1913-30, junior members roll 1919-59; Northampton Society: church minutes and cash account book 1860-74, members book 1861-96; North Manchester Society: church minutes 1905-47, baptismal register 1890-1951, marriage registers 1905-50, members roll 1889-1939, account book 1945-51, misc correspondence nd; Newcastle Society: church minutes 1823-1956, deacons minutes 1887-91, Sunday school minutes 1884-1934, Mutual Improvement Society minutes 1889-1919, library committee minutes 1827-83, Marshall Bequest committee minutes 1884-5, school register 1832-43, Theological School report 1828, burial register 1922-37, members list 1835, trustee appointment 1875, account book 1884-1914, accounts 1885-7, property purchase agreements 1874,1882, copy liturgy 1828, statement of belief 1888, misc correspondence late 19 cent; Norwich Society: church minutes 1819-1924, 'small' minutes 1833-87, report 1924, Swedenborg Society: minutes 1879-88, Sunday school minutes 1879-94, births register 1819, members list 1819-1908, rules and declaration of faith 1908, 'small' membership book 1834, account books 1823-1914, Sunday school subscription and account book 1851-5, Sunday school attendance list 1860, services book 1819, history of society 1908; Oldham Society: minutes 1865-1903, Sunday school teachers minutes 1868-91, education committee minutes 1877-82, baptismal register 1865-1901, members lists 1863-1900, account books 1863-1903, correspondence re property 1866; Oswaldtwistle Society: education committee minutes 1880-92; Pickering Society: members list 1834; Preston Society: marriage register 1927-52; Prestwich Society: baptismal register 1828-43; Radcliffe Society: education committee minutes 1884-92; Ramsbottom Society: education committee minutes 1870-91, marriage registers 1841-1967; St Osyth Society: baptismal register 1815-79; Salford Society: church minutes 1919-40, trustee committee minutes 1822-91, education committee minutes 1863-77 and reports 1828-57, baptismal registers 1811-1939, marriage registers 1837-1939, burial registers 1837-61, sacramental register 1929-38, members roll 1880-1938, accounts 1904-11, cash book 1853-91; Salisbury Society: church minutes 1834-57; Sheffield Society: church minutes 1910-39, Sunday school minutes 1881-94, baptismal register 1853-1940, marriage registers 1915-25, burial register 1915, members roll 1885-1929, junior members roll 1913-18, copy rules and insurance certificates nd; Southport Society: church minutes 1878-1968, members register 1872-1950, members roll 1870-80, junior members roll 1924-51, misc correspondence nd; Stockport Society: church minutes 1851-4, baptismal register 1825-57; Wigan Society: education committee minutes 1888-92; Worsley Society: church minutes 1859-1968, baptismal register 1864-1915, marriage register 1871-1943, members list 1862-1969, junior members roll 1887-1943; York Society: church minutes 1860-1903, baptismal register 1847-1910, account book 1866-96

British New Church Federation: minutes 1903-46; executive committee minutes 1914-46; reading committee minutes 1905-28; dramatic committee minutes 1931-9; roll book 1904-20; papers re Birmingham conference 1925; New Church Doctrinal Research Association constitution and rules 1923

The Scottish New Church Association: minutes 1865-93; copy papers 19 cent

Yorkshire Association: constitution and objects nd; list of preachers 1904-19; programme of service 1910

East Midland District Union: account book 1909-20
Missionary and Tract Society: minutes 1835-1963; preachers meeting minutes 1915-19; committee minutes 1934-45; letter books 1870-1923; misc papers 1821-1929
National Missionary Board: minutes 1858-1924; interim committee minutes 1913-20; copy report 1823-67
National Missionary Institution & Students & Ministers Aid Fund: minutes 1873-98
West of England Missionary Society: minutes 1889-90; account book 1890-7; newspaper cuttings 1899
London Union Coffee Meeting: minutes 1818-36
London New Church Union: minutes 1869-1931; rules nd; account papers 1870-82; misc papers nd
Ministers and Leaders Meetings of New Church Societies in London: minutes 1869,1896,1908,1918
London and District Association of New Church Ministers: minutes 1927-31
New Church Sunday School Union: trustee minutes 1901-47; representative attendance roll 1840-1908; rules 1860-1967; year books 1921-70; bulletins to teachers nd; class book 1871; home reading plans 1947-50; manuals 1865, 1926
London New Church Sunday School Union: general meeting minutes 1876-1968; delegate meeting minutes 1906-38; attendance roll 1915-23; Union roll register 1896-1901
Yorkshire New Church Sunday School Union: minutes 1896-1901
Isolated Receivers: minutes 1888-1937; members roll 1892-1918; baptismal register 1912-24; addresses register nd; lecture notices nd; magazine 1902-08
New Church College: council minutes 1865-1955; building committee minutes 1865-9; joint committee minutes 1881-6; interim committee minutes 1906-33; students reports nd; misc papers nd
New Church Free School Society: school setting up plans 1819-22; reports 1825; cash book 1827-34
London Free School Society: annual reports and proceedings of agms 1823-53
New Church Choir: minutes 1917-19
New Church Women's League: general meeting minutes 1898-1964; committee meeting minutes 1894-1900; annual conference minutes 1906-56
New Church Evidence Society: minutes 1892-1903; lecture notices nd
New Church Temperance Society: minutes 1919-26; annual reports 1888-1919; *Annual* 1908
New Church Theological & Philosophical Society: minutes 1904-20
New Church Historical Society: minutes 1920-1; reports 1885-1921; New Church missionary fund history nd
Swedenborg Reading Society: minutes 1875-88
New Church Press Ltd: directors and general meeting minutes 1913-71; register of members 1913-70; agreements with New Church 1913-14; memo and articles of association 1913; annual reports and accounts 1923

Records (2): at Public Record Office, Ruskin Avenue, Kew, Richmond, Surrey TW9 4DU
Accrington Society: births and baptismal register 1810-37, burial register 1829-37; Bath Society: birth and baptismal register 1830-7; Birmingham Society: births and baptismal registers 1791-1838; Brightlingsea Society: births and baptismal registers 1813-37; Derby Society: births and baptismal registers 1817-39; Little Bolton Society: births and baptismal registers 1828-37; London Societies - Brownlow Street: births and baptismal register 1816-37,

Hatton Garden: births and baptismal register 1797-1837, Lambeth: births and baptismal register 1816-34; Loughborough Society: births and baptismal register 1828-37; Melbourne Society: births and baptismal register 1831-7; Middleton (Greater Manchester) Society: births and baptismal register 1809-38; Newcastle Society: births and baptismal register 1808-37; Norwich Society: births and baptismal register 1819-36; Outwood Society: births and baptismal register 1808-31; Pilkington Society: births and baptismal register 1803-37, burial register 1815-37; Salford Society: births and baptismal register 1811-37, burial registers 1813-37; Salisbury Society: births and baptismal register 1834; Tyldesley Society: births and baptismal register 1830-6

Robert Hindmarsh, *Rise and Progress of the New Jerusalem Church in England, America and Other Parts* (1861)
Carl Theophilus Odhner and others, *Annals of the New Church* 4 Vols (priv pub 1904-76)

141 MONTEVIDEO GAS & DRY DOCK CO LTD

21 Feb 1872
06054
Cavenham House, Millington Road, Hayes, London UB3 4AY
Gas, electricity and ship repairing

History: incorporated in London in 1872 as Montevideo Gas Co Ltd to supply gas to Montevideo, Uruguay. Concession expired in 1887 but company continued to supply gas. In 1897 took powers to generate and deal in electricity and other power sources. Name changed to above in 1919 when acquired by the Maua dock ship-repairing and general engineering works at Montevideo. Gas sales in 1955 were 31 million cubic metres, and in 1966, 24 million cubic metres. Acquired in 1970s by Anglo-Continental Investment & Finance Co Ltd which was subsequently acquired by Generale Occidentale SA, France.

Records: at Montevideo Gas & Dry Dock, Cavenham House, Millington Road, Hayes, London UB3 4AY
board and general meeting minutes 1872-date; correspondence 1936-date; installation photographs late 19 cent

142 EXTEL GROUP LTD

28 Mar 1872
06152
Extel House, East Harding Street, London EC4P 4HB
News agency and financial services

History: incorporated in 1872 as Exchange Telegraph Co Ltd to transmit business intelligence, stock and share prices, shipping news etc from stock or commercial exchanges etc to subscribers to the service. Founded by Sir James Anderson, former captain of *Great Eastern* and an American, George B Field. Leased 17&18 Cornhill, London and obtained licence to carry out its system of telegraphy within a 900 yard radius of Stock Exchanges in London, Liverpool, Manchester, Leeds, Birmingham, Edinburgh, Glasgow and Dublin. Captain WH Davies, former first officer of *Great Eastern* became managing director. Added New York, Paris, Berlin, Vienna and Istanbul Stock Exchange prices to service. Started Parliamentary Service in 1876 and General News Service in 1879. In 1882 acquired MacMahon's Telegraphic

News Co and launched Glasgow Exchange Telegraph Co and Liverpool Exchange Telegraph Co. By 1886 had over 500 subscribers to its Financial Service and over 200 subscribers to its General Service. By 1892 had 74 column printers each capable of delivering 2000 words an hour. Signed Joint Service Agreement with the Press Association Ltd (inc 1868) in 1906. Extended objects in 1913 to include collecting and distributing news worldwide, and undertaking advertising agency business. Acquired new freehold premises at 64 Cannon Street, London in 1918. Started successful Statistics Service in 1919. In 1945 acquired Press Association's interest in Central News Ltd which they had jointly controlled since 1935. Also acquired Thames Paper Supplies in 1948 and Victoria Blower Co (1942) Ltd which operated the 'Blower' telephone service for bookmakers from London and Leeds in 1954. Acquired new head offices between Fetter Lane and Shoe Lane, London in 1954. Closed Foreign Service in 1956 and General Home News and Parliamentary Service in 1965 and withdrew from Joint Law Service in 1965. Formed Extel Communications Ltd in 1957 and Extel Statistical Services Ltd in 1965. Acquired London & Provincial Sporting News Agency (1929) Ltd in 1962, HG Guest (Amplifiers) Ltd (renamed Teletalk Co Ltd) in 1965 and Burrup, Mathieson & Co Ltd (est 1628), printers in 1964. In 1966 changed name to Exchange Telegraph Co (Holdings) Ltd and became holding company of Exchange Telegraph group. Acquired Dorland City Ltd, financial advertising agents and public relations consultants in 1971. Changed name to above in 1980 and re-registered as a public limited company in 1982. In 1981 principal trading subsidiaries were Exchange Telegraph Co Ltd (inc 1966) sporting and financial news services, data and telecommunications systems and engineering; Extel Computing Ltd (inc 1967) computerised information and investment accounting services; Extel Statistical Services Ltd, financial information services; Victoria Blower Co Ltd, racing message service; Burrup, Mathieson & Co Ltd and subsidiaries including Clout & Baker Ltd, Lawrence-Allen Ltd, Robert Stace & Co Ltd, Shaw & Sons Ltd, financial, local government and commercial printers; Royds Advertising Group Ltd, advertising, marketing services and public relations; City Island Property Co Ltd; Mandeville Properties Ltd, property holding; Robophone Ltd, telephone communications systems; and Teletalk Co Ltd, amplifying equipment manufacturers and installers.

Records: at Extel, Extel House, East Harding Street, London EC4P 4HB
directors meeting: minutes 1872-date, agendas 1880-4,1947-73, papers 1947-date, annual reports 1962-date, monthly returns 1945-68, attendance books 1914-70; general meeting minutes 1872-date; agm: proceedings 1885-1979, agendas 1880-date, papers 1896-1963; shareholders: notices 1872-1963, lists 1884-1947, correspondence 1872 on; share: registers 1872-1950, transfer and probate register 1947-62; annual returns: 1877-1975, correspondence 1943-80; memo and articles of association 1872-1980; capital reorganisation papers 1872-1914; agreements, papers and correspondence: GPO private wire, wayleaves and telephone 1872-1973, acquisitions 1888-1979; annual reports and accounts 1872-date; employee reports 1974-date; interim reports 1966-date; directors registers 1914-64; seals register 1954-80; audited balance sheets and accounts 1874-date; expenditure and income accounts 1887-1966; comparison accounts 1872-1909; sundry accounts and schedules 1882-1963; costs statistics 1904-68; ledgers: private c1920-64, costs 1872-1961, personal 1920-7,c1948-64, correspondents expenses c1935-c56, exchange c1928-c59; cash book 1872-3; general and branch expenditure books 1897-1961; income tax returns 1901-23; financial correspondence and papers 1901-78; general services: circulars 1879-1942, tariff rate lists, booklets, correspondence and papers 1891-1961, advertisements and articles 1899-1904,1946-58,

brochures 1970s-date, cost graphs 1910-38, reports and correspondence 1913-60s; subscribers: application register 1879-1918 and forms 1906-51, tariff book 1884-1941; subscription sheets c1889-c1927; election: poll books 1885-1901, service papers and correspondence 1895,1959-66; monarch deaths and coronation instructions, relayed news and correspondence 1910-53; General News Service: tape slips nd, instructions 1908-09, subscribers application register 1879-93; Stock Exchange Service: accounts 1887-1900, reports, papers and correspondence 1872-1962, advertisements and articles 1946-58; Statistical Service: report 1945, correspondence and papers 1916-63, advertisements 1946-58; Sporting Service: subscribers application register 1879-93, reports 1966-71, racing accounts, papers and correspondence 1883-1917,1969-74, Olympic Games copy reports 1928,1932; Joint Service (Press Association): agreements, papers and correspondence 1906-67, joint committee meeting minutes and attendance books 1906-62 and agendas 1918-43, reports 1966-78, pool accounts, schedules, reports and correspondence 1906-66, balance sheets and accounts 1944-63, Law Service accounts 1945-65, and booklets 1951,1960, Combined Service accounts 1945-62, general election results accounts 1910, subscribers ledgers 1906-c50, pool ledger 1927-c60, provincial ledgers 1935-64, cash book 1906, Commercial Service plans 1961-2; engineers reports 1881-90,1932-71; F Higgins, engineer, papers 1870-1916; engineering department papers 1881-1953; patents, specifications and papers 1871-1915; Liverpool telegraph wire consent notices 1882-1901; circuits book 1910-25; Creed System papers and correspondence 1906-41; news tapes 1925-36; broadcasting papers and correspondence 1936-43; GPO equipment correspondence 1951-80; staff: papers and correspondence 1886-1967, provincial record cards 1930s-40s, photographs 1868-1980s, menu cards 1937-9; union agreements 1937-76; time book 1879; Haymarket agency wages book 1896-8; wage comparisons and lists 1885-1939; foreign correspondents reports, papers and correspondence 1927-46; pension fund: trustee meeting minutes 1929-49 and papers 1934-75, trustee officer changes 1943-56, trust deeds and rules 1928-76, circulars 1965,1972-80, annual reports and accounts 1929-date, journal 1929-65, investment ledger 1947, rent roll 1952-72; London and provincial premises leases 1869-date; legal action papers and correspondence 1882-1979; correspondence and papers with other news agencies 1882-1976; staff, directors, offices, functions, equipment photographs 1880s-1970s

Allans (Weston) Ltd: memo and articles of association 1964-72

Associated Industrial Film Services Ltd: directors: and general meeting minutes 1932-68, report 1968, register 1966-9; members register 1932-67; share: certificate book 1932-66, transfer documents 1961-3, correspondence 1960s; memo and articles of association 1932-57; annual returns 1947-68; correspondence: solicitors 1938-57, liquidation 1958-69

Blower Ltd: board papers 1963-9; members register 1928-51; memo and articles of association 1963; annual returns 1963-77; balance sheets and accounts with schedules 1961-6

Breams Printing & Publishing Co Ltd: directors and general meeting minutes 1959-78

Burrup Mathieson & Co Ltd: board meeting: minutes 1949-78, papers 1964-81, reports 1966-78; executive directors meeting minutes 1972-3; directors: attendance books 1960-76, correspondence and papers 1966-71; London factories minutes 1972-5; general meeting minutes 1937-64; members registers etc 1931-66; share: certificate book 1964-6, transfer documents 1923-74; annual returns 1951-81; partnership agreements 1897,1900; memo and articles of association 1923-76; acquisition documents 1954-66; business names registration papers 1953-71; seals registers 1964-80; annual reports and accounts 1942-72; balance sheets and accounts 1959-66; sales literature 1970s; printing licences c1963-70; staff service agreements and correspondence 1961-75; wages and salaries books 1960-8; pension fund papers 1971-3; premises: leases 1956-73, correspondence 1941-56; staff, offices, workshops, equipment and premises photographs c1940-c72; history booklets and articles c1899-c1950

Central News (City Advertising) Ltd: (See summary no 347)

City Island Property Co Ltd: directors and general meeting minutes 1954-79; board papers 1960-81; memo and articles of association 1954-60; annual returns 1958-77; seals register 1957-72; balance sheets and accounts 1958-66; private ledger 1955-63; leases 1950s-71

City Reporting Agency Ltd: corporate papers and correspondence 1956-77; balance sheets and accounts 1967

Column Printing Co Ltd: directors and general meeting minutes 1923-78; board: papers 1947-81, reports 1966-80; share: registers 1924-66, certificate books 1927-64; annual returns 1935-67; corporate documents and correspondence 1923-60s; memo and articles of association 1923-66; seals register 1956-64; balance sheets and accounts 1934-66; private ledgers 1945-66; journal 1940-65; subscribers list 1939

Column Printing Telegraph Syndicate Ltd: prospectus 1889; tariffs 1889-96; corporate agreements and correspondence 1889-c1907

Crawford City Advertising Ltd: directors and general meeting minutes 1960-71; board reports and papers 1972-4; members register 1960-72; acquisition papers and correspondence 1967-9

Days Publications & Services Ltd: directors and general meeting minutes 1946-74; board papers 1974-9; members register 1946-74; annual returns 1974-7

Dorland City Ltd: directors and general meeting minutes 1925-71; board papers and correspondence 1968-79; members register 1925-71; annual returns 1972-7; memo and articles of association 1973; acquisition papers and correspondence 1960s-70; service agreements and correspondence 1934-75; leases 1950s-60s; financial and general correspondence 1967-74

Duchamp Securities Ltd: memo and articles of association 1973; annual returns 1973-7

Exchange Telegraph Co Ltd: board papers 1974-80; memo and articles of association 1966; annual returns 1966; seals register 1966-80

Exchange Telegraph Pension Fund Trust Ltd: memo and articles of association 1955; formation papers 1948-55; seals register 1955-78

Extel Advertising & PR Services Ltd: board papers 1974-9

Extel Advertising & PR Ltd: board papers 1973-80; acquisition papers 1977; annual returns 1972-7; brochure nd

Extel Communications Ltd: board: reports 1966-71, papers 1959-80; agm papers 1977-8; formation correspondence 1957-65; acquisition papers 1972; memo and articles of association 1957; annual returns 1957-77; balance sheets and accounts 1958-66

Extel Computing Ltd: board: reports 1973-8, papers 1976-81; memo and articles of association 1967; annual returns 1972-80

Extel Computing Services Ltd: board papers 1969-79; memo and articles of association 1969; annual returns 1969-77

Extel Engineers Ltd: board: reports 1961-78, papers 1969-79; memo and articles of association 1969; annual returns 1966-77

Extel Financial Services Ltd: board papers 1969-79; memo and articles of association 1969; annual returns 1966-77

Extel Ltd: board papers 1969-79; memo and articles of association 1969

Extel Printing & Publishing Ltd: memo and articles of association 1937-65; annual returns 1964-77

Extel Properties & Investments Ltd: board papers 1969-79; memo and articles of association 1969; annual returns 1969-77

Extel Racing & Sport Services Ltd: board papers 1969-79; memo and articles of association 1969; annual returns 1969-77

Fintel Ltd: board report 1978; memo and articles of association 1972; information pack nd

Fleet Street Group Ltd: board: and general meeting minutes 1945-74, papers 1974-9; share certificate book 1945-8; members register 1945-75; annual returns 1974-9

Frank O'Shanohun Associates Ltd: board: and general meeting minutes 1959-74, papers 1973-9; members register 1959-73; annual returns 1973-7; memo and articles of association 1959; acquisition papers 1973

Frank O'Shanohun Financial Services Ltd: board: and general meeting minutes 1962-72, papers 1974-9; members register 1962-71; annual returns 1973-7; memo and articles of association 1962

Frank O'Shanohun (Overseas) Ltd: board: and general meeting minutes 1965-71, papers 1974-9; members register 1965-71; annual returns 1973-7

Frank O'Shanohun (Trade Advisory Services) Ltd: papers and correspondence 1976-81

Glenhill & Ballinger Ltd: directors and general meeting minutes 1937-65; members register 1937-67; acquisition documents c1954-c68; balance sheets and accounts 1954-66

Green & Welburn Ltd: directors and general meeting: minutes 1938-65, agendas 1964-76; members register 1938-65; acquisition documents 1962-6; memo and articles of association 1938; annual returns 1964-77; balance sheets and accounts 1959-66

Investment Accounting Services Ltd: board: and general meeting minutes 1968-72, papers 1972-9; memo and articles of association 1976; members register c1972; directors register 1968-72; annual returns 1969-77; acquisition documents 1972; pension fund papers 1970-4

B Lawrence Ltd: directors and general meeting minutes 1950-79

Lawrence - Allen Ltd: directors and general meeting minutes 1979-82; corporate papers and correspondence 1979-82; annual returns 1973-82

Lawrence Brothers (Weston) Ltd: minutes, corporate papers and correspondence 1979-82; annual returns 1973-82

Lawrence Press Ltd: directors and general meeting minutes 1934-68; members register 1934-c69; share certificate book 1938-61; annual returns 1952-77; memo and articles of association 1934-70; acquisition documents 1968-71

Lewes Press Ltd: directors and general meeting minutes 1938-68; share transfer documents 1938-69; annual returns 1959-77; memo and articles of association 1938-71; acquisition documents 1968-71; seals register 1969; leases 1908-77

Lewis Coates & Lucas Ltd: directors and general meeting minutes 1976-9

London & Provincial Sporting News Agency (1929) Ltd: directors meeting: minutes 1929-62, papers 1962-9; general meeting minutes 1930-62; agm: proceeding reports, press cuttings and correspondence 1929-38, chairmans statements 1929-39; members registers 1928-63; share certificate books 1950-80; annual returns 1963-77; memo and articles of association 1927; annual reports and accounts 1930-9; balance sheets and accounts 1930-66; ledgers: 1938-64, private 1929-48; journals 1937-63; returns 1964-6; income tax papers 1946-61; Blower service prospectus 1933; racecourse agreements and accounts c1926-68; legal action papers and correspondence 1928-37; correspondence and papers: GPO telephone service 1934-69, racing and racecourse betting 1947-68, advertising 1962-4; acquisition circulars and press cuttings 1962-4; staff: record cards 1940s-50s, wages book 1963-5, endowment association ledgers c1955-61; premises: leases 1940-75, plans c1953-75, papers and correspondence 1940-76; directors, accountants and solicitors correspondence 1940-71; history note 1963

Modern Accounts Ltd: directors and general meeting minutes 1951-79

Pullman Business Machines Ltd: board meeting: minutes 1969-73, papers 1974-80; general meeting minutes c1969-74; members register etc 1969-74; annual returns 1971-9

Robophone Ltd: board: and general meeting minutes 1956-75, papers 1980-1; members register 1956-74; annual returns 1971-80; memo and articles of association 1970-4; acquisition documents 1970s; patent papers and correspondence 1963-71; information pack c1974; pension fund papers 1973-9

Robophone (Facilities) Ltd: board meeting: minutes 1948-74, papers 1964-80; general meeting minutes 1948-69; members registers etc 1958-75; annual returns 1971-7; memo and articles of association 1970-4

Robophone (Holdings) Ltd: board meeting: minutes 1965-71, reports 1974-8, papers 1974-9; general meeting minutes c1965-74; agm papers 1974-6; annual returns 1971-6; memo and articles of association 1971-4

Robophone (Southern) Ltd: board: and general meeting minutes 1955-74, papers 1974-80; members register etc 1955-74; annual returns 1971-7; memo and articles of association 1970-4

Rollco Papers Ltd: board papers 1970; annual returns 1969-73; premises leases, papers and correspondence 1933-60s

Royds Advertising Group Ltd: subsidiaries: memo and articles of association 1970s, annual reports and accounts 1978; brochure 1980; newsletters 1979-80; pension scheme trust deeds and correspondence 1973-8

St Stephen Bristol Press Ltd: directors and general meeting minutes 1940-65

Shaw & Sons Ltd: directors meeting: minutes 1968-79, papers 1980-1; general meeting minutes 1935-80

Sidney Barton Ltd: directors and general meeting minutes 1950-78; members registers etc 1950-77; acquisition documents 1977

Spon & Play (1930) Ltd: directors and general meeting minutes 1914-46; members register etc 1931-65; annual returns 1965-77; memo and articles of association 1930; acquisition documents 1962-6; patent papers and correspondence 1934-8

Stet Syndicate Ltd: board papers and accounts 1946-8

Teletalk Co Ltd: board: and general meeting minutes 1963-5, papers 1965-81; annual returns 1965-77; memo and articles of association 1962-71; balance sheets and accounts 1962-5,1977-8; private ledger 1962-6; service agreements 1965-72; engineering department correspondence 1951-63; equipment papers and correspondence 1965-77

Thames Paper Supplies Ltd: board: papers 1949-73, reports 1966-73; corporate agreements 1948-72; annual returns 1948-72; seals register 1956-73; balance sheets and accounts 1949-64; private ledger 1949-53; personal ledger 1956-62; monthly returns 1964-6; sales literature and advertisement press cuttings 1962-71; supply agreements and correspondence 1958-73; premises and exhibition photographs 1957,c1966

Transtel Communications Ltd: board papers 1978-81; annual returns 1977-81

Victoria Blower Co Ltd: board: and general meeting minutes 1940-61, papers 1955-81; memo and articles of association 1940-2; corporate correspondence 1954-5; acquisition documents 1954-5; annual returns 1954-77; balance sheets and accounts 1954-70; private ledgers 1950-63;

subscribers ledger 1963-7; monthly returns 1964-6; advertising papers and correspondence 1955-64; premises: correspondence 1951-69, photographs 1966-7
Waytime Ltd: directors and general meeting minutes 1963-4; annual returns 1963-77; balance sheets and accounts 1964-6
Wightman & Co Ltd: directors and general meeting minutes 1922-68; prospectus 1898; memo and articles of association 1898-1973; acquisition documents 1968-71; agm and shareholders notices and correspondence 1899-c1968; members registers 1898-c1969; share: certificate books 1936-68, agreements 1919-68, transfer documents 1957-68, correspondence 1929-46; directors registers 1907-69; mortgage register 1901-68; annual returns 1971-7; annual report and accounts 1941; premises leases and correspondence 1855-1947; history booklets, papers and correspondence 1886-1950s
Wigmore Holdings Ltd: board meeting: minutes 1975-9, papers 1979-81; members register etc c1954-76; annual returns 1978-80; memo and articles of association 1970s; acquisition documents and correspondence 1973-9; annual report and accounts 1978; pension fund papers c1973-8; subsidiaries: memo and articles of association 1930s-70s, annual report and accounts 1978
Wodderspoon & Co Ltd: directors and general meeting minutes 1951-61; share: certificate books 1926-64, transfer register 1926-64; memo and articles of association 1926-73; acquisition documents 1962-4; annual returns 1951-77; balance sheets and accounts 1961-6
Wodderspoon (Holdings) Ltd: directors and general meeting minutes 1960-3; members register 1960-5; memo and articles of association 1972; acquisition documents 1962-4; annual returns 1961-77; balance sheets and accounts 1961-6

JM Scott, Extel 100, *The Centenary History of the Exchange Telegraph Company 1872-1972* (1972)

143 LANCASHIRE & YORKSHIRE BANK LTD

1 May 1872
06227
54 Lombard Street, London EC3P 3AH
Banking

History: established and incorporated as above in 1872 when the Manchester branch of the Alliance Bank of London & Liverpool Ltd (est 1862) was freed. By 1888, 15 branches had been opened at Waterfoot, Pendleton, Burnley, Bacup and Blackburn, Lancashire; Sowerby Bridge, Shedehill, Todmorden, Dewsbury and Elland, W Yorkshire; Warrington and Haslington, Cheshire; and Rochdale, Bury and Bowdon, Greater Manchester; and 5 sub-branches at Nelson, Lancashire; Lymm, Cheshire; and Ramsbottom, New Cross and Swinton, Greater Manchester. Acquired Bury Banking Co Ltd (est 1836) in 1888 and Preston Union Bank Ltd (est 1882) in 1894. New head offices were completed in Spring Gardens, Manchester in 1889. By 1899 further branches had been established at Southport, Merseyside; Blackpool and St Anne's, Lancashire; and Hebden Bridge, W Yorkshire. Acquired Adelphi Bank Ltd (est 1862, Liverpool, Merseyside) in 1899, West Riding Union Banking Co Ltd (est 1836) in 1902, and Mercantile Bank of Lancashire Ltd (est 1890) in 1904. Although amalgamation talks had taken place since 1894 with Parr's Bank Ltd and later with Westminster Bank Ltd, merged with Bank of Liverpool & Martins Ltd (est 1918) in Jan 1928. Latter was renamed Martins Bank Ltd in 1928 and merged in 1968 with Barclays Bank Ltd.

Records: at Barclays Bank, 54 Lombard Street, London EC3P 3AH
board minutes 1872-1924; private minutes 1886-1927; agm minutes 1904-28; managers diary 1889; press cuttings re amalgamation 1927; widows and orphans fund minutes 1922-9; house journal 1907-16; branches - Accrington: drafts issued register 1899 on; Preston: authorities book 1894-1912

George Chandler, *Four Centuries of Banking* Vol 1&2 (1964,1968)

144 APOLLO STEELS LTD

17 May 1872
06278
177 Kirkstall Road, Leeds, W Yorkshire LS4 2AQ
Steel, files, saws, and springs manufacturers

History: established by William Ibbotson in Bridge Street, Sheffield, S Yorkshire in 1809. Moved to Bower Spring by 1821 and to Globe Works, Penistone Road in 1825. Was known as Ibbotson & Roebuck by 1821, and Ibbotson Brothers by 1828 when firm was steel converters and refiners, merchants and manufacturers of stove grates, fenders, saws, files, scythes, edge tools etc. Went bankrupt in 1846 but William Ibbotson re-established the Globe Works at Cross Smithfield, moving to Russel Street (later Alma Street) by 1862. Incorporated as Ibbotson Brothers & Co Ltd in 1872. By 1923 specialised in railway products and Globe Works covered 10 acres. Taken over in 1939 by Jonas Woodhead & Sons Ltd of Leeds, W Yorkshire, laminated spring manufacturers. Globe Steel Works was merged in Woodhead Components Ltd in 1971 and company name changed to above.

Records: at Jonas Woodhead & Sons, 177 Kirkstall Road, Leeds, W Yorkshire LS4 2AQ
directors and general meeting minutes 1888-1972; directors: reports 1939-55, attendances 1939-58; shareholders: attendances 1904-47, lists and holdings 1899-1967; memo and articles of association 1872-1939; takeover papers 1939; members register 1899-1933; share certificates nd; share transfer: register 1899-1954, lists 1900-39; dividend and interest book 1898-1937; mortgage register 1879-1910; debenture transfer register 1899-1910; documents sealed list 1941-51; balance sheets 1901-55; annual accounts 1939-55; private: ledger 1939-43; journal 1919-47; general journal 1927-39; bank: cash books 1939-64, pass books 1938-58; petty cash books 1955-65; purchase journal 1970-2; sales day book 1965-72; out letter book re trade-mark infringements 1921-45; steel tube brochure 1930s; salary books 1901-59; wage: agreement 1930, books 1944-72; machinery stock books 1914-39; correspondence with trade associations 1942-62

145 LAWES CHEMICAL CO LTD

23 May 1872
06291
1 Noble Street, London EC2V
Artificial fertiliser manufacturers

History: founded by John (later Sir John) Bennet Lawes who established a factory for manufacture of superphosphate at Deptford Creek, London in 1843. In 1857 bought 100 acres at Barking Creek, London, on which the main factory and workmen's cottages were built. Business purchased from Lawes by group of businessmen in 1872 and incorporated as Lawes

Chemical Manure Co Ltd to manufacture artificial fertilisers, sulphuric acid etc. Branches were established in Scotland, Wales and the Channel Islands, and traded overseas in North and South America, India, New Zealand, Australia, South Africa and the Middle East. Established several subsidiary companies as artificial fertiliser merchants: Gwalia Fertilisers (Briton Ferry) Ltd, Neath, W Glamorgan (inc 1934); A Nightingale & Sons Ltd, Bedford (inc 1937); Thomas Fenn Ltd, Ipswich, Suffolk (inc 1947); Sealright Chemicals Ltd (inc 1967): Jersey Trading Co Ltd (inc 1914) and Jersey Trading Co (1948) Ltd as fruit and vegetable traders. Name changed to above in 1935 and went into liquidation in 1969, the business continuing to trade under the name of Sealright Chemicals Ltd.

Records (1): at London Borough of Barking & Dagenham, Libraries Department, Valence House, Dagenham, Essex RM8 3HT
board and general meeting minutes 1872-1959; shareholders attendance register 1873-1969; register of members 1948-52; register of directors 1931-68; register of directors holdings 1931-67; preference share register 1873-1953; registers of share transfers 1872-1966; share documents 1872-1962; corporate correspondence 1872-1950; memo and articles of association 1888-1950; registers of probates 1880-1959; annual returns 1962-6; annual reports and accounts and proceedings of agms 1873-1966; audited accounts 1933-66; private ledgers 1872-1959; impersonal ledgers 1939-61; nominal ledgers 1968-9; journals 1958-69; customer accounts ledgers c1946-59; bought ledgers 1952-61; bought ledger transfers 1935-57; bought journals 1947-61; purchase ledgers 1965-8; storage ledger 1961; day books 1949-61; cash books 1955-69; plant schedule 1957; bag and bought contracts 1925-60; suppliers correspondence 1925-60; order and delivery day books 1959-61; goods received books 1950-60; stock books and analysis 1962-9; cost book 1948-61; production time book 1965; wages and salary books 1925-59; wage rates 1947-64; staff contracts 1962-8; papers and correspondence re accidents 1966-70; rent book 1942-50; correspondence re workers cottages 1950s-60s; pension scheme: trustee and agm minutes 1951-8, report 1965, accounts 1951-60, contributions 1950-61; plans of factory 1957-67; inventory of works 1945; general correspondence 1924-69
Gwalia Fertilisers (Briton Ferry) Ltd: board and general meeting minutes 1934-51; memo and articles of association and corporate papers 1934-65; audited accounts 1934-69; employee contracts 1964-6
Acides et Superphosphates Standairt Société Anonyme: directors minutes 1929-40; articles of association 1929
Jersey Trading Co Ltd: board and general meeting minutes 1914-49; register of members 1914-41
Jersey Trading Co (1948) Ltd: board and general meeting minutes 1948-61; correspondence and papers re shares 1960-3; audited accounts 1949-62; staff records 1950-62
A Nightingale & Sons Ltd: share certificate book 1937-56; audited accounts 1955-62; private ledger 1937-56; sales and bought ledgers with compound agreements 1955-7
Thomas Fenn Ltd: board and general meeting minutes 1947-61; register of members 1948-52; share certificate book 1947-52; memo and articles of association 1947; annual returns 1949-61; audited accounts 1949-61; ledger 1953-8

Records (2): at Institute of Agricultural History & Museum of English Rural Life, University of Reading, Whiteknights, Reading, Berkshire RG6 2AG
customer ledger 1898-1914; publicity magazine 1930-34,1958-9; specifications and costs of products 1933-50s; sales representatives notes 1937; sales catalogues, trade leaflets, price lists

etc 1864-1960s; advertisements 1834-1965; photographs of exhibition stands 1930s-50s; plan and results of experiments at Rothamstead 1869; map of Lawes Wharf nd; photographs and drawings of works, plant, machinery, products, research and staff 19-20 cent; articles and press handouts on history of company, JB Lawes, Rothamstead and Barking 1871-1968; letters of JB Lawes 1843,1902; misc correspondence and documents 1902-60; trade literature 1906-53
Gwalia Fertilisers (Briton Ferry) Ltd: advertisements 1963; trade literature 1962-3

146 EASTERN TELEGRAPH CO LTD

6 Jun 1872
06338
Mercury House, 110-124 Theobalds Road, London WC1X 8RX
Telegraph

History: founded and incorporated by John Pender, Liberal MP and pioneer of ocean telegraphy, in 1872 with the amalgamation of Anglo-Mediterranean Telegraph Co Ltd (inc 1868), Falmouth, Gibraltar & Malta Telegraph Co Ltd (inc 1869), British Indian Submarine Telegraph Co Ltd (inc 1869) and Marseille, Algiers & Malta Telegraph Co Ltd (inc 1870). Developed the systems of its constituent companies, which provided a direct British telegraph route to India, by doubling and trebling the more important and busier routes, by expanding and extending the existing routes. Laid cable in 1899-1900 from Capetown, South Africa, to St Vincent, Portugal, via St Helena and Ascension Islands, linked to Porthcurno, Cornwall, England, in 1901. Cables of the West African Telegraph Co Ltd (inc 1885), African Direct Telegraph Co Ltd (inc 1885) and Eastern & South African Telegraph Co Ltd (inc 1879) were taken over in 1899 to form part of the Eastern & Associated Telegraph Companies group which consisted of 12 companies by 1929. On recommendations of Imperial Wireless & Cable Conference meeting in 1928, Cables & Wireless Ltd and Imperial & International Communication Ltd were formed, the former acquiring all the ordinary shares of the Eastern & Associated Companies group and the Marconi Wireless Telegraph Co Ltd, and the latter all their communication assets. In 1934 the former was renamed Cable & Wireless (Holdings) Ltd and the latter Cable & Wireless Ltd which became publicly owned in 1946. In 1981 company operated within the UK as a subsidiary of Cable & Wireless Ltd.

Records (1): at Cable & Wireless, Mercury House, 110-124 Theobalds Road, London WC1X 8RX
board minutes 1872-1945; finance committee minutes nd; agm: minutes 1872-c1947, proceedings 1873-1903; corporate papers and documents, including agreements, contracts, leases, concessions etc 1856-1946; memo and articles of association 1872-1929; seal books 1875-1946; annual accounts 1872-1938; balance sheet and accounts 1873-1906; general ledgers 1872-1928; journal 1932-52; cash statements 1873-88; investment ledger 1890-1924; financial memoranda 1872-1907; tariff rates 1887,1925; telegraph code book 1902; cable specifications, prices and statistics c1850-1903; register of cable buoys 1901-59; cable and core returns 1926-8; engineers cable reports 1876-1922; cable lay log books and diaries 1897-1958; photographs of cable lays 1899-1922; correspondence re cable laying and cables 1877-1923; technical papers and literature re cables 1890s-1931; cable route maps 1880s; salary and wage books 1887-1941; staff record books c1870-1949; Porthcurno staff registers 1905-53; cable ships officers and engineers service books 1870-1920; employee agreements 1916,1923; staff rules and

regulations 1883,1923; staff hand books 1920-9; staff photographs 1892-1939; house magazine *The Zodiac* 1907-date; Porthcurno staff quarters plan c1924; letter book and papers re *CS Levant* 1937-46; photographs of company property, stations, cable ships and visits c1890-1967; head office and local letter books 1868-1946; correspondence with and memoranda to stations 1871-93; Sir James Anderson papers re telegraph companies and cable laying c1841-93; general managers papers and correspondence 1926-32; newscuttings, articles and publications re company 1872-1975; climate record book c1890-1917
Anglo-Mediterranean Telegraph Co Ltd: board minutes 1868-1976; corporate documents 1868-70; memo and articles of association 1868; agreements and contracts 1868-71; cable lines sketch map c1868
British Indian Submarine Telegraph Co Ltd: corporate papers, incl memo and articles of association 1869-70; agreements 1869-73; engineers cable report 1870; cable lay log book 1870; list of instruments 1870; cable insurance and payments 1870; proposed staff details c1870
Falmouth, Gibraltar & Malta Telegraph Co Ltd: corporate papers, incl memo and articles of association 1869; correspondence re telegrams 1870; service form 1871; magazine article on cable 1870
Marseilles, Algiers & Malta Telegraph Co Ltd: corporate papers, incl memo and articles of association 1870; tariff report 1870

Records (2): at Science Museum Library, South Kensington, London SW7 5NH
cable contracts and specifications 1873-90; cable lay log book 1927-9; cable laying and repairing journal (Thomas W Bowden, joiner) 1879-82

KC Baglehole, *A Century of Service. A brief history of Cable and Wireless Ltd 1868-1968* (1969)
Hugh Barty-King, *Girdle Round the Earth* (1979)

147 METHODIST INSURANCE CO LTD

19 Jun 1872
06369
Brazennose House, Brazennose Street, Manchester, Greater Manchester M2 5AS
Insurance

History: established in Manchester in 1872 on initiative of the Wesleyan Methodist Conference and incorporated as Wesleyan Methodist Trust Assurance Co Ltd to provide fire insurance for 'connexional' property only, especially chapels and schools. An accident department was added in 1907 and provided cover for voluntary workers and local preachers after 1948. In 1933, shortly after the merger of the 3 branches of British Methodism, it merged with Primitive Methodist Insurance Co Ltd, founded in 1866 at York, and United Methodist Church Guarantee Fund, created in 1910 by the merger of Methodist New Connexion Trustees Mutual Guarantee Fund (est 1860), Bible Christians' Fire Insurance Society (est 1881) and Free Methodist Fire Insurance Fund (est 1888), to form the above. A single-office company, its net profits have always been distributed as grants to Methodist Church funds. Total insurance funds grew from £37,000 in 1933 to nearly £1 million in 1981. In 1983 moved from 51 Spring Gardens to Brazennose Street, Manchester.

Records: at Greater Manchester Record Office, 56 Marshall Street, New Cross, Ancoats, Manchester, Greater Manchester M4 SFU

directors: meeting minutes 1871-1941, report 1876; committee meeting minutes 1873-1971; agm minutes 1872-1920; share register 1922-81; memo and articles of association 1872-1978; corporate documents and correspondence 1871-1933; amalgamation papers 1931-2; annual reports and accounts 1873-1970; audited accounts 1872-1947; insurance: prospectus 1874, specimen forms, renewal receipts and brochures c1900-70; policies 1877-1923; war damage claims: register 1941-6, correspondence 1947-55
Methodist New Connexional Trustees Mutual Guarantee Fund: insurance policy 1879
Primitive Methodist Insurance Co Ltd: directors meeting minutes 1866-1933; general meeting minutes 1887-1934; shareholders lists 1890s; insurance: policies lists 1867-1916, endorsement register 1894-1916, liabilities list 1895-1901, policies 1894-1922; Chapel Aid Association minutes 1869-99

W Russell Shearer, *Century of Service 1872-1972* (priv pub 1972)

148 GIRLS PUBLIC DAY SCHOOL TRUST

26 Jun 1872
06400
26 Queen Anne's Gate, London SW1H 9AN
Schools

History: founded and incorporated in 1872 as the Girls' Public Day School Co Ltd in order to establish junior day schools for girls of all classes. Schools were established where sufficient local demand existed and local people took up shares in the company. The trust's council appoints headmistresses and maintains overall financial control. Headmistresses manage their schools in conjunction with local governors. The first school was established in 1873 in Chelsea with 16 pupils. 9 schools had been opened by 1875 attended by 1000 pupils and 38 schools with 7100 pupils were being maintained in 1901. 15,000 pupils were attending the 22 senior and 23 junior schools situated in Bath, Birkenhead, Brighton, Greater London, Ipswich, Liverpool, Newcastle upon Tyne, Norwich, Nottingham, Oxford, Portsmouth, Sheffield and Shrewsbury in 1981. Many of the schools had teacher training departments (now closed) and the trust also ran Clapham Teacher Training College between 1900 and 1949. The company was reconstituted as a trust in 1905 in order to qualify for local education authority grants and the schools were 'direct grant schools' from 1945 until 1976 when the scheme was phased out. The schools were then run on an independent basis and from 1981 have taken pupils under the Assisted Places Scheme. The company was reconstructed and its share capital reduced in 1950 when it obtained charitable status.

Records (1): at Girls Public Day School Trust, 26 Queen Anne's Gate, London SW1H 9AN
council and committee minutes 1874-date; council regulations 1893-1980; finance committee minutes 1933-40; teachers committee minutes 1927-39; share transfer ledgers 1872-1950; debenture stock transfer and redemption registers 1950 onwards; legal documents, papers and correspondence re shares and stock 1913-63; corporate documents 1888-1950; memo and articles of association 1875-1979; register of premises and mortgages 1873 on; legal documents, papers and correspondence re loans, mortgages and the sinking fund 1897-1979; probate register 1941-78; statements of accounts 1880,1887-1940; summarised schools income and expenditure accounts 1924-32; general ledger 1931-58; building fund accounts 1914-23; cash books 1955-70; misc financial papers and correspondence 1912-77; correspondence re direct grants 1974-8; combined schools ledgers c1930s on; local governors: meeting minutes

1944-59, correspondence nd; correspondence and papers re war damage c1945-66; examiners reports 1879-96; correspondence with Department of Education 1960s; school leavers files c1960s; correspondence and papers re scholarships and prizes 1879-date; teachers provident fund legal documents, correspondence and bank books 1885-1900; title deeds, legal documents and correspondence re trust property 19-20 cent; Friends of the GPDST: lists of investments and legal documents 1952-62; copy correspondence 1972-7; Bath High School: memoranda and correspondence re scholarships and prizes 1927-70; ledger 1922-43; title deeds to property in Bath 1785-1808; Birkenhead High School: memoranda and correspondence re scholarships and prizes 1932 on; ledger 1922-43; inventory of furniture and fittings c1901; Blackheath High School: memoranda and correspondence re scholarships and prizes 1895 on; title deeds, property documents and correspondence 1879 on; Brighton & Hove High School: memoranda and correspondence re scholarships and prizes 1918 on; ledger 1922-43; Bromley High School: memoranda and correspondence re scholarships and prizes 1930 on; Clapham High School: memoranda and correspondence re scholarships and prizes 1915 on; property documents and correspondence 1900 on; Croydon High School: memoranda and correspondence re scholarships and prizes 1913 on; governors ledger 1914-43; cash books 1922-46; title deeds, property documents and correspondence 1878 on; Ipswich High School: memoranda and correspondence re scholarships and prizes 1913 on; title deeds, property documents and correspondence 1758 on; Kensington High School: memoranda and correspondence re scholarships and prizes 1935 on; title deeds, property documents and correspondence 1859 on; Belvedere School, Liverpool: memoranda and correspondence re scholarships and prizes 1893 on; ledger 1922-42; title deeds, property documents and correspondence 1847 on; Central Newcastle High School: memoranda and correspondence re scholarships and prizes 1910 on; ledger 1922-43; title deeds, property documents and correspondence 1897-on; Norwich High School: memoranda and correspondence re scholarships and prizes 1946 on; ledger 1922-43; title deeds, property documents and correspondence 1858 on; Nottingham High School: memoranda and correspondence re scholarships and prizes 1919 on; ledger 1922-43; title deeds, property documents and correspondence 1852 on; Notting Hill & Ealing High School: memoranda and correspondence re scholarships and prizes 1897 on; title deeds, property documents and correspondence 1930 on; Oxford High School: memoranda and correspondence re scholarships and prizes 1898 on; ledger 1922-43; title deeds, property documents and correspondence 1866 on; Portsmouth High School: memoranda and correspondence re scholarships and prizes 1913 on; ledger 1922-43; title deeds, property documents and correspondence 1885 on; Putney High School: memoranda and correspondence re scholarships and prizes 1930 on; title deeds, property documents and correspondence 1869 on; Sheffield High School: memoranda and correspondence re scholarships and prizes 1926 on; ledger 1922-43; title deeds, property documents and correspondence 1900 on; Shrewsbury High School: memoranda and correspondence re scholarships and prizes 1925 on; ledger 1922-43; title deeds, property documents and correspondence 1884 on; South Hampstead High School: memoranda and correspondence re scholarships and prizes 1922 on; title deeds, property documents and correspondence 1881 on; Streatham Hill & Clapham High School: memoranda and correspondence re scholarships and prizes 1922 on; property documents 1938 on; Sutton High School: memoranda and correspondence re scholarships and prizes 1904 on; title deeds, property documents and correspondence 1867 on; Sydenham High School: memoranda and correspondence re scholarships and prizes 1920 on; title deeds, property documents and correspondence 1855 on; Tunbridge Wells High School: memoranda and correspondence re prizes 1932 on; title deeds and property correspondence 1920 on; Wimbledon High School: memoranda and correspondence re scholarships and prizes 1929 on; cash book 1943-57; title deeds, property documents and correspondence, including All England Old Lawn Tennis ground 1856-on

Records (2): at Wimbledon High School, Mansel Road, Wimbledon, London SW19
council minutes with reports of committees 1872-1930; examination committee minutes 1884-1947; general purposes committee minutes 1875-7; education committee minutes 1875-1933; finance committee minutes 1877-1933; sites and building committee minutes 1877-1940; teachers committee minutes 1879-1927; art teaching: committee minutes 1910-18, advisory board reports and correspondence 1911-42; centenary committee minutes 1970-2; agm minutes 1872-date; share and share transfer registers 1872-1950; share transfer ledgers 1872-1950; stock ledger 1950-65; stock dividend book 1932-4; stock interest book 1950-7; share, share transfers and stock certificates 1873-1960; legal documents, papers and correspondence re: shares 1889-1959, and constitution of trust 1894-1950; legal papers, opinions, evidence and correspondence re Education Commissions and Acts and direct grant status 1894-1975; papers, reports and correspondence re national educational advisory bodies 1909-57; reports and releases of bursaries fund 1978 on; mortgages and sinking fund papers 1909-67; probate register c1875-1941; annual reports and accounts 1872-date; balance sheets 1872-1970; summarised schools income and expenditure accounts 1922-72; general ledger 1877-1957; sinking fund ledger 1906-45; capital expenditure ledger 1945-57; accounts inventory 1900-05; bank pass book 1872-3; financial papers and correspondence re loans and building appeal 1910-19,1950; fee scales and correspondence thereto 1907-80; correspondence and papers re grants, free places etc 1895-1970; local governing bodies and committees of management: regulations 1922-46, member lists 1928-46; correspondence re administration and government of schools 1926-date; internal inspectors and examiners reports 1879-c1900; external examiners reports 1879-1936; headmistresses reports 1906-38; circulars to headmistresses 1876-9,c1888-1910; reports, papers and correspondence with local and national education authorities re examinations, teaching, curriculum etc 1901 on; GPDST publications on curriculum 1889-1931; prospectuses, reports, notices etc 1903-64; misc documents and correspondence re prizes, prize giving and scholarships 1890 on; inter school magazines 1935-8,1968-73; staff register 1872-1931; misc documents and correspondence re staff training and salaries 1897-1970s; teachers provident fund trustee minutes 1886-99; photographs of chairmen, founders and associates of trust c1890s; circulars re boarding houses and school premises nd; photographs of schools 1890-1972; sketches of 26 Queen Anne's Gate c1968; press cuttings re schools and education 1871-1960s; circulars and prospectuses for individual schools and the trust 1880-1977; articles and books on trust's history and women's education with correspondence and papers re centenary publication, misc documents, correspondence, press cuttings, photographs and tape recordings re jubilee and centenary celebrations 1923,1970-2; correspondence and papers, including lectures, addresses and pamphlets of founders, including Mrs W Grey, and supporters of trust and women's education 1870 on; misc papers re trust, schools, staff, pupils etc 1880-date; Friends of the GPDST: printed notes, circulars and bulletins 1975; newsletters 1951-date; Bath High School: pupils admission register 1932-45; fee notices 1932-45; title deeds, legal documents and correspondence re property 1932 on; centenary magazine 1975; prospectuses, press cuttings, inspectors reports etc 1901 on; photographs of school c1950s; Birkenhead High School: pupils admission register

1901-45; property documents and correspondence 1941 on; prospectuses, press cuttings, inspectors reports and correspondence 1901-51; Blackheath High School: pupils admission register 1926-45; property documents and correspondence 1926 on; published histories 1927,1980; prospectuses, press cuttings, inspectors reports etc 1901 on; Brighton & Hove High School: pupils admission register 1925-45; fee notices 1925; property documents and correspondence 1925 on; building appeal papers 1906-11; published history 1953; prospectuses, press cuttings, inspectors reports etc 1899 on; Bromley High School: pupils admission register 1926-45; property documents and correspondence 1946 on; published histories 1933,1958; prospectuses, press cuttings, inspectors reports etc 1887 on; Carlisle High School: prospectuses, press cuttings, inspectors reports etc 1908-69; Chelsea High School: log book 1873-90; Clapham High & Middle Schools: pupils register 1875-1904; pupils admission register 1882-1945; fee notices 1921-5; correspondence re fee scales 1947-9; particulars of grant received 1922-46; statements of accounts 1946-8; prospectuses, press cuttings, inspectors reports etc 1882-1931; Croydon High School: governors reports 1915-49; correspondence re articles of government and free place fees 1914-49; pupils admission register 1925-45; regulations for governor's scholarships and exhibitions 1919-36; inspectors reports on local scholarship examinations 1925-49; income and expenditure accounts 1919-47; property documents and correspondence 1928 on; correspondence, photographs and papers re building and opening of new school 1953-67; published histories 1924,1954; prospectuses, press cuttings, inspectors reports etc 1898 on; Dover High School: staff register 1901-08; Dulwich High School: pupils admission register 1878-83; prospectuses, press cuttings, inspectors reports, correspondence etc 1910 on; Highbury & Islington High School: photographs of pupils and buildings 1894; prospectuses, press cuttings, inspectors reports, correspondence etc 1907 on; Ipswich High School: correspondence re constitution of governing body 1926; articles of government 1941; property documents and correspondence 1931 on; correspondence with boarding house mistresses 1936-40; published history 1978; prospectuses, press cuttings, inspectors reports etc 1899 on; Kensington High School: pupils register 1874-1937; pupils admission register 1890-1945; staff register 1895-1937; correspondence re fees, administration and closure of upper school 1925-51; extra subjects fees record 1925-33; property documents and correspondence 1929 on; furniture and fittings inventories 1905-38; plans and architects drawings of Upper Phillimore Gardens 1943-68; prospectuses, press cuttings, inspectors reports etc 1890 on; Belvedere School, Liverpool: pupils admission register 1906-45; fee notices 1912-25; staff register 1901-12; property documents and correspondence 1929 on; plans, architects drawings of 13-23 Belvidere Road 1882-1980; anniversary magazine 1980; prospectuses, press cuttings, inspectors reports etc 1888 on; East Liverpool High School: register of pupils 1891-1910; Howells School, Llandaff: headmistress report 1979-80; Central Newcastle High School: pupils admission register 1921-45; fee notices 1921-5; property documents and correspondence 1922 on; published history on school and headmistress 1936,1955; school and boarding house prospectuses, press cuttings, inspectors reports etc 1907 on; Norwich High School: pupils admission register 1908-45; fee notices 1919-25; property documents and correspondence 1925 on; plans and architects drawings of school buildings 1931-72; published histories 1950,1975; prospectuses, press cuttings, inspectors reports etc 1882 on; Nottingham High School: pupils admission register 1918-36; fee notices 1919-25; property documents and correspondence 1923 on; published histories 1954,1975; prospectuses, press cuttings, inspectors reports etc 1895 on; Notting Hill & Ealing High School: pupils admission register 1928-45; property documents and correspondence 1930; published history 1973; prospectuses, press cuttings, inspectors reports etc including timetable and scheme of work for Notting Hill & Bayswater High School 1873 on; Oxford High School: pupils admission register 1911-45; property documents and correspondence 1926 on; press cuttings and photographs of building and opening of new school 1955-8; *Ad Lucem* addresses by headmistress 1930; published histories 1960,1975; prospectuses, press cuttings, inspectors reports etc 1894 on; Paddington & Maida Vale High School: prospectuses, press cuttings, inspectors reports and correspondence re school transfer 1889-1912; Portsmouth High School: pupils admission register 1929-45; property documents and correspondence 1938 on; published history 1957; prospectuses, press cuttings, inspectors and headmistresses reports 1868 on; Putney High School: pupils admission register 1921-45; property documents and correspondence 1939 on; building appeal papers 1906-11; prospectuses, press cuttings, inspectors reports 1893 on; Sheffield High School: pupils admission register 1917-45; fee notices 1919-25; property documents and correspondence c1940; centenary magazine 1978; prospectuses, press cuttings, inspectors reports, centenary celebration papers etc 1895 on; Shrewsbury High School: pupils admission register 1907-45; property documents and correspondence 1931 on; plan and architects drawings of school buildings 1924-71; published history 1960; prospectuses, press cuttings, inspectors reports etc 1884 on; South Hampstead High School: pupils admission register 1919-45; fee notices 1919-25; property documents and correspondence 1941 on; plans, architects drawings and photographs of school buildings 1889-1968; published history 1976; prospectuses, press cuttings, inspectors reports etc 1876 on; Streatham Hill & Clapham High School: pupils admission register 1914-45; fee notices 1921-5; property documents and correspondence 1900 on; photographs and correspondence re opening of new school 1952; prospectuses, press cuttings, inspectors reports etc 1887 on; Sutton High School: pupils admission register 1936-45; property documents and correspondence 1924 on; published histories 1934,1964; prospectuses, press cuttings, inspectors reports etc 1895 on; Swansea High School: prospectuses, press cuttings, inspectors reports, correspondence etc 1888 on; Sydenham High School: pupils admission register 1922-45; property documents and correspondence 1910 on; photographs of new gymnasium 1979; published history 1967; prospectuses, press cuttings, inspectors reports etc 1886 on; Tunbridge Wells High School: pupils admission register 1902-40; fee notices 1919-25; local governors meeting minutes 1927-43; correspondence re school closure 1931-40; staff register 1902-26; photographs of pupils and buildings 1891-97; school magazines, published history and Old Girls Association newsletter articles 1894-1944; prospectuses, press cuttings, inspectors reports etc 1891-1940; Weymouth High School: prospectuses, press cuttings, inspectors reports, correspondence etc 1888 on; Wimbledon High School: pupils admission register 1925-c47, playing fields fund papers 1923-45, including ledger 1923-31, cash books 1923-45, and bank books 1923-43; published histories 1980; prospectuses, press cuttings, inspectors reports etc 1887 on; York High School: prospectuses, press cuttings, inspectors reports, correspondence etc c1970; Clapham & Streatham Hill Training College: admission register 1931-48; printed reports, minutes and accounts 1946-8; correspondence and papers re art training, future of college, fee scales, staff appointment, grants etc 1935-52

Records (3): at GPDST Surveyor's Department, Sutton, Greater London
correspondence re the surveyor's department, individual school property and scientific equipment 20 cent; plans, architects drawings etc of buildings: Bath High School with photographs 1932-date, Birkenhead High School 1918-date, Blackheath High School 1936-

date, Brighton & Hove High School with photographs 1891-date, Bromley High School 1979-date, Croydon High School 1964-7, Ipswich High School 1934-date, Central Newcastle High School 19 cent-date, Nottingham High School 1923-date, Notting Hill & Ealing High School 1930-date, Oxford High School 1951-date, Portsmouth High School 1944-date, Putney High School 1918-date, Sheffield High School 1921-date, Streatham Hill & Clapham High School 1893-date, Sutton High School 1931-date, Sydenham High School 1933-date, Wimbledon High School c1920-date

Records (4): at Sun Alliance Insurance Group, Trustee Department, 40 Chancery Lane, London WC2A 1JN
memo and articles of association 1875; mortgages and transfers and assignments of same 1905-79; legal documents and correspondence re mortgages and finance 1909-59; fire insurance policies 1897-1964; title deeds and documents for trust properties 1897-1937; title deeds and property documents; Bath High School 1785-1946, Birkenhead High School 1851-1952, Blackheath High School 1857-1962, Brighton & Hove High School 1819-1980, Croydon High School 1851-1964, Ipswich High School 1885-1958, Belvedere School, Liverpool, 1843-1959, Central Newcastle High School 1893-1957, Norwich High School 1839-1980, Nottingham High School 1852-1946, Notting Hill & Ealing High School 1875-1934, Oxford High School 1880-1950, Portsmouth High School 1799-1934, Putney High School 1870-1963, Sheffield High School 1866-1946, Shrewsbury High School 1769-1958, South Hampstead High School 1880-1956, Streatham Hill & Clapham High School 1857-1932, Sutton High School 1866-1951, Sydenham High School 1861-1979, Wimbledon High School 1885-1931

Josephine Kamm, *Indicative Past: A Hundred Years of the Girls Public Day School Trust* (1973)
The Girls Public Day School Trust 1872-1972. A Centenary Review (1972)

149 WEST'S PATENT PRESS CO LTD

1 Jul 1872
06415
Eagle Star House, 28-36 Carver Street, Sheffield, S Yorkshire S1 4FS
Property (formerly cotton and wool bailing press manufacturers)

History: incorporated in 1872 to acquire the right to use and work West & Co's patent machinery for pressing cotton and other materials. Company traded exclusively in India, cleaning wool and cotton for export to the UK, primarily Manchester and Yorkshire areas. At the height of its success, the company was one of the largest in India, with over 70 stations. From the 1950s the company began to sell its stations to Indians and it subsequently relocated in Sheffield. In 1984 activities were property owning and investment companies, with properties in the Sheffield area.

Records (1): at West's Patent Press, Eagle Star House, 28-36 Carver Street, Sheffield, S Yorkshire S1 4FS
directors and general meeting minutes 1877 on; register of directors 1877 on; share ledger 1877 on, transfer register 1877 on

Records (2): with Mr CF Letch, 16 Gledhow Lane, Oakwood, Leeds, W Yorkshire
share: ledger 1877-1980,transfer register 1909-83; annual returns 1950-9; memo and articles of association 1946; nominal ledger 1955-76; Indian property leases 1887,1941

150 SHEFFIELD ROLLING MILLS LTD

18 Jul 1872
06470
9 Albert Embankment, London SE1 7SN
Steel

History: incorporated in 1872 as Sheffield Forge & Rolling Mills Co Ltd and operated as steel rollers, forgers, tilters and drawers from Millsands Works, Sheffield, S Yorkshire. Subsequently changed name to above. In 1977 had works in Sheffield in Shepcote Lane, Tinsley; Millsands Works; River Don Works, Hawke Street; Hallamshire Steel Works, Bardwell Road; and Toledo Works, Neepsend Lane. Operated as steel rollers, heat treaters, bright drawers, and black and bright alloy and carbon bars, spring steel and wire rod and section producers. Subsequently became part of British Steel Corporation.

Records: at British Steel Corporation, Northern Regional Records Centre, Unit F2, Commerce Way, Skippers Lane Industrial Estate, South Bank, Middlesbrough, Cleveland TS6 6UT

151 BARNAGORE JUTE FACTORY CO LTD

22 Jul 1872
06480
Victoria House, Vernon Place, London WC1B 4DH
Jute products

History: the first jute mill to use power looms in India, was established in 1859 by Borneo Co Ltd, Far Eastern traders, at Barnagore, just outside Calcutta, India. Incorporated as above in 1872, the Borneo Co retaining a shareholding until 1935. New mills built in 1901 and 1906. Managed by a board of directors in London under secretaryship of George Henderson & Sons Ltd, East India merchants, to 1946 and then of Matheson & Co Ltd, merchants, to 1978 when control was transferred to India. Originally purchased jute to make bags but by 1982 various jute products were manufactured.

Records (1): at Barnagore Jute Factory, Victoria House, Vernon Place, London WC1B 4DH
directors meeting minutes 1872-1970

Records (2): at Barnagore Jute Factory, 4 Clive Row, Calcutta, 700 001 India
directors meeting minutes 1970-date; current records

152 SUNDERLAND CLUB LTD

6 Aug 1872
06505
1 Toward Road, Sunderland, Tyne & Wear SR1 2QF
Gentlemen's club

History: established in 1869 as Sunderland Club & News Room to provide reading and billiard rooms and card game facilities for members. Membership was open to gentlemen and military and naval officers on duty in Sunderland, Tyne & Wear. Company incorporated in 1872 as above to take over and run club. Premises were at 25 Fawcett Street until 1959 when they were purchased by Hugh Fraser to extend Binns department store. Purchased Victoria Hall site in

Toward Road and built new premises. Membership in 1870 was about 235, mainly consisting of colliery and ship owners. Fell to an average of 195 in 1930s and in 1983 was about 260.

Records: at Sunderland Club, 1 Toward Road, Sunderland, Tyne & Wear SR1 2QF
directors, committee and general meeting minutes 1928-date; members: register 1911-57, subscription book 1916-41, lists 1869-99; annual reports and accounts 1928-41,1951; rules, regulations, articles of association and by-laws 1869-1910; forces visitors book 1942-57; proposition book 1893-1981; complaints book current; newscuttings 1869; Fawcett Street building photographs 1929,1931

153 NATIONAL BANK OF NEW ZEALAND LTD

14 Aug 1872
06533
8 Moorgate, London EC2R 6DB
Banking

History: incorporated as above in 1872. In 1919 Lloyds Bank Ltd obtained shareholding in company. Became a wholly owned subsidiary of Lloyds Bank Ltd in 1966. In early 1980s head office was in Wellington, New Zealand.

Records: at National Bank of New Zealand, PO Box 1791, Wellington, New Zealand

154 LEICESTER REAL PROPERTY CO LTD

16 Sep 1872
06610
3 Wycliffe Street, Leicester, Leicestershire LE1 5IR
Property and investment

History: incorporated in 1872 as above to purchase land for domestic housing development in Leicester. By 1892 was letting 120 houses. Formed LRP (Investments) Co Ltd in 1962. From 1960s have sold vacant houses and invested proceeds.

Records: at Leicestershire Record Office, 57 New Walk, Leicester, Leicestershire LE1 7JB
directors and general meeting minutes 1891-date; share: ledgers 1872-1960, certificate books 1900-14; dividend warrant books 1957-9; annual returns 1919-29; debenture certificate book 1887-1912; annual reports and accounts 1891-1957; private ledgers 1872-1952; personal ledgers 1886-1930; ledgers 1907-52; cash books 1872-1939; petty cash book 1911-30; rent: summaries 1912-28, ledger 1950s-60s; deed lists 1898-1904; letter book 1911-29

155 DIRECT SPANISH TELEGRAPH CO LTD

8 Nov 1872
06732
1 Berkeley Street, London W1X 6NN
Investment (formerly telegraph)

History: founded and incorporated in 1872 by John Pender, Liberal MP, pioneer of ocean telegraphy and founder of Eastern & Associated Telegraph Companies group, as Falmouth & Bilbao Submarine Cable Co Ltd to connect telegraphically Bilbao, North Spain, with Kennack Cove, Cornwall, and then by land line to Falmouth. From 1921 shore lines were diverted to Porthcurno, Cornwall. Name changed to above by 1874 when land line was laid between Barcelona, Spain, and Marseille, France. Second Bilbao to Porthcurno cable laid in 1925. Never member of Eastern & Associated Telegraph Companies group, although had operations room in Electra House, Moorgate, at Eastern headquarters, but remained private company of Pender family. Operating assets leased to Imperial & International Communications Ltd (became Cable & Wireless Ltd in 1934) in 1933 for £3500 per year for 20 years. Acquired as an investment company by First National Finance Corporation Ltd, then by the Slater Walker Group in early 1970s and since 1977 has been a subsidiary of Trafalgar House Ltd.

Records: at Cable & Wireless, Mercury House, 110-124 Theobalds Road, London WC1X 8RX
agreements 1882-1927; cable lay log book 1925; telegraph staff registers c1873-1932; magazine cutting re messenger girls 1924

Hugh Barty-King, *Girdle Round the Earth* (1979)

156 MALDON IRONWORKS LTD

26 Nov 1872
06772
Riverside Works, Norwich, Norfolk NR1 1EB
Structural steel engineers and joinery manufacturers

History: moved in 1853 by Samuel Warren from Broad Street Green, Heybridge, Essex, to Maldon, Essex, and incorporated as above in 1872. New premises built in Fullbridge, Maldon, in 1875. Acquired in 1947 by John Sadd & Sons Ltd, timber merchants (inc 1889) who were subsequently acquired by Boulton & Paul, engineers of Norwich, Norfolk (est 1797) a subsidiary of British Electric Traction Co Ltd. Continued to operate as agricultural engineering factory of John Sadd group until 1955 when factory was converted into a television/radio cabinet factory managed by Maldon Woodwork Ltd. The premises were closed in 1981 and subsequently sold.

Records (1): at Essex Record Office, County Hall, Chelmsford, Essex CM1 1LX
retail ledgers 1873-1942; wholesale ledgers 1873-1916; warehouse ledger 1873-1936; retail day books 1911-42; wholesale day books 1911-42; warehouse day book 1926-38; cash books 1873-99; bank cash books 1901-45; receipts cash book 1898-1947; petty cash books 1935-47; bank statements 1885-96; order books 1926-43, 1953-4; statistics books 1876-1940; returns day book 1926-38; letter book 1949-51; correspondence journal 1938-41; wages books 1947-51; misc correspondence and insurance papers 1950s

Records (2): at Maldon Museum Association, 71 High Street, Maldon, Essex
retail ledgers 1876-89, 1912-23; wholesale ledger 1884-92; retail day book 1914-15; returns day book 1932-42; cash books 1877-91; bank cash book 1873-1900; order book 1937-41; carriage book 1874-c1936; wages book 1940-6; correspondence journal 1941; letter book 1951

157 MOWLEM CONSTRUCTION (PLANT HIRE) LTD

28 Nov 1872
06775
Westgate House, Ealing Road, Brentford, Greater London TW8 0QZ
Paving contractors

History: incorporated in 1872 as Improved Wood Pavement Co Ltd to acquire patent of Improved Wood Pavement and for laying and maintaining same. Took over business and contracts of Samuel Norris and Benjamin B Hotchkiss, engineers, who had laid pavements in London, Portsmouth Dock Yard and Leeds between 1871 and 1872. Original London offices were at 32 Lombard Street, moving to 46 Queen Victoria Street in 1876 and in about 1922 to Blackfriars House, New Bridge Street. By 1914 were contractors for wood paving, wood block flooring, sawing, creosoting, excavating, concreting etc and had saw mills and works at East Greenwich. Formed Mowlem Paving Co Ltd in 1947 with John Mowlem & Co Ltd, government and public works contractors of Westminster. During 1950s became a wholly owned subsidiary of Mowlems and ceased to operate independently in 1959. Name subsequently changed to above. In 1983 was a subsidiary of John Mowlem & Co PLC through Mowlem Construction Co Ltd.

Records: at John Mowlem, Westgate House, Ealing Road, Brentford, Greater London TW8 0QZ
directors meeting: minutes 1872-1944, attendance books 1907-53; shareholders: meeting minutes 1873-1954, attendance books 1873-1952, address books 1901-24; applications and share allotment books 1872-3; call register 1873; shareholders register 1875-1945; share: ledger c1947-54, transfer register 1872-1907; directors register 1907-42; dividend statements 1874-1952; probate register 1874-1936; balance book 1926-52; impersonal ledgers 1872-1959; sold ledgers 1872-9; bought ledgers 1872-1901,1917-36; customers ledger 1952-6; journals 1872-1902; cash books 1872-1904; cash receipts book 1922-9; petty cash book 1949-54; income tax papers and correspondence 1908-58; accounts rendered 1959

158 MEADOW FOUNDRY CO LTD

29 Nov 1872
06783
Clumber Avenue, Sherwood Rise, Nottingham, Nottinghamshire NG5 1AH
Engineers and ironfounders

History: founded by James Bownes in Littleworth, Mansfield, Nottinghamshire. Meadow Foundry established on Western Avenue, Sheepbridge Lane. Incorporated as above in 1872 to purchase this business and carry on trade of galvanized and wrought iron and general metal manufacturers, engineers and iron founders. In 1977 employed 200 people. Went into liquidation in 1980.

Records: at Spicer & Pegler, Liquidators, Clumber Avenue, Sherwood Rise, Nottingham, Nottinghamshire NG5 1AH
minutes 19-20 cent; annual reports and accounts, staff records and correspondence 1950s on

159 WESTERN TELEGRAPH CO LTD

8 Jan 1873
06886
Mercury House, 110-124 Theobalds Road, London WC1X 8RX
Telegraph

History: founded and incorporated in 1873 as Brazilian Submarine Telegraph Co Ltd to connect by telegraph the main Brazilian ports to each other and to Europe. Worked closely with Western & Brazilian Telegraph Co Ltd (inc 1873), laying cables from Recife southwards, connecting with England in 1874 and Montevideo, Uruguay, in 1875. The two companies merged in 1899 and changed name to above. Became part of the Eastern & Associated Telegraph Companies group which became Cable & Wireless Ltd in 1934 and publically owned from 1946. Continued to operate in Brazil until 1973 and in 1981 still operated in Uruguay as a subsidiary company of the same.

Records (1): at Cable & Wireless, Mercury House, 110-124 Theobalds Road, London WC1X 8RX
board minutes 1873-1939; agm: minutes 1873-1948, reports 1904-28; debenture stockholders minutes 1918-29; agreements, concessions, contracts and articles of association 1873-1929; seal registers 1900-46; annual reports 1873-1970; balance sheet and accounts 1873-1926; half yearly accounts 1907-13; balance book 1900-01; general ledgers 1873-1948; journal 1931-54; engineers cable reports 1873-1925; cable lay log books 1900-21; photographs of cable lay 1911; staff registers: European c1873-1931, local c1898-1930, and cable ships c1902-30; photographs of staff and staff quarters c1927-53; house journal 1883-7; correspondence 1873-87; station instructions 1914-18; press cuttings and releases and articles and notes on history of company 1894-5,1951-68
Western & Brazilian Telegraph Co Ltd: board minutes 1873-99; report to directors 1893; committee meeting minutes 1884-6; agm minutes 1873-99 agreements and concessions 1870-98; legal papers, accounts and costs re various legal cases incl Central American Telegraph Co Ltd 1876-95; annual reports and accounts 1888-99; financial statements 1896-7; counter receipts 1886,1890; Brazilian superintendents memoranda and correspondence 1893-1928

Records (2): at Science Museum Library, South Kensington, London SW7 5NH
cable contracts 1873-83; cable lay log books 1919-25; photographs of cable lays 1919-25;

Records (3): at University College Library, Gower Street, London WC1E 6BT
European staff books nd; staff lists nd; letter books 1883-1949; company history 1934

KC Baglehole, *A Century of Service. A brief history of Cable and Wireless Ltd 1868-1968* (1969)
Hugh Barty-King, *Girdle Round the Earth* (1979)

160 TEESSIDE & DISTRICT CHAMBER OF COMMERCE & INDUSTRY
10 Mar 1873
07056
Commerce House, Marton Road, Middlesbrough, Cleveland TS1 1DW
Chamber of commerce

History: founded in 1863 as Middlesbrough Chamber of Commerce and incorporated as same in 1873 to promote and represent industry, commerce and trade in Teesside and district. Amalgamated in 1928 with Stockton Chamber of Commerce to form Teesside Chamber of Commerce. By 1947 area of influence stretched from Whitby, N Yorkshire to south west Durham and name changed to Teesside & South West Chamber of Commerce. Amalgamated with Hartlepool Chamber of Commerce in 1963 and name changed to Teesside & District Chamber of Commerce. Name altered to above in 1972. First permanent premises were acquired in the Royal Exchange, Middlesbrough, Cleveland in 1921. Moved to 7 Queen's Square in 1928 and to Marton Road in 1936. Published monthly journal between 1923 and 1982. In 1983 services offered to members included import and export advice, information, certificates of origin, translation, telexes, seminars and functions.

Records (1): at Teesside & District Chamber of Commerce & Industry, Commerce House, Marton Road, Middlesbrough, Cleveland TS1 1DW
council, committee and agm: minutes 1906-date, papers and correspondence 1961-79; annual reports and accounts 1906-71; memo and articles of association 1929; cash books 1947-73; members account books 1964-9; day books 1965-72; petty cash books 1965-73; journal ledgers 1951-70; advertising summaries 1960-8; membership: and subscription books 1893-1974, records 1967-74, figures 1946-53, translation records 1965-73; secretarys letter book 1918-22; newscuttings re chamber and Teesside 1936-73; photographs of district, staff, officials and members 1900s-70s; *Teesside Journal of Commerce* 1923-80; publications 1930-63
Northern Chambers of Commerce: council minutes 1958-68
Middlesbrough Railway & Traders Panel: minutes 1923-41

Records (2): at Middlesbrough Central Library, Victoria Square, Middlesbrough, Cleveland TS1 2AY
annual: meeting report and accounts 1917, reports 1963-4; members list and trade index c1961; yearbook and members directory 1977-date; information booklet 1960s; trade and industry statistical reports 1877-1916

161 LONDON MERCHANT SECURITIES LTD

12 Mar 1873
07064
Carlton House, 33 Robert Adam Street, London W1M 5AH
Property and investment

History: incorporated in 1873 as London & Hanseatic Bank Ltd to carry on banking, financial and mercantile business operations, changing name to London Merchant Bank in 1916. By start of WW1 substantial amounts were due from debtors in Germany, Poland, Latvia (USSR), Austria, Italy, Russia and other countries which led to considerable losses. Banking business was suspended on outbreak of WW2 and transferred to Guinness Mahon & Co. Name changed to above and converted into an investment trust. Main activity from 1945 was collecting of foreign debts of which less than 20 per cent were received. With subsequent loss of Eastern European business became effectively a quoted shell company. Acquired by Max Rayne (later Lord Rayne) property financier in 1958. Bought Rayne's property company British Commercial Property Investment Trust Ltd, through which all subsequent developments were carried out. Main property interests are still in London. From 1960 have held substantial shareholdings in industrial concerns, for example The Sanitas Trust Ltd, a pharmaceutical and cosmetic group; Invergordon Distillers (Holdings) Ltd; The Haddon Group Ltd, battery manufacturers; Carlton Industries Ltd; and Century Power & Light Ltd, active in North Sea gas and oil exploration.

Records: at London Merchant Securities, Carlton House, 33 Robert Adam Street, London W1M 5AH
directors and general meeting minutes 1873-date; board papers and agendas 1967-date;

directors attendance book 1966-date; shareholders letters and special resolutions 1969-date; directors interests register 1947-date; directors register 1947-date; memo and articles of association current; charges register 1960-date; guarantee copies 1970-date; seals register 1951-date; annual reports and accounts 1948-date; nominal and cash ledgers 1873-date

162 RTZ UNITED KINGDOM HOLDINGS LTD

29 Mar 1873
07132
6 St James's Square, London SW1Y 4LD
Mining

History: incorporated in 1873 as Rio Tinto Co Ltd to acquire an ancient Spanish mine. 40,000 tons of copper matte were being produced each year by 1900. As the copper content of the ore declined the production of pyrites for the manufacture of sulphuric acid became more important. New investments in copper production were made elsewhere, especially in Zambia in the 1920s. In the 1950s the Rio Tinto mine was sold to a consortium of Spanish banks; a third of the proceeds were invested in the new concern and the remainder in mining activities in other countries. By 1962 the company had developed uranium mines in Canada and Australia, had a copper project in South Africa, and a potential iron ore project in Western Australia. In 1962 Rio Tinto Co Ltd merged with Consolidated Zinc Corporation (formed in 1905 as the Zinc Corporation) to form the Rio Tinto-Zinc Corporation Ltd. The operations of the two companies were restructured with assets in each country being held by virtually autonomous local companies. In 1963 company changed name to RTZ Investments Ltd. In 1967 Capper Pass & Son Ltd, a specialist tin producer, was fully integrated into the group and the following year Borax (Holdings) Ltd was acquired. During 1970 Pillar Ltd with principal interests in aluminium fabricating and light engineering activities became part of the group. In 1978 company changed name to above and is now a wholly owned subsidiary of the Rio Tinto-Zinc Corporation PLC.

Records: at Rio Tinto-Zinc Corporation, 6 St James's Square, London SW1Y 4LD
board meeting: minutes 1873-date, reports 1875-1908, agenda books 1918-date; general meeting: minutes 1873-date, attendance books 1873-date, papers 1959-62; share, mortgage and debenture issue papers 1875-1940; Talons & Coupons specimens 1897; Talons record book 1945-6; seal book 1928-62; annual reports and accounts 1873-1962; committee meeting minutes: management 1949-55, financial 1925-48; finance transfer books 1944-55; reports, plans, contracts, photographs etc re Rio Tinto mines 1873-1954; reports by board deputations and special visits to Spain and Portugal 1876-1963; daily official quotations for copper 1920-39; commercial department contracts 1933-7; product agreements 1937-40; operating committee meeting minutes 1935-49; group co-ordination committee meeting minutes 1938-40; reserves of mineral forecasts 1927-37; staff: committee meetings 1935-44, book 1873-1956, register 1919-29

D Avery, *Not on Queen Victoria's Birthday. The Story of the Rio Tinto Mines* (1974)
CE Harvey, *The Rio Tinto Company. An Economic History of a Leading International Mining Concern* (1982)

163 WEST KENT ESTATES LTD

10 Apr 1873
07146
291 Main Road, Sidcup, Greater London DA14 6QL
Property

History: in the 1870s Joseph Wates, secretary of Woolwich Equitable Building Society, began to invest in house property in Plumstead and Woolwich, London. In 1873 he incorporated West Kent Co-operative Dwelling Co Ltd, with himself as chairman and his son as secretary to administer his property. Tenants had the option of carrying out small repairs on their cottages and then receiving a rebate of a certain proportion of their rent. Wates thought this scheme would be of mutual advantage but it was not a success as tenants abused the system. In 1926 'Co-operative' was removed from the title. Property was acquired in Woolwich, Plumstead, Greenwich, Lewisham, West Ham, Hounslow, Canning Town, Millwall, Deptford and Blackheath, London; and Sidcup and Strood, Kent. During the 1930s tenants were encouraged to acquire the freehold of their premises. By 1935 accommodation was being provided for about 1000 families, and a staff of 25 undertook repairs and collected rent. During the 1950s a number of properties in designated clearance areas were compulsorily purchased by local authorities. To offset this further purchases were made in Lee, Plumstead and Hither Green, London. Registered offices were moved from Woolwich to Sidcup in 1955. Name changed to above in 1956. A subsidiary, West Kent Estates (Builders) Ltd, was formed in 1963. Acquired by Anglo-Metropolitan Holdings Ltd in 1980.

Records: at West Kent Estates, 291 Main Road, Sidcup, Greater London DA14 6QL
directors and general meeting: minutes 1879-1980, agenda book 1942-80; shareholders: register 1884-1979, list 1980; directors list 1926-81; share transfer certificates 1925-79; dividends ledger 1934-80; annual reports and accounts 1873-1980; agm reports 1926-44; consolidated balance sheets 1971-3,1979; private ledger 1885-1955; loan ledger 1885-1949; agency account ledger 1952-69; journal 1959-64; cash books 1920-68; estates account books 1873-1967; rent account book 1873-1963; stock books and deed registers 1872-1950; mortgage register 1936-55; rents and property list 1964; Wates history of company 1942
West Kent Estates (Builders) Ltd: annual reports and accounts 1970,1979-80

164 COWANS SHELDON & CO LTD

10 Apr 1873
07180
NEI House, Regent Centre, Newcastle upon Tyne, Tyne & Wear NE3 3SB
Crane manufacturers

History: founded in 1846 at Woodbank near Upperby, Carlisle, Cumbria by John Cowans and Edward P Sheldon, ex employees of locomotive engineers, Robert Stephenson & Co, Newcastle, Tyne & Wear. Formed partnership with William and Thomas Bouch, civil engineers, who became sleeping partners. Main customers were railway, colliery and dock companies. By 1853 the manufacture of railway wagon wheels and axles had increased beyond capacity of Woodbank and whole of forge business was transferred to Darlington Forge Co, in which partners had financial interests. Expansion continued and in 1857 bought St Nicholas Works with newly built foundries and other plant. Woodbank Works closed in 1869. First firm to make balance on centre turntables; other products included cranes and steam engines.

George Dove, manager of the new works, became a partner in 1863. John Cowans died in 1873. Subsequently the firm was converted to a limited company. In 1881 became established as heavy lifting plant manufacturers and in 1891 erected 130 ton steam jib crane at Finnieston Quay, Glasgow, largest dockside crane in UK. By 1940 recognised worldwide as one of foremost manufacturers of port, railway and heavy industrial equipment. Merged in 1961 with Clyde Crane & Booth Ltd, itself acquired by Clarke Chapman-John Thompson Ltd of Gateshead in mid 1960s. CA Parsons Ltd merged with latter in 1979 to form Northern Engineering Industries Ltd, Cowans Sheldon becoming an NEI unit. In 1981 became NEI Cranes Ltd and in 1982 produced railway cranes, track maintenance equipment, North Sea oil plant and other related machinery.

Records (1): at NEI Cranes, PO Box 9, St Nicholas Works, Carlisle, Cumbria CA1 2PA
board and sealing committee minutes 1892-1955; general meeting minutes 1893-1964; members register 1886-99; articles of association and resolutions 1872-1939; legal reports and counsel's opinion 1886-7; agreement with Clyde Crane & Booth Ltd 1961; seal register 1903-27; balance sheets and capital analysis record 1859-1921; ledger 1847-53; private ledger 1872-90; sales journal 1847-51; letters patent 1906-47; illustrated catalogues 1898-1912; outline history and products range 1961; specifications and estimates book 1859-65; estimate books 1940 on; contract specifications 1940 on; Woodbank order book 1857-64; main order books 1910-65; main order copies 1950 on; material sheets 1933 on; drawing costs notebook nd; cost books 1905-37; contract correspondence 1952 on; sub-contract records and correspondence 1959 on; drawings 1868-90; microfilm detail drawings 1919 on; photographs and artists impressions of completed jobs c1940s-80s; wages book 1921-30; pension and assurance scheme minutes 1940-60; managing directors speeches to staff re centenary 1946; Clyde Crane & Booth Ltd proposals 1961; photographs and paintings of directors and secretaries 19-20 cent; photographs of works c1979; notes on and histories c1946-7,1970s

Records (2): at Northern Engineering Industries, NEI House, Regent Centre, Newcastle upon Tyne, Tyne & Wear NE3 3SB
directors meeting minutes 1955-date; general meeting minutes 1964-date; title deeds and other property documents 19-20 cent

Records (3): at Cumbria Record Office, The Castle, Carlisle, Cumbria CA3 8UR
co-partnership deed 1858; case and opinion on directors qualifications 1886; partnership ledger 1858-72; publicity material 20 cent; order books 1861 on; smith shop books 1861 on; engineering drawings 1862,1888,1899-1962; title deeds and property papers 1623-1873

165 EASTERN EXTENSION AUSTRALASIA & CHINA TELEGRAPH CO LTD

24 Apr 1873
07224
Mercury House, 110-124 Theobalds Road, London WC1X 8RX
Telegraph

History: founded and incorporated in 1873 by John Pender, Liberal MP and pioneer of ocean telegraphy, by the amalgamation of British India Extension Co Ltd (inc 1869), British Australian Telegraph Co Ltd (inc 1870) and China Submarine Telegraph Co Ltd (inc 1869), with the object of extending telegraph communication beyond India to the Far East and Australia. First major project was laying cable from Botany Bay, Australia, to Blind Bay,

Nelson, New Zealand, completed 1876. In 1879 laid 2 cables between Pinang, Malaysia and Singapore; 1880, Hong Kong and Manila, Philippines; 1883, Fuzhou and Shanghai in China; 1891, Pinang and Medan, Sumatra, Indonesia; 1894, Borneo and Singapore and Hong Kong; 1900, Shanghai and Chefoo in China and Mauritius and Rodriguez Islands, Cocos (Keeling) Islands; Fremantle, Perth, Australia; and in 1908 Cocos and Batavia, Java. Became part of Eastern & Associated Telegraph Companies group which became Cable & Wireless Ltd in 1934 and publicly owned from 1946. In 1981 was a non-trading company within the Cable & Wireless group.

Records (1): at Cable & Wireless, Mercury House, 110-124 Theobalds Road, London WC1X 8RX
board minutes 1873-1939; finance committee minutes 1874-97; Great Northern Telegraph Co Ltd joint committee minutes 1886-1926; agm minutes 1873-1948; general meeting report 1882-1929; corporate documents, agreements, concessions, correspondence and articles of association 1868-1929; seal books 1876-1936; annual report and accounts 1882-1929; balance sheet and accounts 1900-24; financial statements 1923-9; general ledgers 1875-1949; journal 1940-50; income tax papers 1903-25; engineers and electricians cable reports 1876-1901; cable lay log books 1914-26; correspondence and data re cable lays 1911-25; photographs of cable lay 1921; cable map c1891; staff registers 1870-1930; staff rules and regulations 1906-15; staff bonus fund account book 1914-23; historical and technical data, articles and press cuttings re stations, branches and cables 1893-1973; photographs of stations, offices and staff 1906-25; title deeds and other property documents 1874-1931
British Australian Telegraph Co Ltd: cable contract 1870; general ledgers 1869-73; engineers cable reports 1871-2; historical notes on company and Australian telegraphs nd
British Indian Extension Co Ltd: prospectus, articles of association and agreements c1870s; cable route map c1870
China Submarine Telegraph Co Ltd: agreements 1870-4; engineers cable report 1871

Records (2): at Science Museum Library, South Kensington, London SW7 5NH
cable contracts 1875-93; cable lay log book 1901,1914; photographs of cable lay 1901-02,1925

KC Baglehole, *A Century of Service. A brief history of Cable and Wireless Ltd 1868-1968* (1969)
Hugh Barty-King, *Girdle Round the Earth* (1979)

166 BOWDON BOWLING & LAWN TENNIS CLUB LTD
28 Apr 1873
07241
Stamford Road, Bowdon, Greater Manchester
Sports club-houses

History: incorporated in 1873 as Bowdon Bowling & Croquet Club Ltd to purchase land in Stamford Road, Bowdon, Greater Manchester on which to form a bowling green and croquet grounds and erect club premises. By 1883 had also laid out cinder and grass tennis courts. Name changed to above in 1909. In 1983 provision of bowling and tennis facilities continued to be main activities.

Records: at Bowdon Bowling & Lawn Tennis Club, Stamford Road, Bowdon, Greater Manchester
directors and general meeting minutes 1885-date; committee lists 1890-2; share: allotment register 1873-6, ledger and members register 1873-date, certificates and applications 1919-65, transfer register 1874-1902, transfer documents 1873-1977; annual summaries 1874-1902; articles of association and correspondence 1942-9; annual reports and accounts 1892,1895,1919,1921-date; club rules 1889-1929; balance sheets 1873-1945; private ledgers 1873-1946; day book 1906-23; cash books 1873-92,1923-69; receipts and vouchers 1891-1901; members: proposal book 1874-date, register 1890-4; subscription: register 1891-1923, circulars 1886-1941; visitors books 1874-date; fete and members photographs 1916-18; correspondence 1880-1949; misc papers 1896-1969

167 HAWTIN LTD

16 May 1873
07317
Metropolitan House, Preston New Road, Blackpool, Lancashire FY3 9TJ
Industrial clothing and property (formerly dental equipment manufacturers)

History: incorporated as Dental Manufacturing Co Ltd in 1873 to manufacture dental equipment and artificial teeth. Factory situated at High Barnet, Hertfordshire and by 1923 company had branches in Birmingham, Brighton, Bristol, Cambridge, Cardiff, Croydon, Glasgow, Leeds, Liverpool, Manchester, Newcastle, Nottingham, and Reading, UK; Dublin, Republic of Ireland; Moscow, USSR; New York, USA; Rio de Janeiro, Brazil; and Sydney, Australia. In early 1950s, due to fall in demand from the National Health Service, company began to diversify into motor silencers and agricultural equipment manufacturing, house building and transport. By 1966 owned 16 engineering, 2 chemical and plastic, 4 building and construction and 4 transport and general subsidiaries. Sold dental business to Amalgamated Dental Co Ltd in 1968 and changed name to Hawtin Industries Ltd. Sold motor silencer business in 1970 and changed name to above. Established Hawtin & Partners for banking and financial services in early 1970s but after secondary banking crisis Hawtin & Partners was sold to Gilwise, subsidiary of Gulf & Western Associates, USA, in Dec 1974. Sold banking business in 1976 and became property owners and protective clothing manufacturers. In 1983 principal activity was that of holding and management company for subsidiary companies involved in manufacture of specialised knitted fabrics, industrial gloves and clothing; wholesale of industrial gloves, clothing and safety equipment, and chemist sundries; property development, and investment.

Records: at Hawtin, Metropolitan House, Preston New Road, Blackpool, Lancashire FY3 9TJ
directors and general meeting minutes 1936-date; share registers 1889-date; annual reports and accounts 1936-date; Barnet factory: plant inventory and valuation 1945, blue prints 1941
Dental Manufacturing Co (Brazil) Ltd: directors and general meeting minutes 1915-35

168 MANCHESTER JOINT STOCK BANK LTD

21 May 1873
07331
Poultry, London EC2P 2BX
Banking

History: founded in 1836 as a private bank, Robertson, Fraser & Co, in High Street, Manchester, by WM Fraser, formerly of Sewell & Nephew, Manchester, and the National Bank of Scotland. Incorporated with limited liability in 1873 as above. Head offices were moved to Pall Mall in 1875, leaving High Street as a branch, and again in 1879 to King Street. By 1892 had opened 11 branches, all within Manchester. Had abortive amalgamation discussions with other small Lancashire banks and finally amalgamated in 1892 with London & Midland Bank Ltd, renamed London City & Midland Bank Ltd in 1898, London Joint City & Midland Bank Ltd in 1918 and Midland Bank Ltd in 1923.

Records: at Midland Bank, Poultry, London EC2P 2BX
board minutes 1873-92; committee minutes 1882-93; shareholders minutes 1873-92; shareholders list 1890-2; shareholders register 1873-92; share allotment 1873-91; share application register 1873-92; share transfer register 1873-92; proxy register 1892; amalgamation papers and correspondence 1892; half-yearly balance sheets 1873-93; general ledger 1873-92; salaries ledger 1873-85; private letter book 1873-94; correspondence re account 1878

WF Crick and JE Wadsworth, *A Hundred Years of Joint Stock Banking* (1936)

169 PROTECTOR LAMP & LIGHTING CO LTD

30 May 1873
07348
Protector Works, Lansdowne Road, Monton, Eccles, Greater Manchester M30 9PH
Lamp and gauze filter manufacturers

History: incorporated in 1873 to acquire the business and patent rights of WE Teale, oil and lamp manufacturer of Manchester. In early 1890s factory moved to Eccles, Greater Manchester. Manufactured miners' safety, oil, gas and electric lamps and sold lamp oil and spirit under the 'Colzalene' trade name. Established an electric lighting department which in 1884 was converted into Simplex Electric Light & Patent Co Ltd (liquidated 1888). In 1891 patented the successful improved miners' safety lamp developed by Joseph Prestwich, the company's manager. Began to diversify in the 1890s and by 1897 was producing safety valves and water closets. From about 1900 was manufacturing motor vehicles (ceased in 1906) and established an enamelling department which took over the London based Patent Letter & Enamel Co, advertisement sign manufacturers. Also produced brass hinges and other castings. After 1918 flame safety lamps in mines were being replaced by battery lamps although they remained important for methane gas detection. The enamelling business ceased in 1939 and safety lamp demand fell again after 1945. Production of heavy brass hinges and citadel door and window fasteners continued after WW2 but main manufacture was in gauze filters for aircraft and motor industries.

Records: at Protector Lamp & Lighting, Protector Works, Lansdowne Road, Monton, Eccles, Greater Manchester M30 9PH
directors and general meeting minutes: 1882-1935,1960s on, agenda books 1922-40; mortgage register 1900-26; debenture stock: trust deed 1900, allotment lists 1899, certificate book 1900-20, transfer register 1906-19, and documents 1906-15, ledger 1899-1926, interest journal 1900-26; annual reports and accounts 1884-1910; balance sheets and accounts 1898-1906,1909-13; ledger 1876-1906; private ledgers 1891-1912,1940-54; sales ledger 1898-1954; journals 1899-

1922; cash book: 1920-36, petty 1940-8; bank pass book 1925-7; wage books 1900-45; accident book 1939-50; departmental instructions 1903-20; patents list 1911; letter books 1895-1926; easement agreements 1893-1906

Philip Heyes, *The Protector Lamp and Lighting Company Limited 1873-1973: the first hundred years* (priv pub 1973)

170 LEICESTER COAL CONSUMERS CO LTD

4 Jun 1873
07355
15 Loseby Lane, Leicester, Leicestershire
Coal and coke merchants

History: incorporated in 1873 as above to carry on business as coal, coke, fuel and firewood merchants. Registered offices were established at 12 Horsefair Street, Leicester and sites were obtained at Humberstone Road, Westbridge and Soar Lane Wharves. In 1877 purchased site in King Richard Street for new stables, workshop and house. This was sold in 1904 and new stable accommodation bought in Soar Lane. Offices moved to 23 Hotel Street in 1888, and to 15 Loseby Lane in 1958. Purchased coal merchant businesses of THV Allsop, Burton Overy, Leicestershire, and HS Whitehouse Ltd, Belgrave Road, Leicester in 1958. Sold property in Soar Lane in 1959. Went into liquidation in 1983.

Records: at Leicestershire Record Office, 57 New Walk, Leicester, Leicestershire LE1 7JB
directors meeting minutes 1873-1910; share: ledger 1873-1983, certificates and transfer documents 1907-81, dividend warrants 1899-1901; prospectus 1873; memo and articles of association c1948; annual reports and accounts 1875-1926,1945-81; balance sheets and profit and loss accounts 1914-72; management accounts 1968-72; coal account ledgers 1910-73; general ledger 1956-66; cash receipt books 1912,1939,1942; sales record 1958-81; coal: orders 1918-1919, delivery tickets 1942-3, weighing machine vouchers 1912, carriage rates 1920-1, supply licences 1945-6; coal merchant business acquisition correspondence 1957-8; delivery lorry photograph 1930s; Mrs M King (clerk) personal correspondence, papers and family photographs 1918-40s

171 SOWERBY & CO LTD

5 Jun 1873
07362
Cowick Hall, Snaith, Goole, Humberside DN14 9AA
Linseed oil manufacturers

History: incorporated in 1873 as above by group of Humberside farmers and merchants to carry on business of bone crushers and manufacturers of linseed and other cake and oil. Original offices were at River Head, Grimsby, Humberside. Purchased Norfolk Mills, Grimsby in 1902. By 1926 owned the Riverhead Buildings, East Marsh Mill, (given up 1957), Dial Square Mill (dismantled 1954) and Haven Mill (sold 1947) in Grimsby and premises at Boston and Sutton Bridge, Lincolnshire. United Premier Oil & Cake Co Ltd were appointed company's managers in 1930. Seed crushing ceased in about 1954, efforts being concentrated on merchandising fertilizers and manures. Acquired in 1967 by Croda Organisation Ltd and subsequently ceased to trade.

Records: at Croda International, Cowick Hall, Snaith, Goole, Humberside DN14 9AA
directors and general meeting minutes 1891,1914-63; members registers and share ledger 1873-1982; share transfer documents 1874-80; annual returns 1903-17; memo and articles of association 1919-20; partnership agreements 1894,1919; mortgages and charges register 1956; financial statements and reports 1919-55; private ledgers 1915-49; traffic agreements 1854,1902; premises title deeds, documents and correspondence 1854-1914,1951

172 HALLAMSHIRE STEEL CO LTD

19 Jun 1873
07399
9 Albert Embankment, London SE1 7SN
Steel rollers

History: incorporated in 1873 as Hallamshire Steel & File Co Ltd, operating as steel rollers etc from the Hallamshire Works, Sheffield, S Yorkshire. By 1931 products included wire rods, sheets, and all sections of special steels and files. Subsequently changed name to above and became part of British Steel Corporation.

Records: at British Steel Corporation, Northern Regional Records Centre, Unit F2, Commerce Way, Skippers Lane Industrial Estate, South Bank, Middlesbrough, Cleveland TS6 6UT

173 TUTTLE & SON LTD

27 Jun 1873
07420
1 Welbeck Street, London W1A 1DF
Drapers and furnishers

History: formed in 1813 when Benjamin Harvey opened a linen store on the corner of Lowndes Terrace and Sloane Street, Knightsbridge, London, later trading as B Harvey & Co. On his death in late 1850s, business went to his daughter Elizabeth on the condition that she took Colonel Nichols, a silk buyer, into partnership. Harvey Nichols & Co Ltd was incorporated in 1873 to acquire the business and property of Benjamin Charles Harvey on the death of his partner. Company became a fashionable retail house specialising in linens, silks, furnishings and carpets. In about 1900 a new building was opened at 109-125 Knightsbridge and 208-212 Sloane Street. In late 1919 merged with Debenhams Ltd (est 1788) of Wimpole Street, London. Store was redeveloped between 1973 and 1976 but company ceased to trade in 1975. Name changed to above in 1980 and became a finance company.

Records: at Debenhams, 1 Welbeck Street, London W1A 1DF
board meeting minutes 1873-1973; general meeting minutes 1874-1975; share and share transfer registers 1875-c1928; directors register c1940-50s; mortgage registers 1904-36; annual reports and accounts 1934-55; balance sheets 1874-1918; staff committee meeting minutes 1921-8

Maurice Corina, *Fine Silk and Oak Counters Debenhams 1778-1978* (1978)

174 GLOBE INVESTMENT TRUST LTD

11 Jul 1873
07465
Electra House, Victoria Embankment, London WC2R 3HP
Investment

History: formed and incorporated as Globe Telegraph & Trust Co Ltd in 1873 by John Pender, Liberal MP, pioneer of ocean telegraphy and founder of the Eastern & Associated Telegraph Companies group, in order to spread the short term risk of cable laying over a number of companies. Shares in the company were offered in exchange for shares in submarine telegraph and associated companies which were exchanged in 1929 for shares in Cables & Wireless Ltd (later Cable & Wireless (Holdings) Ltd), the company set up to run, through Imperial & International Communications Ltd (later Cable & Wireless Ltd), the overseas telecommunications of the British Empire. Acquired Cables Investment Trust Ltd (became Electra Investment Trust Ltd in 1975) as a subsidiary in 1935. In 1946 when Cable & Wireless Ltd was nationalised, owned a third of the issued capital of Cable & Wireless (Holdings) Ltd which was converted into an investment trust, renamed Cable Trust Ltd in 1971 and merged with Globe in 1977. Since 1948 have been involved in general investment business and in 1981 was one of the largest investment trusts in the UK, holding British and overseas investments. Name changed to above in 1977. Member of the Electra House group of companies.

Records: at Globe Investment Trust, Electra House, Victoria Embankment, London WC2R 3HP
board minutes 1873-date; board papers 1949-date; agm minutes 1873-date; incorporation papers 1873; annual returns 1881-date; misc correspondence 1949-date

KC Baglehole, *A Century of Service. A brief history of Cable and Wireless Ltd 1868-1968* (1969)
Hugh Barty-King, *Girdle Round the Earth* (1979)

175 NEUCHATEL ASPHALTE CO LTD

29 Jul 1873
07512
PO Box 8, Ettingshall, Wolverhampton, W Midlands WV4 6JP
Asphalt

History: incorporated as above in 1873 to take over certain concessions from Neuchatel government, originally held by Neuchatel Bituminous Rock Co Ltd (inc 1871) to work the Val de Travers mines in Switzerland, to acquire the undertakings of Neuchatel Rock Paving Co Ltd; Anglo-Austrian, Anglo-German, Anglo-Hungarian and Belgian-Dutch Bituminous Rock Paving Companies Ltd and South American Val de Travers Rock Paving Co Ltd and obtain and sell rock and mastic asphalt. South American agency was sold in 1875. During 1880s and 1890s contracts were obtained for supplying asphalt for paving the streets of large continental towns. Acquired Belgian Neuchatel Asphalte Co Ltd (est 1879 to execute pavings) in 1890 and the Abruzzi asphalt mines in Italy in 1895. Faced serious problems during WW1 and WW2 as many mines were in enemy hands. Acquired sole concession to Val de Travers asphalt mine in Seyssel, France in 1949. By 1957 had the following UK subsidiaries: Cray

River Sand & Gravel Co Ltd: Mendip Stone & Concrete Co Ltd; Neuchatel Asphalte Co (Overseas) Ltd; and Neuchatel Anti-Corrosion Ltd, and others in Australia, France and West Germany. Acquired in 1965 by Derbyshire Stone Ltd (inc 1935) which merged in 1968 with Tarmac Ltd and William Briggs & Sons Ltd to form Tarmac Derby Ltd, renamed Tarmac Ltd in 1971.

Records: at Tarmac, PO Box 8, Ettingshall, Wolverhampton, W Midlands WV4 6JP
directors meeting minutes: 1873-1969, private 1945-64; general meeting minutes 1873-1969; 4 per cent debenture stockholders meeting minutes 1944-66; annual reports and accounts 1874-1968

176 JOHN TUCKEY & CO LTD

3 Sep 1873
07618
20 Brook Street, Mayfair, London W1
Linen wholesalers and retailers

History: reputedly founded in 1764, trading as House of Tuckey from Duke Street, Mayfair, where it remained until 1908 when it moved to Wigmore Street. Moved to its present address in the 1940s. Manchester branch dealt mainly with the wholesale business until John Tuckey (Wholesale and Export) Co Ltd was incorporated in 1949 as a subsidiary to manage the export trade. Taken over in 1957 by the National Linen Co Ltd.

Records: at National Linen, 20 Brook Street, Mayfair, London W1
directors and general minutes 1873-date; royal appointments 1892, 1907; sales catalogue c1955

177 STAFFORD COAL & IRON CO LTD

10 Sep 1873
07638
Cockshutt Lane, Broseley, Salop TF12 5NN
Coal and iron manufacturers

History: incorporated as above in 1873 to exploit minerals in Great Fenton, Stoke on Trent, Staffordshire. Acquired adjoining mineral area and surface lands in 1913 and further mineral area and surface lands. Taken over by National Coal Board at nationalization of coal mining industry in 1947.

Records: Staffordshire Record Office, County Buildings, Eastgate Street, Stafford, Staffordshire ST16 2LZ
papers re costs, absenteeism, output, manpower, equipment, shifts, trading accounts, district comparisons, profits, coal charges 1932-46; correspondence 1904; colliery papers and correspondence incl plans 1935-42; salary books 1923-46; North Staffs Colliery Owners Association papers and correspondence 1931-9

178 GRAMORS LTD

15 Sep 1873
07651
NEI House, Regent Centre, Gosforth, Tyne & Wear NE3 3SB
Investment (formerly saltpetre refiners)

History: incorporated in 1873 as East London Saltpetre Works Ltd to purchase saltpetre (nitrate of potash) refining business of Benjamin Thomas Simmons, manufacturing chemist at Henry Street, Mount Pleasant, Limehouse, along with the goodwill, plant and premises. S Tudor & Sons acted as sole agents and shippers of company's saltpetre to Portugal and Spain. Name changed to above in 1958, and acquired by Brandram Brothers & Co Ltd, white lead, paint and saltpetre manufacturers of Rotherhithe, London. Objects were changed in 1967 to stock and share underwriters and dealers. By 1976 was subsidiary of International Combustion (Holdings) Ltd which in 1981 was a subsidiary of Northern Engineering Industries Ltd. In 1981 company acted as investment and property dealers. Liquidator appointed in Dec 1981.

Records: none survive

179 BRIGHTON COLLEGE

18 Sep 1873
07663
Eastern Road, Brighton, E Sussex BN2 2AL
School

History: founded in 1845 and opened in Portland Place, Brighton, with 47 boys attending in 1847. Moved into buildings designed by Sir George Gilbert Scott in Eastern Road in 1849, which were greatly expanded in the 1880s. Despite serious financial problems in the 1890s and 1930s, the college has catered continuously for the education of boys of all ages, the majority being boarders. After WW2 a rapid recovery took place and in 1973 almost 400 boys were at the college, which also admitted girls during the 1970s. It was incorporated as a charitable institution with limited liability in 1873.

Records (1): at Brighton College, Eastern Road, Brighton, E Sussex BN2 2AL
council minutes 1845-date; council agendas 1873-1951; finance committee minutes 1887-95,1933-68; scholarships and prize endowments trustee minutes 1901-71; building and standing committee minutes 1913-27; general purposes committee 1955-68; centenary endowment and war memorial fund minutes 1955-71; rules and regulations 1846-83; list of proprietors 1874-89; share register 1846-1936; share transfer register 1873-1946; share and share transfer certificates 1874-1958; register of debenture interest payments 1910-34; register of mortgages and bonds 1873-c91; legal documents, papers and correspondence re founding of college and mortgages 1841-1950; legal papers and correspondence re incorporation of college 1862-1957; memo and articles of association 1873-1973; grant of arms 1920; annual returns 1935-57; annual reports 1864-1918; audited accounts 1884-1970; general ledger 1846-1935; nominal ledger 1913-34; building fund ledger 1928-65; personal ledger 1931-49; building ledger 1956-62; fees ledger 1906-63; junior school fees ledger 1946-8,1965; notices re fees 1930s-70s; journals 1910-56; tuition fees account book 1847-54; treasurers account book 1848-78; boarding fees account books 1930-9; income account book 1952-7; building fund account

book 1956-62; bursars cash book 1929-39; Dawson Memorial Fund cash book and correspondence 1938-40; secretarys petty cash book 1849-60; petty cash book 1907-20; bills and receipts 1845-1968; correspondence, minutes, reports, surveys etc re building fund appeal 1928-80; college: registers 1847-1969, rolls 1886-1981; class lists 1858-1905; junior school rolls and registers 1957-79; house rolls 1914-80; scholarship rolls 1925-48; legal documents, reports, papers and correspondence re scholarships and examinations 1863-1980; Old Brightonian Association: minutes 1892-1923, account book 1928-39, visitors book 1926-51; correspondence and papers re houses, pupils and the OBA 1851-date; board of education inspectors reports 1911-61; correspondence and papers: re college library 1849-1979; teaching of science 1955-70s; correspondence, newscuttings, membership cards, programmes, results, publicity photographs etc re sporting and other clubs 1848-date; *Brighton College Magazine* 1858-date; junior school, house and unofficial magazines 1921-80; salary scales 1937-51; papers and correspondence re staff appointments and salaries 1930s-78; salaries account books 1936-64; staff tenancy agreements 1887-1964; staff pension scheme: minutes 1924-44, accounts 1925-43, legal documents and correspondence 1908-50s; correspondence and papers of George Long, classics master 1840s, and GP Burstow, history master and vice-principal 1924-75; misc staff papers 1872-1970; title deeds and correspondence re college premises and land 1849-1929; correspondence and papers re building of college 1845-93; inventories of buildings and furnishings 1881-1948; documents and correspondence re insurance 1882-1954; college plans c1863-1971; legal documents, papers and correspondence re chapel and choir 1847-1980; chapel baptism, marriage and confirmation registers 1903-80; letter books 1845-89; headmasters correspondence and papers 1845-date; secretarys correspondence 1848-99; bursars correspondence 1953-75; general correspondence 1882-1975; correspondence register 1875-82; photographs of college buildings, staff, pupils and council members 1848-1980; *Brighton College Year* (film) 1950s; notes, histories and articles on the college 1883-1972; newscuttings re the college 1847-1977; college and junior school calendars 1922-80

Records (2): at Griffith, Smith, Dodd & Riley, 47 Old Steine, Brighton, E Sussex
title deeds and legal documents re college land 1848-92

GP Burstow, MB Whittaker and SC Roberts, *A History of Brighton College* (1957)

180 LONDON & COUNTY GLAZING CO LTD

10 Oct 1873
07710
1 Bartholomew Lane, London EC2N 2AB
Insurance

History: incorporated in 1873 as London & County Plate Glass Insurance Co Ltd to carry on business of insuring plate glass against damage and other insurance business except life assurance. Original registered offices were at 4 St Paul's Churchyard, London, moving to Ludgate Hill, in 1885, and to Edward Street, (renamed Chancel Street) Blackfriars, in 1919. Acquired by Sun Fire Office Ltd in 1909 and became its plate glass insurance department. Changed name to London & County Insurance Co Ltd in 1929 and to above in 1973. Sun Insurance Office merged with Alliance Assurance Co Ltd in 1959 to form Sun Alliance Insurance Group and with the London Assurance in 1965 to form Sun Alliance & London Insurance Group. Company carries out plate glass replacement in the UK on behalf of other companies in Sun Alliance & London Insurance Group.

Records: at Sun Alliance Insurance Group, 1 Bartholomew Lane, London EC2N 2AB
current records

181 RYLANDS & SONS LTD

25 Oct 1873
07748
PO Box 99, 3 Dale Street, Manchester, Greater Manchester M60 1XA
Textile manufacturers and general warehousemen

History: established in 1823 by John Rylands (1801-88) in Manchester as warehousemen, cotton spinners, manufacturers, bleachers, dyers etc. A London office was opened in 1849 and firm was incorporated as above in 1873. By 1923 had offices in New High Street, Manchester, 55 Wood Street, London, and Lime Street, Liverpool; warehouses in Manchester, London and Liverpool, Sydney and Melbourne, Australia and Cape Town, South Africa; factories including cotton spinning and weaving mills in London, Manchester, Gorton, Wigan and Swinton, Greater Manchester, Heapey and Chorley, Lancashire; and about 8000 staff. Products included floor oilcloths, waddings, clothing, underclothing, furniture and bedding. Acquired in 1953 by Great Universal Stores Ltd. By 1957 owned Dacca Mills Ltd (formerly Rylands & Sons (Overseas) Ltd), Lintex Ltd, Vyse Sons & Co Ltd and Stapley & Smith Ltd. Wholesaling trade was transferred to Dacca Ltd in 1966 and company subsequently ceased to trade.

Records: at John Rylands University Library of Manchester, Deansgate, Manchester, Greater Manchester M3 3EH
directors meeting: minutes 1873-1956, attendances 1899-1956, information 1873-1918; governors minutes 1873-88; general meeting minutes 1874-1913; co-partnership articles 1860; memo and articles of association 1873; purchase agreement 1873; prospectus 1874; debenture prospectus 1889; annual reports and accounts 1902-13,1924-59; works: profit and loss accounts 1847-54, and ledger 1811-44, ledger 1824-41; balance sheets 1873-1950; petty ledger 1827-47; loan documents 1879-89; trade-mark: album 1879-1957, register 1886, correspondence 1933-5; catalogue and price lists 1908-39; mill production policy conference papers 1921; wages ledger 1870-80; traveller agreement 1927; staff: club rules 1892, consideration fund conditions 1920-3; estates capital accounts 1942-68; property: plans c1860-1960, register c1860-1960, title deeds, documents and papers 1742-1969, valuation 1921, photographs 1930 on

182 LIVERPOOL STORAGE CO LTD

6 Nov 1873
07787
165 Queen Victoria Street, London EC4V 4EE
Storage

History: established and incorporated as above in 1873 as warehouse owners in Birkenhead and Liverpool for the storage of lubricating and burning oils. First depots were at Wallasey, Merseyside, and then at Manchester with smaller ones in other northwest Lancashire towns. It was the first company in the north of England to specialise in bulk oil storage. First storage tanks, built in 1885-6, were still in use in 1981. Registered offices were at 13 Rumford Street,

Liverpool, until 1957 when company was acquired by Stevenson, Hardy & Co. The Manchester and Liverpool depots were closed between 1957 and 1969 and the working sites are now at Eltham, Wirral and Wallasey and Birkenhead, Merseyside. In 1969 Jessel Securities Ltd took over the company which was subsequently bought by Panocean Shipping & Terminals Ltd in 1972.

Records (1): at Liverpool Storage, 165 Queen Victoria Street, London EC4V 4EE
directors minutes 1881-4; general meeting minutes 1892-1943

Records (2): at Panocean Storage & Transport, Power House Road, Eastham, Wirral, Merseyside
directors minutes 1873-80,1884-1957; finance committee minutes 1900-39; agenda book 1885-1902; register of shareholders 1883-1927; share ledger 1902-20; share transfer ledger 1951-7; memo and articles of association 1949; annual returns 1942-8; annual reports and accounts 1951-78; rough ledger 1959-66; journal 1968-70; cash books: Birkenhead 1916-47, Liverpool 1909-39, Manchester 1919-56; costings and budgeting papers 1971-2; tank books 1897-1972; handling charges book 1964-73; custom entries book 1966-71; technical notes on tanks 1930s; tank diagrams 1971; staff pension scheme trust deed 1960; leases of Liverpool office 1919-32; schedule of title deeds 1873-1957; land and tank plans c1940-69; inventory and valuations of sites and plant 1920-65; lists of tanks, buildings and fittings 1959-72; photographs of plant, premises, pipeline and staff c1900-67; company history notes 1973

183 MITCHELL'S AUCTION CO LTD

8 Nov 1873
07796
Fairfield House, Agricultural Hall, Cockermouth, Cumbria CA13 9PY
Auctioneers, valuers and estate agents

History: established at Cockermouth in 1860 by Robinson Mitchell, ex journeyman shoemaker who became an auctioneer and appraiser in 1849. First premises were near the Fairfield and in 1865 the Agricultural Hall, the first auction mart in Cumbria was opened. Known as Mitchell, Bowe & Mitchell until incorporation as above in 1873. Sales of real estate, furniture and farming stock etc continued to be undertaken by R&JR Mitchell, later known as JR Mitchell & Sons. This business purchased by company in 1947. Also purchased Farmers' Auction Co Ltd (est in Cockermouth in early 1870s) in 1921 and the Whitehaven & West Cumberland Auctioneering Co Ltd, owners of the Whitehaven Mart, in 1960. Cockermouth Auction Mart was remodelled in 1904 with alterations carried out in 1950s, an abbatoir built in 1963 and a restaurant built in 1964. In 1982 had premises in Whitehaven, Workington and Cockermouth.

Records: at Mitchell's Auction, Fairfield House, Agricultural Hall, Cockermouth, Cumbria CA13 9PY
directors meeting minutes 1903-date; general meeting minutes 1922-date; share ledger and registers 1873 on; annual reports and accounts 1921-date; hand bills re auctions 1826-68; photographs: sheep sales 1875-1920s, directors 19-20 cent, sales rings and marts 20 cent; history 1973

Centenary 1873-1973 of Mitchell's Auction Company Limited (priv pub 1973)

184 RIVERS STEAM NAVIGATION CO LTD

12 Nov 1873
07806
40 St Mary Axe, London EC3A 8EU
Shipping

History: founded in 1862 as New Rivers Co by Capt JH Williamson, tea merchant, to transport passengers and goods on the River Ganges. Soon expanded into Assam. Changed name to Rivers Steam Co in 1865. Incorporated in London as above in 1873 with the Macneill and Mackinnon families, who were to form the basis of the Inchcape group of companies, as the prominent shareholders. Begg, Dunlop & Co were the company's managing agents from 1865-72, being succeeded by Macneill & Co. Known as the Joint Steamer Companies along with India General Steam Navigation Co (est 1844) after a joint agreement of 1889. The company provided steam navigation in Iraq as well as India during both World Wars. The partition of India after WW2 led to the division of the fleet and other serious difficulties. In 1959 the Pakistan River Steamers Co Ltd was incorporated to operate the Pakistani fleet of the joint companies from 1 Jan 1961. The company took over the Indian assets of the IGSN Co Ltd in 1962 and incorporated the Rivers Steam Navigation Co (Holdings) Ltd to consolidate their Pakistani interests. In 1965 the Indian assets were sold to the Indian government for £1. The Indo-Pakistan war caused further problems, culminating on 26 Mar 1972 with the nationalization by the Bangladesh government of Bangladesh River Steamers Ltd, the renamed PRS Co Ltd.

Records: at Inchcape, 40 St Mary Axe, London EC3A 8EU
board and general minutes 1887-1956; financial statements presented to board 1910-16; papers re administrative reorganisation 1951-7; register of members 1874-1935; share ledger 1935-42; register of transfers and probates 1873-1934; share, stock and share transfer certificates 1874-1949; dividend register 1930-54; correspondence re shares 1891-1967; debenture: register 1880-1935, receipt books 1921-45, lists and interest coupons 1910-53, summary book 1939-49; memo and articles of association 1873-1918; reconstruction papers 1946-67; power of attorney 1869; copy letters, agreements and minutes with railway companies, re transport 1906-27; correspondence and documents re legal cases 1892-1910; seal register 1909-48; annual returns 1906-57; audited accounts 1906-57; half yearly accounts: general 1915-48, Calcutta 1938-57, Pakistan 1952-7, India 1952-5; statements of accounts 1924-42; statements of estimated expenditure 1949-54; accounting working papers 1918-58; ledgers 1873-1961; Calcutta account books 1916-28; journals 1876-1964; cash book 1928-37; ships sailing reports 1891-3; joint passenger service time tables 1935-59; route maps 1893-1948; fleet lists c1910-28; fleet register 1938-61; wear and tear schedules 1944-50; river traffic survey reports 1938-60; traffic register 1955; Pakistani and Indian superintendent engineers reports 1952-60; Calcutta inland steamer exports register 1954; final trip data 1924-40; correspondence: re Indian and Pakistani mail 1957-62, Assam coal contract 1959-63, traffic, vessel repair, buildings and accidents and reorganisation 1922-64, impressment of vessels 1939-47; plans and specifications of vessels 1939-65; photographs of deep sea barges and repair of *TSMV Sangola* 1948-55; inventory of tools and machinery 1950s; premises depreciation ledger 1950-60; property notes c1950; staff provident institution: directors report 1947,1960, statement of accounts 1952-3; historical notes on personnel c1953; notes on London letters 1875-1900; letter book 1909; correspondence and papers re agms, agendas,

agreements, finance, tours, transport, staff and buildings 1906-67; correspondence and press cuttings re Pakistani political and economic situation 1953-60; historical notes on company and partition 1928-42
Pakistan Rivers Steamers Co Ltd: proposals and prospectus 1959; memo and articles of association 1958-9; annual report and accounts 1962; catamaran water bus specifications 1965
Rivers Steam Navigation Co (Holdings) Ltd: memo and articles of association 1962; dividend lists and annual report and accounts 1957-62

Sir Percival Griffiths, *A History of the Inchcape Group* (1977)

185 CHESTER DIOCESAN BOARD OF FINANCE

18 Nov 1873
07826
Diocesan House, Raymond Street, Chester, Cheshire CH1 4PN
Church finance

History: formed in 1871 as Chester Diocesan Fund Association to collect, receive and distribute funds for diocesan societies and to act as trustees of money or property given or bequeathed to the Church of England within the diocese. Incorporated in 1873 as a company limited by guarantee. First offices were at 3 Union Court, Castle Street, Liverpool. In 1880 the Diocese of Liverpool was formed. The Liverpool Diocesan Fund Association was set up in 1883, the older association moving to Chester. Name changed to above in 1927.

Records (1): Chester Diocesan Board of Finance, Diocesan House, Raymond Street, Chester, Cheshire CH1 4PN
board: meeting minutes 1936-date, sub-committee meeting minutes 1963-date, annual meeting minutes 1937-date; committee meeting minutes: emergency 1939-45, benefices augmentation fund 1945-59, spiritual aid fund 1946-59, pastoral reorganisation 1953-9, press and publication 1955-68, pastoral 1957-date; Queen Victoria Jubilee Clergy Pension Fund meeting minutes 1887-1914,1954-7; ordination candidates fund meeting minutes 1931-55; Warrington Institutions Widows & Orphans meeting minutes 1939-72; diocesan: pensions fund board meeting minutes 1946-57, conference minutes 1905-69, council and bishops council meeting minutes 1967-date, and association organisation reports 1873-date, calendars 1941-date, conference handbook 1926-32; Cheshire churches planning committee meeting minutes 1964-70

Records (2): at Cheshire Record Office, The Castle, Chester, Cheshire CH1 2DN
general committee meeting minutes 1873-1936; sub-committee meeting minutes: finance 1873-1938, investment 1879-1917, assessment appeals 1927-34; annual reports 1955-68; balance sheets 1941-55; general ledgers 1875-1951; ledger 1937-55; diocesan church aid fund ledger 1957-9; investments 1881-1958; securities record 1888-1934; journal 1905-46; cash books 1917-59; appeal fund: ledger 1937-44, statements and papers 1937-49, cash book 1937-56; thanksgiving appeal: meeting minutes 1945-56, ledger, cash book, statements, correspondence and leaflets 1945-53

186 GREENCOAT INDUSTRIES LTD
22 Nov 1873
07836
North West House, 119-127 Marylebone Road, London NW1 5QB
Gas, chemicals

History: incorporated in 1873 as Gas Purification & Chemical Co Ltd to deal in products used in purification of gas, chemicals and other materials. Offices were at 160-162 Palmerston Buildings, Old Broad Street, London. From 1950s acted as holding company, being taken over in 1967 by British Industrial Holdings Ltd which was taken over by Greenbrook Securities Ltd in 1977. Name subsequently changed to above and was a dormant company in 1981.

Records: at Greenbrook Securities, North West House, 119-127 Marylebone Road, London NW1 5QB
certificate of incorporation 1873; memo and articles of association 1954; correspondence re duplicate keys 1874

187 CANTRELL & COCHRANE (NORTHERN) LTD
12 Dec 1873
07900
Club House, Hamworth Road, Sunbury, Surrey TW16 5DF
Soft drinks

History: incorporated in 1873 as Apollinaris Co Ltd, whose main business was natural mineral water importers. Offices in early 1890s were at 19 Regent Street, London, moving to 4 Stratford Place, Oxford Street, in 1895. Purchased by Cantrell & Cochrane Ltd, Irish soft drinks manufacturers (est 1852) in late 1920s/early 1930s. Name changed to Forward Industries (Mineral Waters) Ltd in 1963 and to Cantrell & Cochrane (Soft Drinks) Ltd in 1965. Amalgamated in 1969 with soft drink companies of Courage, Barclay & Simonds Ltd, Schweppes Ltd and Watney Mann Ltd to form Cantrell & Cochrane (Great Britain) Ltd. Company's name changed to above and became trading company of new concern in north England and Scotland, all links with original Irish company terminating except in use of trade-marks. Head office and factory were situated in Stockport, Greater Manchester. In 1981 was registered as a private company and was a dormant member of Watney Mann & Truman Brewers Ltd, a subsidiary of Grand Metropolitan Ltd.

Records: at Coca-Cola Southern Bottlers, Club House, Hamworth Road, Sunbury, Surrey TW16 5DF
board minutes 1971-80; corporate documents incl memo and articles of association 1971-80; audited accounts 1970 on; employee agreement 1934; photographs of vans, staff etc 1929 on; label books 1930 on
Chemists' Aerated & Mineral Waters Association: minutes 1882-1961

188 BIRKBECK SECURITIES LTD

27 Jan 1874
08032
Cemetery Lodge, Elmers End Road, Beckenham, Kent BR3 4TD
Cemetery

History: incorporated in 1874 as Crystal Palace District Cemetery Co Ltd to establish a cemetery on 41 acres of land fronting Elmers End Road, Beckenham, Kent, bought in 1868 by the London & Suburban Land & Building Co Ltd. The latter company was established in 1852 to purchase freehold land, its shareholders being offered shares in the cemetery company. Cemetery was opened in 1876. The number of burials fell sharply after WW2 and by 1951 the company was seeking permission to convert a cemetery chapel into a crematorium. In 1953 work began on the crematorium which was opened in 1956. In 1970 283 burials and 2212 cremations took place. Name changed to Beckenham Crematorium Ltd in 1970 and to above in 1979.

Records: at Birkbeck Securities, Cemetery Lodge, Elmers End Road, Beckenham, Kent BR3 4TD
general meeting minutes 1874-1981; prospectuses 1873; memo and articles of association 1873-1970; corporate documents 1874,1970,1979; annual reports and accounts 1886-1981; financial notebook 1876-1904; fees scale 1883; cemetery authorisation letters 1870-6; title deeds, mortgage and property documents 1868-1963; cemetery plans 1872-5,1918; burial registers 1876-date; cremation registers 1956-date

189 JESSEL TRUST LTD

3 Feb 1874
08057
6 Vincent Square, London SW1
Investment

History: incorporated in Manchester in 1874 as Manchester Bonding Warehousing Co Ltd. Changed name to above in 1971 following reorganisation as a holding company for a group of investment companies.

Records: at Jessel Trust, 6 Vincent Square, London SW1
board and general meeting minutes 1971-date; share papers 1971-date; memo and articles of association 1971; annual reports and accounts 1971-date; accounting working papers 1971-date

190 CAPITAL GUARANTEE SOCIETY LTD

23 Feb 1874
08092
1 Noble Street, London EC2V 7DA
Finance

History: incorporated in 1874 as General Expenditure Assurance Co Ltd and renamed as above in 1881. Proposed to operate 'a system of investment for the redemption of capital, applied to trade, commerce and financial undertakings, as well as to domestic expenditure of all kinds.' Coupons of any denominated value were sold at 5 per cent of their face value to tradesmen, who sold them to their customers at a discounted price on their denominated value. Customers then used the coupons for purchases from the distributing tradesmen. The company guaranteed to pay the customer the difference between the denominated value and the discounted price when the coupons had been exchanged for purchases. This payment was financed by the proceeds of and interest earned on sales to tradesmen. Branch offices were established in Dublin, Edinburgh, Glasgow, Liverpool and Paris. The company ceased trading in 1883, was then placed in liquidation but not removed from the register.

Records: enquiries to Business Archives Council, 185 Tower Bridge Road, London SE1 2UF meeting minutes: directors c1870-82, shareholders 1874-91, general and committee 1874-9, finance 1875-83; register: directors attendance 1878-83, members 1874-80; share: list of holders 1878, warrant books 1874-5, dividends 1880, and transferred certificates 1875-82; mortgage debentures 1880-1943; correspondence re shares and shares, bond and policy holders 1875-8; documents and papers re liquidation 1883-1909; liquidators returns 1883-1913; bonds: and shareholders claims c1883-1943, list of holders 1875-6, register c1871-81, sold and rebated 1875-83, certificates and receipts 1875-82; coupons issued, received and returned 1876-81; lists of contributors, certificates and bonds 1883-7; articles of association 1877; corporate agreements 1874-8; ledger balances and balance sheets 1882-4; draft accounts and statements 1893-1909; journal and ledger 1875-83; stock journal c1877-83; trial balances and accounts 1877-81; coupon: accounts 1874-84, day books 1875-7; cash books 1874-81; bank pass book 1883-92; invoice copy book 1876-80; accounting papers 1875-83; monthly sales summaries and advertisements 1874-80; trade list tables and order books 1875-6; letter books: 1874-80, liquidators 1883-95; postage and parcel book 1874-80; correspondence 1875-8; clerks salary book 1875-7; canvassers book c1876-9; London office inventory and valuation 1883

191 WARRINGTON LAND & PROPERTY CO LTD

27 Feb 1874
08118
31 Bold Street, Warrington, Cheshire
Property investment

History: incorporated in 1874 as Warrington Loan Land & Property Investment Co Ltd to buy, sell and deal in land and to lend money. Original registered offices were at 68 Buttermarket Road, Warrington, Cheshire, moving to Bewsy Chambers in 1885, 41 Leigh Street in 1921 and to 31 Bold Street in 1947. Name changed to above in 1881. From 1968 also held quoted investments. Went into voluntary liquidation in 1971.

Records: none survive

192 COUNTY ESTATE & LAND CO LTD

25 Apr 1874
08298
254 Oldham Road, Grotton, Oldham, Greater Manchester OL4 5SE
Property

History: incorporated as above in Oldham, Greater Manchester in 1874 to purchase building land and buildings which were to be improved and let. The original registered offices were at 2 Clegg Street, Oldham. By 1907 had purchased 157 dwelling houses and 3 shops at Oldham and Royton, Greater Manchester. In 1975 the offices of the company moved to 254 Oldham Road and company's business was the management of cottage properties and investment of securities. Voluntary liquidation commenced in 1979 and the company dissolved in 1982.

Records: none survive

193 HYDRAULIC ENGINEERING CO LTD

29 Aug 1874
08308
Charles Street, Chester, Cheshire CH1 3HL
Manufacturers hydraulic plant

History: incorporated as above in 1874 to take over the business of mechanical engineers carried on by Johnson & Ellington of Chester (founded 1869). In 1886 had offices at 9 Bridge Street, Westminster, London and a factory at Charles Street, Chester. By 1890 company had supplied hydraulic equipment to the Mersey Docks and Harbour Board and Bolton and Birmingham Corporations. Between 1904 and 1908 premises and buildings were extended. During both WWs the factory was given over to government work. By 1923 had branches in Hull, Humberside, Cardiff and Newcastle upon Tyne. A new market was found in the export of machinery for cleaning with sisal, leading to the formation of a subsidiary, Decorticators Ltd in 1930. In 1957 became a subsidiary of Esanes Ltd. In early 1980s was still involved in the production of hydraulic machinery.

Records: at Hydraulic Engineering, Charles Street, Chester, Cheshire CH1 3HL
board, committee and general meeting minutes with annual accounts 1886-1977; directors register 1901-77; preference share book 1892-1966; memo and articles of association 1874,1950; seal register 1884-1984; machinery registers 1877-1984; drawing office order book 1911-26; order number scale drawings c1920 on; plans: new offices 1906, works 1921,1927; Brook Street boundary on 1940
Decorticators Ltd: share ledgers 1930-40

194 MERSEYSIDE CHAMBER OF COMMERCE & INDUSTRY

5 May 1874
08324
1 Old Hall Street, Liverpool, Merseyside L3 9HG
Chamber of commerce

History: founded as Liverpool Chamber of Commerce in Feb 1850, with 473 individuals and firms joining in first year. Membership reached 610 by 1865 and 807 by 1900. Registered as company limited by guarantee in 1874 as Incorporated Chamber of Commerce of Liverpool to promote and protect trade and manufacturers in Liverpool, Merseyside. From 1902 published monthly journal. First offices were in Exchange Buildings, moving to Old Hall Street (rebuilt 1964) in 1936. Changed name to Liverpool Chamber of Commerce & Industry in 1965 and to above in 1972. In 1981 acted as a business centre, giving information, help and advice to its members.

Records (1): at Merseyside Chamber of Commerce & Industry, 1 Old Hall Street, Liverpool, Merseyside L3 9HG
council, general, committees, country and trade section meeting minutes c1925-date; special committee reports 1854-76; annual reports and accounts 1850-date; members lists 1850-1914,1947-date; monthly journal 1902-date; misc papers 19-20 cent

Records (2): at Liverpool Record Office, City Libraries, William Brown Street, Liverpool, Merseyside L3 8EW
council and general meeting minutes 1860-1925; committee meeting minutes: arbitration 1914-45, commercial law 1897-1922, executive 1902-25, finance, library and members 1871-1909, general purposes 1882-1925, local Mersey district 1917-19, merchants executive 1917-22, motor transport 1917-28, special 1894-1925, port trade 1903, traffic 1919-20, misc 1923-7; light railways committee report 1898; trade section minutes: African 1902-25, American, South and Central 1917-24, East India and China 1891-1930, Greece and Levant 1919-24, Italian 1919-21, Russian 1902-24, West India and Cuba 1902-12, animal and meat trades 1903-12, canned goods 1906-25, coal 1916-80, hide and leather 1918-30, iron and general metal 1896-1920, iron, steel, tinplate and metal merchants 1918-34, motor 1918-33, tea 1917-20, timber 1917-20, tobacco 1890-1918, toy and fancy 1916-19; directors register nd; members register nd; accounts 1905-22; subscriptions books 1913-22; monthly magazine cash book 1905-26

195 HOLYWELL TEXTILE MILLS LTD

20 May 1874
08384
Upper Mill, 29 Greenfield Street, Holywell, Clwyd, CH8 7NU
Woollen cloth manufacturers

History: incorporated in 1874 by Urias Bromley and William Brown of Browns of Chester Ltd as Welsh Flannel Manufacturing Co Ltd to acquire business of Richard Baldwin & Co Ltd, flannel manufacturers in Holywell, Clwyd. Installed new machinery in the existing mills which soon had 80 water powered looms producing 60 pieces of cloth per week. Demand for flannel declined in 1890s. By 1914, when name was changed to above, new products had been developed such as union shirtings, Welsh tweeds and blankets. Survived slump of early 1920s and by 1925 more than 200 looms were in operation. After WW2 products again changed, womens' coating cloths being manufactured for London and foreign markets, and the woollen upholstery and curtain material trade being developed. The textile depression of the 1950s effected the company badly and in 1957 a private investment company acquired its shares in order to keep the mill in operation. Products again changed to tapestry and honeycomb bedspreads and blankets and travel rugs, only the manufacture of a few Welsh flannel and velour cloths being retained. In the late 1960s Welsh blankets, tweeds, flannel and travel rugs, and tapestry cloths proved popular and in the early 1980s company concentrating on high quality woollen cloth.

Records: at Holywell Textile Mills, 29 Greenfield Street, Holywell, Clwyd, CH8 7NU
board and special committee meeting minutes 1899-1964; corporate documents and papers 1899-1958; share and share transfer documents 1891-1950; dividend accounts 1944-52; memo and articles of association 1877-c1950; mortgages and bonds register c1886-95; debentures register c1922; annual returns c1949-57; directors reports and balance sheets 1895-1955; statement of accounts with working papers 1886-1924,1936-48; draft accounts 1957,1960-2;

trade-mark litigation papers 1960-4; buildings, plant and machinery valuation and inventory 1941; machinery supply correspondence 1909-26; title deeds and other property documents and correspondence 1857-1980; works fund draft constitution nd; employees welfare fund subscribers accounts list nd; correspondence re war service deferment of LM Harris 1941-3

Welsh Shirt Manufacturers Association: minutes 1917-22

196 HOLBORN VIADUCT LAND CO LTD

29 May 1874
08414
4 Carlton Gardens, Pall Mall, London SW1Y 5AB
Property

History: incorporated in 1874 to take over the building leases of several pieces of ground on north and south sides of Holborn Viaduct, London granted to Richard Tress in 1872. Registered offices were established at 19&20 Holborn Viaduct. Acquired in about 1959 by Central & District Properties Ltd which was acquired in about 1974 by Town & City Properties Ltd.

Records: at Town & City Properties, 4 Carlton Gardens, Pall Mall, London SW1Y 5AB
current records and registration papers

197 HULL STEARINE & WAREHOUSING CO LTD

3 Jul 1874
08528
Lever House, Bebington, Wirral, Merseyside
Stearine manufacturers and warehousemen

History: incorporated as Kingston upon Hull Stearine Co Ltd in 1874 to carry on business of stearine (a mixture of fatty acids used for candles) manufacturers, warehousemen, especially of oil and turpentine, and manufacturers, merchants, distillers and refiners of turpentine, mucilage, grease, pitch, oleine and other products. Offices were in Cleveland Street, Hull, Humberside. Changed name to above in 1906. Taken over in 1908 by British Oil & Cake Mills Ltd (est 1899) which amalgamated with Lever Brothers Ltd, soap manufacturers, in 1925. Has not traded since 1939 although works continued operating until 1952. In 1981 was dormant company within Unilever Ltd.

Records: at Unilever, Unilever House, Blackfriars, London EC4P 4BQ
directors and general meeting: minutes 1874-date, agendas 1947-53; shareholders ledger 1874-1939; members and share transfers register 1874-1954; directors register 1940-54; share documents 1906-58; memo and articles of association 1906-date; bonds and mortgages register 1876-1917; audited balance sheets, trading and profit and loss accounts 1938-40

Harold W Brace, *History of Seed Crushing in Great Britain* (1960)

198 SHREWSBURY TOOL & DIE CO LTD

31 Jul 1874
08614
Harlescott Lane, Shrewsbury, Salop SY1 3AS
Engineering (previously safe manufacture)

History: Thomas Milner supplied strong boxes etc prior to establishing a safe manufactory in Liverpool in 1830. He was joined by his son, William and in 1874 Milners' Safe Co Ltd was incorporated to take over the business of Thomas Milner & Son. Absorbed Milners' Safety Cycle Co Ltd (inc 1896) in 1898 and formed a subsidiary Milners' Safe Co (South Africa) Ltd in 1900. By 1923 was specialising in fire and thief resisting safes, strong rooms, and steel office furniture and fittings from its head office in Moorgate, London and Phoenix Works, Liverpool. A new factory at Speke, Merseyside was built between 1938 and 1940. Produced tanks, armoured turrets, shells and Mulberry harbour units during WW2. Closed 2 of its subsidiaries in 1954: Mincing Lane Safe Deposit Co Ltd (inc 1896) and Whitfields Safe & Door Co Ltd (est c1857, inc 1926). Had sales offices in Glasgow, Manchester, Bristol, Leeds and Liverpool. Acquired in 1955 by British Reinforced Concrete Engineering Co Ltd, a member of the Hall Engineering Group of Shrewsbury, Salop and integrated with Chatwood Safe & Engineering Co Ltd of Bolton, Greater Manchester. The latter was incorporated in 1864 as Chatwoods' Patent Safe & Lock Co Ltd and reconstructed in 1909 as Chatwood Safe Co Ltd having been run from at least the 1900s by members of the Hall family. The company was renamed Chatwood-Milner Ltd in 1956 and purchased the undertaking of Chatwood Safe & Engineering Co Ltd. In 1958 the security part of its business was sold to Chubb & Son Ltd (inc 1882 as Chubb & Sons Lock & Safe Co Ltd) and its name was changed to Hall Engineering Ltd. It operated from the Shrewsbury Works and during the 1960s designed and manufactured specialist machinery and equipment for the electrical, chemical, confectionery, metal working and nuclear industries, in sound resisting, blastproof and air lock doors and had die making and fixture shops for the motor car industry. By 1980 name had changed to above and in 1983 manufactured automated assembly equipment and fixtures, sheet metal pressings and assemblies, water saver systems and pallets.

Records (1): at Shrewsbury Tool & Die, Harlescott Lane, Shrewsbury, Salop SY1 3AS
board meeting minutes 1874-1956; finance committee meeting minutes 1913-21; share: registers and ledgers 1895-1955, transfer register 1874-1956, and documents 1938-55, certificate books 1898-1955, cancelled register 1940-56, and exchange books 1874-1941; probate registers 1915-54; executors requests 1933-55; memo and articles of association 1951; agreement with Chatwood-Milner Ltd 1956; debenture stock deed 1950; balance sheet and accounts 1955; general ledgers 1911; returns book 1940-9
Milners' Safe Co (South Africa) Ltd: memo and articles of association 1900
Milners' Safety Cycle Co Ltd: directors meeting minutes 1896-8
Chatwood Safe & Engineering Co Ltd: directors meeting minutes 1930-63; memo and articles of association 1945-50; sales ledgers 1945-9; sales catalogues c1950,nd; price lists 1936-7; product photographs 1925-6; work sheets 1931-48; cost: stock account 1920-49, journal 1924-50; branch costs 1939-48; plant, machinery and premises inventories 1922-40; letters patent 1875; staff photographs c1924,c1930; Shrewsbury premises photographs 1926-30; history articles c1918,nd

Chatwood-Milner Ltd: directors meeting minutes 1956; memo and articles of association 1956; sales literature 1966-7

Records (2): at Chubb & Son, Manor House, Manor Lane, Feltham, London TW13 4JQ corporate guard books 1899-1938, documents 1898; memo and articles of association 1875-1951; debenture stock deed 1950; annual report and accounts 1875-1955; Liverpool: sales ledgers 1937-41, depot ledgers 1929-37; equipment testimonials 1885-94; newscuttings 1941-56; catalogues, price lists and sales literature 1878-1958; lock register 1870-83; key registers 1887-1954; letters patent 1857-65; product: plans, drawings, specifications and papers 1910,1947-60, photographs c1940-58; apprentice leaflet 1951; staff and directors photographs 20 cent; works photographs 1930s; history booklets, articles and notes 1866,1938-54
Thomas Milner & Son: day book 1859-61; order book 1857-61
Milners' Safe Co (South Africa) Ltd: directors meeting minutes 1901-54; general meeting minutes 1901-58; memo and articles of association 1900; annual reports and accounts 1950-5
Milners' Safety Cycle Co Ltd: memo and articles of association 1896; catalogues and advertisements c1896-1900
Mincing Lane Safe Deposit Co Ltd: memo and articles of association 1896; liquidation notes 1955
Whitfields Safe & Door Co Ltd: memo and articles of association 1926-44; order: book 1871-4, instruction sheets 1857-74; catalogues, price lists and sales literature 1874-1947; history article 1888
Chatwood Safe Co Ltd: corporate documents 1864,1909; safe register indices nd; publicity material c1914-77; advertisements 1924-6; catalogues 1872-1958; product: instructions c1937-c57, plans, specifications and papers c1930-58, photographs 1925-57; legal case papers 1881-92; works progress book 1898-1929; safe registers c1864-c1958; lock registers 1875-1956; letters patent 1876-96; agency catalogues and product photographs c1925,c1950; staff photographs nd; history articles and notes c1894-1983
Chatwood-Milner Ltd: sales catalogues and literature 1956-8; exhibition and sales conference photographs 1956-8; doors progress 1956-8; plans, specifications, drawings and operating instructions 1956-8

199 FRANCIS (CLOCKS) LTD

4 Aug 1874
08657
50 Bloomsbury Street, London WCIB 3QT
Clock retailers (formerly cotton spinners)

History: incorporated in 1874 as Cotton Hall Spinning & Manufacturing Co Ltd to build a mill and carry on business of cotton spinning and manufacturing. Cotton Hall Mill in Darwen, Lancashire was erected by 1877. Changed name to Cotton Hall Manufacturing Co Ltd in 1930 and to Cotton Hall (Holdings) Ltd in 1953. Due to poor state of cotton trade went into receivership in 1956 and its subsidiary, Cotton Hall Manufacturing Co Ltd went into liquidation. Ownership changed and registered offices moved to Manchester in 1957. Sole selling agency agreement was signed in 1958 with John D Francis Ltd to retail clocks and name changed to above. Objects were also changed to that of light engineers and dealers in electrical apparatus and chronometers and horological instruments. Registered offices moved to London in 1962 and company was purchased by Crater Controls Ltd of Knaphill, Woking,

Surrey, manufacturers of low current switchgear and time devices. Went into liquidation in 1980.

Records: at Surrey Record Office, County Hall, Penrhyn Road, Kingston upon Thames, Greater London KT1 2DN
directors and general meeting minutes 1954-80; members register 1958-80; share certificate books 1962; annual returns 1950-7; annual reports and accounts 1949-56; ledger 1962-80; journals 1962-80; cash books 1975-80

200 WILLIAM BIRTWISTLE TRADING LTD
29 Aug 1874
08705
Osprey House, Queen Victoria Street, Blackburn, Lancashire BB2 2QC
Cloth merchants (formerly cotton manufacturer)

History: registered in 1874 as John Fish Ltd to acquire Waterfall and Primrose cotton mills and associated buildings at Livesey, near Blackburn, Lancashire, owned by John Fish, cotton spinner, dyer and finisher. Nominal capital was £200,000 in 4000 shares of £50 each. By c1900 company was under leadership of Birtwistle family. Name changed in 1953 to John Fish (Holdings) Ltd and to above in 1979. By 1983 its principal activity was the sale of cloth in the textile industry and was a subsidiary of Hawkins Steeple Group Ltd which was owned by Grandston Ltd.

Records: at Lancashire Record Office, Bow Lane, Preston, Lancashire PR1 8ND
directors meeting minutes 1874-1947; share: ledgers 1897-1947, transfer register 1875-1948; memo and articles of association c1900; quarterly accounts 1907; nominal ledger 1945-57; yarn sales book 1953-71; cloth order books 1929-52; bale purchase book 1938-50; loom patent declaration and diagram 1852-3; wages book 1964; insurance ledgers and schedules 1919-48; air shelter plans 1939-40; out letter book 1902-07

201 BRISTOL CHAMBER OF COMMERCE INDUSTRY & SHIPPING
16 Sep 1874
08752
Dyrham Lodge, 16 Clifton Park, Clifton, Bristol, Avon BS8 3BY
Chamber of commerce

History: founded as Bristol Chamber of Commerce & Shipping by group of merchants and manufacturers in Bristol, Avon, in 1823 to protect and promote their interests. It was suspended from 1826 during the lifetime of Free Port Association but was reformed in 1853. Became a founder member of Association of Chambers of Commerce in the UK and was incorporated as a company limited by guarantee in 1874 as Bristol Incorporated Chamber of Commerce & Shipping. Name changed to above in 1975. Meetings first held in the Commercial Rooms, then in the Merchants Hall, before offices were established in the Guild Hall in 1882. Moved to Old Council House, Corn Street, in 1957 and bought present offices in Clifton in 1966. In 1981 promoted interests of members locally, nationally and internationally, represented views on legislative measures affecting same, provided trade information and other services to members, and published a monthly news-letter and quarterly magazine.

Records: at Bristol Record Office, Council House, College Green, Bristol, Avon BS1 5TR
chamber, directors and committee meeting minutes 1823-6; general and committee meeting: minutes 1859-date, attendance record 1859-84; annual reports and proceedings 1823-date; correspondence 1823-89; rules and regulations 1823,1853; signed accounts 1949-75; ledgers 1946-75; subscriptions and donation receipts 1941-74; pension scheme trust deed 1950; property agreements 1965,1972; monthly journals 1921-date; year book 1913; directories 1965-77; publications on Bristol 1901-8,1968; photographs of presidents, members, exhibitions etc c1880-date; newscuttings and documents re history 1822-1948; incl M Whitwell's report of Social Science Conference, Glasgow 1874
Western Counties Association of Chambers of Commerce: minutes 1967-75

202 ST ANNE'S ON THE SEA LAND & BUILDING CO LTD

15 Oct 1874
08831
128 Queen Victoria Street, London EC4P 4JX
Property

History: incorporated as above in 1874 to purchase, improve and let land and property in and around St Anne's on the Sea and Lytham, Lancashire. By the 1970s, when it was taken over by Amalgamated Investment & Property Co Ltd, the company's sole object was to collect ground rents. It went into liquidation with its parent company in 1976 and was placed in creditors' voluntary winding up in 1979.

Records: at Joint Liquidators, PO Box 207, 128 Queen Victoria Street, London EC4P 4JX
directors and general meeting minutes 1948-77; memo and articles of association 1949; certificate of incorporation 1874

203 BRITISH MEDICAL ASSOCIATION

21 Oct 1874
08848
Tavistock Square, London WC1H 9JP
Professional association

History: founded as Provincial Medical & Surgical Association in 1832 by a group of medical men with the object of diffusing medical knowledge and maintaining the interests of the medical profession. Holds annual meetings in various towns throughout Britain. Changed name to above in 1855 after formation of London branch and was incorporated as a company limited by guarantee in 1874. It is the professional body for doctors in the UK and is a trade union under the Trade Union & Labour Relations Act 1974. Has published *British Medical Journal* since 1840.

Records (1): at British Medical Association, Tavistock Square, London WC1H 9JP
council: minutes, agenda and documents 1864-date, attendance register 1886-1970, committee and sub-committees minutes 1868-1974, and attendance register 1945-77; minutes, agenda and documents of c325 committees 1872-date; annual meeting: minutes 1834-1932, reports 1903-date, programmes and delegates lists 1872-1930; memo and articles of association 1854-1972; handbooks 1904-79; year books 1950-62; calendars 1962-70; balance sheets 1866-1907; statements of account 1866-1920; general ledgers 1879-1952; superannuation ledgers 1920 on;

trust correspondence and documents 1880-1930s; *British Medical Journal* 1857-date; publications 19-20 cent; correspondence with members, branches etc re litigations etc 1900s-date; branch agreements 1897 on; division and branch: reports 1930-77, circulars 1930-75; Metropolitan counties branch: minutes, agenda and documents 1923-75; Advisory Hospital committee minutes and correspondence 1922-4; general correspondence 1924-32; policy statements, circulars etc 1937-9; annual reports 1952-8

British Medical Guild: trustee minutes 1949-57; committee minutes, agenda and documents 1948-57; cash book 1949-76

Dain Fund: committee minutes, agenda and documents 1954-66; cash books 1940-69

General Medical Services Defence Trust: committee minutes, agenda and documents 1949-date; cash book 1949-62

Hospital Medical Staffs Defence Trust: committee minutes, agenda and documents 1950-78; cash book 1951-8

National Insurance Defence Trust: minutes 1919-47; financial reports 1934-64; general ledgers 1928-47; cash books 1919-61

Public Health Service Defence Trust: committee minutes, agenda and documents 1950-67; cash books 1950-68

Records (2): at Barnes Medical Library, Birmingham University, Edgbaston, Birmingham, W Midlands B15 2TT
Birmingham branch: pathological and clinical section minutes 1901-40

Records (3): at Dundee University Library, Dundee, Tayside DD1 4HN
Dundee branch: misc records c1894-1917

Records (4): at Glamorgan Archive Service, County Hall, Cathays Park, Cardiff, S Glamorgan CR1 3NE
South Wales & Monmouthshire branch: Swansea division minutes 1903-70

Records (5): at Warrington Library, Museum Street, Warrington, Cheshire WA1 1JB
Warrington branch: minutes 1903-45

Records (6): at Southampton University Library, Southampton, Hampshire SO9 5NH
Wessex branch: minutes and attendance book 1907-75

Records (7): at Cumbria Record Office, County Offices, Kendal, Cumbria LA9 4RQ
Westmorland branch: minutes 1903-75; correspondence and financial papers 1959-75

Records (8): at E Sussex Record Office, The Maltings, Castle Precincts, Lewes, E Sussex BN7 1YT
Sussex branch: minutes 1913-51, Brighton division minutes 1911-50

Paul Vaughan, *Doctors' Common: A Short History of the British Medical Association* (1959)
Ernest Muirhead Little, *History of the British Medical Association 1832-1932* (1932)
E Grey-Turner and FM Sutherland, *History of the British Medical Association, Vol II, 1932-1981* (1982)

204 CALCEDON INVESTMENTS LTD

27 Oct 1874
08862
Station Tower, Station Square, Coventry, W Midlands CV1 2GR
Colliery proprietors

History: founded in 1851, and incorporated in 1874 as Pope & Pearson Ltd to carry on business of same name, of colliery proprietors at Altofts, near Normanton, W Yorkshire. Coal business was carried on until nationalization in 1947 although land containing deposits of material suitable for brick manufacture was retained and a brickworks erected on the site. Brick manufacturing business was subsequently transferred to a wholly owned subsidiary, Altoft Brickworks Co Ltd. Between 1947 and 1950 acquired other brickmaking companies including Newbrick & Tile Co (Newhay) Ltd, Rochdale, Lancashire and Wilson's Sandel Brickworks Ltd, Wakefield, W Yorkshire as well as Richard Haighton Ltd, foundry company, which was sold in 1970. Acquired AN Cooke & Co Ltd, textile waste processors of Dewsbury, W Yorkshire in 1965. Acquired in 1973 by Coltness Group Ltd which was subsequently acquired by Aurora Holdings Ltd, constructional, general and precision engineers. Changed name to above in 1973.

Records: at Calcedon Investments, Station Tower, Station Square, Coventry, W Midlands CV1 2GR
directors meeting minutes 1875-date; general meeting minutes 1875-date; share: ledgers 1874-1955, allotment book 1955, transfer register 1875-1965, and documents 1928-56; brickworks acquisition papers 1973; directors resignations 1953,1960; annual reports and accounts 1875-7,1892-1929; balance sheets and accounts 1877-8; accounting sheets 1969-74; private ledgers 1956-74; journals 1942-73; cash book 1959-74; West Riding and Silkstone collieries valuation and correspondence 1879

205 PROVIDENT MUTUAL LIFE ASSURANCE ASSOCIATION LTD

29 Oct 1874
08870
25-31 Moorgate, London EC2
Insurance

History: established in London in 1840 as Provident Clerks' Mutual Benefit Association & Benevolent Fund. Originally a friendly society, it also provided endowment and benefit insurance, and from 1846, the first recorded 'group' staff insurance scheme. Paysheet deductions for 'group' schemes were first provided for the Post Office's employees in 1859 and for the major railway companies in the 1860s. Renamed Provident Clerks' Mutual Life Assurance Association & Benevolent Fund in 1849 and Provident Clerks' Mutual Life Assurance Association in 1864. Name changed in 1903 to Provident Clerks' & General Mutual Life Assurance Association and to present title in 1917. Business dominated originally by insurance of clerks and average values insured in first 20 years were less than £200. In 1862 amalgamated with Consols Insurance Association (est 1858). Incorporated in 1874, when the association also acquired Citizens' Assurance Corporation (est 1866). A sister company, Provident Clerks' & General Guarantee Association was established in 1865 and another, Provident Clerks' & General Accident Insurance Co in 1876. Established offices in Manchester (1874), Liverpool (1889), Leeds (1903) and Bristol (1905). Other local offices opened in the 1920s. The association now has interests in life assurance, annuities, group and personal pensions, group life assurance and pension fund management.

Records (1): at Guildhall Library, Aldermanbury, London EC2P 2EJ
board meeting minutes 1840 on; local accounts 1925-54; balance sheets 1873-1903; balances: weekly 1939-59, monthly 1939-47, summaries 1932-56; branch accounts 1923-37; cash books 1938-56; petty cash: books 1907-37, vouchers 1961-4; list of financial commitments 1920; dividends due 1892-1911; interest earned account 1883-97; capitalised accounts 1922-54; instalments 1888-1923; journals 1841-5,1944-57; ledgers: general 1841-87,1938,1949,1956-62, agents general and investments 1888-96, agents, mortgages and staff 1897-1946; medical fees cash book nd; actuarial: calculation work book 1897-1908, special calculations 1914-24; agents: accounts 1923 on, outstanding premiums and commissions 1910-52; group schemes: alterations accounts 1944-53, debit and credit accounts 1916-57, exit accounts 1938-52, lapses and withdrawals 1934-62, Electric & Telegraph Co premium list 1864-8, Post Office premium list 1860-70, Cox & King savings accounts 1944; investments lists 1898-1913; securities list 1912; loan: books 1851-61, register c1898 on, lists to 1955, accounts 1890-1939, lapse account 1939-43, repayments accounts 1923-54, securities c1898 on; mortgage: registers 1851-1921, investment lists 1890-1901, reversions list 1912, investment repayments 1886-1921; reversions and policies for sales 1894-98; policy: register 1841-1949, paid up 1860-1911, railway offices 1865-1908, holders address books 1930 on, account books 1941-64, alterations account 1945-53, annuities due for payment 1887-1920, annuity cash books 1940-67, assignment registers 1851-93, bonus books 1892-1951, bonus cheques, cards and lists 1923-61, claims account register 1866-79, claims in suspense account 1921-42, claims cash book 1923-56, death registers 1846-1919, war register 1939-45, probate register 1893-1954, deaths account 1917-63, lapsed 1890-1958, monthly and daily lapsed accounts 1921-54, maturities accounts 1917-58, maturities cash books 1955-66, new business cash books and alterations 1938-60, nomination registers 1943-80, premiums accident account 1933-49, renewal and committed commission cash books 1946-61, surrenders account 1917-56, specimen proposal and claim papers 1841 on; salaries account 1899-1903; benevolent fund: minute book 1911-69, balance sheets 1841-83, cash book 1922-49, ledger 1937-52, registers 1856 on, securities list 1924-45, subscriptions and donations register 1923-51, special reports 1957 on

Records (2): at Provident Mutual Administration Centre, Wedgwood Way, Stevenage, Hertfordshire SG1 4PU
policy files: deaths 1924-date, lapses 1906 on, maturity 1929 on, surrenders 1929 on, policies and proposals 1841-1908

FH Sherriff, *From then till now: being a short history of the Provident Mutual Life Assurance Association 1840-1940* (1940)

206 WORKING MEN'S COLLEGE CORPORATION

4 Nov 1874
08894
Crowndale Road, London NW1 1TR
Education

History: founded in 1854 by FD Maurice and Charles Kingsley in association with other Christian socialists, Lowes Dickinson, George Tansley, JM Ludlow, Thomas Hughes and FJ

Furnivall, to arrange evening classes in the humanities and sciences for working men. Registered as above as a company limited by guarantee in 1874. First premises were in Red Lion Square, then in Great Ormond Street, both in London, and in 1906 moved to present college buildings at Crowndale Road, Camden, designed by WD Caroe. Women were not admitted as full members until 1965 although the Frances Martin College, founded for working women in 1874 by Maurice's inspiration, moved to the college in 1957. Since 1965 a close association has existed between the two institutions. Has playing fields at Edgware and formed Clubs' Association in 1924 to co-ordinate the activities of its various clubs and societies.

Records: at Working Men's College, Crowndale Road, London NW1 1TR
reports 1889-date; correspondence: founders 19 cent, official c1880-1928, registers c1880-1928; student registers 1854-date; accounts 1854-date; prospectuses, press cuttings, examination papers etc 1854-date; minutes and papers of clubs and societies 19-20 cent; college magazine 1859-61; college journal 1890-date; photographs of college buildings, events and personalities 19-20 cent

207 GROVE MILL PAPER CO LTD

12 Nov 1874
08912
Oakwood Road, Romiley, Stockport, Greater Manchester SK6 4DY
Paper

History: incorporated in 1874 as Langford & Lancaster Ltd to acquire Grove Mill, Disley, Cheshire and the business of paper stainers carried on at the mill by AF Langford & Co whose surviving partner was George Chambers, commission agent. Commenced business as paper makers, stainers, printers, embossers, dealers and merchants. Name changed to above in 1880 and company moved to New Mills, Stockport, Greater Manchester. In 1940s and 1950s specialised in papers for foodstuffs and confectionery industries. Acquired by Cope Allman International Ltd in about 1968 and by Sonoco UK Ltd in 1982. Ceased paper making in 1975 and ceased trading in 1977.

Records: at Sonoco UK, Oakwood Road, Romiley, Stockport, Greater Manchester SK6 4DY
certificate: incorporation 1874, change of name 1880, statutory records current

208 JOSHUA HEAP & CO LTD

23 Nov 1874
08950
Oldham Road Works, Ashton under Lyne, Greater Manchester OL6 8NG
Screwing machine and tool manufacturers

History: incorporated as above in 1874 by a group of Oldham businessmen to manufacture Joshua Heap's patent screwing machines. Acquired Albion Steel Works in Oldham, Greater Manchester and renamed them Oldham Road Works. Heap left the company in 1876 and Martin Hall who subsequently acquired 80 per cent of the shareholding became manager. By 1900s was manufacturing pipe and bolt screwing machines and tools for engineers, plumbers and gas and steam fitters. During 1960s the old works were demolished and smaller premises built on the site. In the early 1980s the company was a machine tool maker and still run by the Hall family.

Records: at Joshua Heap, Oldham Road Works, Ashton under Lyne, Greater Manchester OL6 8NG
directors and general meeting minutes 1875-date; members register 1881; allotment book 1880; dividend book 1876-98; share: certificates 1880-1931, documents 1925, transfer register 1881-97, transfer documents 1887-1952; annual returns 1894-8,1904; balance sheets 1874-95; balances book 1899-1929; nominal ledgers 1899-date; cash books 1926 on; catalogues and price lists 1895-1920s; exhibition certificates 1876-82; works plans 1917,1958; Hall family papers and documents 1916-46; competitors catalogues and price lists 1897-c1909

209 WERNETH RING MILLS LTD

14 Dec 1874
08985
Henley Street, Featherstone Road, Oldham, Greater Manchester OL1 2NQ
Cotton and synthetic yarn spinners

History: incorporated in 1874 as Werneth Spinning Co Ltd to carry on business as cotton spinners at Featherstone Road, Oldham, Greater Manchester. By 1899 the mill contained 80,000 spindles and employed 230 people. Name changed to Werneth Spinning Co (Holdings) Ltd in 1953 and to above in 1959. Company was controlled by Thorley family until it was acquired by Oxley Threads Ltd (est 1870) in the 1970s. In 1981 processed raw cotton and synthetic yarns in preparation for twisting, dyeing etc.

Records: at Oldham Local Interest Centre, Greaves Street, Oldham, Greater Manchester OL1 1DN
directors: and general meeting minutes 1873-8,1893-1966, meeting agendas 1912-75, meeting notes 1920-45; members register 1970 on; directors registers 1874-1974; mortgage register 1892-1905; debenture trust deeds 1894; stock: register 1946-51, transfer register and documents 1960-73; loan-holders ledger summaries 1911-19; share indemnities 1900-14; memo and articles of association 1874-1959; annual reports and accounts 1899-1959; trade and profit and loss account balance book 1948-74; accounting papers 1940s on; income tax papers 1901-28; impersonal ledger 1941-6; production: register 1949-58, study papers 1967; time books 1951-8; cotton: purchase books 1954-75, stockbook 1924-58, cover positions book 1952-60; yarn and waste journals 1947-66; stock reports 1950-76; stock taking books 1906-78; order books 1951-6,1970-2; outward trade: ledger 1954-61, journals 1951-6; inward trade: ledger 1944-54, journals 1956-75; salaries and wages books 1940-70; pension fund papers 1963-9; staff retirement correspondence 1930; insurance policies 1929 on; mill valuations 1912-13; water and electricity supply papers 1901-45; plant maintenance papers 1950s on; secretarys correspondence 1946-7; legal: opinion 1896, correspondence 1901; yarn articles 1930-3; Bolton Master Cotton Spinners Association statistics, circulars and correspondence 1933
Werneth Spinning Co Ltd: directors: and general meeting minutes 1953-9, meeting agendas 1953-9; members register 1953-9

210 HYTHE PIER CO LTD

15 Dec 1874
09029
Hotspur House, Hythe, Southampton, Hampshire SO4 6AU
Pier

History: incorporated in 1874 as Hythe Pier & Southampton Ferry Co Ltd to construct a light iron pier at Hythe, Hampshire to accommodate the ferry service across Southampton Water to Southampton, Hampshire, as facilities at Hythe Hard were inadequate. In 1878 royal assent was given to an order permitting the construction of the pier, which was built between 1879 and 1881 by Bergheim & Co of London under the direction of John Dixon, engineer. Local landowners including Lord Henry Scott MP, later Lord Montagu of Beaulieu, were leading promoters. Derived income from leasing out pier tolls to the ferry boat owner which from 1887 was the Percy family. James Percy in 1915 sold his ferries to General Estates Co Ltd (est 1900), London, which subsequently acquired control of the company. Since 1945 numbers using the ferry have decreased. In 1983 pier was also used for cruise departures.

Records: at Hythe Pier, Hotspur House, Hythe, Southampton, Hampshire SO4 6AU
directors and general meeting minutes 1924-82; members registers and share ledgers 1924-81; cash book 1879-1953; pier correspondence and plans 1921-30; notes and newscuttings re company and shareholders 1923-36

Alan Titheridge, *Hythe Pier and Ferry - A History* (1981)

211 CALDERDALE CHAMBER OF COMMERCE & INDUSTRY

29 Dec 1874
09069
36 Clare Road, Halifax, W Yorkshire HX1 2JB
Chamber of commerce

History: incorporated as a company limited by guarantee in 1874 as Halifax Chamber of Commerce to promote and protect commercial interests in Halifax, W Yorkshire. In 1970 became affiliated to Bradford Chamber of Commerce and by 1980 all administration was dealt with at Bradford except certification of export documents. Meetings continue to be held monthly in Halifax. Changed name to above in 1977 to show that it acted for the whole of the Calderdale area.

Records: at Bradford Chamber of Commerce, Commerce House, Cheapside, Bradford, W Yorkshire BD1 4JZ
papers 1970-date

212 FIRMIN & SONS LTD

4 Jan 1875
09081
100 Crawford Street, London W1H 1AN
Button and military uniform accoutrements

History: founded in c1677 by Thomas Firmin at 3 King's Court, Lombard Street, London. By 1702 business was carried on at the sign of the Red Lion in the Strand. Subsequently moved to

153 Strand in 1760, St Martin's Lane in 1894, 8 Cork Street in 1915 and then to Crawford Street. Between 1760 and 1915 branches were opened in London and elsewhere, the most important being Globe Works, Villa Street, Birmingham, in 1892, where the manufacturing side of the business took place. A small branch also operated in Portsmouth, Hampshire in 1970s. Company received its first royal warrant from George II in 1754 and have been similarly honoured since then by every British sovereign. Incorporated as above in 1875 and members of the founding family have maintained a majority among the board of directors. Amalgamated in 1970 with William Dowler & Sons Ltd, button manufacturers.

Records: at Westminster City Libraries, Archives Department, Victoria Library, 160 Buckingham Palace Road, London SW1W 9DU
directors minutes 1875-1948; general meeting minutes 1883-1961; register of members 1875-1901; share ledger 1875-1908; transfer register 1875-1969; debenture register 1898-1907; dividend account books 1875-1942; notices re shares and meetings 1881-1910; partnership and corporate documents 1749-1875; memo and articles of association 1875-1969; annual returns 1875-9; partnership accounts 1836-77; accounts summary 1871-2,1959-63; general ledgers 1876-1902; private ledgers 1831-1933; bought ledger 1839-40; Birmingham factory ledger 1907-42; private journal 1935-54; cash account book 1926-51; cash books 1836-44,1935-71; bank books 1845-61; accounting papers 1874-5; order books 1754-1818; sales account book 1846-1957; commission account book 1846-1957; travellers dissection book and sales summaries 1952-62; copies of bills 1811-13; royal warrants and advertisements 1796 on; die books 1893-1927; pattern books 1799-1937; family crest book nd; stock and job receipts 1811-72; title deeds and property correspondence 1638-1941; legal accounts 1836-41; letter book 1875-82; family legal papers and correspondence 1688-1896; newscuttings re company and family 1875,20 cent; premises photographs 1920s-70s

213 ALBERT BOWLING CLUB LTD

16 Jan 1875
09117
39-41 Old Lansdowne Road, West Didsbury, Greater Manchester M20 8PA
Sports club-house

History: incorporated as above to purchase land in Lansdowne Road, Albert Park, Didsbury, on which to lay out a bowling green and erect club premises. In 1984 the main activities were bowling, tennis, snooker, table tennis and darts.

Records: at Albert Bowling Club, 39-41 Old Lansdowne Road, West Didsbury, Greater Manchester M20 8PA
directors and general meeting minutes 1900 on; memo of association 1875; articles of association 1883; annual accounts 1891 on; presidents photograph album 1885 on

214 KIRKLEES & WAKEFIELD CHAMBER OF COMMERCE & INDUSTRY

22 Jan 1875
09141
Commerce House, New North Road, Huddersfield, W Yorkshire HD1 5PJ
Chamber of commerce

History: founded in 1853 and incorporated in 1875 as Huddersfield Incorporated Chamber of Commerce as a company limited by guarantee to promote and protect domestic and overseas trade and commercial interests in Huddersfield, W Yorkshire. Originally main interest was affairs of textile trade but has greatly diversified since late 1960s. Merged with Spen Valley Incorporated Chamber of Commerce in 1967, Batley & Birstall Chamber of Commerce in 1974 and Wakefield Chamber of Commerce in 1977. Name changed to Huddersfield & Spen Valley Incorporated Chamber of Commerce in 1967, to Kirklees Chamber of Commerce in 1975 and to above in 1977. Published monthly journal plus business and export bulletins and information sheets. In 1981 was controlled by council of 36 with permanent staff of 15 and membership of c1300.

Records (1): at Kirklees & Wakefield Chamber of Commerce & Industry, Commerce House, New North Road, Huddersfield, W Yorkshire HD1 5PJ
minutes 1977-date

Batley & Birstall Chamber of Commerce: annual reports and accounts 1910-69

Records (2): at Kirklees Libraries & Museums Service, Central Library, Princess Alexandra Walk, Huddersfield, W Yorkshire HD1 2SU
minutes 1853-1977; travelling studentship minutes 1938-66; directors and managers particulars 1930-67; annual reports 1893-1964; discussion documents 1975-7; year book 1918, newscuttings 1919-38

Huddersfield Chamber of Trade: minutes 1964-71

Cleckheaton Chamber of Commerce: minutes 1878-1923

Heckmondwike Chamber of Commerce: minutes 1909-23

Cleckheaton & Heckmondwike Incorporated Chamber of Commerce: minutes 1923-32

Spen Valley Incorporated Chamber of Commerce: minutes 1932-67; attendance register 1959-67; directors register nd

Batley & Birstall Chamber of Commerce: minutes 1960-73

215 TYNE & WEAR CHAMBER OF COMMERCE & INDUSTRY

22 Jan 1875
09143
4 St Nicholas Buildings, Newcastle upon Tyne, Tyne & Wear NE1 1RR
Chamber of commerce

History: established in about 1866 to protect and encourage commerce and industry in Tyne & Wear. Incorporated as above in 1875 as company limited by guarantee.

Records: at Tyne & Wear Archives Department, Blandford House, West Blandford Street, Newcastle upon Tyne, Tyne & Wear NE1 4JA
council: meeting minutes 1866, reports 1878-1908; attendance book 1956-66; committee meeting minutes 1908-67; annual returns 1930-52; accounts 1909-18,1930-63; cash book: 1870-1910, petty 1935-9; financial analysis book 1955-8; subscriptions 1919-29; membership books 1927-47; correspondence 1819-22; newscuttings 1929

216 BELIZE ESTATE & PRODUCE CO LTD

26 Feb 1875
09246
Lee House, London Wall, London EC2
Landowners and timber

History: incorporated as above in 1875 to acquire the assets of British Honduras Co Ltd (in liquidation), owners of about 1 million acres in British Honduras, Central America, from which it had produced and exported mahogany and logwood and worked 4 sugar estates. Latter were abandoned in 1877 but timber operations, cattle rearing and sawmills continued. A railway was also built and bananas, coconuts and chicle gums were exported, and many goods were imported for resale. Purchased by Albert Gliksten of J Gliksten & Son Ltd, London timber merchants, in 1944. After amalgamation with several other timber companies, in 1970 Gliksten became a subsidiary of International Timber Corporation Ltd. Company was sold to WF Belote, Dublin, Georgia, USA, which had large timber interests in South America and USA.

Records: with WF Belote, Minter Naval Stores, 212 Calhoun Street, Dublin, Georgia, 31021 USA
board meeting: minutes 1875-1958, agendas 1953-63; general meeting: minutes 1875-1944, agendas 1959-63; share transfer register 1877-1920; dividend books 1882-1926; shares, debentures and mortgages documents and correspondence 1875-1947; mortgage register 1875-1912; directors register 1901-47; corporate documents 1875-1939; annual returns 1935-8; annual reports and accounts 1876-1956; balance sheets and accounts 1918-49; financial documents, working papers and correspondence 1931-65; ledgers 1875-1951; purchase ledger 1890-3; journals 1897-1959; cash books 1895-1959; loan documents and correspondence 1924-42; costs and statistics sheets 1967-70; agreements, papers, accounts and correspondence re log deliveries, mining rights, chicle, cohune nuts, coconuts, pines, railway concessions and rubber 1899-1930; insurance policies and correspondence 1941-54; mahogany and cedar: sales book 1935-57; production book 1953-7; Belize mill production book 1962-4; production costs papers and correspondence 1907-58; diaries, reports, notes and correspondence of visitors to Belize estates 1904-39; service agreements, references, correspondence etc 1910-54; staff register and salary agreements c1948-65; photographs of houses, huts, staff, equipment, natives etc c1912; property and estate plans 1868-1910; land, works and estate schedules, land title lists, papers and correspondence re company property 1865-1961

217 KENDAL & DISTRICT INCORPORATED CHAMBER OF COMMERCE

2 Mar 1875
09263
9 Highgate, Kendal, Cumbria
Chamber of commerce

History: founded in 1857 as Kendal Chamber of Commerce to promote trading interests of Kendal, Cumbria and district. Became member of Association of Chambers of Commerce in 1862. Registered as company limited by guarantee in 1875 as Kendal Incorporated Chamber of Commerce & Manufacturers. Changed name to above in 1967.

Records (1): at Kendal & District Incorporated Chamber of Commerce, PO Box 27, Exchange Chambers, 10B Highgate, Kendal, Cumbria
council minutes 1857-date; agm minutes 1925-date; memo and articles of association 1875; annual reports and accounts 1898,1925-date; members list 1932; newscuttings 1925-date

Records (2): at Barclays Bank, 9 Highgate, Kendal, Cumbria
accounting records 19-20 cent

218 ROACH BRIDGE PAPER CO LTD

15 Mar 1875
09307
Roach Bridge Mill, Samlesbury, Nr Preston, Lancashire PR5 OUB
Paper manufacturers

History: incorporated in 1875 as Roach Mill Paper Co Ltd to acquire buildings and land on which to erect works for manufacture, printing and sale of paper. Purchased site of Roach Mill (a cotton mill est 1780s) in Apr and changed name in Jul 1875 to above. Rebuilt mill and produced first paper in 1876. Specialised in MG tissue. Changed hands in 1954 and extensively modernised. Between 1960 and 1964 was a wholly owned subsidiary of Harper Paper Group Ltd. Became independent in 1965.

Records: at Roach Bridge Paper, Roach Bridge Mill, Samlesbury, Nr Preston, Lancashire PR5 OUB
directors and general meeting minutes 1901-date; corporate documents 1875; balance sheets and accounts 1875-date; mill: sale particulars 1867,1875, correspondence and papers 1873-4, title deeds 1875 on; staff and premises photographs 1870s-1975

Roach Bridge Paper Co Ltd 1875-1975 (1976)

219 TAMESIDE PROPERTIES LTD

19 Mar 1875
09321
Booth Street Chambers, Ashton under Lyne, Greater Manchester OL6 7LQ
Property

History: incorporated in 1875 by group of local businessmen including James Eaton, architect, as Ashton under Lyne Estate & Building Co Ltd to acquire building land in Ashton under Lyne, Greater Manchester. Name changed to above in 1960s.

Records: none survive

220 MANCHESTER LITERARY & PHILOSOPHICAL SOCIETY

22 Mar 1875
09330
55 Brown Street, Manchester, Greater Manchester M2 2JG
Learned society

History: founded in the 1770s by gentlemen of Manchester, the first formal meeting held in Feb 1781. Half of the 25 original members were physicians, surgeons or pharmacists to

Manchester Infirmary. Meetings were held in Cross Street Chapel and by 1782 membership had reached 53. John Dalton (1766-1844) chemist, natural philosopher and originator of the atomic theory of matter joined in 1795 and was president from 1817-44. He influenced the society's emphasis on science to almost the complete exclusion of literature until an arts section was formed after 1950. In 1799 society bought 36 George Street where Dalton had his laboratory. Members included: James Prescott Joule (1818-89) physicist, president in 1860; Blackett; Bohr; Bragg; Thomas Henry (1734-1816) chemist, first secretary in 1781 and president in 1807; Jevons; Mosely; Roscoe; Rutherford; and Schunk; and engineers: Sir William Fairbairn (1789-1874); James Nasmyth (1808-90); Sir Joseph Whitworth (1803-87); and Wilde. Incorporated as above as a company limited by guarantee in 1875. George Street house was destroyed in an air raid in 1940 and a new building on the site was opened in 1960. It proved too costly to maintain and was subsequently sold, the society moved into office accommodation in the centre of Manchester in 1980 and holds meetings in various venues. In 1981 it had 400 members and continued to encourage interest in cultural and scientific subjects, but excluding religion and politics which, being 'controversial', fell outside its constitution.

Records: at Manchester City Archives Department, Central Library, St Peter's Square, Manchester, Greater Manchester M2 5PD
Daltonian professorship and monument committee minutes 1844; memo and articles of association 1875; list of members 1781-1896; membership diplomas 1785,1804; rules 1782,1852-61; leaflets 1863; *Memoirs* 1785-1887; *Proceedings* 1857-88; library catalogues 1840-75; leases, mortgages and papers re 36 George Street 1797-1951; conversazione programme 1919; syllabus 1921; historical account 1783

221 COCKER BROTHERS LTD

17 Apr 1875
09413
Fitzalan Works, PO Box 125, Effingham Road, Sheffield, S Yorkshire S9
Spring manufacturers

History: established in 1752 as Cocker & Son and incorporated in 1875 as above to carry on business as steel and coil and laminated spring manufacturers. Purchased Fitzalan Works, Effingham Road, Sheffield, S Yorkshire in 1888 from Marriott & Atkinson Ltd (est 1785). From 1929 manufactured collision guards for motor vehicles. Acquired in early 1970s by Woodhouse & Rixson Ltd, steel product manufacturers of Sheffield. In 1982 was principal subsidiary of Woodhouse & Rixson (Holdings) Ltd.

Records: at Cocker Brothers, Fitzalan Works, PO Box 125, Effingham Road, Sheffield, S Yorkshire S9
minutes 1908-73; share: register 1875-94, certificates 1875,1917-49, transfer register 1918-48; memo and articles of association 1875; annual reports and accounts 1875-86; balance sheets and trading accounts 1882-1917; plant accounts 1896-1974; French, Swiss, Irish and Italian ledger indexes 1890s; BF Cocker cost price book 1874-88; private invoices: journal 1935-74, and addition to fixed plant, machinery and buildings 1934-63; purchase invoice book 1962-73; financial correspondence 1916; trade-mark correspondence 1888-1964; catalogue c1890; premises purchase agreement 1888; patent documents 1925-9; water supply agreements 1911,1916

222 SINGLETON BIRCH LTD

23 Apr 1875
09433
Melton Ross Quarries, Barnetby le Wold, Humberside DN38 6AE
Limestone

History: founded in 1815 by William Singleton Birch, mineral merchant, who developed warehouses and distribution centres in Lancashire. Took over Earl of Yarborough's lease of mineral rights and a small whiting works at Chalk Hill, Melton Ross, Barnetby le Wold, Humberside in 1856. Developed the works with his 2 sons, WA and TH Birch and in 1875 became suppliers of fluxing stone to Scunthorpe Iron Works. Incorporated in 1875 as W Singleton Birch & Sons Ltd with offices in Upton Street, Manchester and Effingham Road, Sheffield, S Yorkshire. After TH Birch died in 1920 many of the company's assets were sold including china clay mines at Rosvear, St Austell, Cornwall, but lease of Melton Ross was retained. By 1939 annual quantity of stone mined exceeded 100,000 tons. From late 1950s lime kilns were installed to produce burnt lime for new steel making techniques. Yarborough lease, covering 412 acres was extended for another 60 years in 1973. By 1979 the company was third largest lime producer in UK with a capacity of 260,000 tons of burnt lime annually.

Records: at S Humberside Area Record Office, Town Hall Square, Grimsby, Humberside DN31 1HX
directors meeting minutes 1921-65; members registers 1875-1963; share ledgers 1875-1935; directors register 1928-63; share: prospectuses 1890, agreements 1879-91, certificates 1884-1920, transfer certificates 1875-1915,1928; debenture: certificates 1877-1907, holders list 1920, issue papers 1906,1917; correspondence and papers re proposed winding up and reincorporation 1890; memo and articles of association 1875-1927; agreements, papers and correspondence re: Cornish clay holdings 1888-1919, Marple Mineral Co 1875, Frodingham Iron & Steel Co Ltd; balance sheet, trading and profit and loss accounts 1945-9; private ledgers 1922-65; impersonal ledger 1922-30; nominal ledgers 1930-55; ledger 1962-7; sales ledger 1967-71; journal 1955-67; invoice books 1960-70; cash book 1958-71; solicitors bills 1902-03; Rosvear bank book 1887-9; sales: correspondence 1920-46, agreements 1938-9; wages books 1929-64; payroll 1964-71; staff agreements 1876-1902; sick club rules 1928-37; agreements, papers, plans and correspondence re Melton Ross quarries c1851-1955; haulage books 1960-73; deeds, documents, papers, plans and correspondence re property at Louth, Manchester, Sheffield and Fleetwood 1839-1933; WS Birch will 1881; John Wallace will and codicils 1872,1878

Elsham Lime Products Co Ltd: directors and general meeting minutes 1930-65; share certificates 1952-64; members, share transfer, directors register 1931-40; annual returns 1941-63; ledgers 1930-64; sales ledger 1967-71; skips record 1961-5

Hurley & Co: nominal ledger 1954-66; bought ledger 1965; purchase day book 1947-66; cash book 1966-8

Kentops Ltd: directors and general meeting minutes 1944-64; share certificates 1944-62; members, directors, share transfer register 1944-55; impersonal ledger 1960-5; petty cash book 1949-62; sales daybook 1961-5

North Ormsby Lime Ltd: directors and general meeting minutes 1938-64; members, share transfer, directors registers 1938-54; nominal ledgers 1955-66; sales ledger 1966-71; cash book 1962-5

223 MATTHEW BROWN & CO LTD

27 Apr 1875
09446
Lion Brewery, Blackburn, Lancashire BBI 5NH
Brewing

History: traces its origins to 1830 when Matthew Brown (1807-53) inherited his father's brewhouse at Preston, Lancashire (est 1820s). In 19 cent built and acquired numerous public houses. Matthew retired in 1875 when his business was producing £8000 per year. The above was then formed to acquire the business with Matthew's sons Joseph and Richard becoming joint managing directors. Walter Bibby, late Mayor of Preston, was chairman. By 1900 Matthew's grandsons managed the business. In 1910 they undertook to supply beer etc to customers and tenants of Hall Hale & Co Ltd of Preston, this company being acquired by Browns in 1920. In 1913 acquired Cunninghams & T&W Thwaites Ltd of Blackburn, brewers and wine and spirit merchants (inc 1897) and W Sharples Ltd of Preston. Through these acquisitions public houses were acquired at Clitheroe, Walley and Accrington, Lancashire. Acquired Richard Holden Ltd (inc 1898) of Blackburn, brewers, and W Unsworth of Hindley, Greater Manchester, brewers, in 1924. J Dalzell's Parton & Harrington Breweries Ltd of Whitehaven, Cumbria, was acquired in 1925, bringing the total number of public houses controlled by this company to 260 in addition to 40 off-licence shops. Expanded brewing capacity in mid 1920s through acquisition of Nuttall & Co (Blackburn) Ltd (est 1847). Nuttall's Breweries Ltd was established in 1927 to manage this brewery and to acquire Whittle Springs Brewery Ltd, near Chorley in 1929, with houses in Chorley, Leyland and Preston. Brewing at Preston discontinued in 1928 and alterations and extensions were effected at Preston brewery between 1928-38. Purchased Victoria Hotel Co (Southport) Ltd (inc 1863) and Cleator Moor Brewing Co Ltd (inc 1896) in 1947. Brewing ceased at Cleator Moor, Cumbria in 1968. Purchased JW Brockbank & Sons, brewers, Millom, Cumbria in 1954, Thornton & France Ltd (est c1717), wine merchants, Preston in 1964, and Workington Brewery Co Ltd (inc 1891) in 1975. By 1981 'Slalom Lager' was brewed at Blackburn and all other beers were produced at Workington. The company then owned or managed c530 public houses, hotels and restaurants.

Records: at Matthew Brown, Lion Brewery, Blackburn, Lancashire BBI 5NH
directors and general meeting minutes 1875-date; shareholders notices 1875-1920; chairmans speeches 1928-75; prospectus 1875; shareholders list 1896; annual report and accounts 1876-date; legal, financial and directors correspondence 1876-1935; invoice 1852; general memoranda book 1881-1939; public house lists 1882,1901; estimates for painting hotels and public houses 1882; Cavendish Hotel, Barrow in Furness, Cumbria stock list 1881; tenancy documents c1900; newscuttings 1881-1939; photographs of Brown family, directors, workmen, plant, premises, transport, floats, production, advertisements etc 19 cent-1970s; history articles and booklets c1895-1976
Birkenhead Brewery Co Ltd: annual reports and accounts 1882
Bothwell & Mills Ltd: directors meeting minutes 1900-61; memo and articles of association 1900
Cleator Moor Brewing Co Ltd: general meeting notices 1896,1946; letter to shareholders 1946; retail price list nd; trade advertisements c1904

Little Harwood Brewing Co Ltd: prospectus 1875; memo and articles of association 1875; annual report and accounts 1875
Nuttall & Co (Blackburn) Ltd: photograph of Ellis Nuttall nd; staff correspondence 1919; list of company men killed in WW1; particulars and conditions re sale of Little Harwood Brewery 1892; sketch of brewery nd; photographs of float pre 1927
Nuttalls Breweries Ltd: annual report and accounts 1945; newscuttings re ex employee 1934
Paitsons Brewery Co Ltd: registration papers 1875; letter re general meeting 1884; papers re let of Royal Oak Inn, Egremont, Cumbria 1875
Victoria Hotel Co (Southport) Ltd: directors meeting minutes 1916-30; memo and articles of association 1919
Henry Spencer & Co Ltd: general meeting minutes 1891-1967; shareholders notices and letters 19-20 cent; annual reports and accounts 1958-67
Thornton & France Ltd: price lists c1910-37; photographs of Fishergate, Preston c1887 and John France with transport 1890
Workington Brewery Co Ltd: general meeting minutes 1891-1975; annual reports and accounts 1892-1974

224 GROVER & CO LTD

29 Apr 1875
09453
Britannia Engineering Works, Carpenters Road, Stratford, London E15 2EB
Engineers and perforating and dye embossing machinery manufacturers

History: established and incorporated as above in 1875 at Britannia Iron Foundry, Regent's Canal, London by John William Grover, a railway engineer. In 1873 he had patented improvements in spring washers or nut locks chiefly used for securing fish plates to railway lines. Company patented 'Grover' washers throughout Europe and quickly extended its product range to include spring dowel pins, lead glazing strips and thumb-screw bottle openers. Became renowned for the manufacture of machines for perforating and dye embossing postage stamps. Moved to Britannia Engineering Works, Stratford in 1915.

Records: at Grover, Britannia Engineering Works, Carpenters Road, Stratford, London E15 2EB
directors and general meeting minutes 1875-1980; corporate agreements, share papers and correspondence 1876-1939; printed annual reports and accounts 1876-1980; private ledgers 1875-1980; sales: statistics 1883-7, agreements and correspondence 1900-51; price lists, catalogues, printed descriptions and advertisements 1885-1959; specifications, patents and production correspondence 1873-c1936; paper pin sizes, master dyes and perforated plates 1920s-1980; engineering drawings 1880s-1980; photographs of products and works c1900-1970s; correspondence and papers re staff appointments and insurance 1880-1936; JW Grover general election speech 1886; leases, plans and correspondence re premises 1862-1943; newscuttings re the company 1915

225 BRITISH MUTUAL BANK LTD

3 Mar 1875
09467
54 Lombard Street, London EC3P 3AH
Banking (formerly investment)

History: founded in 1857 as British Mutual Investment Loan & Discount Co. Renamed British Mutual Investment Co in 1869, registered as limited company in 1875 and changed names again in 1876 and 1877, becoming British Mutual Banking Co Ltd in 1882 and finally in 1945 to the above. Premises moved in 1876 from 17 New Bridge Street, Blackfriars, to St Bride Street and later to Ludgate Circus. Opened first branch in St James's Street, London in 1950 and also operated first cross-channel bank on Dover-Calais service. Amalgamated in 1951 with Martin's Bank Ltd (est 1712) which itself amalgamated with Barclays Bank Ltd in 1969.

Records: at Barclays Bank, 54 Lombard Street, London EC3P 3AH
board minutes 1923-50; prospectus, shareholders letters, press cuttings, annual reports 1857 on; balance sheets 1915-50; ledgers: general 1940-51, impersonal 1896-1930s, customer 1910-43, deposit account 1906-43, discount 1913-32

George Chandler, *Four Centuries of Banking* Vol 1 (1964)

226 REDCAR RACE CO LTD

14 Jun 1875
09592
Liverton Lodge, Loftus, Saltburn by the Sea, Cleveland
Racecourse

History: incorporated in 1875 as Redcar & Coatham Grand Stand Co Ltd. Racing held prior to 1850 at seaside, moved in 1870 to Redcar, Cleveland where a 21 year lease was secured. Additional land was leased in 1879 from Lord Zetland which enabled the creation of the straight mile course. Spring and summer meetings were held and ground let to local organisations during the year. During both WWs ground was occupied by military. In 1920 company changed name to above and in 1939 bought the ground for £6000. New grandstand opened in 1964 and by 1967 applied for fifteen days racing. In 1984 the company ran meetings at Redcar.

Records: at Redcar Race, Race Course, Redcar, Cleveland TS10 2BY
directors and general meeting minutes 1875-1967; memo and articles of association 1878-1959; racecourse leases, conveyances and plans 1923-68; history c1950

J Fairfax-Blakeborough, *Redcar Race Course* (priv pub c1950)

227 SHORTHORN SOCIETY OF THE UNITED KINGDOM OF GREAT BRITAIN & IRELAND

15 Jul 1875
09597
4th Street, National Agricultural Centre, Stoneleigh Park, Kenilworth, Warwickshire CV8 2LG
Breed society

History: society was formed in 1872 to take over the running of *Coates Herd Book*, printed since 1822. Society purchased Herd Book in 1874 for £500 and company was incorporated as above as company limited by guarantee in 1875. Issued herd book, maintained breed register, awarded medals and issued importation certificates. In 1935 amalgamated with Dairy Shorthorn Society and included entries from Lincolnshire Red Shorthorn Association in *Coates Herd Book*.

Records: at Shorthorn Society, 4th Street, National Agricultural Centre, Stoneleigh Park, Kenilworth, Warwickshire CV8 2LG
council: and general meeting minutes 1875-1977, agendas 1907-27, attendance books 1947-77; committee meeting minutes: formation 1872-4, general purpose 1875-1936, arbitration, general purposes, judges, 1875-1933, editing 1875-1939, special 1875-1943, finance and administration 1936-49, rules and discipline 1936-8; committee agendas 1931-7; reports: economy committee 1935, amalgamation with Dairy Shorthorn Society 1935, company formation 1874; prospectus 1874; memo and articles of association 1875; members: proposed at council meetings 1878-1936, elected 1962-7, rules and by-laws 1880-5,1936-55; copyright assignment 1875; Lincolnshire Red Shorthorn Association agreement 1935,1943; *Coates Herd Book* 1822-date; show and sale meeting minutes 1936-9; register: entries and inspections 1947-68, inspections 1952-64; propaganda 1936-43; prize offers 1967-9; sale catalogues 1810,1838-date; newscuttings re cattle, shows and sales 1864-79,1923-33; staff agreements 1935-49; superannuation fund trust deed and papers 1947-66; Shorthorn publications 1835-date; visitors book 1920-57
Shorthorn Breeders Club: committee meeting minutes 1879-1964, dinner and membership cards 1894-1963
Dairy Shorthorn Association: council and general meeting minutes 1926-43
Lincolnshire Red Shorthorn Association: committee meeting minutes 1936
National Dairy Herd Association: memo and article of association 1953
Breeders of Bate's Shorthorns: dinner and membership cards 1888-1902

228 HULL INCORPORATED CHAMBER OF COMMERCE & SHIPPING

16 Jun 1875
09604
Samman House, Bowlalley Lane, Hull, Humberside HU1 1XT
Chamber of commerce

History: although meetings of a 'chamber of commerce' were held in Hull, Humberside in 1784, Hull Chamber of Commerce was not properly established until 1837. Membership consisted of merchants, bankers, manufacturers, shipowners, underwriters and other businessmen, with its main objects being to protect the commerce of Hull. Amalgamated in 1847 with Hull Shipowners' Society, (est late 17 cent) to form Hull Chamber of Commerce & Shipping. First meetings held in Old Hull Exchange, moving to the premises of Hull Exchange Co in 1865 and in 1919 to present offices in Bowlalley Lane. In 1860 was prime mover and founder member of Association of British Chambers of Commerce. Incorporated as above in 1875, as a company limited by guarantee. Between 1890 and 1914 separate trade associations were formed for specific trades. Junior Chamber of Commerce formed in 1948. In 1981 main activities were export documentation, verification and certification, provision of full information services and general representation of local business.

Records: at Hull Incorporated Chamber of Commerce & Shipping, Samman House, Bowlalley Lane, Hull, Humberside HU1 1XT
council meeting minutes 1837-date; shipping committee meeting minutes 1847-date; annual reports and accounts 1838-date; Hull general current price lists 1853-1959; press cuttings 1900-35; trade association (affiliated and non-affiliated) minutes 1890s-date

William J Hope, *Hull Incorporated Chamber of Commerce and Shipping* (priv pub 1976)

229 ASSOCIATION OF BRITISH CHAMBERS OF COMMERCE

28 Jun 1875
09635
Sovereign House, 212-224 Shaftesbury Avenue, London WC2
Chamber of commerce

History: founded in 1860 by a group of chambers of commerce to act as a national voice to influence the government and disseminate information to its member chambers. Established offices and an agent in London at 30 Parliament Street, Westminster. Registered in 1875 as company limited by guarantee as Association of Chambers of Commerce and subsequently changed name to above. By 1900 comprised of 90 chambers, rising to 101 by 1914, and achieved many amendments to commercial legislation in interests of members. In 1960 had 99 member chambers in UK and 15 affiliated British overseas chambers. Moved premises to Adam House, Queen Anne's Gate, around 1920, to 68 Queen Street, London (headquarters of London Chamber of Commerce) in 1960, and subsequently to Sovereign House, Shaftesbury Avenue, London.

Records (1): at Association of British Chambers of Commerce, Sovereign House, 212-224 Shaftesbury Avenue, London WC2
executive council meeting minutes 1953-date; committee meeting minutes 1953-date

Records (2): at Guildhall Library, Aldermanbury, London EC2P 2EJ
executive council: meeting minutes 1860-1953, papers, correspondence, reports, memoranda, circulars etc 1876-1949; committee meeting minutes: finance and taxation 1921-52, with papers, correspondence, circulars, reports etc 1921-39, foreign and colonial affairs 1921-52, general purposes 1956-61, home affairs and transport 1921-51, with agendas 1922-30, and papers, memoranda, correspondence etc 1922-30, presidents advisory 1921-8, postal 1925-39, special and misc 1921-45; sub-committee minutes 1921-39; reports on gold reserves, banking, currency and metallic resources c1908, associations work 1923; executive meeting proceeding reports 1914-60; annual meeting proceeding reports 1861-1960; laws and rules and regulations 19 cent; subscriptions lists 1919-21; newscuttings c1876-1949

AR Ilersic and PFB Liddle, *Parliament of Commerce: The Story of the Association of British Chambers of Commerce 1860-1960* (1960)

230 WOOD STREET MILL CO LTD

9 Jul 1875
09668
Beech Mill, Pimhole, Bury, Greater Manchester BL9 7EQ
Cotton spinners and cloth manufacturers

History: incorporated in 1875 as James E Worsley & Co Ltd to acquire Springfield Mill at Elton, Greater Manchester from James E Worsley and to carry on the spinning, weaving and manufacturing of waste cotton and other products. Worsley remained managing director until 1879. Bought Beech Mill, Pimhole, Bury, Greater Manchester in 1877 and changed name to above in 1880. Sold Springfield Mill in 1935. In late 1970s the company was a spinner of condenser and other allied yarns, and a manufacturer of cloth products including decorated dust sheets, curtain linings, tea towels, dusters, aprons and flannelette sheets. By 1981 was a wholly owned subsidiary of Radwise Ltd whose holding company was Royal Westminster Investments NV, incorporated in the Netherlands.

Records: at Wood Street Mill, Beech Mill, Pimhole, Bury, Greater Manchester BL9 7EQ
directors and general meeting minutes 1875-date; shareholders registers 1883-date; share transfer documents 1931-date; annual returns 1929-date; memo and articles of association 1875-1949; annual reports and accounts 1888,1937-date; balance sheets and accounts 1889-1900,1916,1924-72; private ledger 1875-1960; fire damage invoices 1957-9; employee accident reports 1922-60; factory registers 1956-79; staff pension fund trust deed and rules 1961; fire insurance: papers 1959-date, policies 1950s, schedules c1930-50s; mill: plans 1931,1973, fire photographs 1957; new weaving shed papers 1919-26; humidity register 1966,1980; letter book 1921-2; goods exhibition photograph 1920s

231 ARDEN & COBDEN HOTELS LTD
31 Jul 1875
09725
257 Hagley Road, Birmingham, W Midlands B16 9NA
Hotel

History: incorporated in 1875 as Birmingham Artisans' Clubhouse Co Ltd to provide teetotal club-houses in various parts of Birmingham. William White, Quaker and philanthropist, was first chairman. Purchased St George's Club (founded in 1874), ran Bordesley House, Watery Lane from 1875 to 1878. Name changed in 1877 to Birmingham Coffee House Co Ltd and opened first coffee house in 1877 at 1 Stafford Street. By 1883 had opened 23 coffee houses, including Cherry Street Coffee House. In 1885 Cobden Hotel was built by James Moffatt to the designs of W Doubleday and JP Osbourne. By 1895 another 5 coffee houses and cafes were opened. In 1896 land was leased in New Street on which Hen & Chickens Hotel and cafe was built. Hen & Chickens Hotel was modernised and extended in 1930s, renamed Arden Hotel in 1938, further modernised in 1950s, sold in 1972 and demolished in 1973. In 1948 purchased a private hotel at 263-265 Hagley Road and named it Norfolk Hotel, which was then expanded by purchasing houses in Hagley Road and St Augustine's Road. Cobden Hotel closed in 1959, but new Cobden Hotel was opened in Hagley Road next to Norfolk Hotel. Company name changed to above in 1940. In 1977 its hotels were still unlicensed and contained over 500 beds.

Records (1): at Arden & Cobden Hotels, Norfolk Hotel, 257 Hagley Road, Birmingham, W Midlands B16 9NA
directors reports and annual returns 1933-40; general meeting minutes 1945-80; share transfer register 1878-1979; dividend: register 1903-43, account books 1908-64; mortgage register 1882-1940; annual share summaries 1887-1901; ledgers 1930-67; cash account summaries 1934-70; cash received book 1958-73; inventory valuations of Arden and Norfolk Hotels 1958;

photographs of staff, premises, old Cobden Hotel, Norfolk Hotel, Hen & Chickens Hotel, chairman 1920s-78; articles, notes, correspondence, press releases, newscuttings, guest lists, menus and centenary history c1880-1978

Records (2): at Birmingham University Library, Special Collections Department, Main Library, PO Box 363, Birmingham, W Midlands B15 2TT
directors: meeting minutes 1877-1946, reports 1877-1943, executive committee minutes 1880-90; general meeting minutes 1874-1949; share ledgers 1876-c1931; annual returns 1912-31; annual reports and accounts 1874-1949; profit and loss accounts 1903-36; trading accounts 1914-38; quarterly balances 1930-40; purchase: ledgers 1909-37, journals 1915-37, day book 1942-3, book 1934-7; cash account summaries 1884-1909; general cash book 1913-36; petty cash book 1910-37; payment books 1921-9; accounts paid book 1929-36; cash received book 1939-48; sales journals 1900-47; stock book 1910-37; mutual improvement society records 1883-7; hospital Saturday collection list 1894-1938; contact book 1915-38; newscuttings 1876-1918
Birmingham Restaurant Co Ltd: directors and general meeting minutes 1886-1902

AL Enfield, *90 Years Young: A Brief History of Arden & Cobden Hotels Ltd* (priv pub 1977)

232 OLD RADNOR TRADING CO LTD

3 Aug 1875
09732
Conyngham Hall, Knaresborough, N Yorkshire HG5 9AU
Dormant (previously lime manufacturers)

History: registered in 1875 as Old Radnor Lime, Roadstone & General Trading Co Ltd to acquire the lease of lime kilns and lime and stone quarries at Old Radnor, Powys, the property of Sir GF Lewis Bt of Harpton Court. The capital of £10,000 was in 100 shares of £100 each. In 1900 name changed to above. Ceased to trade in 1974 when assets were acquired by Tilling Construction Services Ltd of Knaresborough, N Yorkshire.

Records: no records survive

233 SOUTHAMPTON CHAMBER OF COMMERCE

30 Aug 1875
09806
53 Bugle Street, Southampton, Hampshire SO9 4WP
Chamber of commerce

History: founded in 1851 following a meeting of merchants and traders of Southampton, having been recommended by Trade Committee of Southampton Town Council. Incorporated as above as a company limited by guarantee in 1875 to promote trade, commerce, shipping and manufactures of town and port of Southampton. Encouraged railway development, North Atlantic shipping trade and mail packet services and initiated a reciprocal trading scheme for blitzed traders during WW2. Issued own journal from 1952. Formed Junior Chamber of Commerce in 1959. Offices located in Corn Exchange 1850s-1874; Hartley Institution 1874-1904; 79 High Street 1904-07; small Philharmonic Hall 1907-31; Blue Peter House, Portland Terrace 1931-7; Cumberland Place 1937-57; Bugle Street 1957-date.

Records: at Southampton Chamber of Commerce, 53 Bugle Street, Southampton, Hampshire SO9 4WP
general and committee meeting: minutes 1851-1981, notices, agendas and attendances 1946-70; chamber proceedings 1872 on; memo and articles of association c1890s; freight origin certificates registers 1964-74; newscuttings re incorporation and Southampton trade, commerce and reconstruction 1875,1938-51; *Southern Gateway*: 1952-date
Southampton Junior Chamber of Commerce: general and committee meeting minutes 1959-68
Southampton War History Committee: minutes and press cuttings c1948-52
Southern Fruit & Potato Merchants' Association: minutes 1942-63; accounts for Outspan scheme 1965-7
Traders Panel for Southampton Area: minutes 1925-7; press cuttings re trade 1936-42

234 PRINCE OF WALES HOTELS LTD
2 Sep 1875
09821
72 King Street, Southport, Merseyside PR8 1LG
Hotel

History: incorporated as Prince of Wales Hotel Co, Southport, Ltd in 1875 to carry on the business of hotel keepers and wine and spirit merchants; to continue an existing agreement to pull down Union Hotel, Lord Street, Southport and to erect a new hotel and dwelling houses. Prince of Wales Hotel was subsequently erected in Lord Street. Name changed to above in 1972 and by 1979 the company had acquired 7 hotels in Southport, Merseyside; Blackpool, Lancashire; Chester, Cheshire; Windermere, Cumbria; Brighton, E Sussex, and Harrogate, N Yorkshire. From the 1970s the company also promoted popular music concerts.

Records: with Company Secretary, 91 Lord Street, Southport, Merseyside PR8 1SA
board meeting minutes 1940-date; general meeting minutes and papers 1913-82; register: directors holdings 1918-82, share transfers and certificates 1945-67; share papers 1936-69; memo and articles of association 1875; accounts 1949-68; ledger 1936-56; monthly statements 1951-69; stock taking reports and papers 1955-71; excise and weekly returns 1952-9; salary books 1963-70; hotel register 1970-1; menus, press cuttings, correspondence and papers 1950-70

235 SHEFFIELD DISTRICT INCORPORATED LAW SOCIETY
11 Sep 1875
09844
8 Campo Lane, Sheffield, S Yorkshire S1 2EF
Law society

History: founded in 1873 by Sheffield solicitors and incorporated as above in 1875 as a company limited by guarantee with a membership of 48 attorneys, solicitors and notaries practising in Sheffield or within a 20 mile radius. Main objects were protection and support of solicitors, consideration of alteration or administration of the law, formation of a law library and encouragement of the study of law. Took over old law library in Castle Buildings and housed it in own premises in Aldine Court, High Street. By 1878 had 110 members. In 1882 office moved to Hoole's Chamber, Bank Street and to 8 Campo Lane by 1983.

Records: at Sheffield District Incorporated Law Library, 8 Campo Lane, Sheffield, S Yorkshire S1 2EF
committee: and general meeting minutes 1878-date, reports 1914-16; papers, bulletins and circulars 1980-date; agm proceedings 1933-64; memo and articles of association 1908,1936; debenture: holders register 1929-45, papers and certificates 1928-34; annual reports 1875-1948; circulars and annual dinner cards 1875-1920; hon treasurers papers 1882-1927; members: list 1875-1969, subscription registers 1922-36, newscuttings 1920-38; library book register 1927-52; law society papers 1906-29; new law and legal case papers and correspondence 1925-30,1976; general correspondence 1925-8; students society: committee and general meeting minutes 1910-51, annual reports 1910-30, newscuttings and annual dinner menus 1930-51

236 MIDLAND PRINTING CO LTD

15 Sep 1875
09850
583 Moseley Road, Birmingham, W Midlands B12
Printers

History: incorporated as above in 1875 as general printers and school stationery manufacturers. Company has always been closely associated with Midland Educational Co Ltd (inc 1870) and was acquired by latter in 1919. Original premises were in Simpson Street, Oldbury, W Midlands, moving to new works at Blackheath in 1961. In early 1980s company manufactured scholastic stationery and acted as general printers for parent company.

Records: at Midland Educational, Burnt Tree House, Tipton, W Midlands
share: ledger 1912-62, certificates 1912-date; annual report and accounts 1902-04; private ledger 1950-61

237 NOTTINGHAMSHIRE LAW SOCIETY

23 Sep 1875
09872
Bromley House, Angel Row, Nottingham, Nottinghamshire NG1 6HL
Law society

History: founded and incorporated as above in 1875 as a company limited by guarantee to promote fair and honourable practice in the law profession in Nottingham and district, and to protect the interests of its members. Has maintained a law library ever since. In 1875 membership numbered 57 rising to 132 by 1889, 244 by 1963 and 383 by 1974.

Records: at Nottinghamshire Law Society, Bromley House, Angel Row, Nottingham, Nottinghamshire NG1 6HL
council and general meeting minutes 1912-date; history 1975

238 PLATT & CO LTD

24 Sep 1875
09874
Skull House Lane, Appley Bridge, Wigan, Greater Manchester
Brick and tile manufacturers, stone merchants and quarry owners

History: incorporated as above in 1875 to take over the stone quarries and clay lands at Appley Bridge of Platt & Son and the clay lands at Newburgh, Lancashire of Platt & Mangnall, brick makers and stone merchants. Brown Edge brickworks was disposed of in 1916 and Appley Bridge quarry was no longer in use by 1980.

Records: at Wigan Record Office, Town Hall, Leigh, Greater Manchester WNY 2DY
minutes (rough) 1924-56; share certificate books 1875-1951; memo and articles of association 1875; annual returns 1934-55; annual reports and accounts 1949-57; trading and profit and loss accounts 1900-57; analysis credit journal 1935-53; cash books 1903-59; bank book 1944-55; sales book 1931-49; stock book nd; explosives issue book 1956-9; workmen time book 1956-9

239 HYDE CLUB LTD

9 Oct 1875
09918
Bowling Green Street, Hyde, Greater Manchester
Sports club-house

History: incorporated as above in 1875 to purchase land in order to erect and maintain a pavilion and bowling green. Initially the company ran the bowling club, but it later leased the premises to Hyde Club. In 1886 the club premises were valued at £150 and included a bar, card room, billiard room, cellar, pavilion and grounds. In the early 1980s the company continued to lease the premises.

Records: at Hyde Club, Bowling Green Street, Hyde, Greater Manchester
directors and general meeting minutes 1883-date; register of members and share ledger 1875-1980; memo and articles of association 1875; cash book 1895-1973; inventory and valuation 1886; mortgages 1887-1912

240 BINGLEY EXHIBITION HALL CO LTD

11 Oct 1875
09922
Great King Street, Birmingham, W Midlands B19 2XF
Property

History: first national exhibition was staged in Bingley Hall, Broad Street, Birmingham in 1849. The site was leased to George Branson and Edwin Gwyther in 1850 for 99 years. The above company was incorporated to acquire the property, let the hall and hold cattle and other livestock exhibitions. Birmingham Agricultural Exhibition Society sub-leased the hall and organised the exhibitions. After the lease terminated in 1949 the society bought up the company's shares. In 1956 Lucas Industries Ltd acquired the company which was dormant by 1983. Bingley Hall was run by Bingley Hall Exhibition Centre in 1983.

Records: at Lucas Industries, Great King Street, Birmingham, W Midlands B19 2XF
directors meeting minutes 1916-57; general meeting minutes 1876-1941; share ledger c1946-56; directors register 1913-52; share certificate book 1876-c1956; stock papers 1936-7; memo and articles of association 1903; annual: returns 1954-6, reports and accounts 1876-1943,1954-6; balance sheets 1954-6; accounting papers 1952-7; private ledger 1927-1956; Bingley Hall: proprietors list 1852, leases 1878-1934

241 GEORGE WOSTENHOLM & SON LTD

4 Dec 1875
10064
65 Garden Street, Sheffield, S Yorkshire S1 4BJ
Cutlery manufacturers

History: founded in 1745 by George Wolstenholm, Sheffield cutler. Succeeded by son and grandson, another George who dropped 'l' from firm's name. Incorporated as above in 1875 to continue cutlery manufacturing business. Purchased Washington Works, Sheffield, S Yorkshire in 1850. By 1923 had agents in USA, Canada, Australia and New Zealand. In 1958 had 2 subsidiaries Christopher Johnson (Cutlers) Ltd and Champion (Mexborough) Ltd. Acquired in 1972 by Richards of Sheffield (Holdings) Ltd, cutlery, pen knife, scissors and stainless steel tableware manufacturers. Acquired in 1984 by Meteor Industries Ltd.

Records: at Sheffield City Libraries, Archives Division, Central Library, Surrey Street, Sheffield, S Yorkshire S1 1XZ
shareholders list nd; share and share transfer agreements and papers 1875-90; memo and articles of association 1875; ledgers 1950-65; invoices 1971; credits 1970-1; purchase tax documents 1943-52; New York agency agreements, reports, accounts and correspondence 1926-31; stock records nd; advertising: correspondence 1895-1911, plans 1935-9; price lists 1810-1960s; trade-mark documents 1876-7; knife machinery papers 1918; suppliers correspondence 1935; order forms and summaries 1949-60; staff: undertaking forms 1860-84, legacy deed 1877, register nd; wages books 1936-50; overtime notebooks 1939-41; war: payment book 1939-47, savings record nd; union papers 1877-1918; fire insurance claims, accounts and rebuilding correspondence 1914; office reorganisation report and papers 1915; USA factory correspondence nd; scissors correspondence: plant 1929-30, quality 1935; USA letter book 1895-6; overseas correspondence 1929,1931-52; Board of Trade correspondence 1930-8,1941; trade associations correspondence and papers 1943-52; chairmans photograph nd; overseas visit notebooks nd
Christopher Johnson (Cutlers) Ltd: price lists 1948-60s
Champion (Mexborough) Ltd: price lists 1960s

242 JESSOP SAVILLE LTD

14 Dec 1875
10094
Smithfield House, Sheffield, S Yorkshire S1 2AS
Steel manufacturers

History: established at Sheffield, S Yorkshire, in 1774 by William Jessop. Incorporated in 1875 with a nominal share capital of £400,000 to acquire the business of William Jessop &

Sons, iron masters, smelters, engineers, iron founders and steel manufacturers. The business was then one of largest makers of crucible steel in Sheffield and was one of the first to make steel castings. For example it was the first to cast, in one piece, stern frames for ships. In the 1880s it was amongst the first to produce nickel steel alloys for use in the making of armour plate. In 1902 it constructed a works at Pennsylvania, USA, and in 1904 acquired a half interest in JJ Saville & Co Ltd, steel manufacturers of Sheffield. By 1908 it had offices at Toronto and Johannesburg. Prior to 1920 it was acquired by Birmingham Small Arms Co Ltd (BSA) and in the 1920s the business claimed to be the largest manufacturer of high-grade crucible steel in the world. In 1959 on the reorganisation of BSA's Sheffield steel interests, its name was changed to above. In c1971 the company was acquired by Thos Firth & John Brown Ltd, subsequently known as Johnson & Firth Brown PLC, and by 1978 it had ceased to trade.

Records: at Thos Firth & John Brown, Smithfield House, Sheffield, S Yorkshire S1 2AS
board reports 1973; acquisition documents, papers and correspondence 1967-70; rationalization papers 1969; pension scheme booklets and papers c1973; annual accounts 1967-8; correspondence and papers 1967-71

243 STRATFORD UPON AVON INVESTMENT CO LTD

24 Dec 1875
10134
1 John Street, Stratford upon Avon, Warwickshire
Property

History: incorporated as Stratford upon Avon Labourers Dwellings Co Ltd in 1875 to build and administer property in the Stratford area for labourers. By 1878 possessed 27 cottages in the town but latterly also had property in Warwick and Leamington Spa, Warwickshire; Malvern Link, Hereford & Worcester; and Birmingham, W Midlands. Name changed to Stratford upon Avon Land Investments Co Ltd in 1950 and to above in 1959. Went into liquidation in 1980.

Records (1): with the Liquidator, PA Jones, 17 Greenhills Street, Stratford upon Avon, Warwickshire CV37 6LF
directors and general meeting minutes 1950-80; ledger 1950 on; rent book 1950 on

Records (2): at Shakespeare Birthplace Trust, Shakespeare Centre, Stratford upon Avon, Warwickshire CV37 6QW
directors and general meeting minutes 1876-1950; members register 1876 on; share transfer register 1876-1942; corporate documents 1878-1959; share documents 1876-7; annual reports and accounts 1876,1891-9; statements of account 1949,1965

244 CARDIGAN MERCANTILE CO LTD

24 Dec 1875
10139
58 Pendre, Cardigan, Dyfed
General merchants and ironmongers

History: established in 1785 by David Davies, shipowner, as general merchants and ironmongers. Incorporated as above in 1875. Opened first retail outlet at Cross Street, Cardigan High Street, Dyfed, after WW2. In 1977 had retail shop in High Street, Haverfordwest, Dyfed, and offices and shop in Pendre, Cardigan.

Records (1): at Cardigan Mercantile, 58 Pendre, Cardigan, Dyfed
minutes 1965-date; members register 1876-date; share: transfer register 1955-date, certificate book 1961-date, and transfer and dividend certificates 1950-75; directors register nd; annual returns registers 1876-1942; annual return 1972; annual accounts 1968-date; audited accounts 1936-70; invoices 1971-date; leases 1959-68; photographs of company properties nd

Records (2): at Pembrokeshire Area Record Office, The Castle, Haverfordwest, Dyfed
minutes 1932-65; subscribers list 1875; annual return 1876; annual accounts 1906-60; general ledgers 1938-57; papers re borrowing powers 1957-67; receipts, bills and accounts 1813-81; business correspondence 1790-1904; press advertisement 1928; accident book 1924-45; property agreements and correspondence 1894-1912; cargo insurance policy 1914; plans 1834,1903; notes and articles on history 1960s-70s

245 SEA INSURANCE CO LTD

30 Dec 1875
10150
1 Bartholomew Lane, London EC2N 2AB
Insurance

History: established in Liverpool in 1813 by William Jones, insurance broker as William Jones & Co. Known as Jones & Hodson from 1834, Jones, Younghusband & Co from 1847, Jones, Palmer & Co from 1853 and WH&S Jones & Co from 1868. William H and Edward S Jones joined their father's business in 1850 and 1868 respectively. Incorporated as above in 1875 with underwriting of marine insurance as its main business and WH Jones as its chairman. Undertook marine insurance in Europe and North America after 1883, offered fire and accident insurance from 1923 and general insurance after 1930. By 1936 had branches in London, Birmingham, Cardiff, Glasgow, and Manchester in UK; New York, USA; Sydney, Australia; Cape Town, South Africa; Bogota, Colombia; and Toronto, Canada. Amalgamated with Beacon Insurance Co Ltd (inc 1883) in 1953. Acquired in 1960 by London Assurance Corporation which had merged with Sun Insurance Office Ltd in 1959 and Alliance Assurance Co Ltd in 1965 to form Sun Alliance & London Insurance Group. Offices in 1814 were at 22 Exchange Buildings and in 1974 were at Derby House, Exchange Buildings, Liverpool.

Records (1): at Sea Insurance, Derby House, Exchange Buildings, Liverpool, Merseyside L2 3QH
directors meeting minutes 1921-65; annual reports and accounts 1875-date; nominal and private ledger 1923 on; agency agreements and powers of attorney 1883 on; staff: register 1924-45, appointment book c1920-51

Records (2): at Liverpool Record Office, City Libraries, William Brown Street, Liverpool, Merseyside L3 8EW
directors: meeting minutes 1875-1922, reports to shareholders 1877-1922; staff: attendance

register 1854-7, salary list 1890-1917, income tax returns 1910-14; *SS Gunga* log book 1845; voyages and time risk book 1864-6; policies casualty book 1876-7

246 UNION LIGHTERAGE CO LTD

5 Jan 1876
10165
4 Carlton Gardens, Pall Mall, London SW1Y 5AB
Lighterage

History: incorporated as above in 1876 to carry on business of lightermen on the River Thames. Registered offices were situated at 16 Philpot Lane, London. Also owned Anchor Bay Slipway, Erith, Kent until it was closed in 1970. Acquired in 1960s by Butler's Wharf Ltd which was acquired by Town & City Properties Ltd in c1980.

Records: at Southwark Local Studies Library, John Harvard Library, 211 Borough High Street, London SE1 1JA
directors: and general meeting minutes 1923-38, reports 1963-70; management meeting minutes 1971-2; balance sheets and accounts 1928-70; financial statements and reports 1966-72; creditors ledgers 1963-70; debitors ledger 1967-71; tankers ledger 1966-70; journals 1968-71; depreciation registers: property 1908-66, vessels 1950-67; vessel contracts 1909-70; accidents register 1965-71; staff: registers c1920-40, engagement forms 1918; wages book 1960-6; pension fund: meeting minutes 1964, trust deed 1967, register 1947-63, rule books 1947-64, balance sheets and accounts 1965-71; Erith Yard and Anchor Bay Slipway title deeds, documents, plans and correspondence 1951-71

247 FINE ART SOCIETY LTD

10 Feb 1876
10262
148 New Bond Street, London W1Y 0JT
Fine art society and art gallery

History: based at 148 New Bond Street since its incorporation as above in 1876, the society has held over 2000 exhibitions. Major artists and architects with which the society has been connected include EW Godwin, GF Faulkner, Ruskin, Lord Leighton, Whistler, Sickert and New English Art Club. An Edinburgh branch was opened in 1973.

Records (1): at Fine Art Society, 148 New Bond Street, London W1Y 0JT
directors meeting minutes 1876-1926; shareholders register 1876-1909; share: allotment book 1876-1974, ledger 1876-1919; mortgage register 1876-1924; debenture register 1932-44; share notices and correspondence 1870s-1932; annual report and balance sheets 1895-1942; private ledger nd-1966; ledger 1942-61; journal c1889-1963; receipts cash book 1926-72; payments cash book 1926-66; cash book 1938-56; sales day books 1905-79; bought day books 1927-71; on sale books 1939-71; oil and watercolour stock ledger 1921-67; prints published stock ledger 1919-42; misc stock ledger 1945-66; Frank Brangwyn etchings stock ledger 1941-51; engravings stock ledger 1948-9; etchings stock ledger 1932-5; private stock book nd; retail department ledger 1927-31; stock summaries 1946-58; uncollected stock 1970-5; bound

catalogues of exhibitions 1878-1979; correspondence with Rev RW Wilson 1963-8; and Scottish Arts Council 1960s

Records (2): at Glasgow University Library, Whistler Collection, Glasgow, Strathclyde G12 8QQ
correspondence between Marcus Huish, Ernest Brown and JM Whistler 1878-1910

Records (3): at Royal Institute of British Architects Library, 21 Portman Square, London W1
correspondence between Marcus Huish and EW Godwin, architect 1881

Fine Art Society Ltd, *1876-1976 Centenary*, Centenary Exhibition Catalogue (1976)

248 SHEFFIELD & HALLAMSHIRE PROPERTY CO LTD

17 Feb 1876
10300
Knowle House, 4 Norfolk Park Road, Sheffield, S Yorkshire S2 3QE
Property

History: incorporated in 1876 as above as a property development company in Sheffield and district. In 1933 owned properties in Moorhead, Devonshire Street, Powell Street, Brookhill, Fulney Road, Frickley Road and Attercliffe Road, Sheffield, S Yorkshire. Went into voluntary liquidation in 1983.

Records: at S Yorkshire County Record Office, Cultural Activities Centre, Ellin Street, Sheffield, S Yorkshire S1 4PL
directors and general meeting minutes 1876-1934; members register 1930-81; share ledgers 1903-81; annual summaries and returns 1911-40; memo and articles of association 1876; annual reports and accounts 1877-1981; balance sheets and profit and loss accounts 1876-1965; nominal ledgers 1876-1960; impersonal ledger 1935-58; cash books: 1925-38,1956-60, petty 1954-64; yearly rental summaries 1904-15; rent registers 1926-40; Devonshire Street premises valuation and report 1965

249 BRITANNIA STEAMSHIP INSURANCE ASSOCIATION LTD

19 Feb 1876
10340
Southwark Towers, 32 London Bridge Street, London SE1 9SU
Insurance

History: founded in 1855 for the protection of shipowners against liability claims, collision and harbour damage claims and other risks. Incorporated as above in 1875. Subsequently provided war risks strike and freight demurrage and defence insurance. In 1984 managed by Tindall, Riley & Co.

Records: at Britannia Steamship Insurance Association, Southwark Towers, 32 London Bridge Street, London SE1 9SU
board, committee and general meeting minutes 1876-1958; rough meeting minutes 1928-63; secretarys meeting minutes and correspondence 1900-18; letter books 1904,1918; members: register 1876 on, address book 1898; club rules 1916-40; owners files 1936 on; average and loss books 1903-54; policy calls compromised 1950; claims: 1945-55, outstanding 1918-48; risk

books: 1876-1920,1944-71, indemnity club 1931-50, oriental 1870-7, war 1917-18,1939-42, protection club 1931-50, sailing protection club 1887-1904, ships books 1899-1920 on

250 **LONDON STEAMSHIP OWNERS MUTUAL INSURANCE ASSOCIATION LTD**
19 Feb 1876
10341
17 Crosswall, London EC3N 2AT
Mutual marine insurance

History: founded as a mutual insurance club in 1866 by Sir F Hodgkinson and incorporated as above in 1876. GE Hodgkinson & Son continued as managers until 1891 when A Bilbrough & Co Ltd were appointed. During 1930s had branch offices in Cardiff, S Glamorgan, Newcastle upon Tyne, Tyne & Wear and Swansea, W Glamorgan.

Records (1): at London Steamship Owners Mutual Insurance Association, 17 Crosswall, London EC3N 2AT
rules and regulations 1876 on

Records (2): at A Bilbrough, Walsingham House, 35 Seething Lane, London EC3N 4DQ
committee meeting agendas and papers 1946-54; ledgers: 1938-c69, private c1882-c1906, reinsurance and sundries 1927-45, impersonal 1929-c45, principals 1931-3; cash books 1910-73; entry forms: 1882-1911,1955-75, books 1914-19, special terms c1914-48; British members: ledgers 1932-42, registers 1937-52; foreign members: ledgers 1928-41, indexes 1931-47; claims: registers 1904-19, notices 1921-57; legal advice, opinions and papers 1890-1930; war risks: premium registers 1938-58, entry registers 1937-53, members register 1962-73, ledgers 1931-49, journals 1925-57, cash books 1937-51, papers 1937-43; lake steamers: premiums books 1942-5, claims notices 1931-45; American reinsurance pool: premium registers 1942-56, members register 1944-51; American agencies claims notices 1945-64; foreign reinsurance: registers 1946-57, tonnage entry registers 1946-57, index 1934-9, ledgers 1930-9, claims notices 1931-69; Danish claims index 1927-60; Norwegian mission claims notices 1941-6; stevedores indemnity register 1959-66; call: entry guarantees 1910-47, journals 1920-56; tonnage capital 1949-61; premium: journals 1939-61, cash book 1942-6; reinsurance: entry index 1920-33, recoveries 1948-54, tonnage capital 1954-61; releases 1965-74; out letter books 1932-9
War Risks Associations: London group meeting minutes 1914-38; financial statements: London group 1940-57, Liverpool & London 1941-57, North of England 1941-58
Shipowners Equitable Mutual Assurance Association Ltd: liquidation papers and accounts 1887-93
A Bilbrough & Co Ltd: directors and general meeting minutes 1911-63; members register c1960-6; directors holdings register c1967-71; balance sheets and accounts, annual reports and accounts, annual returns and agm correspondence 1940-55; private ledgers 1921-57; cash books 1959-71; Paris supplement registers 1924-6; LVR registers 1948-58; call journal 1940; out letter books: private 1896-1912, semi-private 1920-52; salaries ledgers 1911-57

Records (3): at A Bilbrough, 46 High Road, Orpington, London
committee: sub-committee and agm minutes 1876-1971, agendas and notes 1940-6, attendance

books 1944-76; annual reports and accounts 1890-1923; claim statistics 1889-1957; protection and indemnity clubs secretarys and managers meeting minutes 1900-62
Shipping Interest Association Ltd: committee and agm minutes 1912-39
Empire Steamship Assurance Association Ltd: directors and agm minutes 1905-25

251 PENRITH FARMERS' & KIDD'S LTD

1 Mar 1876
10553
Agricultural Hall, Penrith, Cumbria CA11 7HX
Auctioneers and estate agents

History: formed and incorporated as Farmers' Auction Co Ltd in 1876 to carry on the business of an auction mart at Penrith, buying the existing Penrith Auction Mart in the same year. Bought the auctioneering business of Thornborrow & Co in 1907 and Appleby Auction Co Ltd in 1922. Amalgamated with Kidd's Auction Co Ltd in 1922 and became Penrith Farmers' & Kidd's Auction Co Ltd, and acquired Kirkby Stephen Farmers' Auction Co Ltd in 1933. Name changed to above in 1970. In 1981 owned auction marts in Cumbria at Penrith, Lazonby, Appleby, Kirkby Stephen and Troutbeck, estate, furniture and insurance offices in Penrith, Keswick and Kirkby Stephen, and Agricultural Hotel in Penrith. Operated own slaughter houses until the 1940s and owned Southwaite auction mart until it was closed in the 1960s.

Records: at Penrith Farmers' & Kidd's, Agricultural Hall, Penrith, Cumbria CA11 7HX
directors and general meeting minutes 1876-date; shareholders list and share allotment 1931-3; correspondence re shares, profits and tolls 1907-14; annual reports and accounts 1877-8,1884-7,1906-date; revenue account and balance sheets 1909-22; particulars of sales 1900-02,1911-13; invoices 1882-93; land and income tax papers 1909-17; staff bonus and pension scheme papers 1920,1934-5; photographs of winning stock 1940s-50s
Thornborrow & Co: revenue account and balance sheets 1909-22
Kidd's Auction Co Ltd: directors and general meeting agenda and minutes 1908-09; correspondence re weighing machine maintenance, trade, shares and accounts 1908; commission and charges figures 1904-07;
Kirkby Stephen Farmers' Auction Co Ltd: list of shareholders and shares 1932

252 EDGBASTON HIGH SCHOOL FOR GIRLS

25 May 1876
10631
Westbourne Road, Edgbaston, Birmingham, W Midlands B15 3TS
School

History: formed by initiative of George Dixon, Birmingham industrialist, later Lord Mayor and MP for Edgbaston North and incorporated as Edgbaston High School for Girls Ltd in 1876. Leased a private residence in Edgbaston, W Midlands to house the school. 76 girls were admitted in 1877 and numbers doubled by 1878 causing a lease to be taken on new premises in Hagley Road. During the 1880s a hall and 6 classrooms were built and in 1896 Edgbaston School House for Girls Ltd was incorporated to acquire and then run a boarding house. A preparatory department opened in 1913. From 1922 no dividends were paid as all profits were directed to educational purposes. During the depression, numbers fell to 200 but rose to about 400 by 1939. School was evacuated to Stroud, Gloucestershire in 1939 where it shared premises with the local girls high school but its numbers fell to 100. Returned to Edgbaston in 1940 and amalgamated in 1941 for the rest of the war with Edgbaston Church of England College for Girls and numbers rose again to 200. By 1950 numbers stood at 600. 'Ltd' was removed from its title in 1957. Extensive building work was undertaken during the 1950s but the site was cramped and suitable for commercial development. In 1960 the lessors, Calthorpe Estate, offered a new site in Westbourne Road, Edgbaston on which a new school was built. The school had over 900 pupils in the mid 1970s.

Records: at Edgbaston High School for Girls, Westbourne Road, Edgbaston, Birmingham, W Midlands B15 3TS
school committee meeting minutes 1875-8; council: meeting minutes 1876-date, annual reports and accounts 1877-1955, members list 1833-1933; finance committee: meeting minutes 1876-1959, reports 1930-71; house committee: meeting minutes 1890-1957, reports 1930-71; bursary committee: meeting minutes 1932-54, reports 1935-71; boarding house committee meeting minutes 1906-28; education sub-committee meeting minutes 1894-5; building appeal committee papers 1946-50; development and maintenance committees reports 1930-71; general meeting: minutes 1896-date, attendance book 1896-1971; share: ledger 1876-1981, certificates 1877-1920, circulars 1877-1909, correspondence 1922-3; memo and articles of association 1876-1957; reconstruction papers and correspondence 1956-7; school: prospectuses and advertisements 1876-1958, circulars 1877-1909; headmistress reports 1877-1909; examiners reports 1881-1918; mistresses, holidays and term lists 1876-1921; admission register 1895-8; new pupils registers 1936-48; pupil: nominations 1877-1909, statistics 1887-1931; income and expenditure statistics 1887-1928; financial correspondence 1940-1; salary lists 1878-1918; leaving notes 1886-1912; property leases and agreements 1792-1896,1951-64; building contract 1884; school house: prospectus nd, register 1897-1942, rules 1926; letters from Charles Dodgson re: *Alice in Wonderland* 1883-94; press cuttings 1877-1909
Edgbaston School House for Girls Ltd: directors meeting minutes 1896-1902; memo and articles of association 1896; annual reports and accounts 1900-01

Janet Whitcut, *Edgbaston High School 1876-1976* (priv pub 1976)

253 COSENS & CO LTD

10 Jun 1876
10673
50 Commercial Road, Weymouth, Dorset
Marine engineers

History: established in 1845 by Captain Joseph Cosens who operated pleasure steamer trips along the south coast. Incorporated as above in 1876 after Captain Cosens' death. From 1881 acquired Bournemouth business of Bournemouth & South Coast Steam Packet Co Ltd (est 1868). Became known as Buff Funnel operators. Acquired by Red Funnel Group, Southampton, Isle of Wight & South of England Royal Mail Steam Packet Co Ltd in 1947. Owned 6 steamers in 1960 but subsequently concentrated on ship repairing and marine engineering. In 1962 owned 2 paddle steamers, 34,000 cubic feet of cold storage (including the offices of 4 local meat wholesalers) and 2 slipways at Weymouth, Dorset. Operated in 1982 as marine and general engineers, steel fabricators and boilermakers.

Records: at Cosens, 50 Commercial Road, Weymouth, Dorset
directors: meeting minutes 1868-1966, attendance books 1951-70; general meeting minutes 1868-1959; members list 1882-5; share: certificates 1911-51, transfer documents 1949-70; debenture stock transfer register 1908-37; corporate documents 1901-27; memo and articles of association 1876-98; annual reports and accounts 1880-1908; account statements 1923-68; ledgers 1876-1973; journals: 1943-74, stewarding 1904-06; day books 1951-67; expenses correspondence and statements 1876; sailing timetables 1852,c1910; vessel: illustrated guides 1920s-50s, overhaul agreements 1956-65, bills of sale, logs, surveys 1876-1951, inventories and check lists 1946-56, insurance details 1930-1,1967-8, photographs and postcards 1880-1960s; passengers carried 1931-61; hired labour book 1909-12; salary book 1962-81; apprenticeship indentures 1928-60; employment agreement 1964; staff and directors: photographs c1900-60s, dinner menus 1914,1926; property agreements and papers 1947-70; Bournemouth & South Coast Steam Packet Co Ltd correspondence 1901-10; newscuttings and misc working papers 1957-62; articles on history 1962-c70

254 TENBY & COUNTY CLUB CO LTD
11 Jul 1876
10747
The Croft, Tenby, Dyfed
Social club-house

History: incorporated in 1876 to establish a gentleman's club in Tenby, Dyfed. Built the club-house on freehold land on The Croft. Due to new legislation a separate Tenby & County Club was formed in 1894 to run the club. Since 1894 the company's principal activity has been the ownership of the premises rented and run by Tenby & County Club which in 1984 had around 100 members.

Records: at Tenby & County Club, The Croft, Tenby, Dyfed
directors and general meeting: minutes 1876-date, agendas 1887-1905; share: allotment list 1876, registers 1876-date, transfer register 1877-1936, ledger 1930s on; annual lists and summaries 1877-date; directors: lists 1887-1905, register 1930; annual reports and accounts 1878-date; accounts statements 1935-55; ledgers 1879-94; cash book 1887-94; purchase ledger 1888-92; billiard table: takings book 1891-3, correspondence 1887-93; hon secretarys out letter books 1876-1907; club: committee meeting minutes 1894-1912, suggestions book 1887-8, officers and members subscription lists 1888-9, members lists pre 1894, tenancy agreements 1894,1963

255 REDLAND TRAFFIC SYSTEMS LTD
26 Aug 1876
10841
Redland House, Reigate, Surrey RH2 OSJ
Dormant (previously road building material manufacturers)

History: incorporated as Mountsorrel Granite Co Ltd to take over the lease of stone quarries near Mountsorrel, Leicestershire and to manufacture tarred granite and slag for use in road building. By 1930 had subsidiaries also concerned in producing material for road building: John Ellis & Sons Ltd, Enderby & Storey Stanton Granite Co Ltd and Mountsorrel Tarred Macadam Co Ltd. In 1960 share capital was increased, name was changed to Mountsorrel Holdings Co Ltd and company became a non-trading holding company. In the same year Redland Holdings Ltd acquired the company, and integrated the activities of the subsidiary companies into the group. In 1970 name changed to above and by 1984 company was dormant.

Records (1): at Redland, Redland House, Reigate, Surrey RH2 OSJ
meeting minutes: directors 1960-83, general 1927-82; members register 1960-80; annual returns 1964-82; memo and articles of association 1960; annual report and accounts 1963-82

Records (2): at Leicestershire Record Office, 57 New Walk, Leicester, Leicestershire LE1 7JB
sales particulars of quarries in Leicester 1859; valuation, rental and papers 1875-88

256 NORTHUMBERLAND WHINSTONE CO LTD

8 Nov 1876
10982
Whinstone House, 1 Station Road, Benton, Newcastle upon Tyne, Tyne & Wear NE12 8YX
Stone quarry owners

History: incorporated in 1876 to purchase Barrasford, Greenhead, Longhoughton and Littlemill quarries in Northumberland and stock and plant belonging to William Barkus and Thomas A Gledstaines and to work and sell stone and minerals from quarries. Lease of Littlemill quarry terminated in 1896. Gunnerton quarry was acquired in 1899-1900 and Fontburn quarry in 1917. Sold 59,285 tons of stone in 1917. In 1940s lost use of number 2 face of Greenhead Wall Town quarry which was situated next to Hadrians Wall. Output in 1934 consisted of 195,800 tons of whinstone and 21,800 tons of limestone. In 1971 was also manufacturing concrete products and had 2 subsidiaries - Northumberland Concrete Co Ltd and North West Granite Ltd. Acquired in 1972 by Tarmac Ltd and Longhoughton and Greenhead quarries were subsequently closed. In 1984 Barrasford quarry was largest operating roadstone quarry in Northumberland.

Records: at Northumberland Whinstone, Whinstone House, 1 Station Road, Benton, Newcastle upon Tyne, Tyne & Wear NE12 8YX
directors meeting: minutes 1876-1951, agendas and rough minutes 1942-55, papers 1941, attendance book 1876-1936; general meeting: minutes 1876-1953, agendas and rough minutes 1942-55; agm: chairmans speeches 1947-51, directors reports 1926-47; memo and articles of association 1876-1954; share: applications 1876, certificates 1878, transfer documents 1877-1972, allotment returns 1950; annual reports 1878-1972; balance sheets and accounts 1877-1911; general ledgers 1876-83,1905-11; journals 1876-83,1901-06; cash book 1876-86; stone

costs statements 1895-1901,1927-37; work, pay and costs book 1875-80; quarry leases, papers, correspondence and plans 1870-1905; head office photograph nd
North West Granite Co Ltd: memo and articles of association 1961

257 TOLLESBURY & MERSEA NATIVE OYSTER FISHERY CO LTD

15 Dec 1876
11066
Coast Road, West Mersea, Nr Colchester, Essex CO5 8PA
Oyster fishing

History: incorporated as Tollesbury & Mersea (Blackwater) Oyster Fishery Co Ltd in 1876 to restore and cultivate the oyster fishery in the River Blackwater, to give employment to local dredgermen, and to acquire rights of fishery in certain parts of the river. Two classes of share were offered, 'A' shares available to anyone and 'B' shares which could only be held by dredgermen and their sons residing within the precincts of the fishery. The fishery was managed by a jury of local dredgermen. Name changed to above in 1912. In 1983 the company was unable to employ full time staff, mainly due to disease affecting the oysters.

Records: at Essex Record Office, County Hall, Chelmsford, Essex CM1 1LX
directors and general meeting minutes 1877-1939; register: directors 1901-35, members 1876-95; share: ledger 1876-1984, register 1877 on, allotment book 1879-96, holders address book 1877 on, certificates 1879-1926, list c1910, transfer register 1879-1924, transfer certificates 1879-1921; option 1886, annual list 1877-1910; memo and articles of association 1876,1924; letters of indemnity 1897-1925; by-laws 1879-90; prospectus 1877; annual report and accounts 1879-1960; balance sheets 1919-36; ledger: 1931-59; private 1877-1972, bought and sold 1879-1914, sales 1915-19; journal 1879-1975; cash book: 1877-1973, petty 1922-45; day book 1879-1961; stock book 1879-96; legal bills 1979-92; *SY Violet* plan and correspondence 1897; wages: 1943-56, dredgermen 1912-37, watchmen 1919-43; agreement re special constables 1889; fishing grounds: correspondence 1879,1904, plan c1900; company transactions c1900-50; Fishery Order and Act 1868,1878; poor rate legal papers 1922-3
Growers of Nature Oysters: draft rules 1897
Blackwater River Oyster Fishery Co Ltd: memo and articles of association c1875

258 BSC FOOTWEAR LTD

20 Dec 1876
11076
Sunningdale Road, Leicester, Leicestershire LE3 1VR
Footwear

History: established in 1870 by Edward Wood who began manufacturing boots and shoes in Leicester, trading as Edward Wood & Co. Incorporated as Freeman Hardy & Willis Ltd in 1876 to manufacture and deal in leather boots, shoes and other articles. Wood was a director along with his traveller, his factory manager, William Freeman, and Arthur Hardy, an architect. Trading began in 1877 from 39 Portland Street. First retail outlet opened at Wandsworth, London in 1877, followed by shops at Banbury, Oxfordshire, Coventry, W Midlands and Leamington Spa, Warwickshire. By 1921 when Sir Edward Wood retired as chairman, company owned 428 shops. Acquired Rabbits & Sons Ltd, boot and shoe retailers,

Newington Butts, London in 1903; Kettering Boot & Shoe Co Ltd (inc 1879) in 1913; and Leavesley & North Ltd, wholesale boot and shoe manufacturers, Leicester in 1925. Acquired in 1927 by J Sears & Co (True-Form Boot Co) Ltd (inc 1912) of Northampton but all trading activities remained under company's control in 1954. Became nucleus of British Shoe Corporation formed in 1956 by Charles Clore (later Sir Charles) who had taken over J Sears & Co in 1953. BSC subsequently took over several boot and shoe manufacturers and retailers: Manfield & Sons Ltd, Northampton (est 1840); Dolcis Ltd (formerly Upsons Ltd, inc 1921); Lilley & Skinner Ltd, London (inc 1894); Curtess & Saxone Shoe Companies; and Stratford Court Hotel Ltd. In 1967 company changed name to above, the title of a dormant subsidiary, and to British Shoe Corporation Ltd in 1980. In 1982 it was the largest retail shoe store chain in Europe having 551 branches.

Records (1): at British Shoe Corporation, Sunningdale Road, Leicester, Leicestershire LE3 1VR
directors meeting minutes 1940-date
Lewis's Group: pension scheme trustee minutes 1958-70
Lewpen Nominees Ltd: directors and general meeting minutes 1952-70
AL Scott & Son Ltd: memo and articles of association 1922; powers of attorney 1960s; journal 1931-61
J Sears & Co (True-Form Boot Co) Ltd: ledger 1930-66

Records (2): at Leicestershire Record Office, 57 New Walk, Leicester, Leicestershire LE1 7JB
directors meeting minutes 1928-40; share: register 1953-6, transfer register 1956-7; balance sheets and profit and loss accounts 1912-46; trading accounts 1933-9; shop accounts and expenditure 1939-46; agreement re sales competition 1897; pension scheme members register 1962-5; war damage accounts 1940-45; property documents: Leicester 1698-1947, Bedford 1815-85, Bristol 1782-1900, Lancaster 1810-71, Oxford 1906-27, Preston 1815-1915, Salisbury 1806-19, Scarborough 1743-1883, Great Yarmouth 1734-1819
Active Modern Shoes Ltd: members register 1955-68; share register 1954-7; memo and articles of association 1953
Arch Preserver Shoes Ltd: members register and share ledger 1954-64; share register 1954-7; memo and articles of association 1953
CW Barron & Co Ltd: directors meeting minutes 1908-55; members register 1908-49; general ledger 1896-1908
Alexander Boyd (Ayr) Ltd: memo and articles of association 1929
Frederick Cork Ltd: memo and articles of association 1934
Dolcis Ltd: directors and general meeting minutes 1921-57; members register and share ledger 1921-37; share and share transfer register 1928-57; directors register 1951; private ledgers 1905-30
Dolcis Shoe Co (Ireland) Ltd: minutes 1935-55
Dutton & Thorowgood Ltd: members and share register 1957-68; memo and article of association 1905
Easy Goer Shoes Ltd: members register and share ledger 1954-68; share register 1954-7; memo and articles of association 1953
Edward Lloyd Ebbern Co Ltd: members register and share ledger 1951-68; share registers 1932-57; memo and articles of association 1932

Freeman Hardy & Willis (Kettering) Ltd: directors meeting minutes 1879-1935; general meeting minutes 1880-1935; debenture trust deed 1900; memo and articles of association 1879; accounts statements 1894-1912
Leavesley & North Ltd: general meeting minutes 1920-35
Lilley & Skinner Ltd: memo and articles of association 1894-1949
Manfield & Sons Ltd: directors meeting minutes 1943-50; articles of association 1950; annual returns 1954-67; private ledger 1938-68; employees trust fund deed 1922,1927; pension scheme minutes 1951-67
G&W Morton Ltd: memo and articles of association 1923, 1950
Porter & Co Ltd: memo and articles of association 1903
AL Scott & Son Ltd: share register 1931-61; debenture register 1953-5; seal register 1963-8; memo and articles of association 1922
J Sears & Co (True-Form Boot Co) Ltd: members registers and share ledgers 1912-16; share ledger 1930-66; memo and articles of association 1912; private ledgers 1932-57; shop front plans, Coventry, Dundee, London and Manchester 1912-36
Selbrite Shoes Ltd: members register and share ledger 1952-68; share certificate book 1954-7; memo and articles of association 1953
Stratford Court Hotel Ltd: private ledgers 1936-58
True-Form (Dublin) Boot Co: premises plans 1917-c22; sale documents 1926-7
Tru-Poise Ltd: members register and share ledger 1954; memo and articles of association 1953
Vari-Tred Shoes Ltd: minutes 1959-65; members register and share ledger 1954-68; share register 1954-7; memo and articles of association 1953; annual returns and correspondence 1959-65; mortgages and deed re land in Suffolk 1733-1889

259 PALATINE ENGINEERING CO LTD

3 Jan 1877
11106
491 Hawthorn Road, Bootle, Liverpool, Merseyside L20 9DD
Waste water meter manufacturers

History: incorporated in 1877 as Waste Water Meter Co Ltd to purchase from and carry on under the patent rights of George F Deacon (civil engineer and engineer to Liverpool Water Undertaking), the business of manufacturing and selling waste water meters. Had offices in Blackstock Street, Liverpool in 1908. Name subsequently changed to above. Went into liquidation in 1980.

Records: at Merseyside County Archives, 64-66 Islington, Liverpool, Merseyside L3 8LG
minutes 1877-1978; patents, sales catalogues and advertisements 1876-1913; results record 1898-1901; sectional drawings nd; water article 1882

260 CABLE & WIRELESS (WEST INDIES) LTD

9 Jun 1877
11116
Mercury House, 110-124 Theobalds Road, London WC1X 8RX
Telegraph

History: formed in 1869 as West India & Panama Telegraph Co to establish with Cuba Submarine Telegraph Co (est 1870) telegraph communication from Cuba through Jamaica to Colon, Panama, and to Georgetown, Guyana via the eastern Caribbean islands. First cables opened in 1870, connected Batabano, south Cuba, to Jamaica via Cienfuegos and Santiago, Cuba. By 1871 cables had been laid to connect San Juan, Puerto Rico, St Thomas, St Kitts, Antigua, Guadeloupe, Dominica, Martinique, St Lucia, St Vincent, Barbados, Grenada, Trinidad and Georgetown. Jamaica and San Juan were linked in 1872 and Jamaica with Colon in 1873. St Croix connected to Puerto Rico, St Thomas and Trinidad in 1875. Became an associated company of Imperial & International Communications Ltd in 1929 (Cable & Wireless Ltd from 1934 and publically owned from 1946) and taken over by them in 1932. In 1935 took over operating assets of Direct West India Telegraph Co Ltd (inc 1897), Halifax & Bermudas Cable Co Ltd (inc 1889) and Cuba Submarine Telegraph Co Ltd and changed name to above in 1938. Operated in 1981 as the West Indian subsidiary of Cable & Wireless Ltd.

Records: at Cable & Wireless, Mercury House, 110-124 Theobalds Road, London WC1X 8RX board meeting minutes 1869-1938; committee meeting minutes 1883-1926; shareholders meeting minutes 1869-1938; dissenting shareholders register 1933-60; allotment book 1877; share ledger 1870-1911; second preference shareholders register 1874; preference share ledger 1873; debenture holders register 1872-1924; directors registers 1901-33; agreements, cable leases and related papers 1868-1927; legal court papers re Cuba Submarine Telegraph Co 1900-01; seal registers 1869-1936; annual reports 1869-1970; general ledgers 1871-1936; revenue ledger 1944-50; London journals 1870-1938; cash book 1944-62; clerks and cleaners staff record books 1908-30; local staff rules and regulations 1951; premises leases 1870-8; photographs of cable offices and other property 1928-9; articles, press releases, notes etc re history of company and communications in West Indies 1869-1977
Cuba Submarine Telegraph Co Ltd: board meeting minutes 1869-1944; shareholders: lists 19 cent, ledger c1877-1925; contracts, agreements, deeds and related corporate papers and correspondence 1867-1920s; annual reports 1874-1943; general ledgers 1870-1937; cable lay and repair logs and diaries 1873-95; cable rates 1889; Havana station staff rules and regulations 1879
Direct West India Telegraph Co Ltd: board meeting minutes 1897-1961; shareholders: meeting minutes 1897-1966, ledger 1897-1966; share transfer ledger 1898-1966; annual reports 1898-1966; ledger 1897-1901; general ledger 1910-61; journal 1935-55; cash book 1930-67; traffic notes c1890-1918; maps, correspondence and notes re laying of West Indian cables c1950; staff rules and regulations c1900; staff book c1905-30; photographs of Bermuda office c1900
Halifax & Bermudas Cable Co Ltd: board meeting minutes 1889-1966; shareholders: meeting minutes 1889-1966, register 1947-65; share: transfer register 1889-1966, ledger 1889-1965; debenture: application and allotment register 1889-97, ledgers 1889-1909; mortgages and charges registers 1889,1897; directors and managers registers c1890-1964; annual reports 1891-1966; general ledgers 1889-1951; journal 1922-58; traffic notes c1890-1918; staff rules and regulations c1900; staff book c1905-30; photographs of Bermuda office c1900

KC Baglehole, *A Century of Service. A brief history of Cable and Wireless Ltd 1868-1968* (1969)
Hugh Barty-King, *Girdle Round the Earth* (1979)

261 CV HOME FURNISHINGS LTD

19 Jan 1877
11136
39 Well Street, Bradford, W Yorkshire
Manchester warehousemen

History: established in 1840 by JF Roberts who was joined by his brother H Roberts in 1842. Partnership was incorporated as JF&H Roberts Ltd in 1877, the business of manufacturing and selling Manchester goods continuing from 21 Portland Street, Manchester. By 1923 had mills at Foulridge, Lancashire and Oxenhope, W Yorkshire; branch warehouses at 15 Watling Street, London; Melbourne and Sydney, Australia; agencies in New Zealand and Montreal, Canada; and was specialising in tailors trimmings and linings, woollens, dressmakers linings, flannelettes and calicoes. Acquired in 1962 by British Van Heusen Corporation Ltd which was itself acquired in 1963 by Viyella International Ltd (later Vantona Viyella Ltd). Name subsequently changed to Dorma Sheets Ltd and to above in 1973. In 1977 was operating as textile manufacturers, merchants and exporters handling terylene/cotton bed linen under the 'Dorma' trade name. Has been based at Swinton, Greater Manchester since mid 1970s.

Records: at CV Home Furnishings, PO Box 7, Newton Mill, Lees Street, Swinton, Greater Manchester M27 2DD
directors and general meeting minutes including prospectuses, correspondence, share material, circulars, directors reports and accounts, stocktaking resolutions, lease and premises documents, articles of association, etc 1877-1966; customer account book 1910-17; Antipodean branch reports and correspondence 1912-20
John Duckworth & Son (Blackburn) Ltd: directors and general meeting minutes 1953-64
WL Sandbach Ltd: directors and general meeting minutes 1931-62, managing directors reports 1938-45; general ledger 1929-33; balance sheets and trading accounts 1929-45
Wakefield Mill Ltd: members register and share ledger 1920-41

262 DOOM DOOMA TEA CO LTD

15 Feb 1877
11212
Thames House, Queen Street Place, London EC4R 1DH
Tea

History: incorporated as above in 1877 to acquire tea estates in Upper Assam, India which were developed and managed by the Warren family of tea planters. By 1921 owned 14,390 acres, 5717 acres of which were under cultivation and in 1957 owned 15,826 acres with 6202 acres under cultivation. Subsequently acquired by Brooke Bond Liebig Ltd.

Records (1): at Osmond Aerosols, S Humberside Industrial Estate, Grimsby, Humberside
directors meeting minutes 1877-82

Records (2): at Brooke Bond Liebig, Thames House, Queen Street Place, London EC4R 1DH

263 UNICORN INDUSTRIES-UK LTD

20 Feb 1877
11222
24 Queen Anne's Gate, London SW1H 9AR
Grinding machines and abrasive wheel manufacturers

History: incorporated in 1877 as Slack's Emery Wheel & Machine Co Ltd to purchase Samuel Slack's emery wheel and emery wheel machinery manufacturing business. Robert Luke was a founding director and Mountford Spencer and Eli Spencer acquired financial interests and became directors. Samuel Slack sold his share in 1882 and name changed to Luke & Spencer Ltd in 1885. First manufacturing site was at Lime Bank Street, Ardwick, Manchester, moving to site bordered by the Manchester Road, Bridgewater Canal and Atlantic Street (then Central Road) in Broadheath, Altrincham, Greater Manchester with the canal providing a means of easy access. The factory initially operated on gas engines transferring to electricity in 1914. Involved in commercial development of synthetic abrasives and resins required in emery wheel manufacture. Produced grinding wheel machinery until 1973 when it became uneconomical. Established agents in Australia and Egypt in mid 1920s. In 1960 was acquired by Unicorn Industries Ltd, industrial group (including Universal Grinding Wheel Co Ltd with whom company had abortive amalgamation talks in late 1930s) engaged in diamonds, abrasives and hard material technology. Name changed to above in 1973 and Broadheath factory closed in 1981 and site sold for redevelopment. Unicorn Industries Ltd subsequently became a subsidiary of Foseco Minsep Ltd.

Records: at Unicorn Industries-UK, Doxey Road, Stafford, Staffordshire ST16 1DZ
directors and general meeting minutes 1877-1958; articles of association 1877-1961; secretarys letter book 1884-1913; share certificate book 1961-72; annual reports and accounts 1935-57; balance ledger 1901-63; audited balance sheets and accounts 1939,1954-61; service agreements 1898,1909; staff records 1968-81; training profile and report 1979; employers provident fund policy and schedules 1937-52; pension fund: management committee minutes 1955-71, members register and contribution record c1954-66, ledger c1955-65; pension scheme papers and correspondence 1965-81; photograph of factory and transport fleet
Fascut Products Ltd: directors and general meeting minutes 1949-57; annual reports and accounts 1952-7; corporate papers and correspondence incl subsidiaries 1949-76; deed schedule 1949-63; licences, patent and trade-marks schedule 1951-67; photograph of exhibition stand 1960s; retirement benefits plan: staff register 1975, works register 1975, papers and correspondence 1970-5

Luke and Spencer Ltd 1877-1977 Centenary Year, 100 Years of grinding wheel manufacture (priv pub 1977)

264 IBSTOCK BRICK CATTYBROOK LTD

15 Mar 1877
11298
Cattybrook Works, Almondsbury, Bristol, Avon
Brick manufacturers

History: founded in 1864 by Charles Richardson, Bristol & South Union Railway Co engineer, who obtained lease of Cattybrook brickfields, Almondsbury, Bristol, Avon. Entered into partnership in 1871 with Ernest E Street, civil engineer, and Edward Grover. Incorporated in 1877 as Cattybrook Brick Co Ltd and operated from Cattybrook and Lawrence Hill, Bristol, manufacturing bricks and agricultural drain pipes. Purchased in 1903 Shortwood Brick & Tile Co Ltd which owned the mineral rights at Shortwood, Mangotsfield, Bristol. Purchased by Ibstock Johnsen Ltd, brick manufacturers of Ibstock, Leicestershire in about 1972 and changed name to above in 1973.

Records: at Ibstock Johnsen, Leicester Road, Ibstock, Leicestershire LE6 1HJ
directors and general meeting minutes 1872-1972; Shortwood board meeting minutes 1903-71; share: certificate book 1895-1972, transfer certificates 1882-1972; debenture trust deed 1905; memo and articles of association 1877-1969; corporate papers and correspondence 1877-1948; annual: returns 1901-72; reports and accounts 1908-67; balance sheets 1877-1922; revenue accounts 1894-1926, Shortwood works 1912,1915; brochure 1906; stock returns 1918-19; patent papers 1877-84; glazed brick recipe 1888; boiler insurance policies 1906-21; wages: book 1927-51, negotiations 1919-56; works manager agreement 1925; employers liability policies 1906-21; inventory and valuation of Cattybrook 1895,1965, and Shortwood 1965; property papers, correspondence and agreements re Almondsbury, Cattybrook and Shortwood 1859-1968; fire insurance policies 1906-21
Shortwood Brick & Tile Co Ltd: correspondence re purchase and liquidation 1902-03; annual: return 1900, reports and accounts 1895,1898; title abstract, surface rights agreements and correspondence 1889-99

265 NORTHWICH VICTORIA CLUB CO LTD

16 May 1877
11462
Chester Way, Northwich, Cheshire
Social club-house

History: incorporated as above in 1877 by a group of Northwich businessmen to establish a gentleman's club and lease Victoria Hall, Northwich, Cheshire. Purchased freehold in 1896-7.

Records: at Northwich Victoria Club, Chester Way, Northwich, Cheshire
directors and general meeting minutes 1877,1898-1930,1948-date; members register 1903-45; share certificate and transfer documents 1890-1963; annual returns 1934-63; debenture stock correspondence 1896,1943; memo and articles of association 1877; annual reports and accounts 1878-1963; balance sheets 1903-06,1912-59; general ledgers 1903-53; journal 1903-53; cash books: 1894-1947, petty 1907-12; mortgage repayment correspondence 1937; subscription books 1887-93,1907; stock books 1902-28; visitors book 1877-date; steward agreement 1948; leases 1909-38; car park plan and correspondence 1966-8

266 CROMPTON & EVANS' UNION BANK LTD

26 May 1877
11487
Iron Gate, Derby, Derbyshire
Banking

History: incorporated as above in 1877 as a joint stock bank with the amalgamation of the banking firms of Crompton, Newton & Co of Derby and Chesterfield (est 1685) and WS Evans & Co of Derby (est 1771). In 1879 it took over the greater portion of the business of Chesterfield & North Derbyshire Banking Co (est 1833) and the business of Wilson & Son of Alfreton, Derbyshire (est 1853) and James Taylor & Sons of Bakewell, Derbyshire (est 1846). In 1918 amalgamated with London, County & Westminster Bank Ltd, a predecessor of National Westminster Bank Ltd, at which time it possessed 19 branches and 27 sub-offices.

Records: at National Westminster Bank, 41 Lothbury, London EC2P 2PB
board meeting minutes 1905-13; minutes 1877-1913; committee meeting minutes 1895-1914; agendas 1896-1918; share allotments 1877-96; prospectus and articles of association 1877; amalgamation papers 1913-14; annual reports 1882-1914; balance sheets 1888-9; profit and loss account memoranda 1877-84; customer weekly memoranda 1886-96; investments and advances memoranda 1906-13; salary books 1897-1913; clerkship application registers 1891; staff instructions 1883; directors correspondence 1911-14; head office instructions to branches 1879-1914; branches - Bakewell: half yearly returns 1879-1913; Chesterfield: profit and loss account 1880, list of overdrawn accounts 1882, general ledger balances 1896-1913; Hathersage: half yearly returns 1892-3

TE Gregory, *The Westminster Bank Through A Century* Vol 2 (1936)

267 BRITISH XYLONITE CO LTD

3 Jun 1877
11530
Buchanan House, 3 St James's Square, London SW1Y 4JS
Plastics

History: established in about 1862 when Daniel Spill began to use 'Parkesine' (a type of plastic invented by Alexander Parkes) at his brother George's waterproofing works in Hackney Wick, E London. Parkes founded Parkesine Co Ltd with Daniel Spill as works manager in 1865 but it went into liquidation in 1868. Spill founded Xylonite Co Ltd in 1869 to manufacture 'Xyloidine' at the old premises of Parkesine Co. This company was liquidated in 1874 and Spill then founded Daniel Spill & Co Ltd at 124 High Street, Homerton, where he produced Xylonite (celluloid) and 'Ivoride' knife handles, brooches and decorative trinkets. In 1876 he was joined by LP Merriam and expanded into 122 High Street. In 1877 with the agreement of 3 businessmen, EB Bennett, HL Bennett and Alexander Mackay, the above was incorporated to manufacture Xylonite, with EB Bennett as managing director. Homerton Manufacturing Co Ltd was formed to run Merriam's part of the business but the two companies merged in 1879 under the name of Xylonite Co Ltd. Business became successful after Lewis L Hyatt, collar and cuff manufacturer from France, joined the company in 1885 and began production in Benwell Road, Holloway, London. The Homerton factory was badly damaged by fire in 1885 and new premises were built at Brantham, Suffolk in 1887. New plant and premises were opened at Hale End, Walthamstow and Homerton factory closed in 1896. A new collar factory was built at Hale End and Benwell Road factory closed in 1900. Employed 29 workers in 1877, 500 in 1888, 1160 in 1902 and 2000 in 1923. From 1921 'Lactoid' (casein formaldehyde) was manufactured at a new factory at Larkswood, Chingford, London and British Xylonite Co (Canada) Ltd was incorporated in 1922. In 1931 acquired Cascelloid Ltd, Abbey Lane, Leicester, plastic hair slide and jewellery manufacturers which opened a plastic doll and toy manufactory in Owen Street, Coalville, Leicestershire in 1937 and a third factory in West Street, Stamford, Lincolnshire in 1939. British Xylonite (Australia) Pty Ltd was incorporated in 1931. By 1937 Brantham factory was producing Bexoid (cellulose acetate plastic) but Xylonite was still the main product. Hale End manufactured goods such as tooth and hair brushes, combs, knife handles etc from Xylonite, Bexoid and synthetic resins such as phenol-formaldehyde and urea-formaldehyde. Two subsidiaries were formed in Jan 1939: BX Plastics Ltd which took over the raw material factories at Brantham and Larkswood, and Halex Ltd which took over manufacture at Hale End. In 1939 Distillers Co Ltd became owners of a half-interest in the company. BX Plastics Ltd acquired Expanded Rubber Co Ltd of Croydon, London, manufacturers of Rubazote and Onazote (soft and hard rubber) in 1943 and a new factory in Dundee, Tayside for manufacturing Bexoid moulding powder and polyvinylchloride sheets, extrusions and compounds in 1945. It also formed Plastic Cutters Ltd to distribute Xylonite knife handles and Bexford Ltd (in conjunction with Ilford Ltd) to manufacture photographic film and film base in 1945; Scintillex Ltd to manufacture artificial jewellery in 1946; and British Xylonite Inc in the USA in 1948. The company in 1951 bought back the manufacturing businesses from its wholly owned subsidiaries Halex Ltd, Cascelloid Ltd and Scintillex Ltd, which became selling companies. In 1963 Bakelite Xylonite Ltd, controlled jointly by Distillers Co Ltd and Union Carbide Corporation of New York, was formed from Bakelite Ltd (est 1926), British Xylonite Co Ltd, BX Plastics Ltd and other UK plastics interests of Union Carbide Corporation. In 1973 Distillers transferred its shares in this company to Union Carbide Corporation. In 1978 Bakelite Xylonite became a wholly owned subsidiary of British Petroleum Co Ltd. In 1983 British Xylonite Co Ltd was a dormant subsidiary company of BP Chemicals Ltd through BXL Plastics Ltd. Xylonite manufacture continues at Brantham site, now owned by Bernard Wardle Group.

Records (1): at BXL Plastics, Buchanan House, 3 St James's Square, London SW1Y 4JS
board minute extracts 1903-19; group organisation circulars 1954-64; annual reports and accounts 1919-38; balance sheet and accounts 1939; catalogues 1928-39; publicity department reports 1949-64; patent specifications 1924-5; house magazines 1922-65; Manningtree, Essex property papers and correspondence 1887,1894; Homerton factory sale particulars c1893-8; factories, machinery, products and personnel photographs 1890s-1970s; history booklets, articles, notes etc 1900s-82; visitors book 1894-1911

Bakelite Ltd: trade-mark agreements 1928-56; process agreements 1959-62; annual reports and accounts 1928-63; profit and loss accounts 1929-46; catalogues and sales brochures and literature 1936-60s; trade magazines 1946-60s; press release 1932; plant plan nd; house magazines 1958-75; factory, plant and staff photographs 1930s-70s; press cuttings 1948-57; history articles, notes and interview tapes 1928-70

Bakelite Xylonite Ltd: corporate agreements 1966-70; merger papers 1977-8; annual reports and accounts 1965-date; sales literature 1970s; advertisements 1963-7; trade magazine 1965-9; factory, products and directors photographs 1960s-70s; safety posters nd; house magazine 1965-70

Bexford Ltd: house magazine 1969-75

BXL Plastics Material Group Ltd: corporate agreements 1970; sales brochure 1969; house magazine 1967-9

BX Plastics Ltd: Brantham factory: production figures 1887-1965, statistics 1938-59, plans nd, photographs 1940-63, fire records 1940-63; future forecast 1955; staff progress booklets 1953-8; bombing maps etc 1940; historical notes 1959-62

Cascelloid Ltd: catalogues and technical and sales literature 1959-66; Leicester and Stamford works photographs c1946; historical notes c1973
Damard Lacquer Co Ltd: corporate agreements 1917-27; patent specification and experiment results and reports 1902-16; travellers notebook 1908; 'gormbook' 1914-15; sales brochure nd; James Swinburne papers and photographs 1890s-1960; historical articles and notes 1930-50s
Expanded Rubber Co Ltd: Croydon and Dundee factory photographs 1940s; historical booklet 1957
Halex Ltd: sales catalogues and price lists 1939-58; factory, exhibition and staff photographs 1920s-40s
Warerite Ltd: house magazine 1955-9

Records (2): at Hackney Archives Department, Rose Lipman Library, De Beauvoir Road, London N1 5SQ
directors meeting minutes 1877-1925; general meeting minutes 1884-1932; corporate agreements 1877-1917; shareholders: register 1877-80, ledgers 1887-1927, list 1935; share certificate book 1883-4; dividend payments 1904-16; members register etc 1920-30; directors registers 1901-30; capital reorganisation papers 1930; debenture: documents and correspondence 1880-1911, stock trust deed 1933, interest accounts 1933-8; annual reports and accounts 1878-1959; balance sheets and profit and loss accounts 1878-80; annual accounts 1886-1906; general ledgers 1877-1911; agents ledger 1910-13; bought ledger 1934-9; financial papers c1877-c1917; sales: agreement and papers 1885-8, statistics 1888-1918; plant books 1893-1918; production costs and sales statistics book 1893-1934; papers c1877-c1917; patent papers and reports c1872-c1917,1933-9; trade-mark papers c1877-c1917; Japanese camphor report and papers 1897-1901; stocktaking book 1908-30; staff papers c1877-c1917; factory sales particulars 1896-9; property papers c1877-c1917
British Tortelloid Ltd: directors and general meeting minutes 1932-8
British Xylonite (Australia) Pty Ltd: directors and general meeting minutes 1931-45; memo and articles of association 1931; annual accounts 1932-43,1950; sales analysis 1932-41
British Xylonite Co (Canada) Ltd: annual accounts 1922-39
British Xylonite Co New York Incorporation: directors meeting minutes 1914-27
British Xylonite Co Nurnberg GmbH: general meeting minutes 1908-14; corporate papers c1908-c17
British Xylonite Co Wien GmbH: general meeting minutes 1908-14; corporate papers c1908-c17
Cascelloid Ltd: directors and general meeting minutes 1931-5; annual reports and accounts 1931-50; annual accounts 1932-45
Homerton Manufacturing Co Ltd: directors and general meeting minutes 1877-9; memo and articles of association 1877; corporate papers 1877-9
Paper Drying Co Ltd: correspondence 1894-1910
Parkesine Co Ltd: history report 1919
Daniel Spill & Co Ltd: prospectus nd
Xylonite Co Ltd: price list 1869; history report 1919

Records (3): at Suffolk Record Office, Ipswich Branch, County Hall, Ipswich, Suffolk 1P4 2JS
directors meetings with Foster Sproxton minutes 1932-42; annual reports and accounts 1888-1933,1945-62; general ledger 1965-9; Larkswood factory cost ledger 1965-7; Brantham: machinery notes and buildings registers 1908-37, manager plant recommendations 1933-6;

output summary and cost book 1881-1961; production statistics batch record books 1869-87,1928-34; laboratory: books late 1870s-c1937, temperature and humidity record 1924-42; analyses and reports 1887-95; formulae books nd; staff: deputations and petitions 1894,1912-16; wages books 1899-1928; time and wages books 1877-1937; work study 1936-7; sick fund accounts 1892-1936; savings bank: ledgers 1908-37, cash books 1928-31; war bank ledgers 1914-18; war savings certificate registers 1917-22; house magazine 1922-70; safe deposit register 1918-63; fire reports, notes, correspondence, photographs and insurance schedules 1888-1939; photographs: Hale End, Brantham, Melbourne, Australia and directors 20 cent; letter books: general 1888-1936, company 1883-1935, directors 1880-1936, benefit club 1912-34, cottages 1888-9, wages department 1936-8, Bexoid 1932-7, laboratory 1898-1938, statements 1888-1936, costs 1909-30, Hale End 1936-8, make department 1936, firms 1936-8; papers, articles, notes and correspondence on company history and plastics 1880-1976
BX Plastics Ltd: Brantham: board reports 1939-58, managers committee minutes 1942-53; production statistics 1946-64; output and cost statistics 1947-60; technical and sales literature c1961; staff wages books 1948-54; work study 1939-42; sick fund accounts 1944-58; savings certificate registers 1948-51; fire reports, notes and photographs 1940-63; photographs 1946-56
Cascelloid Ltd: Leicester works photographs 1927-39
Homerton Manufacturing Co Ltd: correspondence 1877-9
Paper Drying Co Ltd: letter book 1894-1911

Records (4): at Waltham Forest Libraries & Arts Department, Vestry House Museum, Vestry Road, Walthamstow, London E17 9NH
catalogues and price lists 1896-1915; house magazine 1933,1962-4; ex-employee interview tapes 1977,1980; Rolls cottage plan 1950; museum product photographs c1880-c1940; newscuttings nd; history notes and booklets 1886-1965
Halex Ltd: price list nd

M Kaufman, *The First Century of Plastics: Celluloid and its Sequel* (priv pub 1963)

268 OCEAN ACCIDENT & GUARANTEE CORPORATION LTD

21 Jun 1877
11543
1 St Helens, Undershaft, London EC3P 3DQ
Insurance

History: formed and incorporated in 1877 as Ocean & General Guarantee Co Ltd by Ocean Railway & General Accident Assurance Co Ltd incorporated in 1871 as Ocean Railway & General Travellers' Assurance Co Ltd specialising in issue of insurance tickets for railway and sea passengers and professional mariners. Company offered fidelity guarantees for the honesty of persons in positions of trust. Both companies shared same management and premises at Mansion House Buildings, Poultry, London and were merged under above title in 1890. Acquired Commercial Guarantee Insurance Co Ltd (est 1874), Railway & General Insurance Co Ltd (est 1876) and Star Accident Insurance Co Ltd (est 1877) in 1878; Imperial Union & Accident Assurance Co Ltd in 1894; General Accident Guarantee & Indemnity Insurance Co Ltd (est 1879) in 1898; Security Insurance Co Ltd (est 1889) in 1899; Employers' Indemnity Insurance Co Ltd (est 1898) in 1901; and accident insurance business of Lion Life & Accident Insurance Co in 1883, Economic Fire Office Ltd in 1894, Mortgage Insurance Co in

1895 and Lancashire Insurance Co in 1900. Moved to new headquarters in Moorgate, London in 1893. Premium income exceeded £700,000 by 1898. By 1910 was largest British company specialising in accident insurance, with premium income of nearly £1.5 million. Acquired by Commercial Union Assurance Co Ltd in 1910 but continued to operate under its own name and management.

Records (1): at Commercial Union Assurance, 1 St Helens, Undershaft, London EC3P 3DQ
board meeting minutes 1940-65; committee meeting minutes 1962-5; general meeting minutes 1890-1965; share: registers 1908 on, transfers 1905-64; seal books 1962 on; investment ledger 1891 on
Ocean Railway & General Accident Assurance Co Ltd: general meeting minutes 1888-90

Records (2): at Guildhall Library, Aldermanbury, London EC2P 2EJ
board meeting minutes 1877-1940
Ocean Railway & General Accident Assurance Co Ltd: board minutes 1871-90

Edward Liveing, *A Century of Insurance: The Commercial Union Group of Insurance Companies 1861-1961* (1961)

269 KEMPTON PARK HOLDING CO LTD

29 Aug 1877
11675
PO Box 207, 128 Queen Victoria Street, London EC4P 4JX
Racecourses

History: incorporated in 1877 as Kempton Park Racecourse Co Ltd to purchase Kempton Park at Sunbury on Thames, Surrey on which to establish and maintain a racecourse and hold races. Name subsequently changed to above. In 1970 became part of United Racecourses Ltd group, joining Sandown Park Ltd and Epsom Grandstand Association Ltd, when purchased by Metropolitan & Country Racecourse Management & Holdings Ltd. In 1982 was dormant subsidiary company of the Horserace Betting Levy Board through the latter company.

Records (1): at United Racecourses, Kempton Park Racecourse, Sunbury on Thames, Surrey
directors and general meeting: minutes 1915-date, agenda 1901-49, attendance book 1878-1969; memo and articles of association 1877-1948; annual reports and accounts 1915-date; ledgers 1921-54; journal 1928-67; cash books 1937-54; petty cash book 1927-69; race card accounts 1931-61; meetings: analyses 1932-52, records 1937-72, comparisons 1933-55; staff agreement nd; racecourse inspection reports 1948-69; leases 1878-1962; inventory and valuation 1959; stable plan 1964; Tote and catering agreements and contracts 1930s-40s; insurance papers 1930s-60s; correspondence: re premises development 1948-71, with Racecourse Association 1950s on, general 1950s on
Kempton Park Freehold Land Co Ltd: agenda book 1885-1949; directors register 1901-47; annual reports and accounts 1940s; secretarys out letter book 1933-50
Kempton Park Club: royal suite visitors book 1950-8

Records (2): at United Racecourses, Epsom Racecourse, Racecourse Paddock, Epsom, Surrey KT18 5NJ
share certificate counterfoils 1968-74; Tote buildings schedule 1938

270 CLIFTON HIGH SCHOOL FOR GIRLS

12 Sep 1877
11701
College Road, Clifton, Bristol, Avon BS8 3JD
School

History: founded and incorporated as above in 1877, as an unlimited company to provide education for girls in Bristol, opening in Pembroke Road, Clifton, with 67 pupils in Jan 1878, rising to 160 by autumn of that year. Numbers reached 200 in 1913, 490 in 1933, dropped during WW2 to 298 but rose again to 583 in 1945, 669 in 1955 and 726 in 1962. Was in receipt of Board of Education grant from 1908 to 1920 when it was placed on direct grant list but has been independent since 1946. Has preparatory, junior and senior departments.

Records: at Clifton High School for Girls, College Road, Clifton, Bristol, Avon BS8 3JD
council meeting minutes 1877-date; house committee meeting minutes 1877-date; finance committee meeting minutes 1892-date; general meeting minutes 1877-date; share, share transfer and shareholders register 1877-date; pupil nomination book 1877-99; secretarys letter book 1878; memo and articles of association 1918; annual reports and accounts 1878-date; statements of account 1940-50; general ledger 1919-date; cash book 1944-60; petty cash book 1877-1939; luncheons cash book 1886-7; details of house expenses 1889-1957; teaching staff salaries book 1924-46; examination reports 1881-96; scholarship book 1930-51; property title deeds 19-20 cent; plans of school property 20 cent; photographs of staff, pupils and buildings 19-20 cent; newscuttings and articles on school 20 cent

Nonita Glenday and Mary Price, *Clifton High School 1877-1977* (priv pub 1977)

271 ULVERSTON & NORTH LONSDALE AUCTION MART CO LTD

22 Sep 1877
11717
North Lonsdale Road, Ulverston, Cumbria LA12 9AU
Auctioneers

History: incorporated in 1877 as above to carry on business as auctioneers and salesmen. Re-registered as public limited company in c1981.

Records: at Ulverston & North Lonsdale Auction Mart, North Lonsdale Road, Ulverston, Cumbria LA12 9AU
directors and general meeting minutes 1877-date; members register and share ledger etc 1890s-1940s; memo and articles of association 1877-1974

272 GREAT GRIMSBY HIDE, SKIN & FAT MARKET CO LTD

29 Sep 1877
11730
Gilbey Road, Pyewipe, Grimsby, Humberside DN31 2SJ
Hide and skin market

History: incorporated in 1877 to protect the butchers of Grimsby by establishing a market for the sale, purchase or exchange of hides, skins, fat and offal. Only butchers were allowed to be shareholders. Moved from centre of Grimsby to a new industrial estate at Pyewipe in late 1960s.

Records (1): at Great Grimsby Hide, Skin & Fat Market, Gilbey Road, Pyewipe, Grimsby, Humberside DN31 2SJ
directors and general meeting minutes 1900-80; members and share transfer register 1877-1982; directors registers 1902-73; shareholders list 1951; annual returns 1922-64; share: certificates 1907-71, transfer documents 1878-1970; memo and articles of association 1877,1932; annual report and accounts 1949-54

Records (2): at Humberside Area Record Office, Town Hall Square, Grimsby, Humberside DN31 1HX
deeds 1694-1915

273 DERBY LAND BUILDING & INVESTMENT CO LTD

1 Oct 1877
11734
112 Green Lane, Derby, Derbyshire DE1 1RY
Property

History: incorporated in 1877 as above to acquire and develop property. Purchased Fir Estate in Derby and laid out Leicester, Hall, Faire, Raven, Westbury, Dean, Harrison, Wood, Boyer and Warner Streets. By 1883, 68 cottages, 2 shops and a builder's house had been erected by the company and other land had been auctioned to builders. By 1891, 106 houses and shops had been built. Purchased 28 cottages and 8 villas in Normanton district of Derby in 1906 along with other properties in other parts of the town. In 1951 owned 143 houses and shops in Warner, Boyer, Leman, Harrison, Westbury, Dean, Leicester, Moss, Grosvenor and Holcombe Streets and Havelock, Cameron, St Thomas' and Walbrook Roads. During the 1950s sold properties where possible and invested proceeds in stocks. By 1969 owned 58 houses on the Fir Estate and 15 houses on the Normanton Estate. In 1984 still owned properties in Derby.

Records: at Derby Land Building & Investment, 112 Green Lane, Derby, Derbyshire DE1 1RY
directors and general meeting minutes 1877-date; chairman agm remarks 1958-9; memo and articles of association 1887,1961; directors and managers register 1901-c36; annual reports and accounts 1907-68; balance sheets 1891-1903; private ledgers 1909-57; audit book and financial papers 1921-date; income tax returns, papers and correspondence 1938-date; plans 1894,1912; rent: book 1968-72, and rates statistics 1963-71; share, tenant, repair, investment and property correspondence and papers 1958-date

274 BROUGHTON AUCTION CO LTD

20 Oct 1877
11771
Auction Mart, Broughton in Furness, Cumbria
Auctioneers

History: incorporated as above in 1877 to establish an auction mart in Broughton in Furness, Cumbria and to carry on trade as general auctioneers and salesmen. Company still operates for the same purpose in 1985.

Records: none survive

275 BERTHON BOAT CO LTD

26 Oct 1877
11785
Shipyard, Lymington, Hampshire SO4 9YL
Shipbuilding

History: incorporated as above in 1877 to carry on the manufacture of patent Berthon canvas and other boats designed by the Rev EL Berthon, Vicar of Romsey. Lord Dunsany was the first chairman, and the original shipyard was at Romsey, Hampshire. Agencies set up in Southampton and Portsmouth, Hampshire, Ireland and New York. By 1881 the new Duplex boats had been approved by the Admiralty, and had been bought by both British and French governments. Financial problems in 1917 brought about the transfer of property and assets to the May family, already running a shipyard at Hythe, Hampshire. In 1920 Romsey shipyard closed and work was transferred to Lymington, Hampshire. In 1943 the value of work was £116,777 and by 1953 a substantial volume of work was undertaken for the Admiralty. From the late 1950s the company concentrated on trading in the construction and maintenance of pleasure yachts. In the early 1980s the company bought pre-made hulls for further construction, and carried out refits, alterations and repairs.

Records: at Berthon Boat, Shipyard, Lymington, Hampshire SO4 9YL
board and general meeting minutes 1877-1966; directors register 1928-33; share: ledger 1919-67, summary 1908-27, certificates 1919-82; memo and articles of association 1918; private ledger 1920-73; journal 1950-73; bills payable 1918-37; sales literature and reprints from journals nd,c1930-68; day book 1840-61; costs books 1891-1951; register: plant machinery and fittings 1919-65, motor steam yachts 1936-8; plant inventory 1942; construction details 1935-45; specifications: and alterations 1920-60, inshore minesweeper 1949-53, and blueprints 1938-55; wages book 1959-66; factory regulations and certificates 1938-51
Agamemnon Boatyard Ltd: share ledger 1958-65
Lymington Marine Ltd: 'G' ledger 1958-63

276 LEIGH CONSERVATIVE CLUB BUILDING CO LTD

8 Nov 1877
11820
Railway Road, Leigh, Greater Manchester
Political club-house

History: established in 1875 and incorporated as above in 1877 to acquire land in Leigh, Greater Manchester on which to erect premises for the use of Leigh Conservative Club & Assembly Room which had its roots in the Conservative Working Men's Reading Room (est c1868). Purchased land, formerly covered by the Prince of Wales Theatre, fronting Railway Street, and built club building to designs of JJ Bradshaw, Bolton, architect. Club was opened in 1879 and by Oct 1880 had 384 members. From 1889 trustees have held shares in the company on behalf of the club which had nearly 800 male members in 1979.

Records: at Leigh Conservative Club Building, Railway Road, Leigh, Greater Manchester directors and general meeting minutes 1875-date; share: ledger 1878-c1903, certificate book 1883-1977; memo and articles of association 1877 on; annual lists and summaries 1883-1926; trustee appointments 1889-1978; balance sheets 1943-date; ledger 1928 on; account book 1905-date; soiree balance sheet 1905; Working Men's Reading Room picnic account 1879; building: accounts 1878, extension costs 1893, plans 1879-1932, leases 1931-5

LA Goodfellow, *Leigh Conservative Club 1879-1979. The Centenary Celebration* (priv pub 1979)

277 FENLAND LAUNDRIES (GRANTHAM) LTD

3 Dec 1877
11872
Roman Bank, Skegness, Lincolnshire PE25 1SQ
Laundry

History: incorporated in 1877 as Grantham Steam Laundry Co Ltd to establish a steam laundry business at Grantham, Lincolnshire. Authorised share capital was £8000. In 1944 company was acquired by Skegness Steam Laundry Co Ltd, (subsequently known as Fenland Laundries (Skegness) Ltd). Name changed to above in 1958.

Records: at Fenland Laundries (Skegness), Roman Bank, Skegness, Lincolnshire PE25 1SQ directors and general meeting minutes 1936-79; share: ledger 1956-81, transfer book 1879-1977; dividend: register 1882-1946, account book 1956-65; balance sheets c1946-date; ledgers: private 1946-70, general 1964-9; inventory 1944

278 TAMWORTH HERALD CO LTD

13 Dec 1877
11898
10 Aldergate, Tamworth, Staffordshire B79 7DP
Newspaper

History: incorporated in 1877 to purchase the *Tamworth Herald* and printing and publishing business from D Addison. The newspaper was first published in about 1867 and its circulation averaged 2400 copies weekly by 1877. Leased premises at 14 Silver Street, Tamworth, Staffordshire, purchasing freehold in 1892. Acquired new premises in 1899 for printing and publishing departments in Halford Street. Established bookbinding and embossing departments at Silver Street in 1901 and commenced a circulating library in 1903. Acquired a controlling interest in *Lichfield Mercury* in 1933. *Tamworth News* incorporated with the *Herald* in 1936. Acquired Lomax's, printers, stationers and booksellers of Lichfield, Staffordshire in 1942. Opened new printing works at Aldergate in 1958 and Silver Street premises were sold in 1959. New offices were completed in 1965. By 1966 published 3 newspapers - *Tamworth Herald* , *Atherstone Herald* and *Coleshill Chronicle*. In 1966 acquired remaining shares in Baxters of

Atherstone Ltd, first shares having been purchased in 1941. In 1979 launched a fortnightly free publication *Midweek Market* which was replaced in 1980 by the weekly *Herald Midweek Extra*.

Records (1): at Staffordshire Record Office, County Buildings, Eastgate Street, Stafford, Staffordshire ST16 2L2
directors and general meeting minutes 1877-1934; share: ledgers 1877-1959, transfer documents 1878-1925; members registers 1877-88,1920-59; annual list and summary 1877-1938; prospectus 1877; annual reports and accounts 1878-9,1885,1890 on; balance sheet and accounts 1884-99; private ledgers 1877-92; wages book 1894-1912; staff, production, insurance, tax, machinery note book 1890-1905

Records (2): at British Library, Newspaper Library, Colindale Avenue, London NW9 5HE
Tamworth Herald 1870-date; *Lichfield Mercury* 1830-3,1877; *Tamworth News* 1934-6; *Atherstone Herald* 1884-6,1946-59; *Coleshill Chronicle* 1874-date

279 SPP GROUP LTD

1 Jan 1878
11943
Oxford Road, Reading, Berkshire RG3 1JD
Pump manufacturers

History: established in 1875 by John E Hodgkin, engineer who purchased the patent rights of an American steam pump 'The Pulsometer' and formed a partnership with Matthias Neuhaus to manufacture the pump at small works in Battersea, London with offices at 61&63 Queen Victoria Street. Incorporated as Pulsometer Engineering Co Ltd in 1878 to take over the business and to carry on as manufacturing engineers. Agents were appointed in France in 1878 and German and Russian agencies were set up in 1879. Leased Hayle Foundry Wharf Works, Nine Elms from 1880 until 1901 when company moved to Oxford Street, Reading, Berkshire. Opened branch offices in Leeds, W Yorkshire in 1894 and Liverpool in 1898. Began manufacture of 'Hydrotrope' boiler feeders in 1876, American 'Deane' steam pumps in 1882, refrigeration machinery in 1887 and centrifugal and turbine pumps and sirens. In 1909 acquired business of Easton & Anderson Ltd, 11 Tothill Street, London which added high duty pumping engines for water, drainage and sewage works, waterwheels, turbines, superheaters, tunnel shields and explosives and cartridge manufacturing machinery to company's products. By 1923 had also opened branches in Glasgow, Manchester, Birmingham and Cardiff. In 1951 acquired Joseph Evans & Sons (Wolverhampton) Ltd, established in 1810 as manufacturers of reciprocating pumps and later of turbine and centrifugal pumps and in 1957 Skyhi Ltd, hydraulic pump manufacturers, Isleworth, London and GS Tett & Co Ltd, water softening plant manufacturers. Acquired by Booker McConnell Ltd in 1961 and merged in 1962 with Sigmund Pumps Ltd, Gateshead, Tyne & Wear (est 1869 in Czechoslovakia) to form Sigmund Pulsometer Pumps Ltd. Name subsequently changed to above. Fire protection division was set up in 1968, offshore oil division in early 1970s and series pump division in 1975. SPP Systems Ltd was formed in 1973 to specialise in irrigation projects. SPP Controls Ltd was formed at Thatcham, Berkshire to design and manufacture control equipment in electric, electronic and pneumatic systems. Robot Pompen NV, Dutch manufacturing specialists in submersible and other pumps joined the group in 1979. In 1982 SPP Group Ltd was the holding company for 9 subsidiary companies. In 1983 it was acquired from Booker McConnell PLC by a consortium led by Guide House Ltd and became an independent company.

Records: at SPP Group, Oxford Road, Reading, Berkshire RG3 1JD
directors meeting: minutes 1878-1968, agenda 1919-39, attendance books 1878-1962, salaries 1937 on; general meetings minutes 1876-1964; share summaries 1902-33; prospectus 1877; memo and articles of association 1877-1958; corporate correspondence and papers 1878-1926; dividend: account 1899, receipts 1905-11; debenture agreements and correspondence 1919; takeover agreements and correspondence 1877-1957; seal books 1878-1953; annual reports and accounts 1900,1922-35; balance sheets and accounts 1878-1919,1962-8; accounts: statement c1875, summaries 1891-1909; correspondence 1900-09; debtors: and creditors list 1917, correspondence 1881-90; customer ledger 1881-6; sales statistics: 1893,1908-10, 'Electro' pumps 1913-56; sales, agent and agency agreements and overseas manufacturing licences 1879-1960; price lists, catalogues, advertisements and sales literature 1875-c1965; patent agreements, specifications papers and correspondence 1872-1903; press cuttings and articles on products, works and company 1879-1965; products and works photographs 1883-c1970; orders received 1909,1934-58; production: contract 1888, statistics 1934-43; cost sheet queries 1899 on; working instructions books 1900-27; block illustration and number book 1958; insurance policies and inspection contracts 1957-60s; pump drawings 1875-6; stationery book 1920s on; works committee meeting minutes 1939-48; staff: character register 1900-19, service and retirement agreements 1876-92,1922-59, testimonials 1887-9, apprenticeship brochures 1950s, photographs c1900-70; buildings and machinery inventory and valuation 1941,1969; premises: agreements and leases 1875-1902,1953, plans 1900,1907; misc correspondence 1875-93
Easton & Anderson Ltd: boilers and pumping machinery specifications 1888
Joseph Evans & Sons (Wolverhampton) Ltd: directors meeting minutes 1947-51; pumps: sales catalogue 1947, photographs 1950s-60s
William Evans & Co Ltd: directors meeting minutes 1962-78; general meeting minutes 1921-77; memo and articles of association 1970
Sigmund Pulsometer Pumps Ltd: directors meeting minutes 1961-9
Sigmund Pumps Ltd: patent and manufacture agreements and correspondence 1947-55
Sigmund Pumps (Great Britain) Ltd: directors meeting minutes 1940-6, acquisition agreement 1947; pump photographs 1940s
GS Tett & Co Ltd: product photographs 1950s-60s

280 LIVERPOOL COMMERCIAL SALE ROOM CO LTD

26 Jan 1878
11998
Melbourne Building, 19-21 North John Street, Liverpool, Merseyside L2 5QU
Property (formerly sale room)

History: promoted by the 4 member firms of Liverpool Fruit Brokers Association (est 1877) - James Adam Son & Co, Dart & Rogers, JC Houghton & Co and Woodall & Co and incorporated in 1878 to erect a building later known as Commercial Sale Room Building at 1 Temple Court, Liverpool and to establish an auction sale room there. Continued to operate the auction sale room until 1925 when the new Fruit Exchange, Victoria Street was opened. The Commercial Sale Room Building was reconstructed for office accommodation which was leased. Acquired 3 Temple Court in 1978. Acquired by Mersey & Metropolitan Investment Co Ltd in 1980.

Records (1): at Liverpool Commercial Sale Room, Melbourne Building, 19-21 North John Street, Liverpool, Merseyside L2 5QU
current records

Records (2): at Tanyard Farm, Hooe, Battle, E Sussex TN33 9EL
sale documents, incl prospectus and photographs c1981; balance sheets and accounts 1979; newscuttings 1982; history booklets 1936
JC Houghton & Co: brochures 1920s; premises postcards nd; history 1952

281 OLD SWAN HOTEL (HARROGATE) LTD

8 Feb 1878
12028
1 Worship Street, London EC2A 2AB
Hotel

History: incorporated in 1878 as Harrogate Hydropathic Co Ltd to run a hotel in Harrogate, N Yorkshire. Changed name to above in 1957 and to Leisuretime International PLC in 1983. In early 1980s owned a holiday subsidiary, Preston Travel Ltd and holiday villas in Majorca, Canary Islands and Spanish mainland.

Records: at Leisuretime International, 1 Worship Street, London EC2A 2AB
memo and articles of association 1878; title deeds 19-20 cent

282 CORNISHMAN NEWSPAPER CO LTD

16 Feb 1878
12053
Leicester Harmsworth House, 65 New George Street, Plymouth, Devon PL1 1RE
Newspapers

History: incorporated as above in 1878 to establish a newspaper in Penzance, Cornwall and carry on business of printers. *Cornishman* was published on Thursdays and Saturdays from offices in Parade Street and by 1896 weekly circulation was c8000. Between 1896 and 1904 purchased Cornish Post & Morning News Ltd (est 1889) which published the weekly newspaper of the same name from its offices in East Charles Street, Camborne, Cornwall. In 1908 purchased Cornish Telegraph Newspaper Co Ltd which published the weekly *Cornish Telegraph* (est 1851) and evening *Cornish Tidings* from its offices at 16 Chapel Street, Penzance. Merged *Cornishman* and *Cornish Telegraph* and purchased *Helston Advertiser* and *Redruth Effective* during 1909, *St Ives Summary* (est 1890s) in 1910 and *Hayle Mail* in 1911 which were all merged by 1922 into *Cornishman* and *Cornish Telegraph*. Acquired in 1944 by Western Morning News Co Ltd, of Plymouth, Devon which was subsequently acquired by Associated Newspapers Group Ltd. In 1984 former still published *Cornishman* on Thursdays.

Records (1): at Western Morning News, Leicester Harmsworth House, 65 New George Street, Plymouth, Devon PL1 1RE
directors and general meeting minutes 1904-69; share transfer documents 1895-1941; private ledgers 1944-76

Records (2): at Associated Newspapers Group, Carmelite House, Carmelite Street, London EC4Y OJA
memo and articles of association 1878-1913; annual returns 1947-70

Records (3): at British Library, Newspaper Library, Colindale Avenue, London NW9 5HE
Cornishman 1878-date; *Cornish Tidings* 1870 on; *Cornish Telegraph* 1852-1915; *Cornish Post and Mining Times* 1899-1944; *Helston Advertiser* 1910-18; *Hayle Mail* 1913-18; *St Ives Summary* 1890,1898-1918; *Redruth Effective* 1909-15

283 HEREFORD HERD BOOK SOCIETY

5 Mar 1878
12100
3 Offa Street, Hereford, Hereford & Worcester HR1 2LL
Breed society

History: incorporated as above as company limited by guarantee to maintain the purity of and improve the Hereford breed of cattle. Continued the issue of *Eyton's Herd Book of Hereford Cattle* which was closed in 1885, and the registration of pedigrees, noting transfers, sales and deaths. By 1890 had 234 life members and 263 annual members, granted export certificates and awarded prizes at major agricultural shows. From the 1880s its offices have been in Offa Street, Hereford and in 1983 it was a registered charity with a membership of over 2700.

Records: at Hereford Herd Book Society, 3 Offa Street, Hereford, Hereford & Worcester HR1 2LL
council meeting minutes 1878-date; general meeting minutes 1890-date; committee meeting: minutes 1878-date, reports 1890 on, agendas 1933-49; rules 1911; private ledgers 1907-51; general: ledgers 1928-36, cash books 1916-57; journal 1917-39; cash books 1925-71; members: list 1888-97, registers 1878-1955, attendance book 1915-40; subscription ledgers 1920-52; sales: ledgers 1942-72, and show purchase book 1916-30, day book 1946-53; export certificate registers 1890-date; herd register c1950-60; sale catalogues 1843-date; press releases 1965-date; *Herd Book* 1859-date; other publications 1923-date; letter book 1929-43; office photographs c1923

284 WEST AUCKLAND BREWERY CO LTD

14 Mar 1878
12117
Greenbank Offices, Lion Brewery, Hartlepool, Cleveland TS24 7QS
Brewing

History: established in 1840 under deed of settlement as West Auckland Joint Stock Brewing Co. By 1859 was under control of John JH Tamplin, brewing premises were situated at West Auckland Farm and owned public houses in and around Darlington, Durham, at Framwellgate Moor, Wingate Grange, Kelloe, Witton Park, South Church, Newfield, Aycliffe and East Hetton. Business went into liquidation in 1877. Bought in Jan 1878 by group of brewers and maltsters including John W Cameron of West Hartlepool, William Cunningham of Drem, Lothian, William Standish of Darlington, and Henry Rudd of Thirsk, N Yorkshire, to form a limited company which was incorporated as above in Mar 1878. In 1959 acquired by JW Cameron & Co Ltd (inc 1894) of Lion Brewery, West Hartlepool, Cleveland, ceasing to brew around 1962, and premises sold in 1978. The former was acquired by Ellerman Lines Ltd in 1978-9.

Records (1): at JW Cameron, PO Box 21, Hartlepool, Cleveland TS24 7QS
directors and general meeting minutes 1950-date; corporate papers 1960s; members registers and share ledgers c1915-date; directors registers 1902-date; share and share transfer documents 1909-date; shareholders circulars 1953-61; memo and articles of association c1961; annual returns 1915-16; annual report and accounts 1920; balance sheet and accounts 1959; title deeds and other property documents 1841-1980

Records (2): at Durham County Record Office, County Hall, Durham, Co Durham DH1 5UL
minutes 1840-1907; private ledgers 1879-1920; rent ledger 1934-8; personal and impersonal accounts 1878-85; cash books 1837-73

285 ROYAL SCHOOL OF NEEDLEWORK

16 Apr 1878
12192
25 Princes Gate, Kensington, London SW7
Craft school

History: formed in 1872 as School of Art Needlework to improve the standard of art in embroidery and to create employment for penurious gentlewomen. First president was Princess Christian of Schleswig-Holstein and has had a royal president ever since, the 'Royal' prefix being granted in 1876. Incorporated as a company limited by guarantee in 1878 as Royal School of Art Needlework, 'Art' being dropped in 1922. Originally had 20 young ladies working as embroiderers and apprentices, by 1903 had risen to 100 and later reached 150. Embroidered many robes etc for royal occasions from Queen Victoria's coffin pall to Queen Elizabeth II's coronation robe. First premises were above a bonnet shop in Sloane Street, Knightsbridge, moving to 31 Sloane Street in 1873, to Exhibition Road in 1875 where custom-built premises to display their wares opened in 1903. School moved to Princes Gate premises in 1948 and furnishing and lingerie departments closed. In 1981 held day and evening classes as well as enrolling 6 new apprentices per year for a 2 year certificate course, repaired historic works, and designed and executed commissions. Registered as a charity and was non-profit making, funds coming from commissions, classes, a shop, voluntary contributions and a 'Friends Scheme'.

Records: at Royal School of Needlework, 25 Princes Gate, Kensington, London SW7
council meeting minutes 1873-date; general meeting minutes 1878-date; committee meeting minutes: advisory 1908-09, art 1875-83, executive 1885-1965, finance 1875-85, agendas 1896-1916, teaching branch 1899 on; council and committee agendas 1885-96; council, agm and committee attendance book 1935-63; members register and share ledger 1878-82; share certificates 1878-1972; legal documents 1874-1922; articles of association and resolutions 1878-1922; balance sheet and accounts 1891-3; general ledgers 1902-26; ledger balances 1909-44; journal 1927-55; cash books 1952-60; petty cash book 1932; monthly statements of receipts

and payments 1876-7; customer accounts summary cash books 1950-61; monthly cash summaries 1948-60; students admission books c1872-1912; gifts and articles on loan book 1951-8; salaries books 1946-59; staff hours notebook 1958-61; students club account book 1954-60; work room docket books 1950 on; coronation robe specifications 1937; title deeds, leases and other property documents 1874-1915; inventory and valuation of school 1947; secretarys letter book 1907-29; correspondence c1894-1930; press cutting books 1872-date; photographs of royalty, special orders, exhibitions, ecclesiastical work, school work room and premises 20 cent
Royal School of Art Needlework Associates: subscriptions and printed reports 1934-73; supplementary fund account book 1902-12

Winefride Jackson and Elizabeth Pettifer, *The Royal School of Needlework - Today and Yesterday* (1981)

286 GREEN MOUNT ESTATE CO LTD

11 May 1878
12255
Hollins House, Cottesmore Gardens, Hale Barns, Altrincham, Cheshire WA15 8TS
Property

History: incorporated in 1878 as above by local businessmen to purchase part of Greenmount Estate near Christ Church, Harpurhey, Manchester. By 1887 owned 22 houses in Church Lane, 26 houses in Palatine Street, 12 shops in Rochdale Road and 17 houses and shops in Albert Edward Street which were all leased to tenants. In 1936 purchased whole of business property of Crumpsall Estate Ltd. In 1977 freehold properties had a market value of £100,000. From 1950s domestic property was sold where possible to tenants, the proceeds being invested. In 1984 owned about 20 properties and was managed by Hollins Murray Group Ltd, the Hollins family having been connected with the company since its inception.

Records: at Green Mount Estate, Hollins House, Cottesmore Gardens, Hale Barns, Altrincham, Cheshire WA15 8TS
directors and general meeting minutes 1908-date; members registers and share ledgers 1889-1966; annual lists and summaries 1900-34; memo and articles of association 1931,1976; annual report and accounts 1946-9; balance sheets and accounts 1897-9,1928-date; financial statements 1922-5; nominal ledgers 1899-1943; capital ledger 1899-date

287 HAUNCHWOOD-LEWIS BRICK & TILE LTD

11 May 1878
12258
Western House, 303 Western Bank, Sheffield, S Yorkshire S10 2TL
Brick and tile manufacturers

History: established in 1875 as Haunchwood Brick Co by co-partners George Fowler, civil and mining engineer, William Mattby, surgeon and John W Fowler, gentleman, to manufacture bricks, tiles and earthenware. Partners sold their brick and pipe making business to Haunchwood Brick & Tile Co Ltd (inc 1878). Company had 3 works in Nuneaton, Warwickshire: Haunchwood Road, Stockingford, Heath End Road and Bermuda Road. Manufactured 'Haunchwood' blue engineering bricks, facing rustic bricks, chimney pots, quarry tiles, sewer pipes, land drainage pipes, hollow floor bricks, common building bricks etc. Merged in 1968 with associated company GW Lewis Tileries Ltd (inc 1896) which had works at Cheslyn Hay and Walkmills, Cannock and Essington, Staffordshire and manufactured 'Rosemary' clay roofing tiles, rustic facing bricks and blue engineering bricks. Changed name on merger to above. Went into voluntary liquidation in 1973.

Records (1): at Warwick County Record Office, Priory Park, Cape Road, Warwick, Warwickshire CV34 4JS
directors: meeting minutes 1878-1910, register nd; general meeting minutes 1903-75; share registers 1878 on; annual returns 1960-72; memo and articles of association 1878 on; Stockingford title deeds 1885; lease and agreements book 1899-1940; rent book nd; plans c1890-1963; Haunchwood works aerial photographs nd

Records (2): at Leicestershire Record Office, 57 New Walk, Leicester, Leicestershire LE1 7JB
co-partnership agreements 1875,1878; memo and articles of association 1878; employee work notebook 1904; workers output statistics 1956-60; land leases and correspondence 1874-80; plant and machinery photographs nd; kiln and machinery plans 1883-1961; site maps and plans 1893-1958; products: catalogues 1930s, illustrations c1905, diagrams 1948-53
GW Lewis Tileries Ltd: works: lease 1904, plan 1884,nd, bore holes findings 1905
Gilbert Tucker & Son Ltd: works plans nd,1960-7; buildings and product photographs c1930-60,nd

Records (3): at Staffordshire Record Office, County Buildings, Eastgate Street, Stafford, Staffordshire ST16 2LZ
GW Lewis Tileries Ltd: directors: meeting minutes 1896-1932,1947-78, register nd; general meeting minutes 1896-1973; members registers 1896 on; memo and articles of association 1896-1959; annual returns 1960-72

288 CUNARD STEAM-SHIP CO LTD

23 May 1878
12286
2 Chalkhill Road, Hammersmith International Centre, London W6 8DN
Shipping

History: established in 1840 as British & North American Royal Mail Steam Packet Co by Samuel Cunard (prominent merchant and shipowner of Halifax, Nova Scotia, Canada who had obtained the British government's contract and subsidy for carrying mails by sailing vessels across the North Atlantic in 1839); Robert Napier, Clyde shipbuilder; George Burns, shipowner; and David MacIver, Burns's partner. First 4 mail and passenger ships were wooden paddle-wheel vessels. The Atlantic mail service was doubled in 1847 and under a new contract a vessel sailed from Liverpool to New York or Boston on alternate Saturdays. Yearly subsidy of £80,000 was raised to £173,340. Cunard Co introduced screw propellers in ships of the Mediterranean auxiliary service which commenced in 1852. The 1867 mail contract stipulated weekly Saturday sailings from Liverpool to New York calling at Queenstown for the mails. Subsidy was reduced to £80,000 and further reduced to £70,000 per year in 1868. After contract was renewed in 1875, remuneration was made according to weight of mails. The Mediterranean and Atlantic fleets were amalgamated in 1878 and the above was incorporated. 13 of the company's fleet of 26 ocean going steamers were lost by enemy action during WW1.

Acquired Port-Line Co Ltd (formerly Commonwealth & Dominion Line Ltd) in 1916. The company ran into financial difficulties in the early 1930s and the government provided funds for the construction of the *Queen Mary* which was launched in 1934 and the *Queen Elizabeth* which followed in 1938. The condition was that Cunard and White Star Line amalgamated to form Cunard-White Star Co Ltd in 1934. Cunard-White Star Co Ltd became a wholly owned subsidiary of the above in 1949. Thomas & John Brocklebank Ltd were acquired in 1940 and HE Moss Tankers Co Ltd in 1964. In 1965 owned 20 ships with a gross tonnage of 377,000 BRT. The *Queen Elizabeth II* was launched in 1967. Headquarters moved to Southampton, Hampshire in early 1960s. In early 1970s also owned Cunard House Ltd, Cunard Properties Ltd, Cunard Properties Canada Ltd, property companies; Cunard-White Star Co Ltd (est 1934); Cunard Insurance Ltd; Cunard Stevedoring Ltd; Chas Howson & Co Ltd, ship repairers; and Finch Edge & Co Inc, shipping agents. Acquired by Trafalgar House Investments Ltd in 1969-70, then renamed Trafalgar House Ltd in 1977.

Records (1): at Liverpool University Archives, PO Box 147, Senate House, Abercromby Square, Liverpool, Merseyside L69 3BX
directors meeting minutes 1878-1941; executive committee meeting minutes 1880-1948; finance committee meeting minutes 1880-1934; general meeting proceedings 1880-1950; annual reports and accounts 1880-1950; members and share ledgers, share transfer and certificate and stock registers 1880-1949; seal registers 1885-1946; chairmen: out letter books 1909-53, correspondence files and papers 1909-53; directors out letter books 1885-1946; secretarys out letter books 1878-1952; vessel: construction correspondence 1905-14, abstract journals 1890s; movement books 1895-1965; passage books 1848-1953; average speed books 1917-61; oil consumption book 1930-66; mails carried book 1915-22; passenger lists 1872-1967; launch brochures, illustrated leaflets, menus etc 1945 on; ships, sea and shore staff, passenger activities, premises etc photographs 1900s on; notes, newscuttings etc on company, history and ships 1945 on; North Atlantic Conference minutes and committee circulars 1917-19
Cunard House Ltd: records 1929-68
Cunard-White Star Co Ltd: directors meeting minutes 1934-41; executive committee meeting minutes 1934-62; out letter books 1934-53
Port Line Co Ltd: directors meeting minutes 1914-52; correspondence files 1890-1950; out letter books 1915-50
Tyser Line: directors meeting minutes 1889-1915; agenda books, members, mortgage and contract registers and voyage summary books 1891-1919
White Star Line: passage book 1871-89

Records (2): at Merseyside County Archives, 64-66 Islington, Liverpool, Merseyside L3 8L6
technical committee meeting minutes and papers 1921-6; voyage data books 1874-1949; steam ships log abstracts 1858-1930; naval architects records 1911-59; vessel: specifications 1898-1962, plans and drawings 1840-1954, correspondence 20 cent; misc papers 1914-69

NRP Bonsor, *North Atlantic Seaway* (1967)
T Stephenson, *A History of the Cunard Line from 1840-1902* (1902)
FE Hyde, *Cunard and the North Atlantic 1840-1933: A History of Shipping Management* (1975)

289 SHIRE HORSE SOCIETY

11 Jul 1878
12383
East of England Showground, Alwalton, Peterborough, Cambridgeshire PE2 0XE
Breed society

History: incorporated as a company limited by guarantee as English Cart Horse Society of the United Kingdom of Great Britain in 1878 to improve the breed and promote the breeding of English cart horses. Earl of Ellesmere was first president and Prince of Wales became its patron. First offices were those of its secretary at Wherstead Hall near Ipswich, Suffolk. First annual breed show was held in London in 1880 and first stud book issued that year. Changed name to Shire Horse Society of the United Kingdom of Great Britain & Ireland in 1883 and moved offices to 11 Chandos Street, Cavendish Square, London in 1884. From 1892 awarded prizes at local agricultural shows for shire classes. During 1890s formed London Cart Horse Parade Society to encourage the drivers to take a humane interest in their animals and this amalgamated with Van Horse Parade to form London Harness Horse Parade in 1966. From 1894 the society leased 12 Hanover Square, London and by 1901 membership had reached 3029, rising to 4199 in 1914. By 1900 the stud book was registering about 5000 new animals per year. Numbers declined during 1920s and 1930s as horses were replaced on roads and farms by motor transport and after 1939, when the government's Heavy Horse Breeding Scheme grants ceased, subscriptions fell drastically. Between 1948 and 1958 the annual show was held at Derby Racecourse. From 1960 it was incorporated with Percheron Society and held at the National Heavy Horse Show at Peterborough Agricultural Society Showground. In 1963 offices were moved to 12 Priestgate, Peterborough, Cambridgeshire when membership was 1079, falling to 803 by 1966 after which slow recovery occurred. Name shortened to above in 1963. By 1968, when offices moved to the new Alwalton showground of East of England Agricultural Society, show entries were the highest since the early 1950s. Membership rose by 912 between 1970 and 1977. In 1974 the liaison with Percheron Society was ended and the National Heavy Horse Show was renamed the National Shire Horse Show.

Records: at Shire Horse Society, East of England Showground, Alwalton, Peterborough, Cambridgeshire PE2 0XE
council minutes 1878-date; stud books 1880-date; correspondence re history 1964-75

Keith Chivers, *The Shire Horse: A History of the Breed, the Society and the Men* (1976)

290 SWAN LAUNDRY (NORWICH) LTD

1 Aug 1878
12428
Holland Court, The Close, Norwich, Norfolk NR1 4DY
Laundry

History: incorporated as Norwich Steam Laundry & Baths Co Ltd in 1878 to purchase an estate in Heighan, Norfolk comprising 2 acres with dwelling houses known as Nortons, late Tinklers Bath Houses, and to carry on the laundry and bathing business. Name changed to above in 1932. By 1975 registered office was at 3 Princes Street, Norwich. Employed 103 people with principal activities of launderers and dry cleaners centred mainly on the domestic market. In 1978 the dry cleaning business and goodwill was sold and the company went into voluntary liquidation in 1979.

Records: at Norfolk Record Office, Central Library, Norwich, Norfolk NR2 1NJ
directors meeting minutes 1931-49; reports to board 1950-60; general meeting minutes 1878-1970; share register 1879-1918; declarations of trust 1927-33; memo and articles of association 1878-1954; ledger: private 1917-45, general 1879-1945, bought 1929-51; register: customers complaints, motor accident claims etc 1937-54, plant and depreciation 1930-6; managers contracts 1918-43; inventory and valuation 1938; commemorative booklet 1943; articles 1970
Wymondham Laundry Co Ltd: directors meeting minutes 1935-64; share ledger 1914-52; report on company with memo and articles of association 1914-52; sale of goodwill 1912; annual report and accounts 1948-65; balance sheets 1948-65; nominal ledger 1933-69; cash books 1941-55; register of customer complaints, accidents to employees etc 1937-54; price list nd; census of production 1949; staff contracts and undertakings 1915-58; premises: Fakenham agreement 1914, Wymondham, Surrey 1925; inventory and valuation 1942; plan 1932; insurance policies 1912-22

291 JAMES WARREN & CO LTD

13 Sep 1878
12515
Welton House, Kiln Lane, Welton, Daventry, Northamptonshire NN11 5JN
Food, insurance and property (formerly merchants, agents and secretaries)

History: founded by James Warren, tea planter and incorporated in 1878 as Planters' Store & Agency Co Ltd to acquire the business of Planters' Stores Co Ltd, an Indian undertaking. Operated in India as merchants, agents and secretaries. Name changed to above in 1949. By 1957 had branches in London, Calcutta, Assam, Bangladesh, Singapore, Malaysia and Kenya. Acquired business of Begg Roberts & Co in 1951. In 1969 acted as secretaries for Amgoorie Tea Estates Ltd, Darjeeling Co Ltd, Deundi Tea Co Ltd, Jetinga Valley Tea Co Ltd, Jorehault Holdings Ltd and Tara Tea Co Ltd and for its associated companies: Warren Rubber Holdings Ltd (inc 1960 to acquire capital of Allagar Rubber Plantations Ltd, Cairo (Malay) Rubber Co Ltd, Eow Song Rubber Co Ltd, Escot Rubber Estates Ltd and Sungei Chinoh Rubber Co Ltd); Warren Tea Holdings Ltd (inc 1963 to acquire the capital of Dekharic Tea Co Ltd, Eastern Assam Tea Co Ltd and Pabbojan Tea Co Ltd); Kiboko Coffee Co Ltd; Kithavan Estates Ltd; Gadek Rubber Estates Ltd (inc 1910); Bobbins Ltd; James Warren & Co (India) Ltd; and James Warren & Co (Malaysia) Sdn Bhd. In 1972 had following subsidiaries: James Warren & Co (Africa) Ltd (inc Kenya) merchants, engineers and agents; James Warren & Co (Tanzania) Ltd, merchants; and James Warren & Co (Uganda) Ltd, James Warren & Co (Malaysia) Sdn Bhd, and James Warren & Co (Singapore) Pte Ltd, merchants and engineers. Acquired Mahawale Holdings Ltd in 1972 and changed its name to Warren Securities Ltd. Sold Malaysian and Singapore subsidiary companies in 1973 and purchased Provincial Garden Cities Ltd (inc 1925) and Leas Properties (Folkestone) Ltd. Acquired Clark's Bread Co Ltd of Hove, E Sussex (inc 1903) in 1974. Offices moved from City of London to Ashford, Kent in 1975-6 by which time it was a holding company. Its main activity was the manufacture of frozen and chilled dairy products operated by its subsidiary Dairy Tops Group Ltd. Other interests through subsidiaries were food wholesaling and distribution, insurance broking and property. In 1978 acquired by Talbex Group Ltd (inc 1933 as New G&S Processes Syndicate Ltd) an investment holding company whose main group interests were aerosol packaging and manufacture and installation of ductwork. Warren food interests were subsequently sold.

Records (1): at Talbex Group, Welton House, Kiln Lane, Welton, Daventry, Northamptonshire NN11 5JN
directors and general meeting minutes 1973-9; corporate agreements and papers 1972-8; memo and articles of association 1973; directors register c1969-79; Talbex acquisition papers 1978; guardbook 1964-77; annual report and accounts 1945-76; audited accounts: 1976-81, subsidiaries 1973-8; annual accounts papers 1972-81; consolidation accounts 1974-8; ledgers and cash book 1970-4; London journals 1970-4; staff papers 1966-82; European staff provident fund: meeting minutes 1950-75, London clerical provident staff fund ledgers 1942-74; UK property agreements 1970s
Anstey Galleries Ltd: directors and general meeting minutes 1973-8; corporate documents and papers 1971-9; members register 1949-79; annual accounts 1974-8
Burlington Insurance Services Ltd: directors and general meeting minutes 1969-73; annual acounts 1974-8
CB Properties Hove (1954) Ltd: directors and general meeting minutes 1954-79; account statements 1955-72; annual accounts 1974-8; ledger 1954-78
Clark's Bread Co Ltd: directors and general meeting minutes 1960-79; corporate agreements 1972-7; annual reports and accounts 1972-6; annual accounts 1974-80; purchase ledger 1974-6; cash books 1974-7
Gigins Ltd: directors meeting minutes 1960-75; general meeting minutes 1968-74; managers meeting minutes 1972-3; annual accounts 1976-8; ledger 1975
Hoggetts Food Products Ltd: directors and general meeting minutes 1975-80; members register 1957-78; annual accounts 1976-7; nominal ledger 1975-6; cash book 1974-6
Mahawale Holdings Ltd: directors and general meeting minutes 1969-73; memo and articles of association 1959; annual reports and accounts 1969-73; cash book 1960-75
Maser Ltd: directors and general meeting minutes 1973-9; memo and articles of association 1964; annual accounts 1976-8; ledger 1964-74; cash book 1964-75
Redman Pamix Ltd: directors and general meeting minutes 1970-9; corporate documents 1970-9; members register 1970-8; annual accounts 1976-8
Pelmadulla Holdings Ltd: directors meeting minutes 1975-9; annual report and accounts 1960-74; annual accounts 1975-8; ledger 1960-75; cash book 1960-76
Provincial Garden Cities Ltd: directors and general meeting minutes 1973-5; annual accounts 1971-7; ledger 1966-78
RB Chambers & Co Ltd: directors and general meeting minutes 1935-68,1974-8; annual returns 1972-9; members register 1935-78; annual accounts 1976-8
United Services Mutual Insurance Agency Ltd: directors meeting: minutes 1951-71, attendance book 1914-65; general meeting minutes 1967-71; annual accounts 1971-8
Warren Rubber Holdings Ltd: directors and general meeting minutes 1974-9; corporate agreements 1972; directors register 1960-74; annual reports and accounts 1970-3; annual accounts 1975-8; ledger 1971-6

Records (2): at Osmond Aerosols, S Humberside Estate, Grimsby, Humberside
directors meeting minutes 1878-1973; agm: minutes 1879-1973, reports 1921-73, papers 1972-5; corporate: agreements 1870s-1970s, guardbook 1939-64; securities register 1940s-60s;

annual and half yearly reports and accounts 1879-1976; balance sheets and accounts 1873-8; UK and overseas companies accounts 1970-3; overseas companies valuation 1960s-70s; ledgers: 1956-70, private 1900-10, purchase 1908-12; London journals 1958-70; cash books 1959-70; taxation papers 1953-71; staff: service agreements 1940s-70s, salary papers c1948-c69; European staff provident fund: meeting minutes 1938-50, trust deed and rules 1939, annual accounts 1969-73; London clerical provident staff fund: meeting minutes 1949-71, trust deed and rules 1948, annual accounts 1969-73; India and London property documents 1870s-1970s; Chittagong Station, property plans and photographs 1950s-60s; Kuala Lumpur branch manager correspondence 1964-7
Clark's Bread Co Ltd: directors and general meeting minutes 1903-60; agm minutes 1929-68; members register c1924-37; corporate documents 1908-36; merger papers 1974-6; annual returns 1936-71; annual reports 1950-76; factory reorganisation papers 1973-8
Doom Dooma Tea Co Ltd: directors meeting minutes 1877-82
Gigins Ltd: directors meeting minutes 1923-60; general meeting minutes 1932-68; members register 1906-42; annual returns 1924-70; papers 1974-6
Jetinga Valley Tea Co Ltd: London ledger 1937-49; estates ledger 1945-55
EP King (Bognor) Ltd: directors and general meeting minutes 1951-67; private ledger 1951-6
Limbuguri Tea Co Ltd: directors and general meeting minutes 1906-26
Mapalagama Rubber Co Ltd: share registers 1933-61
Redman Pamix Ltd: annual accounts 1973-5
Pelmadulla Holdings Ltd: annual accounts 1973-5
Provincial Garden Cities Ltd: directors meeting minutes 1925-73; general meeting minutes 1925-72; members register etc 1925-50; memo and articles of association 1925; takeover papers 1973; annual accounts 1935-74; ledgers 1925-50; journal 1925-48; cash books 1925-64
United Services Mutual Insurance Agency Ltd: directors meeting minutes 1914-51; general meeting minutes 1915-66; members register 1914-64; annual reports and accounts 1915-62
Warren Rubber Holdings Ltd: directors and general meeting minutes 1960-74; guardbook: corporate agreements, share papers etc 1960-73; annual returns 1963-8; annual reports and accounts 1960-73; ledger 1961-71; journal 1960-70

292 PENMAENPOOL BRIDGE CO LTD

26 Sep 1878
12537
Bridge Street, Dolgellau, Gwynedd LL40 1AT
Toll bridge proprietors

History: incorporated as above in 1878 with the object of constructing and maintaining a bridge across River Mawddach near Penmaenpool Bridge Station, Gwynedd on the Cambrian Railway and road approaches from Dolgellau to Towyn High Road on the south side of the river and from Dolgellau to Barmouth on the north. The bridge, built by George Owen, engineer of Cambrian Railway Co, was opened in the summer of 1879. The bridge tolls were collected by the railway company until 1909 when a toll collector was appointed. Due to falling income bridge was closed during winter of 1982-3. Company went into liquidation in 1984.

Records: Penmaenpool Bridge, Bridge Street, Dolgellau, Gwynedd LL40 1AT
directors and general meeting minutes 1878-1984; members registers 1952-date; annual

returns 1952-4; financial papers 1960s on; bridge tolls and ferry leases with correspondence 1878-1928

293 GUILD OF ST GEORGE

25 Oct 1878
12583
Hope Orchard, Castle Morton, Nr Malvern, Hereford & Worcester WR13 6JB
Learned society

History: initiated in 1871 by John Ruskin and incorporated as above in 1878. Conceived as a vehicle for publicity and putting into effect Ruskin's ideals for the reform of society into one based on a proper relationship between man and man, between man and his work and the material world in which he lives. On receiving corporate status, the guild's aims were to determine and institute in practice the wholesale laws of labourers and craftsmen in science and literature; the acquisition by gift or purchase of plots of land; the acquisition and erection of schools, museums and other educational establishments; the acquisition of pictures and sculptures, books and objects of art and natural history; and the erection of houses for agricultural labourers. By 1879 the guild had established a museum at Sheffield, housing what came to be the Ruskin collection; prepared an elementary school book on history; and developed a library. In the early 1880s the guild was clearing small plots of waste ground and by 1881 had an interest in a small rural woollen mill. By 1900 had land and cottages at Barmouth, Gwynedd; 20 acres of land at Bewdley, Hereford & Worcester; 13 acres of land at Totley, S Yorkshire; a small plot of land at Claughton, Lancashire; and a woollen mill. In 1900 it established a school to teach Ruskin's views on education. It modified its aims only slightly over the years and in the early 1980s it continued to promote the advancement of education and training in the field of rural economy, industrial design and craftmanship, and the appreciation of the arts. In 1984 Sheffield City Council approved expenditure on a scheme to house the Ruskin collection at a city centre site.

Records: at Guild of St George, Hope Orchard, Castle Morton, Nr Malvern, Hereford & Worcester WR13 6JB
directors meeting minutes 1975-84; general meeting minutes 1879-1983; report: J Ruskin 1881, master 1908; memo and articles of association 1926,1970; annual report and accounts 1879-1983

294 WINDERMERE HYDROPATHIC CO LTD

7 Nov 1878
12608
2 The Calls, Leeds, W Yorkshire LS2 7JU
Hotel

History: incorporated as above in 1878 to purchase freehold mansions called 'Rockville', 'Rockfield House' and 'Rockfield' at Bowness, Windermere, Cumbria, to enlarge them and convert them into a hydropathic establishment and sanatorium. Became hoteliers in 1947 operating the renamed Hydro Hotel. Acquired in 1980 by Mount Charlotte Investments Ltd of Leeds, W Yorkshire.

Records: at Windermere Hydropathic, 2 The Calls, Leeds, W Yorkshire LS2 7JU
members register 1878-date; debenture holders register 1888-date; current records

295 LIVERPOOL REVERSIONARY CO LTD

16 Nov 1878
12631
1 Threadneedle Street, London EC2R 8BE
Investment

History: incorporated as above in 1878 to undertake business in the purchase of and loan on reversions and life interests. Office in the 1930s was at 51 North John Street, Liverpool, Merseyside. Acquired in 1920 by Eagle, Star & British Dominions Insurance Co Ltd which was renamed Eagle Star Insurance Co Ltd in 1937.

Records: at Eagle Star Insurance, 1 Threadneedle Street, London EC2R 8BE

296 QUELLYN ROBERTS & CO LTD

20 Dec 1878
12697
13 Watergate Street, Chester, Cheshire CH1 2JX
Wine merchants and hotel

History: founded in 1863 by alderman Quellyn Roberts. Incorporated in 1878 as Colwyn Bay Hotel Co Ltd by group of Chester businessmen to establish a hotel at Colwyn Bay, Clwyd. Shares were acquired in 1927 by Quellyn Roberts & Co, wine and spirit merchants and hotel keepers of Chester. In 1931 company acquired undertaking of same by amalgamation and changed name to above. By 1938 owned Westminster Hotel, Rhyl (sold 1947) and Colwyn Bay Hotel in Clwyd; Queens Hotel, Llandudno, George Hotel, Criccieth, West End Hotel, Pwllheli and Castle Hotel, Harlech (sold 1947) in Gwynedd; and Royal George Hotel, Rugby, Warwickshire. Purchased wine and spirit business of W Bannister at Prenton, Merseyside. Opened branch shop at West Kirby, Merseyside by 1960s. Transferred wine merchant side of business to Quellyn Roberts (Wine Merchants) Ltd in 1982.

Records: at Quellyn Roberts, 13 Watergate Street, Chester, Cheshire CH1 2JX
directors meeting minutes 1893-date; general meeting minutes 1894-date; share ledgers and members registers 1878-1980; annual returns 1901-62; debenture and mortgage register 1913-58; memo and articles of association 1927-58; annual reports and accounts 1879-date; balance sheet 1901; and accounts 1913-date; profit percentage 1897-9; general ledgers 1917-49; journal 1949-77; cash book 1927-35; hotel balance sheets: Belvoir 1902-26, Royal George 1910-48, Wilmslow 1923-6, Castle 1926-47, George 1927-44, West Kirby 1931-66; agents day book 1908-14; crypt sales, purchases and balance sheets 1931-55; trade-mark papers 1890-1901; stock totals 1939-49; advertisements 1957-76; premises documents 1878-1900; rent book 1916-33; tenancy agreements 1930-66; insurance policies and correspondence 1873-1906; misc hotel papers 1891-1939

Quellyn Roberts & Co: monthly totals: till 1874-95, accounts 1888-9; expenses summary 1890-1; stock book 1892-1915; hotel beer book 1896-1903; bills register 1896-1915; port receipts 1841-1936; hotels summary and correspondence 1900-30; price lists 1884,1902-37; manager applications 1916-18; premises photographs c1890,c1920; advertisements 1841-1937; scrapbooks 1841-1937
R Bolland & Sons Ltd: memo and articles of association 1901; restaurant correspondence, papers, menus, price lists and advertisements 1944-51

297 PHILOLOGICAL SOCIETY

2 Jan 1879
12722
University of London, Malet Street, London WC1
Learned society

History: established in 1842 as a learned society consisting partly of members of a society of same name formed at University of London in 1830 to investigate and promote the study and knowledge of the structure, affinities and history of language. Incorporated as above in 1879 in order to facilitate negotiations with Clarendon Press to complete and publish its English dictionary which society members had been compiling since early 1860s. Dr James AH Murray, the society's president in 1878, was appointed editor of the dictionary. The first volume of *A New English Dictionary on Historical Principles* ('Oxford English Dictionary') was published in 1884. The final volume was published in 1928. In the 1980s the society holds 7 meetings per year, and publishes its *Transactions* and other works.

Records: at Philological Society, Hon Secretary, School of Oriental & African Studies Library, University of London, Malet Street, London WC1
council meeting minutes and papers 1868-date; ordinary meeting minutes and papers 1872-date; secretarys: reports 1922-49, correspondence and papers 1878-1957; treasurers reports 1910-15,1931; officers and meeting lists 1870-1950; incorporation papers 1878-9; memo and articles of association 1879,1920; balance sheets 1930-49; accounts 1871-1924; financial correspondence 1870s-1950s; publishing papers and correspondence 1878-1940s

298 BOLTON INCORPORATED LAW SOCIETY

10 Jan 1879
12738
20 Wood Street, Bolton, Greater Manchester
Law society

History: founded in 1831 and incorporated as above in 1879 as a company limited by guarantee to promote the honourable practice of the legal profession and to protect the interests of solicitors in Bolton, Greater Manchester. Offices were in Wood Street previous to 1909.

Records: at Bolton Incorporated Law Society, 20 Wood Street, Bolton, Greater Manchester
general meeting proceedings 1909-71; committee meetings 1929-70; members lists 1831-1927; memo and articles of association 1879; ledger 1932-72

299 SKEGNESS PIER CO LTD

11 Jan 1879
12745
Grand Parade, Skegness, Lincolnshire
Pier

History: formed in 1877 and incorporated as above in 1879 by a group of local businessmen to construct a pier at Skegness, Lincolnshire, a seaside resort developed largely by the local landowner, the Earl of Scarborough. Construction began in 1879 and the pier was completed in 1881. The builders were Head Wrighton & Co Ltd of Stockton on Tees, Cleveland and the designers were Clarke & Pickwell of Hull, Humberside. The pier, costing £22,000 was 1843 feet long and the fourth largest in Britain. It had a theatre and steam boat trips were arranged from the pier head. Between 1909 and 1913 the company was in financial difficulties and Lord Scarborough became sole shareholder and chairman from 1914, having already subscribed for many debentures. The Scarborough family sold their interest in 1971 to a syndicate of local businessmen who built a new leisure centre on the pier head at a cost of £100,000. In 1976 RG Mitchell Ltd gained a controlling interest in the company. The pier was severely damaged by storms in 1978.

Records: enquiries to Business Archives Council Library, 185 Tower Bridge Road, London SE1 2UF
directors and general meeting minutes 1877-date; register of members and share ledger 1880-1982; cash book 1947-67; plans 1936; article on pier 1971

300 FOREIGN & COLONIAL INVESTMENT CO LTD

15 Mar 1879
12901
1-2 Laurence Pountney Hill, London EC4R 0BA
Investment

History: established as Foreign & Colonial Government Trust in 1868 to specialise in overseas government bonds and operate as a common law trust. Issued five series of certificates by 1889 and formed American Investment Trust specialising in American railway bonds. Incorporated in 1879 and formed Foreign, American & General Investment Co Ltd in 1883. From 1890s allowed to invest in mortgages, corporation bonds and debentures and moved into industrial securities, removing 'Government' from title. From the mid 1920s invested in equities, having 35 per cent of its funds in preference shares by 1939, 38 per cent in equities and 27 per cent in bonds, and of those 46 per cent was in the UK, 17 per cent in British Dominions, 25 per cent in USA and 12 per cent in South America. Lost American investments during WW2 and faced many defaulted foreign bonds but post-war boom led to explosive growth in capital and revenue in 1950s, especially in North America. By 1949 had 54 per cent of portfolio in equities - 69 per cent in UK shares, and 12 per cent in North America, but by 1959 had 86 per cent in equities - 53 per cent in UK and 33 per cent in North America. Merged in 1959 with its 2 sister funds, American Investment & General Trust Co Ltd (as American Investment Trust Co Ltd renamed in 1919) and Foreign, American & General Investment Trust Co Ltd sharing same directorate and management. In 1981 held investments in 428 companies based worldwide and owned 7 subsidiary companies. Owned F&C Management Ltd (inc 1953) which managed investments of the trusts in F&C Group and others.

Records: at Foreign & Colonial Investment Trust, 1-2 Laurence Pountney Hill, London EC4R 0BA
directors meeting minutes 1879-date; financial board papers 1966-date; merger papers 1959; general meeting minutes 1879-date; shareholders letters, notices etc 1913-29; directors register c1901-19; trust and corporate documents 1868-79; memo and articles of association 1879-date; seal books 1960-72; annual reports and accounts 1880-date; journal 1949-63; petty cash book 1956-63
American Investment & General Trust Co Ltd: directors meeting minutes 1879-1960; general meeting minutes 1879-1959; shareholders letters, notices etc 1911-31; directors register c1901-c19; trust and corporate documents 1879-1912; mortgages register c1888-1930; memo and articles of association with resolutions 1879-1919; annual reports and accounts 1880-date; journal 1944-58; petty cash book 1956-63
Foreign, American & General Investment Co Ltd: directors meeting minutes 1883-1959; general meeting minutes 1883-1959; shareholders letters, notices etc 1884-1929; memo and articles of association with resolutions 1883-1913; prospectus 1883; directors register c1901-c19; mortgage register c1884-1952; annual reports and accounts 1884-date; journals 1941-71; petty cash book 1956-63
F&C Management Ltd: directors and general meeting minutes 1953-66; memo and articles of association 1953 on; annual reports and accounts 1954-date; profit and loss accounts and balance sheets 1953-66; ledger 1963-5; cash books 1953-71; petty cash book 1956-63

Donald Last, *A Centenary Review 1868-1968* (priv pub 1968)

301 COMBINED ESTATES CO LTD

26 Mar 1879
12929
25 Bloomsbury Square, London WC1A 2PL
Property

History: incorporated as above in 1879 to provide improved dwellings for the industrial classes. Original architect and surveyor was Alfred B Rooke, Bedford Row, London. Purchased dwelling houses and shops throughout London and Surrey which were rented out. Became a property investment company in 1981.

Records: at Combined Estates, 25 Bloomsbury Square, London WC1A 2PL
directors and general meeting minutes 1960-date; share: and dividend ledgers 1880-1958, transfer register 1879-1942; shareholders register 1879-1958; mortgage register 1879-1939; directors register 1900-58; annual summaries 1879-1901; memo and articles of association 1879-1981; current files 1960-date

302 WATTS & CO LTD

31 Mar 1879
12934
7 Tufton Street, Westminster, London SW1P 3QB
Church furnishers

History: founded and incorporated as above in 1879 by George F Bodley, Thomas Garner and George G Scott junior, ecclesiastical, domestic and collegiate architects, to produce furnishings (needlework, textiles and wallpapers) for their Gothic revival designs which no other company could provide. Bodley and Garner had been in partnership since 1868 and had founded the firm of Burlison & Grylls to produce glass and painted decoration. All 3 founders designed the furnishings with Bodley designing most of the wallpaper. Many leading architects employed the company including Sir Edwin Lutyens, Sir Giles Scott and Sir Robert Lorimer. Wallpapers and fabrics hand made to the original designs, have been used in new and restoration work. In the 1970s work included Royal Opera House, Covent Garden, National Theatre and House of Commons. Although renowned for secular and ecclesiastical embroidery and needlework, especially in altar frontals and vestments, the company also design metal ware to custom and restore fabrics and antique furnishings. Original premises were in Baker Street, moving to Dacre Street, in the 1950s and subsequently to Tufton Street, Westminster.

Records (1): at C Hoare, 37 Fleet Street, London EC4P 4DQ
directors meeting minutes 1879-1957; general meeting minutes 1879-1946,1950-5; standing orders, resolutions and notices re meetings and shares 1880-1960; register of members, shares and share transfers 1879-1951; list of directors, shareholders and issued dividends 1930-40; share and share transfer certificates 1879-1963; correspondence re shares, dividends and directors appointments 1888-1947; corporate legal documents 1879-1950; seal book 1949-64; annual returns 1924-56; audited accounts 1879-1962; journal 1929-55; textiles and metals sales day books 1952-8; sub-contractors account book 1954-5; cash books 1952-7; petty cash books 1953-6; legal accounts and correspondence with accountants re results, setting up and running company 1879-85; stock: list 1887, book 1938-50; staff list 1954; wages and salary books 1949-58; correspondence 1938; legal property documents 1877-88; correspondence and reports on property repairs and tenancy 1929-57

Records (2): at Watts, 7 Tufton Street, Westminster, London SW1P 3QB
directors meeting minutes 1957-date; general meeting minutes 1946-date; catalogues 1962,1980; advertisements with costs 1950-61; stock book 1951-65; fabric pattern stock book 1955-date; order books: vestments and soft furnishings 1939-date, retail 1953-80, metal and woodwork 1957-80, wallpaper 1960-4, assorted 1965-71; estimates book 1954-68; work room progress book 1953-date; inscription book 1973-8; pattern books 19-20 cent

303 OVERSTONE ESTATES LTD

1 Apr 1879
12939
90 Abington Street, Northampton, Northamptonshire NN1 2BX
Property

History: incorporated in 1879 as Wellingborough Public Coffee House Co Ltd to carry on business as teetotal general refreshment housekeepers in and around Wellingborough, Northamptonshire. Registered offices were originally at 47 Oxford Street, Wellingborough. Ran Granville Coffee House, Midland Road, Wellingborough from at least 1921. Name changed to Granville Hotel (Wellingborough) Ltd in May 1927 and to above in 1963 when it owned land at Overstone, Northamptonshire. Subsequently went into liquidation and was dissolved in 1983.

Records: none survive

304 CITY OF PORTSMOUTH MASONIC HALL LTD

17 Apr 1879
12980
10 Guildhall Walk, Portsmouth, Hampshire PO1 2DD
Masonic hall

History: founded by freemasons and incorporated in 1879 as Borough of Portsmouth Freemasons Hall & Club Co Ltd to purchase the Roman Catholic schools in Spring Gardens, Landport, Portsmouth, Hampshire and adapt them for meetings of masonic lodges and to purchase 79 Commercial Road, Landport, with attached ground on which to erect suitable premises for a masonic club. Club opened in 1880 with a membership of 10 rising to 270 by 1881. Rooms were let to other masonic lodges and local chamber of commerce. Billiard tables were installed in 1890. 4 masonic lodges bought the premises in 1904 and acquired the company's shares. Premises were entirely reconstructed and refurbished during 1928. Name changed to above and reopened in 1929.

Records: at City of Portsmouth Masonic Hall, 10 Guildhall Walk, Portsmouth, Hampshire PO1 2DD
directors meeting minutes 1914-date; general meeting minutes 1879-date; share: ledgers and registers of members 1879-date, certificates 1880, transfer certificates 1902-12; annual: returns 1918-23, reports and accounts 1879-1940; general ledger 1912-17; club rules, reports and balance sheets 1881-6

305 BERGER, JENSON & NICHOLSON LTD

6 May 1879
13033
Berger House, Berkeley Square, London W1X 6NB
Paint

History: established in 1760 by Lewis Berger, colour chemist from Frankfurt, West Germany, manufacturing dry pigments in Shadwell, London. Moved to Homerton, Hackney, London in 1780 and also established City offices in Well Court. By 1790 was producing 19 colours. Business subsequently managed by his 3 sons and 2 grandsons. Incorporated as Lewis Berger & Sons Ltd in 1879 and acquired lead works in Sheffield, S Yorkshire. Trade expanded into India, Australia and North America, and further improvements and expansions were made at Homerton. However financial performance was indifferent until 1905 when company was sold to Mr Cottingham, vice president of Sherwin Williams & Co, American paint manufacturers. Formed several subsidiary companies, in Australia 1916; New Zealand 1923; Peintures Berger SA, France 1926; Ireland 1935; and Jamaica in 1956. In 1960 merged with Jenson & Nicholson Ltd (est 1821 as coach paint manufacturers) when name changed to above. Subsequently formed Berger Traffic Markings Ltd in 1960, companies in South Pacific in 1967 and Barbados and Trinidad in 1968. Acquired MacGregor Wallcoverings Ltd in 1966 and British Paints Ltd in 1969, formed in 1930 from merger of J Dampney & Co Ltd of Cardiff (est 1867) and British Antifouling Co Ltd of Barking, Essex (est late 1890s). Taken over in 1970 by Hoechst AG, chemical company of Frankfurt, West Germany. Formed companies in Bangladesh in 1970 and Angola in 1971, acquired company in South Africa in 1973 and Arthur Johnson (Paper) Ltd, wallpaper manufacturers (est 1926), in 1975. In 1977 Berger Group had 35 companies and divisions running 46 factories with 10,000 employees in 25 countries. In UK had factories at Chadwell Heath, Dagenham, Essex; Stratford, E London; Hengrove, Bristol; East Kilbride, Strathclyde; and Newcastle upon Tyne, Tyne & Wear; research centres at all factory sites except East Kilbride; main warehouses at Chadwell Heath, Hengrove and Middleton, Manchester; and employed over 4000 people.

Records: at Berger, Jenson & Nicholson, Berger House, Berkeley Square, London W1X 6NB directors meeting minutes 1879-1960; attendance book 1931-60; general meeting minutes 1926-67; agm reports 1926-38; shareholders: registers 1882-1929, circulars 1947 on, lists 1926-37; share: registers 1926-c41, allotment book 1920-6, ledgers 1879-1929, transfer registers 1926-35, certificates 1897-1905; dividend account book 1923-42; mortgage and debenture registers 1879-1958; debenture papers 1902-12; directors register 1928-36; probate register 1926-40; corporate documents, papers and correspondence 1816-1970s; seal registers 1931-51; annual reports and accounts 1926-54; Berger Group annual accounts 1948-date; draft trading account 1898; stock ledger and abstracts of accounts 1804-10; town ledgers 1800-03; private ledger 1947-64; ledger and accounts sheets 1960s-70s; journal 1940-1; cash books 1807-09; private cash book 1900-02; accounts notebook 1803-04; bank credit book 1940 on; press cuttings re profit reports 1951-60; misc financial papers 20 cent; order book 1787-1808; Indian: paint market report 1939, stock receipt book 1940-3; press advertisements 1959-67; paint recipes 1819-96; dry colour striking book 1815-18; colour: ledger 1900-10, cost books 1890s, manufacture notebook c1885-94; formula cards 20 cent; raw material lists c1905-08; contracts notebook 1840-94; English vermilion manufacture report 1906; letters patent 1950 on; memoranda, data and technical drawings re boiler installation 1835-6; plan, specifications and patent for French paint mixer and packer 1878; equipment correspondence 1932-8; negative photographic film of technical operations c1940s; staff salaries 1868-97, 1940-9; depot salaries 1945-54; piece work and wages investigation report 1929; pension fund documents 1960s on; report and valuation: Homerton works 1892-1944, Birmingham, Liverpool, Manchester and Newcastle upon Tyne branches 1944; documents, papers and correspondence re Sheffield lead works 1878-1907; title deeds, plans and property documents and correspondence re Homerton works and Hackney 1717-1960s; copy deeds re Dublin premises 1935; out letters 1881-1907; Lewis Berger will 1814; press cuttings re paint manufacturing and company 1953-61; company histories 20 cent

Jenson & Nicholson Ltd: corporate documents 1859-1917; balance sheet and profit and loss accounts 1873-1941; profits and expenses statements 1882-91; monthly summaries 1903-33; factory accounts 1886-9; sales analysis 1896-1901; varnish sales and returns record book 1885-6

Lewis Berger Australia Ltd: minutes nd; directors register nd; members register and share ledger 1914 on; corporate correspondence 1921

Lewis Berger & Sons (Australia) Proprietory Ltd: board meeting minutes 1931-8; agm minutes 1931-7

Lewis Berger & Sons of America Ltd: minutes 1899-1900; members register and share ledger 1899
Établissements Lewis Berger & Sons SA: statutes 1925
Lewis Berger (Scotland) Ltd: correspondence and agreements re mutual assistance pact 1940
Lewis Berger & Sons (New Zealand) Ltd: board meeting minutes 1931-6; agm minutes 1931-7
Lewis Berger & Sons (Ireland) Ltd: minutes 1935-6
Lewis Berger & Sons (South Africa) Ltd: board meeting minutes 1921-34; agm minutes 1922-36
Conrad W Schmidt (FA Glaeser): balance sheets and profit and loss accounts 1877-1907
John Hall & Sons Ltd: minutes c1941
Sherwin Williams Co (Ireland) Ltd: board and agm minutes 1935-7
Sherwin Williams Co (New Zealand) Ltd: board and agm minutes 1935-7
Sherwin Williams Co (South Africa) Proprietory Ltd: board and agm minutes 1934-5
Sir WA Rose & Co Ltd: minutes 1917-48

Thomas B Berger, *A Century and a half of the House of Berger 1760-1910* (1910)

306 THETFORD MOULDED PRODUCTS LTD

16 May 1879
13067
Mill Lane, Thetford, Norfolk IP24 3DA
Plastic moulding (previously pulpware manufacturers)

History: incorporated in 1879 as Patent Pulp Manufacturing Co Ltd to acquire patents and assets of E Vickers & Co for treatment and application of vegetable and animal pulps for the manufacture of hollow or moulded articles. Factory at Thetford, Norfolk produced variety of goods including pith helmets for the army and later 'hard hats' for use in mines and shipyards. Pulp became obsolete in the 1950s and was replaced by polythene and polypropylene. Company subsequently changed name to above and acquired its first injected moulding machines in 1967. Changed from manufacturing pulpware to plastic moulding concentrating on the crash helmet market.

Records: at Thetford Moulded Products, Mill Lane, Thetford, Norfolk 1P24 3DA
board meeting: minutes 1879-86,1902-25,1935, agendas 1879-88; general meeting minutes 1888-1926; share: certificates 1879-1922, transfer documents 1879-1983, papers and correspondence 1913-36; annual reports and accounts 1900,1902-06; balance sheets and revenue and profit and loss accounts 1879-1925; general ledger 1909-20; bank books 1879-1937; investment notebook 1923-4; sales contracts, papers and correspondence 1882-1931; agency agreements and correspondence 1887-1933; patent agreements and correspondence 1870-1938; trade-mark papers and correspondence 1889-1945; catalogues, price lists, brochures and advertisements 1881-c1950; stock sheets 1880-6; mill manager reports 1884-91; production: notebooks c1930-5, costs 1883,1951-5, papers and correspondence 1886-1929, photographs c1960; plant plans 1897; wages: sheet 1919, cards 1943-8; employee agreements and correspondence 1882-1925; staff and directors photographs c1930-c69; property: schedules 1879-1916, insurance policies, papers and correspondence 1887-1966, fire damage

papers 1897, plans 1888-1971; works photographs c1900-30; official correspondence 1917-18; water rights papers 1897-1928; legal case papers 1928-31
E Vickers & Co: bankruptcy cash accounts 1879

100 Years Thetford Moulded Products Limited 1879-1979 (priv pub 1979)

307 EQUITABLE REVERSIONARY INTEREST SOCIETY LTD

28 May 1879
13101
4 Coleman Street, London EC2R 5AP
Investment

History: established by deed of settlement in 1835 with share capital of £300,000 with the object of purchasing reversionary property, life interests and annuities. Incorporated under 1856 Companies Act in 1865 and under 1862 Act in 1879 as above. Offices were located in West End of London. Purchased by Equitable Life Assurance Society (est 1762) in 1920. Assets were sold to fellow subsidiary Reversionary Interest Society Ltd (est 1823) in 1976.

Records: at Equitable Life Assurance Society, 4 Coleman Street, London EC2R 5AP
directors meeting minutes 1837-date; settlement deed 1837

308 LAMBETH ESTATE CO LTD

12 Jun 1879
13141
4 Carlton Gardens, Pall Mall, London SW1Y 5AR
Property

History: incorporated as above in 1879 to acquire and manage Roupell Street Estate, parish of St Mary, Lambeth, London. By 1892 possessed 140 houses in Roupell Street, Broadwall, Cromwell Road, Hatfield Place and Whittlesey Street and a factory (later called Crown Engineering Works) in Whittlesey Street. Acquired in 1960 by Charlwood Alliance Properties Ltd, subsidiary of Charlwood Alliance Holdings Ltd which became part of Town & City Properties Ltd in 1971.

Records: at Lambeth Archives Department, Minet Library, 52 Knatchbull Road, London SE5 9QY
directors and general meeting minutes 1879-1949; annual reports and accounts 1879-1943,1957-8; memo and articles of association 1879

309 THOMAS GREEN & SON LTD

14 Jun 1879
13151
PO Box 498, 12 Booth Street, Manchester, Greater Manchester M60 2ED
Horticultural engineers

History: founded in 1835 by Thomas Green to manufacture grass mowers and incorporated as above in 1879. Products included lawn mowers, garden rollers, steam road rollers and motor rollers. Had factory at Smithfield Iron Works, North Street, Leeds, W Yorkshire which closed in 1975, and show rooms, stores, repair works and offices at New Surrey Works, Southwark Street, London which closed after 1958. Exported worldwide. In 1982 was a dormant subsidiary of Finance for Industry Ltd.

Records (1): at Leeds Archives Department, Chapeltown Road, Sheepscar, Leeds, W Yorkshire LS7 3AP
board papers and agency agreements 1956-9; directors attendance book 1944-62; agm attendance book 1923-63; shareholders lists 1919-34; shareholdings register 1879-1937; articles of association 1904; insurance policies register 1881-1901; accounts and balance sheets files 1932-70; cash books 1948-59; correspondence re capital reorganisation 1951; sales catalogues 1905-71; publicity photographs 20 cent; testimonials 1881-99; order book 1875-92; costings and parts book 1938-41; machinery records sheets 1940-5; drawings indices c1882-1941; patents 1856,1872; trade-mark certificates 1908-09; house magazine 1949-56
Hudswell Badger Ltd: articles of association 1969

Records (2): at Institute of Agricultural History & Museum of English Rural Life, University of Reading, Whiteknights, Reading, Berkshire RG6 2AG
sales catalogues 1883,1935

310 HULL INCORPORATED LAW SOCIETY

15 Aug 1879
13295
Imperial Chambers, Bowlalley Lane, Hull, Humberside
Law society

History: founded in 1818 by a meeting of attorneys and solicitors practising in Hull, Humberside, to encourage fair and honourable practice within the profession and to protect interests of members. Hull Law Library was established in 1835 and transferred to the society in 1856, and Hull Law Student Society was established in 1861. In 1982 had its own premises at Imperial Chambers, Bowlalley Lane, which housed law library and where educational and social functions were held.

Records: at Hull Incorporated Law Society, 5 Parliament Street, Hull, Humberside HU1 2AZ
society meeting minutes 1818-22; agm: minutes 1852-date, agenda, memoranda, attendances etc 1965-78; council meeting minutes 1879-date; committee meeting minutes 1852-1935,1950-7; directors attendance register 1952-65; members register 1937-68; directors register 1954-7; mortgages register 1946-51; memo and articles of association with correspondence 1946-67; annual returns 1965-78; annual reports and accounts 1880-1962; auditors report and financial statement 1966-8,1977; members list 1849-72,1889-1917,1966-7; property documents c1949-70; Willis Mills prize trust deed 1948; papers and correspondence re services to members 1975-date; memo, reports and draft bills on legal matters c1917-69
Hull Law Library Society: minutes 1835-56; winding up resolution 1879
Hull Law Students Society: rules 1881,1926; liaison committee report 1968

311 SEFTON NEWSPAPERS LTD

16 Aug 1879
13297
PO Box 48, Old Hall Street, Liverpool, Merseyside L69 3EB
Newspapers

History: established by Robert Johnson (1807-88) printer and bookseller of Lord Street, Southport, Merseyside who first published *Southport Visiter* in May 1844. Until 1852 when it became a permanent weekly, the newspaper was published on Saturdays from May to Oct. From Apr 1860 it became a bi-weekly and from May 1877 a tri-weekly, issued on Tuesdays, Thursdays and Saturdays. Johnson sold the *Visiter* and the printing business in 1879 to newly incorporated Robert Johnson & Co Ltd. Albert F Stephenson managed the newspaper and subsequently became its proprietor. New building was completed in 1889 at present premises, 26-32 Tulketh Street. Sir Albert Stephenson retired in 1933 and was succeeded as managing director and managing editor by his son WH Stephenson whose nephew Albert F Stephenson became general manager on the latter's retirement in 1967. Acquired *Southport Journal* (est 1882) in 1933 and *Southport Guardian* (est 1882) in 1956. Company's name changed to Stephenson Newspapers Ltd in 1961 and to above in 1975. Acquired by Liverpool Daily Post & Echo Ltd in 1965. By 1969 company published *West Lancashire Visiter*, *Southport Journal Visiter*, *Saturday's Southport Visiter*, *Crosby Herald*, *Formby Times*, *Bootle Times Herald*, *Maghull Times Herald* and *North Liverpool Times*, and in 1984 *Tuesday Visiter*, *Formby Times*, *Thursday Visiter*, *Bootle Times*, *Walton Times*, *Maghull Times*, *Crosby Herald* and *Southport Visiter*.

Records (1): at Sefton Newspapers, 26-32 Tulketh Street, Southport, Merseyside PR8 1BT
directors and general meeting minutes 1879-date; shareholders ledger 1879-1965; share: allotment register 1886-93, certificates 1895-date, transfer register 1880-1965, dividends and interest book 1883-90; directors: register 1900, attendance and fee register 1884-1964, list and summary 1894-1908; memo and articles of association 1935; annual reports and accounts 1882-1908,1950-date; balance sheets 1879-81; cash account book 1879-89; postal book 1879-82; loans register and ledger 1891-8; salary: and wages book 1885-90, books 1950s on; time book 1879-92; premises plan c1934; Hesketh estate: rents ledger 1885-96, tenants and wages book 1894-6; history articles 1939,1944; *Southport Visiter* 1846,1881,1926

Records (2): at British Library, Newspaper Library, Colindale Avenue, London NW9 5HE
Southport Visiter 1844-date; *Southport Journal* 1904-65; *Southport Guardian* 1959; *West Lancashire Visiter* 1965-date; *Crosby Herald* 1895-date; *Formby Times* 1894-date; *Bootle Times* 1878-date; *Maghull Times* 1958-date; *North Liverpool Times* 1963-5; *Walton Times* 1919-date

312 CHAPMAN & HALL LTD

6 Jan 1880
13655
11 New Fetter Lane, London EC4P 4EE
Publishing

History: founded in 1830 by Edward Chapman and William Hall at 186 Strand, London as a bookselling business with publishing as a secondary interest. Published works of many well-known authors, including Charles Dickens, William Thackeray, Thomas Carlyle, Charles

Kingsley, Mrs Gaskell, Robert and Elizabeth Browning, Anthony Trollope, HG Wells, Arnold Bennett, and Alec and Evelyn Waugh. By the 1860s the firm moved to Piccadilly and in 1880 moved to Henrietta Street, Covent Garden. Was incorporated as above in 1880. Published technical books in 1914, merged with Methuen & Co Ltd, educational publishers (est 1889) in 1938 and amalgamated with Eyre & Spottiswoode (Publishers) Ltd, general publishers (est 1769) and E&FN Spon Ltd, technical publishers and booksellers (est 1830) in 1954. Took name of Associated Book Publishers Ltd in 1955. The last novel with a Chapman & Hall imprint was published in 1965 and the last general book in 1970. Subsequently formed the scientific and technical book division of ABP Ltd.

Records (1): at Associated Book Publishers, 11 New Fetter Lane, London EC4P 4EE
royalty and author contracts 1850s on

Records (2): at Associated Book Publishers, North Way, Andover, Hampshire SP10 5BE
directors and general meeting minutes 1880-1956; directors meeting: agendas 1931-4, attendance book 1955-63; agm reports 1895-1936; share: allotment register 1880-1, certificate book 1936-9; directors: register 1901-50, and managers particulars 1926-54; corporate and share documents 1879-1948; memo and articles of association 1880; correspondence re foundation of company 1879; annual returns 1920-38; annual report and accounts 1880-1956; balance sheet and accounts 1931-2; trading and profit and loss account 1963; private ledger 1944-65; accounts for Charles Dickens works 1870-5; legal account 1912; agency agreements and correspondence 1894-1928; register of titles 1960-4; advertising and publication ledger 1966; advertisements 1938-63; legal documents and correspondence re copyright of various works 1858-1914; publication register 1937-62; production costs 1946-62; stock: books c1870s-1964, valuations 1935-62; correspondence with Evelyn Waugh 1942-59; staff employment agreements 1888-1936; travellers salaries and expenses cash book 1944; photographs of managing director 1920s; title deeds and property documents 1875-1945; fire insurance policies 1880-1922; cleaning agreements 1922-51; history leaflet 1980

313 CAPITAL & COUNTIES BANK LTD

31 Jan 1880
13729
71 Lombard Street, London EC3P 3BS
Banking

History: formed as Hampshire & North Wilts Banking Co in 1877 on merger of Hampshire Banking Co (est 1834) and North Wilts Banking Co (est 1835), name changing to Capital & Counties Bank in 1878. Registered in 1880 as above. Acquired the banking business of Willis Percival & Co (est 1670) of London in 1878; Sutton, Leach, Bevan & Read (est 1775) of Devizes, Wiltshire and Haydon & Smallpiece (est 1765) of Guildford, Surrey, in 1883; Gloucestershire Banking Co (est 1831) and Knight, Jenner & Co (est 1806) of Farnham, Dorset, in 1886; Northamptonshire Banking Co Ltd (est 1836) and Western Counties Bank Ltd (est 1864) in 1890; Garfit, Claypon & Co (est 1754) of Boston, Lincolnshire, and Watts & Co (est 1840) of Teignmouth, Devon, in 1891; Mollersh & Co (est 1808) of Godalming, Surrey, and Wells, Hogge & Lindsell (est 1807) in 1893; Toomer, Bunney, Slocock & King (est 1791) of Newbury, Berkshire, in 1895; St Barbe & Co (est 1788) of Lymington, Hampshire; Margesson, Henty, Henty & Hopkins (est 1808) of Worthing, W Sussex; Thomas Wheeler & Co (est 1812) of High Wycombe, Buckinghamshire, in 1896; Eliot, Pearce & Co (est 1791) of Weymouth,

Dorset, in 1897; Glamorganshire Banking Co (est 1836) and Wright & Co (est 1760) of Nottingham in 1898; Oakes, Bevan, Tollemache & Co (est 1795) of Bury St Edmunds, Suffolk, in 1900; Lacon & Co (est 1791) of Yarmouth, Norfolk; Moore & Robinson's Nottinghamshire Banking Co Ltd (est 1802) in 1901; Cornish Bank Ltd (est 1771) in 1902; Payler, Hammond, Simmons & Gipps (est 1788) of Canterbury, Kent, in 1903; Foster & Co (est 1804) of Cambridge in 1904; Bacon Cobbold & Co (est 1786) of Ipswich, Suffolk, in 1905; Berwick & Co (est 1772) of Worcester in 1906; and Eyton, Burton & Co (est 1792) of Shrewsbury, Salop, in 1907. Merged with Lloyds Bank Ltd in 1918 by which time had 473 branch offices plus London head office at 39 Threadneedle Street.

Records: at Lloyds Bank, 71 Lombard Street, London EC3P 3BS
private minutes 1876-1924; chairmans agenda book 1889-1917; general memoranda book 1878-1918; directors register 1900-18; articles of association 1908-18; amalgamation papers 1880-1924; annual reports 1878-1918; bad and doubtful debts 1916-17; memoranda and instruction book 1905; premises ledger 1880-1902; private letter books 1891-1918; head office circulars 1877-1917; managers instructions 1908; branches - Aldershot: security register 1890s; Basingstoke: security registers 1883-1918; Brighton: security registers 1873 on; Gloucester: security register 1889-1920, authorities book 1872 on, character book 1897 on; Haslemere: profit and loss account 1918, security ledgers 1900 on; Hastings: memoranda book 1880s-90s; Llandeilo: coupon register 1898-1918, security register 1900-20; Piccadilly, London: letter books 1890-1916; Luton: security registers 1898-1918; Northampton: minutes 1892; Ryde: security registers 1890-1921; Skegness: security registers 1880-1920; Southampton: private ledger 1887 on, security registers 1887-1921, staff book 1909-18; Stow on the Wold: security register 1886-1922; Sudbury: circular book 1877-90; Ventnor: security ledgers 1904-18, and registers 1900 on; Westcliff on Sea: security ledgers 1901-20; Wirksworth: security ledger 1902-27, and register 1901-22; Woking: security ledger 1908-20, and registers 1893-1920, record books 1907-17; Woolwich: balance book 1915-17, signature books 1880-1918, deposit accounts ledger 1876-1916, security ledger 1894-1905, and registers 1891-1918; Wootton Bassett: letter book 1890-1926; Worcester; letter books 1906-20

RS Sayers, *Lloyds Bank in the History of English Banking* (1957)

314 LEAMINGTON & WARWICK TRANSPORT CO LTD

18 Feb 1880
13780
Midland House, 1 Vernon Road, Edgbaston, Birmingham, W Midlands B16 9SJ
Bus operators

History: incorporated in 1880 as Leamington & Warwick Tramways & Omnibus Co Ltd, to construct and run tramways. In 1901 British Electric Traction Co Ltd purchased a majority of the company's shares in order to reconstruct and electrically equip the lines. In 1902 name changed to Leamington & Warwick Electrical Co Ltd and objects widened to carry on the business of electrical engineers and to undertake Warwick Electric Lighting Order of 1901. In 1929 company abandoned the tramways and replaced them with an omnibus service and purchased Blue Motor Service, Stratford upon Avon. In 1935 electrical undertaking was sold to Midland Electric Light & Power Co Ltd and company was bought by Birmingham & Midland Motor Omnibus Co Ltd changing name to above. By 1984 held the town services operated by Midland Red (South) Ltd, a member of National Bus Co.

Records (1): at United County Omnibus, Bedford Road, Northampton, Northamptonshire NN1 5NN
directors and general meeting minutes 1947-81; general meeting minutes 1902-81; registers: directors 1901-75, debentures and charges 1908-35, deeds 1881-1943; memo and articles of association 1902,1969; agreement for sale of business 1929,1935; annual report and accounts 1901,1913-80; balance sheets 1913-80; financial schedules 1974-80; Tramway Orders, Transport Acts and notes 1900-67; working agreements 1930-7; indemnity insurance scheme papers 1930-6; advertising space agreements 1924,1932; pay rates agreement 1937; lease Emscote, Warwickshire 1936

Records (2): at Warwick County Record Office, Priory Park, Cape Road, Warwick, Warwickshire CV34 4JS
directors meeting minutes 1880-1930; impersonal ledgers 1905-30

315 OLDHAM JOINT STOCK BANK LTD

19 Feb 1880
13782
Union Street, Oldham, Greater Manchester
Banking

History: formed and incorporated with limited liability as above in 1880 by group of cotton industrialists, opening for business in Yorkshire Street, Oldham, Greater Manchester. Absorbed business of Rochdale Joint Stock Bank Ltd (est 1861) in 1882 and built new head offices in Union Street in 1892. By 1897 had 7 branches and 3 sub-offices in Oldham district. Amalgamated in 1898 with London & Midland Bank Ltd, renamed London City & Midland Bank Ltd in 1898, London Joint City & Midland Bank Ltd in 1918, and Midland Bank Ltd in 1923.

Records: at Midland Bank, Poultry, London EC2P 2BX
board meeting minutes and agenda 1880-98; share registers 1880-98; summary of capital and shareholders 1898; prospectus 1880; reports and balance sheets 1880-98; general ledger 1882-92; securities registers 1881-98; building society accounts ledger 1883-98; investment register 1880-6; investment ledger 1883-98

WF Crick and JE Wadsworth, *A Hundred Years of Joint Stock Banking* (1936)

316 BETTS & CO LTD

18 Feb 1880
13787
Avenue Works, Walthamstow Avenue, London E4
Capsule manufacturers

History: founded in 1841 when William Betts, brandy distiller with his 3 brothers at Smithfield Bars, London, obtained the British rights to Dupre's tin capsule and started to manufacture capsules. Patented tin-coated lead capsules in 1849. In 1856 he left the family distilling business to concentrate on capsules and developed tinfoil rolling for tea chests. In about 1858 he purchased Batavia Mills, Holloway Road, London and by 1880 was also established at 1 Wharf Road, City Road; at Moor Green Rolling Mills, Pershore Road, Birmingham; and Bordeaux, Marseille and Paris, France. Also carried out business under name of Alexander

Robertson & Co at Holloway Mills, Holloway Road, London. Company incorporated as above in 1880 on semi-retirement of William Betts. Manufactured collapsible tubes from 1884. Formed Betts British Foil Factories Ltd in 1915, and Betts & Co (Canada) Ltd in 1919. Acquired Vollman Bros Ltd, manufacturers of specialist industrial finishes, paints etc, and Neville & Co, makers of stopper cork etc in 1957. By 1958 owned 3 factories - 2 in London and 1 in Colchester, Essex, and was leading producer of capsules in UK. Acquired in 1958 by Group Developments Ltd, a subsidiary of Courtaulds Ltd, and became part of the packaging and later of the plastics divisions of the latter. In 1982 was a dormant subsidiary company of Courtaulds PLC through Courtaulds Acetate Ltd although the business continued in the name of Betts & Co.

Records (1): at Courtaulds, PO Box 16, 345 Foleshill Road, Coventry, W Midlands CV6 5AE
directors meeting minutes 1880-8; members registers 1880-1934; annual returns 1880-1934; mortgage register 1880-1944; memo and articles of association 1880-1948; seals register 1880-1949; annual reports and accounts 1936-62; balance sheets and accounts 1913-61; trading and profit and loss accounts 1880-99,1913-47; financial breakdown 1945-57; private ledger 1896-1903; invoices 1895-8; sales data 1852-1929; manufacturing notes and correspondence 1905-06; foil composition records 1860-1915; production: data 1852-1929, agreements 1947-58, reports 1959-60; patent: register 1947-58, specifications 1936-61, correspondence 1939-1961, infringement papers 1862,1868; factories and product photographs 1950s,nd; staff papers 1903-09; property deeds, papers and correspondence 1853-99; misc correspondence 1847-1932; press cuttings, articles and notes on history 1900-22; William Betts: diaries and notebook 1829-38, trust records 1887-1906
Betts et Cie: correspondence and papers 1867-1947

Records (2): at Betts, 50 Ipswich Road, Colchester, Essex
directors and general meeting minutes 1888-1904; general meeting minutes 1935-60

317 GEC (MANAGEMENT) LTD
21 Feb 1880
13795
1 Stanhope Gate, London W1Y 6AA
Telegraph, telephone and electric cable manufacturers

History: established by William T Henley (1814-82) in 1837 when he opened his first workshop in Hayden Street, Minories, London for the manufacture of electro-magnetic machines. Took premises in Clerkenwell, and later at Enderby's Wharf, East Greenwich, making electrical instruments and insulated wires. In 1859 built works at North Woolwich. Between 1868 and 1873 manufactured 12,000 miles of submarine cable and land line of 260,000 tons weight. Went bankrupt in Apr 1875 and WT Henley & Co Ltd was incorporated in Jul 1875 to carry on the business vested in Robert Fletcher, his trustee under the liquidator. This company was wound up in 1877 and the final liquidation report was made in 1881. WT Henley's Telegraph Works Co Ltd was incorporated in 1880 to take over the running of the business with WT Henley as managing director. From 1890s made gutta percha golfballs as well as submarine cables, galvanic batteries, magnetic machines and galvanized wire stands. In 1904 formed Henley's (South Africa) Telegraph Works Co Ltd and in 1906 built works at Gravesend, Kent for the manufacture of telephone cables and golfballs. The development of the Grid Scheme and the construction of power lines led to the formation of another subsidiary, Holborn

Construction Co Ltd, civil and electrical engineers. During WW2 developed and manufactured with Siemens Brothers Ltd, PLUTO, the 'pipeline under the ocean' which supplied the Allies with petrol. Acquired by Associated Electrical Industries Ltd (inc 1899) in 1959 and became part of AEI Group, producing paper insulated cables at Gravesend works while North Woolwich works was gradually run down. The AEI Group was acquired by General Electric & English Electric Cos Ltd in c1968. In 1984 AEI Henley manufactured cable joints and accessories at Gravesend.

Records: at GEC Henley, Gravesend, Kent DA11 9DA
directors and general meeting minutes 1880-1966; general meeting papers 1948; agm press cuttings 1931-59; purchase agreement 1880; debenture stock trust deed 1905; annual returns 1933-65; annual reports and accounts 1886-1966; research papers 1930 on; patents drawings 1857-64; Box department reports, papers and correspondence 1905-10,1931-3; Engineering department reorganisation papers 1930-6; *SS Orsted* cable laying log book and photograph 1898; technical handbook 1951; sales catalogue (Finnish) 1897; illustrated: brochure 1953, price lists 1907-17; staff pension fund trust deeds 1916-51; staff benefit fund: committee meeting minutes 1953-63 and agenda and papers 1956-70s, documents and correspondence 1960s-70s, ledgers 1927-77, journals and cash books 1927-74; house magazine 1919-58; out letter book 1880-1; annual company history documents, newscuttings, articles, circulars, photographs, correspondence 1880-1959; Henley and company history articles, notes and booklets 1859-1950s; works plans 1862-1951; directors, staff, premises, products, transport and cable laying photographs 1880s-1950s
GEC (Cable & Equipment) Ltd: corporate documents and cash book 1966 on
Hackbridge Cable Co Ltd: directors and general meeting minutes 1917-65; members register etc 1917-68; directors register 1969-77; corporate records 1960s on; seal registers 1918-76
Henley's (South Africa) Telegraph Works Co Ltd: directors and general meeting minutes 1903-30; annual returns 1933 on
WT Henley's Telegraph Works Co India Ltd: directors and general meeting minutes 1957-70s; members register 1960-7; directors register 1957-70s; memo and articles of association 1956; corporate documents 1968-78; seal book 1971 on
Liverpool Electric Cable Co Ltd: directors meeting minutes 1950-65; general meeting minutes 1956-64; members register etc 1901-69; directors register 1902-77; memo and articles of association and corporate documents 1960s-70s; seal register 1926-68
Lydbrook Cables Ltd: directors and general meeting minutes 1925-9
Mitcham Motor Co Ltd: directors and general meeting minutes 1947-70s; members register 1923-70s; corporate documents 1930s-70s

E Slater, *One Hundred Years 1837-1937: The History of Henley's* (priv pub 1937)

318 WILLIAM CLOWES (BECCLES) LTD

26 Feb 1880
13814
15 Cavendish Square, London W1M 0HT
Printing and publishing

History: founded in London in 1803 at 20 Villiers Street by William Clowes (1779-1847), printer, Chichester, W Sussex. Expanded premises in 1804 and moved to 7 Northumberland Court in 1807. Supplied stationery to the army during Napoleonic wars, and in 1815 opened a military bookshop at 14 Charing Cross. Became printer to Royal Academy of Arts in 1824. In 1826 moved to premises in Duke Street (later Duchy Street), and in 1827 opened what was reputedly the largest printing works in the world. From 1832 printed periodicals for Society for the Diffusion of Useful Knowledge. By 1839 the firm was known as William Clowes & Sons and had over 600 employees. Duke Street had 20 steam presses operating and another works for small jobs had been opened in Charing Cross Road after Northumberland Court was closed. William Clowes junior (1807-83) and George Clowes (1814-86) took over the business on their father's death in 1847. Produced the catalogues of Great Exhibition of 1851, opened works near South Kensington Museums and printed their catalogues until the 1890s. Printed for many learned societies, including Institution of Civil Engineers and Royal Society. In 1865 printed first *Law Reports* for Council of Law Reporting in England & Wales. WCK Clowes and WA Clowes formed partnership in 1870 with William Moore, proprietor of Caxton Press at Beccles, Suffolk to establish cheaper printing works outside London. Management was left to Moore until he absconded with the firm's money, but Clowes & Clowes survived and by 1876 possessed 15 power-driven presses. London firm became publishers and printers of *Hymns Ancient and Modern* in 1875. London and Beccles firms were amalgamated in 1879 and incorporated in 1880 as William Clowes & Sons Ltd. In 1881 started to produce *General Catalogue of Printed Books in the British Museum Library*. Opened a code office in Fenchurch Street, in 1885 and began publishing *Brassey's Naval Annual* in 1886. In 1900 jobbing printing works opened in Great Windmill Street (closed in late 1930s). Installed litho plant at Duke Street in early 1900s. Absorbed Gilbert & Rivington (est 1750), non-Roman alphabet specialist printers, in 1907. After 1918 the Beccles premises expanded and specialised in book printing while London premises specialised in periodicals and general printing. Published *Army Quarterly* in 1920 and ran advertising agency from 1924-39. Duke Street premises were destroyed by bombing in 1941 and offices were taken in Arlington Street. In 1946 merged with McCorquordale & Co Ltd and London offices and publishing department moved to Little New Street. In 1953 Beccles factory of 175,000 sq ft produced over 4 million bound books per year. By 1977, name had changed to above, employed 718 people and operated typesetting, lithographic printing and book binding services. In 1983 was a subsidiary of McCorquordale PLC through McCorquordale Books Ltd.

Records: at William Clowes, Beccles, Suffolk N34 9QE
directors: and general meeting minutes 1880-1959, attendance book and correspondence 1902-53; members register and share ledger 1880-1956; share certificates, papers and correspondence 1880 on; interest and dividend ledger 1918-57; debenture stock: application and allotment book 1904, register 1904-46, transfer register 1905-48, papers and correspondence 1904 on; customers ledgers 1822-1928; bought ledgers 1872-1958; profit and loss ledgers 1872-1950; general ledgers 1872-1957; supplementary ledger 1877-8; sales ledgers 1908-56; printing ledger 1914-36; binding ledger 1924-58; sundries ledger 1914-c20; publishing department ledger c1959-c67; Little New Street small ledger accounts 1932-41; misc accounts analysis ledgers 1881-1958; journals: 1879-1971, Beccles 1880-1954, Duke Street 1880-1958, purchase 1837-50; cash books: 1932-58, London 1929-69, Beccles 1934-54, printing 1938-51; balance books 1875-83,1924-49; day books 1918-60; discount book 1929-58; departments weekly costs 1920-74; charges and costs job book 1947-63; Duke Street plant invoices c1923-c40; inventory and valuation: Duke Street 1879,1921, Great Windmill Street 1921, Beccles and Great Yarmouth premises 1967; type foundry returns 1921-38; order book 1915-26; stock:

books and papers 1934-53, reports 1948-64; wages summaries 1885-1968; wages book 1938-41

WB Clowes, *Family Business 1803-1958* (priv pub 1958)

319 LONDON & PROVINCIAL MARINE & GENERAL INSURANCE CO LTD
26 Feb 1880
13816
Beckett House, 36-37 Old Jewry, London EC2R 8BQ
Insurance

History: established as London & Provincial Marine Insurance Co at Royal Exchange Buildings, London, in 1860, with JF Rougemont as underwriter. Liverpool office opened in 1867. Incorporated in 1880. Underwrote general insurance after 1890, when it took present title. Significant shareholding was taken by World Marine Insurance Co Ltd (est 1894) but entire share capital sold to Yorkshire Insurance Co in 1913. Continued to underwrite in own name under management of Leslie & Godwin. Yorkshire Insurance Co and its subsidiaries became a subsidiary of General Accident Fire & Life Assurance Corporation Ltd in 1967.

Records: at London & Provincial Marine & General Insurance, Beckett House, 36-37 Old Jewry, London EC2R 8BQ
meeting minutes: board 1861-1941, general 1864-91, proprietors 1880-1941; deed of settlement 1860; registers: members 1906 on, transfers 1908-11; annual report and accounts 1860-1935; ledgers 1933-62; journals 1946-61; cash books 1947-62

320 WEST YORKSHIRE BANK LTD
3 Mar 1880
13841
71 Lombard Street, London EC3P 3BS
Banking

History: established in 1829 as Halifax Joint Stock Banking Co and incorporated in 1880. It amalgamated with Halifax & Huddersfield Union Banking Co (est as Rawson & Co 1807) in 1910 and was renamed the following year as above. In 1919 it amalgamated with Lloyds Bank Ltd, at which time it possessed 34 offices.

Records: at Lloyds Bank, 71 Lombard Street, London EC3P 3BS
chairmens minutes 1887-1921; directors meeting minutes 1888-1920; board: meeting minutes 1915-22, agenda 1900-15; minutes 1887-1919; deed of settlement with supplement 1829-89; amalgamation papers 1919; Halifax branch misc customer ledgers and registers from c1900; Huddersfield branch private memoranda from 1884

RS Sayers, *Lloyds Bank in the History of English Banking* (1957)

321 SOVEREIGN MARINE & GENERAL INSURANCE CO LTD

8 Mar 1880
13855
10 Trinity Square, London EC3P 3AX
Insurance

History: incorporated in 1880 as British & Irish Glass Insurance Co Ltd by a group of manufacturers and merchants in Bristol, Avon to undertake plate glass insurance. Head office was established at 35 Corn Street, Bristol, the office of its secretary, Henry L Riseley, insurance agent. By 1880, 23 agencies had opened and 308 policies had been effected. London manager was appointed in Nov 1880 and by 1884, 159 agencies had opened including one in Belfast. A very successful Irish agency opened in Dublin in 1887. In 1900 premium income was £1764 and company took powers to undertake other insurances. Despite falling business, Henry L Riseley & Sons continued to manage the company and after merger in 1922 with Willis Faber & Co, insurance brokers of London, the latter acquired an interest in the company. Name changed to British & Irish Insurance Co Ltd in 1928 after which plate glass business continued at Bristol with marine business operated by Willis Faber in London. By 1933 plate glass business had proved unprofitable and was transferred to Cornhill Insurance Co Ltd, another Willis Faber company. Name changed to Lombard Insurance Co Ltd in 1939 and subsequently to Lombard Marine & General Insurance Co Ltd. From 1933 to 1952 only marine business was undertaken although an unsuccessful non-marine business operated from 1952 to 1966. Name changed to above in 1954 and aviation business was added in 1959. Re-entered non-marine market in 1972 and 50 per cent of gross premium income of £22 million came from non-marine business, 30 per cent from marine and 20 per cent from aviation in 1979. Approximately 10 per cent of business came from UK, the remainder being split between overseas business offered in London and by foreign agents in Belgium, Canada, Denmark, France, West Germany, Hong Kong, Norway, Saudi Arabia and USA.

Records: at Sovereign Marine & General Insurance, 10 Trinity Square, London EC3P 3AX
directors and general meeting minutes 1880-date; members register etc 1922-date; annual reports and accounts 1918-28,1948-date

322 REVERSIONARY INTEREST SOCIETY LTD

12 Mar 1880
13877
4 Coleman Street, London EC2R 5AP
Investment

History: established by deed of settlement in 1823 with a share capital of £500,000 to purchase reversionary and life interests under wills and settlements and grant loans on security of such interests. First company of its kind to be formed and by mid 19 cent a large part of its business was the purchase of life policies. Incorporated under 1862 Companies Act as above in 1880. Purchased by Equitable Life Assurance Society (est 1762) in 1919. Purchased assets of fellow subsidiary Equitable Reversionary Interest Society Ltd (est 1835) in 1976. Sold all reversions and loans to Equitable Life Assurance Society in 1979 leaving life interests valued at £432,089.

Records: at Equitable Life Assurance Society, 4 Coleman Street, London EC2R 5AP
directors meeting minutes 1826-date; proprietors: meeting minutes 1824 on, directors reports 1824 on, list 1860; settlement deed 1823; business conduct report 1838

323 LONDON & WESTMINSTER BANK LTD

13 Mar 1880
13878
41 Lothbury, London EC2P 2BP
Banking

History: promoted in 1833 as a joint stock bank by William Douglas, a London based Scottish merchant, with other London businessmen. Offices at 38 Throgmorton Street and 9 Waterloo Place (West End office) opened in 1834, and branches in Bloomsbury, Whitechapel, Marylebone and Southwark, London were added in 1836. Headquarters moved to 41 Lothbury, London in 1841. James Gilbart, first general manager, emerged as an acknowledged leader in banking practice and theory over the next 30 years. In addition to numerous publications, he initiated the Gilbart Lectures on Banking at King's College, London. Acquisitions were Commercial Bank of London (est 1840) in 1861, London & Middlesex Bank (est 1862) in 1863, and Jones Loyd & Co (est c1771) in 1864. Although the bank's prestige was always high, only 37 branches had been opened by 1909, with deposits valued at nearly £27 million. Incorporated as above in 1880 and in that year merged with London & County Bank Ltd to form London County & Westminster Bank Ltd.

Records: at National Westminster Bank, 41 Lothbury, London EC2P 2BP
meeting minutes: board 1833-1909, private 1836-90, daily committee 1846-1907, establishment committee 1875-1909, general 1835-1909; prospectus 1833; proprietors list 1838; settlement deed 1834; articles of association 1897; capital increase papers 1836-80; Leamington Bank papers 1837-8; solicitors reports 1860-6; secretarys memoranda book 1861-1911; annual report and accounts 1835-1919; balance sheets 1834-82; statements: weekly 1837-1940, net profit 1840-8, loan accounts and balances 1845-8; signature books 1841-61; country bank agreements 1835-9; undertakings book 1836-7; register: country securities 1859, county and overseas accounts 1860; current account statistics 1871-1909; past due bills list 1937; Coutts & Co ledger 1833-4; North of England & Newcastle Joint Stock Bank failure memoranda book 1846-7; stock book 1845-8; staff: details 1834-1920, appointments 1834-55, list 1830; officers: appointment registers 1835-81, register 1836-1909; secrecy declarations 1846-85; correspondence 1833-40; letter books: 1833-6, sundry board 1834-9, State of Victoria Loan 1859-79; head office circulars 1834-60; country managers 1864-9; branch: circulars 1836-1928, head office instructions 1862-71, accounts statistics 1845-8; branches - Bloomsbury: officers ledger 1836 on; Lothbury: general ledgers 1834-1909, loan ledger 1834-57, customer ledger 1834, deposit ledger 1842-6; Marylebone: minutes 1836 on, general order book 1840 on, staff book 1834 on, customers out letters 1836-9; Southwark: diary 1839, general balance book 1844-8, general ledger 1836-42, customer ledger 1836, officers ledgers 1837 on, letters received 1858 on; Temple Bar: officers ledger 1837 on; West End offices: local minutes 1834; Westminster: minutes 1834-45, day book 1834, customers ledgers 1834-5

TE Gregory, *The Westminster Bank Through a Century* (1936)

324 WESTON SUPER MARE MASONIC HALL CO LTD
30 Mar 1880
13882
Boulevard, Weston super Mare, Avon
Masonic hall

History: incorporated in 1880 as above to run and maintain a masonic hall in Weston super Mare, Avon.

Records: at Weston super Mare Masonic Hall, Boulevard, Weston super Mare, Avon
directors and general meeting minutes 1892-date; articles of association 1935; share certificates 1953-82; annual reports and accounts 1936-8,1950-81; balance sheets 1979,1982; renovation papers and correspondence 1967-80; general correspondence 1968-82

325 CITY BANK LTD
16 Mar 1880
13893
5 Threadneedle Street, London EC2
Banking

History: incorporated by royal charter in 1855 and with limited liability in 1880. By 1898 and its amalgamation with London & Midland Bank Ltd to form London City & Midland Bank Ltd, it had opened 21 branches in London and its suburbs. Its head offices in Threadneedle Street were the head offices of London City & Midland Bank Ltd, renamed London Joint City & Midland Bank Ltd in 1918 and Midland Bank Ltd in 1923, from 1898 until 1930.

Records: at Midland Bank, Poultry, London EC2P 2BX
board meeting minutes 1854-98; shareholder meeting minutes 1856-98; committee meeting minutes 1856-98; deeds of settlement 1855-81; charter of incorporation 1856; amalgamation papers 1898; balance sheets 1855-98; foreign banks arrangements 1862-98; securities book 1888-1901; staff appointment list 1855-8; staff regulations nd; rules for branch managers 1874; branch accountants reports 1884-91; Holborn branch security registers 1879-99; Old Street branch deposit receipt book 1894-8; Paddington branch journal, cash book and letter book 1873-1903

WF Crick and JE Wadsworth, *A Hundred Years of Joint Stock Banking* (1936)

326 YORKSHIRE BANKING CO LTD
19 Mar 1880
13907
Poultry, London EC2P 2BX
Banking

History: founded in 1834 as Yorkshire District Banking Co, a joint stock bank with its head offices in Leeds, W Yorkshire, to establish a branch banking system throughout Yorkshire. Took over business of Perfect & Co, private bankers of Leeds and Pontefract, W Yorkshire almost immediately and amalgamated in 1835 with N Yorkshire banking firms of Dresser & Co (est 1820) and Britain & Co, both of Thirsk, N Yorkshire and Coates, Meek & Carter of Knaresborough (est 1804). Had established 20 branches throughout Yorkshire by 1837-8.

Suffered financial difficulties in 1840s which led to liquidation of bank and formation of Yorkshire Banking Co in 1843 to carry on business with 13 branches and 12 agencies. Registered with limited liability in 1880 and represented by 60 branches and agencies in 1901 when it amalgamated with London City & Midland Bank Ltd. Renamed London Joint City & Midland Bank Ltd in 1918, and Midland Bank Ltd in 1923.

Records (1): at Midland Bank, Poultry, London EC2P 2BX
board: meeting minutes 1834-1901, agenda 1891-1901; committee of investigations notebook 1843; shareholder meeting minutes 1835-1901; share registers 1892-1901; directors register 1901; deeds of settlement 1834-65; prospectus 1843; amalgamation papers 1901; liquidation papers 1901-02; profit and loss accounts 1843-1902; half yearly: balances 1843-88, reports 1843-1901, statements 1880-6; letter books 1878-95; head office circulars 1880-98; auditors branch reports 1844-1901; branches - Beverley: general ledgers 1838-52; Doncaster: declarations of secrecy 1835-1914; Goole: general ledgers 1838-73; Guiseley: letter book 1899-1912; Huddersfield: general ledger 1860-71; Leeds: general ledgers 1866-76; Pontefract: deposit receipt ledgers 1843-82; Ripon: general ledgers 1843-69; Thirsk: general ledgers 1861-73; declarations of secrecy 1835-1922; Wetherby: reference book 1870

Records (2): at Leeds Archives Department, Chapeltown Road, Sheepscar, Leeds, W Yorkshire LS7 3AP
deed of settlement and papers re formation 1834; securities register 1834-51; securities and securities papers c1901; legal papers re claims on bank 1833-48

WF Crick and JE Wadsworth, *A Hundred Years of Joint Stock Banking* (1936)

327 ENSOR HOLDINGS LTD

3 Apr 1880
13944
Pool Works, Woodville, Burton upon Trent, Staffordshire DE11 8FU
Building products (formerly firebrick manufacturers)

History: incorporated in 1880 as Ensor & Co Ltd to acquire the business of E&HL Ensor (est 1826), firebrick manufacturers of Ashby Woulds, Woodville, Derbyshire. The latter had acquired FE Hoffman's patents for the improvement of brick kilns etc. Woodville Works was built next to local clay pits and quarries. By 1895, products included firebricks, chimney pots, drain and land pipes, air bricks, ornamental vases etc. Sales offices were opened in Sheffield, S Yorkshire and London in 1898. The latter was subsequently formed into Ensor Sales (London) Ltd. Operated a factory at Polesworth, Warwickshire from 1947 to 1971. Name changed to above in 1965. In early 1980s was a holding company for subsidiaries engaged in manufacture, supply and distribution of specialised building products, and building and contract work.

Records (1): at Derbyshire Record Office, County Offices, Matlock, Derbyshire DE4 3AG
members registers and share ledgers 1880-1965; share: transfer registers 1880-1946, certificates 1920-64; directors registers 1901-45; annual returns 1880-1945; dividend cash book 1927-67; memo and articles of association 1887; directors reports, balance sheets and accounts 1936-65; balance sheets 1890-1929; private ledgers 1890-1938; class ledgers 1880-1912, 1937-47; general ledger 1940-51; ledger balances 1937-50; cash books: 1930-50, general 1937-59, bank 1926-65; monthly sales accounts 1928-32; mine report 1921; fire clay leases correspondence 1904; stock

books 1895-1952; returns books 1936-41; day book 1958-62; production agreement 1933; clay workings plans 1944,1947; history c1935

Records (2): at Ensor Holdings, Pool Works, Woodville, Burton upon Trent, Staffordshire DE11 8FU
directors and general meeting minutes 1964-date

328 CARDIFF CHAMBER OF COMMERCE & INDUSTRY

8 Apr 1880
13961
101-108 East Wing, Exchange, Mount Stuart Square, Cardiff, S Glamorgan CF1 6RD
Chamber of commerce

History: incorporated as above in 1880 as a company limited by guarantee to promote trade and industry in Cardiff. In 1982 operated enquiry, export documentation and trade information services and organised seminars.

Records: at Glamorgan Archive Service, Glamorgan Record Office, County Hall, Cathays Park, Cardiff, S Glamorgan CF1 3NE

329 WESTMINSTER BANK LTD

5 Apr 1880
13977
41 Lothbury, London EC2P 2BP
Banking

History: established as a joint stock bank in 1836 as Surrey, Kent & Sussex Banking Co in Southwark, London. Head office was transferred to Lombard Street, London in 1837 and name changed to London & County Banking Co in 1839. By 1845 the bank had over 40 offices in the Home Counties and 30 years later its 150 offices comprised the largest branch network in the UK. Amalgamations included Hove Banking Co (est 1876), in 1891 and F Burt & Co, Cornhill, London (est 1872) in 1907. Incorporated as London & County Bank Ltd in 1880. In 1909 merged with London & Westminster Bank Ltd to form London County & Westminster Bank Ltd, which was one of the largest clearing banks with deposits of £70 million and 300 branches. In 1913 formed London County & Westminster Bank (Paris) Ltd, which later opened branches in Bordeaux, Lyon and Marseille, France. Parent bank opened branches in Madrid and Barcelona, Spain in 1917. The Ulster Bank Ltd, established in Belfast in 1836, became a wholly owned subsidiary in 1917. Merged with Parr's Bank Ltd in 1918 to form London County Westminster & Parr's Bank Ltd, renamed as above in 1923. Became a constituent part of National Westminster Bank, with 1400 branches by 1968.

Records: at National Westminster Bank, 41 Lothbury, London EC2P 2BP
board meeting: minutes 1836-date, agendas 1839-43, standing orders 1841-93;1911; directors attendance and fees register 1863-75; instructions: managers 1839-1911, board to general manager 1841-62; committee meeting minutes: 1838-9, general purposes 1839-41, daily 1848-1909, daily agendas 1904-05, special 1842-9, special rough 1863, Lombard Street 1864-9, head office 1896-1914, foreign discount 1918, foreign business 1918-39, agm minutes 1838-1905; half yearly meeting notes 1840-59; general meeting: reports 1860-1908, agendas 1867-1954; general memoranda 1856-62; shareholders list 1887; directors: list 1836-1905, register 1909-21;

deed of settlement 1836; articles of association 1909-date; amalgamation papers 1909-23; annual report and accounts 1837-date; general accounts 1836-8; general statistics 1868-1911; signature books 1867-80s; authorities to prove debts 1874-1909; deposit receipt book 1837; bad debts register 1838-1971; mortgaged property register 1850s; information books: general managers 1865-85, managers 1908-32; salary book 1914-54; staff: records 1873-1942, register 1917-47, rules 1853,1908, statistics 1937; letter book 1877-1919; head office circulars 1909-29; branch: committee meeting minutes 1839-48, inspectors letter book 1841-6, authorised expenditure 1862-1905; branches - Ashford: minutes 1841-58; Aylesbury: minutes 1900-31, information book 1878-1932; Bakewell: profit and loss statements 1918-33; Bishop's Stortford: salary sheets 1867-1911; Braintree: quarterly returns 1858 on, annual returns 1872 on; Brentford: information books 1885-1936; Brighton: minutes 1852-1926; Buckingham: quarterly returns 1856 on; Buxted: premises papers 1921-2; Cambridge: minutes 1845-1900, profit and loss statements 1910-31; Chelmsford: letter book 1843-7; Chesham: profit and loss statements 1923-45; Chester: profit and loss statements 1918-37, salary book 1914-54; Croydon: minutes 1878 on; Dorking: half yearly returns 1909-18; Godalming: quarterly returns 1877; Halstead: quarterly returns 1874,1907; overdraft reports 1872; Hastings: quarterly returns 1848; Hertford: managers letters 1879-1909; Hitchin: status reports 1883-98; Hoddesdon: minutes 1898-1903; Leighton Buzzard: deposit account ledger 1837; Barnet: letters 1889-1926; Bloomsbury: minutes 1910-20; Chancery Lane: minutes 1911-29; Finsbury Park: half yearly returns 1920; Greenwich: minutes 1845-75; Hammersmith: minutes 1901-08, profit and loss statements 1910-36; Hanover Square: head office correspondence 1868-72; Harley Street: profit and loss statements 1910-27; Holborn: minutes 1874-1914; Kensington: information books 1878-1904; Lombard Street: minutes 1910; Marylebone: minutes 1904-14,1910-22; Regent Street: profit and loss statements 1910-27; St Mary Axe: minutes 1906-16; Southwark: bad and doubtful debt returns 1910; Upper Clapton: minutes 1901 on; Maldon: bad debts memo 1866; Milbourne Park, Feltham, Greater London: head office correspondence 1910-29; Newbury: quarterly returns 1851; Peterborough: premises press cuttings 1933; St Albans: correspondence registers 1848 on; Salisbury: half yearly returns 1922-59; Selborne; head office correspondence 1916-31; Teddington: minutes 1905-26, returns book 1923-8, impersonal ledger 1905-15, letter book 1925-8; Uckfield: business papers 1923-30, premises correspondence 1925-30; Weston super Mare: profit and loss statements 1918-30; Windsor: premises correspondence 1853-89, staff correspondence 1858-1900, opinion letters 1867-75, memoranda 1889-1908

TE Gregory, *The Westminster Bank Through a Century* (1936)

330 CARLISLE CITY & DISTRICT BANKING CO LTD

27 Apr 1880
14015
Poultry, London EC2P 2BX
Banking

History: opened for business in Carlisle, Cumbria in 1837 as Carlisle City & District Banking Co, having already absorbed the embryo Borough Bank and with it the Carlisle banking business of J Connell & Co (est 1825) and contrary to original intentions issued its own notes. Also absorbed business of Joseph Sanderson, solicitor-banker at Cockermouth, Cumbria (est 1829) in 1837. Established 8 Cumbrian branches by 1878 at Workington, Maryport,

Brampton, Haltwhistle and elsewhere (latter 2 came from defunct business of solicitor-banker William Carrick). Had financial difficulties in 1878 due to frozen loans in local granite industry and troubles in iron industry and had abortive amalgamation discussions with Cumberland Union and Carlisle & Cumberland banking companies before re-registering the bank with limited liability in 1880. Amalgamated in 1896 with London & Midland Bank Ltd, renamed London City & Midland Bank Ltd in 1898, London Joint City & Midland Bank in 1918, and Midland Bank Ltd in 1923.

Records: at Midland Bank, Poultry, London EC2P 2BX
board: meeting minutes 1879-80; agenda 1885-96; shareholder meeting minutes 1880; deed of settlement 1837; articles of association 1881; amalgamation papers 1896; balance sheets 1837-96; fidelity bonds and guarantees 1837-81

WF Crick and JE Wadsworth, *A Hundred Years of Joint Stock Banking* (1936)

331 UNION BANK OF AUSTRALIA LTD

1 May 1880
14031
71 Cornhill, London EC3 3PR
Banking

History: established as a co-partnership in Old Broad Street, London in 1837 and opened first branches at Launceston, Tasmania in 1838 and Sydney, New South Wales, Australia in 1839. Incorporated as above in 1880, when it had 41 branches in Australia, New Zealand and Fiji and operated with paid-up capital of £1.5 million. It was 1 of only 9 banks not to suspend during 1893 banking crisis in Australia. In 1951 merged with Bank of Australasia (est 1835) to form Australia & New Zealand Bank Ltd, which in turn merged with English, Scottish & Australian Bank Ltd (est 1852) to form Australia & New Zealand Banking Group Ltd in 1970.

Records: at Australia & New Zealand Banking Group, Collins Place, 55 Collins Street, Melbourne, Victoria 3000, Australia
London board and committee meeting minutes 1880-1951; general meeting reports 1880-1951; correspondence re business in Australia, New Zealand and UK 1880 on; Australia, New Zealand and UK staff records nd; bank note designs nd; photographs and drawings of bank buildings nd; account book, branch ledgers and returns nd

332 DAIRY SUPPLY CO LTD

3 May 1880
14045
Unigate House, Western Avenue, London W3 0SH
Dairy equipment

History: founded in 1866 by George Barham (founder of Express Dairy Co Ltd) and others to trade in dairy equipment invented by himself and others, from Express headquarters in Museum Street, Bloomsbury, London. Incorporated as above in 1880 and from 1888 held a royal warrant. By 1890s had expanded and set up branches in Edinburgh, Belfast and Cork. In 1893 George Barham handed management of his companies to his sons Arthur Barham (Dairy Supply) and George Titus Barham (Express) and in his will left 50 per cent shareholding in both to each of his sons. In 1912 Dairy Supply acquired new premises in

Cumberland Avenue, Park Royal, and gradually acquired the wholesale milk distribution of Express. During WW1 the company, Great Western & Metropolitan Dairies of Praed Street, Paddington, and Wiltshire United Dairies of Albert Embankment, London, began to operate closely together, and merged in 1917 to form United Dairies Ltd with Arthur Barham as managing director. Dairy Supply continued to manufacture and sell utensils but its wholesale milk business was merged with the new company, which made Express's position difficult. After abortive amalgamation talks in 1920 the 2 Barham brothers swapped shares in each other's companies in 1921. Dairy Supply remained an autonomous company within United Dairies Ltd, manufacturing and selling dairy and ice-cream making machinery from Park Royal. Ceased to trade in mid 1970s and in 1983 was a dormant subsidiary of Unigate PLC.

Records: at Unigate, Unigate House, Western Avenue, London W3 0SH
directors and general meeting minutes 1975-date; share register etc 1948-date

333 BRITISH DENTAL ASSOCIATION

3 Jun 1880
14161
64 Wimpole Street, London W1M 8AL
Professional association

History: established at a meeting in 1879 called by Dental Reform Committee of the Odontological Society of Great Britain and incorporated as above in 1880 as a company limited by guarantee to represent the interests of the profession and encourage improvements in the standards of dental health. Between 1880 and 1902 absorbed existing provincial associations and societies which became branches. Amalgamated in 1949 with Incorporated Dental Society (est 1892 as Society of Extractors & Adaptors of Teeth) and Public Dental Service Association (est 1923) to consolidate the profession's negotiating machinery. Membership numbered 10,000 in 1949 and 11,000 in 1957. In 1975 had 21 branches throughout UK. In early 1980s published a bi-monthly journal, maintained a library and museum and represented the profession at national and local level.

Records: at British Dental Association, 64 Wimpole Street, London W1M 8AL
council meeting minutes 1919-57; committee meeting minutes: executive with documents 1949-67, general purposes 1905-19, finance 1881-1956, penal cases 1904-37, law and ethics 1932-54, publishing 1880-1904, journal 1881-1904, editorial 1920-71, library and museum 1920-74; representative board meeting: committee minutes 1879-1957, business committee minutes 1879-1904, journal committee minutes 1879, attendance registers 1939-64; National Dental Service Committee meeting minutes 1912-47; Public Dental Officers meeting minutes: group minutes 1935-67, committee 1962-8; London County Division and committee meeting minutes 1933-66; Hospital Group meeting: minutes 1948-65, committee minutes 1947-64, South Western division minutes 1948-54; ad hoc and sub-committee meeting minutes, agenda and papers 1903-67; agm: minutes 1879-1960, notices, programmes, papers read, handbooks and press cuttings 1904-77; members: nomination papers 1879-1901, list 1938; legal case papers and correspondence 1884-1940s; memo and articles of association and rules 1879-1975; annual reports and accounts 1879-date; cash books 1932-9,1965-6; benevolent fund donors and subscribers list 1884-1938; founders correspondence 19 cent; dentistry, events and personalities photographs 20 cent; dentistry and association newscuttings 1855-date; publications pre 1880 on; history and dental health pamphlets, notes and leaflets 1818-1974;

branches - Berkshire, Buckinghamshire and Oxfordshire: council meeting minutes 1951-69, general meeting minutes 1951-67, conference committee meeting minutes 1956-69, annual reports and accounts 1951-69; Central Counties: council meeting minutes 1884-1971 and attendance registers 1884-96,1940-67, general meeting minutes 1884-1939, accounts 1951-63, cash book 1940-63, Nottingham, Leicester and Derby section meeting minutes 1904-26, Birmingham council meeting minutes 1935-8; Eastern Counties: council and general meeting minutes 1882-1951, Cambridge section committee meeting minutes 1936-7, balance sheets and accounts 1938, members list nd, correspondence 1911-14, Stoke on Trent section meeting minutes 1951-63; East Midlands: Derby and District Dental Group meeting minutes 1946-57, Derbyshire section meeting minutes 1956-61 and correspondence 1950-61; Metropolitan: council meeting minutes 1929-61, general meeting minutes 1890-1972, Lambeth and Southwark section meeting minutes 1952-6, Eastern section meeting minutes 1934-51, Northern and North West section meeting minutes 1927-58, Western section meeting minutes 1906-14 and annual reports and accounts 1890-1926; Midland Counties: council meeting minutes 1880-1913, out letters 1890-1902, reports 1905-13, by-laws and members lists c1890-1900, Worcester section meeting minutes 1963-75, Birmingham and Warwickshire dental emergency committee meeting minutes 1939-48; Northern Counties: council and general meeting minutes 1905-66; North Midland: council meeting minutes and reports 1913-19, agm minutes 1913-15, general meeting programmes 1905-13, dental education committee meeting minutes 1902-15, law and ethics committee meeting minutes 1902-15, procedure rules c1902-05, Leeds dinner papers 1900; Southern Counties: council meeting minutes 1891-1966 and reports 1902-18, executive committee meeting minutes 1935-66, general and presidential meeting minutes 1912-62, account statements c1912-45, rule books 1905,1924, BDA annual meeting notices, programmes and accounts 1889,1903,1926, Brighton and Hove District section meeting minutes 1886-1953, committee meeting minutes 1904-65, accounts 1897-9,1930-9, and rules 1920s; Wessex: meeting minutes 1944-50, rules 1934,1961, Bournemouth and District section meeting minutes 1926-48; Western Counties: council meeting minutes 1879-1946, general meeting minutes 1883-1946, account book 1879-1968, by-laws 1893, Bristol and District section general and committee meeting minutes 1911-55, East Cornwall section meeting minutes 1951-66, Torquay and District section meeting minutes 1920-61, North section meeting minutes 1933-63; West Lancashire and West Cheshire: council meeting minutes and reports 1920-43, general meeting minutes 1919-43, law, ethics and public appointment committee meeting minutes 1920-5, rules 1920

British Dental Association, Incorporated Dental Society & Public Dental Service Association: committee meeting minutes: standing and documents 1925-9, Plymouth Joint Dental Committee general and reports 1939-47, Sheffield and District Joint Dental Committee meeting minutes, dinner balance sheets, correspondence and press cuttings 1933-45; Dental Wartime Association co-ordinating committee meeting minutes 1941-8

Incorporated Dental Society: meeting minutes: council 1934-49, general 1896-1949; branch representative board 1919-22, finance committee 1934-49, general purposes committee 1936-49, parliamentary and legal committee 1911-25; history articles c1921,1949

Odontological Society of Great Britain: dental reform committee meeting minutes 1876-9; secretarys notebook 1888

Public Dental Service Association: council meeting minutes 1940-5, committee meeting minutes: central 1923-49, emergency 1923-6, executive 1923-49, public dental service 1924; committee papers and correspondence 1912-21; general meeting minutes 1923-6; members list

1938; directors register 1923-47; balance sheets and accounts 1923-42; history articles c1949
School Dentists Society (Dental Group of Society of Medical Officers of Health): council and general meeting minutes 1898-1974; reports 1937-8, members lists 1920s; dental health committee meeting minutes 1962-71
Society of Dental Anaesthetists: council and general meeting minutes 1915-58; London and Southern Counties Branch meeting minutes 1945-56

SH Coplans, *The Seven Ages of the British Dental Association 1856-1956* (1973)

334 LEICESTERSHIRE BANKING CO LTD

5 Jun 1880
14167
Poultry, London EC2P 2BX
Banking

History: opened for business in Leicester as a joint stock bank in 1829. Opened branches at Hinckley in 1831, Market Harborough in 1838, (both Leicestershire) Atherstone, Warwickshire in 1840, Melton Mowbray, Leicestershire in the 1840s, Kettering, Northamptonshire in 1856, Swadlincote, Derbyshire in 1865, Nuneaton, Warwickshire in 1874, Peterborough, Cambridgeshire and Grantham, Lincolnshire in 1883, and Northampton and Wellingborough, Northamptonshire and Burton, Lincolnshire in 1889. Other banks were absorbed, namely: Fisher, Simmonds & Mammatt (est 1790) of Ashby de la Zouche, Leicestershire, and Miller & Co (est 1814) of Leicester in 1835; the Market Harborough branch of Northamptonshire Banking Co (est 1836) in 1838; Weaver & Co (est 1790) of Atherstone in 1840; Coventry Union Bank, Atherstone branch in 1845; and Middleton, Cradock & Middleton (est 1790) of Loughborough, Leicestershire, and Hardy & Co (est 1819) of Grantham in 1895. Original premises were in Friar Lane, Leicester, and moved to new site in Granby Street in 1840s which was substantially enlarged in 1874. Registered with limited liability in 1880 and amalgamated in 1900 with London City & Midland Bank Ltd, renamed London Joint City & Midland Bank Ltd in 1918 and Midland Bank Ltd in 1923.

Records (1): at Midland Bank, Poultry, London EC2P 2BX
board meeting minutes 1829-1900; shareholder meeting minutes 1845-1898; shareholders resolutions 1895; deed of settlement 1829; amalgamation papers 1900; weekly balance sheets 1890-4; balance sheets abstracts 1894-9; profit and loss ledgers 1829-1900; general ledgers 1842-1901; discount ledger 1895-1901; bills of exchange diaries 1877-99; note circulation ledger 1878-1900; bill register 1895-1901; returned bills book 1879-85; bill balance book 1885-96; country bills for collection 1888-1900; foreign bills for collection 1897-1908; general managers memoranda 1874-9; deeds of covenant 1836-73; security books 1873-90; customers bills discounted 1878-1900; loan register 1883-99; declarations of secrecy 1829-96; staff list 1871-99; general manager letter book 1876-1900; branch receipts and expenditure 1896-1905; branches - Ashby de la Zouche: board minutes 1837-57; Grantham: general ledger 1883-96; Hinckley: general ledger 1848-53

Records (2): at Leicestershire Record Office, 57 New Walk, Leicester, Leicestershire LE1 7JB
shareholder meeting minutes 1900; prospectus 1829

WF Crick and JE Wadsworth, *A Hundred Years of Joint Stock Banking* (1936)

335 SKINNINGROVE IRON CO LTD
8 Jun 1880
14171
9 Albert Embankment, London SE1 7SN
Iron and steel

History: incorporated as above in 1880 as iron and steel manufacturers operating from Carlin How, Saltburn by the Sea, Cleveland. Acquired by Iron & Steel Holding & Realisation Agency under Iron & Steel Act 1953 and became part of British Steel Corporation in 1967.

Records: at British Steel Corporation, Northern Regional Records Centre, Unit F2, Commerce Way, Skippers Lane Industrial Estate, South Bank, Middlesbrough, Cleveland TS6 6UT

336 EXPRESS DAIRY CO LTD
9 Jun 1880
14172
430 Victoria Road, South Ruislip, Greater London HA4 0HF
Dairy products

History: founded in 1864 as Express Country Milk Supply Co by George Barham who had started a dairy in Dean Street, off Fetter Lane, City of London, in 1858. By 1860s was using railways to transport milk into London from outlying farms. Opened new premises in Museum Street, Bloomsbury in 1864. In 1866, concern with the chilling and transportation of milk led to setting up of a subsidiary, Dairy Supply Co, to trade in dairy equipment. Incorporated in 1880 as Express Country Milk Supply Co Ltd with several retail premises and a distribution network handling half a million gallons of milk per year. Name changed to above in 1882 and head offices moved to Bloomsbury Mansions. Opened College Farm, Finchley, as a dairy showpiece in 1883. Established branch dairies in London at Montpelier Vale, Blackheath and Hampstead in late 1880s and at Herne Hill and Muswell Hill in 1890s. Tea shops were introduced around 1900 and 21 branches and shops, and 31 tea shops had been opened by 1904. Moved to new headquarters in Tavistock Place in mid 1900s. George Barham retired in 1893, handing management of Express Dairy to his sons, the tea shop and retail concern, to George Titus and Dairy Supply, the utensils and wholesale concern, to Arthur. This led to conflict after his death in 1913 as both had a 50 per cent share in the other's company. In 1917 Dairy Supply merged with the other large wholesale dairies in London to form United Dairies Ltd with Arthur Barham as managing director. Despite amalgamation talks the brothers exchanged shares in 1921 and the 2 companies went their separate ways. First dairy concerns purchased were Buscot & North Berkshire Dairy Co and Marshalls Dairies Ltd, with many other creameries and farmers co-operatives especially in Sussex area acquired in 1920s. Milk-collecting depot was established at Billinghurst, W Sussex and tuberculin tested and bottled milk was introduced in early 1920s. New branch dairies were established in late 1920s at Chiswick and Cricklewood in London, a bottling plant at Bollo Lane, Acton, London in 1934, new creameries in the midlands and north in the 1930s and in the west country in 1940s. Amalgamated with Lord Rayleighs Dairies in 1929 acquiring its 13 branches. In early 1930s TH Lewis Ltd, coach builders (est 1850) of Camden Town, London became fully owned subsidiary and subsequently changed name to Express Dairy Foods Ltd. Went public in 1938 and acquired in London, Vicarage Farm Dairy Ltd of Kentish Town

1939, and CM Robarts & Sons of Northwood and Moon & Southdown Dairies of Wimbledon in 1942. After WW2 built 3 new bottling centres in London at Bromley, Eltham and Brentford. Acquired Dairy Farmers Milk Supply Ltd in 1945, Henry Edwards & Sons Ltd in 1950, City of London Dairies Ltd in 1951, several London retail rounds and 2 cheese factories in Salop. All 6 northern companies of Express group, including Chatsworth Dairy Co, Sheffield, S Yorkshire, Manorcroft Dairy Co of Dewsbury, W Yorkshire and Yorkshire Wholesale Dairies Ltd, were reincorporated in 1947 as Express Dairy (Northern) Ltd, 6 more companies having joined by 1950. New concerns in Yorkshire and Greater Manchester were added at an average of 1 per year in 1950s. From late 1940s introduced self-service shops and later supermarkets. Opened new bottling plant at South Morden, London, new cheese factory at Appleby, Cumbria and developed South Ruislip site in 1950s. Set up Express Dairy Products Ltd in 1955 to promote sales of 'Eden Vale' products and in 1959 acquired Independent Dairies Ltd with 8 country creameries. In 1960 acquired Tower Holdings Ltd with its Mitcham Foods and Goldhanger Fruit Farms factories, Hornby & Clarke of Richmond, Surrey and Spiers & Pond Ltd, consisting of 12 hotels, 12 restaurants and a chain of licensed buffets. Also opened 2 new creameries in Crediton, Devon and Staplemead, Somerset and a sterilised milk centre at Battersea, London in early 1960s. By 1964 group consisted of 25 companies, 255 shops and supermarkets, 17 food factories employing more than 17,000 people, handling 250 million gallons of milk, blending 10,000 tons of butter, packing over 150 million eggs annually. Acquired by Grand Metropolitan Ltd in 1969 and subsequently moved its registered offices to South Ruislip.

Records (1): at Express Dairy, 430 Victoria Road, South Ruislip, Greater London HA4 OHF board and general meeting minutes 1953-date; committee meeting minutes: group executive 1957-70, hotels management 1965-70, group policy 1965-7; corporate documents 1958-80; share register 1960-5; preference share dividend account book 1925-33; stock registers c1947-c70; powers of attorney 1952 on; memo and articles of association 1960,1974; share purchase agreements, allotment letters, transfer deeds and other documents re purchase of companies 1923-77; seals register 1962-70; annual reports and accounts 1880-1918,1934-date; balance sheets and audited accounts 1956-80; branch accounts 1956-70; financial working papers 1960s; creamery ledger: cash books 1951-65, milk products journal and day books 1954-66; expenses, purchases and sales ledgers 1950-70; farm milk ledgers 1952-60; branch accounts ledgers 1960-76; misc ledgers 1948-61; journals 1955-78; day books: milk purchases 1956-60, dairies 1958-60, misc 1945-61; cash received book 1960-1; cash books: 1955-66, branches 1958-65, creameries 1951-9; account books: egg depots 1953-9, haulage 1959-66, Milk Marketing Board accounting records 1955-67; statistical books 1960-4; branch sales figures 1962-3; market research reports c1955,1967,1974-80; royal warrant papers 1895-1956; trade-mark and production agreements etc 1965-73; list of dairies 1943; illustrated sales literature c1950-66; milk price margins book 1919-39; photographs: and slides of products and publicity material 1960s-70s, transport and production methods 1900-79, staff and employees 1900s-70s, plant, College Farm, shops, dairies, refreshment depots, factories and supermarkets 1900s-70s; plant and machinery accounts 1965-7; vehicles registers 1951-60; railway analysis books 1953-66; stock books 1951-60; milk: intake book 1957-64, sample report books 1949-64, products movement books 1957-68; dairy complaints 1948-63; technical manuals c1970; staff publications on milk production etc 1958 on; union meeting proceedings 1937-43; wages books 1959-70; salaries books 1947-61; pension payment registers 1956-63; career and safety booklets 1960s; house magazine 1956-date; long service association: annual reports 1958-69, award presentation programmes 1953-66; property ledgers: 1956-70, transfers 1945-63; freeholds ledger 1950-2; rent cash book 1958-63; booklets, articles and notes on history of company 1950-70s; press cuttings re company, dairy products, dairies etc 1954-62,1973

Andover Creameries Ltd: members register 1946-67

Anglo-Saxon Condensed Milk Co Ltd: private ledger 1958-70

Bladen Dairies Ltd: members register 1927-c60; private ledgers 1943-75; sales ledger 1957-60; journals: 1958-75, cheese sales 1959-64

R Bowyers & Sons Ltd: milk analysis cash book 1947-8; wages books 1956-63

Brent Bridge Hotel Ltd: annual accounts 1967

Brighton Grand Hotel Co Ltd: share ledgers 1942-60; directors registers 1948-70; seals register 1947-71; annual reports and accounts 1965-71; annual accounts 1964-7; staff correspondence and papers 1967-8

Bull Hotel (Gerrards Cross) Ltd: annual accounts 1967

Chessington Dairies Ltd: private ledgers 1951-61

Chorleywood Dairies Ltd: private ledgers 1951-61

City of London Dairies Ltd: private ledgers 1960-1; milk samples report book 1950-64

John Clark (Hainault) Ltd: private ledgers 1950-61

Dairy Farmers Milk Supply Ltd: members register 1926-65; balance sheet and accounts 1967-8

TE Davies Ltd: members and share register 1925-67; private ledger 1958-65

Drapers Dairies (Woodford) Ltd: private ledgers 1946-61

East Kilbride Dairy Farmers Ltd: share register 1965-9; annual reports and accounts 1967-9

Eden Vale Ltd: members register etc c1955-66; milk samples report book 1950-63; stock book nd; sales booklet 1981

Empire Hotel Ltd: directors shareholding register 1949-60

J Evans Dairies (Black Lion Yard) Ltd: private ledger 1951-6

Express Dairy (Caterers) Ltd: ledgers 1950-7; cash books 1951-62; wages ledgers 1950-64; property list nd; catering complaints 1954-8

Express Dairy Co (London) Ltd: directors and general meeting minutes 1949-56; partnership minutes 1949-50; members register 1949-66; seals registers 1966-75; private ledger 1956-61; ledgers 1959-71; purchase journal 1956-67; branch: accounts 1964-5, profit and loss books 1950-72, ledgers 1973-5, cash books 1969-75; milk samples report books 1949-55; dairy complaints books 1958-61; wages: ledger 1952-8, cash book 1970-3; salaries book 1953-60; property: ledgers 1971-5, list nd

Express Dairy Foods Ltd: directors and general meeting minutes 1956-65; members registers etc 1955-6; private ledger 1952-8; revenue and gross profit book 1958-60; expenses books 1956-9; cash books 1957-61; staff publications on production methods c1958 on

Express Dairy (Northern) Ltd: pilot costings 1957-65

Express Dairy (Northern Ireland) Ltd: directors and general meeting minutes 1937-71; ledger: members 1959-71, general 1971-2

Express Hotels Ltd: annual accounts 1969

J Good & Sons Ltd: directors and general meeting minutes 1953-64; members register 1958-62

Griffin Dairies Ltd: directors and general meeting minutes 1942-76; members register 1942-64

Hawley's Bakeries Ltd: ledger 1974-8; service agreements 1973

Independent Dairies Ltd: directors minutes 1949-60; share ledger and papers 1950s; directors reports 1955-68; balance sheet and accounts 1959-70

Independent Milk Supplies Ltd: directors and general meeting minutes 1950-61; members register etc c1941-60; private ledgers 1963-75; journal 1961-75; sales book 1959-60
Independent Wholesale Dairies Ltd: balance sheet and accounts 1967-8; milk samples report book 1953-63; mortgage agreements 1954-61
John Kyle Ltd: private ledger 1957-64
George Lewis (Cheese Factors) Ltd: general meeting minutes 1959-76; members register etc 1958-9
Marshalls Dairies Ltd: milk samples report book 1950-63; salaries book 1958-64
Metropolitan Dairies Ltd: private ledgers 1944-60
C Moon & Sons Ltd: private ledgers 1947-60
EW Morgan & Sons Ltd: private ledgers 1947-60
Morgan Dairies (Kingsbury) Ltd: private ledgers 1951-61
Northern Wholesale Dairies Ltd: members register c1941-64; ledgers: private 1942-75, creamery 1958-60, purchase 1957-61; journals: purchase and sales 1955-75, milk and cheese 1957-63; cash books 1958-61
Packing Case & Timber Co Ltd: general meeting minutes 1971-6; members register c1958-71
Palace Dairies (Battersea) Ltd: private ledger 1951-60
Pearceland Dairies Ltd: private ledger 1949-61
Primrose & Len Dairies Ltd: members register 1947-64; share transfer register 1964-6
Queens Hotel Eastbourne Ltd: annual accounts 1967
Reliance Haulage Contractors Ltd: private ledgers 1955-61
Rickmansworth Dairies Ltd: private ledgers 1951-61
Seven Kings Dairies Ltd: private ledgers 1954-61
Sharpleshall Ltd: members register 1948-60; memo and articles of association 1935; private ledgers 1955-61
Sloans Dairies Ltd: marketing report 1969; service agreement 1972
South Harrow Dairies Ltd: private ledgers 1951-60
Spiers & Pond Ltd: dividends 1960; memo and articles of association 1860-7; annual reports and accounts 1965-9; balance sheet 1968; financial papers 1964-7
Spiers & Pond (Caterers) Ltd: memo and articles of association 1957; annual reports and accounts 1966-9; annual accounts 1964-9
Surrey Sterilised Milk Co Ltd: customer rebate books 1956-60; sales and delivery records 1954-60; hours worked book 1957-60
Swiss Milk Products Ltd: directors and general meeting minutes and register of members 1961-3
Tavistock Restaurants Ltd: ledgers 1948-64; salaries book 1946-52
L Thompson Ltd: general meeting minutes 1960-77; members register c1930-60
Towers Holdings Ltd: directors and general meeting minutes 1958-66
Tuxford & Tebbutt Ltd: general meeting minutes 1972-6; members register 1927-76
Vigormilk Co Ltd: general ledger 1955-68; private ledger 1963-75
Walker Gordon Laboratories Ltd: ledger 1936-9
Wickens Dairies Ltd: directors and general meeting minutes 1961-76; members register 1961-4; memo and articles of association 1958; dairies alteration papers with plan 1966-74
Ye Olde Falstaff Ltd: general meeting minutes 1964-76; members register 1959-75
Yogfruit Erat Ltd: directors and general meeting minutes 1936-9

Yogfruit Ltd: general meeting minutes 1957-77; members register 1943-77; trial balances 1963-7; ledger, journal and cash book 1964-6; production book 1963-5
Yorkshire Economic Laundries Ltd: directors reports and accounts 1966-9

Records (2): at Institute of Agricultural History & Museum of English Rural Life, University of Reading, Whiteknights, Reading, Berkshire RG6 2AG
board and general meeting minutes 1880-1953; transport committee meeting minutes 1945-8; partnership minutes with EDC (London) Ltd 1949-50; branch managers meeting proceedings 1946; members share registers and ledgers 1880-1947; share transfer register 1932-42; debenture register c1894-c1937; balance sheets and accounts 1946-54; profit and loss books: branches 1880-1955, dairies 1926-49, farms 1927-41; account summaries 1925-60; branch percentages 1932-8; private ledgers 1892-1959; bought ledgers 1936-60; creamery ledger: journals 1942-57, day books 1942-60; branches capital ledgers 1904-49; party catering ledger 1948-9; transport department journal 1942-7; day books: milk purchases 1936-44, farms 1943-9; dairies 1935-8; cash received books: chief office 1931-43, branch 1931-58; cash books: 1929-50, creameries 1942-6, branches 1935-45; account books: branch capital assets 1929-40, Echo margarine 1938-58; Milk Marketing Board accounting records 1940-3; College Farm invoice books 1938-41; sales registers 1932-6; illustrated sales literature c1892-1945; cost and depreciation schedule 1947; horse registers c1920-59; cattle registers c1921-40; vehicle registers 1921-52; stock books 1939-48; refreshment complaints 1932-63; accident reports 1936-48; wages books 1916-38; salaries books 1922-58; pension and benefit fund: minutes and balance sheets 1939-55, register 1939-61, ledger 1939-69, cash book 1939-61; pensions payments register 1938-55; Barham Benevolent Foundation Fund payments register 1939-61; chairmans address to staff 1945; rent: journal 1940-3, transfer book 1941-6; property: lists 1949-53, charges 1948, tenure particulars 1941, war damage accounts 1943-7; Frome visitors club visitors book 1940-1; booklet, articles and notes on history of company 1890s-1954; guardbooks, internal notices and stationery 1940s
R Bowyers & Sons Ltd: private ledgers 1931-59; cash book 1938-43; CW Jeffs private ledger 1945-8
Express Dairy (Northern Ireland) Ltd: directors and general meeting minutes 1917-35
Grange Farm Dairies (Buckinghamshire) Ltd: private ledgers 1942-61
Hornby & Clarke Ltd: balance sheets 1932-45; branch trading and profit and loss accounts 1927-55; cash book 1955-60
Independent Milk Supplies Ltd: private ledgers 1930-48
Independent Wholesale Dairies Ltd: members register 1939-65; private ledger 1941-6
Industrial Scientific Instruments Ltd: cash book 1945-57
RD Jones & Son (Dairies) Ltd: private ledgers 1940-60
TH Lewis Ltd: electric milk floats commission book 1938-54; historical booklet 1954
Marshalls Dairies Ltd: members register 1903-65; private ledgers 1921-58; cash books 1935-60
Guy Pearce & Co Ltd: ledgers 1934-48; cash books 1934-43
Primrose & Len Dairies Ltd: directors and general meeting minutes 1934-46
Reliance Haulage Contractors Ltd: private ledgers 1932-43
Richard & Bind (Contractors) Ltd: private ledger 1941-50
Robinsons Dairies Ltd: private ledgers 1936-57
Dairy Trade & Can Protection Society: council minutes 1906-17

Bryan Morgan, *Express Journey 1864-1964* (priv pub 1964)

337 LEEDS CHAMBER OF COMMERCE & INDUSTRY

12 Jun 1880
14183
Commerce House, 2 St Alban's Place, Wade Lane, Leeds, W Yorkshire LS1 8HZ
Chamber of commerce

History: founded in 1785 in Leeds to represent commercial interests of members but collapsed in c1793. Established again in 1851 to promote, extend and protect business interests of members. Registered as company limited by guarantee in 1880 as Leeds Incorporated Chamber of Commerce. In 1780s met in Rotation Office, South Kirkgate, from 1851 in Court House, Park Row, from 1884-1914 in Leeds Exchange Buildings, from 1914-48 in Park Row, from 1948-77 in Quebec Street and from 1977 in Commerce House, Wade Lane. Name changed to above after 1951.

Records (1): at Leeds Chamber of Commerce & Industry, Commerce House, 2 St Alban's Place, Wade Lane, Leeds, W Yorkshire LS1 8HZ
minutes 1964-date; annual reports and accounts 1851-date; *Journal* 1924 on; *Members Trade Directories* 1948 on

Records (2): at Brotherton Library, University of Leeds, Leeds, W Yorkshire LS2 9JT
minutes and letter books 1785-93,1851-1964; account book 1857-68; press cuttings 1951-61

MW Beresford, *The Leeds Chamber of Commerce* (priv pub 1951)

338 DISTRICT BANK LTD

1 Jul 1880
14251
55 King Street, Manchester, Greater Manchester M60 2DB
Banking

History: promoted by Joseph Macardy, stockbroker and other Manchester businessmen as Manchester & Liverpool District Banking Co and opened at Norfolk Street, Manchester, in Dec 1829. The business included premises and goodwill of Christy Lloyd & Co (Stockport & Cheshire Bank) of Stockport, Greater Manchester (est 1824). By 1873 it operated 17 branches in Greater Manchester, Cheshire, Lancashire and Staffordshire. Its headquarters were transferred to Spring Gardens, Manchester in 1834 and in the same year it dropped its own bank note issue as a condition of opening a Bank of England account. Acquired Nantwich & Cheshire Bank (est 1839), in 1844 and Loyd Entwisle & Co, Manchester (est c1771) in 1863. Branches numbered 54 by 1880 and London office was added in 1885. Acquired Lancaster Banking Co, the oldest English country joint stock bank (est 1826) in 1907, and Bank of Whitehaven (est 1786) in 1916. Changed name to above in 1924. Took over County Bank Ltd (est as Manchester & County Bank in 1862) in 1935 and was admitted to London Clearing House in 1936. In 1962 became a subsidiary of National Provincial Bank Ltd. In 1968, when it became a constituent part of National Westminster Bank Ltd, was operating through 570 branches.

Records (1): at Archives National Westminster Bank, 41 Lothbury, London EC2P 2BP
meeting minutes: board 1829-1968, directors committee 1896-1959, head office 1897-1923, foreign department 1917-25, Liverpool shareholders 1830; directors: memoranda 1865-99,

and officers instructions 1831; shareholders: list 1873, register 20 cent; deed of settlement 1843; articles of association 1929, 1951; annual report and accounts 1830-96; balance sheets 1914-70; past due bills 1830-96; bills for acceptance 1864-1900; memoranda: bank rate 1880-93, overdraft 1912-16, investments 1849-56, dividends 1851-97; share: ledger 1829-38, register 1837-57; security: register 1893-5, list 1849-73; bankruptcies and liquidations register 1865-1915; staff registers 1846-1920; managers list 1829-1916; declaration of secrecy 1842 on; pension fund: minutes 1889-1918, rules 1889-1962; overseas business correspondence 1892-1941; branch instructions 1859; branches - Alderley Edge: meeting minutes 1896-7, memoranda 1896-1935; Ashton: local board meeting minutes 1831-95, meeting minutes 1886-98, managers opinions 1867-75, signature book 1862-89, expenses book 1833-41, customers ledger 1831-84; Barrow in Furness: meeting minutes 1910-25, advance register 1898-1927, managers letter books 1899-1911; Bury: board meeting minutes 1875-95; Cannock: information book 1883; Cheadle: meeting minutes 1882-1924, managers opinion 1877-1927, information book 1886-1908; Chester: meeting minutes 1908-38; Chorley: managers meeting minutes 1911-31, information book 1907-44; Cornhill: managers meeting minutes 1888-1922, information book 1886-1908; Crewe: meeting minutes 1886-1928; Duckinfield: managers meeting minutes 1898-1909; Fenton: branch meeting minutes 1885-1919, information book 1883-1908, expenses 1875-99, out letters 1874-1923; Fallowfield: managers meeting minutes 1889-1925, information book 1883-1908; Hanley: meeting minutes 1885-1969, information book 1883-91, half yearly returns 1888-1957, abstract and register of bad debts 1839-86, abstracts of customers balances 1907-50, letter book 1911-29; Haslingden: meeting minutes 1885-1906; Knutsford: meeting minutes 1909-40; Levenshulme: meeting minutes 1898-1959; Liverpool: meeting minutes 1844-1970, opinions 1835-42, analysis 1880-1908, register of bankruptcies 1834-8, managers letter books 1836-1931; London: statistics 1842-1908; Manchester: board meeting minutes 1831-76, managers memoranda 1873-95; Maryport: managers opinions 1919-27; Nantwich: routine business correspondence 1870-80; Ramsbottom: meeting minutes 1908-39; Rochdale: expenses 1833-46, managers out letters 1839-72; Stafford: meeting minutes 1886-94, local board minutes 1843-64, balance sheet 1883, expenses account 1839-69, managers diary 1883-5; Stoke on Trent: information book 1883-1908, customer ledger 1877; Ulverston: meeting minutes 1910-24, managers out letters 1907-16; Warrington: bad debt instructions 1839; Whitehaven: deposit ledger 1916-59, managers diaries 1917-20; Wilmslow memoranda 1898-1914; Windermere: out letters 1907-28

Records (2): at Lloyds Bank, 71 Lombard Street, London EC3P 3BS
proposed amalgamation correspondence 1903

339 BRADFORD BANKING CO LTD

1 Jul 1880
14254
Poultry, London EC2P 2BX
Banking

History: established as a joint stock bank in Kirkgate, Bradford, W Yorkshire in 1827. Had no branches outside Bradford. Registered with limited liability in 1880 and in 1910 amalgamated with London City & Midland Bank Ltd, renamed London Joint City & Midland Bank Ltd in 1918, and Midland Bank Ltd in 1923.

Records (1): at Midland Bank, Poultry, London EC2P 2BX
board meeting minutes 1827-1910; shareholder meeting minutes 1828-1910; list of shareholders 1875; abstracts of shareholders wills 1845-97; formation papers 1825-7; amalgamation papers 1909-10; annual reports 1864-96; balance sheets 1868-1908; profit and loss statement 1828; income tax returns 1870-1909; customers private ledger 1827-30; securities register 1827-1909; safe custody register 1855-82; salary book 1871-91; staff register c1890

Records (2): at Bradford Archives Department, Central Library, Prince's Way, Bradford, W Yorkshire BD1 1NN
deed of constitution 1828

WF Crick and JE Wadsworth, *A Hundred Years of Joint Stock Banking* (1936)

340 NORTH & SOUTH WALES BANK LTD
1 Jul 1880
14255
62 Castle Street, Liverpool, Merseyside
Banking

History: established in Liverpool in Apr 1836 and opened 13 branches and 10 sub-branches in north Wales in same year. Acquired R Sankey & Co of Holywell and Denbigh, Clwyd (est 1790) and Benson & Co, Aberystwyth, Dyfed (est 1762) in 1836, 8 branches of Northern & Central Bank of England (est at Manchester 1884) in 1837, and Douglas Smalley & Co of Holywell and Mold, Clwyd (est 1822) in 1839. Business cut back by financial crisis of late 1830s and dividends suspended between 1839 and 1844. Reconstructed with new capital after stoppage in 1847 and several branches were sold or closed. Acquired Davies, Banks & Co, Knighton, Powys (est 1808) in 1856. Town branches opened in Liverpool and region from 1863. Headquarters removed from James Street to 62 Castle Street in 1873. Acquired Williams & Son of Dolgellau and Barmouth, Gwynedd (est 1803), Cassons & Co of Pwllheli, Ffestiniog, Blaenau and Harlech, Gwynedd (est 1847) in 1875 and Bala Banking Co Ltd of Bala and Dolgellau, Gwynedd and Corwen, Clwyd (est 1864) in 1877. The bank's later development was guided by George Rae, successively general manager (1845), managing director (1865), chairman (1873-98), and advisory director (1898 until his death in 1902). Rae was author of the classic textbook *The Country Banker* (1885), a leading figure in Association of Country Bankers (est 1874) and Institute of Bankers (est 1879), and was instrumental in framing 'reserved liability' legislation of 1879. Rae extended 'Wales Bank' branches in Wirral and Mersey regions from 1880s as rural Welsh business declined. In 1901 bank acquired Leyland & Bullins of Liverpool (est 1807) and by 1908 was one of the largest country banks with 108 branches and sub-branches. Deposits had grown from £2 million in 1870 to £10.8 million in 1908. The bank was amalgamated with London City & Midland Bank Ltd in 1908. Renamed London Joint City & Midland Bank Ltd in 1918, and Midland Bank Ltd in 1923.

Records: at Midland Bank, Head Office, London EC2P 2BX
meeting minutes: board 1836-1908, committee 1846-57, shareholders 1836-1908; share: holders registers 1874-89, registers 1836-1905, ledgers 1836-46, transfer register 1836-41;

prospectus 1836; settlement deed 1836; memo and articles of association 1901; amalgamation papers 1908-10; annual report and accounts 1839-1907; abstract of balance sheets 1843-1909; half yearly balance working papers 1879-1908; general ledgers 1836-1907; teller cash book 1836; note registers 1863-1907; own notes issuable 1861-1908; memoranda 1851-1907; security books 1836-70; bad debt books 1837-42; loan books 1868-1904; advances classification 1907; investment rent book 1849-73; staff registers 1845-76; instruction for officers 1849-1900; chairman's private letter book 1880-96; correspondence: re limited liability 1876-9, re projected amalgamation 1893-1907; press cuttings 1894-1908; branch inspection reports 1848-64; branches - Aberystwyth: general ledgers 1836-80, general ledger balances 1846-78, private ledgers 1840-76, deposit receipt ledgers 1836-79, security books 1836-61, bills of exchange register 1869-73, letter book 1836-44, securities registers 1878-1900; Barmouth: general ledger balances 1874-82; Caernarfon: general ledgers 1836-77, deposit receipt ledger 1836-56; Dolgellau: general ledger 1878-1914; Ffestiniog: private ledger 1837-9; Knighton: general ledger balances 1856-1909; Liverpool: managers letter book 1869-93; Liverpool, Castle Street: note ledger 1826-98, note register 1836-57, debts ledger 1848-75, agents correspondence book 1903-07; Liverpool, Markets: letters of procuration book 1882-90, deposit receipt counterfoils 1882-1905, securities register 1899-1923, correspondence book 1904-09; Liverpool, North: general ledgers 1836-78; Liverpool, South: signature books 1863-1916, securities register 1897-1950, procuration books 1874-1945; Llanfyllin: accounts opened 1888-1909; Llangollen: securities registers 1863-1909, signature books 1863-1909; Mold: private ledgers 1838-44, deposit receipt ledger 1834-74; Oswestry: general ledgers 1836-81, letter books 1862-1902, reference book 1874-92; Portmadoc: deposit receipt ledger 1839-42, accounts analysis; Criccieth: accounts analysis ledger 1883-9; Pwllheli: deposit receipt ledger 1836-48; Ruthin: deposit receipt ledger 1838-62; Welshpool: general ledger 1836-9, securities register 1836-74; Wrexham: general ledgers 1836-40, balance books 1837-1909, securities books 1836-1902, character book 1873-85

WF Crick and JE Wadsworth, *A Hundred Years of Joint Stock Banking* (1936)

341 MIDLAND BANK LTD

1 Jul 1880
14259
Poultry, London EC2P 2BX
Banking

History: promoted as joint stock bank titled Birmingham & Midland Bank by Charles Geach, an official at the Bank of England's Birmingham branch, in 1836. Head office was in Union Street, Birmingham, from 1837 until 1869, when it was transferred to New Street. Acquired Bate & Robins of Stourbridge, W Midlands (est 1770) in 1851 and Nichols Baker & Crane of Bewdley, Hereford & Worcester (est 1782) in 1862 but significant expansion was delayed until 1880s. After purchase of Union Bank of Birmingham Ltd (est 1878) in 1884, its acquisitions were mostly joint stock banks rather than private banks. Operated 45 branches by 1890. In 1891 acquired Central Bank of London Ltd (est 1863) and thereby moved head office to Cornhill, London, and was admitted to London Clearing House. Registered as unlimited company in 1873, adopted limited liability in 1880. Renamed as London & Midland Bank Ltd in 1891 and London City & Midland Bank Ltd in 1898. Amalgamations of 22 banks between 1891 and 1918 included City Bank Ltd (est 1855) in 1898, (giving new head office in

Threadneedle Street, London), North & South Wales Bank Ltd (est 1836) in 1908, Metropolitan Bank (England & Wales) Ltd (est 1829) in 1914 and London Joint Stock Bank Ltd (est 1836) in 1918 when name was changed to London Joint City & Midland Bank Ltd. Under Edward Holden, managing director (1898-1919) and chairman (1908-1919), it became the largest commercial bank in the world with 1327 branches and £389 million in deposits by 1919. Renamed the above in 1923 and moved headquarters to Poultry, London, in 1930. Subsidiaries included Midland Bank Trust Co Ltd (est 1909), Belfast Banking Co Ltd (est 1827) in 1917, Clydesdale Bank Ltd, Glasgow (est 1838) in 1919, North of Scotland Bank Ltd, Aberdeen (est 1836) in 1924, the finance house, Forward Trust Ltd (est 1929) in 1958, Northern Bank Ltd, Belfast (est 1824) in 1865, the merchant bank Samuel Montagu & Co Ltd (est 1853) in 1967, Thomas Cook Travel Group (est c1841) in 1972, and banking subsidiaries in France, Germany, Switzerland and USA. Renamed Midland Bank PLC in 1982, when it had 3364 branches in England and Wales and total deposits of £44,231 million.

Records: at Midland Bank, Poultry, London EC2P 2BX
board meeting: minutes 1836-1960, agendas 1891-8; committee meeting minutes: overdraft 1887-91, Birmingham 1891, and papers 1923-54, finance 1885-1949, Liverpool 1908; general meeting: minutes 1836-1957, press cuttings 1879-99; prospectus 1836; deed of settlement 1836; amalgamation working papers 1896-1924; secretarys notebooks 1871-98; annual report and accounts 1837-date; balance sheets: 1847-1908, working papers 1912-45; head office abstract of accounts 1888-1900; ledgers: general 1900-45, deposit account 1836, current account 1836; cash book 1836; doubtful debts summaries 1891-1911; bills risks book 1895; interest rates analysis 1907-15; classification of advances 1933-9; overseas arrangement book 1898-1914; monies held abroad books 1915-19; overseas letter books 1906-09,c1920; Leningrad office reports and correspondence 1917; investment register 1892-9; staff agreements 1894-1905; guarantee fund accounts working papers 1911-19; Mutual Provident Fund reports and balance sheets 1938-43; refreshment club register 1911-19; premises reference book 1900; head office circulars 1900-39; general managers diaries and reference books 1896-1944; branch: balance sheet ledgers 1890-1904,1912-39, abstract of accounts 1886-97, managers instruction book 1890, premises reference book (London) 1890-1900; branches - Angel Court: reference book 1912-31; Barnsley, Market Hill: reference books 1920-32; Barnsley, Peel Square: reference books 1897-1932; Bewdley: general ledgers 1862; Chancery Lane: securities registers 1890-1921; Chiswick: general charges analysis 1899-1951; Cornhill: securities register 1892-1908, salary books 1891-1932, letter book 1905-13; Covent Garden: salary and reference, letter book 1899-1943; Coventry: letter book 1918-30; Dalton in Furness: private ledgers 1918-44, cash books 1922-4; Huddersfield: salary book 1900-37; Lambeth: salary books 1922-53; Leeds, Park Row: letter books 1922-53, salary books 1922-53; Liverpool, Walton: general ledger 1909-77; Lye: private ledgers 1890; Morley: securities register 1891-1902; Stourbridge: general ledger 1882; Wednesbury: securities register 1877-84, open and closed book 1877-1905

WF Crick and JE Wadsworth, *A Hundred Years of Joint Stock Banking* (1936)
Edwin Green, *The Making of a Modern Banking Group* (priv pub 1979)

342 NATIONAL PROVINCIAL BANK LTD

1 Jul 1880
14260
Drapers Gardens, 12 Throgmorton Avenue, London EC2
Banking

History: founded as a joint stock bank in 1833 as National Provincial Bank of England by Thomas Joplin to be the first London bank with the specific purpose of providing a centrally controlled banking system throughout England and Wales on the successful Scottish model. First branch was opened at Gloucester in 1834 and by 1835 another 14 provincial branches, some with sub-branches, had been established. Acquired Northern & Central Bank of England branch, Bristol, Avon and North Devon Bank, Barnstaple, in 1835; Skinner & Co (est 1815) of Stockton, Cleveland and Darlington, Durham in 1836; Rugeley, Tanfield & Lichfield Joint Stock Bank in 1837; Husband & Co (Devonport General Bank) Devon (est 1810) in 1839; Harris & Co (Dartmouth Bank) Devon (est 1806) and Fryer, Andrews & Co, Wimborne, Poole, Blandford Forum, Dorset (est 1790) in 1840; Dover Old Bank, Kent (est 1700) in 1841; Cole, Holroyd & Co (Devon County Bank) Exeter (est 1807) in 1842; Bideford Old Bank (Ley & Co) Devon (est 1790), Pretor & Co (Sherborne and Dorsetshire Bank) (est 1740) and Loveband & Co, Torrington, Devon in 1843; Isle of Wight Joint Stock Bank, Newport (est 1842) in 1844; Stockton and Durham County Bank, Stockton and Guisborough, Cleveland (est 1838) in 1846; Kennersley & Sons, Newcastle under Lyme, Staffordshire (est 1780) in 1854; William Moore's Bank, Stone, Staffordshire (est 1810) in 1858; Crawshay, Bailey & Co, Newport, Dyfed, Monmouth and Abergavenny, Gwent (est 1837) in 1857; Carmarthen Bank (David Morris & Sons) (est 1790) in 1871; Bank of Leeds Ltd (est 1864) in 1878; County of Stafford Bank Ltd, Wolverhampton (est 1836) in 1899, and Knaresborough & Claro Banking Co Ltd, N Yorkshire (est 1831) in 1903. Had acquired premises at 112 Bishopsgate, London in 1839-40, which opened for banking business in 1866, by which time the bank had 122 offices and over 2000 shareholders. Registered as a limited liability company in 1880. Amalgamated in 1918 with Union of London & Smiths Bank Ltd (est 1839) to become National Provincial & Union Bank of London Ltd. Changed name to above in 1924. Acquired W&J Biggerstaff, Smithfield, London (est 1790) in 1918; Bradford District Bank Ltd (est 1862) incorporating Bradford Commercial Joint Stock Banking Co Ltd (est 1833) and Sheffield Banking Co Ltd (est 1831) in 1919; Northamptonshire Union Bank Ltd (est 1836), Richards & Co, Llangollen in 1920; Dingley & Co, Launceston, Cornwall (est 1855) and Dingley, Pearse & Co, Okehampton, Devon (est 1856) in 1922; Guernsey Banking Co Ltd (est 1874) in 1924. The business of Coutts & Co was affiliated from 1920. In 1951 the bank had 1261 branches and over 45,000 shareholders. Isle of Man Bank Ltd (est 1865) became a subsidiary in 1961 and District Bank Ltd (est 1829) in 1962. In 1968 National Provincial, Westminster and District Banks agreed to combine their banking groups and in 1968 the whole of the issued share capital of the company and of Westminster Bank Ltd (est 1834) was acquired by National Westminster Bank Ltd. From 1970 the businesses of the 3 constituent banks were merged into the latter and they ceased to trade.

Records (1): at National Westminster Bank, 41 Lothbury, London EC2P 2BP
court minutes 1828-78, private 1904-20; chairmans books 1873-8; committee meeting minutes: rotation 1833-78, finance 1879-1915, salaries 1862-87; correspondence department meeting minutes 1878-1966; general meeting: proceedings books 1834-1939, minutes 1908-20,

attendance lists 1870-89, press cuttings 1919-41; directors registers 1901-23; share registers 1833-64; legal opinions re shareholders 1859-85; annual returns 1879-83; prospectuses 1829-30; deed of settlement 1833; proprietors list 1840-53; law books 1870-1949; amalgamation papers 1918; annual reports 1834-1968; balance sheet and profit and loss books 1856-81; incidental charges book 1859-68; bank notes: issue licences 1835-56, issued registers 1833-97, cancelled and destroyed register 1844-55, outstanding register 1897 on, indemnity books 1845-79; assignments re debts due 1839-53; staff: agreement books 1886-1916, payment scales 1860, senior salary book 1877-1920, guarantee fund circulars 1869-86, holiday fund committee minutes 1925-51; managers list 1836; papers re general manager 1836-43; apprenticeship candidate books 1867-1918; probationer regulations 1929; secretarys letter book 1833; head office and agent circulars 1838-1936; private letters 1899-1918; bank history c1850; branch: committee minutes 1843-5,1889-1916, balance sheets 1860-77, instructions to directors and managers 1840, information book 1834, premises history 1905-20, opening papers 1918; branches - Bangor: managers letter book 1861-93; Beaumaris: character books 1878-1906; Birmingham: character book 1887-1914; Bournemouth: staff information book 1946-65; Bridgend: bill registers 1835-57, character books 1898-1922; Bristol: loan book 1911-24, advances and discounted bills analysis 1936-48, character books 1876-1921, interview books 1892-1908; letter book 1902-03; Bristol: premises plans Corn Street 1889-90, Redlands 1889-1927; Conway: character book 1878-1929; Dartmouth: drafts issued book 1876-1966; Dolgellau: managers drafts 1846-52, general ledger and cash book 1861-2, cash on hand 1855-9, daily payments in 1842-63; Ledbury: customer ledger 1835-43, deposit ledger 1835-80; Leeds: character book 1878-84; Lichfield: character books 1877-1908, security register 1834-72; Llandudno: character books 1876-1900; London: Dartford letters with head office 1850-66, Hackney managers letters 1904-24, Lombard Street information book 1908-48, Paddington profit and loss account book 1904-37; March: character books 1875-1952, interview books 1913-26; Scarborough: managers letters 1902-26; Sherborne: character books 1874-1929, interview book 1930-5, letter books 1862-1929; Totnes: information book 1843-68; Wolverhampton: information book 1899-1918, statistics 1899-1926; Wotton under Edge: minutes 1834-74

Records (2): at Liverpool City Record Office, William Brown Street, Liverpool, Merseyside L3 8EW
Llangefni branch managers papers 1850-86

H Withers, *National Provincial Bank, 1833-1933* (priv pub 1933)

343 LINCOLN & LINDSEY BANKING CO LTD

13 Jul 1880
14296
High Street, Lincoln, Lincolnshire
Banking

History: opened for business in Lincoln in 1833 and all subsequent branch developments were within Lincolnshire. Soon opened offices at Louth, Gainsborough, Horncastle, Lincolnshire and Brigg, Humberside with weekly attendances at the markets of Spilsby, Market Rasen and Caistor, Lincolnshire. In 1839 head offices were moved to High Street, Lincoln. Took over the premises and business of the Boston banking firm of Thomas Gee & Co (est 1788) in 1874 and the Gainsborough business of Nottingham & Nottinghamshire Bank Ltd in 1892. Branches were opened at Grimsby, Humberside in 1892 and at Spalding, Lincolnshire in 1898. Registered with limited liability as above in 1880 and amalgamated in 1913 with London City & Midland Bank Ltd, renamed London Joint City & Midland Bank Ltd in 1918 and Midland Bank Ltd in 1923.

Records: at Midland Bank, Poultry, London EC2P 2BX
board meeting minutes 1833-1914; shareholder meeting minutes 1833-1913; deed of settlement 1833; memo and articles of association 1902; amalgamation papers 1913; balance sheets 1834-1912; half-yearly balances 1877-1907; registers of deeds 1834-84; branches - Barton upon Humber: general ledger 1835-43; Gainsborough: business agreement 1878; Louth: board minutes 1833-78; Spilsby: profit and loss book 1869-1900

WF Crick and JE Wadsworth, *A Hundred Years of Joint Stock Banking* (1936)

344 BUCKS LAND & BUILDING CO LTD

28 Jul 1880
14335
5 Temple Square, Aylesbury, Buckinghamshire HP20 2QA
Property

History: incorporated as above in 1880 to purchase real and personal property, to resell same, advance money on mortgage or other securities and to let premises. Formed by group of Aylesbury businessmen led by G Butcher of Butcher & Son, and was an adjunct to Howard & James, solicitors.

Records: at Bucks Land & Building, 5 Temple Square, Aylesbury, Buckinghamshire HP20 2QA
directors and general meeting minutes 1880,1893,1900,1906-date; share: certificate book 1899-1956, transfer documents 1892-1950; memo and articles of association 1880-1962; account book: loans 1932-8, deposit 1959-69, stocks and shares 1934-6, R Jewell 1909-20; cash book 1880-1957; mortgage: agreement c1880, register 1932-55; deposit books 1882-1953; investment service: advertisement c1907, prospectus 1966; title deeds and property documents 1884-1901; land value duties 1910-15; repair schedules 1938

345 DERBY & DERBYSHIRE BANKING CO LTD

4 Aug 1880
14352
21 Corn Market, Derby, Derbyshire
Banking

History: established in 1833 and opened for business in Derby in 1834. Incorporated with limited liability as above in 1880 and amalgamated with Parr's Bank Ltd in 1898, which itself amalgamated with London County & Westminster Bank Ltd in 1918 to form London County Westminster & Parr's Bank Ltd. At the time of amalgamation the bank had 8 branches - Belper, Litchurch, Long Eaton, Matlock Bath, Matlock Bridge and Melbourne, Derbyshire; Crick, Northamptonshire; Driffield, Humberside

Records: at National Westminster Bank, 41 Lothbury, London EC2P 2BP provisional committee meeting minutes 1833; deed of settlement 1833; amalgamation agreement 1898; customer ledger 1835

TE Gregory, *The Westminster Bank Through A Century* Vol 2 (1936)

346 CRAVEN BANK LTD

17 Aug 1880
14382
54 Lombard Street, London EC3P 3AH
Banking

History: established as Birkbecks, Alcock & Co (also known as Craven Banking Co) at Skipton, W Yorkshire and Settle, N Yorkshire, in 1791. Renamed Birkbecks, Alcock, Peart & Moffat in 1812. Acquired Chippendale Netherwood & Carr of Skipton in 1826 and renamed Birkbecks, Alcocks, Birkbeck & Robinson in 1833. Renamed Alcocks, Birkbeck, Robinson, Birkbeck & Stansfield in 1844, Alcock, Birkbeck & Co in 1858, and Birkbecks, Robinson & Co in 1873. Registered with reserved liability as above in 1880 by which time had opened branches at Clitheroe, Lancashire (c1791), Burnley, Lancashire (c1824) and Keighley, W Yorkshire. By 1906 had 15 branches and deposits of £3.5 million. In 1906 was acquired by Bank of Liverpool Ltd (est 1831), which merged with Martin's Bank Ltd (est 1712), in 1918 to form Bank of Liverpool & Martins Ltd, known as Martins Bank Ltd in 1928. Became part of Barclays Bank Ltd in 1968.

Records (1): at Barclays Bank, 54 Lombard Street, London EC3P 3AH
agm minutes 1906; declaration of confidence 1826; shareholders list 1881,1892; prospectus 1880; articles of association 1880; annual report and accounts 1880-1905; half yearly balances 1816-44; partnership accounts 1825-1911; customer: ledger 1791-1803, account balances 1827-36; diaries of Thomas Dixon with notes on customers and records of business 1866-91; stock ledger 1806-36; branches - Barnoldswick: drafts book 1898-1909; Colne: security registers 1876-1902; Clitheroe: security ledger 1900-20; Settle: general balance abstracts 1834-40, private ledger 1813-30, stock book 1800s, note register 1844-70

Records (2): at Pig Yard Museum, Castle Hill, Settle, N Yorkshire
partnership deed 1859; general balances pre 1805; customer ledgers 1802-06; Birkbeck family correspondence 1830

Records (3): Leeds Archives Department, Chapeltown Road, Sheepscar, Leeds, W Yorkshire LS7 3AP
William Birkbeck: bank business letters and papers 1773-1823

347 CENTRAL NEWS (CITY ADVERTISING) LTD

26 Aug 1880
14404
Extel House, 1 East Harding Street, London EC4P 4HB
News agency

History: founded in London by William Saunders and his brother-in-law Edward Spender as the Central Press news agency which from 1863 offered a daily service of 8 columns of general and foreign news and leading articles, parliamentary sketches, late corn trade and agricultural market reports, law cases etc, sent by evening trains to provincial towns. Saunders (1823-95) a journalist and politician, had started the *Plymouth Western Morning News* in 1860 and *Eastern Morning News* (Hull) in 1864. Also an original member of the committee of management of Press Association Ltd (founded 1868 to supply telegraphic news to provincial papers). He resigned after a conflict of interests over Central Press, and in 1871 formed Central News to sell his own telegraphic news. This ensured competition between the 2 agencies until the 1940s and especially fierce price cutting in the 1880s. In 1880 he formed Central News Ltd and sold same his Central News agency which operated from 107 Fleet Street, London. Company also competed for business with Exchange Telegraph Co Ltd, leading on many occasions to court cases, but continued as a main home and foreign news agency from its offices at 5 New Bridge Street, Ludgate Circus, London. Column Printing Co Ltd (est 1889 as Column Printing Telegraph Syndicate Ltd) was an associate before becoming a wholly owned subsidiary in 1900s, operating a betting and sports service. Company was eventually squeezed out by its 2 rivals, shares being jointly bought by Press Association and Exchange Telegraph in 1935. The latter bought the former's shares in c1947 and took over Central News's advertising agency, while the Press Association took over its photographic library and parliamentary service. Changed name to above in 1966.

Records (1): at Extel, Extel House, 1 East Harding Street, London EC4P 4HB
directors and general meeting minutes 1880-1979; board: papers 1947-78, reports 1966-72; attendance books 1928-80; shareholders notices and correspondence 1896-1927; members registers 1880-1939; share ledgers 1880-1947; share certificate and share transfer documents 1886-1966; memo and articles of association 1880-1966; correspondence and documents re takeover 1946; annual returns 1880-1977; balance sheets and profit and loss accounts 1896-1966; private journal 1955-60; monthly returns 1964-6; correspondence, papers and circulars re services and tariffs 1888-1909; tariffs 1905,1914; agreements and licences with correspondence 1907-37; agency and advertising correspondence 1959-71; staff records and correspondence 1959-67; leases 1890-1954; legal action correspondence and papers 1889-1937; jubilee press cuttings and histories 1921
Column Printing Co Ltd: prospectuses 1889; correspondence and papers re setting up company 1888-1903; tariffs, papers and correspondence re services 1889-1909; legal action papers 1889-97

Records (2): at Press Association, 85 Fleet Street, London EC4P 4BE
memo and articles of association 1880,1934; general ledger 1947-53; day books 1940-53; subscriptions journal 1936-47; parliamentary service: general ledgers 1936-53, journal 1947-53, cash book 1947-9, petty cash book 1947-53; petty cash vouchers 1947-50; Company v Press Association report 1883
Column Printing Co Ltd: memo and articles of association 1889

348 FRANCES MARTIN COLLEGE
10 Sep 1880
14445
Working Men's College, Crowndale Road, London NW1 1TR
Education

History: founded in 1874 as College for Working Women based on ideas of FD Maurice, founder of Working Men's College Corporation. Registered as a company limited by guarantee in 1880 and subsequently changed name to above in honour of its first warden. First premises were at 29 Queen Street, London. Subsequently moved by 1880 to Fitzroy Street, London and to Working Men's College in Crowndale Road in 1957. Admission of women as full members of Men's College from 1965 fostered link between the two institutions.

Records: at Working Men's College, Crowndale Road, London NW1 1TR
correspondence 1874-date; student registers 1874-date; accounts 1874-date; misc college and societies records 19-20 cent; photographs of college buildings, events and personalities 19-20 cent

349 LINCOLNSHIRE LAW SOCIETY

11 Sep 1880
14447
3-5 St Swithins Square, Lincoln, Lincolnshire LN2 1HB
Law society

History: founded in 1879 as Lincolnshire Incorporated Law Society to promote fair and honourable practice in the law profession and to protect interests of its solicitor members. Incorporated as a company limited by guarantee in 1880. Membership in 1981 numbered c300. Maintained library from 1900 until 1953. Changed name to above in 1961-2.

Records (1): at Lincolnshire Law Society, 3-5 St Swithins Square, Lincoln, Lincolnshire LN2 1HB
general and committee meeting minutes, accounts and notices to members 1879-date

Records (2): at Lincolnshire Archives Office, The Castle, Lincoln, Lincolnshire LN1 3AB
agendas, reports, accounts, letters, draft articles of association, jubilee banquet programme, minimum scale of conveyancing charges 1929-49

350 GREENALL WHITLEY & CO LTD

4 Oct 1880
14504
Wilderspool Brewery, Warrington, Cheshire WA4 6RH
Brewing

History: traces origin to 1762 when Thomas Greenall (1735-1805) built a brewery at St Helens, Merseyside. In 1786 he acquired interests in brewing business at Wilderspool, Warrington, Cheshire and Liverpool in 1788. In 18 cent and 19 cent with his family he developed many other business interests in nailmaking, cotton spinning, coal mining, banking (Parr Lyon & Co) and glass making (Pilkingtons). In 1791 Wilderspool Brewery was rebuilt and in 1814 the Liverpool brewery was closed. In 1805 Thomas was succeeded in business by 3 of his sons, Edward, William and Peter, but for most of the 19 cent the business was dominated by Gilbert (later Sir Gilbert) Greenall, a grandson of the founder. In 1856 the St Helens Brewery was rebuilt and in 1859 Wilderspool Brewery became fully owned by the Greenall family. John Whitley, Gilbert's nephew, joined the business in the 1850s, beginning his family's important connection. The assets of the 2 independent businesses, Greenall & Co of Warrington and Thomas & Gilbert Greenall of St Helens were acquired by the above in 1881. Sir Gilbert

Greenall was first chairman and Peter Whitley was senior director. Sir Gilbert died in 1894 and was succeeded as chairman by his son, Sir Gilbert Greenall, later Lord Daresbury. In 1896 Spring Brewery at Hough Green was acquired and in 1923 a major interest in the distilling and wine and spirit merchants business of Gilbert & John Greenall Ltd was purchased. In 1930 GF&A Brown, Brewers of Nantwich, Cheshire was acquired followed by the acquisition of John Summer & Co Ltd, brewers at Haigh, Greater Manchester in 1931. Acquired Chester Northgate Brewery Co Ltd in 1949; Shrewsbury & Wem Brewery Co Ltd in 1951; JE Price Ltd, wine and spirit merchants, together with their subsidiary Cambrian Table Water Co Ltd (known as Cambrian Soft Drinks Ltd in 1975) in 1954; Magee Marshall & Co Ltd, brewers of Bolton, Greater Manchester in 1958; and Groves & Whitnall Ltd, brewers of Salford, Greater Manchester in 1961. Became a public company in 1952. In 1961 rebuilt the distillery of Gilbert & John Greenall Ltd which subsequently produced Warrington Dry Gin and Vladivar Vodka. In 1950s hotel and catering interests were combined into Compass Hotels Ltd. Chester, Bolton, Salford and St Helens breweries were closed between 1969 and 1976 when brewing was concentrated at the rebuilt Warrington brewery.

Records: at Greenall Whitley, Wilderspool Brewery, Warrington, Cheshire WA4 6RH
directors meeting minutes 1880-date; board report notebooks 1932-48; register: members 1880-1936, directors 1901-47; mortgage, charges and transfers 1891-1958; share transfer deeds, certificates, correspondence etc 1898-1948; debenture interest journal 1895-1912; papers re dissolution of partnership nd; seal book 1972-8; ledgers: 1781-1865,1948-73, profit and loss 1878-80, Wilderspool 1880-1913, St Helens 1880-90, collection, private and sundries 19-20 cent, private 1805-80, general c1915-53, advances 1907-71, free trade account 1949-54, duty, stock and purchase 1870-1, purchase 1912-71, purchase and sales 1957-63, clubs and societies 1848-68, nominal 1960-71, debt and credit 1923-70, petty 1930-66, monthly balances 1923-58; journals: 1791-1800, purchase 1963-73; cheques paid 1973-4; account book 1784-92; statements of account and stock 1788-1880; stock account book 1863-71; transport and distribution control account 1971-2; expenditure account summaries 1967-71; Wilderspool coal yard accounts 1800; meat purchase accounts 1847-53; general accounts, notebooks and papers c1803-1924; cash books: 1814-1963, received 1962-75, private 1919-67, managed houses payments 1966-72; debts book 1790-1837; incidental expenses book 1872-9; credit transfers 1927-68; bottling department: general ledger 1939-44, ledger balances 1913-68, free trade day book 1956-8, sales day book 1938-72, production and stock returns 1958-65, transfer book 1933-71; sales ledger: 1954-70, beer 1876-80, analysis 1964-9; sales: returns 1956-9, daily sheets 1955-9, day books 1878-82,1954,c1968; quarterly tied trade analysis 1967-70; customer order book 1951-4; public house postcards c1930s; stock book: 1789-1814, Wilderspool 1788-1972, St Helens 1815-1937, Liverpool 1786-1807, cotton works 1792-3, malt, barley and hops 1798-1811, coals, charcoal, malt and hops 1795, summaries 1881-1970; British stock delivery book 1798-1803; Wilderspool tied trade beer stock sheets 1959; beer returned 1758-61,1792-3,1877-9; labels and advertising material c1919-60; carters barrel delivery notebooks 1900-43; cartering expenses notebook 1804-13; barley: and malt purchases book 1874-1938, malting book 1869-1937; brewing notebooks: 1786-1884, Wilderspool 1920-39; St Helens waste books 1787-92,1814-57; trade returns: St Helens 1876-96, Wilderspool 1910-67; wages book: 1922-64; incidents analysis book 1896-1949; leases book c1888-1921; estates ledgers: Wilderspool 1922-53, balances 1922-69; property ledger 1935-69; rates and licences ledger 1939-59; estates cash book 1908-42; rent: list c1908-30, ledger 1785-1832, notebook 1824-74, book 1930-56; houses owned list 1923; houses offered for sale 1882-1918; valuation of property 1929; fixtures

and fittings: ledger c1949-60, register c1860-1900,1950-68; brewery building charges 1791-9; St Helens: estates repairs book 1879-1904, property accounts diary 1869-89; assessment book 1939-44; deeds out book 1887-1948; letter book: c1880-1929, St Helens: 1782-1817, Wilderspool 1794-1804; Greenall family accounts, correspondence and papers 1790-1916
Allied Vintners Investments Ltd: general meeting minutes of subsidiary companies 1967-71
Beverage Investments Ltd: meeting minutes: directors 1963-5, general 1967-70s
Chester Northgate Brewery: (See summary no 664)
Drew & Co (Oswestry) Ltd: directors meeting minutes 1953-67, share papers 1969
Gilbert & John Greenall Ltd: directors meeting minutes 1966-70; register of mortgages 1898,1949; annual returns 1943-4; annual report and accounts 1894-5
Gilbert Greenall: stock book 1867-76
Thomas & Gilbert Greenall: stock book 1802-80
Groves & Whitnall Ltd: meeting minutes: directors 1899-1975, general 1899-1971; register: members c1941-60, share transfers 1941-61, debenture stock 1968-9; share ledgers, registers, cash books and papers 1899 on; seal book 1899-1978; nominal, impersonal, private ledgers and cash books 1899 on; property and rent ledgers and registers 1899 on
Hardshaw Colliery: ledger 1802-16; waste book 1802-19; letter book 1805-16
Hardshaw Kiln: account book 1762-75; waste book 1762-75
Keysell & Co Ltd: directors meeting minutes 1939-68; share: ledgers, registers etc c1928-64; ledger 1952-63
Lyon & Greenall: wages book 1819-27; private letter book 1790-1807
Magee Marshall Ltd: (See summary no 604)
OD Murphy & Sons Ltd: share ledgers and registers, etc c1953-66
Newalls of Manchester: stock books 1812-31
St Helens Building Society: minutes 1836-42; papers 1837-40
Shrewsbury & Wem Brewery Co Ltd: directors meeting minutes 1964-7
Tinsley & Co Ltd: cash book 1871
Tinsley & Glover: stock book 1801-58
T Trott Ltd: cash book 1958-63
David Williams & Co Ltd: directors meeting minutes 1957-64; share ledgers, registers and papers etc 1954; annual list 1935-55; nominal ledger 1971-3

J Norman Slater, *A Brewer's Tale* (1980)

351 PARE'S LEICESTERSHIRE BANKING CO LTD

12 Oct 1880
14521
41 Lothbury, London EC2P 2PB
Banking

History: established in 1800 by Thomas Pares the younger in St Martin's, Leicester as Pares & Heygate. Became a joint stock bank in 1836 as Pare's Leicestershire Banking Co and was incorporated as above with limited liability in 1880. The bank had its own London agency until 1830 and opened branches in Leicestershire at Ashby de la Zouche, Hinckley, Loughborough and Lutterworth along with 10 sub-branches. In 1902 it amalgamated with

Parr's Bank Ltd which itself amalgamated with London County & Westminster Bank Ltd in 1918 to form London County Westminster & Parr's Bank Ltd.

Records (1): at National Westminster Bank, 41 Lothbury, London EC2P 2PB
board meeting minutes 1836-1902; agm minutes 1837-1902; share transfer notices 1889-1902; deed of settlement 1836; amalgamation papers 1902; annual reports 1836-1902; balance sheets 1897-1901; monthly balances 1844-1902; private ledgers 1836-1902; private cash books 1880-1902; customer ledger 1800-06; bad and doubtful debts schedule 1902; stock register 1860-83; Hinckley branch customer ledger 1826-7

Records (2): at Derby City Library, Derbyshire Library Service, Local Studies Department, Derby Central Library, The Wardwick, Derby, Derbyshire DE1 1HF
correspondence between Thomas Pares and his son 19 cent

TE Gregory, *The Westminster Bank Through A Century* Vol 2 (1936)

352 ELAC INSURANCE CO LTD

25 Oct 1880
14558
1 St Helens, Undershaft, London EC3P 3DQ
Insurance

History: incorporated in 1880 as Employers' Liability Assurance Corporation Ltd in anticipation of Employers' Liability Act 1880. Employers' liability insurance offered an indemnity against employee damages claims and provided insurance against third-party accident claims. Said to have been the most successful office in its field. Premium income exceeded £254,000 by 1889 and £342,000 by 1905. Took over business of National Employers' Accident & General Assurance Association (est 1882) in 1884, and acquired Merchants' Marine Insurance Co Ltd (est 1871) in 1919. Amalgamated in 1960 with Northern Assurance Co Ltd, which became part of Commercial Union Assurance Co Ltd in 1968. Name changed to above in 1970.

Records (1): at Commercial Union Assurance, 1 St Helens, Undershaft, London EC3P 3DQ
directors: meeting minutes 1939-65, seal books 1962 on; finance and general purposes committee minutes 1881-2; general meeting minutes 1930-64; shares purchased 1919; policies class index 1887 on

Records (2): at Guildhall Library, Aldermanbury, London EC2P 2EJ
directors meeting minutes 1884-1939

353 BRITISH ENGINE INSURANCE LTD

18 Nov 1880
14644
Longridge House, Manchester, Greater Manchester
Insurance

History: established in King Street, Manchester as Engine & Boiler Insurance Co Ltd in 1878. Promoted by Robert B Longridge, previously chief engineer of Manchester Steam Users' Association from its inception in 1854 until 1859 and Boiler Insurance & Steam Power Co Ltd from inception in 1859 until 1878. Undertook preventive inspection and insurance of engines, boilers, and from 1904, electrical and other engineering plant. Also manufactured safety devices for boilers and engines. Incorporated as Engine Boiler & Employers' Liability Insurance Co Ltd in 1880 and changed name to British Engine Boiler & Electrical Insurance Co Ltd in 1904 on being united with British Steam Users' Insurance Society. Acquired British Steam Users' Association (est 1889) in 1896 and Manchester Steam Users' Association in 1932. In 1912 became a subsidiary of Royal Insurance Co Ltd (est 1845). In 1914 offices moved to premises in Fennel Street, and in 1959 to Longridge House, Manchester. In 1971 Qualitest Division was established, providing integrated technical inspection services for all sections of industry world-wide. In 1976 was granted Queens Award for Export Achievement. In 1978 name changed to above. In 1983 the engineering insurance services of Royal Insurance Group merged with those of the parent company and company now trades as 'British Engine - the Technical Services Division of Royal Insurance (UK) Ltd.'

Records: at British Engine Insurance, Longridge House, Manchester, Greater Manchester
directors meeting minutes 1878-1982; shareholders meeting minutes 1879-1981; acquisition papers 1964; prospectus 1878; memo and articles of association 1880-1919; seal book 1936-81; accounts: annual 1879-1972, revenue sheets 1906-27, statistical record and analysis sheets 1909-73; income analysis 1928-35; thrift fund balance sheets 1911-23; sales brochures 1928-70s; correspondence: business development 1919-49, other agencies 1921,1943; overseas: list 1935-6, reports 1949,1966; policy, proposal and report forms 1896-1921; underwriting notes 1933-4; guarantee certificates 1899-1902; inspection procedure, summary and correspondence 1916-47; technical reports 1921-32; electrical classification sheets 1917-36; lift and crane department: statistics 1926-50, standard descriptions 1960, leaflets 1928,1932,1950; salary book 1904; staff correspondence 1914-63; pension trust fund deeds 1914-53; staff: bonus 1928, office organisation charts 1957-64,1974, statistics 1923-36; office methods 1916-65; expenses record 1864-1968; sports and social club news-letters 1932-62; staff photographs c1940-70; articles, photographs, correspondence, papers Longridge family 1898-1973; premises: photographs, newscuttings, correspondence c1912-70, circular letters and correspondence 1922-70; notes and historical information, articles and photographs 1914-76
Boiler Insurance & Steam Power Co Ltd: shareholders meeting minutes 1877-80; reports, accounts and balance sheets 1860-87; reports by RB Longridge on boiler explosions 1863,1874; correspondence 1874-78
British Steam Users' Association Ltd: report of directors 1893,1895
Engineering Offices Association: tariff electrical rates 1925,1957, engines 1925,1954, boiler 1925,1954, lifting machinery 1948; general regulations 1961
Manchester Steam Users' Association: meeting minutes 1854-5; committee: meeting minutes 1855-75, reports 1855,1911-31; constitution 1902; inspection reports 1855-1927; agreements, pension fund papers reports and correspondence 1853-1932; historical sketch 1905
Royal Insurance Co Ltd: accounts and press cuttings 1916-79; staff group reports 1954-67; takeover correspondence 1912-51

N Edwards, *100 Years of British Engine* (1978)

354 NOTTS & DERBYSHIRE TRADERS ASSOCIATION LTD

25 Nov 1880
14661
4-6 New Street, Leicester, Leicestershire
Traders association

History: established in 1861 as Nottinghamshire & Midland Merchants Traders Association through the initiative of alderman Robert Mellors of Nottingham, to protect the interests of traders by recovering debts for members; preventing, investigating and prosecuting fraud; supporting useful and resisting damaging commercial legislation; enquiring into the worthiness of traders; and issuing particulars of bankruptcies etc. By 1864 had branches at Newark, Bingham and Mansfield, Nottinghamshire; Derby, Chesterfield and Belper, Derbyshire; Leicester and Loughborough, Leicestershire; and Lincoln and Grantham, Lincolnshire. By 1865 membership stood at 1000, rising to 1200 by 1866 but falling to 852 by 1899. Incorporated as Nottinghamshire & Midland Merchants & Traders Association Ltd in 1880 and changed name to above in 1908. Membership fell to around 550 in 1920s and stood at 650 in 1938. Taken over by Leicester Trade Protection Society Ltd (est 1854) in 1969 and dissolved in 1980.

Records: at Leicestershire Trade Protection Society, 4-6 New Street, Leicester, Leicestershire
committee, general and finance sub-committee meeting minutes 1863-7; directors, general and committee meeting minutes 1882-1952; annual reports and accounts 1882-1944; circulars and newscuttings 1863-7,1882-1908; balance sheets and accounts 1863-7,1909-67
Leicester Trade Protection Society: committee and general meeting minutes 1854-1909; annual reports and accounts 1854,1866-1909; circulars and petitions 1864-1909; bank books 1850-70; petty cash book 1872-1941; strong-room papers and correspondence 1886
National Association of Trade Protection Societies: secretarys meeting minutes 1850-1921; special committee meeting minutes 1920-1; register 1899-1940

355 NEWCASTLE UPON TYNE LIBERAL CLUB

30 Nov 1880
14678
Ridley House, Regent Centre, Gosforth, Tyne & Wear
Political club-house

History: founded as Newcastle upon Tyne Junior Liberal Club in 1879 to provide a club for Liberals in Newcastle. First premises were at Alliance Hotel, Charlotte Square, Newcastle, Tyne & Wear, moving in 1880 to former Roach's Chop House in Grey Street. Incorporated in 1880 as company limited by guarantee. Social activities grew rapidly and in 1882 amalgamated with 'older' Liberals and changed name to above. In 1884 club moved to own premises at 98 Pilgrim Street. In the 1920s provided dining, reading, billiard and games facilities, held social events and ran a golfing society for its members as well as supporting the Liberal cause. Club declined as the Liberal Party's fortunes waned. Premises in Pilgrim Street (listed building) were sold in 1968 and company dissolved in 1982.

Records: at Tyne & Wear Archives Department, Blandford House, West Blandford Street, Newcastle upon Tyne, Tyne & Wear NE1 4JA
general committee: minutes 1936, report 1960; committee and officer lists and attendances 1879-1905,1926-60; committee resolution 1892; agm notices and agendas 1879-1905,1935-40;

memo and articles of association c1890; prospectus c1930; annual reports and accounts 1879-1937; account statements 1928-37; ledger 1931-47; visitors account book 1938-46; subscription and wage books 1931-44; petty cash books 1941-5,1950; receipts analysis 1945-60; receipt books 1942-59; banking books 1942-51; financial correspondence 1936-7; employees worksheet register 1950; club constitution and rules 1879-1920s; membership: application papers 1917-37, registers 1913,1921-45; social event programmes, tickets, menus etc 1879-1910; visitors register 1925-45; library register 1891; meals register 1950; bridge competition register and rules 1944-6; newspaper article on club 1896; misc correspondence 1879-1905

356 ASSOCIATED ENERGY HOLDINGS LTD

1 Dec 1880
14685
14 Moorfields Highwalk, London EC2Y 9BS
Water supply

History: incorporated in 1880 as Antwerp Waterworks Co Ltd to acquire the 50 year water supply concession granted by the municipal authorities of Antwerp, Belgium. Easton & Anderson, waterworks engineers of Erith and Whitehall Place, London, negotiated the concession and in 1879 began building Waelhem Waterworks to intake and process water from the River Nethe. Water supply commenced in 1881. A second pumping station was built at Luythagen and opened in 1906. In 1930 a Belgian company, Intercommunale Vennootschap Antwerpsche Waterwerken NV, was formed to run the waterworks. The shareholders of this new company were the City of Antwerp, Antwerp Waterworks Co Ltd, and the Antwerp communes. Both WWs presented the company with serious problems. Company shareholding was sold to the City of Antwerp in 1965 and name changed to above in 1966. Acquired in 1969 by Imperial Continental Gas Association (est 1824). Since 1931 has been a holding company.

Records: at Associated Energy Holdings, 14 Moorfields Highwalk, London EC2Y 9BS
general meeting minutes 1881-1971; directors papers 1929-45; memo and articles of association 1880,1930-6; papers, documents and correspondence re setting up IV Antwerpsche Waterwerken NV 1929-36; German occupation papers 1939-45
IV Antwerpsche Waterwerken NV: statutes 1930; annual reports and accounts 1936-45,1966-7

357 R McDOUGALL & CO LTD

13 Dec 1880
14729
91 Allerton Road, Liverpool, Merseyside L18 2DD
Funeral directors

History: incorporated as above in 1880 to purchase undertaking business (est 1859-60) of Ronald McDougall at 25 Great George Place, 11&13 Renshaw Street and 117&118 St Anne Street, Liverpool. By 1888 fleet of vehicles consisted of 11 black coaches, 9 broughams, 2 coffin vans, 6 hearses and a gig. Leased 98 Vauxhall Road as a branch shop in 1893. In 1902 due to street improvements in St Anne and Great Richmond Streets, company received Liverpool Corporation stables in Breck Road, Everton as compensation and reconstructed their premises fronting Cazneau Street. Continued to operate 5 offices in Liverpool, 164 Breck Road being the only office operating by 1983. Acquired in 1976 by Pearson Collinson Funeral Service Ltd (est 1915) but continued to operate under own name.

Records: at Pearson Collinson, 91 Allerton Road, Liverpool, Merseyside L18 2DD
directors and general meeting minutes 1887-date; members register and share ledger 1947-50; directors register 1948-50; share transfer register 1947-50; annual returns 1946-51; memo and articles of association with papers 1906-35; order book and customers ledger 1894-1907; premises correspondence 1921-2; city coroner contract 1893; pension fund: trust deed and rules 1931, papers 1938

358 ASSOCIATED ELECTRICAL INDUSTRIES (WOOLWICH) LTD

28 Dec 1880
14777
1 Stanhope Gate, London W1A 1EH
Telegraph and electrical engineers

History: established as Siemens Brothers Ltd, an associate company of Siemens & Halske of Germany by William and Karl Siemens in 1858. Woolwich factory established c1858, manufacturing telegraphy equipment, dynamo-electric machinery, electric lighting and cables. Projects included Malta-Alexandria and Indo-European telegraph lines and submarine cables between Rio de Janeiro, Brazil, and Montevideo, Uruguay. The *SS Faraday*, designed by William Siemens and launched in 1874, laid a transatlantic cable that year. Provided electric lighting equipment for Royal Exchange, Royal Albert Hall and British Museum. Manufactured automatic telephone exchanges from 1913. Acquired by Custodian of Enemy Property in 1917 and sold to C Birch Crisp, who sold Siemens Dynamo Works at Stafford to English Electric Co Ltd. Acquired by Associated Electrical Industries Ltd in 1956 and merged in 1957 with Edison Swan Electric Co Ltd to become Siemens Edison Swan Group. Name changed to above in 1959. Became a subsidiary of General Electric Co Ltd in 1967.

Records: at GEC-Henley, Gravesend, Kent DA11 9DA
directors meeting: minutes 1880-1965, agendas and papers 1959-63, attendance books 1955-65; committee meeting: minutes 1957-65, agendas and papers 1960-3; general meeting minutes 1880-1965; share ledger 1881-c1918; members registers 1880-1918,1955-60; share transfer: registers 1880-1918, documents 1880 on; directors registers 1901-77; annual returns 1881-

1964; mortgage register 1900-35; debenture prospectus 1918; memo and articles of association 1880-1959; annual reports and accounts 1899-1965; seal registers 1909-80; balance sheets and accounts 1881-98; ledgers: 1953-5, private 1913-c43; memoranda: 1881-1908, incl accident reports 1881-99, officials lists 1881-1906, profit 1881-99, cable buying personnel 1874-1908, pay rates 1881-98; agreements: cables 1929-60s, managing directors 1918-50s, Newcastle works water and gas supply 1950-60s; Edison integration papers and correspondence 1957; employees journal 1930-49

AEI Cables Ltd: directors and general meeting minutes 1920-69; members register etc c1928-64; annual returns 1936 on; directors registers 1949 on; share transfer documents 1930s on; memo and articles of association 1920; annual report and accounts 1964-78; seal register 1935-79; corporate documents 1960s-70s; ledger 1935-52

Edison Swan Cables Ltd: directors meeting minutes 1926-31; general meeting minutes 1926-48

Edison Swan Electric Co Ltd: directors meeting minutes 1883-1957; management committee meeting minutes 1895; annual reports and accounts 1904-55

Edison & Swan Electric Co (India) Ltd: directors meeting minutes 1913-64; general meeting minutes 1957-64; members register 1913-33; directors registers 1957-77; annual returns 1933-63; memo and articles of association 1913-56; agreements 1940s-50; corporate documents 1960-70s; annual reports and accounts 1950s; seal register 1957-75; balance sheet and accounts 1957-9; ledger 1913-33

Manchester Edison & Swan Co Ltd: directors meeting minutes 1893-6

Power Cable Ltd: corporate documents and correspondence 1960s

Siemens Brothers Dynamo Works Ltd: directors and general meeting minutes 1906-39; directors register 1906-23; annual reports and accounts 1906-39; seal register 1906-08

Siemens & English Electric Lamp Ltd: directors and general meeting minutes 1920-52; management committee meeting minutes 1920-1; annual reports and accounts 1924-39; seal register 1920-50

Swan Electric Appliances Ltd: directors and general meeting minutes 1902-07, annual report and accounts 1902-07

Swan United Electric Light Co Ltd: directors and general meeting minutes 1882-94; annual report and accounts 1883

Tamplin Andmakovski Ltd: minutes 1933-65; corporate documents 1933-60s; accounts 1930s-60s

JD Scott, *Siemens Brothers 1858-1958* (1958)

359 LILLESHALL CO LTD

31 Dec 1880
14802
St George's, Telford, Salop TF2 9BQ
Coal, iron, steel, brick makers and constructional and mechanical engineering

History: established as Earl Gower & Co in 1764 and incorporated as above in 1880. Worked mines over a 2 miles radius of Priors Lee Hall, near Shifnal, Salop until collieries were vested in the National Coal Board in 1947. Erected an engineering establishment at St George's, Salop in 1860. Established a steel plant in about 1884 and in 1888 took over the iron works of Snedshill Iron Co Ltd. In 1923 specialised in coal and ironstone mines, pig iron, engineering production including steam and gas engines, Bessemer and Siemens steel, bar iron and bricks.

By 1958 manufactured glazed bricks and tiles, sanitary ware, glazed pipes, building and fire bricks and concrete products and were constructional, mechanical and general engineers. Owned Lilleshall Iron & Steel Co Ltd and Fairmile Engineering Co Ltd. By 1981 the Lilleshall group of companies were engaged in steel stockholding and distribution of engineers' tools; machining and press work, galvanizing, fencing, rerolling of steel products and alloy steels; shot blasting and protective finishing, distribution of air compressors and equipment; industrial estate managers, lessors and contractors. Principal subsidiaries were Full Force Compressors Ltd, Lilleshall Engineering Ltd, Lilleshall Estates Ltd, Lilleshall Steel Ltd, Lilleshall Stockholders Ltd and Shotclean & Painting Ltd. Throughout the company's history, the Leveson Gower family have been major contributors of capital and management expertise.

Records: at Ironbridge Gorge Museum, Ironbridge, Telford, Salop TF8 7AW
meeting minutes 1840,1878; partnership agreements and papers 1764-1878; memo and articles of association 1878-80; corporate documents 1880 on; debenture documents 1888-1928; profit and loss accounts 1951-3; costs ledger 1890-4; brick making ledger 1850-80; ironstone: account book 1764-1805, pits reckoning book 1805-13; sinking accounts 1818-35; misc accounts 1794 on; invoice book 1954-70; sales book 1956-9; catalogues 1882-1980; business agreements and contracts 1883-1932; patent documents 1892-1909; engine plans 1907-12; production book 1922-3; mill rollings record book 1950-7; laboratory record book 1943; Donnington brick works: day book 1886-93,1906-28, wages book 1905-17, correspondence 1893-1933, illustrations 1923-30; hot metal analysis 1909-20; stock control analysis 1948-55; management files 1951-3; mining note books 1879-80; factory registers 1936-7; accident report 1953; wages book 1937-8; age book 1920-50; service agreements 1900-29; employee letters 1963-5; workers rules and regulations 1937-8; profit sharing scheme papers 1937-44; coal and iron mines, land and property title deeds, documents and papers 1660-1938; premises plans 1767-1945; property valuations 1817-41; local mines and mining press cuttings 1937-47
Snedshill Iron Co Ltd: corporate and share documents 1884-7; partnership deed 1856; title deeds and documents 1883-7; amalgamation report 1888; accounts statement 1888

WKV Gale and CR Nicholls, *The Lilleshall Co Ltd. A History 1764-1964* (1979)

360 MARINE INSURANCE CO LTD

1 Jan 1881
14809
1 North John Street, Liverpool, Merseyside
Insurance

History: established in Birchin Lane, London in July 1836, when objectives included marine insurance of eastern shipping previously dominated by East India Co. Under Theophilus Burnand, underwriter from 1839 to 1870, it was one of the most successful marine insurance companies. Entered agency arrangement with Peninsular & Oriental Steam Navigation Co in 1841. Moved to 20 Old Broad Street, London in 1854. In 1874 acquired London & Oriental Steam Transit Co and established agencies in Amsterdam, Paris, Hamburg and New York between 1881 and 1884. Purchased underwriting business of Ismay Imrie & Co of Liverpool in 1887 and acquired Northern Marine Insurance Co of Dundee (est 1868) in 1892. Premium income averaged £200,000 under Frederick White's management and then grew to £340,000 by 1913 and over £2.8 million in 1917. Became subsidiary of London & Lancashire Insurance

Co Ltd (est 1861) in 1917 but continued to underwrite in own name, even after London & Lancashire was acquired by Royal Insurance Co Ltd in 1961.

Records (1): at Marine Insurance, 15-18 Lime Street, London EC3M 7JX
board meeting: minutes 1836-1939, agendas 1931-4, attendances 1939-70, private meeting minutes 1838-53; committee reports 1906-38; deed of settlement 1836,1839; general meeting attendances 1897-1900; legal proceeding papers 1894; share transfers 1917-70

Records (2): at National Maritime Museum, Romney Road, Greenwich, London SE10 9NF
accounts records 1917-69; agents correspondence 1929-66; claims records 1933-69; policy registers c1930-70

The Marine Insurance Company Ltd 1836-1936 (priv pub 1936)

361 KING & CO LTD

3 Jan 1881
14814
Northgate, Darlington, Durham DL1 1QY
Ironmongers

History: founded in 1744 by Henry King from Wensleydale, N Yorkshire, on purchase of the plane and other toolmaking and ironmongery business of William Southern of Church Lane, Hull, Humberside. Purchased larger premises at 59 Market Place, Hull in 1746. Henry's son Samuel King joined the firm in 1770 and also operated as wharfinger and agent for the Scottish iron company of Carron Co. John Spence of York was a partner from 1781-90, Henry retiring in 1776 and Samuel in 1815. Samuel's nephew Henry King joined in 1806. Purchased 53-54 High Street, Hull in 1815 which became the main workshop site managed by John Turner, a new partner and local iron merchant. In 1830 acquired business of Robert Peach, ironmonger and iron merchant. Henry's son William became a partner in 1843. Purchased 58 Market Place in 1853 and from 1860s became largest distributors of stoves, ranges and fireplaces in England. William King retired in 1866 and sold 80 per cent of his business to 4 leading local ironmongers but continued to act as an adviser. Purchased land in South Church Street and Vicar Lane in 1870s on which workshops, warehouses, showrooms and offices were built to William Botterill's designs. High Street and Market Place premises were vacated between 1877-9. Incorporated as above in 1881 when activities included those of iron merchants, ironmongers, marble masons, tinners, braziers, smiths, plane makers, hot water engineers, engineers, contractors etc. New premises were built in 1890 and in 1891 became first electrical contractors in Hull. Wood plane works were run down from 1905. Acquired adjoining works of Holders Bros Ltd in 1914, opened branch showroom in Hull shopping centre in 1918 and acquired old established business of Thomas James engineering foundry at Northgate, Darlington, Durham in 1924. Purchased premises and business of Young & Peck of Jameson Street, Hull in 1927 and new premises in Mytongate on south side of Hull works in 1941. Shop fronts at Hull and Darlington were redesigned in 1952-4 and present Darlington premises occupied in 1967. Purchased by Ferguson Industrial Holdings Ltd in 1972 and registered offices moved to Darlington. South Church Street offices and warehouses were vacated and business moved to a new industrial estate in Hull, managed by Ferguson Humberside Ltd, and old premises became property of Hull City Council in 1981.

Records (1): at King, Northgate, Darlington, Durham DL1 1QY
board meeting minutes 1881-date; share transfer register 1960-71; memo and articles of association 1881-1949; corporate papers (incl setting up and purchase of company) 1881-1972; annual reports and balance sheets 1882-1944; catalogues and price lists c1910-30s; newscuttings and advertisements 1965-80; photographs of marketing exhibitions, staff, shops exterior and interior, stock rooms c1960s-80; Darlington premises building schedule 1965; history notes 1940s

Records (2): at Hull City Record Office, 97 Lowgate, Hull, Humberside HU1 2AA
partnership agreements and other documents 1807-47; shop quotations 1966; cost sheets nd; supplies and customers correspondence 1966; heating department: contract books 1927-49, cost books 1953-66, invoice books 1915-51, schools heating accounts 1954, drawings 1862,1910-64, jobs lost papers 1961, individual job files 1951-62, general correspondence 1965; building contractors: quotations files 1970-1, works contract books 1938-55; title deeds for South Church Street premises 18-19 cent

AE Spring, *The Bicentenary of the House of Kings* (priv pub c1946)

362 GUARDEX INVESTMENT CO LTD

25 Jan 1881
14887
Royal Exchange, London EC3V 3LS
Investment (formerly plate glass insurance)

History: established in 1866 as Liverpool Plate Glass Insurance Co in Liverpool, Merseyside. Incorporated in 1881, took over Globe General Plate Glass in 1884, and renamed Liverpool & London Plate Glass Insurance Co Ltd in 1894. Acquired by State Assurance Co Ltd in 1908 and subsequently acquired by Royal Exchange Assurance (est 1720) in 1924. Subsequently ceased to underwrite insurance in its own name and took present title in 1969, following formation of Guardian Royal Exchange Assurance Ltd in 1968.

Records (1): at Guardian Royal Exchange Assurance, Royal Exchange, London EC3V 3LS
board and general meeting minutes: 1935-72, agendas 1915-63; register: directors holdings 1967-8, members 1947-53; annual report and accounts 1923-71; takeover agreement 1908

Records (2): at Guildhall Library, Aldermanbury, London EC2P 2EJ
board and general meeting minutes 1880-1925

363 NORTHAMPTON TRADESMEN'S CLUB CO LTD

3 Feb 1881
14916
Woolmonger Street, Northampton, Northamptonshire NN1 1PU
Social club-house

History: incorporated as above in 1881 to acquire rooms suitable for a club-house. Probably original premises were at 96 Bridge Street, Northampton, moving to present site in 1911. Premises were rented until 1930 when the company purchased them for £1650. By 1984 the company was still providing social facilities for its 200 members.

Records: at Northampton Tradesmen's Club, Woolmonger Street, Northampton, Northamptonshire NN1 1PU
directors and general meeting minutes 1930-83; register: directors and secretarys 1881-1960, members and share ledger 1927-68; share certificates 1902-27,1957; annual returns 1963-7; memo and articles of association 1881,1970; annual report and accounts 1963-72; balance sheets 1966-9; cash book 1961-6; subscription receipts 1954-64; wages book 1948-68

364 RELIANCE MARINE INSURANCE CO LTD

8 Feb 1881
14931
Royal Exchange, London EC3V 3LS
Insurance

History: incorporated as above in Liverpool in 1881. Originally offered marine insurance only but subsequently added fire insurance. In 1917 acquired by Guardian Assurance Co Ltd (est 1821), a constituent of Guardian Royal Exchange Assurance Ltd which was formed in 1968, but continued to underwrite in own name.

Records: at Guardian Royal Exchange Assurance, Royal Exchange, London EC3V 3LS
meeting minutes: directors 1881-1973, general 1881-1911,1946-1972, finance 1950-63, underwriting and general business 1946-63; agenda: directors 1952-60, underwriting 1959-63; directors: register 1949-63, attendance 1892-1948; register of members 1932-70; annual report and accounts 1911-79; powers of attorney 1916-38; memo and articles of association 1881-1957; pension fund trustees meeting minutes and agendas 1942-66; fire department: ledger 1927-54, journal 1949-60, agency appointments 1916-27

365 GLAMORGAN INVESTMENTS LTD

23 Feb 1881
15002
St John's Chambers, High Street Arcade, Cardiff, S Glamorgan CF1 2BD
Property

History: founded and incorporated in 1881 as Glamorganshire Workmen's Cottage Co Ltd by F de Courcy Hamilton, Cardiff solicitor who acted as secretary to several Cardiff property companies to supply suitable dwelling house accommodation for the labouring classes in Cardiff and other towns in south Wales. Cottages were mainly built in and around Cardiff, S Glamorgan and from 1960s were sold when leases expired. Proceeds used for purchase of commercial property. Name changed to above in 1962.

Records: at Glamorgan Investments, St John's Chambers, High Street Arcade, Cardiff, S Glamorgan CF1 2BD
directors and general meeting minutes 1880-date; agenda book 1961-72; share ledger 1881-1960; share transfer ledger 1883-1975; directors register 1940s-60s; debenture and mortgage register 1882-1935; prospectus 1880; seal book 1900-57; annual reports and accounts 1881-date; general ledger 1901-68; journal 1915-60; cash book 1942-62; weekly rentals payment book 1930-64; income tax papers 1967; incoming letters 1958-70; directors records: ledger

1901-69, journal 1916-59, cash book 1948-71, ground rents assignments notices 1890s-c1918, ground rents book 1917-27, weekly rentals payment book 1923-76, out letter books 1918-22, incoming letters 1956-7,1964-76

366 J&J HAYES LTD

1 Mar 1881
15028
1 Portland Street, Manchester, Greater Manchester M60 3AP
Cotton spinners

History: established by two brothers William and James Hayes at Westleigh Mill, Leigh, Greater Manchester in about 1820. They separated in 1836, William becoming a founder of the cotton doubling firm of Isherwood & Hayes (later Carrington Mills, Kirkhall Lane, Leigh) and James continuing to operate by himself until 1844 when he moved to Barlow's factory and was joined by his brother John. His brother-in-law Robert Thorp joined the partnership which was known as Thorp & Hayes from 1846. In 1855 the factory was burnt down and the original Victoria Mills built on the site in 1856. In 1874 Alfred and James Thorp, sons of Robert, entered the partnership which was known from then on as J&J Hayes. Incorporated as above in 1881 with James Hayes as chairman. Subsequently became a subsidiary of Hayeshaw Ltd. In 1964 became a branch of Courtaulds Ltd (Spinning Division).

Records: at Wigan Record Office, Town Hall, Leigh, Greater Manchester WN7 2DY
memo and articles of association 1881; capital account statement 1881; ledger: 1833-86, private 1843-56; wear and tear account book 1881-1946; cash books: 1827-49, petty 1843-88; invoices 1836-8; cloth sales record 1818-22; order book 1831-44; day books 1818-86; account books: stock 1823-36,1845-1950, machinery 1875-80, costing 1903, wages 1857-63; staff photographs 1900; family papers 19 cent; James Hayes: will abstracts 1885, obituary 1887; John Hayes executorship: and income ledger 1886-1907, general ledger 1886-1907, cash book 1902-14; insurance report and proposals 1844-6; title deeds: abstract 1834-43, agreement 1844, schedule 1857-1931; mill photographs 1900; misc correspondence 1825-48; history booklets 1952-60; Victoria Institute rules and minutes 1868-71

367 HULL & EASTERN COUNTIES MUTUAL PLATE GLASS INSURANCE CO LTD

3 Mar 1881
15040
Wellington House, 108 Beverley Road, Hull, Humberside HV3 1XA
Insurance

History: incorporated as above in 1881 by local gentlemen to operate mutual plate glass insurance. Original offices were at Cogan House, Bowlalley Lane, Hull, Humberside, moving to 1 Posterngate in 1885. By 1887 agencies had been opened in all towns and many villages of Lincolnshire and East Riding of Yorkshire. By 1932 had moved to 10&11 Silver Street and in 1962 moved to George Street, Hull. Acquired in about 1960 by Oughtred & Harrison (Insurance) Ltd and moved to present address.

Records: at Hull & Eastern Counties Mutual Plate Glass Insurance, Wellington House, 108 Beverley Road, Hull, Humberside HV3 1XA
directors and general meeting minutes 1881-date; members registers and share ledgers 1881-date; share: register 1881 on, certificate books 1889-1978; directors registers 1901-51; dividend lists 1881-1980; annual reports and accounts 1882-1969; investment register 1887-1979; proposal forms 1881; delayed claims register 1895-1983; war damage claims 1940-51

368 STURTON TOWN LIBERAL HALL CO LTD

1 Mar 1881
15057
85-89 Mill Road, Cambridge, Cambridgeshire
Political club-house

History: incorporated as above in 1881 to provide a club-house for the Liberal working men of Sturton town and district. Site in Mill Road was purchased for £735 and a public hall, club and reading rooms costing £1150 were erected. The public hall was let out for entertainments, later becoming a cinema and bingo hall. By 1984 the company's main activity was property owning, leasing a portion of the premises as shops.

Records: at Sturton Town Liberal Hall, 85-89 Mill Road, Cambridge, Cambridgeshire
directors meeting minutes: 1881-1983, agendas 1943-64; general meeting minutes 1881-1983; committee meeting minutes: executive 1882, building 1882; share: application book 1881-3, register 1881-9, ledger 1881-1964, certificates 1881-1959, transfer certificates 1881-1952, dividend ledger 1943-64; annual summaries c1900-63; memo and articles of association 1881; balance sheets 1891-1941; general, revenue and working account 1882; Cambridge working mens club account and vouchers 1882-4; ledgers 1886-1983; cash accounts 1883,1893-9; rent receipt book 1881-95; title deeds etc and papers 1863 on

369 ABNEY PARK CEMETERY CO LTD

19 Mar 1881
15108
Greenwood House, 4-7 Salisbury Court, London EC4Y 8BT
Cemetery proprietors

History: established by deed of settlement in 1839 to purchase Abney Park, Stoke Newington, London and to form and maintain cemeteries at Abney Park and elsewhere. Incorporated as above in 1881. Subsequently acquired Hendon Park Cemetery, Greenford Park Cemetery, Woodgrange Park Cemetery and Chingford Park Cemetery, all of which were in London. The first 3 cemeteries were sold prior to 1960 and Abney Park and Chingford Park Cemeteries were disposed of in 1979. The company was a subsidiary of Albion Securities Ltd by 1963 when it was acquired by Anglo Metropolitan Holdings Ltd. Ceased to trade in 1979.

Records (1): at Anglo Metropolitan Holdings, 53 Upper Brook Street, Grosvenor Square, London W1Y 1PG
settlement deed 1839

Records (2): at Hackney Archives Department, Rose Lipman Library, De Beauvoir Road, London N1 5SQ
minutes 1861-79; general meeting reports 1896; board meeting accounts 1951-3; memo and

articles of association 1897-1946; corporate papers 1920-64; share: certificates 1897-1960, transfer documents 1963-4; debenture: certificates 1927, holders register 1927-32; annual reports and accounts 1885-1917,1955; interment accounts: 1918-52, summary 1840-1963; burial: registers 1840-1927, certificates 1929-63; grave: registers 1840-60s, upkeep records 1950s, details note book c1961, index 1915, list c1950, papers 1919-21; memorials: notebook c1973, and burial regulations 1948, papers 1938-73; cremations: list 1940-55, charges scales 1930-56; insurance register and papers 1921-67; wages: list 1895, agreement 1935, correspondence 1957-63; employee: list 1895, papers and correspondence 1923,1959-64, service agreements 1964-9; cemetery report 1903, schedule c1890, upkeep correspondence 1923-68, photographs and plans 1933-68; chapel report 1921; legal case papers 1850,1916-19; newscutting 1950; misc correspondence and papers 1896-1967; Chingford Mount Cemetery: report 1883, specifications 1907, burial certificates 1936-52, interment charges 1918-20,1956, accounts 1906, cash book 1918-19, staff papers 1914-20, property papers 1907-30, burials and memorial correspondence 1937-73; Greenford Park Cemetery: interment charges 1918-66, burial certificates 1933-47, stock list 1966, map nd; Hendon Park Cemetery: burial register 1931-44, upkeep and burial service papers and correspondence 1900-55, burial certificates 1926-52, property papers and correspondence 1898-1957, chapel papers and correspondence 1902-40, crematorium papers, photographs and correspondence c1900-52; Woodgrange Park Cemetery: directors meeting minutes, reports and correspondence re liquidation of cemetery company 1919-20, memorial correspondence 1927, burial correspondence 1972-3

370 BUILDERS ACCIDENT INSURANCE LTD

12 Apr 1881
15228
31-32 Bedford Street, London WC2
Insurance

History: incorporated as above in 1881 by leading builders as a company limited by guarantee on the mutual basis to insure employers liability and public liability risks in the building trade. Original offices were at 27 King Street, Covent Garden, London moving to 31 Bedford Street, by 1892. In 1884 had premium income of £7115. Established Crystal Glass Insurance Co Ltd in 1889. Started underwriting contractors all risks at beginning of 1983 and turnover (premiums written before deduction of reinsurance) was over £9.5 million that year.

Records: at Builders Accident Insurance, 31-32 Bedford Street, London WC2
directors meeting: minutes 1898-1958, agenda books 1930-40,1964-8, attendance book 1958-64, list 1881-1964; general purposes committee meeting minutes 1898-1916; London committee meeting minutes 1888-98; Liverpool (Northern) branch committee meeting minutes, reports, accounts and correspondence 1881-98; Bristol (Western) branch committee meeting minutes, reports, accounts and correspondence 1884-6; annual reports and accounts 1884,1892; balance sheet and accounts 1895-8; ledgers: 1881-c92,1903-22, private 1882-99, nominal 1881-5,c1962-c72; journals 1881-1900; cash books:1881-97, branches 1881-4, general 1935-42, summary 1947-56; daily cash journals: payments 1913-57, receipts 1903-54; agents commission accounts 1949-55; members register 1920s-50s; renewal register 1977-8; risk books 1924-35; workmens risk: proposals book 1954-64, ledgers 1947-54, accident notice register 1931-69; public risk accident notice register 1941-6; paid claims particulars 1940-56; wages book 1944-50; press cuttings 1942-59

Crystal Glass Insurance Co Ltd: board and general meeting minutes 1889-1933; directors register 1901-18; annual list and summary 1916

371 PRUDENTIAL ASSURANCE CO LTD

1 Jun 1881
15454
142 Holborn Bars, London EC1N 2NH
Insurance

History: established as Prudential Mutual Assurance, Investment & Loan Association in 1848. Originally undertook ordinary life assurance business but from 1854 it also offered industrial life assurance through an agency network. Under Henry Harben, secretary from 1856 to 1877, annual premium income grew from £3709 to £907,444. Renamed British Prudential Assurance Association in 1860 and British Prudential & Consolidated Assurance in 1865. Took present title in 1867 and was incorporated in 1881. Acquisitions included the British Industry Life Assurance Co (est 1852, amalgamated 1860); Consolidated Assurance Co (est 1846, amalgamated 1865); British Mutual Life Assurance Co (est 1844, amalgamated 1868); International Life Assurance Society (est 1837, business transferred 1870);and British Widows Assurance Co Ltd (est 1902, amalgamated 1936). George May, secretary from 1915 to 1931, supervised Prudential's major contribution to war finance in WW1 and was mainly responsible for raising company's assets from £95 million to £256 million between 1915 and 1931. Company provided general insurance after 1919 and entered overseas markets in 1921. In 1977 controlled assets of £424 million and held life assurance funds of £4259 million.

Records: at Prudential Assurance, 142 Holborn Bars, London EC1N 2NH
directors meeting minutes 1847-1964; general meeting minutes 1847-1907; Harben papers 1860-1902; directors register 1907-53; share: ledgers 1849-1911, register 1872-88,1912, certificates 1854,1865 on, transfers 1861-1923, sub-division 1912; head office memoranda books 1848-1911; deed of settlement 1848; annual report and accounts 1848 on; balance sheets 1851-77; cash books 1848-60; probate register 1929; bonus statement counterfoils 1882; policy registers 1846-68; reversions and policies 1906 on; agreements, policies, prospectuses 1848-date; premium receipt books nd; investments, dependant on lives 1874-1915; securities: foreign government nd, stock exchange 1901 on; victory bonds registers and transfers 1920 on; rent ledgers: ground 1917-42, rack 1923 on; deeds and transfers 1901 on; letter book 1901-9
British Industry Life: minutes 1859-60; prospectuses 1853 on
British Mutual Life: minutes 1844-8; accounts 1844-68; policy register 1844-51
British Widows Assurance Co Ltd: shareholding agreements 1936; memo and articles of association 1902; district cash, industrial branch and ordinary accounts 1918-55; ledgers 1923-36; journal 1925; investments cash book 1936
Consolidated Assurance Co: minutes: 1852-66, loan and general purpose committee 1862-5, record books 1858-65
Hercules Insurance Co: prospectus 1862; policy register 1863-8
International Life Assurance Co: prospectus 1864; liquidity agreement with Prudential 1869-71; special reports 1869-71
London & Westminster Assurance Corporation Ltd: policy register 1863-5
Prince Fire Co: minutes 1862-6

Prudential Approved Societies: minutes: 1912-35, executive committee meeting 1913-38; attendance book 1912-28; registers: medical referees 1914-48, members fined etc 1935-46
Universal Building Society: minutes 1866-84; financial reports 1883-4
Church of England & General Permanent Benefit Building Society: minutes 1852-8; share register 1853-4; cash book 1850-4

RW Barnard, *A Century of Service. The Story of the Prudential 1848-1948* (1948)

372 THOS FIRTH & JOHN BROWN LTD

15 Jun 1881
15531
Smithfield House, Sheffield, S Yorkshire S1 2AS
Steel

History: Thomas Firth & Sons was founded in Sheffield in 1843 by Thomas Firth and his 2 sons, Mark and Thomas. The business started in a small way as manufacturers of crucible steel of the highest quality. The first works, named Portobello Steel Works, was situated in Charlotte Street, specializing in cutlery, spear and tool steels. Mark Firth made sales tours throughout the country, and very soon agencies were established all over the world, particularly in USA. Between 1849 and 1851 the firm built Norfolk Works, in Saville Street. In the early 1850s the firm diversified into the manufacture of ordnance and shells. A gun works was built further down Saville Street and Clay Wheel Forge at Wadsley Bridge acquired. During the 1870s the guns forged rose in weight from 35 to 100 tons. Mark Firth died in 1880 and the following year the firm was incorporated as Thomas Firth & Sons Ltd. In 1902 the firm exchanged shares with John Brown & Co Ltd, and Bernard Firth, the chairman of the company joined the John Brown board. In 1930 the company acquired John Brown's steel interests, as part of a nationalization programme. In 1934 Firth-Vickers Stainless Steels Ltd was formed in association with English Steel Corporation to exploit the patents for 'Staybrite' steel. After WW2 the company name was changed to above and became a subsidiary of John Brown & Co. It was nationalized in 1950. When the steel industry was denationalized John Brown & Co refused to take it back and Iron & Steel Holding & Realisation Agency floated it as an independent concern. In 1957 the company acquired the Glasgow steel and armaments manufacturers William Beardmore & Co. By then the whole of the output of above consisted of special steels. Jessop Saville Ltd, steel manufacturers acquired in c1971. Jessel Securities Ltd (see summary no 182) acquired above in 1973 and amalgamated with the old established firm of Manchester wire drawers Richard Johnson & Nephew Co Ltd to form Johnson & Firth Brown Ltd. When Jessel Securities Ltd collapsed in 1975 the share in Johnson & Firth Brown was sold to a number of institutions. The company continues to specialize in special steels.

Records: at Thos Firth & John Brown, Smithfield House, Sheffield, S Yorkshire S1 2AS
directors meeting minutes 1881-1969; board: papers 1899-1922, reports 1889-91,1934-70; managing directors: committee meeting minutes 1934-54, and papers 1952-3, reports and papers 1930s-51; share transfer committee meeting minutes 1944-51; morning conference papers 1932-82; general meeting minutes 1881-1975; partnership articles 1858-75; memo and articles of association 1935-49; share: allotment book 1907, agreements and notices 1947-72; debenture trust: deeds 1903-37, papers 1930s-72; proposed and merger papers 1929-34; directors fees and papers 1930-70s; annual reports and accounts 1956-73; balance sheets and accounts 1901-70s; trading and profit and loss accounts 1936-69; financial reports 1945-69;

various accounts 1887-1900s; private ledgers 1859-c67,1882-1936; nominal ledgers 1881-1952; private journals 1881-1947; works journal 1931; cash books: 1841-4, private 1881-8,1900-33,1956-c68; bank pass books 1842-8,1881-1911; taxation papers 1935-66; stocktaking, production, costs and sales memo book 1881-8; costs book 1946-52; stock books: 1843,1845, Whittington 1881-6; general stocktaking: books 1881-1940, papers 1917-53; Salamander works ledger 1903-09; development reports 1945-65; production: reports 1931, tonnage book 1967-73; estimates book 1921-2; patents register and papers 1909-43; agreements: register 1900s-61, papers 1931-47, BSC 1968-72; cartel papers pre 1936; sales reports 1953-62; wages and salary books 1844-6,1859 on; employee: agreements 1859-60s, register 1880s-1920s; staff society: council meeting minutes 1921,1946-70, section minutes and papers 1946-69; general committee and sub-committee meeting minutes and papers 1946-70s; staff pension fund papers 1941-72; Atlas and Norfolk Works: benevolent society papers 1944-70, sports club papers 1939-62; title deed register 1850s-1930s; title deeds and property agreements 1880s-1970s; property ledger 1889-c1934; plans: Rotherham property 1875, Saville Street with sketches and correspondence nd,1950s; Norfolk Works: inventories 1887,1892,1942, valuations 1886-8,1946-7; works visits: photographs 1934,1967-72, brochures 1939,1954; visitors book 1915-28; press cuttings 1964-72; luncheons and visits papers, programmes etc 1938-65; history booklet 1937; research laboratories brochure c1954; plant, staff, financial, trades and national associations, sales, production, branch offices, premises, works, branch offices and subsidiary and overseas companies papers and correspondence 1920s-1970s

Agence Acieries Firth Sheffield Ltd: board papers 1959-61; annual accounts 1953-71; correspondence and papers 1949-64

Alloy Steel Rods Ltd: board meeting minutes 1963-70; committee meeting minutes 1963-8; annual accounts 1963-70; correspondence and papers 1963-70

GS Baigent & AD Bird (Stainless Steel) Ltd: directors meeting minutes 1968-70; purchase agreements, papers and correspondence 1968-9

William Beardmore & Co Ltd: directors meeting minutes 1957-71; reports 1961-4; annual accounts 1955-71; financial statements 1966-71; annual reports and accounts 1956-63; press cuttings 1957; papers 1954-73; correspondence 1960-71

John Brown & Co Ltd: (See summary no 50)

Thos Firth & John Brown Ltd: board meeting: minutes 1960-9, secretarys reports 1962-70; memo and articles of association 1960; reorganisation papers 1962; annual accounts 1962-8; papers 1960-72

Firth Brown Engineers Ltd: annual returns 1949-69; agency agreements 1947-56; correspondence 1946-52; financial statements 1946-59

Firth Brown Steels Ltd: directors meeting minutes 1947-9; general meeting minutes 1947-9; formation and winding up papers 1947-9; financial statements 1946-50

Firth Brown Tools Ltd: board and general meeting minutes and papers 1946-51; formation, management and sales papers 1946-51; annual report and accounts 1947

Firth-Brearley Stainless Steel Syndicate Ltd: directors and general meeting minutes 1917-52; secretarys board reports 1939-51; finance committee meeting minutes 1929-47; members register 1917-51; memo and articles of association 1917-26; debenture issue documents and papers 1926-52; annual returns 1918-51; merger papers 1917-c27; directors salaries and fees 1917-51; annual reports and accounts 1918-51; balance sheets and accounts 1917-51; ledger 1917-46; journals 1917-52; cash books 1917-52; liquidation papers, accounts and correspondence 1951-2; Krupp returns and agreements 1928-52; Italian trade-mark papers

1923-33; patent agreements 1917-48; Harry Brearley papers and correspondence 1916-33; Brown Bayley Steel Works Ltd papers and correspondence 1916-29; press cuttings 1924-5; stainless steel booklets c1918-34; correspondence and papers 1915-c52

Firth & Derihon Stampings Ltd: board meeting minutes 1952-66; annual accounts 1953-72; financial correspondence 1953-72; papers 1919 on

Thos Firth & John Brown (South Africa) (Pty) Ltd: annual accounts 1953-66

Firth-Stahl Verkauf AG: board meeting minutes 1951-6; agreements and papers 1918-60; annual accounts 1952-68; staff benevolent fund papers 1952-6; financial correspondence 1952-72

Firth-Vickers Stainless Steels Ltd: board meeting: minutes 1944-69, reports 1945-73; balance sheets and accounts 1935-73; agreements 1959-63; general arrangements 1934-70; Shepcote Rolling Mills: report c1954, annual accounts 1954-71

Jessop Saville Ltd: (See summary no 242)

Nicholson & Rhodes Ltd: annual returns 1947-71; annual accounts 1960-8

Nitralloy Ltd: directors meeting minutes 1935-44; annual returns 1936-50; ledger 1950-7; papers and correspondence 1932-49

100 Years in Steel - Firth Brown Centenary 1837-1937 (priv pub 1937)

373 STERLING TRUST LTD

18 Jun 1881
15543
122 Leadenhall Street, London EC3V 4QR
Investment trust

History: incorporated in 1881 as Alabama, New Orleans, Texas & Pacific Junction Railways Co Ltd to acquire control of railways which could be advantageously associated with Alabama Great Southern Railway Co Ltd (inc 1877), namely New Orleans & North Eastern, Alabama & Vicksburg, and Shreveport & Pacific Railways. Defaulted on interest payments in 1887 and receiver and liquidator were appointed. In 1890 a scheme of reorganisation was carried through. Holdings in New Orleans & North Eastern Railroad and South Western Construction Co were sold in 1916 and proceeds invested in Exchequer Bonds. Name changed to above in 1917 and company became an investment trust. Managed by Robert Fleming Investment Management Ltd. Name changed to Fleming American Investment Trust PLC in 1982.

Records: at Robert Fleming Services, 122 Leadenhall Street, London EC3V 4QR
board meeting minutes 1881-date; executive committee meeting minutes 1881-2; general meeting minutes 1881-date; seal books 1881-1974; guardbooks incl agreements, correspondence, memo and articles of association, share documents and papers, tenders, annual returns, traffic tables, annual reports and accounts 1881-date; general ledgers 1922-67; cash books 1880s-1966

374 WILLIAM SUGG & CO LTD

30 Jun 1881
15604
Thorn EMI House, Upper St Martin's Lane, London WC2H 9ED
Gas light and heating appliance manufacturers

History: established in 1837 by William Sugg and incorporated as above in 1881. Specialised in manufacture of incandescent gas burners, lamps and lights, gas cooking stoves, fires etc. First offices leased at 1-2 Grand Hotel Buildings, Charing Cross, London, with Vincent Works in Regency Street, Westminster. By early 1880s established a branch in Paris and agencies in Germany, New Zealand, Australia, Belgium and Sweden. By 1900 goods were being exported worldwide. Vincent Works extended in 1887 and Ranelagh Works, Chapter Street, Westminster established by 1923. Former sold in 1965 as manufacturing business had been moved to Crawley, W Sussex. Acquired Thomas Matlock & Co Ltd (inc 1944) Kingston upon Thames, Surrey in 1956, changing name to William Sugg Export Ltd, and Castlenau Instruments Ltd of Crawley (name changing to Kendare Castlenau Ltd) in 1965. Acquired by Thorn Electrical Industries Ltd in 1969 when main activity was supply of gas central heating appliances to building industry. Trading activities merged in 1970 with Thorn Heating Holdings Ltd to form Thorn Heating Ltd - central heating division of Thorn Group. In 1982 was dormant subsidiary company of Thorn EMI Ltd through Thorn Heating Ltd.

Records: at Thorn EMI Heating, Team Valley Trading Estate, Gateshead, Tyne & Wear NE11 0PG
directors meeting minutes 1881-1907,1964-date; general meeting minutes 1970-date; members register 1969-date; share transfer documents 1910-60; corporate documents and correspondence 1966-date; memo and articles of association 1955; annual reports and accounts 1969-date; pension fund documents and correspondence 1966-70s
William Sugg Export Ltd: directors and general meeting minutes 1944-date; members register 1944-date; corporate documents and correspondence etc 1964-77; memo and articles of association 1944; annual reports and accounts 1972-4
Kendare Castlenau Ltd: directors and general meeting minutes 1954-date; members register 1965-date

375 WILLIAMS DEACON'S BANK LTD

1 Jul 1881
15607
20 Birchin Lane, London EC3P 3DP
Banking

History: established as Manchester & Salford Bank in 1836, as a joint stock bank in King Street, Manchester. Head offices completed in 1838 in Mosley Street with new offices being built between 1858-62. Branches opened in Greater Manchester at Salford in 1862 and Stockport in 1864. Acquired Heywood Brothers & Co Ltd of St Ann Street, Manchester (est 1788) in 1874, Hardcastle, Cross & Co of Bolton, Greater Manchester (est 1818) in 1878 and Clement Royds & Co of Rochdale, Greater Manchester (est 1819) in 1881. Registered in 1871 and with limited liability in 1881. In 1890 acquired Williams Deacon & Co of Birchin Lane, London (est 1771 as Raymond, Williams, Vere, Lowe & Fletcher), London agents of the bank from 1836, and changed name to Williams Deacon & Manchester & Salford Bank Ltd, shortened to above in 1901. In 1906 acquired the Yorkshire based Sheffield & Rotherham Joint Stock Banking Co Ltd, established in 1791 as Walker & Co. Acquired by Royal Bank of Scotland (est 1720) in 1930. Rebuilt London offices between 1934-36 and new Manchester offices opened in 1963. Branches numbered 46 in 1890, 102 in 1907, 173 in 1922, 208 in 1948 and 287 in 1970. Business merged with that of Glyn, Mills & Co Ltd, London, and National Bank Ltd (est 1835 as National Bank of Ireland) to form Williams & Glyn's Bank Ltd, a subsidiary of Royal Bank of Scotland Group Ltd in 1970.

Records: at Williams & Glyn's Bank, 20 Birchin Lane, London EC3P 3DP
board meeting minutes 1836 on; London directors meeting minutes 1933 on; shareholders list 1838; agm: minutes 1836 on, proceedings 1890 on; general managers notebook 1840s; settlement deeds 1836-81; articles of association 1901 on; annual reports 1837 on; balance sheets 1836-1900; working papers 1900 on; profit and loss accounts 1881-1916; private ledgers 20 cent; reserves ledger: c1850-80, details 1917-33; charges accounts 1875-1917; journal 1836-46; information books 1890-1922; interview book 1889-1901; managers customers record 1894-1920; salary: papers 1845-1920, ledger and record book 1900-25; staff bonus papers 1919-25; property ledger 1887-90; London office rebuilding papers 1932-5; private letter books 19 cent; general managers: out letters 1902-04, department private letter books 1908-68; London: general letters 1902-05, letter books 1902-40, office correspondence 1925-50; head office circulars 1888-1970; West End office correspondence 1925-46; general correspondence 1900-62; branch progress reports 1899-1929; branches - Heywoods: profit and loss accounts 1871-1913, business summaries 1880-5; Mosley Street: information books 1870s; Rochdale: accounts opened books 1880s, information books 1880-1913, private letter book 1914-34; Sheffield: managers customer accounts records 1907-23

Williams Deacon's 1771-1970 (priv pub 1971)

376 SAINT MARY STREET BUILDINGS LTD

5 Jul 1881
15623
22 Cyncoed Avenue, Cardiff, S Glamorgan
Property

History: incorporated in 1881 as Saint Mary Street Buildings Co Ltd to finance the building costs of Saint Mary Street Buildings, Cardiff, designed by Walter D Blessley, architect. In 1874 he had obtained the ground lease of site on the corner of Saint Mary Street and Wood Street on which he erected Cardiff's first purpose built theatre, the Theatre Royal, opened in 1876. By 1879 a number of design faults had been discovered. Blessley intended to amend these and provide some commercial development with Saint Mary Street Buildings, which contained 3 retail shops and a new entrance hall, foyer, booking office, bar and dressing rooms for the theatre on Saint Mary Street, and Theatre Chambers, consisting of 4 offices on Wood Street. Both the theatre (transformed into a cinema during WW2) and Saint Mary Street Building were listed as grade II scheduled buildings in the 1980s. In order to keep company active after expiry of the lease in 1975 it was decided in the 1930s to invest capital reserve and other funds in providing accommodation for the middle income bracket. Began purchasing and converting houses in 1934. Company's single-propertied articles of association were altered and name was changed to above in 1936. A shop was added to Saint Mary Street Building in 1950. Portfolio in 1981 consisted of 11 freehold properties, all in Cardiff.

Records: at Saint Mary Street Buildings, 22 Cyncoed Avenue, Cardiff, S Glamorgan
directors and general meeting minutes 1881-date; members register etc 1881-1925; memo and articles of association 1881; ledger 1881-1931; journal 1881-1920; cash book 1881-1922; Prince of Wales Theatre photograph 1940; history with photographs 1981

377 LAND & HOUSE PROPERTY CORPORATION LTD

8 Jul 1881
15633
Pixham End, Dorking, Surrey RH4 1QA
Property

History: incorporated as above in 1881 to acquire lands and buildings for development in London and surrounding country. By 1884 owned 253 private houses and 119 business premises throughout London, mainly in the City and the south western suburbs. Acquired by Friends' Provident Life Office in c1977.

Records: at Friends' Provident Life Office, Pixham End, Dorking, Surrey RH4 1QA
directors meeting minutes 1881-1962; property committee meeting minutes 1881-3; general meeting minutes and papers 1881-1977; share: register c1977, transfer register 1949-60, holders lists 1960s; directors registers 1948-77; annual returns 1943-60; memo and articles of association 1974; mortgage registers 1886-c1976; seal registers 1960-77; annual report and accounts 1883-1951; revenue ledger 1905-27; repairs and complaints register 1957-63; subsidiary: annual returns 1950-63, annual report and accounts 1973-4, memo and articles of association 1972-4, balance sheets and accounts 1972-6
Ashford Development Ltd: directors and general meeting minutes 1962-72
Cotchings Ltd: directors and general meeting minutes 1952-71
Endura Electrical Industries Ltd: directors and general meeting minutes 1972-7
Flintvil Investments Ltd: directors and general meeting minutes 1963-72
Frincon Ltd: directors and general meeting minutes 1962-72
Frincon Holdings Ltd: directors and general meeting minutes 1964-72; loan agreements 1967; takeover papers and correspondence 1970-3
Frincon Investments Ltd: directors and general meeting minutes 1964-72
Frincon (Metropolitan) Ltd: directors and general meeting minutes 1965-72
Greystoke Properties Ltd: directors and general meeting minutes 1955-72; memo and articles of association 1945; annual returns 1955-63
James Sterling (Textiles) Ltd: directors and general meeting minutes 1973-6
Land & House (Croydon) Ltd: directors and general meeting minutes 1973-6
Land & House (Haringey) Ltd: directors and general meeting minutes 1971-7
Maple Cross Properties Ltd: directors and general meeting minutes 1971-7; take over papers 1965
Orchardland Ltd: directors and general meeting minutes 1973-7

378 UNION-CASTLE MAIL STEAMSHIP CO LTD

15 Jul 1881
15671
2-4 St Mary Axe, London EC3A 8BP
Shipping

History: established in 1872 when Donald Currie, whose ships had been engaged in Indian trade, entered the South African trade. Originally known as London Line, Castle Packet Co was formed in 1876 and incorporated as Castle Mail Packet Co Ltd in 1881. All ships were named after castles. In 1900 merged with Union Steam Ship Co Ltd (est 1853), chief competitors for the South African mail contract, to form the above. Control of the company passed to Royal Mail Steam Packet Co and Elder Dempster Co in 1912. In 1913 mail ships provided refrigerated space for fruit trade. In 1932 reconstructed as Union-Castle Line Ltd. By 1950 the mail service was served by 8 passenger ships. In 1956 Union-Castle Line and the long established Cayzer family shipping business of Clan Line Steamers merged to form British & Commonwealth Shipping Co Ltd. In 1965 the first cargo liners without passenger accommodation entered the mailship service. Last Union-Castle ship carrying mail, passengers and cargo sailed in 1977. Although regular passenger services ceased, cargo and mail services were provided by new British & Commonwealth container ship service in which Union-Castle participated through Overseas Containers Ltd.

Records: at British & Commonwealth Shipping, Cayzer House, 2-4 St Mary Axe, London EC3A 8BP
directors council meeting: minutes 1881-date, resolutions 1910-12, papers 1912-13; managing directors meeting minutes 1936-8,1941-6; managers meeting minutes 1912; finance committee meeting minutes 1953-4; agm: minutes 1881-date, papers 1908; chairmans papers 1912; share purchase documents 1911-12; annual reports and accounts 1905-09,1949-65; mail contracts 1876-1922; shipping lines, service, trade and contract agreements and papers 1886-1951; freight: rates nd, papers 1911-20, sailing notices 1960s; movement lists 1962-5; fares and sailing schedules 1900s-54; fleet: particulars 1923, chart 1960; sailing lists 1890-1940; advertisements: 1900s, expenditure 1909-37; ship: plans 1890s-1960s, photographs 1890s-1976, contracts and costs 1903-25, logs and crew agreements 1890s-1904, passage tickets 1890-1911, menus 1879-1977, passenger lists 1881-1959, entertainment programmes 1890-1947, particulars 1890-1910, service booklets 1890s-1950; captains and voyage numbers 1957-8; officers record books 1877-90; instructions: commanders 1892-1901,1950, officers 1901, pursers 1886, chief stewards 1917, agents 1912,1934, managers 1912,1916, surgeons 1922; steward pay rates 1913; crew roll of honour 1914-18,1939-45; passengers hand books nd; offices, passenger and sea staff photographs 1890s-1950s; letter book 1910; correspondence: 1885-1931, D Currie 1879-99; house magazine nd; newscuttings 1880s-1970s; legal papers and opinions 1890s on; misc papers 19-20 cent; history booklets and articles 1890s-1950s
Union Steam Ship Co Ltd: liquidation papers 1907-09; Castle Line agreements 1883-1900; memo and articles of association nd; Cape mail contracts summary 1857-94; defect list 1866; petty cash book 1853-5; ship: plans 1890s, photographs 1850s-1900s, passage tickets 1895,1902, sale agreement 1897, menus 1881, passenger lists 1882-1905, entertainment programmes 1879,1896, correspondence 1886; second mates diary 1870; house magazine 1894-9; history booklets nd

Marischal Murray, *Union-Castle Chronicle 1853-1953* (1953)

WH Mitchell and LA Sawyer, *The Cape Run, The Story of Union-Castle Service to South Africa* (1984)

379 RIVER & MERCANTILE TRUST LTD

30 Jul 1881
15740
7 Lincoln's Inn Fields, London WC2
Investment trust (formerly mortgage)

History: incorporated in 1881 as River Plate Trust, Loan & Agency Co Ltd primarily to conduct a mortgage business in Argentine. Set up Mortgage Co of River Plate Ltd and River Plate & General Investment Trust Co Ltd in 1888. Took over number of Buenos Aires agencies for British public utility, railway and land companies operating in Argentina and elsewhere including Argentine Southern Land Co Ltd, Argentine Eastern Land Co Ltd, Cordovo Land Co Ltd, Rio Negro Land Co Ltd, Santa Fé Land Co Ltd, Techa (Argentina) Land Co Ltd, Tucuman Sugar Co Ltd, La Plata & Ensenada Tramways Co Ltd, Rosario City Improvements Drainage Co Ltd, Rosario Waterworks Co Ltd, Montevideo Waterworks Co Ltd, River Plate Electricity Co Ltd, Central Railway of Chubut, Cordoba & Rosario Railway Co Ltd, East Argentine Railway Co Ltd and Entre Rios Railway Co Ltd. Name changed to above in 1962. Argentina business was closed down and company became an investment trust.

Records: at University College Library, Gower Street, London WC1E 6BT
directors and general meeting minutes 1881-1960s; annual reports and accounts 1881 on; ledgers 1881-1950s

380 ASSAM RAILWAYS & TRADING CO LTD

30 Jul 1881
15743
Victoria House, Vernon Place, London WC1B 4DH
Railway, tea and timber

History: incorporated as above in 1881 by Dr J Berry White, of Dibrugarh Medical School, fellow tea planters and railwaymen, to construct a light metre gauge railway in Upper Assam, India, linking Dibrugarh on the Brahmaputra River to the last tea estate on the Sadiya road, and to the Makum coalfields near the Dehing River, a previous similar venture, Assam Railway Co Ltd, having failed to attract enough financial support in 1879-80. Also to develop coalfields and timber and petroleum concessions. Benjamin Piercy, railway engineer of Clwyd, also backed the company and acted as consulting engineer while his brother Robert and 3 Italian engineers, the Paganinis, built the railway which was opened to Makum by early 1884 and to Talap on the Sadiya road in 1885. Tea branch extended to Saikhoa Ghat, opposite Sadiya in 1909 and Indian government assumed responsibility for railway in 1942, purchasing it for the state line in 1945. Ledo colliery in Makum coalfields started 1882, British workmen arriving in 1883 and coal being produced by early 1884; Tikak colliery in 1884; Namdang in 1896; Ledo New West in 1903; Tirap and Ledo New East in 1904; Barragolai in 1909; Tipongpani in 1924; and Namdang Dip in 1940. In 1885 total annual output of coal was 75,000 tons, reaching 100,000 tons by 1888 and 200,000 tons in 1899. Established brickworks at Ledo in 1890 and rebuilt sawmill and established plywood factory at Margherita in 1924. Annual output of plywood reached 5 million sq ft in 1951. Established own steamer service, flotilla reaching 5 steamers and 16 flats in 1884-5 but was sold off to Rivers Steam Navigation Co in 1887. Sunk oil wells at Makum in 1887-8 and struck oil at Digboi in 1889, building a refinery at Margherita in 1893. Promoted Assam Oil Co Ltd to take over oil interests of company and Assam Oil Syndicate in 1899, selling its shares in 1921 when Burmah Oil Co Ltd became commercial and technical managers. Obtained and cleared land for Margherita tea gardens in 1890. 78 acres had been planted and garden given to Makum (Assam) Tea Co by 1891, promoted and incorporated by company in 1892. 1000 acres under tea by 1894, further gardens planted in 1898 and 1923. Obtained 2000 acres for tea at Namdang in 1908, forming Namdang Tea Co Ltd in 1916 to manage garden, and absorbed Bogapani garden in 1928. Total area of land under tea in 1951 was 5000 acres and crop was 6.25 million lbs. Calcutta agents were Shaw, Finlayson & Co 1881-3; Barry & Co 1883-6; Macneil & Co 1886-1949; Macneil & Barry Ltd from 1949. In 1957 Assam Trading (Holdings) Ltd was incorporated to acquire and hold all the capital of the company.

Records: at Assam Railways & Trading, Victoria House, Vernon Place, London WC1B 4DH
directors board and committee meeting minutes 1880-1938; board agendas and rough notes 1969-71; local board meeting minutes 1972-3; financial forecast and statement 1884
Assam Trading (Holdings) Ltd: memo and articles of association c1958
Makum (Assam) Tea Co Ltd: directors and general meeting minutes 1892-1960; debenture holders meeting minutes 1916,1921; memo and articles of association with resolutions 1957-72
Makum Tea Co (India) Ltd: directors meeting minutes 1972-7
Namdang Tea Co Ltd: directors and general meeting minutes 1915-66
Namdang Tea Co (India) Ltd: directors meeting minutes 1972-7

WR Gawthrop, *The Story of The Assam Railways and Trading Company Limited 1881-1951* (1951)

381 METAL MARKET & EXCHANGE CO LTD

30 Jul 1881
15744
Plantation House, Fenchurch Street, London EC3M 3AP
Metal market

History: in 1876 London Metal Exchange Co Ltd was incorporated to obtain accurate reporting of metal prices and to set up a governing body to regulate the sale of metal. Premises were acquired at 4 Lombard Court and copper and tin were sold in the Ring. In 1881 there was a call to alter the running of the exchange and from this date a committee was elected annually from the general body of subscribers to control the business. In the same year, in response to needs for larger and centralised premises, a site in Whittington Avenue, London was secured. To finance the new building the above was incorporated in 1881, acquiring the assets of the old company. Formal rules were drawn up and by 1883 there were 367 members. By 1890 the main Ring dealt in copper, tin and pig iron, while lead and zinc were traded in the small Ring. The right to deal in the Ring was restricted to London dealers from 1895, and from 1903 all those dealing in the Ring had to provide guarantees of financial standing. Due to expansion, the exchange moved to Plantation House, Fenchurch Street in 1980. In 1984 exchange traded in copper, tin, lead, zinc, silver, aluminium and nickel, with 21 delivery points throughout Europe and the UK.

Records: at Metal Market & Exchange, Plantation House, Fenchurch Street, London EC3M 3AP
board: meeting minutes 1876-1984, agenda books 1879-1976, notices 1942-58; committee meeting minutes: subscribers 1881-date, joint directors and subscribers 1973-84, finance 1876-8; general meeting minutes 1921-84; registers of directors and holdings 1929-84; share: certificate book 1910-51, transfer register 1881-1968, transfer certificates 1881-1919; cash book 1925-35; members: list 1902-67, register of admissions 1906-69, photographs 1897-1977; list of authorised clerks 1903-58; subscribers register 1933-67; code of rules 1887; prices of metals 1909-68; arbitration award register 1923-84; indenture, circular and plaque re Whittington Avenue 1883,1961; benevolent fund meeting minutes 1946-83; notebook with prices of metals etc 1867

Economist Intelligence Unit, *The London Metal Exchange* (1958)

382 HEATON MOOR & DISTRICT CONSERVATIVE CLUB CO LTD

22 Aug 1881
15813
Heaton Moor Road, Stockport, Greater Manchester SK4 4PB
Political club-house

History: incorporated as above in 1881 to acquire land in Heaton Norris, Heaton Moor, Greater Manchester on which to erect premises for Heaton Moor Conservative Club. Purchased land for £1647 on Heaton Moor Road and built a club building, designed by AW Smith, architect. Extensions to the building were made in 1886, 1893 and 1908. The rent received from the Conservative Club was £160 in 1922, reduced to £140 in 1932. In 1984 the company leased the building to the Conservative Club, also rented rooms to masonic lodges and dancing school.

Records (1): at Heaton Moor Conservative Club, 35 Heaton Moor Road, Stockport, Greater Manchester SK4 4PB
directors and general meeting minutes 1881-1983; share: ledger and register of members 1900-82, certificates 1881-1982; transfer certificates 1936-49; memo and articles of association 1881; annual report and accounts 1900-22,1937-72; balance sheets 1936-83; private ledger 1881-1975; lease of premises 1956-1983

Records (2): Stockport Central Library, Wellington Road South, Stockport, Greater Manchester SK1 3RS
general committee minutes 1883-1916; house committee minutes 1886-1931; membership: nomination book 1895-1924, subscription books 1901-30; cash books 1881-1934: trade ledgers 1883-1927; stock books 1928-36; bank book 1925-30; wage book 1925-7; account books 1873-1971; creditor ledgers 1911-27; purchase ledger 1928-33

383 MANNS NORTHAMPTON BREWERY CO LTD

12 Sep 1881
15868
Lodge Way, Harlestone Road, Northampton, Northamptonshire NN5 7UU
Brewing

History: founded in Towcester, Northamptonshire in 1801 by Pickering Phipps and incorporated in 1881 as P Phipps & Co Ltd. Acquired brewery business of Ratliffe & Jeffrey Ltd of Northampton in 1899; Hipwell & Co of Olney, Buckinghamshire in 1920; T Manning & Co Ltd of Northampton in 1933; Campbell Praed & Co Ltd (inc 1896) of Wellingborough, Northamptonshire in 1954; and merged with Northampton Brewery Co Ltd (inc 1887) in 1957 to form Phipps Northampton Brewery Co Ltd. Purchased 153 licensed houses from Ind Coope Brewery Group and merged with Watney Mann Ltd, brewers, changing its name to Phipps Brewery Ltd in 1959, to Watney Mann (Midlands) Ltd in 1968 and to above in 1978. Original brewery site was in Bridge Street, Northampton, production ceasing there when it was sold in 1974. New site at Lodge Way had been developed in 1973 for the distribution to and administration of the company's licensed houses. Also has depots at Kidderminster, Hereford & Worcester; Loughborough, Leicestershire; and Market Rasen and Spalding, Lincolnshire. Licensed premises numbered 1171 in 1960. In 1981 was a subsidiary of Watney Mann & Truman Brewers Ltd which was owned by Grand Metropolitan Ltd.

Records (1): at Manns Northampton Brewery, Lodge Way, Harlestone Road, Northampton, Northamptonshire NN5 7UU
price list 1953; title deeds 18-20 cent; tariff of Black Bay Hotel, Northampton 1900s

Records (2): at Northamptonshire Record Office, Delapré Abbey, Northampton, Northamptonshire NN4 9AW
directors meeting minutes: 1881-1966, managing 1929-55, executive 1955-7; committee meeting minutes: sales 1957, finance 1957-70, production 1958-64, estate 1961-4, inns 1963-7, architects and surveyors 1963-7; shareholders meeting: minutes 1881-1952, agendas 1905-60, attendance book 1882-1959; shareholders: register 1881-7, list 1953; debenture trust: meeting minutes 1907-56, deeds 1897-1959; memo and articles of association 1881,1950; amalgamation documents, papers and correspondence: Northampton Brewing Co Ltd c1959, Campbell Praed & Co Ltd 1952-6; seal register 1928-51; annual reports and accounts 1882-1957; subscription book 1904-52; papers and correspondence re reorganisation of loan capital 1958-9; pension scheme booklets 1954,1959; title deeds nd; managed licensed premises schedule 1958-60; quit rent book 1902-39; fire insurance schedule 1956-60; maps of licensed houses and locality nd; photographs of hotels, inns and off-sales premises in Northamptonshire, Leicestershire, Buckinghamshire, Warwickshire and Cambridgeshire nd; letter books 1902-50; misc correspondence and papers 1899-1905; addresses to chairman nd; newscuttings 1953-62
RC Allen Ltd: minutes 1950-4; articles of association 1951
Campbell Praed & Co Ltd: directors meeting minutes 1896-1958; shareholders register 1896-1949; directors register 1928-48; mortgage register 1897-1924; deeds register 1930-55; memo

and articles of association 1896,1949; takeover papers 1952-6; property book 1878-1964; engineers service agreement 1948; insurance schedule 1958-60
T Collingridge & Co Ltd: papers 1949
Eady & Dulley Ltd: board meeting minutes 1895-1938; shareholders meeting minutes 1895-1938; trust deed 1895; loans ledger 1882-1925
Eldred Everett & Mills Ltd: minutes 1933-58; articles of association 1933
T Manning & Co Ltd: directors meeting minutes 1889-1939; general meeting minutes 1889-1940; shareholders list 1899-1937; private ledger 1890-1933
Northampton Brewery Co Ltd: directors meeting minutes 1887-1955; board analysis sheets 1937-57; annual meeting: minutes 1887-1953, agendas and chairmen's speeches 1925-35; shareholders register 1887-93; debenture trust: minutes 1890-1924, deeds 1887-1953; memo and articles of association 1887; amalgamation deed 1959; securities register 1872-1913; annual returns 1948-63; annual reports and accounts 1887-1954; general ledgers 1872-1908; ledger 1920-5; loans ledger 1881-1915; bank balances day book 1911-19; clubs loans deeds 1950s; sales summaries 1938-50; barley book 1947-68; stock books 1938-44; production record 1930-8,1948-58; salaries ledgers 1872-1951; staff memo 1907; pension scheme: minutes 1936-59, booklets 1935,1954; hospital fund minutes 1921-48; leases 1930-55; property ledger 1887-98; estate department summaries 1931-58; war damage contribution 1941-5; fore insurance schedule and notices 1950-8; Grand Hotel inventory 1947-55
Phillips Stamford Brewery Ltd: trade records 1915-52; misc papers 1952-5
Robinson & Ridday Ltd: minutes 1942-56; articles of association 1942
Shird Hotel Ltd: minutes 1948-54; articles of association 1948
FG Thompson Ltd: minutes 1943-56; articles of association 1943; share transfer papers 1954
Northants Brewers Association: minutes 1883-1959

384 LONDON CHAMBER OF COMMERCE & INDUSTRY

22 Oct 1881
15993
69-73 Cannon Street, London EC4N 5AB
Chamber of commerce

History: launched at a meeting in Jul 1881 under auspices of the Lord Mayor. Incorporated in Oct 1881 as London Chamber of Commerce, a company limited by guarantee to promote trade, commerce, shipping and manufacture of London and home, colonial and foreign trades of UK. Membership reached 1386 by 1882, 3744 by 1900, 5265 by 1913 and 9000 by 1931. Negotiated modifications to Suez Canal agreement in early 1880s and initiated and convened First Congress of Chambers of Commerce of the British Empire (later Federation of Commonwealth Chambers of Commerce) in 1886. Set up Labour Conciliation Board with Metropolitan Trade Unions in 1889, its own commercial education department to provide examinations in commercial subjects in 1890 and inaugurated London Court of Arbitration with City Corporation a few years later. Published monthly journal from 1882 and during both WWs was involved in control of goods. Offices were at 84-85 King William Street from 1882-6, Botolph House, Eastcheap from 1886, moving to Oxford Court, Cannon Street in 1903. Built own offices, opened in 1934, on corner of Queen Street and Cannon Street, with alterations carried out in 1939 and 1955. Changed name to above in 1971 as numbers of industrial members had increased during 1960s. In 1981 membership stood at over 8500, being largest body of its kind in the world, and its trade sections and committees dealt with most aspects of commerce and manufacture in London. Organised exhibitions, trade fairs and missions, published business reports, dealt in export documentation, verification and certification, ran an extensive library and provided full information service for members.

Records (1): at London Chamber of Commerce & Industry, 69-73 Cannon Street, London EC4N 5AB
council, committee, section etc meeting minutes current; annual reports 1881-date; monthly journal 1882-date; government rules and regulations 1914-18; pamphlets 20 cent

Records (2): at Guildhall Library, Aldermanbury, London EC2P 2EJ
council meeting minutes 1888-1967; committee and sub-committee meeting minutes, reports and correspondence 1885-1967; trade section and sub-section meeting minutes and correspondence 1882-1971; committee members list c1910-30; committees and sections meeting attendance book 1934-77; export group meeting minutes 1940-64; traders conference meeting minutes 1918-39; memo and articles of association 1894-1963; annual reports 1919-20; annual accounts and balance sheets 1923-49; ledger 1956-63; journals 1948-55; day books 1947-60; staff salary books 1911-50; pension and commission book 1941-61; correspondence and papers: staff on national service 1940-2, Charles E Musgrave, secretary 1910-24; subscription registers 1884-1959; new members register 1912-71; resignations register 1910-71; specifications for 69-73 Cannon Street 1933; correspondence: presidents 1964-6, chairmans 1964-6, Bribery & Secret Commissions Prevention League 1930-68, Board of Trade with papers re information services 1942, chambers of commerce re certificates of origin 1935-60, National Defence Committee 1936; war circulars 1914-18,1939-47; addresses by or to members, memoranda, pamphlets, papers, notes and press cuttings, re or by chamber 1911-47; papers re dinners 1906-11 and 75th anniversary banquet 1956
Junior Chamber of Commerce: correspondence and circulars 1961-5
London Chamber of Commerce Building Co Ltd: minutes 1900-34; agendas 1920-34; general correspondence 1920-8

Charles E Musgrave, *The London Chamber of Commerce from 1881 to 1914* (1914)

385 NEWTON CHAMBERS & CO LTD

24 Oct 1881
15997
Thorncliffe Ironworks, Sheffield, S Yorkshire S30 4PY
Iron, coal and chemical manufacturers

History: George Newton (1761-1825) and Thomas Chambers (1771-1814) went into partnership in 1792 establishing the Phoenix Foundry in Sheffield, S Yorkshire. Acquired land at Thorncliffe, near Sheffield in 1793 and 2 furnaces had been completed by 1796, collieries having been acquired nearby to smelt ironstone. By 1801 Newton & Chambers were established smelters and ironfounders. Smelters were reorganised to concentrate on gas production and from 1825 to 1850, the supply of gas works equipment constituted the main business. A large manufacturing business in tank construction and fabrication in steel and cast iron grew out of this development. Business operations were extended and modernised from 1869 and coal output was boosted to 1 million tons per year. Business was incorporated as above in 1881 about which time the carbonisation and distillation of coal was being pioneered. Chemical works were established which produced 'Izal' disinfectants, insecticides, antiseptic soaps and cleaning fluids. Had branches in London, Sheffield, Hull, Manchester, Rotherham and Liverpool by 1923. Family representation on the board of directors continued into the late 1940s. As a result of nationalisation in 1947 collieries were transferred to public ownership and company continued as heavy, light and mobile engineers and chemical manufacturers. Subsequently acquired Colindale Paper Co Ltd and Ransomes & Rapier Ltd (est 1868) railway manufacturers, in 1958. By 1977 had 19 subsidiaries with 3200 employees manufacturing excavators, 'Redfyre' burning fires and back boilers and various disinfectants and polishes. Acquired by Central & Sheerwood Ltd in late 1970s.

Records: at Sheffield City Libraries, Archives Department, Central Library, Sheffield, S Yorkshire S1 1XZ
partnership: meeting memo book 1863-87, agreements 1836-81; directors meeting minutes 1881-1953; works advisory committee meeting minutes 1940-53; secretarys reports 1917-24; auditors reports 1900-22; memo and articles of association 1882-95; administration papers 1940-57; mortgage register 1882-95; balance sheets: 1860-1927, abstracts 1797-1821; annual accounts 1868-1918; private: ledgers, journals 1861-81; cash books 1802-11,1876-1903; goods sold and received accounts 1794-1809,1831; misc vouchers 1795-1830; sales catalogues and price lists 1797-1938; sales ledgers 1793-1806,1871-82; production: reports 1900-13, charts 1810-1972, analysis book 1880-9; foundrymens work book 1817-20; works diaries 1909-12; furnace book 1826-37; pig iron book 1890-1; ballast shippings list 1809-10; railway carriage rates 1865-6,1875-1909; day books: ironworks 1793-1852, heavy castings 1839-42, purchase 1822-6, order 1820-5; delta process papers and correspondence 1937-46,1955; ore and limestone: purchase book 1891, carriage accounts 1805-6; furnaces pig iron receipts 1795-7; orders 1876-8; stock books 1793-1829,1874-81; dispatch ledger 1837; sack book 1839-40; orders 1876-8; William Frogatt: order memo books 1894-1907, letter book 1890-1907, works diaries 1909-15; war effort papers 1939-46; fireplace and mantelpiece prints 19 cent; product drawings and plans 1857-1908; Izal and chemical department: patent papers 1893-1942, trading account 1911-12, trading results 1882-1942, legal case papers and correspondence 1897-1929, letter books 1911-24, sales representatives expense accounts 1913-27, production and distribution papers 1893-1919, staff records 1913-28, marketing papers 1927-32; Thorncliffe Colliery: accounts 1795, coal and coke sales ledger 1827-32, diary 1894-1902; Mortomley Colliery weigh or delivery books 1815-31; Newton Chambers collieries branch: letter book 1916, trading account 1937-46; Silkstone Colliery delivery vouchers 1846-9; 'Tommy' shop: purchase books 1803-41, stock purchase vouchers and correspondence 1801-42, stock books 1803-05,1812-17, reckoning books 1801-44, grocery day books 1840, drapery day books 1830,1836-48; employee terms book 1863-77; wages accounts 1796-1800,1831; Thorncliffe & Chapeltown Ironworks: plans and drawings 1836-1909, royalty plans c1946-8; title deeds and documents 1792-1964; deeds register 1793-1880; ironmasters and coal owners meeting minutes and papers 1820-46; ironworks letter books 1825-1915; misc business papers and correspondence: 1793-1928, gas companies 1826-46, waterworks companies 1833-46, iron foundries 1797-1948; family papers and correspondence 1793-1925; visitors book 1931,1939-47; exhibitions, production, works, plant, offices, collieries, products, staff and activities photographs 1867-1968; newscuttings 1883-1955; archivists papers c1950-4
Hoyland Silkstone Colliery Co Ltd: directors meeting minutes 1888-1926; general meeting minutes 1921-6; directors register 1911-26

Newton Chambers Thorncliffe Collieries Ltd: reconstruction: agreement 1945-7, memo 1944-5; conveyances 1946
Thorncliffe Coal Distillation Co Ltd: partnership agreements and papers 1881-1964; debenture interest list 1892; articles of association 1920; proposed co-partnership and profit sharing papers 1926-7; members list 1954; balance sheets 1945-50; cost books 1922-47; stock: books 1946, papers 1946-9; nationalisation: agreements 1941-6, papers 1945-58; NCB: sales agencies papers 1946-9, correspondence 1941-50, compensation papers 1948-9; valuation report and papers 1947-9; production books 1929-52; estate department papers 1921-33; colliery chemical department, Manchester warehouse and equipment papers 1927-49; employment register 1937-43; plant, equipment and staff photographs 1947-50; misc papers and reports 1928-45

386 WESTINGHOUSE BRAKE & SIGNAL CO LTD

7 Nov 1881
16033
Pew Hill, Chippenham, Wiltshire SN15 1RT
Brake and signal manufacturers

History: incorporated in 1881 as Westinghouse Brake Co Ltd to acquire the business of Westinghouse Continuous Brake Co of Kings Cross, London which had been established by George Westinghouse of Westinghouse Air Brake Co of Pittsburg, USA in 1876. Manufactured railway brakes, lighting appliances for railways, and other railway equipment. A German branch was formed in 1884 and works established at Sevran, France in 1891. In 1898 SA Westinghouse formed at Leningrad, Russia. In 1901 a French company, SA Westinghouse, was formed. An agreement was reached in 1902 with McKenzie & Holland Ltd for manufacture of electro pneumatic signalling and in 1904 terms for the manufacture of Morse Chain were agreed. In following year patent rights for vacuum brakes were acquired. Cia Italiana Westinghouse di Freni was formed in 1906 followed by Westinghouse Brake Co of Australasia Ltd in 1907. Westinghouse Bremsen GmbH was formed in 1912 to acquire German assets. In 1919 Morse Chain business was sold to Westinghouse Morse Chain Co Ltd and in following year the interests of Consolidated Signal Co Ltd were acquired. Company's name changed to Westinghouse Brake & Saxby Signal Co Ltd. In 1926 the manufacture of rectifiers commenced and in 1932 the London works was transferred to Chippenham, Wiltshire. Name changed to above in 1935. The USA company sold its interest in the British company in 1937. In 1948 Westinghouse Garrard Ticket Machines Ltd was formed with Garrard Engineering & Manufacturing Co Ltd. Gresham Craven & Heatly (Holdings) Ltd was acquired in 1953, and Douglas (Kingswood) Ltd in 1954. In 1955 Westinghouse Brake & Signal Co SA (Pty) Ltd formed in South Africa. 50 per cent interest in Hobbs Transmission Ltd purchased in 1960 (fully acquired by 1964) and in following year Westinghouse Brake & Signal (Argentina) SAIYC formed (sold 1967). Westinghouse Brake English Electric Semi-Conductors Ltd formed in 1966 with English Electric Co Ltd (owned outright in 1972). In 1979 the company was acquired by Hawker Siddeley Group.

Records: at Westinghouse Brake & Signal, Pew Hill, Chippenham, Wiltshire SN15 1RT
directors meeting minutes 1881-date; general meeting: minutes 1882-1955, attendance book 1921-73; share summary 1881-1935; memo and articles of association 1972; private ledger, Chippenham & London 1922-1951; London journal transfers 1929-48; specifications:

signalling, metal rectifiers, mining equipment, Westinghouse Brake 1932-c50; photographs: Chippenham works, assembly departments, drills, lathes, presses etc c1930,c1950; staff journal 1949-56; historical notes, articles and slides on company and subsidiaries 1935-73
Douglas (Sales & Services) Ltd: share ledger and register of members 1946-76
Hobbs Transmission Ltd: directors and general meeting minutes 1936-60
McKenzie & Holland Ltd: directors and general meeting minutes 1925-75; share ledger 1925-65
Saxby & Farmer Ltd: board and general meeting minutes 1923-75; share ledger 1923-65; portrait of John Saxby c1810
Westinghouse CVB Ltd: directors meeting minutes 1881-1975; general meeting: minutes 1881-1960, attendance book 1881-1974; register of directors: 1950-73, holdings 1948-73; share: ledger 1924-74, transfer registers and certificates 1892-1974
Westinghouse Ticket Machine Co Ltd: register of members and share ledger 1943-71

387 LIVERPOOL & LONDON STEAMSHIP PROTECTION & INDEMNITY ASSOCIATION LTD

7 Nov 1881
16036
Equity and Law House, 47 Castle Street, Liverpool, Merseyside L2 9UB
Mutual marine insurance

History: incorporated as Liverpool & London Steamship Protection Association Ltd in 1881 as a mutual protection association for British passenger carrying steamship owners. Business began in 1882 with 470,828 tons entered and with Thomas H Ismay of the White Star Line as chairman. 1.5 million tons were entered by 1892 rising to 4.9 million tons by 1925, falling to 139,273 tons in 1945. In 1911 the *Titanic* was entered on its books. In 1975 had 2 million tons entered, of which 5 per cent was foreign and in 1983 with 3.5 million tons entered, 75 per cent was foreign. The association's 46 members include Bibby Line and Cunard and 194 vessels including the *Queen Elizabeth II*. From about 1982 Grayhill Ltd have acted as managers.

Records (1): at Liverpool & London Steamship Protection & Indemnity Association, Equity and Law House, 47 Castle Street, Liverpool, Merseyside L2 9UB
directors and general meeting minutes 1881-date; circulars, annual reports, managers reports and claims statements 1881-date; claims: indemnities 1909-11, guarantees 1910-39; counsel opinion claims books 1883-c1946; rules and regulations 1883-date; memo and articles of association 1883-date; steamers entered lists 1883-date

Records (2): at Merseyside County Archives Service, 64-66 Islington, Liverpool, Merseyside L3 8LG
letter books 20 cent

388 FOLLOWS & BATE LTD

17 Nov 1881
16072
Coleridge Street, Sunny Hill, Derby, Derbyshire DE3 7JT
Horticultural engineers

History: incorporated as above in 1881 to take over existing business in Dutton Street, Manchester. In 1886 moved to new works, costing £5000 in Froxmere Street, Manchester. Range of newly designed lawn mowers were introduced in 1893, and other products included household equipment, chimney cowls and paint mills. Acquired by Qualcast Ltd in 1938, the company continued to produce lawn mowers mainly for export. By late 1950s lawn mowers were designed for non-branded market. Production ended in 1978 and factory in Gorton was leased out in 1984.

Records: at Qualcast, Coleridge Street, Sunny Hill, Derby, Derbyshire DE3 7JT
directors meeting minutes 1882-1939; general meeting minutes 1884-1968; share ledger 1881-1904; register of mortgages 1912-22; memo and articles of association 1881,1949; annual report and accounts 1887-1922; profit and loss account 1887; balance sheet 1938; private ledgers c1905-50; cash book 1938-45; cost analysis 1950s; bills of exchange payable 1914-59; catalogues, price lists and advertisements 1897-1930; land values from 1910

389 CHUBWA TEA CO LTD

29 Nov 1881
16105
52-56 Osnaburgh Street, London NW1 3NS
Tea

History: Chubwa tea estates in Upper Assam, India, near the junction of Dibru and Brahmaputra Rivers were first planted around 1832 as an experiment using Chinese seedlings. The seedlings were subsequently washed away by floods. A new garden was planted on the site by the Chinaman in charge of original estate who subsequently purchased the property. Sold out to James Warren, East India merchant, in 1850 and the Warren family's involvement in its management continued until the 1960s. Chubwa Tea Co Ltd was incorporated in 1881 to raise capital to increase the estates. James Finlay & Co, textile manufacturers and East India merchants of Glasgow, becoming financiers and acting as secretaries. Kellyden and Nonai tea gardens were subsequently owned by Chubwa, Nonai Tea Co Ltd amalgamating in 1893. The tea estates were sold in 1976 to Tata-Finlay Ltd, an Indian rupee company in which James Finlay PLC has had holding. In 1981 was a wholly owned subsidiary of the latter.

Records (1): at Chubwa Tea, 52-56 Osnaburgh Street, London NW1 3NS
correspondence and accounts re tea sales at London auctions 1966-7

Records (2): at James Finlay, PO Box 58, Finlay House, 10-14 West Nile Street, Glasgow, Strathclyde G1 2PP
directors meeting minutes 1881-date; general meeting minutes 1881-date; ordinary share register 1924-51; preference stock register 1951-72; ledger 1952-70; land ledger 1875-81; correspondence re early history and Warren family 1948,1958; photographs of plantations, estates, personnel, recreation, work studies 1890s on

Records (3): at Glasgow University Archives, The University, Glasgow, Strathclyde G12 8QQ
directors fees and commissions 1924-72; accounts etc 1899-1966; journal 1881-2; Calcutta auctions 1951-7

390 WHITEHAVEN NEWS LTD

9 Dec 1881
16157
148 Queen Street, Whitehaven, Cumbria
Newspaper

History: *Whitehaven News* was first published in 1885-6. Company incorporated as above in 1881 to purchase the newspaper, plant, machinery etc and carry on business as printers, publishers and stationers. Robert Foster was manager in 1887 when offices were at 26 High Street, Whitehaven, Cumbria. Began publishing *West Cumberland News* in 1918. Acquired in 1962 by Cumberland Newspapers Ltd which became Cumbrian Newspapers Group Ltd in 1974. *West Cumberland News* merged with *West Cumberland Times* and *Cumberland Star* to form *West Cumberland Times & Star* in 1967. Ceased trading in 1972. *Whitehaven News* currently being published by Cumbrian Newspapers Group Ltd.

Records (1): at Cumbrian Newspapers Group, Newspaper House, Dalston Road, Carlisle, Cumbria CA2 5UA
employees profit sharing scheme booklet 1927; deeds and property documents re Theatre Royal, Whitehaven 1769-1909

Records (2): at Cumbria Record Office, The Castle, Carlisle, Cumbria CA3 8UR
correspondence and papers re proprietor, acquisition, editor, Whitehaven events, advertising 1952-66; annual returns 1944; annual and half yearly accounts 1962-7

Records (3): at British Library, Newspaper Library, Colindale Avenue, London NW9 9HE
Whitehaven News (no 22) 1856 on; *West Cumberland News* (no 1-3584) 1918-67

391 NATIONAL BANK LTD

2 Jan 1882
16252
20 Birchin Lane, London EC3 3DP
Banking

History: formed in London in 1835 by deed of settlement as National Bank of Ireland (The Liberator). Initially aimed to establish semi-autonomous 'branches' in Ireland, as separate companies, with equal share capital being provided by local interests and by the bank. Originally share capital was £1 million of which £200,000 was paid up. First branch opened at Carrick on Suir, Kilkenny, as Carrick on Suir National Bank of Ireland. Within 12 months 11 branches and 18 sub-branches were established. Principle of semi-autonomous local banks gradually discontinued from 1837. Dublin branch was opened in 1845 and London & Dublin Bank was acquired in 1847. In 1854 commenced business in England, opening a branch in the City of London and in 1856 changed its name to National Bank. Joined London Clearing House in 1859 and between 1862-8 opened a further 7 London branches. Incorporated as above in 1882. By 1888 there were 97 branches and sub-branches, rising to 146 by 1911. In 1902-03 first English branches outside London were opened at Manchester and Cardiff. In 1925 acquired R Wharton & Son, Bank & Pay Offices at Salford, Greater Manchester, and Wakefield, W Yorkshire, which strengthened bank's interest in Irish cattle trade. In 1966 Irish business was transferred to a newly formed subsidiary, National Bank of Ireland which was then sold to Bank of Ireland. Simultaneously the share capital of National Bank was acquired by National Commercial Bank of Scotland Ltd. In 1968 this bank merged with Royal Bank of Scotland to form National & Commercial Bank Group. This brought together three London clearing banks, National Bank Ltd, Glyn Mills & Co Ltd and Williams Deacon's Bank Ltd, which amalgamated in 1970 to form Williams & Glyn's Bank Ltd.

Records: at Williams & Glyn's Bank, 20 Birchin Lane, London EC3 3DP
court meeting minutes 1835 on; chairmans statements 1836-60; shareholders list 1907,1920; prospectus 1835; deed of settlement 1835 on; formation correspondence 1834-46; secretarys memo book 1912-25; annual report and accounts 1843-96; balance sheets 1864 on; head office ledger 1921; staff lists 1854,1874; instructions 1840-76,1914,1919; chairmans letter book 1874-87; branches register 1856; branches - Baker Street: signature books 1898 on, loans ledger 1899-1919, safe custody registers 1898-1968, security registers 1920s-30s; Bayswater: signature books 1862 on, loans ledger 1862 on, information book 1876-1950; Camden Town: customer ledgers 1947-67, safe custody register 1872-1962; Cavendish Square: safe custody registers 1881-1956, security registers 1897-1932; Charing Cross: signature books 1904-19, press cuttings 1947-53; Grosvenor Gardens: signature books 1864-1931, deposit account ledgers 1922 on, bills register 1901-58, safe custody registers 1893-1938, security registers 1890-1939, information book 1906-66; Harrow Road: signature books 1882-1962, loan ledgers 1950-63, closed accounts register 1950-63, safe custody registers 1882-1960, security register 1914-48, information book 1882-1967; Holborn: signature books 1920-62, letters of instruction 1920 on, safe custody register 1920-71, security ledgers 1920-54; Islington: half yearly report book 1890-1901, signature books 1881-1960, bills discounted ledger 1912-49, past due bill registers 1898-1940, safe custody registers 1894-1930, security registers 1881-1930; Kings Cross: signature books 1868-1961, managers draft book 1868-1923, deposit receipt books 1905-54, loans ledger 1942-62, safe custody registers 1921-61, security registers 1882-1962; Notting Hill Gate: signature books 1868-1962, safe custody register 1892-1963, security registers 1875-1920, information book 1868-1963, letter books 1922-7; Strand: signature books 1897-1950, safe custody registers 1916-60, security registers 1898-1938, staff circular book 1915-60, letter books 1897-1930; Willesden: signature books 1882-1909, day books 1948-55, loan ledgers 1949-60, safe custody registers 1890-7, security registers 20 cent, customer instruction books 20 cent, information books 1955-60

M Slattery, *The National Bank 1835-1970* (priv pub 1972)

392 CITY CENTRE PROPERTIES LTD

4 Feb 1882
16379
1 Fredericks Place, Old Jewry, London EC2
Property

History: incorporated in 1882 as Mansion House Chambers Ltd, and subsequently changed name to Chesham House (Regent Street) Ltd and then to above. Acquired by Land Securities Investment Ltd in 1968. Managed by Land Securities (Management) Ltd.

Records: at Land Securities (Management), Landsec House, 21 New Fetter Lane, London EC4P 4PY
general meeting minutes 1941-58; annual reports 1967-70; correspondence and papers 1950s on

393 SUNDERLAND MARINE MUTUAL INSURANCE CO LTD

17 Feb 1882
16432
4-5 The Esplanade, Sunderland, Tyne & Wear SR2 7BQ
Marine insurance

History: established as a mutual marine insurance club by group of Sunderland shipowners and incorporated in 1882 with unlimited liability as Total Loss Mutual Steamship Insurance Co. Additional cover was provided for partial loss in 1883 and protection and indemnity in 1884 by forming Steam Tug & Trawlers' Mutual Protecting & Indemnity Association. By 1885 was insuring 127 ships from ports in north east England and Scotland. Established Steam Tug & Trawlers' Mutual Insurance Association in 1892. By 1913, 806 out of the 957 vessels insured were fishing boats from throughout Britain. Established Steam Tug & Trawler Mutual Thirds Indemnity Association in 1925. Membership declined rapidly between WWs falling to 401 vessels insured in 1934 and was not reversed until 1953 when accepted diesel-powered fishing vessel insurance and subsequently rationalized insurance classifications. Changed name to above in 1962 and merged in 1974 with Salvus, Bain & Arnott Ltd, marine underwriting firm, founded by one of employees in 1934, which thereafter acted as company's managers. Re-registered with limited liability in 1976. Acquired business of Anglian Mutual Underwriting Association and Fishing Vessels' Insurance Society in 1979 when company was insuring 2611 vessels valued at £200 million.

Records: at Sunderland Marine Mutual Insurance, 4-5 The Esplanade, Sunderland, Tyne & Wear SR2 7BQ
directors and general meeting minutes: 1882-date; class III 1917-69; corporate documents 1882-1976; memo and articles of association 1922-70s; guardbook 1922-72; annual reports and accounts 1926,1954-date; cash books 1945-59; wages books 1938-65; salaries book 1972-5; rules and entered vessels lists 1897-date; insurance registers 1930-74; premium registers 1969,1974; claims: books 1956-70, registers 1968-74; reinsurance registers 1936-59; contract report 1963; correspondence: insurance brokers 1958-74, Aberdeen branch with reports 1960-2; photographs: manager 1890s, damaged vessel 1904; centenary dinner invitations menus and newscuttings 1982
Steam Tug & Trawlers' Mutual Insurance Association: directors and general meeting minutes: 1892-1924, class II 1903-24, class III 1917-24; guardbook 1922-8; rules and vessels entered lists 1897-1922; annual reports and accounts 1926-28
Steam Tug & Trawlers' Mutual Protecting & Indemnity Association: (See summary no 493)
Steam Tug & Trawler Mutual Thirds Indemnity Association: directors and general meeting minutes 1925-70; memo and articles of association 1925-50; guardbook 1925-72; annual reports and accounts 1926,1954-72; rules and vessels entered lists 1925-62; insurance registers 1955-65; claims books 1956-70

P Beaver, *Sunderland Marine Mutual Insurance, The First Hundred Years 1882-1982* (1982)

394 HALIFAX & DISTRICT CREDITORS ASSOCIATION

1 Mar 1882
16478
1 Union Street South, Halifax, W Yorkshire
Traders association

History: established by local traders in 1880 and incorporated as above in 1882 as a trade protection society in Halifax, W Yorkshire. With a maximum permitted membership of 500, the association circulated information about credit worthiness, assisted in the collection of bad debts, and maintained a watching brief on legislation regarding bad debts. In early 1980s carried out status enquiries and company searches and continued to assist in the collection of bad debts on behalf of members.

Records: at Halifax & District Creditors Association, 1 Union Street South, Halifax, W Yorkshire
directors meeting minutes 1882 on

395 WILLIAM GIBSON & SON LTD

9 Mar 1882
16507
517 Aspley Lane, Nottingham, Nottinghamshire NG8 5RP
Hosiery manufacturers

History: founded in 1779 in premises at junction of Lister Gate and Low Pavement, Nottingham. Incorporated as above in 1882 to continue hosiery manufacturing business of William Gibson & Co. Acquired new offices at 14 Thurland Street in 1895 and by 1898 had 2 factories in Arkwright Street, Nottingham and Castle Donington (closed c1960) and warehouses in Thurland and Lincoln Streets, Nottingham. London office was established in Aldermanbury by 1894. Acquired business and factory of Jonee Woollies at South Kirkby, W Yorkshire in 1963. Head offices moved in 1964 to Cromford Street factory which was scheduled for redevelopment along with Thurston Street property in late 1960s. Factory in Aspley Lane continued to operate. In 1965 products were mens, womens and childrens underwear, mens halfhose, womens and childrens outerwear, T-shirts and sports shirts. Acquired in 1970 by Robert Kitchen Taylor & Co Ltd, knitwear manufacturers and textile merchants. By 1977 employed about 250 people at 2 factories in Aspley Lane and South Kirkby. In early 1980s was knitted underwear and leisurewear manufacturer.

Records: at William Gibson & Son, 517 Aspley Lane, Nottingham, Nottinghamshire NG8 5RP
directors: and general meeting minutes 1966-77, attendance book 1888-1970; annual report and accounts 1883-1912; private ledgers 1927-50; private cash book 1882-3; price lists: London and Manchester stock 1894-1902, retailers 1884-1912; Nottingham premises inventory and valuation 1923; yarn prices 1933-41,1960; stock taking summary 1876-86; cricket club score books 1862-72; premises, plant and directors photographs c1900,c1932; newscuttings 1867-1965
Hine Parker & Co Ltd: directors meeting minutes 1897-1950; annual: meeting reports 1897-1903, report and accounts 1904-50

396 WARWICKSHIRE MASONIC TEMPLE PROPERTIES LTD

20 Mar 1882
16552
1 Clarendon Road, Edgbaston, Birmingham, W Midlands B16 8SB
Masonic hall

History: incorporated in 1882 as Edgbaston Assembly Rooms Ltd to provide assembly and meeting rooms in Edgbaston, W Midlands. Property was purchased on the corner of Hagley and Francis Roads on which the assembly rooms were erected. Company sold to Warwickshire Masonic Peace Memorial Temple Ltd in 1937 to provide a masonic temple. In 1963 purchased lease of Congregational church site adjoining assembly rooms and another 3 acres on which a new masonic temple was built. Name changed to above in 1967. Assembly rooms were sold in 1971 and freehold of Congregational church purchased in 1972. In 1983 the property was let for masonic purposes.

Records: at Warwickshire Masonic Temple Properties, 1 Clarendon Road, Edgbaston, Birmingham, W Midlands B16 8SB
directors meeting minutes 1904-71; sub-committee: finance minutes 1966, new masonic temple report 1964; general meeting minutes 1882-1982; members register and share ledger 1882-1938; share certificate book and transfer certificates 1925-51; memo and articles of association c1942; annual report and accounts 1968-82; mortgage register 1888-1971

397 WELLINGBOROUGH CONSERVATIVE CLUB CO LTD
25 Mar 1882
16579
1A High Street, Wellingborough, Northamptonshire
Political club-house

History: incorporated as above in 1882 to build and maintain the High Street premises of Wellingborough Conservative Club. By the late 1960s the club-house was no longer viable and in the late 1970s the company's property was sold. It was placed in voluntary liquidation in 1981.

Records: at Northamptonshire Record Office, Delapré Abbey, Northampton, Northamptonshire NN4 9AW
directors meeting minutes 1889-1967; register of shares, members and share transfers 1882-1920; share ledgers 1882 on; memo and articles of association 1882; annual list and summary 1882-1920; cash book 1901-05; club members register 1941-6; rules and regulations booklet 1962

398 SPIERS & POND LTD
29 Mar 1882
16590
Grand Metropolitan House, 7-8 Stratford Place, London W1N 0AJ
Catering and hotels

History: established in 1863 by Felix W Spiers and Christopher Pond, 2 Englishmen who met in Melbourne, Australia in the early 1850s and opened cafes and other catering establishments before returning to England and setting up as railway caterers. Opened first buffet at Farringdon Street Station and by 1890s maintained 60 dining cars and over 200 main line buffets. First London restaurant, the Silver Grill, Ludgate Hill, was opened in 1866. Theatre cafes were also established, the first, the Criterion, designed by Thomas Verity in 1873, followed by the Gaiety, Drury Lane, and the refreshment room at Regent's Park Zoo. First hotel, Holborn Viaduct Hotel was designed by Isaacs & Florence and opened in 1874. Baileys

Hotel, Gloucester Road, S Kensington was acquired in 1890 and later became the headquarters of the hotel business which consisted of 12 hotels by 1960. The earliest acquisitions were at seaside resorts in Brighton, Worthing and Eastbourne in E&W Sussex and Scarborough, N Yorkshire, but old coaching inns in Aylesbury and Gerrards Cross, Buckinghamshire, and Exeter, Devon were purchased later. Company incorporated as above after Pond's death in 1882. Spiers retired in 1904 and died in 1910. Acquired in 1957 by Leslie Jackson and Leopold Muller, managers of Chicken Inns (London) Ltd. Chicken Inns (London) Ltd amalgamated in 1960 with Express Dairy Co Ltd, which was acquired by Grand Metropolitan Ltd in 1969. By 1981 all but one of the company's hotels had been sold by Grand Metropolitan.

Records (1): at Grand Metropolitan Hotels, Grand Metropolitan House, 7-8 Stratford Place, London W1N 0AJ
directors and general meeting minutes 1948-date; directors register 1948-date; seals register 1950-date; ledger 1964 on

Records (2): at Express Dairy, 430 Victoria Road, South Ruislip, Greater London HA4 0HF
dividends 1960; memo and articles of association 1860-7; balance sheet 1968; accounts and correspondence 1964-7

Records (3): at Kensington & Chelsea Central Library, Phillimore Walk, London W8 7RX
impersonal ledgers 1890-1911

Bryan Morgan, *Express Journey 1864-1964. A Centenary History of the Express Dairy Company Limited* (1964)

399 FOWEY HOTEL CO LTD

5 Apr 1882
16628
Fowey Hotel, Esplanade, Fowey, Cornwall
Hotel

History: incorporated as above in 1882 by the initiative of local railway companies to lease land, later bought, at Fowey, Cornwall on which to build a hotel to cater for railway passengers.

Records: at Fowey Hotel, Esplanade, Fowey, Cornwall
directors meeting: minutes 1882-1942, attendance book 1893-1972; members register 1882-1937; share: ledger 1882-1925, certificates and transfer certificates 1892-1960; dividend: accounts book 1886-1944; mandates 1897-1943; debenture holders book 1886-1944; mortgage register c1920s; general meeting reports 1882-1949; annual reports and accounts 1882-1949; general ledger 1906-63; expenditure abstract book 1936-76; monthly accounts 1934-71; guests daily accounts 1946,1961-72; cash books 1922-76; guest summaries 1963-5; purchase ledger 1938-50; food purchase journal 1969-72; bar order book 1966-71; bar stock book 1975-8; bin book 1963-4; dining room notebook 1972-7; visitors book 1960-79; Fowey Hotel catalogues, early 20 cent; wages book 1954-70; valuation of furniture c1943; photographs of hotel, Fowey and district, early 20 cent; out letters 1933-48; hotel stationery 1965

400 FALMOUTH HOTEL CO LTD

5 Apr 1882
16705
Falmouth Hotel, Cliff Road, Falmouth, Cornwall TR11 4NZ
Hotel

History: first company was incorporated as above in 1863 by the directors of Cornwall Railway Co to build a large hotel at Falmouth Bay designed by London architects, Kennedy & Rogers, and built by Plymouth (Devon) contractor John Marshall. The hotel opened in May 1865 and additions were completed in 1880, 1898 and 1972. Company went into liquidation in 1882 and a new company was incorporated with the same name to run the hotel. In about 1893 built 'The Pendennis' hotel on Falmouth cliff top drive, taken over by the War Department in 1917, sold in 1926 and later renamed 'The Hydro'. Also built 'The Bay Hotel' on the seafront during the 1900s. Company still ran both hotels in 1982.

Records: at Falmouth Hotel, 15 East Street, Newquay, Cornwall TR7 1DE
share transfer registers 1882 on; directors register 1901-38; articles of association 1882; annual reports and accounts 1882 on; monthly hotel receipts summaries 1885-1972; lease of Falmouth Hotel Tap 1896; photographs of Falmouth seafront and Bay Hotel early 20 cent; Christmas festivities programme 1933

The Falmouth Hotel Company 1882-1982 (priv pub 1982)

401 ANIMAL PRODUCTS CO LTD

8 May 1882
16772
67 Kentish Town Road, London NW1
Food processing

History: founded in Liverpool in 1864, possibly by William Henry King, albumen manufacturer. In 1882 he sold the business to Thomas Gibbons, heating engineer. Above company was registered shortly after to acquire the business. Main objects were to manufacture and deal in animal extracts of serum, albumen, pemmican, pepsine, extract of meat and glycerine, their by-products and albumen substitute. Until 1950s offices were in Benson Street, Liverpool when they moved to Central Markets, Smithfield, London after change in ownership. Objects altered in 1956 to include dealings in frozen and fresh meats, canned goods, provisions, milk products etc. Also owned an abattoir in Chertsey Lane, Staines, Surrey. Went into liquidation in 1982.

Records: at Fordyce Curry, 61 West Smithfield, London EC1
directors and shareholders meeting minutes 1924-72; members, directors, share transfers and charges register and share ledger 1911-73; memo and articles of association 1882-1956; letter re lease 1930; annual returns 1911-57

402 LAW REVERSIONARY INTEREST SOCIETY LTD

16 May 1882
16807
20 Lincoln's Inn Fields, London WC2A 3ET
Investment

History: established in London in 1853 for investment in and lending on the security of reversions and life interests. Was acquired as a subsidiary of Equity & Law Life Assurance Society Ltd in 1912.

Records: at Law Reversionary Interest Society, Amersham Road, High Wycombe, Buckinghamshire HP13 5AL
board meeting minutes 1941 on; general meeting minutes 19 cent on

403 WORCESTER & WORCESTERSHIRE INCORPORATED LAW SOCIETY

26 May 1882
16861
Carlton House, Marlborough Street, Kidderminster, Hereford & Worcester DY10 1BA
Law society

History: founded by Worcester solicitors in 1842 as a law society, renting a room in Natural History Society's buildings in Foregate Street, Worcester for a committee and library room. From the 1850s the rooms were let to Law Students' Society. By 1879 society had 60 members. Incorporated as above as a company limited by guarantee in 1882 to protect and advance the status of solicitors and promote honourable practice, and to raise money to purchase Old City Library Buildings in Pierpoint Street for £1000.

Records: at Worcester & Worcestershire Incorporated Law Society, Carlton House, Marlborough Street, Kidderminster, Hereford & Worcester DY10 1BA
committee and general meeting minutes 1841-1903

404 LONG EATON WEST END MILL CO LTD

8 Jun 1882
16906
49 Derby Road, Long Eaton, Derbyshire NG10 1BN
Room and power

History: incorporated as above in 1882 to acquire land in Long Eaton, Derbyshire on which to erect a factory suitable for the manufacture of lace. Space in the Leopold Street factory was leased to shareholders and other tenants. Has continued to rent out room and power.

Records: at Long Eaton West End Mill, 49 Derby Road, Long Eaton, Derbyshire NG10 1BN
directors and general meeting minutes 1882-date; members registers and share ledgers 1882-date; directors register 1905-date; share: transfer registers 1883-1920, transfer documents 1883-1955, certificates 1883-5; annual lists and summaries 1882-1911; memo and articles of association 1882; annual report and accounts 1907, 1916-57; balance sheets and accounts 1934-71; ledgers 1884-1908

405 LONDON HYDRAULIC POWER CO

29 Jun 1882
16999
Renforth Street, Rotherhithe, London SE16 1JJ
Hydraulic power

History: incorporated in 1871 as Wharves & Warehouses Steam Power & Hydraulic Pressure Co. Hydraulic power was first supplied in the autumn of 1883 over a limited area of the riverside. Power was generated from a pumping station at Falcon Wharf, Holland Street, (Hopton Street) London. General Hydraulic Power Co Ltd was registered in 1882. Primary business was to acquire Wharves & Warehouses Steam Power & Hydraulic Pressure Co and later Liverpool Hydraulic Power Co, incorporated in 1884. In Jun 1884 name of the original company was changed to the above and the area of supply was extended. The name of the holding company was changed to GHP Group Ltd in 1961. During the 1970s the remaining consumers machines were converted to alternative power sources and the company ceased pumping in 1977. GHP Group Ltd was acquired by Low & Bonar Ltd in 1977, who sold 80 per cent of its holdings in the above to NM Rothschild & Sons Ltd.

Records (1): at London Hydraulic Power, Renforth Street, Rotherhithe, London SE16 1JJ
minutes 1882-date; share records 1882-1977; accounts 1882-date; letter books nd
London Hydraulic Power Co: annual statistical reports c1910-77; letter books 1890-1905; circular books 1885-1920; financial records c1930-77; customer: service cards 1885-1977, correspondence, agreements, inspection reports 1950-77; mains: laying inspection reports 1885-1977, laying return book c1900-20, system maps 1885-1925, papers c1920-77, inspectors test sheets c1920-77, and service detail books 1885-1925; machinery inspection reports 1885-1977; plant specification books 1880-1920; plant correspondence, contracts and specifications c1930-77; engine room registers 1885-1977; pumping station building and plant drawings 1885-1977
Liverpool Hydraulic Power Co: annual reports c1910-c77

Records (2): at London Borough of Tower Hamlets, Central Library, Bancroft Road, London E1 4DQ
Wapping pumping station drawings c1885-1977

Records (3): Greater London Record Office, 40 Northampton Road, London EC1R OAB
minutes 1882-1916; annual report and accounts 1882-1960; share: allotment books 1882-1903, stock ledgers 1882-1923, stock transfer registers and documents 1882-1951, annual returns 1882-1905
London Hydraulic Power Co: minutes 1872-1919; annual report and accounts 1882-1960
Liverpool Hydraulic Power Co: minutes 1886-1922; annual report and accounts 1882-1960

406 SHEFFIELD & DISTRICT SOCIETY OF CHARTERED ACCOUNTANTS

29 Jun 1882
17002
2A Rutland Park, Sheffield, S Yorkshire S10 2PD
Accountants' society

History: established in 1837 as Sheffield Institute of Accountants to provide a forum for the discussion of matters relating to the accountancy profession, to promote the education of local accountants, and to provide a code of conduct for competition for work. After the establishment of Institute of Chartered Accountants in England and Wales in 1880 its role was redefined and it was registered as a private unlimited company, Sheffield Incorporated Society of Chartered Accountants with a membership of 28. Subsequently dropped Incorporated from title. Originally members were drawn from within 20 miles of Sheffield Town Hall, but this was eventually expanded to include Doncaster, S Yorkshire; Worksop and Retford, Nottinghamshire; and Matlock, Derbyshire and name was changed to above. Membership grew to 47 by 1900, 72 by 1914, 79 by 1944 and 878 in 1977.

Records: at Sheffield & District Society of Chartered Accountants, 2A Rutland Park, Sheffield, S Yorkshire S10 2PD
committee and general meeting: minutes 1882-date, papers 1882-1949; sub-committees meeting minutes 1948-71; memo and articles of association 1882-1922; annual report and accounts 1883-1920; general ledgers 1877-1970; cash books 1918-72; rules 1877; members lists 1882-1958; subscription register 1958-63; newscuttings 1882-1923; stùdents society committee meeting minutes 1956-61

AM Hoe, *The Sheffield & District Society of Chartered Accountants. The First Hundred Years Centenary 1877-1977* (priv pub 1977)

407 WHITBREAD EAST PENNINES LTD
3 Jul 1882
17030
Exchange Brewery, Bridge Street, Sheffield, S Yorkshire S3 8NL
Brewing

History: established in 1820 in Market Place, Sheffield, S Yorkshire as Proctor & Co and acquired by Edward and Robert Tennant in 1840. Brewery moved to Bridge Street in 1852. Incorporated as Tennant Brothers Ltd in 1882. Acquired Wiley & Co Ltd, wine and spirit merchants of Sheffield in 1904, AH Smith & Co Ltd, Don Brewery, Sheffield in 1916, Strout's Brewery Co Ltd, Sheffield in 1918, Thomas Berry & Co Ltd, Moorhead Brewery, Sheffield in 1924, Nottingham Brewery Ltd, Nottingham in 1944, Sheffield Free Brewery Co Ltd in 1954, Laing & Co Ltd and William Hickling & Son Ltd, both wine merchants of Nottingham in 1954 and 1956 respectively, Clarkson's Old Brewery (Barnsley) Ltd, Barnsley in 1956, and Worksop & Retford Brewery Co Ltd, Worksop, Nottinghamshire in 1958. Incorporated Gold Label Barley Wine Co Ltd in 1958. Acquired by Whitbread & Co Ltd in 1962 when controlled about 700 licensed premises. In about 1970 changed name to Whitbread (Yorkshire) Ltd and shortly after to above. Ceased to be a trading subsidiary and changed name to Whitbread & Co Ltd during 1983.

Records: at Whitbread, Chiswell Street, London EC17 4SD
directors meeting minutes 1882-1983; management committee meeting minutes 1953-69; agm: minutes 1882-1984, attendance book 1946-61, directors registers 1925-68; members registers 1929-81; share: registers 1929-50, ledgers 1943-65, transfer registers 1961-date, transfer documents 1906-26, transfer correspondence 1961-74, certificates 1906-81; memo and articles of association 1958-64; mortgage register 1883-1964; debenture stock: deed 1946, certificates 1920-42; annual: returns 1954-9, reports and accounts 1952-60; balance sheets and accounts 1910-63; private ledger 1936-47; cash book 1955-60; sales: summaries 1950-9, balance books 1956, staff salaries books 1917-24,1942-55, travellers expenses book 1966-9; pension scheme: journal 1950-9, papers and correspondence 1950-69; brewing: books 1928-67, journals 1955-60, disposals book 1959-64, costs books 1955-67; production statistics 1945-72; beer: duty books 1965-75, stock books 1952-73; materials used book 1957-9; bottle and cases collected journal 1957-9; properties: ledger 1930-7, sinking fund book c1930; licensed premises

valuation ledger 1934-7; war damage claims register 1942 on; leases and tenancy agreements 1898-1939; calendar 1959

Gold Label Barley Wine Co Ltd: directors meeting minutes 1958-70; members register 1958-70; share certificate book 1958-68; annual returns 1959-69

408 UNILEVER UK HOLDINGS LTD

8 Jul 1882
17049
Unilever House, Blackfriars, London EC4P 4BQ
Industrial holding company (previously West African merchants)

History: created by George Taubman Goldie in 1879 as United African Co Ltd on amalgamation of various British trading interests on the Niger River, West Africa. Refused royal charter in 1881 but launched new company National African Co Ltd, incorporated in 1882 to purchase and develop business of older company. Founded many trading stations on Niger and by 1884 had bought out the French stations. British government declared Protectorate over large part of southern Nigeria in 1886 and granted company a royal charter. Changed its name in 1886 to Royal Niger Co Chartered & Ltd. Territory stretched from Forcades River to Nun mouth of Niger and extended for almost 1000 miles inland from both banks of the Niger and tributaries. Maintained a constabulary and abolished legal status of slavery in 1897. Surrendered charter in 1899 handing all administrative rights to HM Government, dropping 'Royal' and 'Chartered' from name and became purely a trading company. Made moderate profits up to 1920 slump in raw material prices. Bought by Lever Brothers Ltd, soap manufacturers, in 1920 and underwent reorganisation, many of Levers West African businesses being invested in the company, including Bathurst Trading Co Ltd (inc 1888); Cavall River Co Ltd (inc 1911); Cie Proprietaire du Kouitou Niaire SA (inc 1899); Richard & William King Ltd (est 1690); WB MacIver & Co Ltd (est 1875); Palm Oil Estates Managers Ltd; P Radcliffe & Co Ltd; Sedec SA; John Walkden & Co Ltd (est 1868); Apol Ltd; Bromport Steamship Co Ltd; African Oil Nuts Co Ltd; African Timber Co Ltd (est 1907); British West African Underwriters Ltd; Cie Francaise de la Côte d'Ivoire SA; Continental Overseas Trading Co Ltd; Gambia Trading Co Ltd (inc 1922); Lever Stores Ltd; Niger Mineral Development Co Ltd; Pickering & Berthoud Ltd; Thomas Brothers (Liverpool) Ltd; Trading Association of Nigeria Ltd; T Welsh & Co Ltd; Weeks Transport & Engineering Co Ltd; West African Motors Ltd; Voltaland Ltd. Seychelles Co Ltd and Niger Corporation Inc, USA, were registered in 1922. Merged in 1929 with old rivals African & Eastern Trading Corporation Ltd (est 1889) to form United Africa Co Ltd. In 1929 Lever Brothers Ltd merged with Margarine Unie of Holland to form Unilever Ltd and the Dutch company transferred all its West African trading companies to UAC Ltd which then controlled biggest proportion of West African trade. In 1930-1 capital and management was reorganised, staff reduced and superfluous branches and stations rationalized. By this time was mainly concerned with commodities but was also involved in shipping, river and motor transport, oil palm and rubber plantations, mining royalties, cold storage depots, automobile and agricultural machinery agencies, cotton ginning, tank installations and timber concessions in Nigeria, the Zaire, Togo and Benin and Shana. In 1960s faced with changes in Africa, it altered operations from general to specialised trading and then to manufacturing of timber, coach-building, furniture, beer etc. Name subsequently changed to above when it became holding company for UK subsidiaries of Unilever Ltd. Registered as private company.

Records (1): at UAC, UAC House, Blackfriars Road, London SE1 9UG
directors report 1929; members and mortgage register 1906-09; treaties and land agreements with correspondence and papers 1884-98; charter documents and papers 1884-99; profit pooling and trading agreements 1899-1918; correspondence and papers with banks 1910-14; share correspondence and papers 1914-20; memo and articles of association 1908; regulations and circulars 1882-99; revenue memo 1895; agents reports 1886-8; administrative and commercial circulars 1886-99; trading correspondence 1887-1921; trading memos 1892,1895; plan of Guri and Rabba 1901; steamers and Akassa workshop machinery valuation 1882; papers re river vessels c1890; stations: value and maps logbook 1898-1914, index nd; photographs of stations, staff, bungalows, boats, premises etc c1884-1930; coast staff agreement form c1890; kit instructions nd; staff index nd; administrative correspondence 1885-97; constabulary: men and officers lists and rolls 1886-99, expedition lists 1886-99, Akassa Rising report 1885, Bula Expedition report 1899, Badiko Expedition correspondence 1903-05, proceedings, notes, correspondence and reports on ammunition, guns, promotions, stores etc 1895-9; service reports 1897-1905; applications, correspondence and lists re medal issue 1897-1901; historical notes on company 1884-1951

Records (2): at Unilever, Unilever House, Blackfriars, London EC4P 4BQ
directors and general meeting minutes 1954-73; mortgage and charge register c1901-30; members register and share ledger c1931-61; directors: registers 1920-73, lists 1920-9, administration proclamation 1886; share papers and documents 1933-8; debenture stock papers, documents and correspondence 1925-33; memo and articles of association 1882-1973; annual reports and accounts 1882-1946

Records (3): at Public Record Office, Ruskin Avenue, Kew, Richmond, Surrey TW9 4DU
charter documents, papers and correspondence 1885-99; treaties with local chiefs 1886-98; report and papers re administration of company's territories 1890; memo and articles of association 1882

Charles Wilson, *The History of Unilever: A Study in Economic Growth and Social Change* Vol 1-3 (1954,1968)

409 PROVINCIAL BANK OF IRELAND LTD

10 Aug 1882
17050
Abacus House, 33 Gutter Lane, Cheapside, London EC2
Banking

History: founded by Thomas Joplin in London in 1824 mainly by British subscribers as the best means of introducing British capital into Ireland. Branch banks were established in Cork, Waterford, Eire and Belfast, N Ireland. Incorporated under deed of settlement in 1825, and re-registered as above with limited liability in 1882. In 1952 head office was transferred from London to Dublin, Eire. In 1966 number of branches exceeded 105 excluding sub-offices. In the same year, merged with Munster & Leinster Bank Ltd and Royal Bank of Ireland Ltd (est 1836) to form Allied Irish Banks Ltd.

Records: at Allied Irish Banks, 3-4 Foster Place, Dublin, Eire
meeting minutes: directors 1824-1966, committee 1825-1966; share ledgers etc 1826-1966; registers: seal 1921-66, bonds and deeds 1857-1966; annual report and accounts 1826-1966; profit and loss accounts 1910-66; ledgers 1825-1966; note issue records 1825-1954; premises records nd; officers registers 1825-1966

410 READING & CAVERSHAM LAUNDRY CO LTD

21 Jul 1882
17103
78 George Street, Caversham, Reading, Berkshire RG4 8DJ
Laundry

History: incorporated as above in 1882 by a group of Basingstoke businessmen to build a laundry designed by Thomas & Taylor, architects, in George Street, Caversham, Berkshire. From 1884 undertook carpet cleaning as well as domestic laundry and in 1887 purchased Mr Scull's patent dry cleaning process in conjunction with the laundries in Newbury, Berkshire; Oxford, Oxfordshire; and Basingstoke, Hampshire. Premises were doubled in size in 1895. In early 1980s still undertook domestic laundry and dry cleaning although a third of its business was in contract laundry and garment hire to industry, schools and hotels. Subsidiary of H Tomlins Ltd of Slough, Berkshire.

Records: at Reading & Caversham Laundry, 78 George Street, Caversham, Reading, Berkshire RG4 8DJ
directors and general meeting minutes 1882-1906; annual report and accounts 1885-1905; laundry book, post 1939; advertisements 1940s; photographs of premises, plant, transport, staff, production processes, displays 1910-50s

411 BASMA TRADE PROTECTION SERVICES (INC)

28 Sep 1882
17357
84-88 Great Eastern Street, London EC2V 7DS
Trade association

History: mutual association, incorporated in 1882 as Boot & Shoe Manufacturers Association & Leather Trades' Protection Society as a company limited by guarantee to protect members against persons unworthy of mercantile credit, promote the prosecution of fraudulent debtors, effect the payment of debts due to members, and support legislation for the protection of traders. In 1980 changed name to above and became a trade protection society for all trades with a section for the leather trade. In 1984 had about 1000 members.

Records: at Basma Trade Protection Services, 84-88 Great Eastern Street, London EC2V 7DS
corporate records 1940 on

412 LONDON JOINT STOCK BANK LTD

30 Sep 1882
17361
3 Princes Street, Mansion House, London EC4
Banking

History: formed in 1836 by renowned City men and began business in Coleman Street. New premises built in Princes Street in 1837. Acquired the London agency of several provincial banks and entered into mutual agency agreements with North American banks. In 1840 acquired business of Wright & Co (est pre 1759) of Covent Garden, which became West End branch of bank, subsequently moving to Pall Mall. Opened branches in Chancery Lane in 1866, Southwark in 1870, West Smithfield and Copenhagen cattle markets on purchase of Albion Bank Ltd (est 1864) in 1870, and Paddington in 1872. Incorporated as above in 1882. Imperial Bank (est 1862) was acquired in 1892 and by 1900, 35 new branches had been opened. In 1909 amalgamated with York City & County Banking Co Ltd (est 1830) which added c180 branches and sub-branches to its metropolitan base and took it into the top 10 banks in England and Wales, with over 250 offices. Number of branches in London and Yorkshire was increased, as well as 2 branches being opened in Norfolk and 1 in Portsmouth, bringing total to 310 by 1917. Amalgamated with London City & Midland Bank Ltd in 1918 to form London Joint City & Midland Bank Ltd, which was shortened to Midland Bank Ltd in 1923.

Records: at Midland Bank, Poultry, London EC2P 2BX
board meeting minutes 1836-1917; departments committee meeting minutes 1899-1905; house committee meeting minutes 1909-18; shareholders meeting minutes 1837-1918; deeds of settlement 1836-68; amalgamation and liquidation papers 1918-66; annual reports 1837-1918; profit and loss account ledger 1836-41; balances: daily 1836-55, weekly 1855-79, monthly 1848-65; general ledgers 1908-16; private ledgers 1842-1924; signature books 1836-71; deposit account signature indices 1859-81; country office standing orders 1840-98; counter order books 1842-73; accounts analysis 1909-19; staff regulations 1879-1900; cricket club minutes 1872-1900; leases register 1872-97; Lord Harlech diary extracts 1892; branches - Knaresborough: managers reports 1901-20; Lambeth: directors attendance book 1911-19; Leadenhall Street: salaries register 1889-1920; Limehouse: counter orders 1898-1912, signature book 1898-1923, security register 1909-29; Lothbury: counter orders 1893-1918; Pall Mall: balance sheet abstracts 1864-1911, general ledger 1840-50, mandate book 1841-8, letter book 1859, salary book 1903-20; St Mary Axe: letter book 1901-12; St James's Street: mandates 1902-21

WF Crick and JE Wadsworth, *A Hundred Years of Joint Stock Banking* (1936)

413 MARTINS BANK LTD

11 Oct 1882
17409
54 Lombard Street, London EC3P 3AH
Banking

History: established as Bank of Liverpool in 1831. Registered with reserved liability in 1882. Acquired Arthur Heywood, Sons & Co of Liverpool (est 1773) in 1883; Liverpool Commercial Banking Co (est 1832) in 1889; Wakefield, Crewdson & Co of Kendal, Cumbria (est 1840) in

1893; Craven Bank Ltd of Skipton, W Yorkshire, and Settle, N Yorkshire (est 1791) in 1906; Carlisle & Cumberland Banking Co Ltd (est 1880) in 1911; and North Eastern Banking Co Ltd of Newcastle upon Tyne, Northumberland (est 1872) in 1914. In 1918 acquired Martin's Bank Ltd of Lombard Street, London, which had been founded as Martin & Co in c1712, had been known as Martin, Stone & Co between 1769 and 1851, had been renamed Martin & Co in 1851, and became Martin's Bank Ltd in 1891. Enlarged bank was then renamed Bank of Liverpool & Martins Ltd. Acquired Cocks, Biddulph & Co of Charing Cross, London (est 1757) and Palatine Bank Ltd of Manchester; Greater Manchester (est 1899) in 1919; Halifax Commercial Banking Co Ltd (est 1810) in 1920; Cattle Trade Bank Ltd (est 1920) in 1923; Equitable Bank Ltd of Halifax, W Yorkshire (est 1913) in 1927; and Lancashire & Yorkshire Bank Ltd of Manchester (est 1872) in 1928. Name changed to above in 1928, when there were 560 branches and £83 million in deposits. Acquired British Mutual Bank Ltd (est 1857) in 1951. In 1968 the above was amalgamated with Barclays Bank Ltd.

Records (1): at Barclays Bank, 54 Lombard Street, London EC3P 3AH
board: meeting minutes 1918-68, letters 1920, attendance books 1918-54; partnership agreements 1714-91; articles of association 1918-31; amalgamation papers 1918; annual report and accounts 1918-68; balance sheets: 1731-1842, 1891-1918, weekly 1891-1939; profit and loss books 1755-70; ledgers: general 1796-1873, foreign exchange 1913-20, discount 1909-13, foreign customer account 1911-12, deposit account 1923-30, accepted bill 1920-3; balance books: daily cash 1729-1852, general 1746-82; discount books 1731-5; receipt books 1744-75; signature books 1811-1912; customer: ledgers 1772-1930, weekly balances 1847-71; registers: safe custody 1827-40, security 1896-1932, war loan 1917; bills discounted 1802-15; bad and doubtful debt books 1850-1926; securities 1891-1932; accounts and information books 1812-44; extensive papers re customers, securities, and bankruptcy, including prospectuses, articles of association, legal cases, correspondence etc 19 cent; accounts, papers of Stone family and Blackwell 1862-1909; staff guarantees and letters 1881-1918; clerk registers 1882-1919; staff managers' circulars 1940-5; widows and orphans fund minutes and rules 1922-58; superannuation fund meeting minutes 1940-58; head office building committee meeting minutes 1926-33; plans, deeds and specifications re premises 1748, 1798-1944; letter books 1714-1916; head office circulars 1919-31; Cocks, Biddulph: account ledger 1920, interview book 1930-3, staff letter book 1920-2, head office letters 1920-8

Records (2): at Public Record Office, Ruskin Avenue, Kew, Richmond, Surrey TW9 4DU
papers re amalgamation with Lancashire & Yorkshire Bank and Equitable Bank 1928

414 SUN PAPER MILL CO LTD

13 Oct 1882
17419
83 Piccadilly, London W1A 1EJ
Paper manufacturers

History: incorporated as above in 1882 to carry on the manufacture of paper at Feniscowles, near Blackburn, Lancashire. Acquired in 1960 by Albert E Reed & Co Ltd which became Reed International Ltd in 1970. Ceased to trade in 1963.

Records: at Reed International, 83 Piccadilly, London W1A 1EJ
directors meeting minutes and agendas 1962-date; general meeting minutes 1962-date;

directors register 1972-date; secretarys register 1966-date; mortgage register 1958-date; annual returns 1971-date; articles of association 1955; corporate correspondence 1955-date; annual report and accounts 1978-81

415 MEPC (LIVERPOOL) LTD

19 Oct 1882
17428
Brook House, 113 Park Lane, London W1Y 4AY
Property

History: in 1853 Liverpool Stock Exchange (est 1836) secured the lease on premises on west side of Exchange Buildings which were leased in order to raise funds to build a new Stock Exchange. Bought land in Dale Street and new premises opened in 1879. In 1882 Liverpool Stock Exchange Building Co Ltd was incorporated to take over the land and maintenance of the buildings, its capital being divided amongst members of the exchange who alone qualified as shareholders. Also rented offices, shops and store rooms in the building. Acquired in 1965 by MEPC Ltd for development, and name changed to above. However, planning permission was denied and the building sold.

Records (1): at MEPC, Brook House, 113 Park Lane, London W1Y 4AY
directors and general meeting minutes 1964-date; takeover circular 1964; company registration papers 1964-date

Records (2): at Liverpool Stock Exchange, Silkhouse Court, Tighebarne Street, Liverpool, Merseyside
pension scheme trust deeds 1952-69; tenancy agreements, leases etc for Imperial Buildings 1931-72

416 SALISBURY DIOCESAN BOARD OF FINANCE

24 Oct 1882
17442
Church House, Crane Street, Salisbury, Wiltshire SP1 2QB
Church finance

History: formed to collect, receive and distribute funds for diocesan societies and to act as trustees of money or property given or bequeathed to the Church of England within the diocese. Incorporated in 1882 as a company limited by guarantee.

Records: at Wiltshire Record Office, County Hall, Trowbridge, Wiltshire BA14 8JG

417 LIVERPOOL UNDERWRITERS' ASSOCIATION

7 Nov 1882
17497
Derby House, Exchange Buildings, Liverpool, Merseyside L2 3QG
Underwriters

History: established in Liverpool in 1802, originally as an association of merchants, shipowners, marine insurance brokers and underwriters. Compiled a register of Liverpool shipping from 1815 until 1845 when the register was amalgamated with Lloyd's Register. After

1860 the new Liverpool marine insurance companies were also represented. In 20 cent has provided an information service for the Liverpool marine insurance market, including a statistical service. Affiliated to Institute of London Underwriters in 1971.

Records: at Liverpool Underwriters' Association, Derby House, Exchange Buildings, Liverpool, Merseyside L2 3QG
meeting minutes: committee and general 1802-date, case 1912-44, sub-committee, prizes, and legal bills 1893-1946; committee members details c1802-1963; rules and regulations book 1812-1900; annual report and accounts 1864-date; cash book 1970-81; subscription lists for memorials and charities 1901-79; letter books 1819-1918; McNeill prize trustee announcements, candidates, winners, conditions, papers etc 1908-77; Wallace prize papers 1919-77; strangers introduction book 1887-1956; premises photographs c1937-56; handbook 1892-c1922; history booklet and press cuttings 1901-02; International Union of Marine Underwriters meeting minutes 1946-60

418 SHAW SAVILL & ALBION CO LTD

10 Nov 1882
17518
52 Leadenhall Street, London EC3A 2BJ
Shipping

History: established as Shaw Savill & Co in 1858 by Robert Shaw and Walter Savill, to specialise in the New Zealand trade. Gained part of New Zealand government contract for a regular mail, passenger and cargo service between UK and New Zealand. In stiff competition for many years with Albion Line (est 1834) operated by Robert Henderson and James Galbraith. Firms amalgamated in 1882 to form limited company as above with John Potter (later Lord Ritchie) as manager. Introduced refrigerated ships in 1882. In 1902 became associated with White Star Line run by Oceanic Steam Navigation Co Ltd, a member of International Mercantile Marine Co syndicate and began to operate a joint service. In 1905 became major shareholders, with White Star Line, in Aberdeen Line. Royal Mail Group under Lord Kylsant purchased White Star Line in 1926 and the major shareholding in the company in 1928, but after the group's collapse in 1931, the above became part of Furness Withy & Co Ltd in 1933. Inaugurated a new fast passenger and cargo service to New Zealand via the Cape and Australia in 1939. In the post war era many new vessels were designed without passenger accommodation but in 1955 *Southern Cross* was built solely for passengers, with one-class accommodation, to operate on a new round the world route. Joined by her sister ship *Northern Star* in 1962 and maintained 8 round the world sailings a year until the decline in the passenger trade in the early 1970s. The passenger office in Haymarket, London closed in 1975. In 1977 had fleet of 26 vessels, aggregating 182,800 gross tons.

Records: at National Maritime Museum, Manuscripts Section, Greenwich, London SE10 9NF
correspondence files re new vessel building and trials, ships in service, standard freight rates and routine instructions to masters 1924-65; passage money: summaries and passengers numbers 1900-46, analyses outward 1946-60, 1970-2, analyses homeward 1965-8; refrigerator and engine logs 1956-62; deck logs 1944-65

Alan Mitchell, *Splendid Sisters, A Story of the Planning, Construction and Operation of the Shaw Savill Liners* (1966)

419 GARSON BLAKE & SON LTD

21 Nov 1882
17567
59A North Quay, Great Yarmouth, Norfolk NR30 1JB
Builders' merchants

History: incorporated in 1882 with nominal capital of £5000 to acquire the business of Garson Blake & Son, coal merchant, shipowner and dealer in bricks, lime, cement and other materials, at Great Yarmouth, Norfolk. In 1980s continued to operate as builders' merchants and was still under the leadership of the Blake family.

Records (1): at Garson Blake & Son, 59A North Quay, Great Yarmouth, Norfolk NR30 1JB
general meeting minutes 1883-1978; balances 1917-50; profit and loss account 1927-63; ledgers: private 1914-47, general investment 1927-52; journal: 1941-61, creditors 1930-67, purchase 1954-8, sales 1938-55; cash book: 1914-67, petty 1937-60; daybooks 1937-63; sales: summaries 1921-35, brick 1936-53; catalogues 1921-40; cost price register c1910-24; papers re prices, petrol, supply, brick controls etc 1940-5; insurance: registers 1918-65, ledger 1919-65, cash book 1926-64; staff: correspondence 1934-46, Christmas gifts 1901-72

Records (2): at Norfolk Record Office, Central Library, Norwich, Norfolk NR2 1NJ
ledger 1913-26; coal: truck book 1895-1946, journal 1910-46; sales journal 1918-43; sales accounts 1927-36; day books 1900-02,1927-41; cash sales book 1911-12,1941-63; building materials sold 1913; journal: steamers 1904-6, insurance 1910-28
Great Yarmouth Transport Co Ltd: share ledger 1903-18

420 JOHNSONS-HPL (HOLDINGS) LTD

26 Nov 1882
17581
14 Priestley Way, London NW2 7TN
Photographic materials manufacturer

History: in 1743 Richard Wright established a goldsmith's business in Maiden Lane, London. His apprentice, John Johnson eventually took over the business, becoming the first private and independent assayer in the City of London. In 1829 the business moved to Basinghall Street, and in 1831 George R Johnson, grandson, became assayer to Bank of England and Royal Mint. Johnson & Sons also began to manufacture silver and gold chemical salts for Fox-Talbot photographic process. In 1873 firm moved to Croft Street, Finsbury Circus, becoming incorporated in 1882 as Johnson & Sons, Manufacturing Chemists Ltd, while the assay business was formed into a separate company. By 1900 the popularity of photography was well established and the company supplied both pre-packed solutions, and materials for amateur and professional photographers. With the outbreak of WW1 came a demand for organic developers; the company built a warehouse in Hendon and supplied photographic chemicals to Royal Naval Air Service and Royal Flying Corps. In 1927 the offices moved to the factory in Hendon, and in 1948 company's name changed to Johnsons of Hendon Ltd. In 1940 company acquired the photographic equipment business of Ensign Ltd. In 1953 name changed to Johnsons of Hendon (Holdings) Ltd and became the holding company for Johnsons of Hendon Ltd, Fotoco Ltd, Houghtons (Holborn) Ltd and Kosmos Photographics (Holdings) Ltd. In the early 1970s the group was acquired by Hestair Co Ltd and underwent major restructuring involving the abandonment of chemical production in 1974. In 1977 the group was purchased by Eumig, the Austrian cine camera manufacturer, and in 1981 was bought by its directors. In 1984 the company was known as above.

Records: at Johnsons of Hendon, 14 Priestley Way, London NW2 7TN
directors and general meeting: minutes 1882-1939, agendas 1914-20, meeting reports 1928-31; register: mortgages 1890-1921, members 1882-1920, directors 1901; annual report and accounts 1960-2; ledger: 1914-17, private 1882-c1930, 'M' 1901-09; journal: 1926-7,1953-72, private 1916-24; cash book: 1926-7, building 1890-2; sales accounts 1912-14; price lists and catalogues c1913-55; trade-mark certificates 1902-26; assay: records 1785-1892, fees for analysis 1875, cash journals 1785-6; letter books: private 1876-1918, directors 1908-18, P Maw's 1908-18; Hendon Lodge specifications 1915; sketches of warehouse 1883; photographs: Macclesfield premises 1961-2, processes, staff, social and works 1933-56; visitors book 1933-42

421 JOHN BOYD & CO LTD

13 Dec 1882
17642
Higher Flax Mills, Castle Cary, Somerset BA7 7DY
Horsehair weavers

History: incorporated as above in 1882 to take over business of horsehair weavers established by John Boyd in 1837. Company purchased factory and goodwill for £9000. Machinery included 120 power looms. In 1923 employed 95 staff with branches in London, Glasgow, Manchester, Paris, Oslo and Sydney. In 1950 merged with TS Donne & Sons, also horsehair manufacturers, and production concentrated at Higher Flax Mills. By 1984 had 60 looms and exported cloth to Germany, Italy, France and Japan and were the only horsehair weavers in England.

Records: at John Boyd, Higher Flax Mills, Castle Cary, Somerset BA7 7DY
directors and general meeting minutes 1898-1942; share: ledger 1883-1965, certificates 1890-1954, receipts 1884-1918; prospectus 1882; balance: sheets 1937-54, book 1934-56; private ledger 1956-64; journal 1915-55; cash books 1944-66; sales abstracts 1944-53; day book 1951-6; catalogue c1970; patent 1872; stock lists 1942-56; photographs: machinery and staff c1969
TS Donne & Sons: directors meeting minutes 1926-45; memo and articles of association 1926; annual report and accounts 1958-60; balance sheets 1930s-50s; receipt book 1877-1924; loom catalogue c1900,1935; photographs of trade stands and rope walk 1935-47; stock lists 1924-5,1954; inventory Higher Flax Mill 1941; history 1934,1947; Somerset County Rugby Football Union letter book 1897-1909
Donne & Marsden Ltd: members register 1951-63; balance sheets 1957-60; private ledger 1951-63; cash book 1951-63

422 CHUBB & SON LTD

14 Dec 1882
17652
Manor House, Manor Lane, Feltham, Greater London TW13 4JQ
Security equipment

History: established at Portsea, Hampshire by Charles Chubb (1772-1846) following the granting in 1818 of a patent to his brother Jeremiah for detector lock. Charles moved to London in 1827 to open a shop at 57 St Paul's Church Yard and in 1830 he began manufacturing locks in Wolverhampton, W Midlands, originally in Temple Street, moving to St James's Square in 1835 and to Old Mill Lane, Horsely Fields in 1841. Charles patented his first safe in 1835 and by 1846 the firm's safe manufactory was established at 27 Cow Cross Street, Smithfield, London. Branches were opened in Manchester in 1838 and Liverpool in 1839. John Chubb (1815-72) joined his father in partnership in 1841 and carried on the business after the latter's death. The safe factory moved to Glengall Road, off Old Kent Road, Camberwell in 1867. Wolverhampton lock works moved to Glengall Road works in 1882, returning to the old premises in Horsely Fields in 1889. After John Chubb's death the business was carried on by his executors and his sons John Charles (1846-99) and George Hayter Chubb (1848-1946, later Lord Hayter). The business was incorporated as Chubb & Son Lock & Safe Co Ltd with GH Chubb as chairman in 1882. A new showroom was opened at 68 St James's Street, London in 1874 and in 1877 the head offices were moved to 128 Queen Victoria Street, London, 57 St Paul's Church Yard being re-opened for the sale of ecclesiastical metal work and furnishings by the end of the year. Trading began in South Africa in 1890, Chubb & Maxwell Ltd, being incorporated in 1895. Chubb's Australian Co Ltd was set up in Sydney in 1897. A new lock works was built in Wolverhampton with frontages to Railway Street and Chubb Street and opened in 1899. Auxiliary safe works were built on Railway Street and opened in 1900. A new safe works was built at Wednesfield Road, Wolverhampton and opened in 1909, the London works being transferred north immediately and the Railway Street safe works in 1916. A safe, strong room and bronze work factory was built in Sydney, Australia in 1921. Chubb-France SA was formed in 1922 and Chubb India Ltd in 1926. The Railway Street lock works moved to new lock works at Wednesfield Road in 1938. Enemy action in 1941 totally destroyed the company's head offices which moved to St James's Street and then to 40-42 Oxford Street, London in 1946, 175-176 Tottenham Court Road, London in 1955 and to 14-22 Tottenham Street, London in 1960. Lord Hayter retired in 1940 to be succeeded by his nephew Harry Emory Chubb (1880-1960). The company went public with authorised capital of £220,000 in 1948. Began manufacturing security equipment in Johannesburg, South Africa in 1950 and in Toronto, Canada in 1954. Acquired Hobbs Hart & Co Ltd (est 1852, inc 1887), lock and safe manufacturers in 1956. Its factory at Staffa Road, Leyton, London continued to manufacture locks until Sep 1963 and safes until Dec 1983. HE Chubb retired in 1957 and was succeeded as chairman by George CH Chubb (later Lord Hayter). Purchased security goodwill of Chatwood-Milner Ltd, established in 1955 on the merger of Chatwood Safe & Engineering Co Ltd (est 1854) of Bolton, Greater Manchester and Milner's Safe Co Ltd (est 1830) of Speke, Merseyside and Shrewsbury, Salop. Changed name to above in 1958 and became holding company for whole group. Formed Chubb-Mosler & Taylor Safes Ltd in 1960 on the merger of the 2 largest safe manufacturers in Canada. In 1961 formed New Zealand company which had factories at Wellington and Auckland by 1964 and Zimbabwean company began manufacturing in Harare in 1962. Acquired International Coin Counting Co Ltd (inc 1909) and Middleton Tool & Engineering Co Ltd both of Enfield, Greater London in 1961 and 1962 respectively; Burgot Alarms Ltd (est 1935), audible and silent burglar alarm manufacturers in 1962; Read & Campbell Ltd (inc 1881), fire extinguisher manufacturers of Horsham, W Sussex and Josiah Parkes & Sons (Holdings) Ltd (est 1840), 'Union Locks' doors, door fittings and related hardware manufacturers of Willenhall, W

Midlands in 1965; Pyrene Co Ltd (est 1914), fire protection equipment and detection equipment specialists of Brentford and the oldest Belgian safe manufacturers Laurent Fraigneux SA (est 1835) in 1967; Samuel Jones & Co (Engineering) Ltd (est 1910), fire fighting appliance manufacturers of Peckham, London in 1968; Albert Marston & Co Ltd, aluminium door and window fittings manufacturers of Willenhall in 1969; Lips & Gipsen NV (est 1871), safe and office equipment manufacturers of the Netherlands in 1971; CE Marshall (Wolverhampton) Ltd, car locking mechanism manufacturers in 1972; Marfig Nederland BV, marine fire fighting equipment manufacturers in 1975; Gross Cash Registers Ltd, cash register manufacturers in 1977; L&F Willenhall Ltd, vehicle lock manufacturers in 1977; and Fire Kill International Ltd, sprinkler specialists in 1984. Head offices moved to Manor Lane, Feltham, Greater London in 1980. Ceased cash register manufacture in 1981. Lord Hayter retired in 1981 and was succeeded by the first non Chubb family chairman. Re-registered under 1980 Companies Act as a public limited company in 1982. Acquired by Racal Electronics PLC in Oct 1984.

Records: at Chubb & Son, Manor House, Manor Lane, Feltham, Greater London TW13 4JQ directors and general meeting minutes 1941-date; board reports 1968-75; managing directors conference papers 1957,1968-9; share: registers and papers 1940s-date, correspondence 1883-1903; memo and articles of association 1882-date; corporate agreements and papers 1882-date; agency agreements 1842-1917; annual reports and accounts 1883-date; balance sheets and accounts 1882-date; group ratio accounts 1959-date; ledgers: 1874-82, private 1859-81, sundries 1882-3; day books 1827-30,1917-22; cash books 1882; works cost sheets 1954-77; tax papers and correspondence 1842-80; bank pass book 1840-2; cheques, account statements and bills of exchange 1844-85; order books: 1846,1881-2, factory 1871-1959, branches 1893-1934; sale: reports, correspondence and papers 1879-date, catalogues, price lists and literature c1852-date; test reports and papers 1913-72; exhibition and product photographs 1880s-date; promotional films 1959-c70; salaries books 1877-89; staff: agreements and papers 1845-84,1963-71, directories 1960s-date, training papers 1957-75, photographs c1890-date, dinner menus 1957-71; safe makers strike papers 1897; pension fund reports 1960-date; house magazines and internal memo 1946-date; factory minutes 1871-1925; safe number registers: 1847-66,1951-3, microfilm 1847-date; lock number registers 1819-1936; safe deposit number register 1900-40; manufacturing reports 1960-70; patents and specifications 1820-1976; trade-mark papers and correspondence 1877-1931; title deeds and documents 1814-1979; property photographs 1880s-date; legal case papers 1876-93; collectanea-newscuttings, land bills, correspondence, advertisements and invitations etc c1825-date; Chubb family papers, correspondence, photographs and publications 1843-1981; diaries: Charles Chubb 1837, GH Chubb 1865; HW Chubb letter book 1888-9; competitors sales literature etc 1830s-date; historical articles, booklets and correspondence on company, locks, safe and security 1850-date

Burgot Automatic Alarms Ltd: directors and general meeting minutes 1948-78; members register 1957-82; share certificate book 1945-57; corporate correspondence and papers 1965-82; annual reports and accounts 1977-81; premises plans and leases 1948-60s

Burgot Automatic Alarms (Overseas) Ltd: directors and general meeting minutes 1923-78; members register 1923-82; memo and articles of association 1965-75; corporate correspondence and papers 1965-82; annual reports and accounts 1977-81

Central Station Signals Ltd: directors and general meeting minutes 1954-78; members register 1963-82; memo and articles of association 1969-75; corporate correspondence and papers 1965-82; annual reports and accounts 1977-81

Chatwood Safe Co Ltd: (See summary no 198 - Shrewsbury Tool & Die Co)

Chatwood-Milner Ltd: safe and strong room: specifications and drawings 1958-71, photographs 1958-70s; order book 1968-71; sales catalogues, price lists and literature 1958-75; exhibition photographs 1958-71; sales staff papers and correspondence 1959-68; burglar attack reports 1967-8

Chubb Alarms Ltd: directors and general meeting minutes 1968-78; executive committee meeting minutes and papers 1980-2; members registers 1960-82; memo and articles of association 1977; seal registers 1968-83; annual reports and accounts 1978-81; insurance: register 1976-82, papers 1970s-80s; contract papers and correspondence 1976-80; premises leases plans and papers 1960s-80s; pension papers 1972-80s; photographs 1960s-date; subsidiary companies corporate and financial papers 1969 on; newscuttings and advertisements 1978-date

Chubb Alarms Group Ltd: directors and general meeting minutes 1973-8; members registers 1971-81; memo and articles of association 1977; seals register 1973-83; corporate correspondence and papers 1976-81; annual report and accounts 1977-81; premises leases and plans 1948-60s; pension committee and trustee meeting minutes and papers 1976-81; staff council meeting minutes and papers 1978-80

Chubb Fire Security Ltd: directors meeting minutes 1950s-date; management reports 1972; annual reports and accounts nd; corporate documents 1959-date; catalogues 1960s-date; photographs 1960s on; newscuttings and advertisements 1978-date; history 1981

Chubb Home Protection Ltd: directors and general meeting minutes 1969-82; executive committee meeting minutes 1978-9; memo and articles of association 1969; seal register 1977-81; corporate correspondence and papers 1977-82; annual reports and accounts 1977-81

Chubb India Ltd: annual reports and accounts 1928-35; memo and articles of association 1926; annual returns 1928-36; price lists 1905-13

Chubb & Maxwell Ltd: prospectus 1898,1903; share papers 1903-13; memo and articles of association 1894-1950; agency agreements 1894-1917; annual reports and accounts 1897-1954; balance sheets and accounts 1940-52; summaries: account 1935-48, results 1950-3

Chubb-Mosler Taylor Safes Ltd: sales catalogues, price lists and literature 1950s-74

Chubb Panorama Ltd: sales catalogues 1960s-date

Chubb Security Installations Ltd: sales catalogues 1960s-70s

Chubb & Son Lock & Safe Co Ltd: sales catalogues 1958-date

Chubb & Son Lock & Safe Co (SA) (Pty) Ltd: managing director reports 1974; balance sheets and accounts 1952-66; sales catalogues and literature 1950s-67; house magazine 1965-81; history articles 1966-70; newscuttings 1981-date

Chubb Wardens Ltd: members register 1972-81; memo and articles of association 1972; seals register 1977-82; annual reports and accounts 1977-81; contract papers 1976-80; insurance papers 1970s-80s

Chubb's Australian Co Ltd: annual reports and accounts 1899-1950; assets notes 1947; works report 1975; sales literature 1921-c34; product photographs 1920s; house magazines 1967-8,1981; newscuttings and advertisements 1981-date

Dunhelm Security Services Ltd: members register etc 1974-82; memo and articles of association 1974; acquisition papers 1975-81; annual accounts 1981
Hobbs Hart & Co Ltd: (See summary no 563)
ICC Machinery Ltd: sales catalogues and literature 1960-70; newscuttings and articles 1978-84
Lips & Gipsen NV: sales catalogues and literature 1960s-80s
Milners Safe Co Ltd: (See summary no 198 - Shrewsbury Tool & Die Co)
Minimax Ltd: annual reports and accounts 1920s-60s; sales catalogues 1960s-70s; photographs 20 cent
Josiah Parkes & Sons (Holdings) Ltd: memo and articles of association 1936; reports 1971; sales catalogues and literature 1964-date; history booklets and correspondence 1934-date; newscuttings and advertisements 1981-date
Rampart Engineering Co Ltd: memo and articles of association 1929; balance sheet and accounts 1973; photographs 1940s on; newscuttings 1981-4
Read & Campbell Ltd: annual reports and accounts 1950s-70s; sales catalogues c1960s-70s; photographs 20 cent
Rely-a-Bell Alarms Ltd: directors and general meeting minutes 1961-78; members register 1959-75; share certificates book 1959-71; corporate papers and correspondence 1965-82; memo and articles of association 1921-75; annual report and accounts 1977-81; sales catalogues 1960s; photographs 1940s
Rely-a-Bell Grilles Ltd: members register 1975-82; memo and articles of association 1969-75; annual reports and accounts 1977-81
Steelage Industries Ltd: meeting minutes 1965-6; reports, papers and correspondence 1962-7

Noel Currer-Briggs, *Contemporary Observations on Security from the Chubb Collections 1818-1968* (priv pub 1968)
Chubb Fire Security Ltd, *Ten Years of Chubb Fire, A Background From 1881* (priv pub 1981)

423 OLDHAM & DISTRICT INCORPORATED CHAMBER OF COMMERCE

12 Jan 1883
17772
Civic Centre, Oldham, Greater Manchester OL1 1UT
Chamber of commerce

History: founded largely by the efforts of SR Platt, mechanical engineer, and incorporated as a company limited by guarantee in 1883 as Oldham Incorporated Chamber of Commerce to protect and promote trade, commerce and manufactures in Oldham. By end of first year had 121 members. From inception was involved in training schemes and commercial education and was instrumental in setting up British Cotton Growing Association in 1902. Changed name to above in 1919 and set up Junior Chamber of Commerce in 1928. In 1983 ran information and other services for members as well as certifying export and other documentation, observing legislative developments on behalf of members and acting as an independent voice of local business.

Records: at Oldham & District Incorporated Chamber of Commerce, 94 Werneth Hall Road, Oldham, Greater Manchester OL8 4AX
council and general meeting minutes and papers 1882-date; sub-committee reports 1916-65; memo and articles of association 1883-1949; annual report and accounts 1883-date; general ledgers 1883-1948; cash books 1922-53; members: lists 1883-date, subscription book 1915-46;

Year Book 1918; annual and special dinner menus 1886-date; Junior Chamber of Commerce: meeting minutes and agendas 1937-62, committee meeting minutes 1928-32,1959-65

424 SOUTH EAST HAMPSHIRE CHAMBER OF COMMERCE & INDUSTRY

10 Feb 1883
17877
27 Guildhall Walk, Portsmouth, Hampshire PO1 2RP
Chamber of commerce

History: established in 1879 as Port of Portsmouth Chamber of Commerce to promote trade, commerce, shipping and manufactures of the town. Incorporated as a company limited by guarantee in 1883. Catered mainly for wholesale and retail traders until new manufacturing industries moved into the area after WW2. By the 1970s a third of its members were industrialists and its catchment area stretched over south east Hampshire. Chamber reorganised to reflect changes and name changed to above. Issued bi-monthly news-letters. Original premises in Commercial Road, Portsmouth.

Records (1): at South East Hampshire Chamber of Commerce & Industry, 27 Guildhall Walk, Portsmouth, Hampshire PO1 2RP
directors meeting minutes 1949-date; corporate documents 1883-1975; annual reports and accounts 1949-date; monthly journal 1947-63; *Tradewind* - magazine 1972 on; trade and tourist directories and lists c1915-date

Records (2): at Portsmouth City Records Office, 3 Museum Road, Portsmouth, Hampshire PO1 2LE
directors meeting minutes 1879-1949; management committee meeting minutes 1921-43; sub-committee meeting minutes 1917-50; annual reports and accounts 1879-1949

425 OLD ROAD & LOVE LANE REFORM CLUB LAND & BUILDING CO LTD

19 Feb 1883
17918
45 Old Road, Heaton Norris, Stockport, Greater Manchester SK4 1TD
Political club-house

History: incorporated as above in 1883 to acquire land in Heaton Norris and to erect a club-house for political purposes. Land in Oxford Road was purchased for £400 and club-house rented to Reform Club for £50 per annum. In 1984 company rented premises to Heaton Norris Liberal Club.

Records: at Old Road & Love Lane Reform Club Land & Building, 45 Old Road, Heaton Norris, Stockport, Greater Manchester SK4 1TD
directors and general meeting minutes 1883-1984; share ledger 1884-date; memo and articles of association 1883; private ledger 1884-1983; cash book 1883-1984; receipts 1914

426 IONIAN SECURITIES LTD

3 Mar 1883
17994
64 Coleman Street, London EC2
Investment (formerly banking)

History: formed by bankers and merchants in the City of London in 1839 as Ionian Bank, with a share capital of 4000 shares each of £25. Acted as a deposit and note issue bank in the Ionian Islands then under British suzerainty. Established under both the laws of the Ionian Islands and by charter granted by British Parliament. Opened main office at Corfu in 1840 followed by branches at Zante and Cephalonia. Played an important role in financing local currant and olive oil production and external trade. Agencies opened at Athens and Patras in 1845 and special agents appointed at Venice and Trieste in same year. Bank privilege of note issue renewed in 1860, 1880 and 1905 and ended in 1920. Following ceding of Ionian Islands to Greece in 1864, Athens and Patras agencies converted into full branches and in 1873 Athens became head office of the bank in Greece. From 1864-1920 shared note issue with National Bank of Greece. In 1883 converted into a registered company as Ionian Bank Ltd and charter revoked. In 1907 Alexandria, Egypt branch opened and bank became heavily involved in finance of Egyptian cotton trade. By 1909 seven branches or agencies were established in Egypt. Served military interests in WW1 and opened branches at Salonica, Syria, Chios and Mitylene. In 1922 acquired Guaranty Trust Co of New York's branch at Istanbul (closed 1929). Opened first Cyprus branch, at Nicosia, in 1926. In 1938 formed Ionian Insurance Co and in 1939 acquired two thirds of the capital of Banque Populaire, a major Greek bank and competitor. By 1953 had acquired all capital when the business was entirely merged into that of Ionian Bank. In 1951 established branch at Cairo. By 1958 disposed of its Greek branches to Ionian & Popular Bank of Greece. By early 1970s it had no connection with Greece and Middle East. Its banking business was discontinued in late 1970s when its name was changed to above.

Records: at British Library of Economics & Political Science, 10 Portugal Street, London WC2A 2HD
court: meeting minutes 1839-43,1884-1972, agenda book 1956-61; general meeting minutes 1842-1906; reports 1909-40; committee meeting minutes: 1886-99, issue of small notes and papers 1885-1909; directors: attendance book 1946-57, registers 1902-05; share: holders registers 1839-1955, transfer registers 1879-1919,1951-9, holders letters 1891-1911, annual list and summary 1919-27,1936-45, applications 1924-39; prospectus 1839; deed of settlement 1840; papers: charter, formation and renewal of privileges 1837-1905; articles of association 1886-1950; seal book 1887-1949; annual report and accounts 1841-1975; profit and loss accounts 1898-1918; balance sheets: 1907-27, head office 1928-9, working papers 1919-20; general ledgers 1839-48,1945-58; head office: ledgers 1924-57, journals 1937-48, and major branch yearly accounts c1952-7; branch accounts ledger 1939,1950-6; salaries committee meeting: minutes 1891-1926, agenda book 1891-1923; staff: letters 1916-23, establishment books 1838-67,1880-1906; office general charges register 1936-51; reports: branches 1879, Egypt 1905; note issue papers 1883; Greek branches: reports 1927-55, minutes, correspondence and memoranda c1920s-50s; bank advertisements 1877-1938; history papers 20 cent

427 LIMERICK CLOTHING CO LTD

9 Mar 1883
18012
100 Regent Street, London W1A 2AQ
Wholesale clothiers

History: established in 1850 by Sir Peter Tate and incorporated in 1883 as Auxiliary Forces Uniform & Equipment Co Ltd to supply the auxiliary forces and others with uniforms, clothing and equipment. A clothing factory was established in Limerick, Ireland. The registered offices at 1 Old Bond Street, London moved to Vauxhall Bridge House, and then to 24 Claverton Street, in 1893-4. In 1923 premises covered 6 acres and the company employed 900 people. Changed name to Limerick Clothing Factory Co Ltd in 1890 and to above in 1962. Acquired by Aquascutum Ltd in 1970 and ceased trading in 1974. Named Aquascutum Products Ltd from Jul 1974 to Jul 1975.

Records: at Reynolds Cooper McCarron, 88 O'Connell Street, Limerick, Eire
general meeting minutes 1885-date; share registers current

428 FLORAL PRESS LTD

18 Apr 1883
18184
25 New Street Square, London EC4A 3JA
Publishing

History: incorporated in 1883 as Shipping World Ltd to publish a trade magazine called *Shipping World*. First editor was Major ER Jones, American consul at Newcastle upon Tyne, and subsequently an MP. Purchased by Sir Archibald Hurd in c1926. Acquired in 1962 by Benn Brothers Ltd, who published *Shipping World* until 1981 when the title was sold to Marine Publications International Ltd. Name changed to Benn Graphics Ltd in 1978, to above in 1980, and to Benn Specialist Publications Ltd in 1983. The company ceased to trade in c1977.

Records: at Benn Brothers, Sovereign Way, Tonbridge, Kent TN9 1RW
directors meeting minutes 1883 on

429 LIVERPOOL DIOCESAN BOARD OF FINANCE

10 May 1883
18301
1 Hanover Street, Liverpool, Merseyside L1 3DW
Church finance

History: incorporated as above as company limited by guarantee to collect, receive and distribute funds for diocesan societies and to act as trustees of money or property given or bequeathed to the Church of England within the Diocese of Liverpool.

Records: at Liverpool Diocesan Board of Finance, 1 Hanover Street, Liverpool, Merseyside L1 3DW
board: meeting minutes 1925-36, 1968-date, reports 1925-36, and committee papers 1945 on; committee: meeting minutes and reports 1925-36, finance sub-committee 1893-1906, executive 1978 on; annual reports and accounts 1906-09, 1925-date; memo and articles of association

1926; seals registers 1947-61; ledgers: 1919-66, church house 1897-c1914,1941-57, church aid 1941-57, JR Fund 1941-9, SFAC 1941-9, clergy sustentation 1941-9, BAF clergy, benefit and funds 1949-67, deanery 1950-1, endowments and repairs 1934-58, trusts 1934-58, loans c1936-58, investments 1934-59; journals: 1935-76, clergy sustentation 1941-66, trust 1941-60; cash books: 1883-1937, charities and funds 1941-64, church house 1915-57, clergy sustentation 1941-66, Liverpool Sunday schools 1918-36, diamond jubilee appeal 1922-51; clergy wages and grants books 1952-60; church aid and stipends quota 1944-60; investment registers 1950s; Divinity Board meeting minutes 1956-68; Education Board meeting minutes 1925-36; Evangelistic Work Board meeting minutes 1925-36; Lay Service Board meeting minutes 1925-36; Ministry Board: and committee meeting minutes and reports 1925-36; Ordained Ministry Board: meeting minutes, 1965-76, committee meeting minutes 1966-75; Mission Board account book 1959-70; Moral Welfare Board committee meeting minutes 1925-36; Press and Publicity Board meeting minutes 1925-36; Sites and Buildings Board: meeting minutes 1925-36, clerk of works reports 1930-6, ledgers 1925-c43, cash book 1941-55; Womens Work Board meeting minutes 1925-33; Liverpool Church Congress committee meeting minutes and papers 1903-04; Liverpool Diocesan: conference minutes 1930-6, Church Aid Society cash book 1941-67, building campaign meeting minutes 1927-30, war damage and reorganisation committee meeting minutes 1941-51, papers and correspondence c1945-57, annual reports and accounts 1929-30,1957-82; Liverpool Bishop Fund committee meeting minutes 1907-25; Church Building Society meeting minutes 1917-26; Liverpool Church of England Scripture Readers Society accounts, reports, rules and papers c1913-48; *Diocesan Calendar* 1911-date, *Gazette* 1903-67; St Edmund's College: council meeting minutes 1909-25, financial statements 1935-59, ledgers 1942-71, journals 1942-71, cash books 1930-74; Edge Hill National School management committee meeting minutes 1824-50; St Lukes National School management committee meeting minutes 1889-1940; St Martins National School cash book 1894-1901; Liverpool Diocesan Schools Association: ledgers 1881-1966, cash book 1941-66, papers, correspondence and press cuttings 1897-1907; schools papers and correspondence 1939-65; St Augustines Church trustee minutes 1834; All Saints Church papers and correspondence 1883-1964; churches: war damage papers 1939-46, architects valuation reports, papers and correspondence 1952-8; Clergy Benefaction Fund: ledger 1941-9, cash book 1941-67; Benefices Augmentation Fund: trustee meeting minutes 1883-1925, ledgers 1919-49, journal 1941-64; Walton Glebe Estate Trustees: ledgers 1885-1952, journals 1877-1905, account book 1884-1909, cash books 1915-43; William Edmunds Fund: ledger and cash book 1915-32, annual accounts 1963; Liverpool Exhibition Endowment trustee meeting minutes 1910-61; Clergy Endowment Fund trustee meeting minutes 1835-8; press cuttings 1902-19,1952-66

Old Church Penny Bank: ledgers: 1864-6, depositors 1881-5,1921-49; payment book 1913-52

Liverpool Diocesan Publishing Co Ltd: members registers etc 1948-50; memo and articles of association 1971; ledger 1939-c52; publications 1926-36

Liverpool Diocesan Church House Ltd: memo and articles of association 1957; annual accounts 1957

430 CARDIFF EXCHANGE & OFFICE CO LTD

16 May 1883
18329
St John's Chambers, High Street Arcade, Cardiff, S Glamorgan CF1 2BD
Property

History: founded and incorporated as above in 1883 by F de Courcy Hamilton, Cardiff solicitor who acted as secretary to several Cardiff property companies in the 1880s, to erect a hall to house a mercantile exchange and other offices in Cardiff, S Glamorgan, in the centre of Mount Stuart Square on land leased from the Marquis of Bute. Architects were the firm of James, Seward & Thomas and the exchange was opened in 1886, office blocks being subsequently built on each side of the square. Coal & Shipping Exchange met in the Central Hall and Cardiff Incorporated Chamber of Commerce had offices on the north side. Restaurant, arbitration, auction and reading rooms were also built. Proposed site of the devolved Welsh Assembly (1979). Company sold the building in 1970 and in 1981 owned property in Newport and Abergavenny, Gwent, and Leominster, Hereford & Worcester.

Records: at Cardiff Exchange & Office, St John's Chambers, High Street Arcade, Cardiff, S Glamorgan CF1 2BD
directors and general meeting minutes 1882-date; share: register 1883-1963, ledger 1883-1963, certificate book 1950s; directors register 1940s-60s; annual reports and accounts 1884-date; general ledger 1883-1965; West block ledger 1890-6; journal 1888-1966; North West block journal 1894-1910; rental ledger 1910-61; weekly rentals payments book 1939-70; income tax papers 1967; out letter book 1916-22; incoming letters 1958-70; New Exchange Building: artists drawings c1900, aerial photograph c1970; directors records: ledger 1901-69, journal 1916-59, cash book 1948-71, ground rents assignments notices 1890s-c1918, ground rents book 1917-27, weekly rental payments book 1923-76, out letter books 1918-22, incoming letters 1956-7,1964-76

431 CONSERVATIVE CLUB (PLYMOUTH) LTD

19 May 1883
18341
2 Osborne Villas, The Hoe, Plymouth, Devon PL1 2PU
Political club-house

History: incorporated as above in 1883 by local Conservatives to form and run a Conservative and Unionist club which opened in George Street, Plymouth, Devon. In 1888 the club moved to Union Terrace and in about 1890 to its own newly built premises in Princess Square which were destroyed by enemy action in 1941. Acquired freeholds of 1&2 Osborne Place in 1948. Premises were renovated in the late 1970's.

Records: at Conservative Club (Plymouth), 2 Osborne Villas, The Hoe, Plymouth, Devon PL1 2PU
directors and general meeting minutes 1912-date; memo and articles of association 1948-61

432 ROYAL INSTITUTION OF SOUTH WALES

24 May 1883
18359
Victoria Road, Swansea, W Glamorgan SA1 1SN
Cultural society and museum proprietors

History: founded in 1835 as Swansea Philosophical & Literary Society by George G Francis, antiquarian researcher and later Mayor of Swansea in 1853. Objects were to cultivate and advance study of natural and local history and encourage literature, fine arts and general diffusion of knowledge. First rooms rented in Castle Square for a library and museum had proved too small by 1836. Raised subscriptions to erect present Classical building in Victoria Road, which opened to the public in 1845. Queen Victoria became patroness in 1838 and name changed to above. Accumulated collections of books, maps, newspapers etc, Welsh porcelain, pottery, folk culture and art, as well as natural history, geological and archaeological items, also an art collection relating to the local district. Acted as headquarters to other local societies, arranged own programme of lectures, socials and meetings and assisted in research and investigation. Between 1868 and 1898 held science classes under Science and Art Departments of Council on Education. Incorporated as above in 1883 as a company limited by guarantee. Work has been carried on mainly by voluntary effort, officers and curators being honorary, and main income derived from membership subscription, but has been jointly run by University College of Swansea since 1973.

Records (1): at Royal Institution of South Wales, Victoria Road, Swansea, W Glamorgan SA1 1SN
council, annual and committees meeting: minutes 1835-date, press cuttings 1839-1939, attendance books 1888-1939; buildings committee report 1876; library committee: reports 1877,1914-18,1931,1939, correspondence 1911-20; hon curators: reports 1928-34, correspondence 1922-60; laws 1866; memo and articles of association 1883; annual reports and accounts 1836-1941; balance sheet 1919; ledgers 1888-1959; journals 1930-9; general account: ledger 1939-49, journal 1939-45, cash book 1940-56; objects of interest account: ledger 1933-48, journal 1932-43, cash book 1931-48; account books: treasurers 1838-1940, keepers 1849-63; subscriptions 1863; postages 1934-49; telephone 1889-90; endowment fund cash book 1938-47; petty cash book 1899-1949; papers and magazines sales correspondence and papers 1915-40; bank books 1884-1919; donation lists and papers 1835-1937; receipts, vouchers, invoices etc 1871-1906; financial correspondence 1931-9; library catalogues and indexes 1846-1933; books donated registers 1838-1953; purchases books 1840-1931; purchase recommendation books 1866-1936; issues registers 1845-1948; WH Smith & Sons circulating library registers 1872-82; museum catalogues 1842-1940s; donation registers 1835-1925; visitors book 1835-1942; admission books 1925-41; subscription books 1836-85; members register 1883-92; subscription and membership correspondence and papers 1890s-1960s; notices, tickets, programmes etc for meetings, lectures, concerts, exhibitions etc 1835-1938; correspondence re appointment of keeper 1867, sub-curator 1905-19, and curators 1940s; building: contract 1839, papers and correspondence 1896-1939, schedules for repairs 1946-8; insurance correspondence and policies 1933-48; correspondence with council members and others re enquiries, membership, research etc 1880s-1948; hon secretarys out letters 1905-56; correspondence and notes of GG Francis c1854-90s, JH Vivian c1869-94, Lt Col WV Morgan c1906-26; meteorological registers 1836-7; Swansea trades register 1837-8; press cuttings re exhibitions 1935-43; misc records 1870s-1930s
Swansea School of Science: committee meeting minutes 1882-6; class registers 1872-95; lecture syllabuses 1869-95
Swansea Art Society: invitations to and notices of meetings 1904-15
Swansea Club: visitors book 1900-07
Swansea Field Naturalists Society: committee and agm minutes 1911-34; rules 1920s; *Proceedings* 1927-56; lectures and meetings invitations and programmes 1911-34; correspondence with Royal Institution 1920

Swansea Literary & Scientific Society: committee and agm minutes 1844-1912; rule book 1845; annual reports 1851,1877-99; subscription and account book 1900-19; society and excursion accounts and correspondence 1907-15; receipts and vouchers 1904-21; meeting, excursion, lecture notices and programmes 1846-1939; lecture notes 1844-c51,1912
Swansea Tradesmen & Mechanics' Institution: cash books 1826-8,1839-45; printing ink recipe and meteorological instruments account c1826-8

Records (2): University College of Swansea Library, Singleton Park, Swansea, W Glamorgan SA2 8PP
correspondence, press cuttings and notes: of GG Francis on locality and Royal Institution 1853-96, and WH Jones, former curator of Royal Institution 20 cent

433 PRESTON BANKING CO LTD
2 Jul 1883
18535
Poultry, London EC2P 2BX
Banking

History: established as a joint stock bank in Fishergate, Preston, Lancashire in 1844 and obtained royal charter in 1845. Branches were opened throughout Lancashire and Merseyside, at Lancaster in 1850, Southport and Ormskirk in 1857 and Blackburn in 1863, and offices at Fleetwood, Garstang, Lytham St Anne's and Blackpool in 1864. By 1894 the number of branches stood at 10 with 16 sub-branches. The bank suspended operations for 5 weeks from 19 Jul 1866 due to the effects of the American Civil War on the cotton trade. Registered with limited liability as above in 1883 and amalgamated in 1894 with London & Midland Bank Ltd, renamed London City & Midland Bank Ltd in 1898, London Joint City & Midland Bank Ltd in 1918, and Midland Bank Ltd in 1923.

Records: at Midland Bank, Poultry, London EC2P 2BX
provisional committee meeting minutes and report 1844; board meeting minutes 1844-72; shareholders meeting minutes 1844-60; report 1866; list of shareholders 1844; annual summary of capital and shareholders 1884-92; share transfer register 1845-65; formation, liquidation and amalgamation papers 1844-94; annual reports and balance sheets 1844-94; balance sheets 1845-65; weekly balances 1844-65; customers balance sheets 1868-9; applications for advances 1866-84; security deposit ledger 1878-94; investment ledger 1883-4; expenses salary book 1844-66; specimen contracts 1871-88; letter book 1883-5; Fleetwood branch security registers 1876-97

WF Crick and JE Wadsworth, *A Hundred Years of Joint Stock Banking* (1936)

434 YORK CITY & COUNTY BANKING CO LTD
2 Jul 1883
18538
13 Parliament Street, York, N Yorkshire
Banking

History: established in 1830 as York City & County Bank, a joint stock bank operating from Ousegate, York, opening office in Malton, N Yorkshire. Took over banking offices of Scholfield, Crackson & Clough (1809-31) in 1831, setting up branches at Howden,

Humberside, and Selby, N Yorkshire. Agencies were established at Scarborough, N Yorkshire, and Goole, Humberside. Absorbed N Yorkshire banking businesses of Fletcher, Stubbs, Dew & Stott (est 1804), Boroughbridge and Northallerton in 1833, Farrer, Williamson & Co (est 1801), Ripon in 1837; Richardson, Holt & Co (est 1786), Whitby in 1843; and Frankland & Wilkinson (est 1778), Whitby in 1845. New head offices built in Parliament Street, York in late 1840s. Opened branches at Middlesbrough, Cleveland in 1871 and purchased Thirsk, N Yorkshire branch of Jonathan Backhouse & Co (est 1773) in 1873. Purchased Harding & Co (est 1802), Bridlington, Humberside in 1878 and Darlington District Joint Stock Bank (est 1831) in 1883. Registered in 1883 as York City & County Bank Ltd, changing name to above in 1893. Amalgamated with Hull Banking Co Ltd (est 1833) in 1894 and Barnsley Banking Co Ltd (est 1832) in 1897; absorbed Borough of Tynemouth Trading Bank (est 1885), North Shields, Tyne & Wear in 1897; and amalgamated with Cumberland Union Banking Co (est 1829) in 1901. In 1909 had 90 branches with as many sub-branches and agencies and amalgamated with London Joint Stock Bank Ltd (est 1836) which amalgamated with London City & Midland Bank Ltd (est 1836) in 1918 to form London Joint City & Midland Bank Ltd which became Midland Bank Ltd in 1923.

Records: at Midland Bank, Poultry, London EC2P 2BX
board meeting minutes 1830-1916; shareholders meeting minutes 1894-1909; annual meeting reports 1883-1900; prospectus 1830; deed of settlement 1830; annual reports 1839-1909; quarterly balances 1898-1908; general ledgers 1830-74; profits comparison 1896-1900; branch: managers instructions 1902, memoranda 1841-51, security books 1833-1902, reports and balance sheets 1874-1910; branches - Bridlington: general ledgers 1879-81; Howden: memoranda 1842-70; Ripon: memoranda 1850-75; Scarborough: general ledger 1861-71; Selby: cash books 1832-83

WF Crick and JE Wadsworth, *A Hundred Years of Joint Stock Banking* (1936)

435 JERSEY CATTLE SOCIETY OF THE UK

10 Jul 1883
18573
Jersey House, 154 Castle Hill, Reading, Berkshire RG1 7RP
Breed society

History: established in 1878 as English Jersey Cattle Society by John Thornton who became the first secretary. Incorporated as a company limited by guarantee in 1883 with 184 members rising to 395 by 1891. Issued herd book, maintained breed register, awarded medals and issued importation certificates. Name changed to above in 1957. Membership stood at 5537 in 1957 and at about 1200 in 1984.

Records: at Institute of Agricultural History & Museum of English Rural Life, University of Reading, Whiteknights, Reading, Berkshire RG6 2AG
council meeting: minutes 1885-date, agendas 1962-75, papers 1885-1920; general meeting minutes 1885-date; committee meeting minutes: general purposes 1888-1979, propaganda 1919-33, editing and milk record 1923-81, and agendas 1954-81, publicity with agendas 1946-81, artificial insemination and export 1946-65, sub 1944-72; committee meetings attendance books 1959-79; annual report and accounts 1885-1926; general ledgers 1958-71; journal 1933-

75; members register 1933-40; *Herd Book* 1878-date
English Kerry & Dexter Cattle Society: council and general meeting minutes 1917-31

436 CHURCH SCHOOLS CO LTD
12 Jul 1883
18582
1A Doughty Street, London WC1N 2PH
Schools

History: founded and incorporated as above in 1883 by members of the Church of England to establish day schools for children (mainly girls) of the middle classes where religious education would be adequately taught. Schools were established and run by local committees although financial control and the right to appoint head teachers was vested in the supervisory council in London. 21 schools had been set up by 1893 and in all, 36 schools have been operated by the company in England and Wales. 7 public day church schools were run as independent schools in 1980, namely Eothen School, Caterham, Surrey; Guildford High School, Surrey; Hull High School, Humberside; Atherley School, Southampton, Hampshire; Sunderland Church High School, Tyne & Wear; Surbiton High School, Greater London; and York College, N Yorkshire.

Records: at Church Schools, 1A Doughty Street, London WC1N 2PH
council meeting minutes 1883-date; committee meeting minutes: education with reports 1883-1919, general purposes 1903-04,1924-31; law and finance 1883-1955; general meeting minutes 1883-1949; dividend: register 1892-8, warrants 1903; papers and correspondence re share transfers 1884,1912-18; annual reports and balance sheets 1883-date; general ledgers 1883-date; schools account ledgers 1890-1947; nominal ledger 1946-54; scholarship/prize fund ledger 1946-68; ledger 1958-66; cash book 1942-9; register of leases and insurance c1893-1913; contract notes, agreements and tenancies c1926-40; correspondence re upkeep of playing fields 1928-9; photographs of school buildings, staff and children 1970s

The Church Schools Company 1883-1933 (priv pub 1934)
E Moberly Bell, *A History of the Church Schools Company* (1958)

437 LAW LAND CO LTD
19 Jul 1883
18610
Brettenham House, Lancaster Place, London WC2E 7EP
Property

History: founded by Arthur M Lloyd and incorporated as above in 1883 as a property company. Built Brettenham House, Lancaster Place, London in 1930s and by 1970s the company and its subsidiaries owned leasehold and freehold office property in central areas of London, a large number of shops in the UK, blocks of flats in London's West End, hotels operated by tenants, and a number of factories. Re-registered as a public company in c1980. By 1981 was a subsidiary of Churchbury Estates Ltd.

Records: at Law Land, Brettenham House, Lancaster Place, London WC2E 7EP
directors meeting: minutes 1888-date, chairmans agendas 1885-1925; general meeting minutes 1883-date; members registers 1883-date; share: allotment books 1883 on, transfer registers and

documents 1883-date; debenture stock registers and documents 1900s-date; memo and articles of association 1883 on; corporate documents 20 cent; annual report and accounts 1883-date; seal registers 1955-date; ledgers: main 1883-date, purchase, sales and tenants 1920s-60s; journals: 1883-date, purchase 1930s-60s; day books 1930s-50s; cash books 1883-date; rent rolls 1886-1970s; property leases and agreements 19-20 cent; press cuttings 1925-date

438 REED CORRUGATED CASES LTD

26 Jul 1883
18638
Cobdown House, London Road, Ditton, Maidstone, Kent MF20 6DQ
Paper manufacturers

History: incorporated in 1883 as Thompson & Norris Manufacturing Co Ltd, pioneer corrugated paper manufacturers. Offices were situated in Hayes, Greater London. Acquired in 1954 by Albert E Reed & Co Ltd and name changed to above in 1956. In 1984 was a subsidiary of Reed International PLC.

Records: at Reed International, Reed House, 83 Piccadilly, London W1A 1EJ
general meeting minutes 1945-63; members register and share ledger 1953-64; directors register 1956-63

439 ELWICK CLUB LTD

10 Aug 1883
18707
Church Road, Ashford, Kent TN23 1RD
Social club-house

History: incorporated as above in 1883 to acquire land and erect premises to provide a social club for town and county members. Original premises were in Bank Street, Ashford moving to Tufton Street in 1923. This building, designed by EA Jackson cost £8000. In 1973 the club moved to premises in Church Road. In 1984 facilities included squash court, snooker room, club and dining rooms.

Records: at Elwick Club, Church Road, Ashford, Kent TN23 1RD
directors meeting minutes 1921-date, management and general committee meeting minutes 1923-72; register: directors 1901-27, members, share ledger and transfers 1883-1957, debenture holders 1920-44; share certificates 1883-5,1921-31; annual returns 1942-6; private ledger 1886-1957; cash book 1894-1953; trading accounts 1892-1926; members: list 1883-1904, and subscriptions register 1884-1963; proposal book 1923-79; suggestion book 1884-1968; visitors book 1957-69

440 EXPRESS & STAR LTD

14 Aug 1883
18718
50-51 Queen Street, Wolverhampton, W Midlands WV1 3BU
Newspaper

History: incorporated as Midland News Association Ltd in 1884 to merge ownership of *Wolverhampton Chronicle*, first published in 1789; *Midland Counties Express*, first published in 1861; *Evening Express*, first published in 1874; and *Evening Star*, first published in 1880 on initiative of Thomas Graham, former pork butcher of Tettenhall, Staffordshire, with the support of Andrew Carnegie, the oil, iron and steel magnate of Pittsburg, USA. *Star* and *Express* were merged in 1884 as *Evening Express & Star* and renamed *Express & Star* in 1889. Graham became sole owner and on his death in 1908 control of Midland News Association passed to his sons Norval and J Douglas Graham. Published *Sporting Star*, a Saturday football paper, between 1919 and WW2. After deaths of Norval and J Douglas Graham in 1944 and 1948 became subsidiary of Express & Star (Wolverhampton) Ltd, created as a holding company for the Graham family's newspaper interests in 1950. *Express & Star* circulation increased from 94,000 in 1939 to 196,000 in 1956 and 250,000 in 1979. Launched *Shropshire Star* in 1964, Selster Travel Ltd in 1969, and in 1972 acquired Powysland Newspapers Ltd, publishers of *Shrewsbury Chronicle*, *Bridgnorth Journal* and *Newport & Market Drayton Advertiser*. Established Shropshire Weekly Newspaper Ltd in 1973. Acquired Keith Prowse & Co Ltd in 1979 but sold interest in 1981. In 1984 was printing and distributing newspapers with circulation of over 2 million copies from its plants in Wolverhampton, Telford and Sandwell.

Records (1): at Express & Star, 50-51 Queen Street, Wolverhampton, W Midlands WV1 3BU
board and general meeting minutes 1939-50; directors register c1883-1941; share: ledger 1885-1918, certificates 1883-1964; mortgages register 1888-1904; accounting statistics c1897-1943; private ledger 1889-c1950; private journal: Midland Echo 1883-5, Express 1889-c1950; cash books: central 1884-5, branch offices 1939-46, general 1960-2, petty 1960-3; brochures re office premises and technology 1928-c75; stock book 1925-50; inventory and valuation of plant 1949-67; wages books: 1884-1940, composing room 1901-65, by department 1910-13; wage analysis 1956-73; reporters handbook 1947; training manual 1969; branches: offices premises details 1950s, machinery, staff reports etc c1938-65
Dawley Observer Ltd: share transfer certificates and papers 1967-8
Express & Star (Wolverhampton) Ltd: directors meeting minutes 1950-60
Powysland Newspapers Ltd: directors and general meeting minutes 1936-64; share certificates 1912-63; articles of association 1901; agreement re premises in Bridgnorth 1950
Shrewsbury Chronicle Ltd: directors register 1942-53; memo and articles of association 1919

Records (2): at British Library, Newspaper Library, Colindale Avenue, London NW9 5HE
Wolverhampton Chronicle 1829-1930; *Midland Counties Express* 1867-1930; *Midland Counties Express & Wolverhampton Chronicle* 1931-47; *Wolverhampton Chronicle & Midland Counties Express* 1947 on; *Evening Express* (Liverpool) 1873-1958; *Evening Star* (Wolverhampton) 1880-4; *Evening Express & Star* 1884-9; *Sporting Star* 1919-39,1949 on; *Shropshire Star* 1964 on; *Shrewsbury Chronicle* 1773 on; *Bridgnorth Journal & General Advertiser* 1854-5; *Bridgnorth Journal & South Shropshire Advertiser* 1855-69,1887 on; *Newport & Market Drayton Advertiser* 1969 on

R Seaton, *Malcolm Graham. Sixty Years in the News* (priv pub 1983)

441 PORTSMOUTH HARBOUR FERRY CO LTD
21 Aug 1883
18751
South Street, Gosport, Hampshire PO12 1EP
Ferry

History: incorporated in 1883 by watermen at Portsea, Hampshire, as Port of Portsmouth Steam Launch & Towing Craft Co Ltd to run a steam launch passenger ferry between Portsea and Gosport in competition with Gosport Watermen's Steam Launch Co Ltd (inc 1875 by Gosport watermen) and to tow vessels in and out of Portsmouth Harbour. Towage business gradually reduced in importance. Both companies were in keen competition with each other for many years, despite rationalization of the ferry procedure in 1888 and a subsequent pooling arrangement to share the ferry takings. Changed name to above on 30 Jan 1962 and on following day merged with Gosport & Portsea Steam Launch Co Ltd (as the Gosport company had been renamed in 1913) which was subsequently wound up. The company's offices moved from Ferry Gardens to South Street, Gosport in 1960s and the company had wharf and workshop at Town Quay, Harbour Road, Gosport. Launches of both companies ran cruises and excursions during the summer months, and saw service in both WWs. The Portsea ticket office was closed in 1978, the Gosport office subsequently charging double fares. Company in 1983 operated ferry service with 2 vessels and ran pleasure cruises from Portsmouth, Gosport and Southsea.

Records: at Portsmouth Harbour Ferry, South Street, Gosport, Hampshire PO12 1EP
directors meeting: minutes 1883-5,1916-date, agenda 1946-62, attendance books 1941-62; general meeting: minutes 1883-date, agenda and attendance book 1946-62; members registers and share ledger 1915-60; share transfer register 1947-74; directors registers 1918-80; mortgages register 1956-73; annual returns 1949-62; annual reports and accounts 1883-1974; annual accounts and balance sheets 1937-64; general ledgers 1958-65; account books 1962-5; dividends 1954-74; accounts due 1941-59; cash books 1942-74; passenger statistics 1956-61; ticket books: Gosport 1970-8, Portsea 1976-8; press releases, photographs, descriptions etc of *Ferry Queen* 1966; ferries insurance policies 1961-2; engineer certificate 1914; employers indemnity policy 1915; correspondence re Gosport and Alverstoke UDC Act 1952-63
Gosport & Portsea Steam Launch Co Ltd: directors and general meeting minutes 1901-62; members register and share ledger 1907-50; share: transfer register 1945-61, certificates 1956-61; annual returns 1931-62; indemnity letters 1933-40,1962; shareholders amalgamation circulars 1961; annual reports and accounts 1876,1931-61; accounts statements 1931-50; excursion traffic trading account 1932; investments: value 1932, interest 1946, correspondence 1932; deposit account books 1906-37; revenue account book 1920-32; dividend account book 1923-9; cash receipts 1918-61; invoice book 1937-62; passenger sales breakdown 1933-4; Gosport landing fees 1929-30; ticket registers 1946-61; *Ferry Belle* sale agreement 1962; stock: valuation 1914-56, book 1934-61; vessel insurance policies 1939-60; union wage agreements 1945-55; mortgages, deeds and schedules of land at Forton 1830-71; office, etc leases 1917-55; premises insurance policies 1911-44

PD Childs, *The Gosport Ferry: A Short History. The Centenary of the Portsmouth Harbour Ferry Company PLC 1883-1983* (priv pub 1983)

442 BEACON INSURANCE CO LTD

5 Sep 1883
18801
1 Bartholomew Lane, London EC2N 2AB
Insurance

History: incorporated in 1883 as Blue Ribbon Life, Accident, Mutual & Industrial Insurance Co Ltd and offered premiums at reduced rates to total abstainers. By 1887 district offices had been established in Bradford and Leeds, W Yorkshire and Sheffield, S Yorkshire; London; Glasgow; and Manchester. Its first offices were in Colmore Chambers, Newhall Street, Birmingham moving to City Buildings, Carrs Lane by 1902. Changed name to Abstainers & General Insurance Co Ltd in 1890. Acquired Methodists & General Assurance Society Ltd of London in 1891. By 1907 the company also transacted fire, burglary, health, employers liability and workmens' compensation insurance and had branches in Belfast; Birmingham; Bradford; Bristol, Avon; Carlisle, Cumbria; Dublin; Dundee, Tayside; Glasgow; London (3); Manchester; Newcastle upon Tyne; Northampton; Nottingham; Portsmouth, Hampshire; and Sheffield. New head offices were taken at 142 Edmund Street, Birmingham. By 1923 motor and plate glass insurance had been added to its business. By 1932 new branches had opened in Brighton, E Sussex; Edinburgh; Leicester; Plymouth, Devon; and Reading, Berkshire. Changed name to above in 1933. Moved to new head offices at 1301 Stratford Road, Hall Green, Birmingham in about 1939. Amalgamated in 1953 with Sea Insurance Co Ltd (est 1875) of Liverpool which was acquired in 1960 by London Assurance Corporation which merged with Sun Alliance Insurance Group in 1965 to form Sun Alliance & London Insurance Group.

Records: at Beacon Insurance, 1301 Stratford Road, Hall Green, Birmingham, W Midlands B28 9AP
directors meeting: minutes 1883-1946, reports and papers 1887-1967, attendance books 1888-1911, executive committee meeting minutes 1888-1967; administration department: standing instructions 1940s-50s, minutes extracts 1925-45; agm proceedings 1902-67; share registers and ledgers 1883-1950s; members register 1894-9; share transfer register 1884-1953; dividends ledger 1906-14; annual reports and accounts 1888-91,1907-09; balance sheets and accounts: 1887-1930s, departmental 1909-40; bad and written off debts 1885-1940; ledger 1940-3; valuation reports, accounts and papers 1888-1909; stock ledger c1909-30s; securities register 1891-1916; loan: and insurance policy registers 1939-61, repaid ledgers 1922-69, interest due registers 1950-71, policy ledgers 1930s on, salary deductions 1935-60; paid up policy register 1899-1918; claim registers 1885-1949; surrender registers 1894-1920; head office salaries 1904-27; centenary luncheon programme 1983

443 SHEFFIELD UNION BANKING CO LTD

1 Oct 1883
18890
Poultry, London EC2P 2BX
Banking

History: established as Sheffield Union Banking Co in Sheffield, S Yorkshire as a joint stock bank in 1843, taking over the business of the Sheffield branch of Yorkshire District Banking Co. Purchased Sheffield & Retford Joint Stock Bank (est 1839 as Borough Bank of Sheffield) and the premises and remaining banking business of Parker, Shore & Co of Sheffield (est 1774, failed 1843) in 1846. Suffered severe setbacks in 1870s due to excessive re-discounting. Incorporated as above with limited liability in 1883 and opened branches within Sheffield in 1890s. Amalgamated in 1901 with London City & Midland Bank Ltd, renamed London Joint City & Midland Bank Ltd in 1918, and Midland Bank Ltd in 1923.

Records: at Midland Bank, Poultry, London EC2P 2BX
board meeting minutes 1843-1916; deed of settlement 1843; annual reports and balance sheets 1862-1901; balance sheets: summary 1845-6, tabulated and weekly 1862-1901; current account balances 1846; investment list 1884-97; circulars re liquidator 1901,1907; summary history 1891; press cuttings re amalgamation 1899

WF Crick and JE Wadsworth, *A Hundred Years of Joint Stock Banking* (1936)

444 ECCLESTON BOWLING CLUB LTD
8 Oct 1883
18912
Pavilion, Knowsley Road, St Helens, Merseyside
Sports club-house

History: incorporated as above in 1883 to lay down bowling greens and run a bowling club in Eccleston, St Helens, Merseyside. In 1984 had 488 members.

Records: at Eccleston Bowling Club, Pavilion, Knowsley Road, St Helens, Merseyside
directors and general meeting minutes 1949-date; shareholders list 1884; share transfer documents 1885-date; annual report and accounts 1889; balance sheet and accounts 1884-5; financial records 1970s on

445 TOXTETH REAL PROPERTY & INVESTMENT CO LTD
1 Nov 1883
19009
7 Union Court, Cook Street, Liverpool, Merseyside L2 4SJ
Property

History: incorporated as above in 1883 to purchase land and build houses in Toxteth, Liverpool. Among the original subscribers were local builders and an architect. Company built both residential and commercial properties in Merseyside for lease to tenants. In 1984 the company was managed by Beavan Maples, and continued to invest in property in Liverpool.

Records: at Beavan Maples, 7 Union Court, Cook Street, Liverpool, Merseyside L2 4SJ
directors meeting minutes 1883-91; annual summary 1896-1915; share: dividend book 1884-1907, allotment book 1883-6, call book 1884, current records

446 JAEGER HOLDINGS LTD
10 Dec 1883
19149
Jaeger House, 57 Broadwick Street, London W1V 1FU
Clothing

History: founded in Princes Street, Oxford Circus, London in late 1870s by Lewis Tomalin who obtained the sole agency in England for retailing Dr Jaeger's 'sanitary' underwear, knitwear, dressing gowns, blankets and coats made from undyed animal fabrics, mainly Merino sheep wool. Incorporated as Dr Jaeger's Sanitary Woollen System Co Ltd in 1883 and in 1884 moved to Fore Street, London. Became an integral part of the late Victorian healthy clothing cult. Wholesale company formed by 1889 to supply rapidly increasing UK and overseas agents and by 1900 had 20 retail shops. Name changed to Jaeger Co Ltd in 1920 and during 1920s popularity of 'sanitary wear' diminished. During 1930s converted into leading fashion house by updating styles and innovating matching colour co-ordination. Number of retail shops rose to 44 by 1939. Moved from Oxford Street to present Regent Street shop in 1935. Rented space in Selfridges and became the first shop within a department store. Started manufacturing goods and after 1945 acquired 2 Scottish knitwear companies, English knitting production at Belper, Derby, and Godalming, Surrey, and tailoring factories at Ipswich, Suffolk; Burgess Hill, W Sussex; and London. Name changed to above in 1947 and set up several subsidiary companies. From 1950s non-animal fabrics have been used. By 1978 had 62 retail shops, 12 tailoring and 5 knitwear factories in UK; 20 shops in USA, 4 each in France and the Netherlands, 3 in Sweden, 2 in West Germany and 1 in both Austria and Switzerland. Acquired by Coats Paton Ltd, textile company, in 1967.

Records: at Jaeger Holdings, Jaeger House, 57 Broadwick Street, London W1V 1FU
board and general meeting minutes 1883-date; sealing committee meeting minutes 1960-7; list of directors 1883-1970; list shares issued 1883-1970; share: register 1960 on, transfer register 1937 on; directors holdings register 1917 on; mortgage register 1917 on; probate register 1947 on; corporate documents incl memo and articles of association 1883-1968; correspondence re shares etc 1883-1935; annual reports and accounts 1930-date; cash book 1884-6; sales catalogues 1887-1931; wholesale trade lists 1904-29; newscuttings - advertisements and articles on company 1906 on; staff magazine c1925-30; photographs, correspondence and papers re Henry F Tomalin, chairman c1940-50

Alison Adburgham, *Shops and Shopping 1800-1914* (1964)

447 OLD PARK SILVER MILLS CO LTD

11 Dec 1883
19154
Knowle House, 4 Norfolk Park Road, Sheffield, S Yorkshire S2 2QE
Property (previously non-ferrous metal manufacturers)

History: founded in 1790 by Joseph Hancock at Old Park Rollings Mills, Brightside, Bierlow, Sheffield, S Yorkshire to roll Sheffield plate for other manufacturers. When incorporated as above in 1883, the company was rolling various metals, including silver, German steel, Britannia metal and copper. Water power was used until 1913, when an electric ingot mill was installed. By 1984 the company had ceased to manufacture metal and was a property holding subsidiary of Sheffield Metal Co Ltd.

Records (1): at Old Park Silver Mills, Knowle House, 4 Norfolk Park Road, Sheffield, S Yorkshire S2 2QE
directors meeting minutes 1908-46; general meeting minutes 1884-1983; register: members 1891-1961, transfers 1884-1961

Records (2): at S Yorkshire County Record Office, Cultural Activities Centre, Ellin Street, Sheffield, S Yorkshire S1 4PL
private ledger 1883-1925; wages books 1883-91

448 FOREIGN ANGLICAN CHURCH & EDUCATIONAL ASSOCIATION LTD

15 Dec 1883
19182
15 Tufton Street, Westminster, London SW1P 3QQ
Church management

History: incorporated as above in 1883 as a company limited by guarantee by 9 members of Marbeuf Church Building Committee in Paris under the chairmanship of Alan P Herbert, MD. Committee had been entrusted by the family of the late Rev Lewis Way (who had established the first Anglican place of worship in Paris at the Rue Marbeuf in 1824) with £12,000 paid by the City of Paris as compensation for expropriation of Marbeuf Chapel site in order to undertake street improvements. A new property was acquired by the committee on which a church, St George's, was built. The association held the church and parsonage property and appointed the chaplain. Building began in 1887 and French Byzantine style church was consecrated in 1889. Although Society for the Propagation of the Gospel (SPG) had declined to accept this property in trust, it offered assistance and the association's registered offices were moved to the society's house in London in the late 1890s. From 1904 secretarys of the association have always been SPG staff members. In 1922 accepted the trust of properties acquired by the SPG in Madagascar. In the 1980s St George's Church still functioned as the Anglican Church in Paris.

Records: at Foreign Anglican Church & Educational Association, 15 Tufton Street, Westminster, London SW1P 3QQ
minutes: 1883-4, council meeting 1906-date, general meeting 1901-date; members register 1955-9; memo and articles of association 1883,1950; annual returns 1921-46; annual report and accounts 1930-69; treasurers report and accounts 1899,1903-37; balance sheets and accounts 1908-65; bank pass books 1880-1939; St George's Church: building papers 1872-82, appeal papers and correspondence 1879-1951, service sheets 1937-49, magazines and newsletters 1891-1937; Madagascar property papers and correspondence 1922-60; letter book 1884-1901; SPG papers 1882-1906; Foundation Trust papers and correspondence 1914-58; secretarys correspondence 1925-54; financial correspondence and papers 1920s-60; chaplain correspondence 1925-56; history booklets and articles 1880-1954
Theatre Girls Hostel, Paris (Cardew Foundation) Ltd: memo and articles of association 1926; annual reports and accounts 1920-2,1925; newscuttings 1926; booklet nd

449 SWANSEA CHAMBER OF COMMERCE INCORPORATED

27 Dec 1883
19242
Burrows Chambers, East Burrows Road, Swansea, W Glamorgan
Chamber of commerce

History: founded in Swansea, W Glamorgan in 1846 as Swansea Chamber of Commerce. Incorporated as a company limited by guarantee in 1883 as Swansea Chamber of Commerce &

Shipping to promote and protect the commercial, shipping, manufacturing, mining and agricultural interests of Swansea and district and of the UK home and foreign trades. Mainly concerned with shipping and coal exporting and in the operation of the port, holding a daily coal and shipping exchange from 1900 to 1939. Post 1945 interests widened to include other aspects of industry and commerce and representation on management committees of colleges and secondary schools in Swansea. Swansea Incorporated Exchange (Royal Metal Exchange est 1875) amalgamated with chamber in 1959. In 1980s main activities are authenticating certificates of origin and other documents, answering members enquiries and voicing needs of local industry and commerce. Known as Swansea Chamber of Commerce & Shipping in 1981.

Records: at Swansea Chamber of Commerce & Shipping, Burrows Chambers, East Burrows Road, Swansea, W Glamorgan
general meeting minutes with notices and newscuttings 1873-8; minutes 1950s-date; members list 1881

450 EASTERN COUNTIES NEWSPAPERS GROUP LTD

15 Jan 1884
19300
Prospect House, Rouen Road, Norwich, Norfolk NR1 1RE
Newspapers

History: in 1844 a group of Norwich nonconformists decided to establish a weekly journal based on civil, religious and commercial freedom. *Norfolk News* was first published in Jan 1845, edited until 1847 by Joseph Geldart and then until his death in 1892 by Jacob Tillett, chairman of the board of proprietors. In 1858 printing works were set up in Museum Court, Norwich, Norfolk and publishing offices were opened in Exchange Street. In 1867 proprietors founded a one penny newspaper *The Eastern Weekly Express* (later *Eastern Weekly Press*) and in 1870 *Eastern Daily Press* with E Dawson Rogers as editor. James Spilling took over the editorship in 1873 and that of *Norfolk News* in 1892. Opened offices in Regent Street, Great Yarmouth, Norfolk in 1880 and established *Yarmouth Weekly Press*. Founded *Eastern Evening News* in 1882. Norfolk News Co Ltd was incorporated in 1884 to run the aforementioned newspapers. Opened offices in Lowestoft, Suffolk in 1886 and founded *Lowestoft Weekly Press*. London offices opened in 1887. A Cozens-Hardy became editor of the group of newspapers in 1897. Opened offices in Cromer and King's Lynn, Norfolk in 1900 and 1902 respectively. Moved offices and printing works to nearby premises in London Street and St Andrews Hill, Norwich in 1902. Founded *Eastern Football News* in 1913 and amalgamated *Norfolk News* and *Eastern Weekly Press* in 1919. Name changed to Eastern Counties Newspapers Ltd in 1960s. In 1969 acquired East Anglian Daily Times Co Ltd of Ipswich, Suffolk with its subsidiaries Arthur Fairweather Ltd, Leiston Abbey Press Ltd and Suffolk Press Ltd. Name changed to above in 1977 by which time company had moved to Rouen Road, Norwich and had branches at Cromer, Diss, East Dereham, Fakenham, King's Lynn, North Walsham, Thetford and Yarmouth, Norfolk; Beccles and Lowestoft, Suffolk; Wisbech, Cambridgeshire; and London. Its publications were *Eastern Evening News*, *The Eastern Daily Press*, *Norwich Mercury Series* and *Eastern Football News*. Live subsidiaries in 1980 were East Anglian Daily Times Co Ltd, Eastern Counties Newpapers Ltd and Slade Packaging Ltd.

Records (1): at Eastern Counties Newspapers Group, Prospect House, Rouen Road, Norwich, Norfolk NR1 1RE
committee meeting minutes 1844-78; managing and general committee meeting minutes 1899-1934; directors meeting: minutes 1935-73, papers 1886-1908; directors committee meeting minutes 1943-4; consultative committee meeting minutes 1920-5; inter company expenses committee meeting minutes 1937-9; agm minutes 1854-84; general meeting minutes 1908-73; agenda books 1862-71; shareholders: register 1854-81, list 1882-1918; members registers and share ledgers 1884-1962; directors register 1917; share certificates 1893-1961; partnership deed 1845; memo and articles of association 1908-33; corporate documents and papers 1880-1932; annual reports and accounts 1898-1977; assets and liabilities statements 1845-55; balance sheets 1898-1937; profit and loss accounts 1886-1937,1961-70; proprietors accounts 1846-52; yearly account summaries 1853-1901; financial estimates 1952-6; private ledgers 1864-1963; journals 1902-40s; cash books 1903-38; printing and publishing costs 1961-8; plant account books 1853-1901; editing, publishing, reporting and directing, salaries books 1880-1951; salary lists 1961-70; wages books: 1948-50, printing 1891-1912; private subsidy books 1916-37; employees benefit fund accounts 1916-37; commission accounts 1916-37; reporting expenses and salaries 1916-37; staff wages correspondence 1948; works canteen committee meeting minutes 1945; profit sharing bonus scheme papers 1930-59; staff registers 1962-70; apprentice list c1883-c97; apprenticeship indentures 1948-62; pension fund: papers 1902-39, accounts 1922-67; plant and office inventory and valuation 1936; Norwich property deeds, leases and papers c1650-1952; building photographs 1967; correspondence: Yarmouth Office 1920-40, misc 1902,1937; libel papers 1930-5; history 1932
East Anglian Daily Times Co Ltd: directors meeting minutes 1959-68; share register and correspondence 1950-65; members registers 1910-77; share: ledger 1910-64, certificates 1910-64; seal register 1914-63
Eastern Evening News Co Ltd: directors and general meeting minutes 1926-72; members registers 1926-62; share: ledger 1926-47; certificates 1926-46; memo and articles of association 1926; sale agreement 1926; annual reports and accounts 1961-77; annual accounts 1926-60; balance sheets and profit and loss accounts 1933-50; private ledger 1926-44; journal 1926-49
Arthur Fairweather Ltd: directors and general meeting minutes 1913-64; members register and share ledger 1931-62
Halesworth Press Ltd: directors meeting minutes 1964
Leiston Abbey Press Ltd: directors and general meeting minutes 1929-43, 1957-60; share ledger 1920-60
Norwich Mercury Co Ltd: directors meeting minutes 1872-1903,1935-70; and general purposes sub-committee meeting minutes 1921-7; general meeting minutes 1872-1970; shareholders list 1882-67; members registers 1907-62; share: ledger 1907-48, certificates 1907-47, transfer journal 1933-50; annual returns 1921-6,1930-1; memo and articles of association 1907; annual reports and accounts 1961-1977; annual accounts 1920-60; balance sheets and profit and loss accounts 1907-32; private ledger 1907-30; journal 1928-40; sales analysis book 1929-39; stock book 1928-38; plant inventory and valuation 1927; wages: ledger 1954-61, books 1915-38; salary books 1923-39; employee and misc correspondence c1930-40
Suffolk Press Ltd: directors meeting minutes 1936-63
Suffolk Press Transport Co Ltd: directors meeting minutes 1963; members registers and share ledgers 1950-62

Yarmouth Mercury Co Ltd: directors meeting minutes 1904-70; agm minutes 1933-73; members register and share ledger 1904-39; annual reports and accounts 1961-77; annual accounts 1928-60; private ledger 1925-32; cash books 1937-40; bank books 1932-8; stock book 1933-40; wages books 1915-38; salary books 1938-40; war service payments 1939-46; employee and misc correspondence c1930-40

Records (2): at British Library, Newspaper Library, Colindale Avenue, London NW9 5HE
Eastern Daily Press: 1870-date (except 1912); *Eastern Evening News*: 1882-date (except 1897,1911-12); *Norfolk News*: 1845-date (except 1898,1912); *Norwich Mercury* 1727-1949 (1727-1822 in parts); *Yarmouth Mercury*: 1880-date (except 1898,1912)

451 CARDIFF RAILWAY WORKMEN'S COTTAGE CO LTD
17 Jan 1884
19313
10 Museum Place, Cardiff, S Glamorgan CF1 3BG
Property

History: incorporated as above in 1884 to provide good, cheap cottage accommodation for railway workmen. Purchased land from Mr Crawshaw in Cathay, Cardiff near the Taff Vale and Rhymney Railways, on which 57 houses were built to the designs of architect, John Price Jones. Another 13 houses were built on land to the north of the site and 4 houses were purchased in Cathays Terrace in 1896. By 1940s property was also owned in Minney, Gladys, May, Dalton, and Richards Streets and Woodville Road. Houses have occasionally been sold since 1949.

Records: at Cardiff Railway Workmen's Cottage, 10 Museum Place, Cardiff, S Glamorgan CF1 3BG
directors and general meeting minutes 1883-1904,1945-80; share: ledger 1884-date, transfer register 1885-date; prospectus 1883; annual report and accounts 1891-1979; cash book 1957-75; rent book 1966-79; invoice book 1930-81; current records

452 CHARLWOOD ALLIANCE PROPERTIES LTD
5 Feb 1884
19397
4 Carlton Gardens, Pall Mall, London SW1Y 5AR
Property

History: incorporated in 1884 as East End Dwellings Co Ltd to provide dwellings and tenements in east, south and central London for the industrial and labouring classes. Between 1885 and 1936 erected property in Stepney Green, Whitechapel, Spitalfields, Bethnal Green, St Pancras, Kings Cross, Islington, and Camberwell Green. By 1900 residents numbered 6079, rising to 7207 in 1910, 7227 in 1920 and then falling to 6553 in 1930. Company owned 2207 tenements, 60 shops and workshops and 4555 rooms in 1920, rising to 2273 tenements, 77 shops and 4899 rooms in 1940. Acquired Lambeth Estate Co Ltd (inc 1879) in 1960 and Tenement Dwellings Co Ltd (inc 1887) in 1964. Name changed to Charlwood Properties Ltd in 1955. Merged in 1960 with Alliance Economic Investment Co Ltd (inc 1871) to form the above which was acquired by Town & City Properties Ltd.

Records: at London Borough of Newham, Local Studies Library, Stratford Reference Library, Water Lane, London E15 4NJ
directors meeting minutes 1884-1952; general meeting minutes 1884-1942; agm proceedings 1931; annual report and accounts 1884-1942; dwelling plans: Cromer Street Estate, Thrawl Street and Cartwright Street 1890s

453 JOHNSON GROUP MANAGEMENT SERVICES LTD

12 Feb 1884
19418
Mildmay Road, Bootle, Merseyside L20 5EW
Laundry

History: formed in 1884 as American Steam Laundry Co Ltd at Newcastle upon Tyne by James Joicey (later Lord Joicey) colliery proprietor, William Bird and others, to establish and operate a steam laundry. Acquired laundries at Moor Edge, Newcastle upon Tyne, in 1890; Blyth, Northumberland, in 1899; South Shields, Tyne & Wear where a dyeworks was constructed in 1900; and Scarborough, N Yorkshire in 1902. Changed name to Birds Ltd in 1911. London receiving agency was opened in 1925. By early 1930s had 11 laundry receiving shops and 2 dry cleaning shops. In 1938 acquired Heaton & Benton Laundry Co Ltd with a laundry at Heaton, Tyne & Wear. Closed Blyth laundry in 1929 and sold Scarborough laundry in 1945. Acquired Tynemouth & District Laundry Co Ltd (laundry closed in 1951) in 1949. In 1957 business was acquired by Johnson Group Cleaners Ltd, launders and dry cleaners of Bootle, Merseyside. Expansion in textile rental business from 1960s. Progressively closed laundry receiving shops and opened dry cleaning shops (had 24 in 1984). Heaton works closed in 1965 and South Shields works in 1970. Changed name to Hartonclean Ltd and subsequently to above.

Records (1): at Johnson Group Cleaners, Mildmay Road, Bootle, Merseyside L20 5EW
corporate documents 1884,1911; directors register c1919-60s

Records (2): at Hartonclean, 1 Claremont Road, Newcastle upon Tyne, Tyne & Wear NE2 4AX
directors meeting minutes 1884-1942,1966-71; general meeting minutes 1884-1962; Argentine reports 1914; share: ledger 1900-36, transfer register 1900-36, certificate books 1884-1934, papers 1892-1932; annual summaries 1900-02; memo and articles of association 1911; mortgage register 1894-1934; directors register c1900-36; debenture: holders meeting minutes 1935-60, register 1934 on, papers 1934 on; purchase agreement 1927; annual reports and accounts 1888-1923,1949-61; auditors correspondence 1901-12; accounts notes 1915-23; audited balance sheets and accounts 1898-1981; private ledger 1884-93; capital re-organisation papers 1962-7; creditors ledgers 1903-38; impersonal ledgers 1904-66; journals 1927-65; cash books 1909-14,1926-71; invoice book 1890-1900; price lists 1890s-1904; sales organisation and expansion reports 1935-7; unit shops cost books 1970-1; branch journey book 1922-8; chemical contracts and licences 1929-70; transport: papers 1950s, photographs 1920s; laundry contracts 1945-52; works committee meeting minutes 1942-59; employee: figures 1930-48, list 1949; wages book 1961-4; salesmen agreements 1933,1953-8; pension scheme papers 1930s; Moor Edge: private ledger 1894-c1902, wage summary 1935-6, financial and corporate records 1890s on; Fleetwing records 1950s on; Blyth laundry financial records 1930s on; laundry plan 1898-1939; title deeds, schedules, property documents and papers

1885-1960s; newscuttings 1879-1970s; directors and staff photographs c1884-c1904; yearly diary 1884-1937; history notes 1890s-1982
Hartonclean Ltd: directors and general meeting minutes 1955 on; members register 1927 on; corporate documents and papers 1899-1970s; sale agreement 1930; annual balance sheets and accounts 1935-7,1958-64; financial records 1890s on; property agreements and papers 1890s-1970s; trade union representative minutes 1946; diary 1933; history booklet 1949; menus 1949,1961
Heaton & Benton Laundry Co Ltd: directors and general meeting minutes 1912-38; corporate records 1910s-60s; annual balance sheets and accounts 1928-63; quarterly accounts 1944-64; financial records 1910s-60s
Tynemouth & District Laundry Co Ltd: directors and general meeting minutes 1906-12; corporate records 1900s-60s; annual reports and accounts 1958-66; quarterly trading accounts 1949-50; financial records 1900s-60s

EB Dobson, *Hartonclean 1884-1984. The Story of the First 100 Years* (priv pub 1984)

454 ROCHESTER CONSERVATIVE CLUB LTD
15 Feb 1884
19440
Star Hill, Rochester, Kent ME1 1SE
Political club-house

History: incorporated as above in 1884 to acquire land and erect a club-house for local Conservative association. Site of Rochester Theatre (built 1791) was purchased for £825, theatre was pulled down and the club-house built for £1940. By 1886 had 700 members, additional premises were rented and in 1894 the premises were altered and extended. By early 1950s club membership had fallen and closure was considered. From 1960s company purchased share capital and a programme of modernisation was put in hand which lasted until 1982.

Records: at Rochester Conservative Club, Star Hill, Rochester, Kent ME1 1SE
directors and general meeting minutes 1883-1907,1921-84; share ledger etc 1884-1984

455 ASHTON, STALYBRIDGE, HYDE & GLOSSOP BANK LTD
11 Mar 1884
19546
Croft House, 230 Stamford Street, Ashton under Lyne, Greater Manchester
Banking

History: established in 1836 as a joint stock bank in Ashton under Lyne, Greater Manchester, where it had its only office. Incorporated as above in 1884. Amalgamated with Parr's Bank Ltd in 1900, which amalgamated with London County & Westminster Bank Ltd to form London County Westminster & Parr's Bank Ltd in 1918.

Records: at National Westminster Bank, 41 Lothbury, London EC2P 2BP
board meeting minutes 1836-1902; list of shareholders 1895-9; deeds of settlement 1836-82;

articles of association 1898; amalgamation agreement 1900; half yearly balances 1880-1900; manager memoranda 1875-80; stock register 1836-1900; pledges of secrecy 1836-1900

TE Gregory, *The Westminster Bank Through A Century* Vol 2 (1936)

456 COSALT LTD

28 Mar 1884
19628
Fish Dock Road, Grimsby, Humberside DN31 3NW
Chandlery, net and caravan manufacturers

History: formed in Feb 1873 as Great Grimsby Coal Salt & Tanning Co Ltd by a group of Grimsby smack owners to supply the necessities for deep sea fishing, mainly coal and salt, as cheaply as possible. Purchased business and buildings of Grimsby Barking & Tanning Co which tanned nets and lines and barked sails, and coal business and premises of E Bannister & Co. By 1875 rope, paint, oil and other ships chandlery had been added to the business and in 1877 larger premises were built on Fish Dock Road. Acquired in 1881 the ironmongery and tinners business of Mr Dobson and opened a ships rigging department and net braiding room in 1882. By 1884 the company had reached the limit of its authorised powers and so it was wound up and re-incorporated under the same name with wider powers. A grocers and butchers department was opened in 1885 and an outfitting and boat building department in 1888. Helped form Grimsby Cordage Co Ltd which manufactured trawl twine in 1899. Branches were opened at Aberdeen, Grampian in 1893; Fleetwood, Lancashire 1901; Milford Haven, Dyfed 1907; Brixham, Devon 1909; Lowestoft, Suffolk 1920; and Padstow, Cornwall, and Sheringham, Norfolk by 1923. Agencies were established by 1923 at Nantes, France; Reykjavik, Iceland; Lisbon, Portugal; Huelva and Barcelona, Spain; and Oslo, Norway. In 1980 ships chandlery branches were in operation at Aberdeen; Channel Isles; Felixstowe, Suffolk; Fleetwood; Fraserburgh, Grampian; Granton, Lothian; Kilkeel, Ireland; Lowestoft; Milford Haven; Newlyn, Cornwall; North Shields, Tyne & Wear; Plymouth, Devon; Tilbury, London; and Troon, Strathclyde. Started to manufacture and sell caravans in 1966, receiving a Queens Award to Industry for exports in 1972. Was also involved in air conditioning units and commercial refrigeration which in 1980 was run from Hazel Grove, Stockport, Greater Manchester. In 1981 was manufacturing and selling fishing, industrial, sporting, horticultural and safety nets, synthetic twines and ropes at Kilbirnie, Strathclyde, through its subsidiary W&J Knox Fibres Ltd. Synthetic twines and ropes were manufactured at Annahilt, N Ireland, and caravans at Hull, Humberside and Stroud, Gloucestershire. Name changed to above in 1968.

Records: at Cosalt, Fish Dock Road, Grimsby, Humberside DN31 3NW
directors and general meeting: minutes 1877-date, agenda books 1893-c1940; departmental committee: minutes 1891-2, branch report 1909, conference report 1910; annual meeting papers 1904; directors attendance books 1891-1904,1942-60; share: register 1884-98, ledger and members registers 1889-1945, transfer documents 1876-1910, papers 1896; mortgage, bond and charge registers 1883-1954; dividends 1873-83; transfers 1873-9; debenture papers 1890-1904; prospectus 1873; memo and articles of association 1873-1950; corporate agreements and papers 1873-1908; annual returns 1884-1906; annual reports and accounts 1893-1933; balance sheets and audited accounts 1893-1922; comparative annual results 1912-61; monthly financial statements 1933-62; capital expenditure statements 1873-1918;

subsidiary companies financial statements 1964-5; departmental trading accounts 1922-68; engineering department accounts 1899-1907; capital ledgers 1878-84,1947-56; impersonal ledgers 1908-46; expenses ledgers 1957-64; journals 1943-76; bank books 1927-30; shipping accounts 1898-1910; legal papers, agreements, accounts etc 1894-1922; coal syndicate agreements 1894-1905; sales ledgers 1901-07,1965-8; branch stock sheets 1957-9; profit and pricing papers 1906-40; representatives order books 1899-1902; agency agreements 1899-1911; advertising material including photographs c1890-1960s; catalogues 1912-15; machinery and stock valuations 1907; equipment agreements 1905-c15; patents 1904-06; vessel plans 20 cent; staff: and apprenticeship agreements 1884-1903, papers 1912-18; property leases, agreements, schedules, papers etc 1875-1915; plans and photographs of Grimsby premises 1873-1940; general correspondence 1930s-40s; staff, premises, product photographs 20 cent; press cuttings 1875-1960; articles on company history 1909; branches - Aberdeen: office costs 1900-02, accounts 1900-07, trade and sales reports 1908-09, price lists 1900-03; plans and building specifications 1890-c1902; Fleetwood: accounts 1904-08, plans 1901-44; Brixham: report 1910, opening and publicity material 1910, financial papers 1925, plans 1912; Lowestoft: plans c1906

Abbott & Co (Lancaster) Ltd: minutes 1920-80; members register and share ledger 1920-76; share certificates 1921-76

Grimsby Cordage Co Ltd: directors: meeting minutes 1899-1977, attendance register 1953-68; general meeting minutes 1930-79; members registers 1899-1964; share ledgers 1896-1964; financial statements 1964-5; impersonal ledger 1955-63

Grimsby Cordage Roll Ltd: financial statements 1964-5; ledger 1936-63

Phillips Trawl Products Ltd: members register 1935-63; financial statements 1964-5

Walker Leigh Ltd: impersonal ledger 1931-67

457 PLYMOUTH ATHENAEUM

1 Apr 1884
19639
22 Derry's Cross, Plymouth, Devon PL1 2SW
Cultural society

History: founded in 1810 by Henry Woolcombe, lawyer and later Mayor of Plymouth, to act as a club to discuss social problems. In 1812 became society named Plymouth Institute (later Institution) with membership of 30, which heard lectures on natural philosophy and other subjects. Met from 1812-15 in Plymouth Dispensary, Catherine Street, and then in Frankfort Place Art Gallery. John Foulston designed the building, constructed in 1818, a museum being added in 1829, an art gallery in 1883 and a library in 1901. Devon & Cornwall Natural History Society, founded 1838, joined the institution in 1851 and name changed to Plymouth Institution & Devon & Cornwall Natural History Society. Incorporated as above as a company limited by guarantee in 1884. Plymouth Mechanics' Institute, founded 1827, was merged with the society in 1899. Foulston's building was destroyed in the blitz of 1941 and new building opened in 1961. Name changed to above in 1961. In 1980s lectures on science, arts and technology are given and the building is also used by local dramatic, film theatre, photographic, local history and archaeology, music and art societies and groups. Membership numbered about 500 in 1981.

Records: at Plymouth Athenaeum, 22 Derry's Cross, Plymouth, Devon PL1 2SW
executive, council and committee meeting minutes 1961-date; lecture programmes 1961-date; *Transactions of the Plymouth Institution/Proceedings of the Plymouth Athenaeum* 1830-date; prints of athenaeum interior and exterior 19 cent

M Alison Wilson, 'A Hundred and Fifty Years of the Plymouth Athenaeum', *Proceedings of The Plymouth Athenaeum* Vol 1 (1976)

458 SOHO CLERKENWELL & GENERAL INDUSTRIAL DWELLINGS CO LTD

2 Apr 1884
19647
7 Wolsey Road, East Molesey, Surrey KT8 9EL
Property

History: founded and incorporated as above in 1884 to created dwellings for industrial workers in Soho and Clerkenwell, London. Registered offices were at Lincoln's Inn Fields from 1890s to 1920s. Acquired by Greencoat Properties Ltd and by 1981 had been dormant for many years.

Records: at Greencoat Properties, 7 Wolsey Road, East Moseley, Surrey KT8 9EL
certificate of incorporation 1884; current records

459 CARDIFF & BRISTOL CHANNEL INCORPORATED SHIPOWNERS' ASSOCIATION

4 Apr 1884
19654
101-108E The Exchange, Mount Stuart Square, Cardiff, S Glamorgan CF1 6RD
Traders association

History: formed in 1884 as a company limited by guarantee as Cardiff Incorporated Shipowners' Association in Cardiff, S Glamorgan. Purpose was to carry on the activities of Cardiff Shipowners' Association formed in 1875 to represent the interests of shipowners who were elected to the association by its membership, and who paid an annual membership subscription. In 1912 authorised membership increased from 100 to 200. In 1914 name changed to above. In 1980s continued to represent the interests of local shipowners and those using ports in south Wales.

Records: at Glamorgan Archive Service, Record Office, County Hall, Cathays Park, Cardiff, S Glamorgan CF1 3NE

460 GLOUCESTERSHIRE & WILTSHIRE INCORPORATED LAW SOCIETY

4 Apr 1884
19680
Ellenborough House, Wellington Street, Cheltenham, Gloucestershire GL50 1YD
Law society

History: founded in 1817 by Gloucester solicitors as Gloucester Law Association with annual subscription of one guinea. Principal objects were to protect and advance the status of solicitors and promote honourable practice. Incorporated as above in 1884, when membership exceeded 100. In 1904 took over law library, previously maintained by Gloucestershire Law Library Society, and transferred it to the Shire Hall, Gloucester. In 1970 law library was sold.

Records: at Gloucestershire & Wiltshire Incorporated Law Society, Ellenborough House, Wellington Street, Cheltenham, Gloucestershire GL50 1YD
committee and general meeting minutes 1817-1944; register of members 1884-1984; law library committee meeting minutes 1905-54

461 NEWPORT & GWENT CHAMBER OF COMMERCE (INCORPORATED)

24 Apr 1884
19727
27 Carlton Chambers, High Street, Newport, Gwent NPT 1GE
Chamber of commerce

History: formed in 1870 to promote the interests of local trade, commerce and industry. Incorporated in 1884 as Newport (Monmouthshire) Chamber of Commerce (Incorporated) changing name to Newport & Monmouthshire Chamber of Commerce (Incorporated) in 1948 and to above in 1975. Formed Federation of Welsh Chambers of Commerce in 1965 along with Chambers of Commerce of Cardiff, Chester, Port Talbot, Neath and Swansea. In 1982 services included provision of business information, training course organisation, overseas export missions, the publication of bulletins on home and overseas affairs, export documentation and through the WCC, the representation of local interests at a national level. Original premises were Lloyds Bank Chambers, Newport, Gwent moving to Carlton Chambers in 1920.

Records (1): at Newport & Gwent Chamber of Commerce, 27 Carlton Chambers, High Street, Newport, Gwent NPT 1GE
chamber meeting minutes 1940-date; council meeting minutes 1941-date; annual report and accounts 1891-7,1916-date

Records (2): at Newport Central Library, 5 John Frost Square, Newport, Gwent NPT 1PA
chamber meeting minutes 1870-1939; council meeting minutes 1914-41; chairmans agenda 1915-16; agm presidential address 1928-31; constitution and laws 1870; annual reports and accounts 1884-9,1919-53,1961-7; ledger 1884-1921; cash book 1884-1916; newscuttings 1884-6; publications, reports, observations and notes on various matters 1892-1927

Records (3): at Gwent County Record Office, County Hall, Cwmbran, Gwent NP4 2XH
annual reports 1916-32; balance sheet 1932-9

462 DALGETY LTD

29 Apr 1884
19739
19 Hanover Square, London W1R 9DA
Holding (formerly Australasian merchants, wool brokers, stock, station and shipping agents)

History: established by Frederick Gonnerman Dalgety (1817-94) who arrived in Australia in 1833 and worked in several Sydney merchants houses before going to Melbourne in 1843 to establish a branch of Griffiths Fanning & Co as Griffiths Borrodaile & Co. He established himself in 1846 in a successor firm, Dalgety, Borrodaile & Gore (Dalgety, Gore & Co from 1847) and formed a branch with Charles Ibbotson in Geelong in 1847 as Dalgety, Ibbotson & Co. Firm provided goods for settlers and bought their produce. Gore retired 1851 and Dalgety entered partnership with AR Cruikshank as Dalgety, Cruikshank & Co. When latter died in 1857 he joined with James Blackwood (1820-81) as Dalgety, Blackwood & Co. Established head office in England in 1854 in partnership with Tasmanian merchant, Frederick Augustus du Croz (1821-97). Established branches in New Zealand through his brother Edmund S Dalgety as Dalgety, Rattray & Co in Dunedin in 1859 and Dalgety, Buckley & Co in Christchurch in 1860. They were reorganised as Dalgety Nicholls & Co in 1870-1. Opened branches in Sydney (Dalgety, Moore & Co) in 1878 and Newcastle (Dalgety, Blackwood & Co based on Great Northern Wool Dumping & Shipping Agency Co) in 1883. Incorporated in 1884 as Dalgety & Co Ltd with FG Dalgety as chairman until his death. Further Australian branches were opened in Perth in 1889, Albany in 1890, Rockhampton in 1891, Brisbane in 1894, Townsville in 1896, Adelaide in 1897, Albury in 1908, Wagga Wagga in 1923 and sub-branches in many smaller towns. Acquired the business of WC Hunter (formerly their agents) in Kenya in 1927. Kenyan interests were merged with those of Inchcape & Co in 1966 to form Mackenzie Dalgety Ltd but Dalgety sold their East African interests in 1969. Merged in 1961 with New Zealand Loan & Mercantile Agency Co Ltd to form Dalgety & New Zealand Loan Ltd which became the above in 1970 after a major reorganisation. Major branch operations were transferred to locally incorporated subsidiary companies Dalgety Australia Ltd and Dalgety New Zealand Ltd. Is represented in USA and Canada through Balfour Guthrie & Co Ltd and Balfour (Canada) Ltd. From 1884 to WW2 Dalgety acted as merchants, wool brokers, stock, station and shipping agents in Australasia. From 1945 its activities diversified. In the UK Dalgety Group included several agricultural merchants, pig breeders, stock feed manufacturers, animal vaccine, malt and fine chemical manufacturers, acquiring Spillers Ltd, animal food manufacturers, flour millers etc in 1979. In Australia Dalgety moved into pastoral development through Pastoral Development (Holdings) Ltd, formed 1964, and New Zealand & Australian Land Co Ltd, acquired 1968. Through Bonaire Ltd, purchased as BDH Ltd, deals in refrigerators, freezers and air conditioning equipment. Other group interests included rural land sub-division, coal mining, hybrid seed breeding, shipping agencies, farm and agricultural advisers. In 1984 sold interest in New Zealand.

Records (1): at Australian National University, Archives of Business & Labour Sciences, PO Box 4, Canberra, ACT 2600, Australia
directors meeting minutes 1884-1961; account committee: meeting minutes 1884-1940, letter book 1904-08; general meeting minutes 1884-1961; annual reports and accounts 1885-1946; chairmans, managing directors, colonial superintendents, secretarys, London managers: letter books 1884-1919, correspondence 1898-1940; Chief Australian inspector reports 1931-7; clients: and stations register c1929-49, genealogies nd-c1949; Australasian office and residence photographs nd; newscuttings 1919-51; FG Dalgety: letter books 1848-93, ledgers 1864-94, journals 1871-9, cash books 1873-83
African Mercantile Co Ltd: directors meeting minutes 1915-61; photographs c1950-8

New Zealand Loan & Mercantile Agency Co Ltd: directors: meeting minutes 1865-1946, attendances 1921-44, registers 1925-41, fees 1884-1930; finance committee meeting minutes 1902-40; articles of association and trust deeds 1897
New Zealand & Australian Land Co Ltd: annual meeting proceedings 1885-1926; members register 1969; annual returns 1934-72; memo and articles of association 1956; company secretarys correspondence and papers 1930s-69; share papers 1915-69; annual reports and accounts 1879-1972; underwriters claims book 1936-69; insurance policies 1897-1968; station photographs 1910-20s; history booklets and articles 1915,1918,1968
Henry Franklin Ltd: directors meeting minutes 1934-59; members register 1934-59; debenture register 1934; directors register 1949-59
Howland & Bush Ltd: directors meeting minutes 1927-62
Stuart Kinross & Co: letter book 1858-64
Samuel Page & Son Ltd: directors meeting minutes 1933-61; members, share and directors register 1933-49
Geo H Penney & Co Ltd: directors meeting minutes 1948-63
W Smith & Son (Dickleburgh) Ltd: directors meeting minutes 1942-65
WA Sparrow & Co Ltd: directors meeting minutes 1920-64; general meeting minutes 1948-64
Taylor Bros (Smithfield) Ltd: directors meeting minutes 1933-58
CF Turner Ltd: directors meeting minutes 1948-64
Samuel Wilkerson & Son Ltd: directors meeting minutes 1952-63; general meeting minutes 1953-62

Records (2): at Dalgety, 19 Hanover Square, London W1R 9DA
directors and general meeting minutes 1961 on; annual reports and accounts 1946 on; subsidiary company records 1960s on

463 OXTED GREYSTONE LIME CO LTD
29 Apr 1884
19741
Conyngham Hall, Knaresborough, N Yorkshire HG5 9AY
Lime

History: formed in 1884 to lease quarries in Oxted, Surrey and to construct plant for the manufacture of lime and lime products. Original capital of £5000 was in £10 shares. Acquired in 1981 by Thomas Tilling Ltd and became a subsidiary of Tilcon Ltd of Knaresborough, N Yorkshire. By 1983 was a dormant company.

Records: at Tilcon, Conyngham Hall, Knaresborough, N Yorkshire HG5 9AY
board meeting minutes 1946 on; register of members 1904 on

464 LANCASHIRE & YORKSHIRE REVERSIONARY INTEREST CO LTD
3 May 1884
19770
Winchester House, Fountain Street, Manchester, Greater Manchester M2 2EF
Investment

History: established in Manchester in 1884 for investing in life interests and reversions. In 1921 was acquired by Yorkshire Insurance Co Ltd, which became a subsidiary of General Accident Fire & Life Assurance Corporation Ltd in 1967.

Records: at Lancashire & Yorkshire Reversionary Interest, Winchester House, Fountain Street, Manchester, Greater Manchester M2 2EF
meeting minutes: board 1884-1958, general 1884 on; balance sheets 1898,1906,1918-date; nominal ledgers 1884,1949-date; journals 1944 on; cash books 1936 on; reversions: information books, loans 1889-date, loan ledgers 1928 on, purchase books 1889-date, purchase ledgers 1909 on

465 PROVIDENT LIFE ASSOCIATION OF LONDON LTD

3 May 1884
19772
Provident House, 266 Bishopsgate, London EC2M 4QP
Insurance

History: established in 1877 and incorporated as Provident Association of London Ltd in 1884 to issue endowment bonds and grant advances for purchase of home property. In 1911 acquired Provident Free Home Assurance Co Ltd and name changed to above in 1958. In 1985 principal subsidiaries were United Standard Insurance Co Ltd and Vigilant Assurance Co Ltd and principal business was life and pensions business.

Records: at Provident Life Association of London, Provident House, 266 Bishopsgate, London EC2M 4QP
agents: appointments and business accounts 1887-1959, salary terms 1889 on; bond: registers 1883-1940, and policy holders ledgers 1884-99; collectors account books 1890-1923; registers: endorsement 1888-date, policy 1894-1937, suspensions 1910-22, transfer 1896-8, premium collection 1882-1928; estates ledgers 1908 on; ground rents 1888-1923; loan department: transfers 1911-65, special advances 1888 on

466 INSTITUTE OF BUILDING

8 May 1884
19789
Englemere, Kings Ride, Ascot, Berkshire SL5 8BJ
Professional association

History: founded in 1834 as Builders' Society by a group of leading builders, and was devoted to industrial problems and the setting up of a benevolent fund. Reconstituted in 1884 and incorporated as a company limited by guarantee as Institute of Builders, to promote and represent the building trade and protect the interests of those engaged in it, diffuse information to members, suppress malpractice, and encourage equitable forms of contract and the settling of disputes by arbitration. Promoted educational foundations and studentships in building science and issued standard forms of contract and sub-contract. Became the professional institution for the building industry in 1923. Branches were established in Manchester in 1920; in south Wales and Liverpool in 1921; and in the midlands in 1923. Published a journal, *Building Technology and Management*, from 1937. Name changed to above in 1965. Merged with Institute of Building Estimators Ltd and Institute of Building

Site Management in 1968, Institute of Hospital Building Supervisors in 1972, and Institute of Cost & Production Surveyors in 1981. Original offices were at 31 Bedford Street, London, moving to 48 Bedford Square in 1918, and to Englemere, Ascot, Berkshire in 1972. Received a Royal Charter and became Chartered Institute of Building in 1980 when it was a registered educational charity and had over 26,000 members engaged in building - in managerial, technical, scientific, commercial, educational or administrative positions or undergoing training.

Records: at Chartered Institute of Building, Englemere, Kings Ride, Ascot, Berkshire SL5 8BJ council, agm and committee meeting: minutes 1859-date, agendas 1884-1970; council meeting: papers 1884-1964, committee attendance books 1914-63; committee reports 1927-55; institute meeting proceedings 1887-90,1950-3; licentiated discussion clubs: meeting minutes 1925-65, and reports 1928-59, rules, book catalogues c1948-59, Nottingham conference papers 1965; memo and articles of association 1919-59; annual reports and accounts 1884-date; balance sheets and accounts 1897-1954; ledgers 1886-1950; cash books 1884-1922; petty cash book 1904-22; bank books 1924-9; membership: roll 1884-1935, statistics 1918-23, lists 1868-84,1947-date, subscription books 1885-1956, certificates 1885-1908, conditions, rules etc booklets 1875,1925-66; mature entry theses 1966-76; annual dinner: account books 1902-24, menus, table plans, guest lists, photographs, programmes, speech notes etc 1903,1911-67; benevolent fund: rules c1859-86, account statements 1884-6, audited accounts 1918-68, cash book 1887-1924, bank books 1922-9; building and education reports and papers 1920s; examination papers, reports, syllabuses, pass lists, assessors lists, student forms 1939-date; travelling studentship reports 1938-62; secretarys out letter books 1884-1904; contract and sub-contract correspondence and papers 1901-51; correspondence: with National Federation of Building Trade Employers 1932-51, re Australian branch 1924-8; journal 1937-date; publications 1902-date; president photographs 19-20 cent; press cutting books 1925-58; Royal Institute of British Architects petition papers 1930; mock planning appeal papers 1966; Hong Kong centre photographs 1973; Thomas Fullford account book 1783-91
South East Federation of National Association of Master Builders: minutes 1898-1901
Institute of Building Estimators Ltd: council meeting minutes 1965-8; papers and newscuttings re merger 1952,1968

467 RANSOMES SIMS & JEFFERIES LTD
12 May 1884
19802
Nacton Works, Ipswich, Suffolk IP3 9QG
Engineering (especially agricultural)

History: founded by Robert Ransome (1753-1830) a Quaker from Wells, Norfolk, who set up a brass and iron foundry in Norwich, mainly supplying plough shares to farmers. In 1785 patented a method of tempering cast iron shares. Transferred business in 1789 to Ipswich, Suffolk, where patented 'chilling' method for plough shares, and in 1808 patented manufacture of interchangeable plough parts. By 1809 trading as Ransome & Son on entry of James Ransome. Diversified and extended activities into general engineering, including bridge building and mill wrighting from 1812 with William Cubbitt, civil engineer (left firm in 1826), directing the business. In 1819 constructed plant for gas supply to Ipswich. Known from 1818 as Ransomes & Sons, from 1825 as J&R Ransome, and from 1830 as JR&A Ransome. In 1832 manufactured the world's first lawn mower under Budding's patent, and by 1852 had produced c1500 machines. In 1841 exhibited first steam thrashing machine and in 1842 first self-moving (traction) engine. Also manufactured wide range of agricultural implements. From mid 1830s involved in railway work under direction of Charles May (left firm c1851) which introduced mass production techniques, and between 1847-67 constructed 12,000 miles of rail. From 1846 known as Ransomes & May. By 1849 production was moved to Orwell Works on Ipswich Dockside. Known as Ransomes & Sims from 1852. Co-operated with John Fowler, Leeds agricultural engineer, in mechanical soil tillage equipment, but were mainly involved in portable and later self-moving steam engines rather than steam ploughs. Experimented with production of harvesting machines in 1860s. From 1875 exports grew rapidly, especially to British colonies. In 1869 the railway work had been transferred to another Ipswich company, Ransomes & Rapier, to accommodate expansion, and in 1871 transferred whole of manufacture of food preparation machinery to Hunts of Earls Colne, Essex. In 1872 separate lawn mower works was established. Known as Ransomes, Head & Jefferies from 1881 and in 1884 became a private limited company known as above. Became a public company in 1911. Period from 1900 to WW1 was one of unprecedented prosperity. During WW1, 2000 women supplemented wartime workforce, manufacturing not only agricultural machinery but shell cases, mine sinkers, howitzers and fighter planes. Diversification into production of bus bodies, trolley buses, fairground amusements, electric vehicles and industrial motors and precision tools occurred during 1920s and 1930s. From 1937 lawn mower production, especially gang motors, expanded. During WW2 agricultural output expanded and war contracts, including precision instruments for Rolls Royce Merlin engines, were completed. In 1946 acquired new 250 acre site at Nacton, just outside Ipswich, where construction of new foundry started in 1947, but move from Orwell Works was not completed until 1974. Output diversified in post-war period and by 1973 agricultural and non-agricultural equipment were of equal importance. Manufacture was carried on in 4 divisions: tillage equipment, including crop spraying machinery; harvesting machinery, including potato and sugar - an interest acquired with Johnson's (Engineering) Ltd and Catchpole Engineering Co Ltd in 1968; electric trucks, especially battery fork lifts; and grass machinery, specialising in grass-cutting machinery for commercial use. One third of total sales in 1973 were exports marketed through dealers, and distribution and subsidiary companies, the latter in 1982 consisting of Ransomes Deutschland GmbH, Munster, Germany and Ransomes France SA, Le Chatelet-en-Brie, France. Ransomes Overseas Services Ltd was formed in 1970s to supply consultancy and management expertise, and Ransomes Property Developments Ltd was established in 1972 to deal with property in Nacton and Catchpole, Bury St Edmunds, Suffolk. In 1973 had factory at March, Cambridgeshire, manufacturing grass machinery components; works of Steel Case Co Ltd at Tredegar, Gwent, supplying steel plate and carrying out heat treatment; and component works at Doncaster, S Yorkshire.

Records (1): at Ransomes Sims & Jeffries, Nacton Works, Ipswich, Suffolk IP3 9QG
directors meetings: minutes 1884-date, proceeding reports 1919-date, attendance books 1949-64; directors memoranda 1892-1965; shareholders minutes 1884-date; annual reports and accounts 1883-date; financial statements 1851-1880; capital payments register 1865-83; bad debts notebook 1878-1927; financial memoranda book c1890-1920s; steam engine: order book 1852-84, drawings nd, instruction book c1852-69; patterns register 1849-1918; patents (photocopies) 1783-1847; plough sketch book 1800s; soil type notebook 1879; lawnmower register c1832 on; microfilmed drawings 1950 on; Barcograph drawing negatives c1916-56;

sales statistics 1871-1950; sales: catalogues 1862-8, leaflets 1960-date; price lists c1900; travellers notebook 1897; workmen lists 1793-1841; apprentice indenture abstracts c1840-78; notebooks: clerks c1837-1948, wages 1895-1918, staff 1911-25; office parts duties 1896; war casualties 1939-44; wages book 1859-71; salaries books: clerks 1863-1926, managers and travellers 1863-86; works: payroll 1939, fines account book 1883-1917, notices 1877-1953; foundry estate plan 1823; assessments notebook 1912-17; general memoranda book 1897-1921; photographs, drawings, paintings etc of staff, premises, products, transport, directors etc 1840-1970s; photograph registers pre 1856-date; company publications on history, production, works etc 1862-1964; printed lectures and notes on ploughs and ploughing 1865-1940s; press cuttings and releases 1981 on; misc documents and objects 1807-1950s

Catchpole Engineering Co Ltd: directors and general meeting minutes 1947-71; management committee minutes 1965-8; members register etc 1947-68; share certificates, transfers and register 1960s; corporate agreements 1947-68; memo and articles of association 1947; documents re takeover c1968; pension scheme: trustee minutes 1961-8, deeds 1961-3, rules 1960s; deeds and documents re High Street property 1927-67

Johnson's (Engineering) Ltd: minutes 1941-68; members register etc 1941-68; share certificates and transfer documents c1968; documents re takeover c1968

Johnson's (Implements) Scotland Ltd: minutes 1957-68; members register etc 1957-68; share certificates and transfer documents c1968; corporate documents 1957-68; documents re takeover c1968

Records (2): at Institute of Agricultural History & Museum of English Rural Life, University of Reading, Whiteknights, Reading, Berkshire RG6 2AG

directors: minutes 1884-1937, proceedings 1919-39; partnership deeds and papers 1809-75; shareholders circulars 1922-68; prospectus and trust deeds 1911; share and stock papers 1948-51; stock transfer register 1911-48; memo and articles of association 1884-1937; corporate papers 1884-1937; annual reports and accounts 1941-79; summary balance sheets 1837-50; annual financial statments 1845-1980; private ledgers 1884-1967; capital ledger 1865-83; nominal ledger 1920-39; QQ (PR) 1920-54; bought ledgers 1962-72; general account book 1804-39; memoranda account book 1895-1925; cost accounts analysis 1885,1936-9; summary accounts notebook 1884-1901; outstanding debts list 1920; correspondence: accounts department administration 1901-04, loan 1838; misc invoices 1834-54; cost analysis books 1958-67; sales, output and wage annual summaries 1884-1901; summary and detailed sales books 1877-88,1906-55; order and sales analyses 1871-1976; order books: general 1932-60, turnery 1860-1949, boiler shop 1895-1946, electric trucks 1917-60, electric vehicles 1920-57, dynamos and motors 1922-51, amusement devices 1927-32, petrol engine components 1936-41, crop sprayers 1945-9, WW2 government work 1941-6; correspondence and data re orders 1927-43; dispatch and purchase books 1867-1932; export books: Peru and United States of Columbia 1875-89, Roumania 1866-85, Russia 1861-85; implement agencies books 1914-50; agency: terms books 1940-50s, information sheets 1969; customer registers and indexes 1911-48; customer records: home 1845-1969, foreign 1906-61; correspondence and notes re sales and marketing trips 1804,1839,1875-1961; commercial reports 1942-8; price lists 1800-1968; prices and price fixing notes 1866-1931; publicity notes, press releases, press cuttings etc 1840-1980; illustrated catalogues, instructions, advertising and servicing leaflets 1800-1970s; catalogue order books 1931-58; artwork: albums 1810-25,1850-1969, order books 1931-66; products and machinery photographs and indexes c1856-1969; patent specifications, agreements, papers and correspondence 1785-1934; trade-mark and registered design papers and correspondence 1872-1932; patent register 1942-75; pattern book 1849-88; plough and parts registers 1839-1956; engine and parts registers, lists and papers 1846-1945; electric trucks: register 1920s-80, wiring specifications 1922-61, government authorities register 1940-2, production licences 1943-7, traction gearing register and supply book 1920-48; engine report and registration books 1874-1914; corn mill report books 1881-1910; trolley bus production lists 1925-48; special requirement book 1909-32; internal works forms 1880-1900; production remuneration and transfer details 1955; experiment and trial books and details 1838-1963; manufacturing test log books 1896-1919; engineering notebooks 1881-1930; ploughs and fittings notebook 1833-81; parts schedules 1940-78; grass machinery reports 1964-6; drawing ledgers, registers, sketch books and indexes 1834-1968; Barcograph drawing transparencies 1880s-1974; technical publications 1850-77; printed matter reference books 1918-61; wages analysis sheets 1871-1939; salaries and wages: books 1887-1940, cost notes 1887-1924; staff details 1920-50; apprenticeship: register 1838-72, indentures 1822,1854-6; employee: lists and registers 1835-1966, character reference files 1900,1917; employment contracts 1900,1920s; training memo 1959; staff appointments and conditions correspondence 1840-1969; staff relief fund: members lists and accounts 1817-42, invalids details 1838-49; friendly society rules 1839,1842; staff pension fund rules book 1940; social events records 20 cent; staff photographs 19&20 cents; house journals 1956-77; conveyancing papers 1852; office equipment purchase register 1925-69; property, buildings and plant valuation files 1895-1964; office equipment fault book 1963; prize lists and registers 1807-1926; exhibition: certificates 1851-1976, photographs 1939-75; misc correspondence 1842-1955; typescript histories, working notes, diaries etc 1774-1970s; family notebooks and correspondence 1804-39; competitors catalogues and publicity material 19-20 cent; Aircraft Works: shops, plant and staff details 1916-18; Lawnmower Works: future report 1918; Odessa Branch: financial statements 1892-1919, correspondence re staff nd; Orwell Works: cost accounts system papers 1856-78, goods dispatched analysis books 1861-91, programme of visit and guide 1886, general and detailed plans 1846-60, alteration records 1870-91, lands, buildings and plant particulars 1852, society and sports clubs records 1931-76, Home Guard records 1940-4, press cuttings 1847-1926, typescript history 1928-30; Princes Street Warehouse (Ipswich): general ledgers 1916-47, principal journals 1902-28, cash book 1946-8; Town Warehouse (Ipswich and Bury St Edmunds): annual statements 1909-46, customer accounts statements 1937-54, regulations 1892, auction records 1957

Catchpole Engineering Co Ltd: publications 1948-68; press cuttings 1960s; news releases 1960-9; photographs of products, works, shows etc nd

James & Frederick Howard Ltd: agricultural implement test photographs 1905-15; advertising and servicing publications 1851-c1930; patent specifications, agreements and correspondence 1925-8; registered designs and trade-mark papers 1912-29

Johnson's (Engineering) Ltd: press cuttings 1960s; plant and machinery valuation register 1952-63

D Lorant Ltd: financial statements 1938-51

James Ransome: foundry account book 1805-07

Ransomes Sims & Jefferies (Watford) Ltd: financial statements 1952-60

Ransomes Sociedad de Responsabilidad Limitada: branch balance sheets 1948-56

Ruston & Hornsby Ltd: memo and articles of association c1919-74; WW2 government work order books 1938-44; advertising and servicing publications 1926-34; Barcograph drawing

order books 1938-44; advertising and servicing publications 1926-34; Barcograph drawing transparencies c1919-74; drawings nd
Ruston Proctor & Co Ltd: drawings nd
Saunders Steel Case Co Ltd: private ledger 1953-69
Smyth & Sons Ltd, Peasehall: photographs of products 1960s
Societe Balkanique Commercialle & Industrielle: articles of association 1911; annual reports 1914-22; misc correspondence nd

Records (3): at Suffolk Record Office, Ipswich Branch, County Hall, St Helen's Street, Ipswich, Suffolk IP4 2JS
photographs and printed material re Ipswich trolley and motor buses and vehicles 20 cent

DR Grace and DC Phillips, *Ransomes of Ipswich: A History of the Firm and Guide to its Records* (1975)

468 SHROPSHIRE SHEEP BREEDERS' ASSOCIATION & FLOCK BOOK SOCIETY

13 May 1884
19803
11 Priory Terrace, Leamington Spa, Warwickshire
Breed society

History: in 1882 leading Shropshire breeders formed Shropshire Sheep Breeders & Flock Book Society, publishing its first flock book in 1883. Incorporated as above as company limited by guarantee in 1884. Issued flock book, maintained breed register, awarded medals and issued importation certificates. The first show and sale was held at Shrewsbury in 1917. By 1920 Shropshire sheep were exported to Australia, New Zealand, USA, South Africa, Russia, Europe, Sweden, Greece and Hungary, although after 1922 exports were affected by outbreaks of foot and mouth disease. By 1974 the society had only 22 members, and the possibility of winding up the society was considered. However, with the aid of Rare Breeds Survival Trust, the breed was again considered commercially viable and by 1980s the society's membership was increased.

Records: at Shropshire Sheep Breeders' Association & Flock Book Society, Cattle Market, The Butts, Worcester, Hereford & Worcester
council and general meeting minutes 1921-76; memo and articles of association 1884; balance sheets 1952-60; cash book 1927-67; editing committee: meeting minutes 1883-1952, and breed publicity meeting minutes 1952-61; flock books: 1882-date, New Zealand 1961-83; entrance forms c1920,1930; subscription book 1928-67; export certificates 1939-77; flock returns 1972-80

469 YORK INCORPORATED (CHURCH OF ENGLAND) SUNDAY SCHOOL COMMITTEE INSTITUTED 1786

14 May 1884
19806
18 Blake Street, York, N Yorkshire YO1 2QH
Sunday schools

History: traces origins to 1786 when a meeting was called to consider the establishment of Sunday schools in York for religious teaching to the children of the poor. Ten schools opened in 1786 under the general administration of a Sunday school committee. In 1853 a library for use of teachers was established. By 1884 there were 16 schools and 2548 pupils taught by 225 voluntary teachers. In that year administration was taken over by York Incorporated (Church of England) Sunday School Committee whose objects were to carry on Church of England Sunday schools and the maintenance of a library for teachers. By 1980s the committee used income from investments to purchase materials for and make grants to local Sunday schools.

Records: at York Incorporated (Church of England) Sunday School Committee, 18 Blake Street, York, N Yorkshire YO1 2QH
annual report and accounts 1827-1900; account sheets 1844; pocket book journal 1881-1902; cheque and credit counterfoils 1881-1912; investment vouchers 1846,1858; publications: ledger 1849-55, summary sheet 1851; publications and history articles 1789-1896; insurance papers 1856-81; Walmgate Sunday School plan and papers 1827; Groves proposed school papers 1856; St Margaret's Sunday School correspondence 1889; teachers list 1857; school annual treat programmes, plans, accounts etc 1842-63; absentee papers c1860s; parental attendance forms 1860s; reports, correspondence and receipts 1835-1914; history papers 1887-96

470 MANCHESTER INCORPORATED LAW LIBRARY SOCIETY

21 May 1884
19836
Law Library, 14 Kennedy Street, Manchester, Greater Manchester M2 4BY
Law library

History: founded by a group of barristers and solicitors in 1820 to establish in Manchester a law library to serve both branches of the legal profession. Until headquarters were established in 1835 over Savings Bank on the corner of King Street and Pall Mall, the library was housed in several solicitors' offices. When Manchester Corporation acquired premises in 1844, Law Library sub-let two rooms on the first floor of 4 Norfolk Street, offices of Manchester Law Association (est 1838). In 1865, leased the third floor of 78 Cross Street and rented out a room to Law Association. The above was registered in 1884 as a company limited by guarantee to acquire and maintain the library. Purchased premises in Kennedy Street which were demolished and a new building (grade II listed in 1981) erected to the designs of Mr Hartas was opened in 1885. First catalogue of its books was printed in 1823. By 1838 there were 700 volumes, growing to 15,000 by 1970. In 1981 had about 650 members.

Records: at Manchester Central Library Archives Department, St Peter's Square, Manchester, Greater Manchester M2 5PD
committee: proceedings and agm minutes 1820-1955, reports 1882-4, resolutions 1884-5,1904, election voting papers 1840,1866; agm notices and balance sheets 1859-1939; members and shares register 1868-1956; corporate papers 1884,1903-04; memo and articles of association 1884-1919; annual reports 1885-1950; audited balance sheets 1860-1936; cash books 1820-1953; vouchers 1864-70; rules 1820-84; admission books 1838-88; subscription books 1843-1902; members lists 1823-1922; statistics 1899-1911; hon secretarys letter books 1864-1940; librarian applications 1836,1877; accessions register 1832-1934; proposition books 19-20 cent; property documents, papers and correspondence 1847-1954; mortgage deeds and

correspondence 1884-1956; building tenders 1884; architect and builder accounts 1885-6; plans and designs 1875-1953; light rights agreements papers and correspondence 1885-1953; insurance policies 1941-4; misc papers and correspondence 19-20 cent

Kenneth H Atkinson, *A Short History of the Manchester Law Society 1838-1924* (priv pub 1924)

471 NOTTINGHAM & NOTTINGHAMSHIRE BANKING CO LTD

21 May 1884
19862
Thorland Street, Nottingham, Nottinghamshire
Banking

History: established in Pelham Street, Derby in 1834. Branches opened in Nottinghamshire at Mansfield (1834), Loughborough (1834), Newark (1835), Worksop (1836), Retford (1836), and Southwell (1874), numbering 20 with 18 sub-branches by 1919. Registered with limited liability as above in 1884 and amalgamated with London County Westminster & Parr's Bank Ltd in 1919, which became Westminster Bank Ltd in 1923.

Records: at National Westminster Bank, 41 Lothbury, London EC2P 2BP
board meeting minutes 1834-1918; share capital summary 1880; deeds of settlement 1834,1873; amalgamation papers 1917-18; balance sheets 1907-18; register of notes 1834-1918; investment and property ledgers 1858-80; clerks salary minutes 1872-1901; officers agreements 1873-92; salary book 1901-18; rules book 1893; general managers letter books 1844-61; managers letter book 1897-1909; Newark branch general ledger 1835-42

TE Gregory, *The Westminster Bank Through A Century* Vol 1&2 (1936)

472 INSTITUTE OF LONDON UNDERWRITERS

5 Jun 1884
19900
40 Lime Street, London EC3M 5DA
Underwriters

History: established in London in 1884 as an association of marine insurance companies for 'the advancement of marine insurance and the protection of the interests of marine underwriters'. It superceded the informal meetings of insurance officials, which had been held since the 1850s. Its work included the approval and issue of standard insurance clauses and wordings. With Lloyd's of London it formed Joint Hull Committee in 1910 for the consideration of hull insurance matters; Joint Hull Returns Bureau in 1922 for settling claims for returns of insurance premiums while hulls are laid up; Joint Construction Risks Committee in 1933; and Joint Cargo Committee in 1942 which deals with cargo insurance topics. The institute's committees also included Claims Adjusters' Committee (est in 1921) Technical & Clauses Committee (est 1925) and War Risks Committee (est 1935). In 1984 membership comprised 106 UK and overseas insurance companies with underwriting interests in the London marine, aviation and transport insurance markets.

Records: at Institute of London Underwriters, 40 Lime Street, London EC3M 5DA
committee meeting minutes: and agendas 1884-date, claims 1921-date, joint hull 1910-date,

joint cargo 1942-date, technical and clauses 1925-date, war risks rating 1935-date; members: weekly meeting notes 1884-date, circulars 1884-date; annual reports and accounts 1884-date; chairmens annual statements 1884-date; financial statements 1884-date

C Hewer, *A Problem Shared. A History of the Institute of London Underwriters 1884-1984* (1984)

473 BRYANT & MAY (HOLDINGS) LTD

12 Jun 1884
19925
PO Box 57, Totteridge Road, High Wycombe, Buckinghamshire HP13 6EJ
Match manufacturers

History: established in 1839 when Francis May of London (1803) and William Bryant of Plymouth, Devon (1804-74) became associated in business as Bryant & May, general merchants operating at Tooley Street, London and Philpot Lane, Fenchurch Street, London. Under a partnership agreement of 1851 Bryant stayed in Plymouth while May managed the London business. Under an arrangement with Carl & Johan Lundstrom, match makers of Jonkoping, Sweden, the firms distributed Swedish matches and sent ink and headless uncut wax vestas to the Lundstroms. Francis May acquired British patent for safety matches based on Lundstroms specifications in 1855 and William Bryant leased Fairfield Works, Fairfield Road, Bow, London in 1861. Initially this factory produced safety matches using Swedish splints whilst Bryant & May continued to import Lundstrom 'strike anywhere' matches. William Bryant left Plymouth in 1862 and in 1863 his son, Wilberforce, joined the partnership as manager at Bow, London. In about 1868 Francis May left the business which was incorporated in 1884 as Bryant & May Ltd. In 1885 acquired Bell & Black Match Co Ltd (est 1839) with its 4 factories at Stratford, London, Manchester, Glasgow and York. Amalgamated in 1901 with Diamond Match Co of America which had a factory in Liverpool, 2 factories in South Africa and controlled Irish Match Co Ltd, Belfast. Wilberforce Bryant's death in 1906 saw the end of family participation in the business. New match factories were built by 1911 at Bow, London at Empire Works, Glasgow in 1920 and at Leeds in 1927. Diamond Works at Litherland, Liverpool was completely destroyed in an air attack in 1941. Mersey Works at Garston were subsequently expanded and were still in operation in 1983 along with the Glasgow factory. Production of woodstick matches ceased at Bow, London in 1971 and the remaining book match works was closed in 1979 and subsequently sold. From 1922 to 1960 the company managed an aspen forest estate at Ballochyle, Argyll. Changed name to above in 1966. Acquired by Wilkinson Sword Ltd in 1974 to form Wilkinson Match Ltd (later renamed Wilkinson Sword Group Ltd).

Records (1): at Wilkinson Sword Group, Langley Hall, Station Road, Langley, Slough, Berkshire SL3 8BZ
directors meeting minutes 1884-date; general meeting minutes 1884-date

Records (2): at Hackney Archives Department, Rose Lipman Library, De Beauvoir Road, London N1 5SQ
directors meeting: agenda book 1884, attendance books 1905-74; executive committee meeting minutes 1919-27; stockholders meeting minutes 1913-45; general meeting: notes 1901,1950-2, notices 1918-35, attendance books 1885-1922; members: lists 1884-5, registers

1884-98; share: issue particulars 1885-6, prices and transfers diaries 1884-1902; shareholders papers 1899-1916; annual returns 1929,1933,1939; debenture stock papers 1884-1933; memo and articles of association 1884-1928; seal registers 1897-1959; partnership agreements 1851-63; Francis May: correspondence and accounts 1827-60, diary 1865-6, bank book 1878-80, papers 1840-62, history notes 1955; papers and correspondence: corporate 1870-1959, match making companies and subsidiaries 1884-1957; group conference papers 1968-70; annual reports and accounts 1884-1958; balance sheets: and trading accounts 1886-1952, schedules and accounts 1902-63; account books 1852-82; private ledgers: 1884-1960, balances 1902-69; general ledgers: 1906, Fairfield 1915-53, Diamond 1913-51, Empire 1919-51, Mersey 1923-52, Leeds 1923-52, personal 1913-52, customers 1917-52, bad debts 1911-13, expenses 1920-52, journal 1952; summary ledger 1966-77; advertising ledgers 1900-74; private journals 1884-1970; nominal journals 1932-52; private cash books 1902-68; directors financial statements 1901-40; profiteering accounts 1902-21; trading accounts analysis 1912-21; investment papers and accounts 1908-47; income tax papers 1901-40; subsidiaries balance sheets and financial papers 1949-60; sales: figures 1903-04, Irish figures 1938-44, papers 1895-1967; selling expenses schedules 1927-47; group marketing conference papers 1955-6; royal warrant papers 1912-55; travellers circular letters, price lists, papers etc 1901-59; advertising contracts correspondence 1937-67; marketing papers 1959-72; catalogues and price lists 1872-1940; handbills and advertising material incl photographs 1865-c1970; exhibition: certificates 1875-1938, photographs c1880s-1950s; production: book 1864-71, papers 1953-72; census 1906-39; reports 1948-52; factory statements 1911-22; stock, production and sales statements 1937-51; costs books: 1904,1912-18,1948, factories 1904-09,1947-9, tin box department 1902-08, papers 1912-16; patent: books 1902-35, agreements, licences, specifications and papers 1855-1933; recipes: soap making 1856-62, matches 1856-62; production, machinery, transport and personnel photographs c1890-1956; premises papers 1893-1928; Fairfield Works: property papers 1870-1909, repair correspondence 1940-3, photographs 1874-1944; Merseyside factories: war damage correspondence 1936-52, photographs c1895-1948; Empire Works photographs 1920-42; Leeds factory photographs c1920-56; Ballochyle estate: cash books 1920-59, wage sheets 1952, photographs 1922-51; forestry estates: cash book 1965-8, photographs c1922,1950s; works committee meeting minutes: 1918-47, Glasgow 1938-69; wages: and hours enquiry 1906, sheets 1965-9, papers 1949-c60; personnel files 1953-60s; employee conditions papers 1852-1950; pension fund: rules booklets 1920-59, account books 1914-57; house magazine: 1921-68, correspondence and papers 1959-75; staff and directors photographs 1874-1950s; press releases 1956-72; public relations correspondence c1930,1963-75; factory visit: gramophone recording 1930s, film c1955; history booklets, articles, correspondence and notes 1892-1972; fire making museum: photographs, catalogues, notes, correspondence etc 1920s-70s, advertisements, articles and booklets 1691-c1960; Gilbert Bartholemew, managing director correspondence and papers 1885-1914; AW Bryant correspondence and papers 1888-96; match companies correspondence 1899-1974; directors and staff correspondence 1907-74; newscuttings 1890-1973; misc photographs c1900-61

Brymay Partnership Trust Ltd: management committee: meeting minutes 1920-59, members register 1920-61; general meeting minutes 1920-61; members register and share ledger 1920-55; share: registers 1920-59, transfer registers 1920-34; directors register 1934-53; memo and articles of association 1920; seal books 1920-59; trust deeds, circular letters and notices 1912-35; booklets 1929-39; ledgers 1926-60; cash books 1941-59; allowance book 1950-2; closed accounts 1957-76; Brymay Savings Bank: annual accounts 1948-78, analysis 1926-72

Brymay Athletic Association: ledgers 1925-66; cash book and annual accounts 1920-60; petty cash book 1925-60; correspondence 1911-64; programme 1914; photograph c1900
British Match Corporation: annual meeting reports 1928-49; monopolies commission papers 1973; directors register 1927-50; annual returns 1964-7; annual reports and accounts 1928-60; interim reports 1963-4; trading agreements schedules 1928-39; consolidated accounts and papers 1948-61; group accounts 1966-7; capital ledger 1958-72; general ledger 1958-72; match: trading results 1948-54, prices graphs 1953-62; correspondence 1963-73
Bryant & May Ltd: private journals 1966-77; private cash books 1966-76; overseas interests correspondence 1959-76
Bryant & May (Forestry) Ltd: annual reports and accounts 1969-70; accounts 1961-7; correspondence 1961-70
Wilkinson Match Ltd: company reports 1974-5; trading results and correspondence 1974-6; production papers 1974-7; press cuttings 1973-8
Acton Match Co Ltd: directors and general meeting minutes 1924-63; members register etc 1924-63; share certificates and transfer documents 1924-63; annual returns 1934-61; memo and articles of association 1924; balance sheet and accounts 1928-9; annual accounts 1947-59; ledger 1947-64; correspondence 1926-37
Hulme Patent Advertising Match Co Ltd: general meeting minutes 1936-66; members register etc 1936-60
Alliance Match Co Ltd: directors and general meeting minutes 1932-63; members register etc 1932-63; ledger 1947-64; correspondence 1933-8
R Bell & Co Ltd: directors meeting minutes 1919-63; general meeting minutes 1888-1963; shareholders list 1890; members register etc 1923-63; share certificates and transfer documents 1955-63; memo and articles of association 1887; corporate documents 1887,1923; ledgers 1913,1947-64; patent documents 1885,1911; price list 1880s
Bell & Black Match Co Ltd: rough directors and general meeting minutes 1876-81; corporate papers 1881-3; memo and articles of association 1876,1881; annual report and accounts 1881-3; general ledger 1876-81; balance sheets and accounts 1882-4; bank books 1876-80; patent trade-mark and design documents 1870-84; contracts book 1877-81; production and sales reports and correspondence 1883-4; stock list 1879; price lists 1878-9; premises and plant inventories 1881
Dixon, Son & Evans: patent agreement and correspondence 1877-86; premises and plant inventory 1881; purchase agreement 1881
Bellerby & Son Ltd: premises plan 1882; purchase agreement 1881
John Jex Long: patent 1878; purchase agreement 1881
British Booklet Matches (1928) Ltd: directors and general meeting minutes 1932-67; members register etc 1932-67; mortgage register and papers 1929-31; ledger 1928-64; journal 1928-32; sales brochures 1932; correspondence and papers 1927-33,1961
Diamond Match Co Ltd: directors and general meeting minutes 1897-1963; members register etc 1907-63; seal register 1897-1907; balance sheets and accounts 1897-1901, ledger 1947-64; price lists c1900; history booklets c1900-1926; correspondence 1899-1901,1948-59
Irish Match Co Ltd: general meeting minutes 1897-1967; share certificates 1897-1967
Maguire, Paterson & Palmer Ltd: directors and general meeting minutes 1919-24; members register etc 1919-24; share transfer register 1921-4; directors and shareholders lists 1919-23; annual returns 1921-4; private ledgers 1918-23; premises: photographs 1920-3, plans 1873

Maguire & Paterson (NI) Ltd: directors and general meeting minutes 1923-63; members register 1923-63; purchase papers 1959

Matches Ltd: directors meeting minutes 1945-65; general meeting minutes 1919-65; members register etc 1919-53; share certificates and transfer documents 1913-53

Midland Match Works Ltd: share certificates and transfer documents 1958; works plan 1920; correspondence 1931-57

WJ Morgan & Co Ltd: private ledger 1883-91; ledger 1955-64; works plan 1920

SJ Moreland & Sons Ltd: copy minutes and agendas 1961-72; directors register 1967-9; balance sheets and accounts 1968-72; private ledger 1968-72; correspondence 1931-72; works: plan and specification 1920, photographs 1941-2, outing newscutting 1937

SJ Moreland & Sons (Holdings) Ltd: copy minutes and agendas 1970-2; accounts 1970-2; private ledger 1968-72

Premier Match Co Ltd: share certificates and transfer documents 1916-22; corporate documents 1908-16; liquidation papers 1922-3

Publicity Book Matches Ltd: directors and general meeting minutes 1928-67; members register etc 1928-67; ledger 1947-64

Standard Match Co Ltd: directors and general meeting minutes 1958-66; correspondence 1931-59

Bryant & May (Brazil) Ltd: members registers 1926-50; share transfer registers 1926-50; memo and articles of association 1931; ledgers 1926-53; journal 1926-30; cash book 1926-30

Cia Fiat Lux: directors, staff, exhibitions and factories photographs 1927-60

Cia General de Fosforous Sud Americania: machinery plans and photographs 1930; staff, buildings and directors photographs 1954-8; match factories lands and buildings inventory nd

Bryant & May, Bell & Co (Pty) Ltd, Australia: governing directors meeting minutes 1909-13; foundation papers 1907-10; memo and articles of association 1910; balance sheets and accounts: Melbourne 1910-48, Perth 1932-47; production photographs 1920s; visitors booklets 1924; match composition recipe 1922; Brymay staff provident fund balance sheets and accounts 1935-49; staff photographs 1911-59; Empire Works: specification 1922, photographs c1910-20s,nd; factory booklet c1910s

Bryant & May, Bell & Co (Pty) Ltd, New Zealand: directors meeting minutes 1910-13,1922; foundation papers 1907-10; memo and articles of association 1910; shareholders list 1922; balance sheets and accounts 1910-48; directors photographs 1928-49; factory: papers and newscuttings 1920-2, photographs 1927-30,nd

Australasia Ltd: advisory committee meeting minutes 1909; papers 1906-10; cash book 1907-10

Federal Match Co Ltd: account statements 1920-5,1935-48; works, machinery and staff photographs 1922-45; correspondence 1927-67

Western Australia Match Co Ltd: building, works and plant photographs 1931-50s; correspondence 1930-50

New Zealand Wax Vesta Co: Dunedin factory: plan and blue prints nd, workers and directors photographs 1920s-48

Eddy Match Co Ltd: shareholders list 1957-61; presidents reports 1963-8; correspondence 1943-72

Canadian Splint & Lumber Corporation Ltd: accounts summary 1961; buildings, timber and directors photographs 1948-65; correspondence 1944-69

Lion Match Co Ltd: directors working statements 1927-42; accounts and stock lists 1905-19; photographs: Durban factory c1900-63, and progress reports 1925-8, Cape Town factory c1900-23, Salisbury factory 1948-59, directors and staff c1900-62, South Africa subjects 1906-45,nd; correspondence 1957-66
Rosebank Match Co Ltd: balance sheets and accounts 1900-04; correspondence 1899-1905
Diamond Deutsche Zundholzfabrik AG: board of control meeting minutes 1904-05; balance sheet and account 1902; Rheinau factory photographs 1901-02; correspondence 1902
Transvaal Diamond Match Co AG: board of control meeting minutes 1899-1905; correspondence 1899-1905
Swedish Match Co: agreements and correspondence 1952-9,1884-1910; catalogues 1898,1932-9; photographs 1950,nd; history booklets and circulars 1920-57
Trinidad Match Factory Ltd: factory photograph 1948; press cuttings 1968
Bifuel Carburettors Ltd: directors and general meeting minutes 1918-30
British Basket & Besto Co Ltd: ledgers: 1950-66, private 1949-65; journal 1966-8; payroll 1965-9; correspondence 1933-70
North West Chip Basket Co Ltd: ledgers 1950-71; journal 1960-70
F Gough & Son Ltd: correspondence 1933-70
J&G Cox Ltd: directors: and general meeting minutes 1898-1972, reports 1898-1969; shareholders: register 1896-1966, correspondence 1934-71; annual returns 1898-1969; memo and articles of association 1898-1961; balance sheets and accounts 1897-1969; profits appointment statements 1897-1917; general ledgers 1898-1959; private ledger 1921-49; journal 1939-43; purchases, stores and wages analysis 1964-9; assets revaluation papers 1968-70; gelatine trade-mark patents 1886-1971; production licences 1941-8; jelly strength standardisation scale 1954; purchase book 1964-9; chemicals stock check 1968-9; gelatine advertisement ledger 1924-55; employment contracts 1964-7; payroll 1967-8; personnel file 1968-9; staff photographs 1960; site: and plant valuation 1958, disposal papers 1969-75; Georgie Mills bowling club papers 1969-71; correspondence 1927
Thomas Nimmo & Co Ltd: directors and general meeting minutes 1935-69; members register etc 1935-69; share papers 1950-8; memo and articles of association 1935; accounts statements 1953-69; glue recipe nd; recommendation 1852; newscutting 19 cent,1933-58
Octavius Hunt Ltd: balance sheets and accounts 1928-41; correspondence 1921-65
Jahncke Ltd: directors and general meeting minutes 1893-1961; committee meeting minutes 1894-9; corporate papers 1878-95,1931; members registers 1894-1960; shareholders list 1959-60; directors register 1951-c60; debenture: share registers 1895-1924, agreements 1889-1900; annual returns 1925-53; liquidation papers c1950-60; balance sheets and accounts 1923-60; ledgers: 1936-60, private 1954-60, bought 1922-60, sales 1942-59; journals 1954-60; cash books 1953-62; order books 1954-60; sales daybook 1960; credit notes 1957-61; production line estimate 1950s,nd; colour box plan 1958; wages and salaries journals 1951-60; staff: papers 1951-60, wage receipts 1955-60; injury treatment record 1959-60; staff benevolent fund: trustee meeting minutes 1926-60, ledger 1948-60, cash book 1939-60; bonus records 1936-60; balance sheets and accounts with correspondence 1948-60; title deeds and property papers and correspondence 1822-1960; ink pellet recipe 1887; correspondence 1884-1901
Ideal Vending Machine Co: ledger and journal 1961-75
London & Provincial Automatic Machine Co Ltd: directors and general meeting minutes 1891-3; prospectuses 1892; directors reports 1894-7

Motormaps Ltd: directors and general meeting minutes 1953-68; members register etc 1953-67; annual returns 1958-71
Packel Ltd: photographs: Hammersmith premises 1940-50, South Africa 1950; correspondence 1949-59
Printpack Ltd: directors and general meeting minutes 1958-67; members register etc 1958-67; share certificates and transfer documents 1958-67; annual reports and accounts 1958-67; memo and articles of association 1958; annual accounts and papers 1960-1; ledger 1958-68; cash books 1958-62; wages book 1959-60; correspondence 1958-67
Print & Paper Ltd: directors and general meeting minutes 1958-71; annual returns 1958-71; business name correspondence 1958-71
Wolverhampton Box Co Ltd: memo and articles of association 1957; factory photographs 1958; correspondence 1958-70
Match Control Office: matches administrative committee meeting minutes 1917-19; ledger 1917-19; summary accounts 1917-19; production reports 1917-19; deliveries reports 1917-19; supply notes 1918-19; administrative papers 1917-18; staff files 1917-19; winding up papers 1919
United Kingdom Match Makers Association: minutes 1872-8
British Match Makers Association: meeting minutes 1903-09; advisory committee meeting minutes 1903-05; Fairfield and Liverpool production grosses 1900-04; Belgian safety match sales figures and correspondence 1907; excise tax papers 1916-21; home trade grosses 1917-21; dinner photograph 1911
Society of British Match Manufacturers: accounts with correspondence 1918-50; mechanical lighters: memoranda 1937-46, reports 1953-9; correspondence 1947-60
Joint Industrial Council for the Match Manufacturing Industry: establishment report 1923; meeting minutes: London District Council 1919-22, health and safety committee 1929-46, works committees 1937-52; association joint industrial councils and correspondence 1929-45; pension fund sub-committee 1938-9; accounts 1924-56; wages, holidays, sick pay etc papers 1946-56; unemployment benefit scheme cash book 1948-69; correspondence 1950-6; Glasgow visit photographs 1938

Making Matches 1861-1961 (priv pub 1961)

474 PETER CROOK LTD
26 Jun 1884
19973
Swan Lane Mills, High Swan Lane, Bolton, Greater Manchester BL3 3AQ
Cotton spinners

History: incorporated in 1884 as above to purchase cotton spinning business established in 1870 and carried on by Thomas and Peter Crook at Robin Hood Mills, Lever Street, Bolton, Greater Manchester. In 1938 purchased Drake Spinning Co Ltd, Drake Mill, Farnworth, Bolton. Acquired in about 1973 by Swan Lane Spinning Co (1920) Ltd, Swan Lane Mills, Bolton, which was subsequently acquired by Courtaulds Ltd. Ceased trading in 1977, when it employed about 400 people.

Records: at Courtaulds, 1 Portland Street, Manchester, Greater Manchester M60 3AP
minutes 1884-date; members register 1930-date; share: register 1884-1937, certificate books 1950-date; directors register 1948-date; memo and articles of association 1884-1953; Drake

Spinning Co Ltd sale particulars 1938; balance sheets 1922-37,1953-72; loan ledger 1929-72; stock and balance book 1957-67; private wages books 1907-55; Drake Mill: valuation summary 1963, plan nd

475 SOCIETY OF AUTHORS LTD

30 Jun 1884
19993
84 Drayton Gardens, London SW10 9SB
Professional association

History: established and incorporated in 1884 as Incorporated Society of Authors to represent interests of authors. Changed name to above in 1914. Membership at end of 1884 was 68 rising to 1550 by 1904. Published journal *The Author* from 1890 and established Authors' Pension Fund by 1904. Promoted a copyright bill, advised members generally, contested cases against publishers on behalf of members and circulated technical leaflets, activities which continued in 1980s. Independent trade union.

Records (1): at Society of Authors, 84 Drayton Gardens, London SW10 9SB
management committee meeting minutes and reports 1883-date; general meeting minutes 1885-date; sub-committee meeting minutes: finance 1924-32, cinematic 1914-29, composers 1912-45, copyright 1885-1915, dramatic 1909-15, Gertrude Page 1924-32, minimum basic agreement 1924-32; agenda books 1883-1938; memo and articles of association 1884-1979; status and constitution papers 1930s-76; annual reports and accounts 1885-date; collection bureau ledger 1932-48; agents: correspondence 1920-69, prospectuses pre 1914, proposals 1925; bookselling correspondence 1931-75; broadcasting agreements, contracts newscuttings, correspondence and papers 1925-75; Composers Guild formation papers and press cuttings 1932-70; copyright: convention papers and correspondence 1907-71, legal case papers and correspondence 1907-76; overseas copyright papers and correspondence 1912-74; British copyright council correspondence and papers 1950-77; annual dinners, functions and celebration programmes and papers 1894-1972; general secretarys correspondence and papers 1918-59; journalism correspondence and papers 1913-79; libel correspondence and press cuttings 1936-53; library papers 1949-60; obscenity papers and correspondence 1953-70; patronage papers 1927-79; public lending rights papers and correspondence 1951-68; publishers correspondence 1920-78; state and literature papers 1944-66; taxation: legal cases papers and press cuttings 1904-75, papers 1945-78; theatre fee records, correspondence and papers 1930-70; literary organisations papers 1926-77, survey reports, papers and correspondence 1952-72; legal case papers and correspondence 1890-1967; arbitration panel papers 1921-5; members obituaries 1946-65; regional groups memos, papers and correspondence 1950-78; childrens writers group committee minutes and papers 1948-78; *The Author* 1890-date; manuscripts received register 1912-25; League of Dramatists: executive committee meeting minutes 1945-71, commission account 1961-72; Radio & Television Writers Association executive and general meeting minutes 1947-59; Radio Writers Association meeting minutes, agendas, papers, correspondence and membership lists 1947-53; Screenwriters Association/Writers Guild annual reports, news-letters and correspondence 1937-75; Translators Association papers 1949-60

Records (2): British Library, Department of Western Manuscripts, Great Russell Street, London WC1B 3DG
committee and sub-committee business papers 1909-13; agents sub-committee reports 1916-18; sub-committee meeting minutes: cinematic 1914-17, composers 1917; dramatic sub-committee papers 1912-27; music royalties papers 1924-8; copyright papers 1912-27; performing rights papers 1923-7; League of Dramatists: formation papers 1931, members files 1928-55; legal cases papers and correspondence 1889-1945; library censorship papers 1909-16; membership files: John Masefield 1909-67, George Bernard Shaw 1909-61; RL Stevenson and Lloyd Osbourne estates 1883-1962, others 1908-67; pension fund papers 1909-19; president election papers 1937; general: letter books 1885-1930, correspondence and papers 1879-1966; circular book 1915-22; literary bodies correspondence 1906-50; solicitors correspondence 1903-19; USA legal representative correspondence 1918-20; William G Clifford papers c1879-1945; GH Thrings history and Canadian tour account 1899; manuscripts, plays, novels and film scripts 1912-29; draft royalty agreements 1914-19; paper importation papers 1916

476 DUNSMARK INVESTMENTS LTD

11 Jul 1884
20043
Vencula House, 29-31 Tower Place, London EC3
Property and investment

History: incorporated in 1864 as Wool Exchange Ltd, changing name to Wool Exchange & General Investments Ltd in 1933, to acquire property in the City and West End of London. Acquired in 1959 by City of London Real Property Co Ltd which was itself acquired by Land Securities Investment Trust Ltd in 1969. Name subsequently changed to above.

Records: at Land Securities (Management), 21 New Fetter Lane, London EC4P 4PY
directors meeting minutes 1918-47; general meeting minutes 1929-58; debenture trust deeds 1935,1937; memo and articles of association c1951; annual reports and accounts 1929-58

477 EMERSON WALKER LTD

7 Aug 1884
20133
NEI House, Regent Centre, Newcastle upon Tyne, Tyne & Wear NE3 3SB
Windlass and capstan manufacturers

History: incorporated in 1884 as Emerson Walker & Thompson Brothers Ltd to acquire and consolidate the businesses of Emerson Walker & Co, 11 Leadenhall Street, London (est 1855 by Edmund Walker), GC&A Thompson, Winlaton, near Blaydon, Tyne & Wear, and Thompson Brothers, Dunston, near Gateshead, Tyne & Wear, and carry on as engineers and steam winch and windlass makers. From 1884 the works were at Dunston. Name changed to above in 1928. Acquired in 1964 by Clarke Chapman & Co Ltd (est 1862), general and electrical engineers and boiler makers of Gateshead. Company by 1968 was selling marine engineering products manufactured by, and producing iron castings for, its parent. Iron foundry closed in Dec 1970 and company ceased to trade in 1972. Clarke Chapman & Co Ltd merged with John Thompson Ltd, engineers of Wolverhampton, in 1970, and CA Parsons, engineers of Newcastle upon Tyne, merged with them in 1979 to form Northern Engineering Industries Ltd. The above went into liquidation in Nov 1980.

Records: at Northern Engineering Industries, NEI House, Regent Centre, Newcastle upon Tyne, Tyne & Wear NE3 3SB
share certificates 20 cent; history notes and correspondence 1940s

478 INVICTA INVESTMENT CO LTD

8 Aug 1884
20134
Imperial Life House, London Road, Guildford, Surrey GV1 1TA
Property

History: incorporated as above in 1884 as a property investment company in Maidstone, Kent. Initially invested in property in Maidstone but by 1951 owned property in Gravesend, Tunbridge Wells, Kent and London. By 1973 owned 280 residential, and 50 commercial properties. In 1973 company was acquired by Morgan-Grampian Property Ltd, and by 1984 was a subsidiary of Imperial Life Assurance Co of Canada.

Records: at Imperial Life, Imperial Life House, London Road, Guildford, Surrey GV1 1TA
directors and general meeting minutes 1947-75; share: holders register 1884-1950, ledger 1960-74, transfer register and certificates 1932-80, papers 1927-81; debenture register and papers 1884-1983; dividend book and papers 1960-80; memo and articles of association 1884; annual report and accounts 1884,1935-73; balance sheets 1934-81; ledgers 1920-63; cash books 1912-69; property values 1920-39; investment register 1959-80

479 IPSWICH CHAMBER OF COMMERCE & SHIPPING (INCORPORATED)

27 Aug 1884
20194
21 Museum Street, Ipswich, Suffolk IP1 1HE
Chamber of commerce

History: founded and incorporated in 1884 as company limited by guarantee, as Ipswich Chamber of Commerce Incorporated, to promote and protect trade in Ipswich area. First offices were in Arcade Street, Ipswich, Suffolk, moving to 17 and then 21 Museum Street in 1978. Membership in 1957 numbered 158 but had risen to over 600 by 1979. In early 1980s provided monthly news-letter, magazine, enquiry, translation, telex and export documentation services and organised seminars for members. Name had previously changed to above and changed to Ipswich & Suffolk Chamber of Commerce, Industry & Shipping (Incorporated) in 1980.

Records: at Ipswich & Suffolk Chamber of Commerce, Industry & Shipping, 21 Museum Street, Ipswich, Suffolk IP1 1HE
council: meeting minutes 1884-date, correspondence 1955-date; committee meeting minutes 1930-date; members register 1884-date; annual returns 1955-date; cash books 1884-date; certificates of origin register 1937-date; correspondence and papers re opening of new premises 1978; news-letters 1971-date; newscuttings re chamber and local business 1971-date; history notes c1978

480 RICHARD THOMAS & BALDWINS LTD

23 Sep 1884
20255
9 Albert Embankment, London SE1 7SN
Iron, steel and tin-plate manufacturers, and colliery proprietors

History: established in 1798 at Lydbrook, Gloucestershire and incorporated in 1884 as Richard Thomas & Co Ltd, steel and tin-plate manufacturers and iron, steel and brass founders. By 1923 owned and controlled about 114 tin-plate mills situated in or near Llanelli, Dyfed; Swansea and Neath, W Glamorgan; Cardiff, S Glamorgan; Newport, Gwent; Bristol, Avon; and steel works, engineering department and silica brickworks at Llanelli. Products included iron, steel and brass castings, green copper (as sulphate of iron), coke and charcoal tin-plates, tin and terne-coated sheets, and Canada plates. Amalgamated in 1944 with Baldwins Ltd and changed name to above. Baldwins were iron masters and colliery proprietors incorporated in 1902 on amalgamation of the following iron and steel manufacturers, and colliery and iron ore proprietors - EP&W Baldwin Ltd; Wright Butler & Co Ltd; Alfred Baldwin & Co Ltd; Bryn Navigation Colliery Co Ltd; and Blackwall Galvanised Iron Co Ltd. Acquired Port Talbot Steel Co Ltd in 1915 and Brymbo Steel Co Ltd in 1918. Specialised in 1930s in sheet steel products. Company became part of British Steel Corporation in 1967.

Records (1): at British Steel Corporation, South Wales Regional Records Centre, Gabalfa, Cardiff, S Glamorgan CF4 1XS

Records (2): at British Steel Corporation, E Midlands Records Centre, By-Pass Road, Irthlingborough, Wellingborough, Northamptonshire NN9 5QH

Records (3): at Glamorgan Archive Service, Mid Glamorgan County Hall, Cathays Park, Cardiff, S Glamorgan CF1 3NE
general meeting report 1938; shareholders letter 1940; history articles 1948-9; Tom Griffiths company secretarys papers 1954 on

481 LEICESTER RACECOURSE HOLDINGS LTD

14 Oct 1884
20359
Racecourse, London Road, Leicester, Leicestershire
Racecourse

History: incorporated in 1884 as New Leicester Club & County Racecourse Co Ltd to purchase Leicester Racecourse, run from about 1880 by Leicester Club & County Racecourse Co. In 1889 the straight mile and round courses were improved. Royal Handicap Race started in 1892. Company was reconstructed in 1894 and changed its name to Leicester Racecourse Co Ltd in 1949 and to above in 1968. Leicester Racecourse Co Ltd, a wholly owned subsidiary, was formed in 1969 to lease the racecourse, buildings and land from the company.

Records: at Leicestershire Record Office, 57 New Walk, Leicester, Leicestershire LE1 7JB
directors: meeting minutes 1884-date, signature book 1927-82, agendas 1923-53; general meeting minutes 1884-date; shareholders signature book 1920-83; members register and share ledger 1924-80; directors registers 1924-78; share transfer: register 1887-1982, documents 1887-1930; debenture correspondence 1925; mortgage and bond register 1885-1954; annual: returns 1924-43, reports and accounts 1886-1969; chairmens speeches 1947-50; race meeting accounts statement 1886-1915; profits application statement 1884-1915; betting control agreement 1930; dilapidation correspondence 1941-7; property agreements, plans, papers and correspondence 1880-1961

482 EDWIN DAVIS & CO LTD

15 Oct 1884
20364
6 Wolfreton Drive, Springfield Way, Anlaby, Hull, Humberside HU10 7BZ
Department store

History: incorporated in 1884 as above to acquire the business carried on by Edwin Davis & Co as drapers, silk mercers, warehousemen, upholsterers, furnishing men and general traders at 46-49 Market Place, Hull, Humberside and the premises known as 'Coburg Vaults'. The store was destroyed during WW2 but was re-built at 27-37 Bond Street, London after the war. Company acquired in 1973 by Cattle's (Holdings) Ltd, retail traders and merchants of Hull and store subsequently closed. Company absorbed trading activities of fellow subsidiary, AJ Blackmore Ltd in 1974 and in 1983 still traded as a department store.

Records: at Cattle's (Holdings), 6 Wolfreton Drive, Springfield Way, Anlaby, Hull, Humberside HU10 7BZ
directors and general meeting minutes 1946-date

483 MEERSBROOK BOWLING CLUB LTD

11 Nov 1884
20447
180 Shirebrook Road, Sheffield, S Yorkshire S8 9RG
Sports club-house

History: founded in Oct 1874 as Meersbrook Proprietary Bowling Green Club and incorporated as above in 1884. Purchased land in Victoria (later Shirebrook) Road, Sheffield, S Yorkshire for bowling greens which were opened in 1875.

Records: at Meersbrook Bowling Club, 180 Shirebrook Road, Sheffield, S Yorkshire S8 9RG
committee meeting minutes 1874-85; directors and general meeting minutes 1931-71; members registers and share ledgers 1912-59; share transfer documents c1900-50; memo and articles of association c1912; annual list and summaries 1925-6,1931; annual reports and accounts 1931-date; balance sheets 1926-69; general ledgers 1909-date; journals 1910-68; cash book 1947-65; by-laws 1924-1979; membership ledger 1937-68; visitors book 1905-74; suggestion book 1921-63; property report 1964; premises plans 1956,1980; insurance policies 1923-4

484 LIFE CYCLE FOODS LTD

21 Nov 1884
20486
PO Box 22, Queen's House, Paragon Street, Hull, Humberside HU1 3NY
Sauce manufacturers

History: established in 1880 by George and John Mason, ex employees of A1 Sauce Co. Acquired a factory in King's Road, Chelsea, London and marketed sauce under the 'OK Sauce' label. Incorporated in 1884 as George Mason & Co Ltd. Factory moved to Fulham in 1896. In 1920 opened second factory in Wandsworth, London, and after its modernisation in 1928 the Fulham works was closed. Acquired a controlling interest in Cottslowe Preserves Ltd, owners of a horseradish cream factory in Dover, Kent in 1934 and by 1936 was producing a wide range of sauces. Acquired in 1964 by Reckitt & Colman Holdings Ltd and was wholly integrated with Colman Foods of Norwich, Norfolk in 1968, its products being marketed under the Colman name. Name changed to the above in 1975 and ceased to trade.

Records: at Colman's of Norwich, Carrow, Norwich, Norfolk NR1 2DD
board meeting: minutes 1884-95, 1964-9, agenda books 1900-42
Cottslowe Preserves Ltd: board meeting minutes 1934-63; newspaper advertisements 1937-67; product labels, showcards, sales literature and price lists 1909-63

485 MERCANTILE INVESTMENT TRUST LTD

8 Dec 1884
20537
122 Leadenhall Street, London EC3V 4QR
Investment trust

History: incorporated in 1884 as Mercantile Investment & General Trust Co Ltd as an investment trust. Took over undertaking of American, English & General Trust Ltd in 1910. Name changed to above in 1960 and company acquired the undertakings and assets of United States & Mercantile Investment Trust Ltd, Second Mercantile Investment Trust Ltd and New Mercantile Investment Trust Ltd. Name changed to Fleming Mercantile Investment Trust PLC in 1982. Managed by Robert Fleming Investment Management Ltd.

Records: at Robert Fleming Services, 122 Leadenhall Street, London EC3V 4QR
board and general meeting minutes 1884-date; annual reports, accounts and investment lists 1885-date; share, stock and debenture registers 1884 on; seal books 1905-30s; general ledgers 1884-1970s; journals 1884-1972; cash books 1884-1976
United States Trust & Guarantee Co Ltd: directors and general meeting minutes 1890-1910
United States & South American Investment Trust Co Ltd: annual reports and accounts 1888-1959
Second Mercantile Trust Ltd: annual reports and accounts 1924-59
New Mercantile Trust Ltd: annual reports and accounts 1938-55

486 KIRBY-WARRICK PHARMACEUTICALS LTD

31 Dec 1884
20626
Mildenhall, Bury St Edmunds, Suffolk IP28 7AX
Pharmaceuticals

History: laboratory established in Newman Street, London by Dr EA Kirby in 1866 for the preparation of medicines for medical practice. Incorporated in 1884 as H&T Kirby Ltd, to take over the business of manufacturing chemist founded by Dr EA Kirby for £80,000. In 1894 HE Kirby became general manager of Soden Mineral Produce Co Ltd, acquiring the companys business on its liquidation in 1894. In 1913 moved to Newman House, Willesden Green, London. In 1960s company moved to its present address. In 1979 acquired by Schering Corporation USA and in 1980 changed name to above.

Records: at Kirby-Warrick Pharmaceuticals, Mildenhall, Bury St Edmunds, Suffolk IP28 7AX
share transfer certificates 1952; debenture trust deed 1921; memo and articles of association 1884,1975,1979; annual report and accounts 1890,1893,1907-50; balance sheets 1891-2; war loan papers 1925; debt papers 1937; agreement for sale of Cole & Co patent medicine business 1895; supply agreements 1890-5; pocket pharmacopoeia 1902; advertising ledgers 1884,c1900-50s; medicine case c1910; labels c1900-54; price lists 1900-60s; samples and boxes nd,1904-50; formulae books 1882-1969; packaging examples 1920-72; order book 1879-80; plant examination 1972-4; managers agreement 1892; Kirby family wills, estates duty and papers 1889-1908

487 SANDOWN PARK LTD

1 Jan 1885
20632
Sandown Park Racecourse, Esher, Surrey
Racecourse operators

History: incorporated as above in 1885 to acquire Sandown Park in Esher, Surrey to establish and maintain the racecourse, to hold races, provide stands and stabling, to give or contribute to prizes and to carry on Sandown Park Club. Name changed to United Racecourses Ltd in 1966 but reverted to above in 1976. Purchased in 1966 by Metropolitan & Country Racecourse Management & Holdings Ltd along with Epsom Grandstand Association Ltd, being joined by Kempton Park Racecourse Co Ltd in 1970 to become part of United Racecourses Ltd. In 1982 was dormant subsidiary company of Horserace Betting Levy Board through Metropolitan & Country Racecourse Management & Holdings Ltd.

Records (1): at United Racecourses, Sandown Park Racecourse, Esher, Surrey
directors meeting minutes 1885-date; agenda book 1939-52; general meeting minutes 1885-date; annual reports and accounts 1886-date; race meeting: card 1875, programmes 1879 on, photographs 1920s; Jockey Club and National Hunt Stewards notices 1909-36
Sandown Park Club: election committee minutes 1902-63; rules 1879; licensing return 1905
Sandown Park Estate Co: minutes 1875-6

Records (2): at United Racecourses, Epsom Racecourse, Racecourse Paddock, Epsom, Surrey KT18 5NJ
share: register 1960s, transfers 1904-68; directors registers 1933-72; balance sheets 1947-9; correspondence re unlicensed bookmakers 1911-13; telegraph wire, electricity etc agreements 1889-1919
United Racecourses Ltd: directors registers 1967-72

488 GLYN MILLS & CO LTD

14 Jan 1885
20672
20 Birchin Lane, London EC3P 3DP
Banking

History: established in 1754 as Vere, Glyn & Hallifax, bankers in the City of London, with a capital of £24,000. From 1766 known as Glyn & Hallifax on withdrawal of Joseph Vere. Briefly stopped payment in 1772 but resumed on receiving loans from friends, especially £10,000 from William Mills on condition that he and his nephew Charles joined the partnership. In 1770s and 1780s bank was led by Thomas Hallifax who died in 1789 leaving a fortune of £100,000. Between 1790 and 1830 country bank agencies expanded from 4 to 49, staff numbers rose from 7 to 51 and between 1810 and 1830 profits doubled to £40,000. Most agencies were in Scotland, Northumberland, Yorkshire, Cornwall, Dorset and Kent. Under leadership of GC Glyn (later Lord Wolverton) in 1830s and 1840s acted as bankers to many railway companies, being known colloquially as 'railway bank'. From 1830s to 1890s, with Baring Brothers, were joint financial agents in London for Upper Canada and later Dominion of Canada Governments when issued much government and railway company stock. By 1849 believed to be largest London bank, excluding Bank of England. In 1870s and 1880s was active in promotion of investment trusts and, from 1890s, other business organisations. Absorbed Ladbroke & Co in 1841 and Curries & Co (est 1773) in 1864 when name changed to Glyn, Mills, Currie & Co. From then to 1890s business led by BW Currie. In 1885 was reconstructed as a private limited company as Glyn, Mills, Currie & Co Ltd, with paid up capital and reserves of £1.5 million. Between 1885 and 1889 balance sheet total doubled to £17 million, which meant the bank was one of largest in Britain. Largest private bank in 1920. Absorbed Holt & Co (est 1809), army agents, in 1923 and Child & Co (est c1584) in 1924 when known as the above. Opened first branch outside London, at Oxford, in 1932. Acquired by Royal Bank of Scotland in 1939. Merged in 1970 with National Bank Ltd (formed as National Bank of Ireland in 1835) and Williams Deacon's Bank Ltd (est in 1836 as Manchester & Salford Bank Ltd) which in 1890 had merged with Williams Deacon & Co (est 1771) to form Williams & Glyn's Bank Ltd.

Records (1): at Williams & Glyn's Bank, 20 Birchin Lane, London EC3P 3DP
partnership deeds 1760; profit and loss books 1809-31; balance sheets 1819-85; trustee accounts 1880-1908; register of exchequer bills purchased 1819-60; discount office: collateral security registers 19 cent, weekly returns 1844-1910; loans and discounts daily summary 1874-85; brokers: money at call 1896-1934, outstanding bills 1909-34; customer: balances 1882-1925, quarterly 1841-5, weekly 1864-90; customer: ledgers 1800-01, discounts from ledgers 1824-7, loans 1854-6, and papers 1880-90; bad debts book 1795-1807; guarantee books 1846-1940; advances and management books 1890-1927; security registers 1915-20; unpaid bills

register 1876-90; status enquiries, information books etc 1853-1934; letters of introduction 1914-35; safe custody registers 19 cent; hypothecatican letters 1895-1921; probate ledgers 1897-1914; staff: salary books 1810-48, lists 1815-31, address books 1833-51, indemnity bonds 19 cent, association papers 1941-9, Christmas box books 1754-1925; staff club meeting minutes and papers 1911-54; staff guarantee and provident fund minutes and papers 1880-1948; house journal 1948 on; letter books: private 1848-1919, BW Currie private 1864-81, solicitors 19 cent; papers: country banks 19 cent, Canadian business 19 cent, Glyn, Mills & Hallifax 19 cent; scrap books and press cuttings 1753-1950

Records (2): at Northumberland Record Office, Melton Park, North Gosforth, Newcastle upon Tyne, Tyne & Wear NE3 5QX
papers re financial difficulties 1772

Roger Fulford, *Glyn's 1753-1953. Six Generations in Lombard Street* (1953)

489 ALBION IRON & WIRE WORK CO LTD

21 Jan 1885
20694
56-57 Britton Street, Clerkenwell Road, London EC1M 5NA
Engineering and metalworking

History: founded and incorporated as above in 1885 in Ironmongers Row, Clerkenwell, then moved to Britton Street. In 1970 took over Myerson Kilby Ltd, sheet metal workers (est 1820) and J&W Shale Ltd, constructional engineers (est 1880s). Subsidiary companies in 1982 included Sebry Staircase & Ironworks Ltd, fire escape staircase manufacturers (inc 1930), Lift Cars & Components Co Ltd (inc 1957) and Albion (Norfolk) Ltd (inc 1970). In early 1980s manufactured wire work, staircase lifts, machinery guards, and metal sheeting and ducting.

Records: at Albion Iron & Wire Work, 56-57 Britton Street, Clerkenwell Road, London EC1M 5NA
board meeting minutes 1885 on; members register 1862-1940; share certificates 1885-1950; annual returns 1920-30; sales journal 1936-53; product catalogues nd; order ledger 1925-58; leases and legal documents re property 1890 on
Myerson Kilby Ltd: sales accounts ledger c1910-64; order ledger 1889-1925; orders supplied sheets 1939-62; engineering specifications notebook 1921-42

490 CARDIFF HIGH STREET ARCADE CO LTD

24 Jan 1885
20706
St John's Chambers, High Street Arcade, Cardiff, S Glamorgan CF1 2BD
Property

History: founded and incorporated as above in 1885 by F de Courcy Hamilton, a Cardiff solicitor who acted as secretary to several Cardiff property companies in the 1880s, to carry on the shopping arcade from the High Street to St John's Square, Cardiff, S Glamorgan. When built, the shops were leased, the tenants living above their shops.

Records: at Cardiff High Street Arcade, St John's Chambers, High Street Arcade, Cardiff, S Glamorgan CF1 2BD directors and general meeting minutes 1884-date; agenda book 1960-70; share: ledger 1885-1964, transfer ledger 1886-1975; directors register 1940s-60s; mortgage register 1886-1929; annual reports and accounts 1886-date; general ledger 1885-1967; rent ledger 1922-71; journal 1917-62; cash book 1958-77; income tax papers 1967; tenants particulars 1886; rent increases 1910; incoming letters 1958-70; directors records: ledger 1901-69, journal 1916-59, cash book 1948-71, ground rents assignment notices 1890s-c1918, ground rents book 1917-27, weekly rental payments book 1923-76, out letter books 1918-22, incoming letters 1956-7, 1964-76

491 SOUTH WALES WAREHOUSES LTD

28 Jan 1885
20718
Victoria Wharves, Ferry Road, Cardiff, S Glamorgan CF1 7XQ
Wharfage and warehouse

History: incorporated as South Wales Public Wharf Warehouse & Transit Co Ltd in 1885 to rent wharves, warehouses and land at Cardiff dock and to create an import business with Johnston Line, Liverpool. After disagreement with Cardiff Dock Co took lease in 1887 on land at Ely Tidal Harbour, retaining leased property in John Street, Cardiff near the docks. Constructed wharf and warehouse and handled cargoes, mainly from Rotterdam, Netherlands and France. In 1890 took lease on second site at Ely which included wharf for petroleum storage, and sub-let land to Victoria Petroleum Co which erected storage tanks. In 1903 additional land was sub-let to Ely Oil Storage Co. Business successfully run until clients left in 1906 and 1909 to operate from Bristol, Avon. Property vacant until 1914 when Anglo-American Oil Co (later Esso Petroleum Co Ltd) took a sub-lease on sites. Retained wharf and obtained revenue from dues and wharfage from shipping while continuing warehousing at John Street and the first Ely site. Acquired freehold of former in 1940 and demolished wharf at latter in 1957-8. Name changed to above in 1952. Sold John Street premises in 1962 in order to concentrate operations at Ely Tidal Harbour. Formed a subsidiary company in 1983 for the repackaging, sale and distribution of snack foods.

Records: at South Wales Warehouses, Victoria Wharves, Ferry Road, Cardiff, S Glamorgan CF1 7XQ
directors meeting minutes 1888-date; general meeting minutes 1885-date; share registers and ledgers 1885-date; share transfer: register 1886-date, documents and correspondence 1885 on; calls register 1885-7; directors registers 1902-66; mortgage register 1885-date; debenture register 1890 on; share certificate book 1885-date; corporate correspondence 1886-1900s; memo and articles of association 1885-1950s; annual reports and accounts 1886-date; private ledgers 1885-c1960; ledgers 1886-1961; journals 1886-1974; cash books 1901-1982; ships account book 1936-48; bills receivable 1885-97; bills payable 1887-96; invoices letter book 1946-55; manifest books 1908-69; warehouse warrant book 1920-72; plans, tracings, contracts etc of warehouses, dwelling houses, Ely Tidal Harbour, river, John Street etc 1889-1963; building book 1890s; draft leases, papers and correspondence re insurance, docks and railway 1890-1905; photographs of wharves, warehouses, ships, barges, locomotives, cargoes unloading and storage 1890 on; wages books 1946-51; time book 1946-7; letter books 1912-55; Ely Tidal Harbour cottages rent books 1928-52

492 **STANDARD STEAMSHIP OWNERS' PROTECTION & INDEMNITY ASSOCIATION LTD**
9 Feb 1885
20758
120 Fenchurch Street, London EC3M 5HA
Insurance

History: incorporated as above as a company limited by guarantee in 1885. Acted as protection and indemnity club for marine insurance of members' ships. In 1984 was managed by Charles Taylor & Co.

Records: at Charles Taylor, International House, World Trade Centre, St Katherine's Way, London E1 9UN
corporate records 1940 on

493 **STEAM TUG & TRAWLERS' MUTUAL PROTECTING & INDEMNITY ASSOCIATION**
19 Feb 1885
20807
4-5 The Esplanade, Sunderland, Tyne & Wear SR2 7BQ
Marine insurance

History: incorporated as above as an unlimited company in 1885 by Total Loss Mutual Steamship Insurance Co (inc 1882) of Sunderland, Tyne & Wear to insure against risks not covered by this company. These included loss of life and personal injuries occurring on board members' vessels; one-fourth collision claims previously uninsurable, damage to piers, quays, and jetties; and other shipowners' liabilities. By end of 1885, 34 vessels were insured, membership being open to steam tugs, trawlers, yachts and small passenger steamers. In Jan 1964 all risks covered by the company were transferred to Sunderland Marine Mutual Insurance Co (as Total Loss Mutual had been renamed) and from 1968 there were no outstanding claims left on the company which subsequently ceased to trade.

Records: at Sunderland Marine Mutual Insurance, 4-5 The Esplanade, Sunderland, Tyne & Wear SR2 7BQ
directors and general meeting minutes: 1884-1970, class II 1903-34; memo and articles of association 1950; guardbook 1922-72; annual reports and accounts 1926,1954-72; rules and vessels entered lists 1897-1962; insurance registers 1945-65; claims books 1934-70

494 **SPRATTS PATENT (AMERICA) LTD**
21 Mar 1885
20937
19 Hanover Square, London W1R 9DA
Animal foodstuffs

History: incorporated as above in 1885 by Spratts Patent Ltd (est 1862), animal foodstuff manufacturers, to acquire its patent rights in USA and Canada and the exclusive business of its selling trade throughout North and South America. Spratts Patent Ltd was acquired in

1960 by Spillers Ltd (inc 1887) which was acquired by Dalgety Ltd in 1979. Liquidated in 1983.

Records: at Dalgety, 19 Hanover Square, London W1R 9DA
corporate records 1930 on

495 SPILLERS FOOD SERVICES LTD

21 Mar 1885
20938
19 Hanover Square, London W1R 9DA
Animal foodstuffs

History: incorporated in 1885 as Spratts Patent (Germany) Ltd by Spratts Patent Ltd to operate the latter's patent and selling rights in Germany and to manufacture and deal in animal foodstuffs. Main German offices were in Berlin. Spratts Patent Ltd was acquired in 1960 by Spillers Ltd (inc 1887) which was acquired by Dalgety Ltd in 1979. Name changed to above in 1973 when it became an agent of the food service division of Spillers Ltd. Ceased to trade in 1977 and was liquidated in 1983.

Records: at Dalgety, 19 Hanover Square, London W1R 9DA
corporate records 1930 on

496 CARDIFF & GLAMORGANSHIRE VALLEYS & BUILDING INVESTMENT CO LTD

20 Apr 1885
21054
Old Bank Chambers, Market Square, Pontypridd, Mid Glamorgan CF37 2SY
Property

History: incorporated as above in 1885 to acquire land on which to build houses, shops and warehouses. Land at Ynysybwl, Mid Glamorgan was leased from Lord Windsor, and C Shepperd & Sons were contracted to build 100 cottages on it from which Augustus Street, Paget Street and Archer Street grew. Investment stocks were purchased to provide funds to buy the freehold reversions of the leases on the cottages, an object achieved in 1949. Cottages have been sold from time to time since the 1950s, the company owning 58 in 1975. Company's business in 1980s is one of investment, owning controlled rent cottages and other residential property, and stocks and shares.

Records: at Cardiff & Glamorganshire Valleys & Building Investment, Old Bank Chambers, Market Square, Pontypridd, Mid Glamorgan CF37 2SY
general meeting minutes 1885-1968; share: certificate books and cancelled shares 1885-date, transfer documents and correspondence 1927-date; annual reports and accounts 1948-75; journal 1930-date; rent book 1934-60

497 UNION DISCOUNT CO OF LONDON LTD

24 Apr 1885
21073
39 Cornhill, London EC3V 3NU
Discount bank

History: established in London in 1885 to acquire the discount and bill-broking business of General Credit & Discount Co Ltd (est 1866) and United Discount Corporation Ltd (est as Discount Corporation Ltd in 1867). In 1891 acquired the discount firm of Harwood Knight & Allen of Cornhill, London (est 1863). By 1894 was the largest company in the London discount market. Was represented on Discount Houses' Committee (est 1914) and its successor, London Discount Market Association (est 1944). With other discount houses it continues to act as intermediary between Bank of England and commercial banks in short-term money markets in treasury bills, commercial and local authority bills, government securities, certificates of deposit and other short-term securities.

Records: at Union Discount, 39 Cornhill, London EC3V 3NU

498 DOWNS CREMATORIUM LTD

25 Apr 1885
21079
The Lodge, Hartington Road, Brighton, E Sussex BN2 3PL
Cemetery and crematorium

History: incorporated in Brighton, E Sussex in 1885 as Brighton & Preston Cemetery Co Ltd. Bodies from Union Street Chapel burial ground were transferred in 1904. Crematorium opened in 1941 and in 1972 name changed to above as cremations outnumbered burials.

Records: at Downs Crematorium, The Lodge, Hartington Road, Brighton, E Sussex BN2 3PL directors meeting minutes 1897-date; general meeting minutes 1885-date; share allotment book 1886-94; dividend statements 1886-1916; memo and articles of association 1885-1965; annual reports and accounts 1886-1959; balance sheet 1885; monthly audited accounts 1900-date; ledger 1965-75; vicars fees 1901-16; ministers payments 1975-date; receipt books 1960 on; burial registers and indexes 1866-date; purchased grave registers 1886-date; cremation: registers 1941-date, diaries 1941-date; memorial indexes 1958-66; rose register 1970-date; roses, informal beds, niches, tablets, recordium panels, rockery, trees, seats and monuments and rose renewal indexes, current; Union Street Chapel: copy burial register 1824-57, plan of burials nd

499 NEWCASTLE DIOCESAN SOCIETY

13 May 1885
21135
Church House, Grainger Park Road, Newcastle upon Tyne, Tyne & Wear NE4 8SX
Church finance

History: incorporated as above as company limited by guarantee to collect, receive, and distribute funds for diocesan societies and to act as trustees of money or property given or property given or bequeathed to the Church of England within the diocese.

Records: at Northumberland Record Office, Melton Park, Newcastle upon Tyne, Tyne & Wear NE3 5QX

500 CHESTER LAUNDRY LTD

23 May 1885
21188
Heath Lane, Boughton Heath, Chester, Cheshire CH3 5SS
Laundry

History: incorporated in 1885 as Chester Steam Laundry Co Ltd in Victoria Road, Chester. Increase in business led to extension of premises in 1891 and 1909. In 1914 fire virtually destroyed laundry, and company moved to Heath Lane premises. In 1964 name changed to above. In 1980s provided laundry services for domestic, commercial and industrial customers and workwear rental services.

Records: at Chester Laundry, Heath Lane, Boughton Heath, Chester, Cheshire CH3 5SS
board and general meeting minutes 1885-1936; memo and articles of association 1885; annual reports and accounts 1885-1936; trade creditors list 1888; photographs: staff 1900-c60, premises c1900-25

501 HARRINGTON FACTORY CO LTD

27 May 1885
21205
49 Derby Road, Long Eaton, Derbyshire NG10 1BN
Room and power

History: incorporated as above in 1885 to erect a factory in Leopold Street, Long Eaton, Derbyshire in which space could be leased to shareholders and other tenants for the manufacture of lace. In early 1980s continued to act as room and power company.

Records: at Harrington Factory, 49 Derby Road, Long Eaton, Derbyshire NG10 1BN
directors and general meeting minutes 1885-date; members registers and share ledgers 1885-date; share transfer: register 1885-1907, certificates c1912-58; calls register 1885-96; directors registers c1900-date; debenture: holders register 1910-56, certificates 1910-13; mortgage registers 1885-1933,1966; annual summaries 1885-1957; annual reports and accounts 1949-64; balance sheet: 1915, and revenue accounts 1939-68; ledgers 1908-72; journals 1914-72; cash books 1934-72; wage books 1951-73; rent: ledger 1908-53, accounts 1936-56; economy report 1929; leases 1938,1953; premises plans 1947-61

502 DOOARS TEA CO LTD

27 Jun 1885
21347
2-4 Cayton Street, London EC1
Tea

History: incorporated in 1885 as above to purchase 4 tea estates - Barandanga-Dhina, Tondoo, Ghatia and Nagrakata, in Western Dooars, Bengal, India from their proprietors, and carry on business as tea planters, growers and manufacturers. Purchased Indong Estate in 1887 and Bhogohpore properties and lands in 1892. In 1958 had 7634 acres of land under cultivation and in 1969 owned 14,338 acres of which 6127 acres were being cultivated. Dooars Holdings Ltd was formed in 1962 to acquire all the issued share capital of the company which went into liquidation in 1979.

Records: at Guildhall Manuscripts Department, Guildhall Library, Aldermanbury, London EC2P 2EJ
share prospectuses 1885-92; memo and articles of association 1925,1935; correspondence re preference shares and articles of association 1929-35; shareholders notices 1935

503 DAVIES BROTHERS & CO LTD

29 Jul 1885
21440
Crown Works, Cross Street North, Cannock Road, Wolverhampton, W Midlands WV1 1PR
Galvanized iron

History: founded in 1830s by Edward Davies at Snow Hill, Wolverhampton, W Midlands. One of the first concerns to make corrugated iron sheets. Incorporated as above in 1885 to carry on business of galvanized corrugated and flat sheet iron and galvanized wrought iron holloware, tanks and cisterns, and roofing and general engineers. Premises at Crown Works throughout history. Went into voluntary liquidation in 1981.

Records (1): at Wolverhampton Borough Archives, Central Library, Snow Hill, Wolverhampton, W Midlands WV1 3AX
minutes 1885-1920; corporate documents and correspondence 1885-1908; directors letter book 1902-18; shareholders annual returns 1885-1918,1940-7; share transfer register 1887-1918; mortgages register 1889-1922; debenture mortgages certificates, papers and correspondence 1888-1916; memo and articles of association 1885; balance sheets 1893-1933; annual accounts 1927-53; private ledgers 1886-1951; bad debts ledgers 1892-1965; royalty: ledger 1895-1901, day book 1895-1904; rebates ledger 1935-41; ledger balances 1933-51; private cash books 1885-1950; cash payments register 1943-57; financial papers and correspondence 1890s-1920; customer address books 1880s-1920s; illustrated catalogues and price lists 1900-c23; maintenance, materials and labour registers 1939-56; departmental output summaries 1937-58; patent documents, papers and correspondence 1877-1935; correspondence and papers re orders 1870,1890s-1930s; title deeds and property documents and papers 1870-1950; buildings register 1920s-40s; plant and machinery register 1920s-40s; employment agreements 1881-1905; photographs of office staff and workmen c1890-1939; marine insurance policies 1890s-1930s

Records (2): with the Liquidator, Edmund House, 12 Newall Street, Birmingham, W Midlands B3 3EP
minutes 1920-81

504 BEDFORD CLUB & BOWLING GREEN CO LTD

1 Aug 1885
21455
11 De Parys Avenue, Bedford, Bedfordshire
Social club-house

History: Bedford Club was founded in 1879 and rented premises in Dame Alice Street, Bedford. The members of this private club, leading tradesmen and professional people of Bedford, subsequently purchased their own premises. Company was incorporated in 1885 as above to run the new club building, constructed at 11 De Parys Avenue by contractor Mr Foster to the designs of Anthony & Young. Facilities of the club included billiard tables, dining room, reading room, tennis courts and bowling green.

Records (1): at Bedford Club & Bowling Green, 11 De Parys Avenue, Bedford, Bedfordshire
directors and general meeting minutes 1964-date; shareholders lists 1969-72; members registers and share ledgers 1885-date; directors register 1950; share and transfer: certificates 1956-73, correspondence 1973-7; dividends register 1938-68; annual returns 1929-38; annual reports and accounts 1964-74; balance sheets 1931-8; revenue and dividend accounts books 1964-9; financial correspondence 1971-7; club: membership book 1923-80, members registers 1973-date, visitors book 1923-77, subscription register 1956-66, stock returns 1911-19, wages book 1967-78, cash book 1968-73

Records (2): at CC Bell & Son, 48-50 Harpur Street, Bedford, Bedfordshire MK40 2QT
directors and general meeting minutes 1927; share transfer: certificates 1927-68, correspondence 1928-61; dividend warrants and correspondence 1938-68; annual returns 1948-68; annual reports and accounts 1929-57; financial correspondence, legal charge papers 1964; bowling green turf correspondence and costs 1928; club lease: and inventory 1945, correspondence 1960; repairs and alteration correspondence and papers 1928-64

Records (3): at Bedfordshire Record Office, County Hall, Bedford, Bedfordshire MK42 9AP
proposed shareholders meeting minutes 1879-85; directors meeting minutes 1885-1917; committee meeting minutes 1923-56; members register and share ledger 1885-c1921; club account book 1880-1918

505 COMMERCIAL UNION ASSURANCE CO LTD

8 Aug 1885
21487
1 St Helen's, Undershaft, London EC3P 3DQ
Insurance

History: established by deed of settlement on 28 Sep 1861 following a meeting of merchants opposed to increases in fire insurance premiums following the Tooley Street fire of 22 Jun 1861. Temporary offices were taken at 34 Gracechurch Street, moving to 19 Cornhill, London by end of year. Rate war with old established fire offices raged until Nov 1863 when a revised tariff was adopted by all. Established a life department in 1862 and a marine department at 5 Royal Exchange Avenue, London in 1863. In 1865 branches and local boards were opened in Manchester, Greater Manchester; Belfast, N Ireland; Dublin, Eire; Liverpool, Merseyside and Glasgow, Strathclyde; Edinburgh, Lothian in 1869; Birmingham, W Midlands and Newcastle, Tyne & Wear in 1873; and by 1887 in Aberdeen, Grampian; Bristol, Avon;

Southampton, Hampshire; Warwick, Warwickshire; and London's West End. Overseas agencies were acquired at Hamburg, Germany in 1861; Rangoon, Burma; Colombo, Sri Lanka; Cape Town, South Africa; Kingston, Jamaica; and Bridgetown, Barbados in 1862; Montreal, Canada; Lima, Peru; Valparaiso, Chile; Shanghai, China; Manila, Philippines; Natal and Port Elizabeth, South Africa; Bombay and Madras, India; Karachi, Pakistan; Jakarta, Java; Izmir, Turkey; and Trinidad in 1863. A New York agency opened in 1871 followed by agencies throughout USA during the 1870s. Most overseas business was fire insurance although life and marine business was also conducted in Canada, India and South Africa during the early 1890s. Fire insurance companies in Australia, New Zealand, Singapore and South Africa were also acquired in the 1890s and the business of several American companies in difficulties after the San Francisco earthquake of 1906 were taken over. Nottingham & Midland Fire Insurance Co Ltd (est 1884) was purchased in 1889 and West of England Fire & Life Insurance Co Ltd (est 1807) in 1894. By 1900 had a new head office at 23-27 Cornhill, London and controlled assets of £7.4 million. Principal acquisitions in accident insurance were: Palatine Insurance Co Ltd (est 1886) in 1900; Globe Accident Insurance Co Ltd (est 1890) and Vehicular & General Insurance Co Ltd (est 1892) in 1901; Accident Insurance Co Ltd (est 1867) in 1906; Alliance Plate Glass Insurance Co Ltd (est 1894), Plate Glass Insurance Co Ltd of London (est 1852) and Ocean Accident & Guarantee Corporation Ltd (est 1871) in 1910; and Midland Mutual Plate Glass Insurance Society (est 1896) in 1913. Also acquired 'composite' offices, notably Hand-in-Hand Fire & Life Insurance Society (est 1696) in 1905; Union Assurance Society Ltd (est 1714) in 1907; North British & Mercantile Insurance Co Ltd (est 1899) in 1959; and Northern Assurance Co Ltd (est 1836) in 1968. Other acquisitions included: Economic Fire Office Ltd (est 1886) in 1894; Scottish Country & Mercantile Insurance Co Ltd (est 1897) and Ocean Marine Insurance Co Ltd (est 1859) in 1907; Railway Passengers Assurance Co Ltd (est 1849) in 1910; Scottish Metropolitan Assurance Co Ltd (est 1876) in 1912; Liverpool Victoria Insurance Corporation Ltd (est 1907) in 1913; National Insurance Co of Great Britain Ltd (est 1897) and Fine Art & General Insurance Co Ltd (est 1890) in 1917; British & European Insurance Co Ltd (est 1908) and Edinburgh Assurance Co Ltd (est 1923) in 1918; West of Scotland Insurance Office Ltd (est 1886) in 1924; British General Insurance Co Ltd (est 1904) in 1926; Travellers' Insurance Association Ltd (est 1910) in 1928; and Hibernian Fire & General Insurance Co Ltd (est 1908) in the 1930s. From 1968 headquarters were at 1 St Helen's, Undershaft, London. By 1978 had total premium income of over £1.3 billion with over 70 per cent from foreign business and life assurance business accounting for about 20 per cent of the total. In 1984 there were approximately 30 branches in UK and 200 main overseas branches.

Records (1): at Commercial Union Assurance, 1 St Helen's, Undershaft, London EC3P 3DQ board meeting minutes 1861-date; accident department minutes 1921-9; fire department reports 1885-1902; committee meeting minutes: agency 1863-5, book-keeping 1862-4, building 1930-4, finance 1861-3, foreign 1862-4, general purposes 1938-62, life 1862-1938, special 1875-1930; marine committee meeting: minutes 1924-38, attendance books 1907-11, agenda 1895-1938; foreign: results book c1865 on, branches and agencies c1900, agents lists c1890; New York agency: minutes 1877, loss letters 1902-05; general meeting: minutes 1861-date, reports 1945-date; secretarys: notebook 1865-7, letter book 1902, memoranda 1874-1908; amalgamation agreements 1894-1924; account balance papers 1920-45; ledger 1863-79; general ledgers and journals 1900 on; investment ledgers: 1870 on, life department 1896 on; marine: net loss account 1921-45, quarterly balances 1932-6, weekly returns 1888,1922-9, letter book 1863-5, building risk books 1923-6, Japanese warship correspondence 1877-8, closing ships correspondence 1863, cargo ship correspondence and papers 1880 on, risk book 1939-40, risk agreements *Queen Mary* and *Queen Elizabeth* 1935-49, excess cover rates nd, hull risk statistics 1946-61, insurance journal 1863-5, voyage risk book 1863, time risks, tramps and liners journals 1931, provisional risk books 1947-9, reinsurance recoveries 1918-23, war risks 1925-47, war loss books 1914-18,1939-42, salvage books 1898-1919,1929-33, salvages received 1939-40, owners claims records 1896-1911, loss report books 1880-1910, casualties 1911-49; joint hull underwriting agreements 1912-41; salvage corps correspondence 1865 on; fire: business results 1877-1902, results accounts 1925-40, memoranda 1888-1922, foreign letter book 1904-05; annuities registers 1862-1905,1948-60; earthquake: Jamaica claims correspondence 1907, San Francisco legal papers, press cuttings, photographs, settlement account, loss estimates, correspondence 1906-08, Valparaiso scrapbook nd; policies statement books 1881-8,1899-1902; South and Central American survey reports 1911-12; agents commission accounts 1910-30; foreign agencies: ledger 1910 on, commission accounts 1901-21; staff salaries 1895-1915

Records (2): at Guildhall Manuscripts Department, Guildhall Library, Aldermanbury, London EC2P 2EJ
committee meeting minutes: accident 1894-1921,1930-8, fire 1861-1938, foreign fire 1885-7

Edward Liveing, *A Century of Insurance. The Commercial Union Group of Insurance Companies, 1861-1961* (1961)

506 WARWICKSHIRE CRICKET GROUND LTD

11 Aug 1885
21497
County Ground, Edgbaston, Birmingham, W Midlands B5 7QU
Cricket ground

History: incorporated in 1885 as above to provide a ground for Warwickshire County Cricket Club (founded 1882). By 1888 the ground had been drained and levelled, and a grandstand, pavilion and other buildings erected. The company purchased County Cricket Ground in 1920. In 1983 it possessed 2 leasehold properties in Edgbaston, including the Colts Ground on the east side of River Rea. County Cricket Club holds the majority of the company's shares.

Records (1): at Evershed & Tomkinson, National Westminster House, Colmore Centre, 10 Newhall Street, Birmingham, W Midlands B3
directors and general meeting minutes 1885-1976; members register, share ledger and annual returns 1885-1963; mortgage and transfer registers 1896-1959; directors register 1901-63; share and share transfer certificates and stubs 1885-1957; memo of association 1885; annual reports and accounts 1887-9

Records (2): at Warwickshire Cricket Ground, County Ground, Edgbaston, Birmingham, W Midlands B5 7QU
directors meeting minutes 1952-82; agm: minutes 1935-77, agendas 1935-81; shareholders list c1890; debenture: interest 1911-12, interest certificates 1934-55, transfer certificates 1941-64; annual returns 1912-74; corporate and administrative correspondence 1945-83; annual reports and accounts 1892-1980; balance sheets 1929-82

507 BOSTON FISHING GROUP HOLDINGS LTD

18 Aug 1885
21516
St Andrew's Building, St Andrew's Dock, Hull, Humberside
Fishing

History: incorporated as Boston Deep Sea Fishing & Ice Co Ltd in 1885 to carry on business of deep sea fishing from the port of Boston, Lincolnshire. Offices had moved from 28 Wide Bargate, Boston to Murray Street, Fish Docks, Grimsby, Humberside by 1925. Subsequently changed name to Boston Deep Sea Fisheries Ltd and to above in 1960s. Went into members' voluntary liquidation in 1972 while one of its subsidiaries, Boston Deep Sea Fisheries Ltd continued to carry on business of fishing and allied trades and industries from St Andrew's Dock, Hull, Humberside. The latter was acquired by North British Maritime Group Ltd in Oct 1983.

Records: at Lincolnshire Archives Office, The Castle, Lincoln, Lincolnshire LN1 3AB
directors meeting minutes 1897-1962; general meeting minutes 1939-64; members registers and share ledgers 1885-1912; share: papers 1889-1902, certificates 1886-98, transfer registers 1885-1916, and certificates 1885-1964; annual lists and summaries 1885-1924; mortgage debenture certificates 1886-c1913; mortgage registers 1885-1967; annual report and accounts 1925; orders and correspondence 1930-1; sale bills and vessel purchase agreements 1885-6; trawling vessels building reports, correspondence and papers 1889-98; vessel mortgage certificates 1879-89,1937-62; agent purchase and supplier agreements 1888-1912; slipway rules c1913; manager application 1896; premises leases 1886-1906; misc 1888-1922

508 CATHAYS COTTAGE CO LTD

24 Aug 1885
21531
St John's Chambers, High Street Arcade, Cardiff, S Glamorgan CF1 2BD
Property

History: founded and incorporated in 1885 as Cathays Workmen's Cottage Co Ltd by F de Courcy Hamilton, a Cardiff solicitor who acted as secretary to several Cardiff property companies in the 1880s, to erect suitable dwellings for the labouring classes in Cathays, Cardiff, S Glamorgan. Name changed to above during the 1960s and it became policy to sell house property when leases expired. Proceeds were used to purchase commercial property in the county.

Records: at Cathays Cottage, St John's Chambers, High Street Arcade, Cardiff, S Glamorgan CF1 2BD
directors and general meeting minutes 1885-date; share: ledger 1885-1964, transfer ledger 1888-1975; directors register 1940s-60s; mortgage register 1886-1931; memo and articles of association 1885; annual reports and accounts 1887-date; general ledger 1886-1968; journal 1886-1967; cash book 1959-68; weekly rentals payments book 1921-77; income tax papers 1967; list of properties nd; out letter book 1918-22; incoming letters 1958-70; directors records: ledger 1901-69, journal 1916-59, cash book 1948-71, ground rents assignment notices 1890s-c1918, ground rents book 1917-27, weekly rental payments book 1923-76, out letter books 1918-22, incoming letters 1956-7,1964-76

509 BLUE CIRCLE INVESTMENTS LTD
9 Sep 1885
21576
Portland House, Stag Place, London SW1E 5BJ
Investment

History: incorporated in 1885 as Stone Court Chalk, Land & Pier Co Ltd to acquire a chalk quarry and plant for the manufacture of whiting and bricks, at Stone, Kent. Nominal share capital was £75,000 in £100 shares. A cement manufacturing plant was erected soon after incorporation for the supply of cement to the London market. By 1920s was a subsidiary of Associated Portland Cement Manufacturers Ltd and in 1929 the company was renamed Stone Court Ballast Co Ltd. In 1975 the company became a property investment subsidiary of Blue Circle Industries Ltd, its name being changed to the above in that year.

Records: at Blue Circle Industries, Portland House, Stag Place, London SW1E 5BJ
directors meeting minutes 1914-33; mortgages and debenture register 1885-1910; legal documents 1897-1942; balance sheets 1922-45

510 THIRD ELECTRA FINANCE CO LTD
29 Sep 1885
21626
Electra House, Victoria Embankment, London WC2R 3HP
Investment (formerly telegraph)

History: incorporated in 1885 as West African Telegraph Co Ltd, promoted by India Rubber Gutta Percha & Telegraph Works Ltd, to lay cables along the west African coast. First cable from Dakar, Senegal, to Banjul, The Gambia, to Conakry, Guinea, to Sierra Leone, was laid in 1886, continuing to Grand Bassam, Ivory Coast, to Accra, Ghana, to Cotonou, Benin to Sao Tome Island, to Gabon, to Principe Island, to Luanda, Angola. In 1889 Principe was connected to Bonny, Nigeria, and all cables were taken over to form part of Eastern & Associated Telegraph Companies group along with African Direct Telegraph Co Ltd and Eastern & South African Telegraph Co Ltd. Became part of Electra House Group and its name was changed to above.

Records (1): at Third Electra Finance, Electra House, Victoria Embankment, London WC2R 3HP
board meeting: minutes 1885-date, papers 1949-date; agm minutes 1885-date; incorporation papers 1885; annual returns 1885-date; misc correspondence 1949-date

Records (2): at Cable & Wireless, Mercury House, Theobalds Road, London WC1X 8RX
agreements 1886-1929; engineers cable reports c1902; photographs of property in Africa c1889-96; staff rules and regulations c1883,1923; photographs of staff nd

Records (3): at Science Museum Library, South Kensington, London SW7 5NH
cable specifications 1886-9

KC Baglehole, *A Century of Service. A Brief History of Cable and Wireless Ltd 1868-1968* (1969)
Hugh Barty-King, *Girdle Round the Earth* (1979)

511 LONDON COUNTY PROPERTIES (DEVELOPMENTS) LTD

30 Sep 1885
21629
Brook House, 113 Park Lane, London W1Y 4AY
Property

History: incorporated in 1885 as Cardiff Steam Coal Collieries Co Ltd to carry on trade as colliery proprietors, coke manufacturers, patent fuel manufacturers and miners. Name changed to Cardiff Collieries Ltd in Mar 1911, and to Property & General Investments Ltd in Mar 1958 when the company's business became property investment. By 1962 held land in Worcester and Kidderminster, Hereford & Worcester; Leicester, Leicestershire; Gateshead, Tyne & Wear; Eastbourne, E Sussex; Cheltenham, Gloucestershire; Southampton, Hampshire; and Edinburgh, Lothian; and had 24 subsidiary and associated companies. Acquired by MEPC Ltd, property and development company, in 1969. Name changed to above in Dec 1969.

Records: at MEPC, Brook House, 113 Park Lane, London W1Y 4AY
directors and general meeting minutes 1962-date; members register 1966-date; memo and articles of association 1958-date; annual returns 1970-date

512 P&O STRATH SERVICES LTD

20 Oct 1885
21695
Beaufort House, St Botolph Street, London EC3A 7DX
Shipping

History: incorporated in 1885 by FC Strick as Frank C Strick & Co Ltd, shipbrokers and coal exporters of London, with a nominal share capital of £2000. This was subsequently increased to £50,000 in 1895 and £100,000 in 1903. In 1887 established Anglo-Algerian Steamship Co Ltd (known as Strick Line Ltd from 1913) to own Stricks' first vessel, and also established London & Paris Steamship Co Ltd as a vehicle for raising finance. The company exported coal from Britain to Italy and imported iron ore from North Africa. In 1892 entered the Persian Gulf trade forming Anglo-Arabian & Persian Steamship Co Ltd. By 1900 Stricks owned 15 ships. La Tunisienne Steam Navigation Co Ltd formed in 1909 to operate vessels in the North African trade. By then Stricks also owned bunkering depots in Port Said, Algiers and Oran. In 1919 FC Strick sold most of his shipping interests to Lord Inchcape and in 1923 Strick Line (1923) Ltd was formed to own and operate the new fleet. However Strick continued to own some shipping interests and in 1928 re-acquired a 49 per cent interest in Strick Line (1923) Ltd and in Shahristan Steamship Co Ltd. In 1972 Peninsular & Oriental Steam Navigation Co completed its acquisition of all Strick interests. In 1976 name changed to above and from the 1970s the company did not trade.

Records: at National Maritime Museum, Romney Road, Greenwich, London SE10 9NF
minutes: board 1903-63, general 1903-50; list of subscribers 1885; annual summaries 1922-60; balance sheets and profit and loss accounts 1897-1960; charter parties, disbursement accounts, stores and provisions accounts for individual ships 1969-71; repairs analysis ledger 1964-70; freight agreements 1914; special letter books 1909-18; correspondence re: Gulf ore shipments 1906-42, Persian Gulf trade 1919-21, Strick family 1939-70, company history 1951-71;

information and publicity material 1903-71; photographs of ships, individuals 1928-54; fleet lists 1887-1960s

Anglo-Algerian Steamship Co (1896) Ltd: minutes 1896-1920; memo of association extract 1896; statement of accounts 1912

'Dwina' Ltd: annual returns 1922-65; share ledger and register of members 1907-43; balance sheets and profit and loss accounts 1908-60

Strick Line Ltd: directors reports and statements of accounts 1915-17; register of mortgages and charges 1968-70; notes on results etc 1969

London & Paris Steamship Co Ltd: board minutes 1920-63; share registers 1920-57; share transfer register 1957-65; directors reports 1921-60; annual returns 1953-65

Shahristan Steamship Co Ltd: general minutes 1922-71; annual returns 1923-66; share certificates 1922-63; balance sheets and profit and loss accounts 1924-60

Strick Line (1923) Ltd: general minutes 1924-71; annual returns 1924-65; seal book 1950-75; combined accounts with subsidiaries 1924-58; balance sheets and profit and loss accounts 1924-60

Strick Scott & Co Ltd: minutes 1950-63; minute extracts 1963-72; secretarys papers 1920-31; report and accounts 1921; balance sheets and profit and loss accounts 1920-71

Frank C Strick & Co (Newcastle) Ltd: minutes: board 1931-73, general 1932-75; annual returns 1949-75; memo and articles of association 1931; share certificates 1931-74; balance sheets and profit and loss accounts 1930-74

Frank C Strick & Co (Liverpool) Ltd: board minutes 1955-75; annual returns 1955-74; registers of directors 1972; memo and articles of association 1954; share certificates 1955-74; balance sheets and profit and loss accounts 1956-73

Frank C Strick & Co (South Wales) Ltd (formerly **North Devon Steamship Co Ltd**): annual returns 1931-65; share certificates 1923-48; secretarys papers 1923; balance sheets and profit and loss accounts 1923-60

Strick Gorchs & Co Ltd: annual returns 1938-65; share certificates 1921-5; balance sheets and profit and loss accounts 1932-61

United Ship Supplies Ltd: secretarys papers 1930-40; annual returns 1941-65; balance sheets and profit and loss accounts 1931-60

513 BASS BREWING (TADCASTER) LTD

20 Oct 1885
21696
Tower Brewery, Tadcaster, N Yorkshire
Brewing

History: incorporated in 1885 as Mappin's Masbro' Old Brewery Ltd with offices and brewery at Greasboro' Road, Masbro', Rotherham, S Yorkshire. Name changed to Mappin's Brewery Ltd in 1949. Taken over by William Stones Ltd (inc 1895) of Sheffield, S Yorkshire in 1954. Brewing and bottling stopped at Rotherham and were transferred to Sheffield. William Stones Ltd was acquired by Bass Charrington Ltd in 1968. Company's name subsequently changed to above and in 1983 it was a subsidiary of Bass PLC through Bass Holdings Ltd.

Records: at Bass North, United House, Piccadilly, York, N Yorkshire YO1 1XQ
directors meeting minutes 1938-79; plant and machinery valuation 1949; properties schedule 1969

514 MEDICAL DEFENCE UNION (LTD)

23 Oct 1885
21708
3 Devonshire Place, London W1N 2EA
Medical practitioners legal defence

History: formed by CF Rideal and other non-medical people and incorporated as above in 1885 as a company limited by guarantee to support and protect the interests of medical practitioners residing in the UK; to promote honourable practice; to give members legal advice; and to consider and promote legislative measures likely to benefit the medical profession and oppose measures likely to injure it. Rideal became the first secretary. Over 400 medical practitioners joined in the first 6 months despite suspicion of its lay origin and leadership. Local branches were formed during the first year at Liverpool, Merseyside; Brighton, E Sussex; Manchester, Greater Manchester; Huddersfield, W Yorkshire; Sheffield, S Yorkshire; and Birmingham, W Midlands. Local solicitors were appointed in Newcastle upon Tyne, Tyne & Wear; Wigan, Greater Manchester; Bristol, Avon; Brighton, E Sussex; and Barnsley, S Yorkshire. A medical club was established in London and a library of works on medical ethics and jurisprudence created. In 1887 the union was nearly insolvent. Rideal resigned and Lawson Tait, president of the midland branch of the union, became president. New articles of association were adopted in early 1888 and the union offices were moved to Birmingham. By 1889 membership had reached 531 rising to 1446 in 1890 and 2924 in 1893. The guarantee fund, which stood at £538 in 1888, grew to £4150 by 1893. Branches were discontinued in 1892 and replaced by small local advisory committees formed in towns, 70 being established by 1900. London & Counties Medical Protection Society Ltd was formed in Apr 1892 by dissatisfied union members. Name changed to Medical Protection Society in 1947. Abortive amalgamation talks were held in 1893 and 1900. The offices moved back to London to 20&21 King William Street, in 1894, moving to 4 Trafalgar Square in 1898 and to 49 Bedford Square in 1923. By 1900 the union was firmly established alongside other medical bodies. Members in 1906 stood at 7042 (a fifth of all medical practitioners in the UK), rising to 8727 in 1919, to 16,267 in 1930 and to over 31,000 in 1946. From the mid 1940s dental practitioners were eligible for membership. In 1979 membership was over 80,000, 45,000 of which were dentists. Members were provided with 3 categories of service: the conduct of legal proceedings on their behalf; indemnification wholly or in part against claims for damages and costs; and advice on a wide variety of problems including employment, defamation, professional and technical matters, and educational guidance on medical and medico-legal problems.

Records: at Medical Defence Union, 3 Devonshire Place, London W1N 2EA
council meeting: minutes 1885-date, agenda and documents 1899-date, attendance registers 1936-date; committee meeting: minutes 1894-1972, executive with agenda and documents 1899-1972, council with agenda 1938-47, finance 1894-1977, with agenda and documents 1900-77, general purposes with agenda and documents 1971-date, cases with agenda and documents 1972-date, treasurers with agenda and documents 1972-date, editorial with agenda and documents 1968-date, dental with agenda and documents 1968-date, standing joint Medical Defence Union and London & Counties Medical Protection Society with agenda and documents 1923-4,1934-45, joint co-ordinating committee Medical Defence Union and London & Counties Medical Protection Society and Medical & Dental Defence Union of

Scotland with agenda and documents 1945-date; presidents committee reports 1976-date; sub-committee meeting minutes, agenda and documents 1899-date; agm: minutes 1897-date, agenda 1901-date; elected members meeting: minutes 1891-date, agenda 1899-date; superannuation fund: trustee meeting minutes and documents 1943-date, annual reports 1888-date; memo and articles of association 1888-date; directors register 1892-date; annual returns 1935-date; seal register 1936-date; final accounts 1938-date; ledgers 1895-date; cash books 1888-date; taxation documents 1918-date; membership: application forms 1885-date, analysis 1942-5; investment register 1927-date; reinsurance claims register 1949-70; specimen letters 1938-date; premises and dignitaries photographs 19-20 cent

Robert Forbes, *Sixty Years of Medical Defence* (priv pub 1947)

515 LIGHTFOOT REFRIGERATION CO LTD

31 Oct 1885
21741
275 Abbeydale Road, North Circular Road, Wembley, Greater London HA0 1PX
Refrigeration

History: incorporated in 1885 as British Linde Refrigeration Co Ltd by Thomas Bell Lightfoot, naval architect and designer of refrigerated ships in conjunction with Geschellschaft Fur Linde's Eis Maschienen, a German company. Ice factories and cold stores were erected in Calcutta in 1897, and Bombay in 1912, India; in Brighton and Hastings, E Sussex in 1911 and 1922; and in Birmingham, W Midlands in 1900. During WW1 connections were severed with the German company and its name was changed to above in 1916. Continued to deal in ice and refrigerants, as well as designing, manufacturing and installing industrial refrigeration plant for land and marine use. Acquired in early 1960s by AVP Industries Ltd which was acquired in 1977 by Lonrho Ltd. In 1978 it was integrated into Firsteel Engineering Ltd. In early 1980s was manufacturing refrigeration equipment for freezing and storing food-stuffs, liquid chilling, process cooling, ice making, chemical processing and air conditioning used in dairies, breweries, abattoirs and for drinking water coolers, and had major plant installations throughout the world.

Records: at Lightfoot Refrigeration, 275 Abbeydale Road, North Circular Road, Wembley, Greater London HAO 1PX
share certificates 1916; German agreement 1958; memo and articles of association 1916; sales booklets c1923,nd

516 EDGBASTON CHURCH OF ENGLAND COLLEGE FOR GIRLS LTD

9 Nov 1885
21778
31 Calthorpe Road, Edgbaston, Birmingham, W Midlands B15 1RX
School

History: incorporated in 1885 as above to establish a girls school in Edgbaston, Birmingham, W Midlands with religious teaching as the main objective. School opened with 42 pupils in Calthorpe Road in May 1886. By 1892 numbers had risen to 240 and building extensions were undertaken. Boys were allowed to join the kindergarten in 1919 when total pupils numbered 332. By 1921 there were 380 pupils and 26 staff: 20 full-time and 6 visiting teachers. In that year clergymen's daughters were admitted at reduced fees. The kindergarten closed in 1930 but number of pupils had risen to 395. From 1934 all profits of the company were used for educational purposes, no dividends or bonuses being paid to the shareholders. From Sep 1939 until Dec 1940 some pupils were evacuated to Attingham Park, Shrewsbury, Salop. In 1941 Edgbaston School was requisitioned and pupils amalgamated with Edgbaston High School for Girls in Westbourne Road, Birmingham. Reopened school in Calthorpe Road in Jan 1947 with 91 pupils, rising to 257 by 1948. Shareholders were invited to sell shares to Birmingham Diocesan Trustees in 1951 and by 1981 that body held nearly all the shares. In 1983 the school had about 500 pupils.

Records (1): at Edgbaston Church of England College for Girls, 31 Calthorpe Road, Edgbaston, Birmingham, W Midlands B15 1RX
council meeting minutes and reports 1890-1968; finance committee: meeting minutes 1904-65, reports 1902-04; general meeting minutes 1886-1983; share certificate book 1900-c60; annual reports and accounts 1948-50; balance sheets 1935-46; accounts 1950-63; private ledgers 1938-71; general ledgers 1949-67; cash book 1967-74; education board inspection reports 1921,1930; salary scales 1917,1920-3; staff records 1959-74

Records (2): at Edgbaston High School for Girls, Westbourne Road, Edgbaston, Birmingham, W Midlands B15 3TS
annual reports and accounts 1903-34,1944-64; prospectuses 1930s

Janet Whitcut, *Edgbaston High School 1876-1976* (priv pub 1976)

517 HALLAMSHIRE TENNIS & SQUASH CLUB LTD

11 Nov 1885
21795
Hunters Bar, Sheffield, S Yorkshire S11
Sports club-house

History: incorporated in 1885 as Sheffield & Hallamshire Lawn Tennis Club Ltd to establish a club in Sheffield for the encouragement and practice of lawn tennis, racquets, fives, cricket, football and archery. Built premises on freehold land at Hunters Bar, Sheffield. Name changed to above in 1971. In 1980s provided facilities for lawn tennis and squash racquets.

Records: at Hallamshire Tennis & Squash Club, Hunters Bar, Sheffield, S Yorkshire S11
members register and share ledger 1885 on; prospectus 1885; memo and articles of association 1885

518 HOUSE PROPERTY CO OF LONDON LTD

18 Nov 1885
21813
Eagle House, High Street, Wimbledon, Greater London SW19
Property

History: incorporated as above in 1885. In 1980 was an independent company owning freehold and leasehold house and shop property in London, with one subsidiary, TE Pearson & Co Ltd, builder's merchants of East Finchley, Greater London.

Records: at House Property, Eagle House, High Street, Wimbledon, Greater London SW19 board meeting minutes 1885-1965; minutes 1866-date; list of members 1914-31; share: register 1885-1938, certificates 1933-78, transfer register 1885-date, transfer sheets and certificates 1866-date; dividends 1892-1933; register of seals 1885-1964; secretarys letter book 1931-2; annual reports and accounts 1885-98; balance sheets and accounts 1921-date; general ledgers 1888-1973; rent ledger 1931-72; private ledger 1941-50; ledger balances 1925-52; journal 1927-60; accounts letter book 1931-42; cash books 1934-61; banking summaries cash books 1950-76; bank book 1970-6; petty cash books 1947-57; invoices 1914; register of mortgages 1886-1927; rent books 1913-72; insurance register 1897-1959; property repair registers 1907-77; house property vouchers and correspondence 1965-80; salaries books 1950-68
TE Pearson & Co Ltd: petty cash book 1920-49; salaries book 1949-65

519 H&G SIMONDS LTD

21 Nov 1885
21825
Anchor Terrace, Southwark Bridge Road, London SE1 9HS
Brewing

History: William Simonds, a maltster, began brewing at Reading, Berkshire in about 1768. When his son inherited the business in 1782 it had 4 public houses. Using inherited money and his wife's dowry, WB Simonds opened a new brew-house in Broad Street, Reading and in 1789 commissioned Sir George Soane to design another in Bridge Street, Reading. It cost £6400 and had an annual capacity of 6000 barrels. In 1791 Simonds was a company founder of a Reading bank and in 1814 founded his own banking business. He retired in 1816 by which time his son Blackall Simonds was managing the business. Output rose from 11,100 barrels in 1831 to 15,000 in 1839 when the business was valued at £10,000 and operated 37 houses. In 1834 it was exporting pale ale. In the 1840s the business stagnated but new management restored fortunes in the 1850s so that by 1866 output had expanded to 28,600 barrels per annum. Management was again reorganised in 1868 when Henry Simonds retired and was succeeded by his son Henry. Between 1866 and 1871 output doubled to equal 57,900 barrels and between 1868-74 profits exceeded £10,000 every year. The brewery benefited from the development of a military trade, following the establishment of Aldershot as the 'home' of the British army in the 1880s, which soon led to branches being set up overseas to supply garrisons in the colonies. A lucrative business was also created through supplying the refreshment rooms of railway companies. Tied house numbers grew from 79 in 1872 to 158 in 1896 and after 1876 profits were never below £20,000. By 1872 the capital of the three partners at £71,500, represented about 40 per cent of the £183,000 liabilities. In 1885 when output stood at 115,000 barrels per annum H&G Simonds Ltd was incorporated with a nominal capital of £0.5 million. The number of tied houses doubled between 1896 and 1916, while up to 1913-14 output increased by 83 per cent. In 1919 the business began to expand by acquiring other breweries - Tamar Brewery of Devonport, Devon in 1919; W Rogers Ltd of Bristol, Avon in 1935; Ashby Staines Brewery Ltd and South Berks Brewery Co Ltd in 1936; Cirencester Brewery, Lakeman's Brewery of Brixham; RH Stiles of Bridgend, Cornwall and WJ Rogers Ltd in 1938; and JL Marsh & Sons Ltd of Blandford Forum, Dorset in 1939. The company was transformed into a leading provincial brewery. Between 1945-53 a further six sizable breweries were acquired. In 1953 the chairmanship passed, for the first time, outside the Simonds family and in 1959 a trading agreement was entered into with Courage & Barclay Ltd of London. By

1960 this matured into a full scale merger.

Records (1): at Courage (Central), 32 Bridge Street, Reading, Berkshire RG1 2LX
board meeting minutes 1885-1975; general meeting: minutes 1885-1962, press notices 1953; committee meeting minutes: general purposes 1946-55, debenture stockholders 1929-54; share: ledger and register of members 1885-1951, transfer papers and correspondence 1890-1954, bonus issue papers 1957, certificates 1887-1925; preference stock register 1937-49; debenture stock: register 1932-48, certificates and papers 1940-52, trust deeds 1928-63; register: managers 1902-47, power of attorney 1951-60, directors 1930-62, seal 1915-61; memo and articles of association and papers 1885-1954; financial reorganisation scheme and takeover papers 1936-63; share and investment correspondence and papers 1850-1938; annual report and accounts 1886-95,1935-61; balance sheets 1845-9; account: book 1896-1957, detailed schedules 1961, central area 1962; ledger: 1851-60,1913-58, private 1851-1930; impersonal 1920-30; journal 1931-7,1960-5; private cash book 1954-66; customer account book 1814-21; weekly cellar stock book 1931-54; cask and bottle loans and returns book 1837-1939; delivery orders book 1939-47; sale, agency and trading agreements and correspondence 1889-1946; free trade agreements register c1960; trade-mark agreements and court case papers 1882-1906; advertising agreements 1903-28; advertisements c1930s-c60; price lists and revisions 1892-1958; press cuttings 1952-5; barley book 1771-1806; brewing books 1823-72; beer production costs 1892-8; bottled beer, stock, wine and spirits stock book 1859-1905; brewing stock book 1938-48; malting agreements 1872,1884; hop sales contract 1934; barley purchase licence 1941; equipment supply agreements 1952; horses register 1892-1946; plant photographs c1950; staff salaries committee meeting minutes 1946-62; salary: books 1966-70, private 1939-72, no 2 1949-67; salary sheets, bank lists, tax papers and correspondence 1939-73; service agreements 1864-1951; first-aid centre attendance register 1958-68; staff reports, legal cases and papers 1947-74; house journals 1927-61; directors and staff photographs c1880-c1954; pension fund, contribution cards, trust deeds, ledger, investments lists, papers and correspondence 1950-73; Simonds family papers, portraits and photographs 1818-1952; estates: committee meeting minutes 1938-65, account book 1839-83, particulars 1895-9, inventory 1830,1852; rent: ledgers 1897-1911, cash book 1901-22, payable 1917-50; memo of valuations 1868; schedule of deeds 1873; register: public houses 1875, title deeds 1912, free properties 1939-57, mortgages c1940-50, fire insurance 1947-57; property: lists 1958-60, valuations and photographs 1951-60, agreements, title deeds, mortgages, leases etc c1820-1978; brewery, premises and public house photographs c1882-1960; public house leases, licences and papers 1816-1926; letter books: 1889-1907, private 1853-82; correspondence 1880-1960

Ashby Staines Brewery Ltd: directors attendance book 1934-6; debenture stockholders meeting minutes 1902-37; share certificates 1928-53; liquidation papers 1936-7; compensation fund 1930-1; annual report and accounts 1912; impersonal ledger 1931-7; stock receipts 1948-53; deeds and tenancy agreements 1789-1936

RB Bowley & Co: deeds, leases etc 1706 on

Cirencester Brewery Ltd: acquisition and liquidation papers 1937-49; memo and articles of association 1888,1898

East African Breweries Ltd: list of shareholders, prospectus and formation papers 1949-50; articles of association 1949-56; annual report and accounts 1954-61

John May & Co Ltd: directors meeting minutes 1941-50; acquisition and liquidation papers 1946-50, compensation fund papers 1947-50
Newbury Brewery Co Ltd: trust deed 1930; properties conveyed to Simonds 1931
Octagon Brewery Ltd: board and general meeting minutes 1899-1958; registers: members 1899-1953, dividends 1916-26, debenture stockholders 1924-45, mortgages and bonds 1899-1945; papers re acquisition and liquidation 1954-8; memo and articles of association 1899-1934; seal registers 1939-55; balance sheets 1948-54; ledger: balances 1954, private 1899-1944; machinery and plant additions 1949-54; stock records 1954; wages book 1954-5; managers agreements 1949-54; leases 1780-1920
Phillips & Sons Ltd: directors meeting minutes 1892-1954; acquisition and liquidation papers 1948-55; registers: directors 1942-8, mortgages 1892-1924, seals 1949-54
Pool & Son Ltd: purchase and liquidation papers 1952-4
Queens Hotel (Farnborough) Ltd: memo and articles of association 1920
WJ Rogers Ltd: liquidation papers and agreements 1938-9; conveyance of propery to Simonds 1938
Ship Hotel (Reading) Ltd: liquidation papers 1938
Simonds-Farsons-Cisk Ltd: articles of association 1929-60; balance sheets 1949-50; correspondence 1950-62
South Berkshire Brewery Co Ltd: board meeting minutes 1923-37; shareholders list 1920; share: certificates 1920, debenture 1897-1936; directors register 1897-1933; co-partnership agreements 1878,1899; liquidation papers 1936-7; memo and articles of association 1897-1906; annual report and accounts 1915-36; property: register c1905-53, list 1919-20; deeds, agreements etc 1620-1936
Tamar Brewery: inventory 1941
Wheelers Wycombe Brewery Ltd: directors meeting minutes 1929-50; general meeting minutes 1930-47; registers: members 1898-1937, mortgages 1899-1949, share transfers 1905-48; debenture stock: ledger 1898-1949, journal 1932-45, trust deed 1899, interest journal 1946-9; liquidation papers 1950; annual report and accounts 1932-4; salary books 1937-50; property valuations 1934

Records (2): at Courage, Anchor Terrace, Southwark Bridge Road, London SE1 9HS
ordinary stock transfer register 1957-60; debenture stock trust deed 1936-54

TAB Corley, 'Simonds' Brewery at Reading 1760-1960 *Berkshire Archaeological Journal* (1968)

520 HULL OIL MANUFACTURING CO LTD

1 Dec 1885
21850
Unilever House, Blackfriars, London EC4P 4BQ
Oil extractors

History: incorporated as above in 1885 to purchase business of William Aird, oil extractor of Hull, Humberside, and carry on business of manufacturers and merchants of oils, manures, feeding stuffs and ancillary trades. First to apply solvent washing process rather than hydraulic pressure to extract oil. Taken over in 1922 by British Oil & Cake Mills Ltd (est 1899) which amalgamated with Lever Brothers Ltd, soap and chemical manufacturers, in 1925. Had factory which closed in 1953, offices at Stoneferry, Hull, and London offices in Fenchurch

Street. In 1981 was a dormant company within Unilever Ltd.

Records: at Unilever, Unilever House, Blackfriars, London EC4P 4BQ
directors and general meeting minutes 1920-date; members registers 1919-date; share: transfer registers 1888-date; documents 1921-date; directors register 1948-date; memo and articles of association 1973; annual returns 1939-date

Harold W Brace, *History of Seed Crushing in Great Britain* (1960)

521 SPILLERS FOODS LTD
9 Dec 1885
21886
19 Hanover Square, London W1R 9DA
Animal food-stuffs

History: established in 1862 by James Spratt and later run by Edward Wylam, Charles John Wylam, and George Beetham Batchelor in partnership as Spratts Patent, animal food manufacturers of Henry Street, Bermondsey, London. Incorporated as Spratts Patent Ltd in 1885. Manufactured fibrine dog and puppy cakes; dog, poultry and game foods; bird foods, dog and poultry medicines; appliances and other accessories; and carried on an extensive grain and seed trade. Also incorporated Russian Spratts Patent Ltd, Spratts Patent (America) Ltd and Spratts Patent (Germany) Ltd in 1885 in order to sell products in those countries. Incorporated Dog Sanatorium Ltd, a veterinary sanatorium in 1887. Built animal biscuit factory at Poplar, London in 1894 and by 1957 had another factory in Liverpool, Merseyside. In 1957 owned Adelphi Press Ltd, printers; Caperns Ltd, bird seed packers; Carter Products Ltd, food distributors; Charles Hearson & Co Ltd, biological equipment manufacturers and laboratory contractors; Dog Sanatorium Ltd, quarantine and boarding establishment; Old Calabar Ltd, dog foods etc; Spratts Patent (Germany) Ltd, holding company; William Taylor & Son (Bird Seed) Ltd; Eldin Co Ltd, dog foods etc; Hygienic Wire Works Ltd, bird cage manufacturers; Spratts Patent (Canada) Ltd, dog foods etc; Spratts Patent (Ireland) Ltd, dog foods etc; Société Francaise Spratts Patent; Spratts Patent (America) Ltd; and WG Clarke & Sons (1929) Ltd, dog, game and poultry foods. Acquired by Spillers Ltd (inc 1887), millers and animal food manufacturers, in 1960. Changed name to Spratts Patent (Holdings) Ltd in 1969 and to above in 1972. Acted as manager for human and pet food interests of Spillers Ltd which was acquired by Dalgety Ltd in 1979.

Records: at Dalgety, 19 Hanover Square, London W1R 9DA
corporate records 1930 on

522 ELECTRA INVESTMENTS LTD
11 Dec 1885
21895
Electra House, Victoria Embankment, London WC2R 3HP
Investment (formerly telegraph)

History: formed and incorporated in 1885 as African Direct Telegraph Co Ltd by Eastern Telegraph Co Ltd and Brazilian Submarine Telegraph Co Ltd to lay cables between the main British ports on the west coast of Africa and England. Started cable laying in 1886 from

Banjul, The Gambia, to Sierra Leone, to Accra, Ghana, to Lagos and to Bonny, Nigeria. In 1893 laid cable from Bonny to Cameroon. Cables were taken over in 1889 to form with West African Telegraph Co Ltd and Eastern & South African Telegraph Co Ltd, part of Eastern & Associated Telegraph Companies. Became part of Electra House Group of companies and changed name to above.

Records (1): at Electra Investments, Electra House, Victoria Embankment, London WC2R 3HP
board meeting: minutes 1885-date, papers 1949-date; agm minutes 1885-date; incorporation papers 1885; annual returns 1885-date; misc correspondence 1949-date

Records (2): at Cable & Wireless, Mercury House, Theobalds Road, London WC1X 8RX
agreements, contracts and articles of association 1885-1929; balance sheets and accounts 1892-1921; papers re tax, cables, finances and staff 1902-25; engineers cable reports and papers 1886-1902; cable lay log book 1914; tariff rates 1920; photographs of company property and staff 1890-1929; history of West African cables 1886

Records (3): at Science Museum Library, South Kensington, London SW7 5NH
cable contract 1893; cable lay log book 1912

KC Baglehole, *A Century of Service. A Brief History of Cable and Wireless Ltd 1868-1968* (1969)
Hugh Barty-King, *Girdle Round the Earth* (1979)

523 BOC INTERNATIONAL LTD
26 Jan 1886
22096
Hammersmith House, Hammersmith, London W6 9DX
Manufacturers of industrial gases and welding, health care and carbon graphite products

History: formed and incorporated in 1886 as Brin's Oxygen Co Ltd by the Brin Brothers and Henry Sharp, to produce oxygen by the barium oxide method for use as 'limelight' in theatres and for medical purposes, leasing a factory site at 69 Horseferry Road, Westminster, and offices at Connaught Mansions, Victoria Street, Westminster, London. In 1887 Scottish & Irish Oxygen Co Ltd and Birmingham Oxygen Co Ltd, and in 1890 Manchester Oxygen Co Ltd were granted licences from the company to produce oxygen, the latter companies being taken over in 1899 and the S&IO works at Polmadie, Glasgow, Strathclyde in 1909. Also granted sole rights to operate Brin process in France, Germany and USA to Continental Oxygen Co. By 1900 new processes had been introduced and company took over the Linde patent in 1906 and changed its name to British Oxygen Co Ltd. By 1918 had new Linde oxygen plants in Greenwich and Wembley, Greater London; Birmingham, W Midlands; Manchester, Greater Manchester; Glasgow, Strathclyde; Newcastle upon Tyne, Tyne & Wear; Cardiff, S Glamorgan; Sheffield, S Yorkshire and Coventry, W Midlands. In 1920 took over Sparklets Ltd of Edmonton, London formed in 1896 as Aerators Ltd to manufacture small bulbs of carbon dioxide for aerated drinks, and moved engineering works to that site in 1921. In 1930 merged with Allen-Liversidge Ltd (est 1910) acetylene gas producers, and head offices were moved to their old offices at Victoria Station House, London in 1934. In 1936 moved again to Thames House, Millbank, London and in 1960 to Hammersmith, London. Acquired Quasi-Arc Co Ltd and Ferro-Arc Welding Co Ltd, manufacturers of arc electrodes for welding, in

1936, opening new welding works at Bilston, W Midlands, which closed in 1968; Odda Smelterek A/S, Norwegian carbide producers, in 1937; and Coxeter & Son Ltd and A Charles King Ltd, medical apparatus manufacturers, in 1939. By 1950 had formed subsidiary companies in over 20 countries. In 1967 took over Murex Group of welding and cutting equipment manufacturers, and Edwards High Vacuum Ltd and Bain & Hodge Ltd, haulage contractors, in 1968. Set up BOC-Linde Refrigeration Ltd in 1968 with Linde AG of Germany to manufacture commercial and industrial refrigeration and deep freeze equipment. Owned Batchelors Ltd, Eire, food processors, from 1969-73 and acquired Ace Refrigeration Ltd, deep freeze distributors, and J Muirhead Ltd, quick frozen food suppliers in 1969. Changed name to above in 1975 and formed BOC Ltd to take over bulk of trading in UK. Purchased Airco Inc, American chemical business, and Software Science International Ltd, software computer company, in 1978. In 1981 operated in 45 countries with 4 major subsidiaries generating 90 per cent of total sales: BOC Ltd, UK; Airco Inc, USA; Commonwealth Industrial Gases Ltd, Australia (inc 1935); and African Oxygen Ltd, South Africa (inc 1927).

Records: at BOC International, Hammersmith House, Hammersmith, London W6 9DX
board meeting minutes 1886-date; managing directors reports 1958-60; board correspondence 1958-61; executive management board: meeting minutes 1959-66, papers 1962-7, information reports 1960-1; chairmans committee meeting minutes 1962-70; executive committee meeting minutes 1948-57; managing directors committee meeting minutes and papers 1966; policy committee meeting minutes 1953-7; regional management committee meeting minutes 1965-76; divisional management meeting minutes and papers 1961-7; management: reports 1963-70, bulletins 1966-77; patents department minutes and papers 1945-61; properties sub-committee meeting minutes 1947-8; trouble shooting working party minutes and papers 1960; chairmens and directors correspondence 1953-73; general meeting minutes 1955-75; agm proceedings 1957-60; members register 1938 on; corporate papers and correspondence re: share and take overs 1890-1980, organisation 1930s-1980, monopolies commission 1954-60; memo and articles of association 1886-date; seal book 1957-77; annual reports and accounts 1887-date; divisions and subsidiaries budgets 1961-75; cost report 1957; accountants reports and correspondence 1956-60; investment papers and correspondence 1939-46; group activities summary 1924-31,1944; trading summaries 1955-66; market survey reports 1955-67; sales agreements 1887-1975; departmental sales bulletins 1954-64; general, medical, welding, cutting, aviation and technical services sales catalogues, brochures, price lists etc 1894-1979; public relations and management conference papers and correspondence 1956-74; photographs of products, sales fairs etc 1948-65; sample labels nd; patent and registered design papers and reports 1957-65; product register 1967-76; limestone reports and papers re carbide production 1923-66; photographs of processes, transport, equipment etc c1900-68; technical publications and literature 1911-71; manufacturing drawings, specifications, reports, instruction booklets etc 1889-1980; welding lecture papers 1936-9; safety rules and regulations and works notices 1893-1965; gas division wage papers 1965; pension scheme booklets 1971,1978; staff committee reports 1977-9; personnel department circulars 1947-59; training booklets and programme papers 1960-79; in house and staff magazines 1937-79; annual dinner and 75th anniversary celebration papers and correspondence 1933-76; retirement presentation papers 1933-61; chairmen and staff photographs 1886-1970s; West End offices plans, papers and photographs 1949-63; papers and correspondence: Welsh carbide factory 1936-40, Corby land purchase 1942-7; Hammersmith House papers and photographs 1960-3; plant, offices

and works photographs 1887-1975; misc correspondence and papers 19&20 cent; press cuttings 1893-1960; history articles, notes, booklets and correspondence 1930s-date

African Oxygen Ltd: board: meeting minutes 1937-79, papers 1961,1978-9; managing directors reports 1961,1965-72; executive management committee meeting minutes 1966; share correspondence 1963-9; sales catalogues 1959-60

Airco Inc: annual report and accounts 1968,1977; correspondence 1973-4

Airco-BOC Cryogenic Plant Corporation: board meeting minutes, papers and correspondence 1967-9; management meeting minutes 1967-8; finance meeting minutes 1967-8; operation meeting minutes 1968; supervision and JV board meeting minutes 1968-9; JV policy development meeting minutes 1969; market reports 1967-8; legal documents and correspondence patents, trade-marks etc 1965-9; shareholders reports 1969; accounts 1968; export financing figures 1968; research and development achievements 1968; staff bulletins 1972; correspondence 1967-71

A-L Meterolite Ltd: board meeting minutes 1913-17

Allen-Liversidge Ltd: board meeting minutes 1920-4; procedures book 1929; sales catalogues and price lists 1920s; works photographs 1920s-40s

Allen-Liversidge Portable Acetylene Co Ltd: board meeting minutes 1910-19; corporate papers and correspondence 1910

Anglo-Blackwells Ltd: minutes 1969-76

Artieselskabet Tysselfaldene: board meeting minutes 1948-60

BOC Linde Refrigeration Ltd: minutes 1969-76; seal book 1970-5

Bain & Hodge Ltd: board meeting minutes 1969-71; correspondence: take over 1969, subsidiary companies 1969-72

Batchelors Ltd: board meeting minutes 1969-73; corporate papers and correspondence 1969-74; accounts 1968-72

Birmingham Oxygen Co Ltd: share certificate book 1880s-90s; managing directors reports 1890,1892

British Industrial Gases Ltd: corporate papers and correspondence 1958-67; USA visit report 1958; financial statement 1963; budget estimates 1959-60; sales returns 1956-64; sales catalogues, price lists and press releases 1955-63; technical literature c1961; correspondence and papers 1934-46

British Oxygen Arc Equipment Ltd: board: meeting minutes and agenda 1955-62, correspondence 1955-66; general managers reports 1956-9; share papers and correspondence 1955-63; annual accounts 1955-65; financial correspondence 1955-65; marketing papers 1955-62; sales catalogues 1952

British Oxygen Canada Ltd: board meeting minutes 1949-63; sales catalogues 1956-8; history booklet c1969; correspondence 1949-62

British Oxygen Gases Ltd: board: meeting minutes, correspondence and reports 1958-60, management meeting minutes and correspondence 1959-60; memo and articles of association 1955; circulars 1955-8; papers re: take overs 1957, cost report 1957, Scunthorpe plant 1958, sales organisation 1959; sales catalogues, price lists and information 1957-62; medical cylinder labels and instructions 1959

British Oxygen (Hong Kong) Ltd: board meeting minutes 1947-77

British Oxygen Linde Ltd: board: meeting minutes 1955-61, correspondence and papers 1955-63; general managers reports 1955-61; agm minutes 1955-61; corporate documents 1955-65; annual reports and accounts 1959-64; audited accounts 1955-62; financial papers and correspondence 1955-61; operational manual 1955-6; sales catalogues nd; tenders and contracts 1956-9; misc correspondence 1945-65

British Oxygen Wimpey Ltd: board and general meeting minutes 1956-71; board correspondence and papers 1956-71; memo and articles of association 1956; corporate agreements and share transfer deeds 1956-64; head office staff register 1957

Burma Oxygen Ltd: board meeting minutes 1949-68; managing directors reports 1965-7

Canadian Helium Ltd: board meeting minutes 1962-71

Canadian Oxygen Ltd: board meeting minutes 1961-77; corporate documents 1949-61; financial statements 1963-7,1971-7

Carbide Distributing Agency Ltd: minutes 1943-64; directors register 1950; audited accounts 1943-57

Ceylon Oxygen Ltd: board meeting minutes 1948-76; private minutes 1961-76; general managers reports 1965-76; balance sheet and accounts 1963; sales catalogue 1960; misc correspondence 1960-4

Commonwealth Industrial Gases Ltd: board meeting minutes 1928-77; executive management meeting minutes 1964-7; manufacturing policy minutes 1967; managing directors reports 1975-80; share: registers 1958-61, papers 1965-71; annual reports and accounts 1960-74; sales correspondence and papers 1938-46; technical literature 1940s-74; directors photographs nd

Continental Sparklets Co Ltd: corporate agreement 1907; Brussels factory letter books 1899-1902; technical notebook 1908-35; newscuttings 1888-97

Coxeter & Son Ltd: board meeting minutes and correspondence 1956; debenture papers and correspondence 1937-45; correspondence 1938-47

Croyplants Ltd: minutes and agenda 1957-77; sales literature 1972 on; technical data and literature 1970-1

Davy British Oxygen Ltd: board and general meeting minutes 1957-67; managing directors reports and correspondence 1957-9; policy papers and correspondence 1957-68; organisation manual 1957-8; balance sheets 1964-6; budget and staff requirements 1957; financial correspondence and papers 1957-64

Deloro Stellite Ltd: board meeting minutes and accounts 1971-2; minutes 1971-8

Dinsmore Co Ltd: board meeting minutes 1963-78

Donald Ross & Partners Ltd: board and agm minutes 1946-61; memo and articles of association 1962; accounts 1960-7

East African Oxygen Ltd: board meeting minutes 1956-77; managing directors reports 1965-77; share papers and correspondence 1964-9; sales catalogue 1960

Edwards Alto Vuoto SpA: board meeting minutes 1955-63; yearly accounts 1955-9

Edwards High Vacuum Ltd: advisory council meeting minutes 1963; correspondence re company organisation and industrial disputes 1962-5; trade pamphlets 1956

W Edwards & Co Ltd: board meeting minutes 1940-72; joint managing directors and group reports 1963-5; general meeting minutes 1953-72; members register and share ledgers 1940-8; statutory registers 1962-72; corporate documents and correspondence 1960-70; annual reports and accounts 1954-67; general ledgers 1919-50; petty cash book 1919; sales catalogues 1940s-71; press cuttings and promotional material 1948-75; research reports 1960-2; technical literature 1950s-60s; founder, staff, premises, plant equipment, photographs etc 1940s-71; history booklet and articles 1940s-66; company news-letters 1958-64

Egyptian Oxygen & Acetylene Co Ltd: office expenses 1952-5; misc correspondence and papers 1945-66

Ferry Lane Securities Ltd: minutes 1938-71; share register etc 1938 on; annual report and accounts 1957-76; annual accounts 1938 on; balance sheet 1966
Finagaz SA: board meeting minutes 1965 on
Fusarc Italiana SpA: board meeting minutes 1965-74; take over correspondence 1964-9
Harris Calorific Co Ltd: board meeting minutes 1963-73
High Speed Steel Alloys Ltd: board meeting minutes 1923-42; take over agreements and correspondence 1968-9
Hirst Welding Rectifiers Ltd: management meeting minutes 1965-8; acquisition papers 1964-5; expansion papers 1966-71; share papers 1968-9; quarterly accounts 1965-8
Hong Kong Oxygen & Acetylene Co Ltd: minutes 1962 on; general managers reports 1965-78
Indian Oxygen Ltd: board meeting minutes 1936-78; executive management meeting minutes 1964-7; managing directors reports 1965-77; share correspondence 1957-9; Indian Monopolies Commission correspondence 1964-7; annual reports and accounts 1958-77; sales literature nd; directors photographs 1960; house magazine 1961-2; works photographs 1920s-30s
Industrial Gases Ltd: minutes 1964-77; general managers reports 1964-77
Industrial Gases (Malaya) Ltd: board meeting minutes 1946-72; private minutes 1965-72
Irish Industrial Gases Ltd: board: meeting minutes 1951-77; minutes 1963-72; corporate papers and correspondence 1935-69
A Charles King Ltd: board: meeting minutes 1947-60, correspondence and papers 1952-60; audited accounts 1934-59; account reports 1928-60; misc correspondence 1939-40
Knowles Oxygen Co Ltd: plans, site agreements etc 1909-28
Kosangas (Ceylon) Ltd: board meeting minutes and directors reports 1965-75
Magnesium Metal & Alloys Ltd: board meeting minutes 1934-48; share register 1934-41; memo and articles of association 1934; draft accounts 1934-48
Malayan Oxygen Ltd: board meeting minutes 1961-74; managing directors reports 1965-72; amalgamation correspondence and papers 1964-5; annual report and accounts 1977
Malaysian Oxygen Ltd: minutes 1960-77; managing directors reports 1966-77; balance sheets 1975-7
Medical Gases Ltd: board meeting minutes 1938-57; correspondence 1938-59
Medishield Corporation Ltd: board meeting minutes and reports 1977-8
Metal Industries Ltd: share papers and correspondence 1958; activities summary 1924-31,1944; correspondence 1947-59
Mineral Gases Ltd: minutes, papers and correspondence 1942-8
J Muirhead Ltd: minutes 1969 on
Murex Ltd: board meeting minutes 1913-76; monthly reports 1943-65; agm minutes 1920-66; legal correspondence 1926-30; seal book 1954-78; annual report and accounts and product list 1957-76; audited accounts 1918-75; income tax papers 1917-26; pension fund accounts 1971-2; property deeds schedule 1950s; notes, drafts and correspondence re history 1948-9
Murex (Australasia) Pty Ltd: board meeting minutes 1950-71
Murex Hispania SA: board meeting minutes 1970-2; accounts 1971-2; correspondence 1969-73
Murex Welding Processes Ltd: board meeting minutes 1918-67; monthly reports 1946-64; memo and articles of association 1950; seal book 1958-74; signed accounts 1931-67; sales papers and correspondence 1930-3; technical literature 1961-7

New Zealand Industrial Gases Ltd: board meeting minutes 1957-78; managing directors reports 1965-9,1977; annual report and accounts 1955-77
Odda Smelteverk A/S: board: meeting minutes 1938-77, papers and agenda 1956-61; operating reports 1938-40; production costs 1938-9; correspondence re works, staff, production, directors, shares etc 1924-64; works photographs 1959
Pakistan Oxygen Ltd: board meeting minutes 1949-76; general managers reports 1965-77; annual reports and accounts 1958-65,1974
Prest-O-Lite Ltd: board and general meeting minutes 1949-64; corporate documents 1912-63; audited accounts 1954-62; correspondence 1949-63
Pure Aeration Supply Ltd: board and general meeting minutes 1912-17
Pure Metal Manufacturing Co Ltd: board: and general meeting minutes 1924-43, agendas 1924-36; members register 1926-7
Pyrana Carbonic Syphon Co (New York): H Rushton Reid letter book 1912
Quasi-Arc Co Ltd: board meeting minutes 1930-60; general meeting minutes 1930-61; seal book 1953-77; monthly costs 1917-19; sales: manuals 1956-66, catalogues 1921-67, conference agenda and proceedings 1952-9; product and plant photographs c1930-60; production results and data 1949; technical publications, instruction books, manuals etc 1931-62; staff bulletins 1922-31,1940-7; misc correspondence 1943-7; draft history 1946-67
Rhodesia Oxygen Ltd: board meeting minutes 1956-68; sales catalogue nd
Rivoira SpA: board and general meeting minutes 1963-8; management meeting: minutes 1963-5, report 1963; correspondence re take over, administration and publications 1963-72; history booklet 1963
Saccab SpA: board meeting minutes 1963-76; general meeting minutes 1963; correspondence 1963-70
Scottish & Irish Oxygen Co Ltd: agreement with Brins 1887; annual reports and accounts 1891-7; sales catalogue and pamphlets 1880-c1900; photographs of Rosehill and Polmadie works 1887
Sierra Leone Oxygen Factory Ltd: agm minutes 1963-7; correspondence 1963-70
Singapore Oxygen Air Liquide Pte Ltd: general meeting minutes 1975-7
Singapore Oxygen Ltd: board meeting minutes 1961-74; private minutes 1963-75; managing directors reports 1965-72
Singapore Welding Pte Ltd: board meeting minutes 1960-75
Sparklets Ltd: board and general meeting minutes 1896-1977; shareholders circulars 1920-40; share transfer papers 1935-67; corporate agreements and correspondence 1898-1960; legal papers and correspondence re accident claims 1934-59; user survey 1935; sales catalogues 1899 on; syphons photographs 1895-1935; standing orders book 1909; works magazine 1917-18,1976-8; Edmonton works sales papers 1935-6; works: map nd, photographs 1920s-40
Tanzania Oxygen Ltd: minutes 1966-77
Thermit Welding (Great Britain) Ltd: audited accounts 1959-66
Thorn & Hoddle Ltd: board meeting minutes 1955-60; corporate papers and correspondence 1956-60; sales returns 1938-49
Tonnax Construction Ltd: corporate papers and correspondence 1957-9; audited accounts 1958-69; quarterly and yearly accounts 1963-5
Uganda Oxygen Ltd: minutes 1966-77

Woodside Die Sinking Co Ltd: board and general: meeting minutes 1960-4, correspondence 1955-66
CE Wooldridge & Co (Lye) Ltd: minutes 1970 on
Zambia Oxygen Ltd: board meeting minutes 1956-76; correspondence 1956-7,1962-3

524 RICHMOND ATHLETIC ASSOCIATION LTD

28 Jan 1886
22106
Richmond Athletic Ground, Richmond, Surrey
Sporting association

History: founded in 1885 by Richmond Town Cricket Club who wanted to lease or purchase part of Old Deer Park, Richmond, Surrey from the Crown. Incorporated in 1886 as Richmond Town Cricket Ground & Athletic Association Ltd to acquire and lay out grounds suitable for cricket, football, tennis, archery, cycling, athletics, and other sports and games. A pavilion was built and a running path and new turf laid. In 1888 Old Deer Park became an auxiliary ground to Surrey County Cricket Club's ground at Kennington Oval and unallotted shares were purchased by Surrey County Cricket Club. A new stand, to hold 700 to 800 people, with dressing rooms etc, was erected in 1889. Premises of Grove House Club became association's registered offices in 1890. Old Deer Park became headquarters of Richmond Football Club and staged Surrey Lawn Tennis Championships in 1890. Ground became headquarters of Middlesex Wanderers in 1891 and was the venue of England's rugby union internationals. Richmond (Surrey) Horse Show Syndicate held their annual shows there until 1967. Purchased additional 8 acres of land in 1893 for cricket facilities. Richmond Cycling Club races were held at Old Deer Park from 1897 and in 1899 Royal Horse Show and first Automobile Show were held there. By 1902 had 1250 seats under cover. In 1923 a new bowling green was laid and during 1930s rebuilding and refurbishment took place. Name changed to above in 1946. During 1960s a new stand was built and more renovations undertaken.

Records: at Richmond Athletic Association, Richmond Athletic Ground, Richmond, Surrey directors meeting minutes 1885-date; committee meeting minutes: special sub 1898-1904, finance 1902-63, ground 1895-1954; directors and committee meeting agendas 1930-60; general meeting: minutes 1886-date, newscuttings 1925 on; shareholders: registers c1886,c1930-c50, annual lists and summaries 1896-1917; share: certificate books 1886-1958, transfer register 1887-1939; directors registers 1901-52; memo and articles of association c1889; debenture issue correspondence 1889; annual reports and accounts 1889-1962; balance sheet and profit and loss accounts 1906-48; Surrey Lawn Tennis Championship balance sheet 1890; general ledgers 1887-1969; nominal ledgers 1889,1911-29; journals 1911-32; cash books 1887-92,1950-72; match books 1905-73; lettings: register 1923-30, correspondence 1888,1932-3; rents and programme advertising 1960-72; building and repair specifications 1909-28
Richmond Ground Tenants Club: committee meeting minutes 1931-76; general ledger 1968-9

525 KIRTLINGTON HOLDINGS LTD

29 Jan 1886
22112
60 Mark Lane, London EC3R 7TJ
Sugar, tea and dried fruit merchants

History: established as HH&S Budgett & Co, sugar, tea and dry fruit merchants at 22 Mincing Lane, London in 1857 under direction of James Budgett. Moved to Monument Yard in 1858 and had offices in Bristol, Avon until mid 1860s. Partnership dissolved in 1875, James Budgett & Son being formed to deal in sugar and fruit, and HH&S Budgett & Co continuing in tea. Incorporated as HH&S Budgett & Co Ltd in 1886 with James Budgett as chairman. Moved to 2-4 Idol Lane, Eastcheap, London in 1915 and to 60 Mark Lane in 1972. By 1977 had branches at Nottingham, Nottinghamshire; South Cave, Humberside; and Cardiff, S Glamorgan; and employed 110 persons. Sold sugar business to ED&F Man Ltd in 1980 and changed name to above.

Records: at Guildhall Library, Aldermanbury, London EC2P 2EJ
directors and general meeting minutes 1886-1951; share agreements 1901,1930; general ledger 1858-70; sales ledgers 1857-99; ledger and general balances 1915-47; cheques received books 1974-9; office cash book 1915-80; collections: bought book 1875-1936, sold book 1896-1945; sales and purchases totals books 1880-1930; goods payment guarantees 1883-1910; Christmas boxes book 1895-1951; firms: changes of address, title, personnel etc notices 1872-1913, credit worthiness reports 1857-1913; customers list nd; order correspondence 1930s; wages books 1869-1916; employees: signatures 1880-1900, lists 1914-18, family and active service correspondence etc 1915-20; cricket club: photographs c1890-1910, menu 1899, and fixtures and rule book 1893; directors, employees and premises photographs 1880s-1920s; staff magazine 1909-19; leases: Idol Lane 1850-82, Laurence Pountney Lane with correspondence 1879-1915; history notes 1980

526 NEWCASTLE PROTECTION & INDEMNITY ASSOCIATION

19 Feb 1886
22217
Centro House, 3 Cloth Market, Newcastle upon Tyne, Tyne & Wear NE1 1NT
Marine insurance

History: founded in 1885 as a mutual protection and indemnity association for shipowners, and incorporated as an unlimited company in 1886. At end of first year's business had 239 steamers covered for 205,888 tons protection and 215,504 tons indemnity. From 1890 offered third class of risk, crew strikes, and by 1897 had 323 steamers covered for 481,699 tons. As mutual non-profit making concern operated with entrance fees for each vessel insured and proportionally shared pooling agreements for excess liabilities. Newcastle War Risks Indemnity Association Ltd was formed in 1913 to cover 'war risks'.

Records: at Newcastle Protection & Indemnity Association, Centro House, 3 Cloth Market, Newcastle upon Tyne, Tyne & Wear NE1 1NT
directors: and general meeting minutes 1885-date, attendance books 1903-37; memo and articles of association 1952; pool and war risks agreements 1913-date; annual reports and accounts 1887-date; balance sheets 1949-68; general ledgers 1887-1940; claims ledger 1895-1934; capital books 1906-77; cash books 1937-60; excess premium book 1910-39; reinsurance books 1932-60; insurances register 1891-9; compensation claims: steamers 1908-22, workmens 1907-44; cargo claims agreements 1949; secretarys: letter book 1920-4, notebook 1867-1917, *SS Tynemouth* papers, log books and correspondence 1967-70; *SS Strathdon* legal proceedings c1899; *Rules* 1885-date

Newcastle 100A Steam Ship Association: directors: and general meeting minutes 1927-37, attendance book and fees 1924-37; annual reports and accounts 1927-37; ledger balances 1914-28; cash book 1917-25; settlements book 1908; laid up premium book 1911-31; *Rules* 1877-1936
Newcastle War Risks Indemnity Association Ltd: directors and general meeting minutes 1913-19; memo and articles of association 1913; annual reports and accounts 1967-date; balance sheets, audited accounts and ledger balances 1921-66; cash book 1921-40; insurances register 1913-14; claims book 1914-37; settlements book 1950; *Rules* 1913-date

527 WELSH CALVINISTIC METHODIST ASSURANCE TRUST LTD

4 Mar 1886
22285
Bryn Afon, Segontium Terrace, Caernarfon, Gwynedd
Insurance

History: established and incorporated as above in 1886 with the approval of the general assembly with the object of providing insurance cover for church property of Welsh Calvinistic Methodist Connexion. Has acted for the sole benefit of the church with unpaid directors and no agents and has underwritten insurances for church property of the Presbyterian Church of Wales. Initially business carried on at the premises of its manager and secretary at 67 South John Street, Liverpool. Subsequently moving to Little Sutton, Merseyside; to Colwyn Bay, Clwyd; and to Caernarfon, Gwynedd in 1963.

Records (1): at Welsh Calvinistic Methodist Assurance Trust, Bryn Afon, Segontium Terrace, Caernarfon, Gwynedd
directors and general meeting minutes 1961-date; members register etc c1930-1960s; memo and articles of association 1925-date; annual accounts 1970-date; nominal ledger 1934-80; policy schedules 1887-date

Records (2): at National Library of Wales, Department of Manuscripts & Records, Aberystwyth, Dyfed SY23 3BU
minutes 1935-51; assembly statements 1929-32; annual reports and accounts 1887-date; correspondence 1913-51

528 ACGE INVESTMENTS LTD

5 Mar 1886
22290
Cheapside House, 138 Cheapside, London EC2V 6BL
Landowning

History: incorporated in 1886 as Oriental Bank Estates Co Ltd to acquire from Oriental Bank Corporation (in liquidation) certain properties in Sri Lanka and Mauritius on which coffee, tea, sugar, cocoa, cinchona etc were cultivated. Name changed in 1894 to Oriental Estates Co Ltd and to Anglo-Ceylon Estates Co Ltd in 1897. In 1913 over 14,400 acres were under cultivation and by 1920 19,102 acres were owned, of which 7792 acres were under tea, 1100 acres under rubber, 1113 acres under cocoa, 3048 under sugar-cane and 312 acres under cardamoms. By 1957 had acquired Bois Bros & Co Ltd (inc in Sri Lanka) and Mon Tresor &

Mon Desert Ltd (inc in Mauritius). Owned approximately 33,000 acres of tea, rubber, cocoa and sugar-cane plantations in Sri Lanka and Mauritius. Acquired in 1967 by Lonrho Ltd. Name changed to above in Dec 1976.

Records: at Lonrho, Cheapside House, 138 Cheapside, London EC2V 6BL
minutes and corporate records 1950s on; agreements book 1886-95; probate register 1887-94

529 LONG ING SHED CO LTD

8 Mar 1886
22306
Cloisters House, High Street, Rickmansworth, Hertfordshire WD3 1DG
Room and power

History: incorporated as above in 1886 to purchase land in Long Ing Lane, Barnoldswick, Lancashire on which to erect a cotton mill where looms and space could be rented out to cotton and worsted spinners and manufacturers. By early 1960s was part of cotton manufacturing group S Pickles & Sons (Holdings) Ltd which was acquired in 1971 by Reed International Ltd. Ceased to trade in 1965. Name changed to Home Management Systems Ltd in 1983.

Records: at Reed International, Reed House, 83 Piccadilly, London W1A 1EJ
directors and general meeting minutes 1965-date; members register 1971-date; directors registers 1971-date; share transfers certificates 1940-date; annual returns 1966-date; memo and articles of association 1965,1973

530 DRG (UK) LTD

31 Mar 1886
22419
1 Redcliffe Street, Bristol, Avon BS99 7QY
Paper making

History: traces its origins to John Dickinson who in 1804 set up a business as a stationer in the City of London. In 1809 he developed a patent process for machine made paper and acquired Apsley Mill, Hemel Hempstead, Hertfordshire in order to manufacture paper. He took George Longman into partnership, the business being known as Longman & Dickinson and later as John Dickinson & Co. In 1810 nearby Nash Mills was acquired followed by mills at Batchworth, Hertfordshire in 1818. Dickinson built Home Park Mills, near Nash Mills, in 1826, in which cards for Jacquard weaving were made. In 1829 Croxley Mills, near Watford, Hertfordshire were built and between 1835 to 1837 a mill was built near Manchester for processing waste from cotton mills. By 1833 the balance sheet total reached £144,000 making the business one of largest paper manufacturers in Britain. Most output went to London publishing and printing houses but between 1840 and 1859 'threaded' paper was supplied for *Penny Post*. In 1850 mechanical envelope production began. Ford Works, South Hyton, Tyne & Wear, was established in 1860 for the production of paper using imported esparto grass. A branch was established at Calcutta, India in 1880. The business was incorporated in 1886 as John Dickinson & Co Ltd, a private company with a nominal capital of £250,000. Offices were opened at Manchester, Greater Manchester (1896); Bristol, Avon (1894); Birmingham, W Midlands (1896); Belfast, N Ireland (1897) where a small factory was opened in c1900; Leeds,

W Yorkshire (1905); Nottingham, Nottinghamshire (1908) and Liverpool, Merseyside (1908). Overseas sales expanded in the 20 years before WW1 when offices were opened at Sydney, Australia (1893), Capetown, South Africa (1894) and in Canada (1910). In 1918 acquired Millington & Son Ltd (est 1824) of Tottenham, London, window envelope manufacturers. Manufacturing operations were extended overseas in 1920s and 1930s and range of products widened to include air mail paper, labels, foil, gummed tape, carrier bags, etc. Merged with ES&A Robinson Ltd, a stationery manufacturer established in 1844, in 1966 when the group became known as Dickinson Robinson Group Ltd, the largest manufacturer of stationery in Britain. Company subsequently changed name to above.

Records: at DRG Envelopes, Apsley, Hemel Hempstead, Hertfordshire
plastics division general meeting minutes 1942-4; board permits capital expenditure 1898-1907; share transfer certificates 1886-98; trust deed 1935; employees share applications and lists 1927-31; share papers and correspondence 1882-1921; memo and articles of association 1886; annual report and accounts 1896-1974; profit and loss accounts 1892-1918; accounts: departmental 1930-60, far eastern 1917-19; ledgers: 1879-1925, African 1899-1913; private journal 1885-92; cash books: 1801-1950, petty 1873-5; bills payable 1836-47; receipts 1886-95; bank books 1817-41; sales record: 1879-1911, East India Co 1830-59; label book orders 1892-1902; patent papers 1854-1938; trade-mark letter books, correspondence and reports 1898-1969; price lists, samples and catalogues: 1874-1970, Red Box 1930-70, Lion Brand 1878-1970, book and office department 1936-69, card department 1888-1977, envelope department 1886-1960s, carrier department 1930-50, stationery department 1917-65, packing supply c1930-50, packing supply 1908-23, Home Park productions 1937-50, plastics division 1940s; Nash Mills samples and advertisements 1930-71; card department sales 1904-26; export circulars, samples, price lists, advertisement and sales correspondence 1889-1957; overseas visits: reports, papers and correspondence 1886-1957; sales brochures c1910-c75; mills capital expenditure 1895-1920; stock books: 1817-1908, card department 1906-30, photographic department 1929-35; invention specification 1807; Croxley order book 1899-1937; envelope samples: Apsley nd,1930-73, M&S nd; Upper Mills envelope department record 1886-1939; machinery: catalogue nd, drawing book 1930s; traffic department delivery and route records 1935-66; photographs of goods trains, barges and vans c1880-1960s; wages: 1952-67, card department 1888-1948, transport department 1935-64, representatives 1935-51; order of service brochures, minutes, programmes etc 1910 on; peace medal 1919; coal and general strike papers 1920-6; trade union papers 1915-39; staff: notices 1926, handbook 1938, sports and social club programmes, posters, balance sheets and papers 1890-1939, war service records 1914-45, photographs c1840-1971, house magazine 1937-49; calendars, Christmas cards and New Year messages 1910-63; war damage papers and correspondence 1914-45; Union of House of Dickinson: committee meeting minutes 1926-33, balance sheets 1926-68, charters 1926-49, posters and display cards 1910-55, papers, correspondence and photographs 1926-51; fire brigade: drill book 1891-4, photographs 1910-60, reports 1919-1939, correspondence and papers 1921-75; railway and canal construction papers 1835-1938; papers: envelope department 1933-4, card buildings 1934-40, Apsley Mills 1935-8; insurance papers 1890-1928; London, Bristol and Birmingham leases and title deeds 1891-1925; factory photographs: Apsley Mills 1925, Croxley Mills c1960, South Africa c1920, Nairobi 1954-5, Cape Town c1958, Australia 1950,c1960, Canada c1950; letter books 1882,1909-28; Upper Mills records of events 1914,1949; correspondence and photographs re royal visits etc 1926-77; Apsley Mills visitors book 1891-1925; history articles and papers 1896-1953

SJ Green: memo and articles of association 1927; share correspondence c1930-50; balance sheets 1927-69; trade stand photographs 1937-66
Millington & Sons Ltd: board meeting minutes 1921-51; share transfer register 1908-32; memo and articles of association 1908; partnership and retirement papers 1836,1880-1; amalgamation papers 1918-32; balance sheets 1880,1909-15; trading accounts 1914-22; price lists c1920-32; advertisements and samples c1900-21; envelope machinery papers 1912-22; employees: register 1911-30, annual dinner 1873, photographs 1900-28; Union of House of Millington papers 1927-9; property deeds, valuation and photographs 1869-1910; history 1928

Joan Evans, *John Dickinson & Co Ltd 1804-1954* (1955)

531 NEMS LTD
12 Apr 1886
22482
Trinity House, Trinity Lane, Waltham Cross, Hertfordshire EN8 7EQ
Music and musical instrument dealers

History: established by James Cook Turner and incorporated in 1886 as Turner & Co Ltd to deal in musical instruments and music. Original offices and shop - North End Music Stores - were at 70&72 Walton Road, Liverpool, Merseyside. Name changed to NEMS & Co Ltd in Mar and to above in Jul 1897. By 1926 had a branch at Haydn House, South Road, Waterloo, Merseyside. When acquired by J Epstein & Sons in 1930 was dealing in pianos, gramophones, records, radios and music. In 1937 when the Waterloo branch was closed, television dealing had commenced. Brian Epstein, manager of the Beatles, used the company for some of his management activities. Company was acquired in 1964 by Edward Bullough Ltd, which was acquired in 1966 by Tucana Ltd, a subsidiary of Thorn EMI Ltd, and ceased to trade in 1977.

Records: at Rumbelows, Trinity House, Trinity Lane, Waltham Cross, Hertfordshire EN8 7EQ
directors: and general meeting minutes 1926-78, reports 1955-65

532 JOHN BLAND & CO LTD
16 Apr 1886
22512
Avon Works, Winterstoke Road, Bristol, Avon BS99 7PL
Timber importers and merchants

History: incorporated as above in 1886 to carry on business of timber importers and merchants with premises at East Moors, Cardiff, S Glamorgan; Gloucester, Gloucestershire; and Highbridge, Somerset. Business expanded and at one time had 20 depots in south Wales, the west country and the west midlands. Acquired Perkins & Seward Ltd (est 1916) in 1953. Made substantial losses in late 1960s and underwent rationalisation in 1971 reducing sites to 4 - Cardiff, S Glamorgan; Highbridge, Somerset; Bridgend, Mid Glamorgan; and Craven Arms, Salop. Became a holding company controlling 3 wholly owned subsidiaries: Perkins & Seward Ltd, John Bland (Timber) Ltd, and C Walsh Graham Ltd. Acquired in 1973 by UBM Group Ltd (formerly United Builders Merchants Ltd), a holding company for a group of builders, engineers and plumbers merchants, light and timber engineers, etc. Had ceased trading by 1980.

Records: at UBM Group, Avon Works, Winterstoke Road, Bristol, Avon BS99 7PL
directors meeting minutes 1951-74; general meeting minutes 1952-78; directors registers 1951-72; share ledger and transfer register 1944-71; memo and articles of association 1888,1951,1972; papers and correspondence re takeover 1972-3; directors reports and accounts 1967-80

533 WICKENS PEASE & CO LTD

10 May 1886
22610
Lever House, Bebington, Wirral, Merseyside
Animal waste products

History: founded in London in early 1870s by Robert Pease and incorporated as above in 1886. By 1894 described as 'bone merchants and crushers, manure manufacturers, tallow melters, glue, size, soap and lubricating oil (animal and mineral) makers, animal charcoal burners, tooth, nail, shaving and other brush makers and general bone turners'. London head offices were at 83 Queen Street from 1891-1901 moving to Bermondsey Wharves, Bermondsey. By 1891 had works in Greater London area at Glaucus Street, Bow Common; Garratt Mills, Wandsworth; Green Street, Blackfriars (ceased 1896); Broad Bridge, Shadwell (ceased 1909); Trundley's Road, Deptford (ceased 1909); and Northolt (ceased 1909). New works at Rainham, Greater London from 1909. By 1921 business was that of 'bone boilers and tallow melters' and the only extant works was Garratt Mills. By 1956 were only 'bone merchants'. Taken over by Unilever Ltd and by 1980 was dormant.

Records: at Unilever, Unilever House, Blackfriars, London EC4P 4BQ
fat, offal etc pooling agreements 1949; correspondence re slaughter house fat 1953-4; tenancy agreements 1948; deeds schedule c1937

534 VOKINS & CO LTD

27 May 1886
22690
Kingsgate House, 66-74 Victoria Street, London SW1E 6SR
Lighterage and towage

History: incorporated as above in 1886 to carry out terms of agreement between William Evetts and James W Maude to carry on business as lightermen, wharfingers, warehousemen, shipowners and carriers. Operated in Thames Estuary and in 1890s were agents to Great Northern and Great Eastern Railway companies with offices at Regent's Canal Docks, Commercial Road; GNR depot, Prestons Road, Poplar; GER depot, Pepper Warehouses, East India Dock Road; and head offices at 47 Mark Lane, London. In 1956, head offices were at 35 Seething Lane, London and additional offices were situated at 130 Lower Road, London; Royal Albert Docks, Woolwich Manor Way, London; Crown Wharf, Orchard Place, London; and Durham Wharf and Thames Lock Wharf, Brentford. Acquired by Transport Development Group Ltd in 1973 and placed in liquidation in 1980.

Records: at Transport Development Group, Kingsgate House, 66-74 Victoria Street, London SW1E 6SR
board and general meeting minutes 1886-1979; directors registers 1886-1979; members register and share ledger 1886-1975; share: application and allotment book 1942-66, transfer registers and documents 1928-73; mortgage and charges registers, correspondence, agreements and papers 1886-1973; memo and articles of association 1886-1973; liquidation papers 1979-80; annual returns 1972,1978-9; annual reports and accounts 1970-8; financial correspondence 20 cent; tenancy agreements 1968,1973; pension fund: minutes 1972-4, members register 1967-74, ledger 1965-77, cash book 1967-77, papers 1966-77; life assurance scheme rules 1970s

535 NEWBURY LAUNDRY LTD

31 May 1886
22702
Queen's Road, Newbury, Berkshire RG14 7NS
Laundry

History: incorporated in 1886 as Newbury Sanitary Laundry Co Ltd. Alfred Dowling, who ran laundries in Basingstoke, Hampshire; Oxford, Oxfordshire; and Caversham, Berkshire became first manager and secretary. Bought site and buildings in West Field, York Road, Newbury, Berkshire on which a factory was built. In 1887 purchased Mr Scull's patent process for dry-cleaning, in conjunction with Oxford, Caversham and Basingstoke laundries. Opened first shop in 1928. During 1930s enlarged York Road factory and built another in Queens Road, Newbury. Name changed to above in 1934. Purchased Bicester Laundry, Oxfordshire and Warminster Laundry Ltd, Wiltshire in 1946. By 1961 also ran Andover (Family Laundries), Hampshire. In the late 1960s entered the textile rental market which was its main business in 1983, although it still carried out some domestic laundry and drycleaning, mainly through its 10 shops and laundrettes.

Records: at Newbury Laundry, Queen's Road, Newbury, Berkshire RG14 7NS
directors and general meeting minutes 1886-date; annual reports and accounts 1887-1947; price lists c1934,1960s; advertisements 1936,1950; dry-cleaning book 1935; National Health insurance cards 1914-15; staff, transport, premises, machinery photographs 1900s-80s; union meeting notice 1920s; machinery tender 1935-42; laundry van blueprint nd; laundry and shop plans and elevations 1901-70s

536 CLEVELAND BAY HORSE SOCIETY OF GREAT BRITAIN & IRELAND LTD

6 Jul 1886
22866
York Livestock Centre, Murton, York, N Yorkshire YO1 3OF
Breed society

History: formed in 1884 and incorporated as above in 1886 to encourage the breed of horses known as Cleveland Bay, and to publish a stud book. Also awarded medals and issued importation certificates. In 1898 had 106 members and there were 1500 stallions, 1200 mares registered in stud books. By 1924 Clevelands were exported to Europe, Argentina, Japan and

Turkey. In 1938 amalgamated with Yorkshire Coach Horse Society (formed 1886). In 1980s Cleveland Bays used for show jumping, hunting, police and carriage horses.

Records: at Yorkshire Museum of Farming, Murton, York, N Yorkshire YO1 3OF
council and general meeting: minutes 1950-67, press cuttings 1884-1944; stud: books 1884-1984, cards 1832-1945; show results, reviews and newscuttings 1734-1931; photographs c1906-41

537 OWNERS OF THE MIDDLESBROUGH ESTATE LTD

14 Jul 1886
22906
Queen's Square, Middlesbrough, Cleveland TS2 1AN
Landowners

History: incorporated in 1886 to acquire from the Pease family of bankers, colliery owners and landowners, the Middlesbrough and Saltburn Estates in Cleveland and to develop the resources of the estates including coal, mineral deposits and forestry. The nominal share capital on formation was £420,000 and all shares were held by the vendors of the estates led by Sir JW Pease. In 1984 the activities of the company, which continued to be led by the Pease family, included property ownership and development, the manufacture of timber products such as packing cases and pallets, and through its Cleveland Car Co Ltd subsidiary, vehicle distribution and garage proprietorship.

Records: at Cleveland County Libraries, Archives Department, 81 Borough Road, Middlesbrough, Cleveland TS1 3AA
council year book and diaries 1904-54; handbooks 1950-c60; by-laws 1868; Act of Parliament and papers 1869-1935; printed works, pamphlets and brochures 1889-1955; photographs, painting and postcards 1890-1900,nd; sales particulars 1882-1942; specifications 1869-1903; maps and plans: Middlesbrough 1844-1940, Saltburn 1861-1956, premises in Durham, Cleveland and N Yorkshire 1830-1961

538 FURNISS & CO LTD

17 Jul 1886
22916
15 New Bridge Street, Truro, Cornwall
Biscuits and confectionery

History: incorporated as above in 1886 to acquire biscuit making and confectionery business of John Furniss of Duchy Wharf, (now New Bridge Street) Truro, Cornwall. He also had luncheon rooms in St Mary's Street, Truro, and catered for refreshments at Truro railway station. Business mainly based in south west England, expanding into general UK and export market in 1970s. Taken over by Argyll Foods Ltd in 1979.

Records (1): at Furniss, 15 New Bridge Street, Truro, Cornwall
directors meeting minutes 1965 on; shareholders register 1949 on; cash books 1950s; bank deposit book 1917 on

Records (2): at Cornwall Record Office, County Hall, Truro, Cornwall TR1 3AY
directors meeting minutes 1886-1965; share: and share transfer register 1886-1948, ledger

1886-1949; incorporation papers incl memo and articles of association 1886; annual reports and accounts 1887-96; plan of factory 1919; title deeds and documents and correspondence re property 1738-1900

539 JOHN FOWLER & CO (LEEDS) LTD

13 Aug 1886
23022
Albion Works, Savile Street, Sheffield, S Yorkshire S4 7UL
Agricultural, locomotive and general engineers

History: John Fowler entered partnership in 1850 with fellow Quaker Albert Fry as agricultural implement manufacturers and traders in Bristol. Dissolved in 1856, Fowler moving to Cornhill, London, to act as sole trader with no manufacturing works, using Kitson, Thompson & Hewitson of Leeds, W Yorkshire; Robert Stephenson & Co, locomotive and general engineers of Newcastle, Tyne & Wear; Ransomes & Sims of Ipswich, Suffolk; and Clayton, Shuttleworth & Co of Lincoln to supply him with steam cultivation machinery. In 1860 Kitsons renamed Kitson & Hewitson, became sole suppliers. However, Fowler began to build his own works, Steam Plough Works, Leathley Road, Hunslet, Leeds, W Yorkshire (completed 1862) on land adjacent to and purchased from Kitsons. William Watson Hewitson joined Fowler in partnership as Fowler & Hewitson in 1861. Hewitson died in 1863, Fowler continued to trade as John Fowler & Co, assisted by his brother Robert, manager of London office in Cornhill. He joined John in partnership in Aug 1864. John Fowler died in Dec of that year and Robert continued business in partnership with Robert Eddison, David Grieg, Reginald Wigram, and Bernard Fowler. Incorporated as above in 1886. Had branches and subsidiary companies in Leeds, W Yorkshire; London; Cambridge, Cambridgeshire; and Essex; Melun, France; Barcelona, Spain; Rome, Italy; Magdeburg, East Germany; Prague, Czechoslovakia; Budapest, Hungary; Bombay and Calcutta, India; Manila, Philippines; Johannesburg, South Africa; Sydney, Australia; and Wellington, New Zealand. Merged with Marshall, Sons & Co Ltd of Gainsborough, Lincolnshire, engineers and boilermakers in 1947 to form Marshall-Fowler Ltd. Company purchased by Thos W Ward Ltd in 1970s, production ceased at the Leeds works in 1974, and went into voluntary liquidation in 1981.

Records: at Institute of Agricultural History & Museum of English Rural Life, University of Reading, Whiteknights, Reading, Berkshire RG6 2AG
partnership agreements, papers and correspondence 1863-93; directors papers, correspondence and photographs 1880s-1933; corporate documents and correspondence 1886-1931; share ledger 1886-1900; shareholders: register 1886-1948, list 1937, letters, notices and documents 1929-31; share documents and correspondence 1886-1937; share transfer: registers 1887-1914, documents 1887-1912; mortgages, probates and debentures: registers 1887-1947, documents and correspondence 1886-97; memo and articles of association with resolutions 1886-1951; investment documents, papers and correspondence 1887-1947; administration: book 1914, correspondence 1933; seal register 1886-1974; annual summaries 1886-1922; directors reports 1913-34; audited financial statements: 1887-1937, analysis book 1887-1923, working papers 1915-35; Steam Plough Works accounts 1860-2,1892-1917; patent royalties account 1867-74; profit working papers 1909-13,1925-7; overseas branches and agencies accounting notes 1912-14; price and costs analysis 1913-18; business agreements and correspondence 1879-1935; customer list 1920s; customer enquiries, quotations, contract and

files 1945-68; patents: letters and specifications 1852-95, licences, assignments and agreements 1855-1929, litigation papers and correspondence 1850-85; catalogues price lists and other advertising material 1874-c1965; printing block proofs and artworks 1860s-1940s; photographs of products 1862-1948; suppliers correspondence, literature and drawings 1960s; order book 1863-5; product registers 1895-1968; shop building books 1901-43; engine details books 1893-1923; product particulars and dimensions books 1885-1930; design registers and lists 1883-1963; plough tackle dispatch graph 1868-1917; trial reports and correspondence 1852-1963; product drawings 1860s-c1945; registers and indexes 1860s-1963; drawing office sketch books 1921-66; staff agreements and correspondence 1874-1940s; staff profit sharing scheme documents and correspondence 1903-17; house journals 1948-61,1971-5; works inventory 1895; building report 1926; Steam Plough Works: plans late 19 cent, correspondence, documents and papers re land purchases 1868-1913; agreement and plan re Atlas Works, Pershore, Hereford & Worcester 1908; works photographs 1948; history notes and correspondence 1940s; steam cultivation machinery photographs 1850s-1901; press cuttings re company, competitors, premises, products, personnel, events 1883-1947; branches - Magdeburg: partnership agreements and papers 1871-1931, balance sheets 1915-19, financial statements 1913-19, statistics analysis 1899-1913, acceptances account 1915-19, agency account 1913, accounting and banking method notes 1912-14, liquidation account statements 1920 on, litigation papers 1921-4, business correspondence 1887-1913, advertising booklets and catalogues c1900-c11; Prague: partnership agreement and papers 1920-34, balance sheets 1926-35, financial statements 1919-30, banking arrangements 1928-31, business agreement 1921, real estate agreements, valuations and papers 1913-32; Budapest: partnership papers 1920-40, balance sheets 1926-35, financial statements 1919-34, banking arrangements 1928-31, litigation papers re government supervision during WW1 1924, real estate papers 1913-38; Bombay and Calcutta: balance sheets 1915-21, financial statements statistics analysis 1910-13, accounting and banking method notes 1912-14, business correspondence 1910; Johannesburg: balance sheets 1915-23, farm and trading agency financial statements statistics analysis 1910-13, accounting and banking notes 1912-14, farming agreements 1904,1911, business correspondence 1904-16; Sydney: business correspondence 1889-1901

Cable Cultivating Contractors Ltd: directors and general meeting minutes 1929-40; members, directors and share register 1929-35; share transfers 1932-6; corporate correspondence 1929-35; financial statements 1931,1934

East & West Riding Steam Ploughing Co Ltd: financial statements 1931-2

Essex Tillage Contractors Ltd: memo and articles of association 1933

Gyrotiller Sales & Service Ltd: financial statements 1934-5

Marshall, Sons & Co Ltd: prospectuses 1936,1947; press cuttings re agm 1936; financial statements 1937; servicing and other advertising literature c1955-65; product photographs 1948

Mechanical Cleansing Service Ltd: share transfer 1932; financial statement 1936

Mechanical Tar Spraying & Grouting Co Ltd: financial statements 1922-38

Société Anonyme John Fowler: copy business correspondence 1909-12; balance sheets 1915-26; financial statements statistics analysis 1910-17; accounting and banking notes 1912-14; catalogue 1921; deed and correspondence re house purchase 1923

Société des Établissements John Fowler: correspondence and papers re partner holdings 1930-5; balance sheets 1927-35; catalogues and advertising leaflets 1927-36; real estate correspondence 1930

Estudias y Construcciones Locker SA: financial statements 1931-2; business reports 1931
Societa Anonima 'La Penetrazione': share correspondence and papers 1929-32; memo and articles of association 1928; financial statements 1929-31; correspondence re state of company 1932; advertising leaflets and booklets 1920s
John Fowler & Co GmbH: shareholding correspondence 1930-5; balance sheets 1930-5; financial statement 1930
Fowler-Petz Machine Factory & Iron Foundry Co Ltd: financial statements 1931-2
John Fowler & Co (India) Ltd: memo and articles of association 1922; shareholding papers 1922-33; balance sheets 1922-35
John Fowler & Co (Manila) Ltd: corporate papers 1913; memo and articles of association 1913; balance sheets 1915-26; accounting and banking notes 1914
NV Naatschappy voor Machinale Asphaltatie en Wegenbouw: financial statements 1930-5; management correspondence 1930
Fowler Tar Spraying Co Ltd: shareholding papers 1924-33; financial statements 1925-33
John Fowler & Co (Australia) Ltd: directors and general meeting minutes 1913-38; shareholding papers 1913-38; memo and articles of association 1913; balance sheets 1915-35; financial statements 1930-7; accounting and banking notes 1912-14; business correspondence 1922,1930-2; liquidation papers 1939-40
John Fowler & Co (New Zealand) Ltd: shareholding papers 1927-32; memo and articles of association 1926; financial statements 1929-34; liquidation papers 1936-40

Theo Davis, *John Fowler and the Business He Founded* (priv pub late 1940s)

540 BRITISH STEEL CORPORATION LIAISON SERVICES (INDIA) LTD

6 Oct 1886
23226
9 Albert Embankment, London EC1
Iron and steel

History: incorporated in 1886 as Whitecross Co Ltd to acquire the assets of Whitecross Wire & Iron Co Ltd (inc 1864) of Warrington, Cheshire, wire and iron manufacturers and colliery owners. In 1932 it was acquired by Lancashire Steel Corporation, formed in 1930 as part of the rationalization of the iron and steel industry. This company was subsequently nationalized to form part of British Steel Corporation. In 1972 company's name was changed to Whitecross Co (Overseas) Ltd and to BSCI (Overseas) Ltd in 1973, to Gower Steel (International) Ltd in 1975 and to above in 1978. By 1975 it was a non trading company whose major asset was a 3.52 per cent ordinary shareholding in Usha Martin Black (Wire Ropes) Ltd, an Indian company. By 1980 its function was to maintain offices in Delhi, Bombay, Madras and Calcutta, India for liason work with British Steel Corporation customers.

Records: at British Steel Corporation, E Midlands Regional Records Centre, By Pass Road, Irthlingborough, Wellingborough, Northants NN9 5QH

541 COURAGE OVERSEAS HOLDINGS LTD

6 Oct 1886
23227
Anchor Terrace, Southwark Bridge Road, London SE1 9HS
Brewing

History: established in 1777 at Star Brewery, Eastbourne, E Sussex. Incorporated as Star Brewery Co Ltd in 1886. By mid 1960s owned 48 licensed properties around Eastbourne. In 1965 the company was acquired by Courage Barclay & Simonds Ltd and ceased to trade in 1967. In 1973 the company changed its name to above since when it has acted as an overseas investment holding company.

Records: at Courage, Anchor Terrace, Southwark Bridge Road, London SE1 9HS
share: register 1955-65, certificate books 1947-71

542 ARTHUR GUINNESS, SON & CO LTD

21 Oct 1886
23307
Bodiam House, Twyford Abbey Road, London NW10 7ES
Brewing, retailing, health, health care and publishing

History: established by Arthur Guinness at St James's Gate Brewery, Dublin in 1759. He died in 1803 when the business was inherited by three of his sons, then subsequently by his grandson Sir Benjamin Guinness and in 1868 by his great grandsons Arthur (later first Lord Ardilaun) and Edward (later first Earl of Iveagh). By 1868 annual output reached 350,000 barrels of beer, primarily stout for sale in Ireland. Thereafter the business benefited from an explosive growth of sales in Britain when output reached 750,000 barrels in 1875 and 1.2 million barrels in 1886 when St James's Gate Brewery was reputedly the largest brewery in the world. Between 1868 and 1886 over £1 million was spent on capital projects. The business was incorporated as a public company in 1886, but the Guinness family subsequently retained a substantial interest in the business. The Guinness Research Laboratories were established in the 1890s. In 1936 a brewery was opened at Park Royal, London, for supplying the British market. In 1952 all brewing and marketing operations were vested in subsidiaries, Arthur Guinness, Son & Co (Dublin) Ltd and Arthur Guinness, Son & Co (Park Royal) Ltd. In 1956 marketing in N Ireland was taken over by Arthur Guinness, Son & Co (Belfast) Ltd. In the 1960s and 1970s the company diversified by acquiring a wide range of businesses involved in confectionary manufacture, leisure and catering, retailing and publishing. Many of these businesses were disposed of in the 1980s.

Records (1): at Arthur Guinness (Dublin), St James's Gate, Dublin, Eire
ledgers 1791 on; brewery memoranda 1869-85; charges ledgers nd; specie books nd; brewer's calculation books 1814-73; personal account books nd; letter books late 19 cent; correspondence 1869 on; English agency papers 19 cent; departmental memoranda nd; brewing machinery advertising 1855-70; financial correspondence nd

Records (2): at Arthur Guinness, Park Royal Brewery, London NW10 7RR
directors meeting minutes 1886-date; committee meeting minutes 1942-78; general meeting minutes 1887-date; share: allotment books 1886, transfer registers 1886 on; preference stock: members registers 1887-97, ledgers 1886-7, transfer registers 1887 on; debenture stock

allotment book 1906; prospectus 1886; memo and articles of association 1886-date; annual reports and accounts 1886-date
Arthur Guinness, Son & Co (Dublin) Ltd: directors meeting minutes 1949-date; committee minutes and papers 1942-58
Arthur Guinness, Son & Co (Park Royal) Ltd: directors meeting minutes 1952-date; committee meeting minutes 1942-61
Many other records of subsidiary companies 1934-date

Records (3): at Institute of Agricultural History, University of Reading, White Knights, Reading, Berkshire RG6 2AG
prices of English barley 1894-1904; plot books 1867-1966

Patrick Lynch and John Vaizey, *Guinness's Brewery in the Irish Economy 1789-1876* (1960)

543 LONDON PAVILION LTD

18 Nov 1886
23463
1 Serjeants Inn, London EC4Y 1JD
Cinema managers (formerly theatre proprietors)

History: incorporated as above in 1886 to lease the London Pavilion Theatre, Piccadilly, from the Villiers estate and to carry on the business of music hall and theatrical proprietors and caterers for public entertainments and exhibitions. Old London Pavilion Theatre closed, new Pavilion opened in 1885. Closed for 29 weeks during 1900 and new house reopened in 1901. Rebuilt in 1934 as a cinema, leased to United Artists, and closed in 1981 for redevelopment.

Records: at London Pavilion, Her Majesty's Theatre, Haymarket, London SW1Y 4QL
certificate of incorporation 1886; memo and articles of association 1886; annual reports and accounts 1970 on; yearly profits and dividends paid book 1887-date

544 TRADE MARK OWNERS ASSOCIATION LTD

3 Dec 1886
23558
15 Finsbury Circus, London EC2M 7DL
Trade association

History: founded and incorporated in London in 1886 as Trade Mark Owners Mutual Protection Association Ltd as a company limited by guarantee by leading trade-mark owners to facilitate the registration and protection of their trade-marks. Name changed to above in 1905. Offices situated in Basinghall Street until 1941, Waterloo Place 1941-6, 50 Charing Cross 1946-60, 15 Finsbury Circus since 1960 (all in London). In 1970 members and subscribers numbered over 600, owning between them thousands of trade-marks registered in UK and abroad.

Records: at Trade Mark Owners Association, 15 Finsbury Circus, London EC2M 7DL
management committee: meeting minutes 1886-date, reports 1906 on, members lists 1886-date; subscribers lists 1886-date; memo and articles of association 1886-date; annual reports and accounts 1959 on; profit and loss accounts 1914-27; membership application forms 1886-date; trade-mark registration books 1940s on; salary books 1950-60; correspondence re trade-

mark registration, disputes, membership etc 1950s on; *Trademark Journals* 1876-date

545 **INDEMNITY MARINE INSURANCE CO LTD**
31 Dec 1886
23712
1 St Helen's, Undershaft, London EC3P 3DQ
Insurance

History: formed in London as a joint stock company, the first in marine insurance, in Aug 1824 by John Staniforth, shipowner who devised a complex system of mutual insurance for the company. This scheme was not successful and Staniforth resigned in 1826 being replaced as managing director by William Ellis who converted the company into a more straightforward joint stock form. By the 1850s annual premium income exceeded £60,000. Ellis who was acknowledged as the leading underwriter of the mid 19 cent, was succeeded in 1889 by Henry Haslam who remained in office as underwriter and managing director until 1912. Incorporated in 1886 as above. Acquired in 1917 by Northern Assurance Co Ltd which was acquired by Commercial Union Assurance Co Ltd in 1968 but continued to operate under its own name.

Records (1): at Commercial Union Assurance, 1 St Helen's, Undershaft, London EC3P 3DQ
board meeting minutes 1921-45; general meeting minutes and reports 1907-70; share register 1917-69

Records (2): at Guildhall Library, Aldermanbury, London EC2P 2EJ
board meeting: minutes 1824-1918, attendance books 1875-1917; building and housing committee: meeting minutes 1903-05,1924-7, letter book 1903-05; accounts committee meeting minutes 1829-1904; management committee meeting minutes 1825-38; finance committee meeting minutes 1841-7,1903-11; secret department and special committee meeting minutes 1826-7; daily committee rotation books 1898-1939; proprietors: meeting minutes 1826-1906, private index 1824-33, nominees index c1890-1907, lists 1895-1916, probate extracts 1867-1956, registers 1824-82; deeds: establishment 1824, settlement 1825; share: ledger 1890, transfer registers 1826-36,1853-1917, transfers amalgamation letter book 1917; directors register 1901-17; seal book 1887-1924; letter books: secretarys 1824-56,1876-1916, manager 1887-99, staff and accommodation 1897-1930, underwriter 1889-1917; secretarys: report book 1824-1918, general notebook 1891-1933; balance: sheets 1837-1918, certificate book 1887-1918; general ledgers 1824-1923; accounts supplementary, personal 1891-1948, monthly 1873-1932, summary 1891-1921; weekly settlements 1892-1915; cash books: 1916-17, petty 1895-1915, summary 1903-21; agencies: annual accounts 1940-9, foreign 1908-15; policies: casualties register 1900-06, day entry books 1830-40, large risks books 1827-35, order books 1865-96,1907-15, risk index 1912-13, voyage book 1836-8, total loss and cancellation register 1911-19; investment: books 1841-1949, ledgers 1842-1924, summary book 1858-1921, bank stock book 1873-1952; capital register returns 1881-7

Indemnity Marine Insurance Co Ltd (priv pub 1975)

546 FALKS INDUSTRIES LTD
7 Jan 1887
23743
Abacus House, Gutter Lane, Cheapside, London EC2V 8AH
Lighting and heating appliance manufacturers

History: incorporated in 1887 as Falk Stadelmann & Co Ltd to acquire and carry on the business of Solomon Falk (est 1881), lamp and burner importer, and Jean Stadelmann & Co, gas burner and glass manufacturers, both of 59 Hatton Garden, London and to manufacture and sell lamps, gaseliers, chandeliers, standards, burners, stoves, globes, chimneys etc. Offices moved to 43 Farringdon Road, London and to 83-87 Farringdon Road in 1890. By 1923 had branches in Glasgow, Manchester and Melbourne and Sydney, Australia. Changed name to Falks Ltd in 1962. By 1967 had branches in Brighton, E Sussex; Southampton, Hampshire; Cardiff, S Glamorgan; Liverpool, Merseyside; Newcastle upon Tyne, Tyne & Wear; Belfast, N Ireland; Birmingham, W Midlands; Bradford and Leeds, W Yorkshire; Bristol, Avon; Dublin, Eire; Dunstable, Bedfordshire; Edinburgh, Lothian; Glasgow, Strathclyde; Manchester, Greater Manchester; Nottingham, Nottinghamshire; Stoke on Trent, Staffordshire. Also had a London showroom in High Holborn, and factories at Liverpool, Merseyside; Wandsworth, London; Brighton, E Sussex; Belfast, N Ireland; Banbury, Oxfordshire; Birmingham (2), W Midlands; and Johannesburg, South Africa; owned trading companies in Australia; New Zealand and South Africa, and 6 other subsidiary companies: Stoves Ltd; Switchgear & Equipment Ltd; Wandleside Warren Wire Co Ltd; Smith & Ansell Ltd; Ionlite Ltd; and Raydex Ltd. Name changed to above and company was acquired in 1970 by Jessel Securities Ltd which was placed in liquidation in 1976. Remained a dormant subsidiary of same and went into liquidation in 1981.

Records: none survive

547 MERCANTILE DRY DOCK CO LTD
19 Jan 1887
23794
Benton House, 136 Sandyford Road, Newcastle upon Tyne, Tyne & Wear NE2 1QE
Ship repairers

History: incorporated in 1887 as above to take over the building of a dry dock at Jarrow, Tyne & Wear begun in 1885 by Gavin Smith & Co Ltd and to purchase that company's ship repairing and marine engineering business carried on at Tyne Dock, South Shields, Tyne & Wear. Subsequently added a second and third dock and a fourth dry dock was completed in 1961. Built a light railway of 1.1 kilometres in Jarrow connecting with the Newcastle and South Shields branch of London and North Eastern Railway. Original registered offices were at Tyne Dock, moving to Jarrow in 1890. Became part of British Shipbuilders Ltd through Tyne Ship Repair Group in 1978.

Records: at Mercantile Dry Dock, Curlew Road, Jarrow, Tyne & Wear NE32 3DS
directors meeting minutes 1887-1962; members registers and share ledgers 1888-1945; share transfer registers 1898-1960; directors register 1931-51; corporate agreements and documents 1887-9; memo and articles of association 1904-25; private: ledgers 1885-1947, journals 1899-1940; employee letter books 1901-62; dock: plan nd, tender 1911, photographs 1906-53;

property: extension and improvement papers with plans 1911, agreements, leases, plans, schedules etc 1886-1938; solicitors bill 1892-6; newscuttings re company and shipping 1899-1952

548 NORTHAMPTON BREWERY CO LTD
9 Feb 1887
23925
Brewery, 91 Brick Lane, London E1 6QN
Brewing

History: incorporated as above in 1887 to acquire business of Northampton Brewery Co. Purchased Lion Brewery of Northampton in 1890 and brewery of Choules & Co in 1896. Acquired control of Eady & Dulley Ltd in 1929 (absorbing it in 1938), of Lankester & Wells in 1931 and Phillips Stamford Brewery Ltd with 70 licensed houses in 1952. Merged with old rivals P Phipps & Co Ltd, also of Northampton, in 1957 to form Manns Northampton Brewery Co Ltd, which merged with Watney Mann Ltd in 1959. Ceased to trade separately in 1959 and in 1980 was a subsidiary of Grand Metropolitan Ltd through Watney Mann & Truman Holdings Ltd.

Records: at Northamptonshire Record Office, Delapré Abbey, Northampton, Northamptonshire NN4 9AW
directors meeting minutes 1887-1955; board analysis sheets 1937-57; annual meetings: minutes 1887-1953, agendas and chairmans speeches 1925-35; shareholders register 1887-93; debenture trust: minutes 1890-1924, deeds 1887-1953; memo and articles of association 1887; amalgamation deed 1959; securities register 1872-1913; annual returns 1948-63; annual reports and accounts 1887-1954; general ledgers 1872-1908; ledger: 1920-5, loans 1881-1915; bank balances day book 1911-19; clubs loans deeds 1950s; sales summaries 1938-50; barley book 1947-68; stock books 1938-44; production record 1930-8,1948-58; salaries ledgers 1872-1951; staff memo 1907; pension scheme: minutes 1936-59, booklets 1935,1954; hospital fund minutes 1921-48; leases 1930-55; property ledger 1887-98; estate department summaries 1931-58; war damage contribution 1941-5; fire insurance schedule and notices 1950-8; Grand Hotel inventory 1947-55
Eady & Dulley Ltd: board minutes 1895-1938; shareholders meeting minutes 1895-1938; trust deed 1895; loans ledger 1882-1925
Phillips Stamford Brewery Ltd: trade records 1915-52; misc papers 1952-5

549 SPILLERS LTD
28 Feb 1887
24021
19 Hanover Square, London W1R 9DA
Millers, flour confectioners and animal food manufacturers

History: established in 1829 by Joel Spiller, corn factor and dealer, in St Mary's Street, Bridgwater, Somerset. He went into partnership in 1840 with Samuel Brown and built a warehouse on West Quay and invested in a mill. By 1846 were renting 3 mills in Somerset and subsequently built a mill with a capacity of 1200 sacks per week at West Dock, Cardiff, S Glamorgan. During 1850s bought a biscuit factory in Cardiff and in 1860, as the Cardiff operation had outgrown the Somerset business, headquarters moved to Cardiff. New mills were built, increasing capacity to 4000 sacks per week by 1877 and Cardiff mill was enlarged in 1879 to 10,000 sacks per week. Company was incorporated in 1887 as Spiller & Co Cardiff, Ltd. Merged in 1890 with William Baker & Sons of Bristol, Avon and changed name to Spillers & Bakers Ltd. Built a new biscuit bakery in Cardiff in 1894 and moved into manufacture of dog food, animal foods, poultry farming, bird seed and related products. Acquired Davidson & Sons in 1896. Purchased Phoenix Mills in Newcastle Upon Tyne, Tyne & Wear and opened agencies and depots throughout UK. In 1906 acquired Uveco Cereals Ltd, maize flake suppliers to the brewing industry and cattle feed suppliers, with mills at Newport, Gwent and Wallasey, Merseyside. Formed Spillers Steamship Co Ltd to operate a fleet of 30 lighters and 5 steamers working the Irish and coastal trades. Acquired 2 insurance companies, British Oak Benefit Association Ltd and Domestic Servants Insurance Co Ltd. Moved headquarters to St Mary Axe, London in 1916. Name changed to Spillers Milling & Associated Industries Ltd in 1919 and a new company Spillers & Bakers Ltd being registered to carry on the flour milling business. Merged with W Vernon & Sons Ltd, millers of Birkenhead, Merseyside and London. By 1923 owned FA Frost & Sons Ltd, Chester, Cheshire; Watson Todd & Co (Millers) Ltd, Birmingham, W Midlands; John Jackson & Sons Ltd, Manchester, Greater Manchester; Rishworth, Ingleby & Lofthouse Ltd, Hull, Humberside; Cardiff & Channel Mills Ltd; Spillers Grain Co Ltd; Uveco Cereals Ltd; Turog Brown Flour Co Ltd; Spillers Victoria Foods Ltd; Associated British Flour Millers No 1 Group Ltd; No 1 Milling Group Import Agency Ltd; and No 1 Milling Group Export Agency Ltd. Name changed to above in Dec 1927. Acquired Henry Leetham & Sons Ltd in 1928; goodwill and trade-marks of animal food section of Thames Milling Co Ltd and business of Craighall Milling Co Ltd and John White & Son (Glasgow) Ltd in 1932; and EC Robson & Sons Ltd of Sunderland, Tyne & Wear; Hosken, Trevithick, Polkinhorn & Co Ltd of Plymouth, Devon; Stoate & Sons Ltd of Bristol, Avon; and Hosegood Industries Ltd in 1930s. Built new mills at Cardiff in 1934, Avonmouth, Avon in 1935 and at Newcastle upon Tyne, Tyne & Wear. Acquired Paul Bros Ltd, of Birkenhead and Coventry, 'Homepride' flour manufacturers; Soya Foods Ltd; and J Lucas & Co Ltd in 1949. By 1957 also owned AH Allen & Co Ltd of Croydon, Greater London; ET Baker (Maldon) Ltd and Superise Flour Co Ltd, of Maldon, Essex; Workman Bros Ltd, of Cam, Gloucestershire; Charles Brown Holdings Ltd; and United Bakeries Ltd. Acquired pet food businesses of Spratts Patent Ltd and subsidiaries in 1960 and Scottish Animal Products Ltd in 1964, and produced 'Winalot', 'Kattomeat' and 'Choice Cuts'; animal feed business of British Feeding Mills Ltd in 1963; food canning business of Tyne Brand Products Ltd in 1967. In 1969 purchased Meade-Lonsdale Group Ltd, slaughterers and wholesale and retail meat distributors. Formed Sainsbury-Spillers Ltd in 1970 to run chicken processing plants and egg packing stations which used Spillers feeds. Acquired Entwhistles Ltd and pet food activities of Ranks Hovis McDougall Ltd in 1972. Merged interests in flour milling, baking and animal feeds with those of Co-operative Wholesale Society Ltd and J Lyons & Co Ltd in a new company, Spillers-French Holdings Ltd. Acquired Mario & Franco Restaurants Ltd in 1973, C&G Lecureur Frères, grain traders and silo operators of Rouen, France in 1977, and Modern Maid Food Products Inc, flour based food ingredient manufacturers of USA in 1978. Withdrew from bread-making in 1978 selling and closing all its bakeries and 3 mills. Acquired in 1979 by Dalgety Ltd, international traders with food and agricultural interests in North America, Australia, New Zealand and UK.

Records: at Spillers, 19 Hanover Square, London W1R 9DA
records post 1920s

'150 Years of Spillers 1829-1979', *Milling and Feed and Fertilisers*, Dec 1979 (pp 26-28)

550 178-202 LTD

1 Mar 1887
24028
178-202 Great Portland Street, London W1N 6NH
Advertising agents, printers and publishers

History: incorporated in 1887 as Technical Publications Co Ltd to develop an advertising agents business and to print and publish technical journals, advertisements, periodicals, circulars etc. Original offices were in Deansgate, Manchester, moving to 55&56 Chancery Lane, London by 1912. George Reveirs, of the printing firm of the same name, was appointed receiver in 1921. Acquired in 1960 by Municipal Journal Ltd and changed name to Municipal Publications Co Ltd. In 1975 its business was that of advertising agents and trade journal and handbook publishers. Name changed to above in 1979 and ceased to trade in 1980.

Records: at Municipal Journal, 178-202 Great Portland Street, London W1N 6NH
minutes and shareholding records 1950s on; accounting records 1954 on

551 AUSTRALASIAN UNITED STEAM NAVIGATION CO LTD

4 Mar 1887
24055
40 St Mary Axe, London EC3A 8EU
Shipping

History: incorporated as above in 1887 by the merger of 2 steam shipping companies, Australasian Steam Navigation Co (est 1851) and Queensland Steamship Co (est 1880) who had joined fleets in 1886 to operate a coastal shipping service around New South Wales. Company's first chairman was Sir William MacKinnon, 'founder father' of the Inchcape group of companies. Bought Eastern & Australian Steamship Co in 1920 and in 1921 joined the Associated Steamship Owners pool which managed most of Australia's inter-state shipping for the next 40 years. Due to challenge of the government shipping line and containerisation, the line slowly became unprofitable. By 1955 a 42ship fleet had been reduced to 4. In 1961 Inchcape & Co Ltd, international traders, purchased the company and the remainder of the fleet was sold but the workshops and engineering activities in Sydney and Brisbane were expanded until the late 1960s when the Sydney works closed. Brisbane opened a new workshop in 1971 which was still operating successfully in 1977.

Records: at Inchcape, 40 St Mary Axe, London EC3A 8EU
directors meeting minutes and agenda 1887-1942; general meeting agendas 1887-1938; share ledgers 1887-1954; register of members 1887-1902; register of mortgages 1927-52; debenture stockholders: meeting minutes 1898-1949, register 1898-1927, reports 1901-27; debenture stock: allotment 1898, correspondence 1889-1950; declarations of trust and agreements 1889-

1927; memo and articles of association 1887-98; printed accounts 1887-1959; profit and loss accounts 1887-1927; accounting working papers 1952-60; ledgers 1887-1948; home journal 1887-1928; voyage and foreign journal 1887-1932; cash books 1887-1956; bills of sale for ships etc 1889-1934; title deeds and property schedules 1888-1934; photographs of premises, shipping, personnel, workshops etc in Adelaide and Sydney c1899-1914
Eastern & Australian Steamship Co: directors meeting minutes 1903-16; logbooks of *SS Fort Wangell* 1944-8

Sir Percival Griffiths, *A History of the Inchcape Group* (1977)

552 BLACKBURN & DISTRICT INCORPORATED CHAMBER OF INDUSTRY & COMMERCE

11 Mar 1887
24084
14 Richmond Terrace, Blackburn, Lancashire BB1 7BH
Chamber of commerce

History: founded in 1886 by manufacturers, merchants and traders of Blackburn, Clitheroe, Darwen, Church, Oswaldtwistle, Rishton, Great Harwood and Clayton le Moors, Lancashire. Incorporated as a company limited by guarantee in 1887 as Blackburn Chamber of Commerce to promote and protect the trade, commerce and manufacture of Blackburn and district. During first 50 years was involved in parliamentary trade legislation and sent out pioneering commercial mission to China in 1896-7, financially supported by other chambers of commerce and the textile trade in Lancashire and Yorkshire. Since 1889 has given financial aid to technical and commercial education in Blackburn. Original offices were at 6 Richmond Terrace, moving to 14 (a listed building) after WW2. Name subsequently changed to above. In 1981 was mainly involved in export documentation.

Records: at Blackburn & District Incorporated Chamber of Industry & Commerce, 14 Richmond Terrace, Blackburn, Lancashire BB1 7BH
council minutes 1899-date; committee meeting minutes 1918-27; annual reports 1887-1909; China mission reports 1898

The Blackburn and District Incorporated Chamber of Commerce (priv pub 1937)

553 HUNT & WINTERBOTHAM LTD

23 Apr 1887
24307
Lodgemore Mills, Stroud, Gloucestershire GL5 3EJ
Wool textiles

History: the Hunt family purchased Cam Mills, Gloucestershire in 1851 and Thomas Hunt and Arthur Winterbotham formed a partnership to run the mill in 1859. Incorporated as above in 1887. Post WW1 recess in textile industry forced several Gloucestershire companies to merge: Winterbotham Strachan & Playne Ltd being formed in 1920 from Strachan & Co, Hunt & Winterbotham Ltd and William Playne & Co. In 1965 John & Thomas Clarke and Samuel Salter & Co were also acquired. Although acquired by Illingworth, Morris & Co in 1969, Winterbotham Strachan & Playne Ltd was the parent company of 10 subsidiary companies manufacturing and distributing woollens and worsteds in 1977. For many years the name 'Hunt & Winterbotham' was used by both the manufacturing mill at Cam and by the merchanting company with its headquarters at 12 Golden Square, London. Merchanting company also had retail outlets in Bond Street, London, on transatlantic liners and in USA. It was concerned exclusively with apparel cloths principally for the mens trade, selling in cut lengths and part-pieces to bespoke tailors worldwide. The Hunt & Winterbotham merchanting company moved from Golden Square to the west of England in 1975 where it diversified to include ready-made outer wear. In 1980s main products of the Winterbotham Strachan & Playne manufacturing group included tennis ball cloth, billiard table and casino cloths, piano felts, filter cloths and scarlets for Ministry of Defence.

Records (1): at Hunt & Winterbotham, Cam Mills, Cam, Gloucestershire
directors and general meeting minutes 1914-date; production costs books c1930-70; west country textile industry pamphlets 1957-60

Records (2): at Gloucestershire Record Office, Worcester Street, Gloucester, Gloucestershire GL1 3DW
directors and general meeting minutes 1902-14; mill executive meeting papers 1948; share: register c1920-30, application and allotment book 1887-1912, certificates books 1905-19, summaries and annual lists 1908-29; debentures: register 1916-32, dividends 1897-1932; misc papers and correspondence 20 cent; private ledgers 1859-1933; nominal ledgers 1920-9; sales ledgers 1892-1936; bought ledgers 1893-1926; foreign ledgers: 1919-36, transfers 1909-34; sundries ledger 1925-35; purchase journals: 1925-54, returns 1926-36; private analysis book 1901-03; cash books 1920-54; day books 1927-52; purchase day books 1920-5; sales day books 1936-57; departmental costing accounts book 1913-14; stock taking books 1901-44; stock books: 1913-28, foreign 1907, worsted 1925-9, woollen 1929; private cost and stock book 1895-1905; cost books 1875-9,1910-34; invoice details books 1926-36; returns book 1932-6; manufacturing books 1902-34; weavers books 1890-1950; weaving books 1943-62; spinners books 1861-1925; measuring books 1925-43; pattern books c1878-1955; yarn contract books 1920-45; wool samples nd; wages books 1924-43; wages analysis books 1928-41; poor rate book 1935-42; rents ledger 1935-41; inventories and valuation of mill machinery and buildings 1913,1925; Cam Mills plans c1895; machinery blue prints 20 cent; glass negatives of production processes c1904-11

554 FALMOUTH DISTRICT PILOT BOAT ASSOCIATION

27 Apr 1887
24327
14 Arivenack Street, Falmouth, Cornwall TR11 3JA
Pilotage

History: incorporated as above in 1887 to organise and carry out an improved pilot boat service in Falmouth pilot district.

Records: at Falmouth District Pilot Boat Association, 14 Arivenack Street, Falmouth, Cornwall TR11 3JA
agm and committee minutes 1887-1956; directors register 1887-1902; general ledger 1925-58; ledger 1953-5; cash book 1918-42; pilot cutter committee cash book 1963-72; day book 1927-

39; cash payment summaries 1947-54; pilotage ledger 1934-69; press cuttings and correspondence re foundation and work of association 1863-1954

555 MEADE-LONSDALE (GLOS) LTD

13 May 1887
24421
19 Hanover Square, London W1R 9DA
Butchers (formerly animal boarding establishment)

History: incorporated in 1887 as Dog Sanatorium by Spratts Patent Ltd (est 1862), animal food-stuff manufacturers to undertake and carry on, as successors to Alfred J Sewell, the business of a veterinary sanatorium in connection with doctoring dogs and preparing dogs for show, carried on by Sewell at Larkhall Rise, Clapham, Greater London. By 1957 the company's business was that of a quarantine and boarding establishment. Name changed to Hackbridge Kennels Ltd in 1962. Spratts Patent Ltd was acquired in 1969 by Spillers Ltd (inc 1887) which was acquired by Dalgety Ltd in 1979. Did not trade from 1974 to 1975. Name changed to above in 1976 when business became that of family and general butchers and meat salesmen. Ceased trading in Apr 1977 and was liquidated in 1983.

Records: at Dalgety, 19 Hanover Square, London W1R 9DA
corporate records 1930 on

556 BOLTON CHAMBER OF COMMERCE & INDUSTRY (INC)

18 May 1887
24446
Silverwell House, Silverwell Street, Bolton, Greater Manchester BL1 1PX
Chamber of commerce

History: founded and incorporated in 1887 as Bolton District Incorporated Chamber of Commerce as a company limited by guarantee to promote and protect trade, commerce and manufactures of Bolton, Greater Manchester. First meetings held in town hall, and offices opened at 11 Chancery Lane, Bolton. By 1906 offices were at 23 Acresfield, moving to 19 Hotel Street c1920; Knowsley House 1929; 21 Mawdsley Street 1935 and 27 Mawdsley Street in 1956; and to Silverwell House in 1979. Junior Chamber of Commerce formed in 1929. Name subsequently changed to above. In 1981 membership stood at c400, and activities included publication of annual report and directory and monthly business news bulletin, offering library, information and other services to members, certifying export and other documentation, observing legislative developments and acting as independent voice of local business.

Records: at Bolton Chamber of Commerce & Industry, Silverwell House, Silverwell Street, Bolton, Greater Manchester BL1 1PX
council and committee meeting minutes 1886-date; annual reports 1935-43; annual accounts 1937-66; general ledger 1903-32; debt ledger 1937-50; cash books 1887-1959; published journal 1887
Bolton & District Junior Chamber of Commerce: council and committee meeting minutes 1929-46

557 ROYAL NATIONAL MISSION TO DEEP SEA FISHERMEN

25 May 1887
24477
43 Nottingham Place, London W1M 4BX
Charity

History: founded in 1881 by EJ Mather to minister to the men of the Dogger Bank fishing fleets, with missionary work carried on from a fleet of mission ships which were working fishing vessels. Also supplied warm clothing, tobacco and medical aid. Incorporated as above as a company limited by guarantee in 1887 receiving royal patronage and prefix in 1896. From 1900 has been active in shore based centres in British fishing ports. In 1980 these were at Grampian - Aberdeen, Fraserburgh, Lossiemouth, Peterhead; Highland - Kinlochbervie, Lochinver, Mallaig, Scrabster, Ullapool; Strathclyde - Ayr, Oban; Shetland - Lerwick; Cornwall - Newlyn; Humberside - Bridlington, Grimsby, Hull; Lancashire - Fleetwood; N Yorkshire - Scarborough; Tyne & Wear - North Shields; Suffolk - Lowestoft. In 1892 Dr Wilfred Grenfell was sent by the mission to Newfoundland and Labrador and International Grenfell Association was founded from his work.

Records: at Royal National Mission to Deep Sea Fishermen, 43 Nottingham Place, London W1M 4BX
agm minutes 1886-1967; committee meeting minutes: finance 1890-1953, hospital 1892-1939; 'Inasmuch' committee papers 1930s; members register 1881-date; memo and articles of association 1887; corporate papers 19-20 cent; seal register 1953-60; correspondence re administration, appeals etc 19-20 cent; Yarmouth Mission cash book 1925; tobacco sales sheet nd; correspondence and papers re mission stations 1956-date; plans, leases, legal fees, trust documents, copy wills etc 1738-date; Lloyds Register certificates 19-20 cent; 'Sunday Signals' notes on crews, history, religious texts, signals etc 1960s; press cuttings and notes on historical incidents and individual boats c1920-date; photographs of mission activities, boats and fishing industry c1900 on; pamphlets 19-20 cent; *Toilers of the Deep* magazine, includes annual report and accounts c1881-date
International Grenfell Association: minutes, correspondence and corporate papers 20 cent

558 GREENE KING & SONS LTD

1 Jun 1887
24511
Westgate Brewery, Bury St Edmunds, Suffolk IP33 1QT
Brewing

History: established by Benjamin Greene who formed partnership with William Buck in 1804 and opened brewery at Bury St Edmunds, Suffolk in 1805. By 1833 owned 1 public house but supplied free trade beer as far afield as Newmarket, Suffolk. In about 1836 the brewery came under the management of Edward Greene, Benjamin's third son. During the 1840s and 1850s business expanded ten fold and in the late 1860s public houses began to be acquired. 40,000 barrels were being brewed per annum by 1875 rising to 65-75,000 barrels in 1887 when firm amalgamated with chief competitors FW King & Son of Bury St Edmunds to form the above. By 1902 owned 70 public houses in Bury and 180 in surrounding area. During WW1 output fell by a quarter but by 1919 the company owned 460 houses and 3 breweries and had an annual output of about 100,000 barrels. Acquired Clarke Bros, Risbygate Brewery, Bury St Edmunds in 1917; FC Christmas & Co, Haverhill Brewery, Suffolk in 1918; Oliver Bros, Sudbury Brewery, Suffolk in 1919; Bailey & Tebbutt Ltd, Cambridge, Cambridgeshire in 1925; Ogden & Son, March, Cambridgeshire in 1930; Rayment & Co Ltd in 1931; and Thomas Prentice & Co, Stowmarket, Suffolk in 1933. Output stagnated between the WWs, was buoyant during WW2 but fell back in the 1950s. Acquired Simpson's Brewery Ltd, Baldock, Hertfordshire and Herbert Cawdron & Son Ltd, wine merchants in 1954; JC Mouldon & Son, Sudbury, Suffolk in 1958; and Wells & Winch Ltd, Biggleswade, Bedfordshire and its 287 public houses in 1961. In 1980s was one of the largest independent brewing companies.

Records (1): at Greene King & Sons, Westgate Brewery, Bury St Edmunds, Suffolk IP33 1QT directors meeting minutes 1887-date; managers meeting minutes: 1919-63, public house 1929-57, and travellers and outside representatives 1936-60; general meeting papers 1940,1953-4; share: correspondence 1948-52, transfer registers 1935-66; debenture stock: deeds and agreements 1887-1982, certificates 1890-1901, ledgers 1887-1929, interest payments 1903-29, and mortgage register 1887; memo and articles of association 1887-1954; annual returns 1959-60; seal register 1950-79; Rayment & Co purchase agreement 1923; annual: report and accounts 1927-date, accounts 1925-date; private ledgers 1887-date; general ledgers 1934-60; investment ledger 1936-50; tax statements and subsidiaries accounts 1944-50; sales books 1902-52; trade books 1914-55; price list c1920; brewing: programme 1906, card 1906, books 1923-53; stock books 1888-1969; labour book 1930-4; staff pension fund: trust deed and rules 1929, meeting minutes 1929-70; brewery proportions 1950; plant valuations 1950; public house: valuations 1950, leases c1880-1930; insurance policies and details 1964-5; newscuttings 1880-1950

E Greene & Son: private ledger 1878-86; leases 1868-87

Herbert Cawdron & Son Ltd: directors and general meeting minutes 1936-54; members register 1937-55; share certificates 1936-55; memo and articles of association 1936; impersonal ledger 1936-46; purchase ledger 1936-46; deeds and agreements nd

Greene King (Baldock) Ltd: directors and general meeting minutes 1935-55; shareholders correspondence 1954-5; partnership deeds and papers 1891-1921; balance sheets and accounts 1954-80; brewery insurance policy 1963

Ixworth Cyder Co Ltd: directors and general meeting minutes 1929-57; share certificates and transfer documents 1920-69; memo and articles of association 1928; seal register 1928-69; balance sheets and accounts 1928-79

JC Mauldon & Son: profit and loss accounts 1939-57; rent ledger 1938-57; public house deeds nd

Norfolk Stones Ltd: directors meeting minutes 1945-58; members register 1948-59; share: certificates 1945-58, transfer documents 1955-8

Olivers Brewery: public house: and estate maps and descriptions 1898-1911, photographs nd

Thos Peatling & Sons Ltd: directors and general meeting minutes 1912-56;
general meeting minutes 1912-36,1955-6; members register 1930-3; share: certificates 1925-56, correspondence and transfer documents 1954-6; directors agreement 1934; balance sheets and accounts 1954-81; impersonal ledger 1937-54; deeds and agreement nd

Peatling & Cawdron Ltd: directors meeting minutes 1956-61; share certificates 1956-80

Rayment & Co Ltd: directors meeting minutes 1936-64; general meeting papers 1932; share transfer documents 1926-62; dividend register 1939-59; annual returns 1922-3; memo and articles of association 1912; annual reports and accounts 1973-81; balance sheet and accounts

1933-71; Furneux Pelham Brewery and other properties deeds and documents 1827-1914; premises valuation 1950

Scruby & Co Ltd: directors meeting minutes 1915-30; general meeting minutes 1915-58; members register 1915-54; share: certificates 1915-54, transfer documents 1936; balance sheets and accounts 1937-56

CA Stockbridge & Co: ledgers 1945-56; petty cash books 1949-57

Wisbech Hotels Ltd: directors meeting minutes 1953-60; members register 1932-57; share: certificates 1932-60, transfer documents 1947-60; dividend account book 1937-59; annual report and accounts 1951-8; ledger 1952-60

Records (2): at Greene King (Biggleswade), 1 Church Street, Biggleswade, Bedfordshire

Greene King (Baldock) Ltd: balance sheets and accounts 1935-65; Baldock trade book 1891-1964; brewing book 1960-2; brewery: inventory and valuation 1853, sale catalogues 1903-04; rent books 1917-52; public house register 1855-1962

Greene King (Biggleswade) Ltd: directors meeting: minutes 1899-1957, agendas 1899-1951; share: allotment register 1938, ledgers and transfer registers 1899-1980, certificates 1899-1961; annual returns 1930-51; debenture stock: register 1899-1937, transfer register 1899-1937, holders register 1932-7, certificates 1899-1945; seal registers 1935-59; accounts c1899-1969; private ledger 1899-1955; impersonal ledgers 1922-50; price lists c1920-60; advertising material c1920-60; produce book 1915-19; brewing books 1906-47; breweries: sales catalogues 1898-1919, plans 1901,1947, histories 1970s; brewery, public houses and plant photographs c1920-60

Hudsons Cambridge & Pampisford Breweries Ltd: directors meeting minutes 1902-49; general meeting minutes 1892-1948; share: ledger 1895-1948, transfer documents 1902-38, certificates 1893-1933; debenture: registers 1898-1928, stockholders registers 1932-8; barley book 1897-1934; malt book c1898-1931; brewing book 1927-31

Records (3): at Bedfordshire Record Office, County Hall, Bedford, Bedfordshire MK42 9AP

Greene King (Biggleswade) Ltd: brewery and public house deeds nd

Records (4): at Hertfordshire Record Office, County Hall, Hertford, Hertfordshire SG13 8DE

Greene King (Baldock) Ltd: balance book 1909-20; ledgers: nominal 1927-56, bank 1923-47, petty 1927-53, sheets 1953-8; cash books: 1936-58, petty 1952-61; expenses books 1926-53; expenditure and receipt book 1935-45; publican: beer purchase book 1853, beer and spirits supplied book 1937-53; order book 1859-61; sales books 1891-1957; petty trade: day books 1937-53, receipt books 1935-53; returned beer books 1915-62; production: notebooks 1880,1910-49, analysis books 1924-56; brewing books 1853-60,1931-54; barley: day book 1853-1945, account book 1883-1953; grains account book 1881-1961; plant plans, specifications, correspondence and papers 1886-1926; water analyses 1870-94; wages books 1912-15,1934-60; Baldock brewery: transfer documents 1831-58, alteration costs 1896-9, plans c1900; Simpsons Brewery plan 1959; property papers 1893-1920; rent ledger 1908-27; licensed houses: repairs book 1945-50, list c1900, deeds and papers nd; letter books 1880-1948

RG Wilson, *Greene King A Business and Family History* (1983)

559 BASS BREWING (ALTON) LTD

7 Jun 1887
24542
Manor Park, Alton, Hampshire GU34 2PS
Brewing

History: established in Cardiff, S Glamorgan by Somerset brewer William Hancock who bought Bute Dock Brewery in 1883. Acquired Anchor Brewery, Newport, Gwent and 46 licensed houses in 1884. After his death, company was incorporated in 1887 as William Hancock & Co Ltd. Between 1886 and 1890 acquired Dowson Brothers, Phoenix Brewery, Cardiff; Ackland & Thomas, West End Brewery, Swansea, W Glamorgan; John Biggs, South Wales Brewery, Cardiff; and Joseph Hall & Co, wine and spirit merchants, Swansea. In 1892 took over High Street Brewery, Swansea, and later County, Castle and Canton Cross Breweries at Cardiff. Bute Dock Brewery was sold in 1895 and brewing concentrated at newly constructed Crawshay Street Brewery, Cardiff (complete with mineral water factory and wine and spirit department) and West End Brewery, Swansea. Acquired Risca Brewery, Risca, Gwent in 1901 by which time controlled 100 licensed houses, and Swansea Old Brewery Ltd in 1927. Purchased David Roberts & Sons Ltd, brewers of Aberystwyth, Dyfed. By 1968 had some 600 licensed outlets. Acquired by Bass Charrington Ltd in 1968 and subsequently ceased to brew, its name changing to above. In 1983 was a subsidiary of Bass PLC through Bass Holdings Ltd.

Records (1): at Bass Wales & West, Maes y Coed Road, Cardiff, S Glamorgan
board and general meeting minutes 1907-date

Records (2): at Bass Holdings, 137 High Street, Burton upon Trent, Staffordshire DE14 1JZ
advertisements 1946-52
David Roberts & Sons Ltd: premises valuation 1897-1941

Records (3): at Glamorgan Archive Service, Glamorgan County Hall, Cathays Park, Cardiff, S Glamorgan CF1 3NE
annual meeting reports 1915-67; ledgers and account books nd; annual journals 1949-53; cash book 1871-94; advertisements nd; prize certificate 1932; apprenticeship indenture 1894; deeds and associated papers 19-20 cent; newscuttings 1907-25; jubilee brochure 1937

560 UPPERTON ESTATES LTD

11 Jul 1887
24571
4 Carlton Gardens, Pall Mall, London SW1Y 5AB
Property

History: incorporated in 1887 as Tenement Dwellings Co Ltd to provide houses for the industrial and labouring classes in London. Alfred Hoare, a partner in C Hoare & Co, appears to have been its founder and was chairman for many years. By the 1900s properties in the London area included over 72 houses in Deptford; 4 blocks of tenement dwellings in Bethnal Green; property in Finsbury; Southwark; Weymouth Buildings, Sayer Street; and Ladysmith Buildings, New Kent Road. Over 57 houses were purchased in Highbury in 1925. Changed name to above in 1958. Was acquired in about 1964 by Charlwood Alliance Properties Ltd (inc 1884 as East End Dwellings Co Ltd), which was acquired by Town & City Properties Ltd in 1974. Struck off Register of Companies in Mar 1981.

Records: at Newham Local Studies Library, Stratford Reference Library, Water Lane, London E15 4NJ
directors and general meeting minutes 1901-41

561 HOLDEN & BROOKE LTD

14 Jun 1887
24582
Sirius Works, Haverford Street, West Gorton, Manchester, Greater Manchester M12 5JL
Pump manufacturers

History: founded in 1883 by Harry Holden and Robert G Brooke, fellow ex-employees of Sharpe Stewart & Co Ltd, Manchester steam locomotive manufacturers, to make feed water injectors at St Simons Works, 27 St Simon Street, Salford, Greater Manchester under the name of Broughton Manufacturing Co. Holden retired from the partnership in 1887 and the business was incorporated as above to manufacture injection boiler fittings. Later products included small gas engines, door locks and automatic sweet delivery machines. Moved in 1897 from Salford to Sirius Works, West Gorton, Greater Manchester, which allowed rapid expansion and development to take place. The 'Dual' Oil Separator was put on the market and feed water heaters were introduced. A London office was opened in 1924 and a branch office servicing the midlands and north England was established in 1931. In 1938 another factory, Sharston Works in Bradnor Road, Wythenshawe, Greater Manchester was opened. Acquired in 1950 Frank Pearn & Co Ltd (est 1872), reciprocating pump manufacturers and producers of the pumps for PLUTO (pipe-line under the ocean) during WW2. A Bristol branch was opened in 1956 and by 1977 the company had branches in London; Birmingham, W Midlands; York, N Yorkshire; Glasgow, Strathclyde; Belfast, N Ireland and Dublin, Eire. During 1970s the export business expanded, especially in the Middle East, Africa and the Far East, the company mainly manufacturing centrifugal, reciprocating and vacuum pumps and heat exchangers. Innovations in the 1970s included packaged sets for sealed system pressurisation, water boosting and fire-fighting systems.

Records: at Holden & Brooke, Sirius Works, Haverford Street, West Gorton, Manchester, Greater Manchester M12 5JL
directors meeting minutes 1887-1948; agm notices 1890; articles of partnership 1883; draft agreements re setting up of company 1887; memo and articles of association 1887-1920; directors agreements and papers re same 1890-1923; balance sheets and profit and loss accounts 1888-1926; steam trap agreement 1895; agency agreement book 1883-96; agreements, correspondence and papers re agencies 1921-82; patents and specifications 1884-1926; RG Brooke pump diagram notebook 1880; works committee minutes with correspondence 1918-21; salaries and expenses books 1896-1950; private commissions book 1898-1907; pay rate book 1924-6; staff: book 1922-36, long service fund 1938-45, signatures 1938-52, agreements 1897,1951, photographs 1933-8; *Quarterly Bulletins* 1943-51; property agreements and papers 1884-96; correspondence and papers re alterations to Sirius Works 1896; plan of Gorton premises c1895; plans and papers re war precautions 1939-43; RG Brooke letter books 1882-95; firms logbook 1933-60

Frank Pearn & Co Ltd: memo and articles of association 1894-1955; directors agreements 1894,1919; private ledger and journal 1878-84; impersonal ledger 1887-93; price list 1899; French catalogue c1900; advertisements c1920; correspondence re PLUTO project 1943; salary books 1884-1953

1883-1983 The First Hundred Years (priv pub 1983)

562 PONTYPRIDD FREEHOLD LAND & BUILDING CO LTD

1 Jul 1887
24681
Old Bank Chambers, Market Street, Pontypridd, Mid Glamorgan CF37 2SY
Property

History: incorporated as above in 1887 to acquire freehold land on which to build houses. Acquired Danygraig Freehold Estate in Pontypridd, Mid Glamorgan on which 210 houses were built. In 1890 completed new office building on corner of Taff Street and Market Square which was let as shops and offices and became new registered offices of company. Principal activity in 1980s was still one of property and investment.

Records: at Pontypridd Freehold Land & Building, Old Bank Chambers, Market Street, Pontypridd, Mid Glamorgan CF37 2SY
directors and general meeting: minutes 1936-72, attendances 1891-1983; members register 1887-1915; share: ledger 1887-date, transfer register 1888-1917; annual summaries 1891-1920; mortgage register and papers 1889-1961; prospectus 1887; annual reports and accounts 1887-99,1934; ledger 1907-40; journal 1927-82

563 HOBBS HART & CO LTD

8 Jul 1887
24725
Staffa Road, Leyton, London E10
Locks and safe manufacturers

History: founded in 1852 by Alfred C Hobbs, an American lock dealer, as Hobbs & Co to take over his lock patents and to start manufacturing locks. By 1855 was known as Hobbs, Ashley & Co and had a factory at 33 Lawrence Lane, off Cheapside, London with showrooms at 97 Cheapside. By 1860 was known as Hobbs Ashley & Fortescue changing name to Hobbs Hart & Co when John M Hart took control on Hobbs' death in that year. Hart initiated safe and strong-room door manufacture at new works in Arlington Street, Islington, London. Held a Royal Warrant from 1861 and supplied safes to Bank of England. After Hart's death in 1887 the business was incorporated as above. Product range increased and exports sent worldwide. New works and office premises were opened in Staffa Road, Leyton, London in 1936. Acquired by Chubb & Son Lock & Safe Co Ltd in 1956 and continued to operate until 1983 as one of the 2 safe manufacturing centres of Chubb Group.

Records: at Chubb & Son, Manor House, Manor Lane, Feltham, Greater London TW13 4JQ
partnership agreements 1860-88; directors meeting minutes 1887-1974, executive committee minutes and papers 1956-9; general: meeting minutes 1897-1974, papers and reports 1887-

1908; members registers 1887-1947; share: registers c1944-58, allotment books 1877-c87, transfer documents 1887-1958, certificates 1947-58, corporate documents 1887-1950s; debenture register and documents 1887-1935; memo and articles of association 1887-1955; annual: returns 1888-1968, reports and accounts 1888-1956; balance sheets and accounts 1888-1961; general ledgers 1887-1959; town ledgers 1950s; expenditure ledgers 1887-1908,1950-7; journals 1887-95,1935-60; bills receivable book 1898-1919; cash book 1943-60; salaries, wages and petty cash book 1925-73; staff bonus fund: ledger 1923-45, working papers 1911-40s; ledgers: cost price 1914-45, safes 1902-58, locks 1888-1959; estimate books 1941-59; cost books 1919-59; order books: factory 1880-1959, customer 1894-1958, lock 1939-59, government 1902-05,1924-c38; piecework: books 1929-42, time sheets 1956-7; stores and lock books c1900-30; patent specifications, papers and correspondence 1865-1958; order, estimates, production etc correspondence and papers 1909-59; works posters 1928-35; general managers reports 1956-9; lock picking agreement 1859; production test photographs nd; sales ledgers 1951-8; catalogues, price lists, and sales and trade literature 1884-1950s; agency agreements and correspondence 1894-1914; customer correspondence 1868-1954; sales reports 1890-1903; property deeds, documents, plans and correspondence 1857-1958; machinery: plant valuations, reports, inventories and correspondence 1897-1948, maintenance books 1924-40, insurance policies 1909-48; works council minutes 1957-60; wages: ledgers 1898-1944, journals 1872-98, and salaries books 1944-61; directors salaries 1898-1958; safe makers strike papers 1897; union correspondence 1912,1953-5; staff papers and correspondence 1897,1911-59; sick club minutes and papers 1898 on; benevolent fund minutes and papers 1950-60; pension fund: trustee minutes 1948-68, papers 1948-68, ledger 1949-70, salaries book 1961-5, annual accounts 1949-68; staff, works and product photographs 1880s on; history booklets 1936,1951; misc papers and correspondence 1881-1960

564 JENNINGS BROTHERS LTD

20 Jul 1887
24795
Castle Brewery, Cockermouth, Cumbria CA13 9NE
Brewers and wine and spirit merchants

History: established by the Jennings family in the 1850s at Lorton, Cumbria, producing 'home brew' beer and incorporated as above in 1887 in order to raise money to pay for the building costs of the new brewery at The Castle, Cockermouth. Property then consisted of 2 breweries, 3 maltings and 16 licensed houses. Had working agreement from 1906 to 1923 with Joseph Dalzell's Parton & Harrington Breweries Ltd, Duke Street, Whitehaven, Cumbria, brewers and wine and spirit merchants, registered in 1892. In 1926 acquired Faulder's Brewery Co Ltd (formed 1883) of Browfoot, Keswick, Cumbria. Brewing ceased at Keswick in 1927 and Faulder's was wound up in 1946. In 1981 had over 100 wholly owned licensed houses in Cumbria.

Records (1): at Jennings Brothers, Castle Brewery, Cockermouth, Cumbria CA13 9NE
directors meeting minutes 1945-date; debenture, share and share transfer certificates 1896-1970s; corporate agreements 1887-1947; memo and articles of association 1906; seal register 1884-1927; annual reports and accounts 1922-69; accounting papers 1888-1920; general ledger 1913-66; sales ledgers c1923-66; private trade ledgers 1947-65; returns and allowances book 1940-74; rent ledger 1922-53; bank ledger 1943-69; ledger balances 1937-60; journals 1947-72;

sales day books: beer 1950-60, wines, spirits and general goods 1943-68; sales day sheets 1923-73; cash book: 1951-74, office 1955-74, petty 1932-51; invoice books 1953-71; invoices: brewery 1918-29, wine and spirit department 1922-8; order books: bottled beer department 1956-73, mineral water department 1957-8; stock book: general 1941-51, spirits and brewing departments 1954-62; public houses beer bottles, boxes and premises book 1888-1918; wages books 1957-69; staff holiday fund payments book 1955-67; maps and plans of breweries, hotels and inns c1881-date; repair schedules and papers 1950s-73; land tax returns 1910; photographs of inns and Castle Brewery c1900-60; history c1978

Joseph Dalzell's Parton & Harrington Breweries Ltd: profit and loss accounts and balance sheets 1914-22; financial working papers 1915-22; publicans ledger 1906-23; returns ledger 1929-30

Faulder's Brewery Co Ltd: share and share transfer certificates and correspondence 1880s-1950s; balance sheets and profit and loss accounts 1929-45

Records (2): at Cumbria Record Office, The Castle, Carlisle, Cumbria CA3 8UR

directors meeting: minutes 1889-1945, agendas 1928-38; share ledger 1887-98; members register and share ledgers 1898-1944; share: certificate books 1887,1944-50, papers 1915-17; debenture: papers 1896-1947, application and allotment book 1896, register and transfer register 1896-1946; mortgage etc register 1887-98; directors register 1915-24; memo and articles of association 1887; annual returns 1905-24; annual reports and accounts 1888-1957; papers and working agreements with Joseph Dalzell's Parton & Harrington Breweries Ltd 1906-25; tenants lawsuit papers 1891,1917-43; profit and loss accounts and balance sheets 1896-1957; financial working papers 1914-32; general ledgers 1888-1918; investment ledger 1899-1935; sales ledgers 1857-1949; purchases ledgers 1866-1927; private trade ledgers 1887-1949; creditors ledgers 1888-1948; banking ledgers 1898-1917; rent ledgers 1888-1906,1942-6; journals 1906-35; cash books: 1883-1942, general 1884-1917, capital 1896, office 1914-17, petty 1909-32, wine and spirit department 1917-23; returns and allowances accounts 1890-1924; sales day books: beer 1906-44, wine and spirits 1920-3; invoice books: 1908-45, wine and spirit department 1935-44; wine and spirit bought, sold and delivery book 1886-1950; trade-mark design papers 1888-91; stock books: general 1941-51, managed houses 1939-48; brewing book 1910-11; tunning book 1941-3; wages books 1917-28; employment agreements with drafts 1891-1945; out letter books 1881-1913; in letters 1907-19; deeds, title abstracts, and papers and correspondence re lettings, licences, tenants, rents, managers, properties, repairs etc 1881-1935; land tax returns 1910; boiler house plan 1948; solicitors papers incl draft and original agreements and deeds, draft accounts, solicitors bills re public houses, brewery, licensed premises, tenants, licences, lawsuits, staff, finance, sales, share and debenture issue, agm and board meetings, company formation, memo and articles of association

Faulder's Brewery Co Ltd: directors meeting minutes 1891-1946; members register etc 1889-1939; share certificates: 1890-1944, and title deed register 1884-1927; stock and stock transfer register 1889-1946; memo and articles of association 1888-1909; annual returns 1911-27; purchase and winding up papers 1926-46; lawsuit papers 1894; annual reports and accounts 1911-27; monthly balances 1918-27; ledgers 1888-1946; cash books 1918-34; draft and copy deeds, plans and property papers 1895-1939

Joseph Dalzell's Parton & Harrington Breweries Ltd: working agreements and legal papers 1906-26; annual reports and accounts 1913-22; profit and loss account 1906; sales ledger 1900-10; cask ledger 1906-19; properties repair lists 1915; deeds, plans and property papers 1929-39

565 ENGLISH ELECTRIC-AEI TRACTION PROJECTS LTD

21 Jul 1887
24807
Trafford Park, Manchester, Greater Manchester
Engineering - locomotive

History: traces its origins to 1875 when WG Bagnall acquired a small millwright's business at Stafford, Staffordshire and in the following year began the construction of railway locomotives and rolling stock. In 1887, WG Bagnall Ltd was incorporated to acquire the business. By late 1880s had developed a capability for supplying complete equipment for light railway track, rolling stock and locomotives. At that time the Stafford works had expanded to cover 11 acres. From 1900 the company specialised in building narrow gauge locomotives and during WW1 built locomotives for use on western front. In 1920s completed its first orders for locomotives for main line railway companies, both at home and in India and other British colonies. In 1933 built its first diesel engine under a licence. Rolling stock production declined from 1939 and was replaced by general engineering work. From 1901 the company came increasingly under the leadership of WS Edwards who was chairman and sole owner by the time of his death in 1947. Company was subsequently acquired by Heenan & Froude Ltd of Worcester, then controlled by AP Good who had widespread interests in the railway engineering industry including Brush Electrical Engineering Co Ltd. Brush-Bagnall Traction Ltd was formed in 1951 for construction of diesel locomotives with Bagnall constructing the engines and Brush the electrical gear. When Good died in 1953, the link he had formed was broken. In 1956 Bagnalls withdrew from Brush-Bagnall Traction Ltd which was renamed Brush Traction Ltd. In 1959 Heenan & Froude Ltd sold Bagnall to WH Dorman & Co Ltd of Stafford, diesel engine manufacturers. In 1961 Dormans was acquired by English Electric Co Ltd which concentrated its locomotive building at Darlington, Durham and Newton le Willows, Merseyside. Locomotive building at Stafford subsequently ceased. Known as above following the amalgamation in 1968 of English Electric Co with General Electric Co Ltd.

Records (1): at GEC-Traction Projects, Trafford Park, Manchester, Greater Manchester
memo and articles of association and corporate papers 1887-date

Records (2): at Staffordshire Record Office, County Buildings, Eastgate Street, Stafford, Staffordshire ST16 2LZ
workmans day book 1915-25; glass negatives: India and South Africa c1920-40

AC Baker and TDA Civil, *Bagnalls of Stafford* (priv pub 1973)

566 ECCLESIASTICAL INSURANCE OFFICE LTD

3 Aug 1887
24869
Beaufort House, Brunswick Road, Gloucester, Gloucestershire GL1 1JZ
Insurance

History: established in London in 1887 as Ecclesiastical Buildings Fire Office Ltd for fire insurance of churches and church buildings. Renamed as above in 1895 and extended business to include life assurance and accident and liability insurance for churches, clergymen and churchgoers. Clergy closely involved in direction of company since inception, and traditionally surplus profits were distributed for 'benefit of clergy and church objects'. In 20 cent company extended its insurance business to include universities, independent schools, charitable institutions, hotels and other commercial and industrial risks.

Records: at Ecclesiastical Insurance Office, Beaufort House, Brunswick Road, Gloucester, Gloucestershire GL1 1JZ
board meeting: minutes 1887-date, agendas 1887-1983, attendance books 1887-1984, notes 1893-5; committee meeting minutes and agendas 1888-9; general meeting: minutes 1887-1972, agendas 1894-1920; meeting minutes: private 1905-09, trustees 1927-72; share: ledgers 1887 on, transfer register 1888-1973, holders notices 1887-1937, bonus circulars 1891-1970; Churchman Insurance Office circulars 1902; memo and articles of association 1912,1919; annual reports and accounts 1888-1971; weekly returns 1889-1943; accounts progress 1843-70; cash books 1896-1964; bank account memo book to 1908; investments: certificate registers 1910-70, ledger 1887-96, loans on lives 1904-46; sales registers 1915-29; endorsements: 1888-1906, cycle insurance 1900 on, glass insurance 1888-91, household 1921-7; claims: 1888 on, burglary 1895 on, personal accident 1895 on; fire policies 1888; surveys and plans c1890 on; salary book 1900-01

567 JC&J FIELD LTD
10 Aug 1887
24902
225 Bath Road, Slough, Berkshire SL1 4ET
Soap and candle manufacturers

History: established as candle manufacturers prior to 1642 by Thomas Field, wax chandler at Lambeth Marsh. From mid 18 cent soap was also manufactured. By 1800 was known as John & Charles Field and from 1820 as JC&J Field. When incorporated as above in 1887 was manufacturing at 15 Upper Marsh, Lambeth, London and by 1890 also had leasehold factories at Bermondsey, Battersea and West Moulsey, London. On expiry of Bermondsey lease in 1894 oil and toilet soap manufacture was transferred to Lambeth. Purchased freehold site for factory at Rainham, Greater London in 1903. Began manufacture of household soap in 1907 and subsequently became toiletries suppliers. Acquired in 1958 by E Griffiths Hughes Ltd (est 1756) manufacturing chemists of Manchester, which were acquired in 1959 by Aspro-Nicholas Ltd (est 1915 in Australia, inc 1927 in UK) manufacturing chemists. Company became Aspro's toiletries division. Placed in liquidation in May and dissolved in Sep 1983.

Records: at Lambeth Archives Department, Minet Library, 52 Knatchbull Road, London SE5 9QY
board meeting minutes 1966-83; general meeting minutes 1887-1920,1966-83; members register and share ledger 1958-82; annual report and accounts 1966-82; dividend book 1948-58; laundry diary 1907

568 EMPLOYERS' LIABILITY ASSURANCE CORPORATION LTD
15 Aug 1887
24918
1 St Helen's, Undershaft, London EC3P 3DQ
Insurance

History: incorporated in 1887 as London Amicable Liability Assurance Society Ltd. Acquired in 1894 by Scottish Metropolitan Assurance Co Ltd which was taken over in 1912 by London & Lancashire Life Assurance Co Ltd which was renamed London & Scottish Assurance Corporation Ltd in 1919 and was acquired in 1923 by Northern Assurance Co Ltd which was acquired by Commercial Union Assurance Co Ltd in 1968. Name changed to above in 1970.

Records: at Commercial Union Assurance, 1 St Helen's, Undershaft, London EC3P 3DQ
directors meeting minutes 1887-1951; general meeting minutes 1887-1968

569 OLDHAM HIDE, SKIN & FAT CO LTD

16 Sept 1887
25040
Gas Street, Rhodes Park, Oldham, Greater Manchester
Hides, skins and fats

History: incorporated in 1887 by local butchers to act as dealers in and manufacturers of hides, skins and other animal products at Oldham, Greater Manchester. By 1922 the company had been acquired by Gallagher Brothers Ltd, hide and skin merchants of Wigan, Greater Manchester. By the late 1960s the company was a subsidiary of FMC Products Ltd, meat wholesalers. Ceased to trade in 1980. By 1984 was a subsidiary of Hillsdown Holdings Ltd, a food processing company, following the latter's acquisition of the FMC business.

Records: no records survive

570 GORING ESTATE & PROPERTY CO LTD

22 Sep 1887
25061
Sharrow Head, Sheffield, S Yorkshire S11 8FU
Property

History: incorporated in 1887 as Ecclesall Liberal Club Buildings Co Ltd to purchase freehold land on which to erect buildings for Ecclesall Liberal Association. Purchased land at junction of Ecclesall Road and Sheffield Moor with a frontage to Bridgefield Road, Sheffield, S Yorkshire. The Club Buildings, which opened in Jul 1888, consisted of shops on ground floor with club accommodation on the first and upper floors. Dwelling houses were also built on the land. The property was bombed during WW2. Changed name to above in 1971. In 1984 was subsidiary of Bradbury Construction Group Ltd.

Records: S Yorkshire County Record Office, Cultural Activities Centre, Ellin Street, Sheffield, S Yorkshire S1 4PL
directors and general meeting minutes 1887-date; share: prospectus 1887, issued list 1887, ledger 1887-1956; members register 1887-1935; annual returns 1888-1956; annual report and accounts 1889-1927; balance sheets and accounts 1929-36

571 BRISTOL OMNIBUS CO LTD

1 Oct 1887
25088
Berkeley House, Lawrence Hill, Bristol, Avon B55 0DZ
Bus operators

History: Bristol Tramways Co Ltd was incorporated in 1874 to lease and operate a tramway constructed by Bristol Corporation using 3 horse trams. Further routes were opened and business expanded rapidly. Company's directors launched Bristol Cab Co Ltd in 1886 and amalgamated it with older company in 1887 to form Bristol Tramways & Carriage Co Ltd. Electric tram services were introduced from 1897 and motor bus services from 1906. Constructed own bus bodies from 1907 opening purpose built works in 1913. Branches were opened in surrounding towns from 1909 and by 1914 regular services were operated from Bristol to as far as Cleeve, Oxfordshire; Thornbury and Newton St Loe, Avon; and Berkeley, Gloucestershire. Acquired Clifton Rock Railway in 1912 and purchased in 1928 a controlling interest in Greyhound Motors Ltd which was sold to Western National Omnibus Co Ltd in 1929. Acquired Bath Electric Tramways Co Ltd and Bath Tramways Motor Co Ltd in 1936, Cheltenham District Traction Co Ltd and Birmingham & Midland Motor Omnibus Co Ltd. Purchased tram services in Weston super Mare, Avon in 1937. Bristol Corporation purchased the city's tramways in 1937 and Bristol Joint Services, jointly owned by company and corporation, was established to run the system. Between 1938 and 1941 electric trams were replaced by buses. Under the Transport Act 1947, a controlling interest in the company was vested in British Transport Commission. Name changed to above in 1957 and company was transferred to National Bus Co in 1969.

Records: at Bristol Omnibus, Berkeley House, Lawrence Hill, Bristol, Avon B55 ODZ
board meeting minutes 1961-date; agm proceedings 1888-1942; share: ledgers 1887-1968, transfer summaries and certificates 1940-9, holding documents, papers and correspondence 1896-1936; debenture stock: trust deeds 1888-1908, registers 1890-1936, papers 1901-25, documents 1880,1949-53; dividend: warrants 1895-1952, accounts 1931-49; indemnity certificates 1940-50; annual returns 1940-69; memo and articles of association 1966; resolutions 1919-36; corporate agreements and papers 1886-1937; annual reports and accounts 1887-1958; group annual accounts and papers 1920-74; capital expenditure account: 1898-9, Tramways Department 1875-1937, Carriage Department 1886-1945, statements 1923-73, papers 1929-73; revenue and operating statements 1904-40; cost returns: 1954-67, country services 1940-50, permanent way 1914-39; ledgers: 1930-53, general 1934-58, bought 1943-51, Bristol 1939-52, Cheltenham, Gloucester and Swindon 1947-51, tours 1934-51; bought journal 1953-4; motor car repairs and sales journals 1940-51; deposit account book 1936-8; investment papers nd; financial papers 1947-70; Gloucester services: annual accounts 1935-9, cost returns 1936-62, ledgers 1936-54; bus and tram: takings record 1922-40, private charges c1910-18, service agreements 1891-1940, timetables 1882-1967, fare tables 1939-50, passes, tokens, tickets etc 1930s-60s, tour brochures c1895-c1962, supply and manufacture documents 1887-1946, traffic survey 1966, bus and rolling stock valuations 1929-48,1958; fleet and plant depreciation 1933-6; machinery schedule and details 1925-47; plant register 1947-8; vehicle registers 1956-66; stock sheets 1969-73; fleet lists 1922,1962-79; instruction books and by-laws 1900s-26; power station, transport, staff, premises, routes, outings photographs c1880-c1970; staff: register 1887-1901, rules, regulations and instructions 1885-1975, wage agreements 1948-

61, pay records 1954-70, badges, medals etc 1900s-50s, welfare papers 1922-50, dinner menus 1904,1918, strike log book 1901; superannuation fund: balance sheets 1899-1949, ledgers 1898-1963, cash books 1898-1952, pensions 1904-41; provident society and pension fund: rules 1905,1912, account statements 1903-11; house magazine 1962-72; mortgage registers 1888-1913; deeds and property registers to 1959,1970; property: cost record 1919-37, valuations 1947-64, deeds, leases, documents and papers 1829-1977, plans 1917-66; building contracts 1899,1910-11; Clifton Rock Railway correspondence 1928-39; motor bus driver diary 1908; works manager: diary 1898-1931, misc 1880-1923; newscuttings 1894-1967; company, vehicle and service history booklets, articles and notes 1950s-80s; insurance policies 1940s; legal papers 1880,1916

Bath Electric Tramways Co Ltd: general meeting: reports 1930-5, proceedings 1902-41; share transfer: certificates 1948-52, papers 1936-7; preference share: prospectus 1902, dividends 1941-6; annual returns 1940-65; memo and articles of association 1902-66; mortgage register 1902-67; annual reports and accounts 1904-58; annual accounts and papers 1937-50,1970-4; capital expenditure summaries and papers 1947-69; costs record 1904-19; ledgers: 1902-52, general 1927-35; journals 1902-61; cash books 1902-06,1933-53; timetables 1963; passes, tickets, warrants, badges etc c1965; offices, buses, premises, routes etc photographs c1900-50; rolling stock schedules 1958; transport agreements 1900-38; staff rules and regulations 1904; deeds and property register to 1959; light railways and tramways order book 1903-09

Bath Tramways Motor Co Ltd: share transfer: documents 1948-50, papers 1936-7, annual returns 1940-69; memo and articles of association 1929-66; vehicle and property sale agreement 1937; annual report and accounts 1936-58; annual accounts and papers 1937-50; capital expenditure: summaries 1947-66, records 1947-58; general ledgers 1920-58; journals 1920-61; cash books 1925-53; passes, warrants, tickets, vouchers, badges etc c1956; rolling stock schedules 1958; deeds register to 1959

Birmingham & Midland Motor Omnibus Co Ltd: directors meeting minutes 1904-55

Bristol Cab Co Ltd: share register and ledger 1886-7

Bristol Tramways Co Ltd: share ledgers 1875-87; annual reports and accounts 1876-87

Bristol Joint Services: annual accounts papers 1968-74; capital expenditure and assets records 1937-65; cost returns 1951-8

Cheltenham District Traction Co Ltd: share and share transfer certificates 1911-57; annual accounts: 1913-38, papers 1950,1970-4; capital expenditure: summaries 1948-69, records 1947-58; cost returns 1939-53; accounting records 1944 on; personal ledgers 1949-61; journals 1946-59; cash book 1951-4; sales day book 1946-50; timetables 1946-51; rolling stock schedules 1958; history 1973

Greyhound Motors Ltd: members register and share ledger 1921-32; share certificate book 1921-35; annual returns 1927-35; memo and articles of association 1921; debentures 1921,1928; sale and liquidation papers 1927-36; advertisements and sales correspondence 1922-6; staff service agreements 1927-38; property details and agreements, plant valuations and correspondence 1921-36

B Coope, *The People's Carriage 1874-1974* (priv pub 1974)

572 MORLAND & CO LTD

1 Oct 1887
25090
The Brewery, 40 Ock Street, Abingdon, Oxfordshire OX14 5DD
Brewing

History: traces its origins to John Morland, a maltster at West Ilsley, Berkshire. His son Benjamin inherited his business in 1726 and expanded into brewing. The business was run by successive generations of the Morland family. In 1854 it passed into the hands of EM Morland who, in 1861, purchased a second brewery, Eagle Brewery, at Abingdon, and shortly afterwards a third brewery, Abbey Brewery, in the same town. In 1887 the above was formed to acquire the business of Morland & Co. In 1889 a third Abingdon brewery, Saxby Brewery, was acquired, as well as the brewery of Field & Sons at Wallingford, Oxfordshire. In 1912 a new brewery was erected on the site of Eagle Brewery and all the other breweries were closed. Between the wars Wantage Brewery Co Ltd, Dymore Brown & Sons Ltd and H Hewitt & Co Ltd of Reading, Berkshire and Belcher & Habgood Ltd of Abingdon were acquired. By 1939 the company possessed 250 licensed houses in Berkshire, Hampshire, Surrey, Wiltshire, Gloucestershire, Oxfordshire and Buckinghamshire. In 1943 acquired Ferguson's Ltd, Reading, wine and spirit merchants.

Records: at Morland, The Brewery, 40 Ock Street, Abingdon, Oxfordshire OX14 5DD
directors meeting minutes 1887-1978; general meeting minutes 1888-1932; registers: directors holdings 1948-66, mortgages 1872-97, transfers 1946-59, dividend payments 1946-78; debenture stockholders lists c1944; reorganisation papers 1943-4; seal registers 1912-79; balance sheets 1938-50; ledgers: 1935-53, private 1888-1962, publicans 1913-16, general 1927-61, nominal 1939-52; private journal 1887-1926; cash book: 1961-8, private 1906-45, bank 1941-4; beer advertisements nd,c1915; price list nd; bought book 1928-53; hops purchased book 1947-55; Reading brewery stocks 1957-9; plant and machinery ledger 1953-66; tunroom photographs 1918; salary account 1894; time sheet analysis 1937-49; staff agreements 1892-1934; benevolent fund meeting minutes 1918-48; staff applications 1943-6; employees, drays, carnival, social club photographs c1880-1959; general repairs and estates committee meeting minutes 1940-64; property ledger 1913-46; premises schedule 1946-62; rent: account 1895-6, ledger 1914-51; repairs ledger 1936-60; Bear Hotel, Wantage: trading account, stock, day and cash books 1933-49; Crown Hotel, Benson: trading account 1937-46; Dundas Hotel: cash and day books 1933-44; Queens Hotel, Reading: balance sheets 1944-55; Salutation Hotel, Faringdon: trading accounts, cash book 1933-43; White Hart Hotel, Benson: trading accounts, cash and day books 1933-46; deeds, mortgages, indentures etc of premises in Oxfordshire and Berkshire 1560-1894; public house: inventory and valuations 1947-64, sale catalogues 1848-1959, tenancy agreements 1916-62; insurance papers and correspondence 1950-65; premises and tax correspondence and papers 1940-65; plans, drawings and photographs of brewery and public houses c1890-1977; G Morland letter book 1891-1906; correspondence 1921-53; Spenlove Abbey Brewery barley book 1790-1823; Brewers Society meeting minutes and correspondence 1933-49
Belcher & Habgood Ltd: directors and general meeting minutes 1898-1944; memo and articles of association 1898; annual report and accounts 1942-3
Dymore Brown & Sons Ltd: directors meeting minutes 1902-11; share transfers 1912-27; trust deed 1927; annual report and accounts 1939-52; balance sheets 1905-55; ledger: 1923-30,

private 1930-56; private account book 1926-31; monthly sales 1914-28; annual sales statements 1916-24; public house trade summary 1914-38; assignment of trade-marks 1944-5; wages book 1947-59; staff photographs c1890; rent ledger 1920-48; properties register 1930-52; public house: deeds and agreements, correspondence c1900-30, inventory and valuations 1916-54; letter book 1926-nd; correspondence: debentures, values, premises c1920-45
Ferguson's Ltd: directors: meeting minutes 1961-71, register c1910-61; general meeting minutes 1921-78; share: holders registers 1946-61, certificates 1941-63; seal register 1940-78; balance sheets 1939-49; ledger: private 1950-66, Chisletts 1953-67, Bicester 1963-6; cash book: 1915-68, private 1956-69; advertisements nd; wine lists 1964-7; plant inventory 1946-66; superannuation fund meeting minutes 1959-66; staff, offices photographs c1890-c1960
H Hewitt & Co Ltd: share transfers 1912-39; debenture certificates 1900; declaration of trust 1917-40; balance sheets 1927-37; private ledgers 1893-1911; H Hewitt accounts 1899-1911; cash increase summary 1885-1904; monthly sales 1914-28; weekly trade summary 1930-51; rents payable c1900
Hordeum Products Co: receipts 1934-51; trade-mark assignment certificates 1938-44; plant: schedule 1954-61, correspondence 1909-10
GF Palmer Ltd: directors and general meeting minutes 1929-56; share: ledger 1929-54, certificates 1929-45; memo and articles of association 1929-55; balance sheets 1929-55; ledger: private 1928-37, nominal 1937-44; cash book 1928-39; receipts 1943-55; order book 1940-6; goods inwards c1950-5; daybook 1934-43; premises correspondence 1946-52
Wantage Brewery Co Ltd: directors and general meeting minutes 1865-1940; private ledger 1920-30; cash book 1919-40; staff agreement 1936

573 WELSH COLD STORES LTD

10 Oct 1887
25126
Tresillian Terrace, Cardiff, S Glamorgan CF1 5RJ
Cold storage

History: incorporated in 1887 as Cardiff Pure Ice & Cold Storage Co Ltd to erect ice storage rooms and to establish ice manufacturing business of Joshua J Neale and Henry West, fish merchants of West Canal Wharf, Cardiff. Cold stores and ice making plant were set up in Tresillian Terrace, Cardiff, and by 1923 company had branch stores at West Bute Dock, Cardiff; Shaftesbury Street, Newport, Gwent; No 2 Dock, Barry, S Glamorgan; and Milford Haven, Dyfed. Name changed to above in 1961. Acquired in 1966 by Transport Development Group Ltd. In 1977 acted as cold store properties operating from original premises with stores at Cardiff and Barry, S Glamorgan; Newport, Gwent; and Swansea, W Glamorgan.

Records: at Transport Development Group, Kingsgate House, 66-74 Victoria Street, London SW1E 6SR
directors meeting: minutes 1900-68, agenda book 1946-63; general meeting minutes 1900-65; members register and share ledgers 1920-77; share transfer: register 1958-69, documents 1937-58; annual reports and accounts 1930-65; property papers: Tresillian Terrace 1963-76, Pentwyn 1967-76, Swansea 1969-71

574 CYCLISTS TOURING CLUB

19 Oct 1887
25185
Cottersell House, 69 Meadrow, Godalming, Surrey GU7 3HS
Cycling association

History: founded in 1878 by Stanley JA Cotterell (first hon secretary) and SH Ineson (first hon chairman) of Bradford Bicycle Club as Bicycle Touring Club at a meeting of 50 cyclists in Harrogate, N Yorkshire, to promote touring by bicycle, to help tourists secure companions and to protect members. Name changed to above in 1883 as tricycles grew in popularity. Membership rose from 142 in 1878 to 10,627 in 1883 and to 22,316 in 1886. From 1878 published *Monthly Circular* (*Monthly Circular and Gazette* from 1880) and from 1879 published annual *Handbook and Guide* which provided details of local information officers, hotels and repairers. Also produced guides, maps and road routes. Incorporated as above as a company limited by guarantee in 1887. Promoted touring abroad from 1880 and issued *Continental Handbook* from 1889. The 1895 membership of 60,449 was the highest ever but fell to 8546 in 1918 rising again in the 1920s. From 1910 had a royal patron. The club initiated national events, eg National Bicycle Week since 1923; National Rally, held at York from 1945; triennial veterans ride since 1928; and British Cycle Tourist Competition since 1952. Membership declined during WW2, rose again to post war peak of 53,574 in 1950, fell to 27,300 in 1959, to 18,727 in 1971, but by 1983 had risen to c30,000. Offices moved from Newcastle, Tyne & Wear 1879-81; to Bradford, W Yorkshire 1881-3; 139-140 Fleet Street, London 1883-96; 47 Victoria Street, London 1896-1910; 280 Euston Road, London 1910-27. The freehold of 3 Craven Hill, Paddington, London was then purchased for use as head offices until 1966 when the club moved to Godalming. First district association (Northumberland & Durham) was set up in 1894 and by 1899 there were 14, rising to 20 by 1918. In 1980 there were 50, helping club members at local level. In 1983 the club offered members a wide variety of services and publications and its aims were promoting and assisting the use of cycles on public roads and rights of way.

Records: at Cyclists Touring Club, Cottersell House, 69 Meadrow, Godalming, Surrey GU7 3HS
council meeting: minutes 1879-date, reports 1879-1958, attendance books 1883-1979; committee meeting minutes: finance 1900-53, rights and privileges 1900-66, general purposes 1920-66, district associations 1899-1966, hotels 1908-15, youth rally organisation 1953-78, tenth triennial veteran ride 1955-6, joint standing on cycling 1961-8; committee attendance books 1948-66; conference on road users minutes and attendance book 1913; inquiry committee minutes and papers 1907-08; council members list 1878-1907; membership books and lists 1880s-1969; general meeting: minutes 1888-date, papers 1965-73; annual reports and accounts 1884-1958; district association reports c1906-18; memo and articles of association 1887-date; legal papers 1906; repairers contracts 1890s-1900s; contract hotel lists 1890s-1910s; appointment sign agreements and correspondence 1900s-20s, 1950-9; danger, caution sign lists 1890s-1900s; administrative correspondence and papers 1933-75; investment ledger 1915-30; petty cash book 1927-30; CTC publications 1879-date; posters, advertisements and publicity material 1878-date; letter book 1919-20; Cotterell and others correspondence 1878-1931; legal papers and solicitors costs and correspondence 1888-1900s; staff agreements 1900s-20s; press cuttings re cycling, other outdoor activities, CTC personalities, rallies, competitions 1890s-

1962; photographs, glass slides and negatives of views, 75th anniversary, activities, bicycles 20 cent; uniform rules and regulations 1878-80; consul certificate, members tickets and application forms 19-20 cent; lecture notebooks and scripts 19 cent; history notes, articles etc 1910s-40s; Rose & Crown visitors books 1880-1912

William Oakley, *Winged Wheel. The History of the First Hundred Years of the Cyclists Touring Club* (1977)

575 STUART'S GRANOLITHIC CO LTD

3 Nov 1887
25270
Stuart House, Church Hill, Coleshill, Warwickshire B46 3AF
Concrete flooring

History: founded in Peterhead, Grampian in 1840 and incorporated in 1887 in London as Stuart's Granolithic Paving Co Ltd. Head offices were at Church Row, Limehouse, E London with other premises at Regent's Canal Docks, Commercial Road moving to Regent's Dock, Limehouse in 1896 and to Granolithic Works, Glengall Road, Millwall between 1900-02. Name changed to Stuart's Granolithic Stone Co Ltd in 1895-6 and to above in 1909-10, 'granolithic' being concrete made with crushed granite. Had offices at various addresses in the City of London from 1910 and branches at various times in Belfast, N Ireland; Birmingham, W Midlands; Dundee, Tayside; Edinburgh, Lothian; Exeter, Devon; Glasgow, Strathclyde; Liverpool, Merseyside; Manchester and Stockport, Greater Manchester. Head offices moved to Harrow, Greater London in 1958 and Coleshill, Warwickshire in 1964. In 1982 had branches at Harrow and Edinburgh. Originally specialised in plaster-work, flooring and reinforced concrete; North British Hotel and Jenners' store in Edinburgh being 2 examples of c1900. In 1982 concentrated on industrial flooring and acted as stone restoration specialists and reinforced concrete consultants and constructors.

Records (1): at Stuart's Granolithic, Stuart House, Church Hill, Coleshill, Warwickshire B46 3AF
directors and general meeting minutes 1888-date; annual reports and accounts 1888-date; souvenir brochures illustrating projects in Scotland and England 1901-02

Records (2): at Stuart's Granolithic, 46 Duff Street, Edinburgh, Lothian EHII 2HP
photographs of projects c1925-35; souvenir brochure illustrating same 1901

576 LENAGRANGE LTD

11 Nov 1887
25315
Windsor House, Temple Row, Birmingham, W Midlands B2 5LD
Carpet manufacturers

History: incorporated in 1887 as Childema Carpet Co Ltd to purchase and extend carpet manufacturing business of Henry Fawcett, trading as Henry Fawcett & Co at Green Street, Kidderminster, Hereford & Worcester. Registered offices moved to Foley Park Works, Beauchamp Avenue, Kidderminster in 1971. By 1974 it was a holding company manufacturing carpets with one subsidiary, Empire Carpet Co Ltd. In 1977 the company employed 224 people. Name changed to above in Dec 1979 and went into liquidation on 23 Jan 1980.

Records: none survive

577 COLEMAN & CO LTD

16 Nov 1887
25342
Carrow, Norwich, Norfolk NR1 2DD
Sauce manufacturers

History: established in 1881 by William Coleman, chemist, druggist and wine merchant, of St George's Middle Street, Norwich, Norfolk. Incorporated as above in 1887 to carry on business of manufacturing and selling 'Coleman's Liebig's Extract of Meat & Malt Wine', later sold as 'Wincarnis'. By 1906 was operating from 101-107 Westwick Street, Norwich. Employed about 400 people in 1923. Acquired by Reckitt & Colman Ltd in 1968 and from c1975 business was one of importing mainly in bulk, bottling and distributing wines.

Records: at Colman's of Norwich, Carrow, Norwich, Norfolk NR1 2DD
board meeting minutes 1887-date; share register 1956-date; directors register 1949-date; documents register 1890-date; account books 1899 on; price lists 1932; advertisements and sales literature 1932-68; product, staff and premises photographs 1950-68

578 WHITBREAD DEVON LTD

17 Nov 1887
25346
Monson Avenue, Cheltenham, Gloucestershire
Brewing

History: incorporated in 1887 as Starkey, Knight & Co Ltd on amalgamation of the brewing businesses of Thomas Starkey, Taunton Brewery, and North Petherton Brewery, Bridgwater, Somerset (est 1845) and George and Henry Knight, Northgate Brewery, High Street, Bridgwater (est 1840). Amalgamated with Thomas Ford & Son, Fore Street, Tiverton, Devon (est 1852) in 1895 to form Starkey, Knight & Ford Ltd. Acquired Arnold, Perrett & Co Ltd, Paignton and Barnstaple Breweries, Devon (est 1884 and 1851) in 1897; Furze & Co Ltd (inc 1903); Uffculme Brewery, Devon in 1918; Hanbury & Cotching, Cannon Street Brewery, Taunton, Somerset (est c1877) in 1923; and Holt Brothers Ltd, Burnham on Sea, Somerset (est 1770) in 1954. Acquired by Whitbread & Co Ltd in 1961 at which time controlled 400 tied houses. During early 1970s changed name to above.

Records: at Whitbread Devon, Monson Avenue, Cheltenham, Gloucestershire
directors: meeting minutes 1914-69, committee meeting minutes 1967-9; members register 1887-1913; share transfer register 1915-50; annual lists and summaries 1901-47; seal book 1960-72; purchase agreement 1897; private ledgers 1855-1964; purchase ledgers 1887-1960; beer stocks and sales ledgers 1952-62; private journal 1957-63; purchase journals 1937-53; cash: journal 1964-6, book 1965-6; gross profit accounts book 1920-61; wages books 1915-59;

rent: payable book 1927-54, ledger 1955-67, journal 1955-66, receivable book 1933-66; repairs ledger 1923-40

579 LONGWOOD FINISHING CO LTD

22 Nov 1887
25370
Parkwood Mills, Longwood, Huddersfield, W Yorkshire HD3 4TR
Textile finishers

History: incorporated in 1887 as Parkwood Mills Finishing Co Ltd to operate as woollen scourers, millers, dyers, finishers and London shrinkers. Formed by John Broadbent & Son, (est c1796) woollen cloth manufacturers Parkwood Mills, Longwood, Huddersfield, W Yorkshire. Name changed to above in 1895.

Records (1): at Brotherton Library, University of Leeds, W Yorkshire LS2 9JT
directors meeting minutes 1887-1923; general meeting minutes 1900-23; balance sheets, directors reports and agm papers 1901-19; memo and articles of association 1887; balance book 1896-1901; private ledgers and mill cash book 1887-95; private ledger 1889-98; journals 1905-18; wages books 1896-1911

Records (2): at Kirklees Libraries & Museums Service, Central Library, Princess Alexandra Walk, Huddersfield, W Yorkshire HD1 2SU
directors: and general meeting minutes 1923-53, register 1946-66; share certificate registers 1920-39; annual returns 1946-66; balance books 1902-47; balance sheet and accounts 1947-8; private ledgers 1898-1964; nominal ledgers 1923-56; cash books 1923-71; expenditure analysis books 1957-65; wages books 1911-60; reports: dyehouse operation 1967-8, costs 1973-5; inventories and valuations of plant and machinery 1916-68

580 BRITISH AUTOMATIC CO LTD

25 Nov 1887
25389
7 Hanover Square, London W1R 0PS
Automatic machines

History: founded in 1886 by Hore & Frampton who installed wooden automatic machine 'chocolate boxes' on railway stations in and around London with 452 installed in the first 9 months. Incorporated in 1887 as Sweetmeat Automatic Delivery Co Ltd. By 1903 the chairman was George A Touche, founder of the accounting firm of the same name. Moved offices from 52 Southwark Street, London to 14 Appold Street, London around 1904, and also owned chocolate factory of Reeves Ltd in Barrowfield Street, Bridgeton, Glasgow. Name changed to above in 1909 and was taken over by Associated Automatic Machine Corporation Ltd in 1929 which subsequently centred its activities in Appold Street. By late 1920s began to install weighing machines in various sites eg chemists, chain stores etc. Cie Belge des Automatiques SA, its subsidiary, operated 800 such machines in Belgium. From early 1930s penny amusement machines began to be installed at holiday resorts and other sites. By 1938 had nearly 50,000 machines of all types in operation. In 1945 purchased James Maxwell & Son Ltd, Scottish retail confectioner and tobacconist with a chain of 60 shops. By 1950 owned over

70 confectionery and tobacconists shops and kiosks in London, Manchester, Greater Manchester and south Scotland. In 1951 main works were at Collier Street, Greengate, Salford, Greater Manchester, with a sub-office at 3 Adrian Street, Blackpool, Lancashire, branch offices at 181 Kingsland Road, Bristol, Avon, and 36A North Great George's Street, Dublin, Eire, with a sub-office at GNR Yard, Glengall Street, Belfast, N Ireland. Associated Automatic Machine Corporation Ltd changed its name to Trust Houses Forte Leisure Ltd in 1970 and to Trusthouse Forte Leisure Ltd in 1979. Company is a subsidiary of Trusthouse Forte Ltd through the latter.

Records: at Trusthouse Forte Leisure, 17 Golden Square, London W1R 3AG
general meeting minutes 1903-date; annual report and accounts 1929-45; press cuttings 1929-50; vending machine illustrations 1950-6
London Automatic Machine Co Ltd: directors meeting minutes and reports 1954,1956; general meeting minutes 1935-date
Trusthouse Forte Leisure Ltd: directors and transfer committee minutes 1929-date; general meeting minutes 1950-date; annual report and accounts 1950-63

581 WHITBREAD WESSEX LTD

14 Dec 1887
25502
7 Admiralty Road, Portsmouth, Hampshire
Brewing

History: established by Mew family in early 17 cent at Newport, Isle of Wight. By end of 18 cent Mew & Co also owned breweries at Lymington, Hampshire. Had a large army canteen trade and branches at Aldershot in Hampshire, London, Malta, India and China. During 19 cent William Langton became a partner of Mew Brothers. Granted royal warrant to supply Queen Victoria at Osborne, Isle of Wight in 1850. Incorporated as WB Mew, Langton & Co Ltd in 1887. Built new malt-house at Royal Brewery, Crocker Street, Newport in 1898 and began manufacture of mineral water. Acquired William Stephens, Solent Brewery, Lymington, Hampshire in 1887; CJ Dashwood, Carisbrooke Brewery, Newport (est c1877) in 1910; and HC&W Sweetman, George Street Brewery, Ryde, Isle of Wight (est 1848) in 1920. Added tobacconist's business in 1931. Acquired in 1965 by Strong & Co of Romsey Ltd (est c1778), Romsey, Hampshire which was acquired by Whitbread & Co Ltd in 1968. Subsequently changed name to above.

Records (1): at Whitbread, Romsey, Hampshire
directors meeting minutes 1887-1930; share: ledger 1888-1937, transfer register 1948-66; probate register 1945-67; annual report and accounts 1961,1966; mainland properties lease 1966

Records (2): at Isle of Wight County Record Office, 26 Hillside, Newport, Isle of Wight PO30 2EB
records 20 cent

582 BODDINGTONS' BREWERIES LTD

15 Dec 1887
25516
Strangeways Brewery, Manchester, Greater Manchester M60 3EL
Brewing

History: traces its origins to 1778 when Caister & Fry was formed to establish a brewing business at Strangeways, Manchester. The business was known as Hole & Harrison in 1835 and in 1842 as John Harrison & Co. In 1848 Henry Boddington, who had worked in the brewery since the 1830s, was admitted as a partner and in 1853 he became sole proprietor. Boddington's family have continued to run the business ever since. By the early 1860s output reached almost 17,000 barrels per annum, rising to 50,000 in 1874 and to almost 94,000 in 1876 when it was Manchester's largest brewery. In 1874 Bridge Brewery, Burton upon Trent, Staffordshire, was acquired (sold 1912) and in the 1880s Strangeways Brewery was rebuilt. The business was acquired by Henry Boddington & Co Ltd, a private company, incorporated in the early 1880s, with a nominal share capital of £200,000. Reconstructed as above in 1887. In 1907 it acquired Isle of Man Brewery, subsequently reconstructed as Boddingtons' Brewery (Isle of Man) Ltd, and later acquired Hull's Brewery at Preston, Lancashire. By 1914 assets exceeded £1 million for the first time. Strangeways Brewery was extended and modernised between the wars but destroyed by bombing in 1940. In 1962 Richard Clarke & Co Ltd, brewers at Stockport, Greater Manchester, was acquired and in 1971 the public houses and off licences of JG Swales & Co, of Levenshulme, Greater Manchester were purchased.

Records (1): at Boddingtons' Breweries, Strangeways Brewery, Manchester, Greater Manchester M60 3EL
directors and general meeting minutes 1883-1977; share: ledger 1883-6, register 1910-22, and debenture certificates 1883-1955; dividends register 1895-6; annual returns 1933-8; memo and articles of association 1883-1922; directors agreement 1887; annual report and accounts 1890-1902; balance sheets 1880-1963; ledgers: private 1867-1920, general 1870-4, impersonal 1871-95; cash book: 1947-64, private 1887-1914; investment society: ledger 1873-94, cash book 1873-1915; production memo books 1851-77; brewers summary 1862-80; sales record 1873-86; trade summary 1874-86; gratuities appeal papers 1919; salary books 1873-1914; registers: employees 1863-1911, family trade 1887-1902, injuries 1895-1938; job applications 1880-1958; registers: property 1888-1970, deeds nd; public houses log books 1902-1950; tenancies: assignment 1888, transfers 1888-1956; loans book 1892; mortgages and assignments 1849-1946; brewery photographs c1935; coat of arms grant 1890; smoke summaries 1901-38; history articles 1926-c40

Records (2): at Oldham Brewery, Albion Brewery, Coldhurst Street, Oldham, Greater Manchester
Oldham Brewery Co Ltd: directors and general meeting minutes 1873-date; share: registers 1873 on, certificates, transfers etc c1890 on; dividend: book 1873-88, and loan summary book 1899-1959; annual report and accounts c1890 on; ledger: balances 1893-1913, impersonal payments 1894-1956, impersonal receipts 1896-1968, sales balances 1936-70, sales 1903-10, sundry sales 1901-20, inward trade 1904-30, loan 1873-1962, public house 1936-45, wine and spirit 1936-47; journal: 1889-96, accounts 1929-64, cash 1902-71; outstanding accounts 1953-61; cash book: 1878-1966, rough 1931-6, accounts passed 1910-14; bank book 1913-37; loan withdrawals 1873-6; bank summary 1885-90; tax paid 1896-1903; summary: sales book 1899-

1959, bottle sales 1926-73, barrel sales 1959-62, barrels tied trade 1926-65, bottles tied trade 1936-64, mineral department weekly 1938-77; bottled sales credit book 1939-77; bottling department sales and returns 1938-40; returns book 1874-1972; table water entry book 1937-43; cask order book 1934-7; purchase book 1904-14; stock book 1918-58; inward goods: mineral department 1933-43, brewery 1947-59; day book 1933-4; bottling: record 1940-2, department returns 1956-7; wages books: 1951-73, mineral department 1935-44; employees insurance register 1912-75; rent: book 1895-1901, ledger 1898-1975, chief rents payable 1900-55; ledgers: repairs 1922-59, rates and taxes 1903-52; public house inventories and valuations c1900 on

Michael Jacobson, *200 Years of Beer. The Story of Boddingtons' Strangeways Brewery 1778-1978* (priv pub 1978)

583 TRUSTEES CORPORATION LTD

16 Dec 1887
25526
Mermaid House, 2 Puddle Dock, London EC4V 3AT
Investment trust

History: incorporated in 1887 as Trustees, Executors & Securities Insurance Corporation Ltd to act as trustees, agents, executors and administrators and to undertake the safe custody of securities deposited with the corporation, to undertake the issue of foreign, colonial and municipal loans and to manage private financial affairs. Changed name to above in 1917. Trustee department operated until 1978 when principal business became that of an investment trust. Changed name to TR Trustees Corporation PLC in 1982. Managed by Touche Remnant & Co.

Records: Touche Remnant, Mermaid House, 2 Puddle Dock, London EC4V 3AT
board meeting minutes 1887-date; committee meeting minutes: 1887-8, general purposes and finance 1888-94, standing with agendas 1888-93, trustee 1889-94, rebuilding 1903-04, transfer 1905-44; general meeting: minutes 1888-date, proceedings 1889-1904,1965-71; annual reports and accounts 1904-date; share ledgers 1954-68; corporate documents and papers 1887-1955; share papers and correspondence 1900-71; debenture stock: trust deed 1894, holders register 1954-62, papers and correspondence 1946-72; balance sheets and accounts 1888-97; general ledgers 1888-1974; journals 1937-79; cash books 1898-1904,1933-78; investment: and loan ledgers 1895-1975, valuations 1972-8, documents, papers and correspondence 1890-1970s; private trust fund ledger 1922-5; securities and trust deeds list 1894-5; Winchester House safe deposit: rent books 1888-1933, probate books 1888-1965, property vault registers 1888-1964, access books 1943-64, application registers 1888-1964, lease registers c1915-64, securities register 1956-62, leases c1922-55, property and safe return register 1954-65, documents register 1937-75, rent receipt books 1954-64, letter books 1961-4, papers and correspondence 1889-1965; staff pension fund: register 1952-5, ledgers 1913-55, investment ledger 1938-55, cash books and journal 1913-55; trustee department: deeds schedules 1894-1954, purchases and sales book 1964-78; estates cash book 1925-8; house department: cash books 1946-65, rent roll 1948-58, wages book 1958; correspondence 1958-70s; agreements trust deeds, leases 1892-1952

584 3M(NSPS) LTD

23 Dec 1887
25562
3M House, PO Box 1, Bracknell, Berkshire RG12 1JU
Advertising

History: incorporated in 1887 as Broomfield & Co Ltd to acquire business of Broomfield & Son, advertising contractors, who published and printed billposters throughout the Potteries. Name changed to North Staffordshire Billposting Co Ltd in 1890, to Stoke on Trent & North Staffordshire Bill Posting Co Ltd in 1910, to North Staffs Poster Services Ltd in 1955, and to NSPS Ltd in 1971. Acquired by 3M United Kingdom Ltd in 1973 and in 1975 company was manufacturing signs and emblems. Name changed to above in 1976 and ceased to trade in 1977.

Records: at 3M United Kingdom, 3M House, PO Box 1, Bracknell, Berkshire RG12 1JU
directors and general meeting minutes 1964-date; members register 1964-date

585 BATH & PORTLAND GROUP LTD

27 Dec 1887
25579
20 Manvers Street, Bath, Avon BA1 1LX
Stone quarry

History: incorporated in 1887 as Bath Stone Firms Ltd, to acquire 7 Bath stone quarrying businesses in the district of Bath, Avon. The businesses were Corsham Bath Stone Co Ltd; RJ Marsh & Co Ltd; Samuel Row Noble; Pictor & Sons; Stone Brothers Ltd; Isaac Sumsion; and Randell Saunders & Co Ltd. The company's objects were to quarry and deal in stone, lime, cement, bricks and terracotta. Quickly expanded into the Portland stone business by acquiring quarry lands and quarrying businesses in the Portland area of Dorset. In 1898 acquired an interest in John Pearce Portland Stone Co Ltd (totally amalgamated in 1948) and in 1900 acquired Stewards & Co Ltd, an old established business which had supplied stone for the building of St Paul's Cathedral, London. In 1904 purchased the assets of Easton Stone Saw Mills Co Ltd of Portland. In 1909 extended its Bath stone business through the acquisition of Marsh Son & Gibbs Ltd. By 1911 was a leading supplier of Bath and Portland stone when its name was changed to Bath & Portland Stone Firms Ltd. In 1927 Manu Marble Co Ltd of Gloucester, Gloucestershire, manufacturers of imitation marble, was acquired (assets disposed of in 1943). In 1929 the assets of Elm Park & Corsham Down Bath Stone Co Ltd were purchased, followed in 1935 by those of Ham Hill & Doulting Stone Co Ltd. In 1960 South Western Stone Co Ltd, a major competitor, was acquired, when company's name was changed to above. The London buildings for which it supplied stone in the 1920s and 1930s included Lloyds Bank head office, Daily Telegraph building, Broadcasting House, Thames House and Cunard House.

Records: at Wansdyke Security, Neston, Corsham, Wiltshire SN13 9TL
board meeting minutes 1887-1964; share ledgers 1887 on

Norman Bezzant, *Out of the Rock* (1980)

586 HALL & SONS LTD

30 Dec 1887
25594
1 Welbeck Street, London W1A 1DF
Footwear

History: incorporated in 1887 as above to carry on boot and shoe making business of Matthew Hall & Sons of 57 Bishopsgate Street, London. Also had premises off the Strand, London and a shop at 5 Stoke Newington Road, London. Continued to lease various shop properties in the City and West End until it was acquired by Debenhams Ltd in 1974. Ceased to trade in 1975.

Records: at Debenhams, 1 Welbeck Street, London W1A 1DF
directors and general meeting minutes 1926-74; share certificate book nd; annual reports and accounts 1926-34

587 NORTH COUNTRY BREWERIES LTD

9 Jan 1888
25647
The Brewery, Silvester Street, Hull, Humberside HU1 3HT
Brewing

History: John Ward founded a brewery in Dagger Lane, Hull, Humberside in 1765. The business was continued by his sons Thomas and John and in 1826 Robert Gleadow, the latter's son in law, acquired the brewery. He was succeeded by his son, Robert Ward Gleadow in conjunction with TW Dibb who owned a brewery in Mill Street, Hull which was subsequently closed. The brewery moved to a larger site in Silvester Street in 1868. The business was incorporated in 1888 as Hull Brewery Co Ltd. Acquired brewing business of Martin Cross and wine and spirit business and licensed houses of Hy Willford & McBride in 1888; Robert Hunt Breweries in 1889; Moffat Breweries and brewery and bottled beer business of John Tate of Hull in 1896; H&JG Smithson's Brewery, Hull in 1901; brewery and licensed houses of Glossop & Bulay Ltd, Hull and Robert Stephenson & Son, Beverley, Humberside; wine and spirit business of Brodrick & Peter, Hull and Sutton Beam & Co Ltd, Brigg, Humberside with 17 licensed houses in 1925; wine and spirit merchants, Lamberts, Parkers & Gaines (Hull) Ltd (est 1740) in 1941; Southerns (Hull) Ltd in 1945; and brewery and licensed houses of Hartley's Brewery Co, Cowick, Humberside in 1957. Acquired by Northern Foods Ltd in 1972 and name changed to above in 1974 to reflect expansion of trading area. By 1981 had about 250 tied houses in Humberside, Lincolnshire, Nottinghamshire and Yorkshire.

Records (1): at North Country Breweries, The Brewery, Silvester Street, Hull, Humberside HU1 3HT
directors meeting: minutes 1888-date, agendas 1888-1964, attendance books 1888-1942; general meeting: minutes 1880-date, agendas 1884-1964, chairmans speeches 1934-53; share and debenture: application and allotment books 1888-1917, documents 1897-1917; memo and articles of association 1924; papers and correspondence 1888-1919; annual reports and accounts 1895-1905, 1941-2; bank book 1935-49; solicitors bills 1867-87; sales and advertising agreements 1917-41; beer price correspondence 1931; brewing: book 1895, costs and sales statements 1895-1902; RW Gleadow brew memo book 1888; brewery stock book 1897-1926; malt statements 1928-49; hop book 1940; purchase and excise duty books 1910-15; duty diary

1922-49; production: licenses 1859, process photographs c1920; public house: leases 1870,1883, plans 1882 on, photographs 1900 on; title deeds registers 1914-32; property: lists 1935-7, agreements, leases, papers and related correspondence 1882-1956; brewery plans 1889; history articles 1924,1965
Hull Federated Bottlers Association: committee meeting minutes 1900-33

Records (2): at Hull City Record Office, 79 Lowgate, Hull, Humberside HU1 2AA
debenture stock papers 1891 on; annual reports and accounts 1938-42; annual accounts 1888-1954; ledgers 1923-71; financial: resume 1888-1921, correspondence 1893-1900; brewery commissions 1890-1903; bottling department: accounts 1890-1900,1906, stock book 1912-64; staff superannuation fund: committee and general meeting minutes 1901-30, cash book 1903-44, rates 1901-30, membership applications 1901-07; pension fund accounts 1902-64; licence application and renewal papers 1891-2; property: revaluation schedules 1890,1897, list 1941

588 BASS HOLDINGS LTD

13 Jan 1888
25675
High Street, Burton upon Trent, Staffordshire
Brewing

History: traces its origins to William Bass who established a brewing business at Burton upon Trent, Staffordshire, in 1777. By 1800 the business was producing 2000 barrels of beer per annum and after 1821 did a large export trade, especially to India. Michael Bass gained control of the business in 1827 when it was producing 9700 barrels a year. By 1837 it was known as Bass, Ratcliff & Gretton when output reached 31,500 barrels. Stimulated by the development of railways, a national trade in Burton ales was established. Output grew from 140,000 barrels in 1852 to 600,000 barrels in the 1860s, to 900,000 barrels in 1876 when it was the largest brewing business in Britain. Until the 1860s it did not own public houses, and thereafter owned relatively few; concentrating on supplying other breweries and the free trade. Incorporated in 1888 as Bass, Ratcliff & Gretton Ltd with a share capital of £2.7 million. Output exceeded 1 million barrels per annum in 1891 and reached 1.35 million barrels in 1920 but thereafter fell off. In 1926 merged with its chief competitor, Worthington & Co Ltd of Burton upon Trent, but the two continued to operate as separate businesses. In the 1950s acquired other breweries including Wilson & Walker Ltd, Wenlock Brewery Co Ltd, William Hancock & Co Ltd and Hewitt Brothers Ltd of Grimsby, Humberside. In 1961 merged with Mitchells & Butlers Ltd of Birmingham to form a new company, Bass, Mitchells & Butlers Ltd. In the 1960s the new business acquired Sidney Fussell & Sons Ltd of Rode, Somerset; Hunt, Edmunds & Co Ltd of Banbury, Oxfordshire and Bents Brewery & Co Ltd of Liverpool, Merseyside. In 1967 it merged with Charrington United Breweries Ltd of London. By 1980s Bass, Ratcliff & Gretton Ltd had been renamed the above and was a subsidiary of Bass Investments Ltd.

Records (1): at Bass, 137 High Street, Burton upon Trent, Staffordshire DE14 1JZ
partnership meeting minutes and correspondence 1869-79; directors: meeting minutes 1886-1954, agenda 1929-60, conference minutes 1948-54, registers 1901-64; managers committee meeting minutes 1949-50; agm programmes 1950-1; share: ledgers 1888-1948, certificates 1888-1901, papers 1933-59; debenture stock: registers 1940-50s, deed schedules 1888,1913, prospectuses 1897, ledgers 1888-1963, journals 1898-1916, trust deeds 1927,1942, transfer registers 1929-65, holders registers 1890,1915; annual lists and summaries 1880-6,1961; memo

and articles of association 1888-1958; corporate papers 1880 on; probate etc registers 1883-1967; merger agreements and papers 1926-37,1970-1; seal registers 1931-65; annual reports and accounts 1949-62; balance: books and ledgers 1836,1843-57, sheets and accounts 1843-1967; accounts: group 1953-65, agencies 1901-15, statistics 1901-07; ledgers: 1918-25,1952-8, customer 1810-13,1953-60, private 1841-50,1893-1964, purchase 1876-97,1920-38, continental 1928-38, sales 1957-62, loans 1887-1915,1927-8, output 1952-7, ale and porter 1805-07,1826-30, analysis book 1961-3; journals: private 1924-44, daily 1962-3; account book: 1744-56, general 1791-1805; cash books: 1821-9,1956-64, cask 1783-91; bank pass books 1881-1938; taxation papers and correspondence 1920s-67; financial papers 1920-70; day books: 1760-70, ale 1797-1807; ale sales and costs 1914-16; agency: sales comparisons 1881-1954, Birmingham terms book 1929, Hull terms book c1929-34, Cambridge terms book 1931-6, Plymouth staff register 1914-19, loan account 1914-46, travelling expenses 1925-33, leases 1916-20, cash book 1948-63; trade: tied book 1875-1924, town book 1917-23; sales summary 1927-8; order books 1790,1941-55,1968-9; bottle beer prices book 1921-53; price list c1950; trade-mark: agreements 1838-1939, registration particulars 1855-90, legal papers 1901-36; sales booklets 1880-c1964; plant: account book 1919-68, utensil inventories 1860,1866; machinery plans 1866-c1920; chief engineer reports 1928-44; equipment and raw materials account book c1900-19; joiners department goods received book 1926-37; cooperage and sawmills journal 1931-3; warehouse clearance book 1960-6; stock books: allowance house 1894-1966, carpenters and joiners 1923-8, electric, cooperage and stave yard 1965-70, loco department 1876-83,1949-67, plate layers railway 1919-60, harness rooms 1921-33, horse 1934; railway dispatch register 1889-1909; carriage journal 1919-26; Bass railways photographs 1881-1926; stable department purchase invoice book nd; Shire horse photographs nd; Burton brewers: meeting minutes 1909-10, and workers union meeting minutes 1914-19; production committee meeting minutes 1961-4; group quality control committee meeting minutes 1968-9; production: and duty book 1937-9, record 1962-9; brewing: comparative statements 1901-19, summaries 1967-8, journals 1802-03,1874-5,1959-70, books 1930-68, notebook 1892-4, notes 1922-6,1945-55, room diary 1926, process photographs 1907,1960s; experimental brewings: journals 1919-21,1947-69, record c1907-60, report books nd, notes 1879-81, cellar samplings 1952-66; forced beers book 1877-8,1881; gyle: book 1965-7, and brew analysis 1966; gravity record books 1896-1966; water: analysis books 1886-1954, well depth 1929-37; couch book 1879-80; malt: analysis 1905-45, book 1930 on, and maize supply 1937-71; hops: received memo 1812-73,1897-9, books 1906-82, brew quantities 1924-36; wort book 1966-8; blend: books 1898-9,1910-13, quality book 1937-8; stock books: brewery 1860-1,1939-73, spirits 1876-99, industrial spirits 1940-54, beer 1955-65; cask: department directory 1867, ownership opinion 1879-98, taken out book 1924, memo books 1924-c30, dimensions c1954, books 1962-70, sketch nd, production photographs c1950; laboratory reports, papers, notes and correspondence 1880-1970; journals and publications 1877-1979; service agreements 1939-56; time books 1877-1900; wages books 1886-1964; salaries cash books 1918-24; employee: lists 1849-1967, registers 1873-1970; pension fund papers 1962-72; disabled persons circulars 1921-52; accident report books and forms 1897-72; staff: correspondence 1919-64, excursion brochures 1893-1913, photographs 1870-1926, regulations 1916-37; fire brigade call book 1917-23,1953-69; Bass Worthington clubs - bowls: agm reports 1935-41, cash book 1930-55, papers 1934-53; cricket: general and committee meeting minutes 1912-32, scoring books, rules fixtures etc 1865-1974; netball: committee meeting minutes 1949-51; football: fixture papers and correspondence 1940-53; lawn tennis: committee and members lists 1940-53, expenses book 1934-55, and requisition book 1947-55; Bass social club: committee meeting minutes 1867-1966, rule book 1946, visitors books 1939-57, suggestion book 1952, journal 1934-66, expenses abstract 1923-45, cash books 1915-62; letter books 1782-1904; brewery premises: plans 1859-1976, descriptions 1889, particulars 1933-59, deeds 1815-82, rent ledger 1952-63; public house: deeds, papers and correspondence 1850-1970s, securities register 1890-1930, photographs c1900-70s; newscuttings and advertisements 1870-1970s; labels 1870-1909; information books 1916-37; brewery visit papers 1902-63; visitors books 1902-68; William Bass will 1787; complaints book 1960-1; subsidiary companies misc records 1860-1960

Diver & Son Ltd: accounts 1959; loans book 1938-9; staff promissory notes 1939-64; property documents and papers 1931-58

Duncan & Daglish Ltd: balance sheet and accounts 1958-9

James Eadie Ltd: directors and general meeting minutes 1893-1935; agm programmes 1950-1; share: ledgers and registers 1896-1965, papers 1933-43; debenture stock: allotment book 1896, holders register 1896, ledgers 1896-1931, registers 1940-50s; directors register 1901-64; annual returns 1958-66; memo and articles of association 1896; seals register 1898-1933; probate registers 1896-1966; annual reports and accounts 1942-64; balance sheets and accounts 1929-41; accounts: annual 1954-66, agm 1951-66, analysis 1955-66, management 1953,1967; private ledgers 1896-66; tax papers 1951-65; spirit ledgers 1878-89,1910-17; supplies ledger 1952-8; blends record 1941; sales ledger 1958; salaries and wages particulars 1940; property: deeds and papers 1850-1968, plans 1930s; mortgage register 1893-1933; deeds register 1908-33; licensed house photographs nd

John Joule & Sons Ltd: takeover papers 1970-1; brewery inventory and valuation 1899; public house photographs 1920 on

Thomas Salt & Sons Ltd: Albion Brewery Ltd deeds, agreements and conveyancing papers 1878-1908; trade-marks 1927-33

Wenlock Brewery Co Ltd: memo and articles of association 1919; debenture stock trust deeds 1896-1931; annual reports and accounts 1952; licensed houses list 1936

Henry Wilson & Son Ltd: minutes: 1894-1920, directors meeting 1930-69; accounts 1959; salaries and wages particulars 1939-59; staff correspondence 1945-61; property deeds and papers 1897-1919

Worthington & Co Ltd: (See summary no 655)

Bass, Mitchells & Butlers Ltd: shareholders correspondence 1969-70; memo and articles of association 1961; annual reports and accounts 1962-3; sales reports 1964-8

Bentley's Old Brewery Rotherham Ltd: newscuttings 1929-57

Charrington United Breweries Ltd: board meeting papers 1964-9

Cornbrook Brewery Co Ltd: brewing book 1949-51; wages book 1890-3

JH Ellis Ltd: share and directors register 1916-30; members register 1917-22; salaries book 1920-31

Highgate Walsall Brewery Co Ltd: private ledger 1904-12

William Hancock & Sons Ltd: (See summary no 559)

Thomas Hoyle & Sons (Plymouth) Ltd: general meeting minutes 1916-34; members registers: 1916-58, and share ledger 1934-58; share and directors register 1930-47; trade ledger 1947-8

Mitchells & Butlers Ltd: (See summary no 590)

Olivers (1913) Ltd: directors and general meeting minutes 1913-64; members registers and share ledgers 1913-49; share and transfer documents 1914-47; balance sheets and accounts 1954-60; cash books 1960-3; salary book 1920-30; salaries and wages particulars 1941-52; staff

correspondence 1941-59; premises deeds and papers 1917-44; public house photographs 1920-65
Webbs (Aberbeeg) Ltd: brewing books 1950-65; stock books 1923-61; order books 1959-65
Burton upon Trent Philanthropic Society of Journeymen Coopers: rules 1912,1932; balance sheets 1892,1946; price: lists 1890-1921, books 1929,1961
Joint Industrial Council of the Cooperage Industry: midland area district council minutes 1920-56
Burton Brewers Cricket Association: general meeting minutes 1894-1965; day book 1923-59; bank cash book 1923-48; address book 1973-8

Records (2): at Bass North, PO Box 3, United House, Piccadilly, York, N Yorkshire YO1 1XQ
Bass Charrington (Northern) Ltd: minutes 1968-74
Bentley & Shaw Ltd: directors meeting minutes 1949-61; general meeting minutes 1892-1961
Bentley's Old Brewery Rotherham Ltd: public house tenant applications 1933-62; tied trade managers notebook 1935-55; deeds register 1933; estates register c1933; properties: report 1956, plans c1892-1957, family notes c1951-9
Grieves & Co Ltd: directors and general meeting minutes 1922-61
Hammonds United Breweries Ltd: board meeting minutes 1951-68; general meeting minutes 1890-1946; debenture register 1898-1957; seals register 1962-8
Hammonds United Breweries (North-Eastern) Ltd: directors meeting minutes 1959-69
Hewitt Brothers Ltd: (See summary no 602)
GS Heath Ltd: directors and general meeting minutes 1956-71
Hills Cromford Brewery Co Ltd: directors meeting minutes 1896-1904
RH Inman Ltd: directors and general meeting minutes 1945-68; seals register 1958-62
Joseph Johnson Ltd: minutes 1917-47
Littleborough Brewery Ltd: directors meeting minutes 1946-66; general meeting minutes 1944-69
Moors & Robsons Ltd: board and committee meeting minutes 1888-1979; general meeting minutes 1903-30; directors notebooks 1900-65; memo and articles of association 1888,1950-65; correspondence 1956-67
Offilers Brewery Ltd: directors meeting minutes 1899-1941,1961-79; general meeting minutes 1899-1941; seal book 1924-70; annual reports and accounts 1899-1941
William Stones Ltd: directors meeting minutes 1895-1970; debenture: register 1898-1954, transfer documents 1924-33; articles of association 1895-1917; annual reports and accounts 1918-36; mortgage register 1895-1919; title deed: schedules 1895-7, registers 1895-c7; licensed properties register c1910-51; properties report 1968
Tadcaster Tower Brewery Co Ltd: partners diaries 1879-95; agendas 1893-1903; sales summaries 1893-1912; brewing produce books 1883-92
United Yorkshire Breweries Ltd: minutes 1963-8
Victoria Bottling Co Ltd: minutes 1930-63; members register 1930-61; directors register 1948
Henry Wilson & Son Ltd: minutes: 1894-1920, directors meeting 1930-69

KH Hawkins, *A History of Bass Charrington* (priv pub 1978)

589 UNITED SHIPOWNERS' FREIGHT, DEMURRAGE & PROTECTIVE ASSOCIATION LTD

16 Jan 1888
25691
52 John Street, Sunderland, Tyne & Wear
Mutual insurance association

History: registered as above in 1888 as a company limited by guarantee for the mutual and individual protection, indemnification, benefit and assistance of its members, mainly in respect of costs incurred in connection with matters concerning freight and demurrage. By 1934 had solicitors upon whom members could call at Sunderland, Tyne & Wear; West Hartlepool, Cleveland; London; and Cardiff, S Glamorgan. Also had agents throughout the world at disposal of members. After Furness Withy Shipping Group left the association for administrative reasons in 1968, the number of ships registered with the association was nearly halved. In 1973, 54 vessels were registered, falling to 35 in 1979. Because of the small number the association began winding up in 1979 and a liquidator was appointed in 1983.

Records: at Snowball, Worthy & Lowe, Solicitors, 52 John Street, Sunderland, Tyne & Wear directors and general meeting: minutes 1934-83, attendance book 1937-81; draft and directors annual reports and accounts 1934-83; directors and secretarys registers 1940s-83; memo and articles of association 1888-1979; *Rules* 1946,1965; register of members and vessels 1888-1978; membership application and vessel entry forms 1888-1982; ledger 1927-83; journals 1932-83; cash book 1937-83; petty cash book 1940-83; call book 1955-82

590 MITCHELLS & BUTLERS LTD

26 Jan 1888
25755
Cape Hill Brewery, PO Box 27, Birmingham, W Midlands B16 0PQ
Brewing

History: incorporated in 1888 as Henry Mitchell & Co Ltd in order to raise money to purchase public houses for Henry Mitchell's brewing business based at Cape Hill Brewery, Smethwick, W Midlands, built 1878-9. The business was started with his father, Henry senior, in 1854 at Crown Inn, Oldbury Road, Smethwick. The younger Henry developed 'Light Mild Ale' and in 1866 built Crown Brewery next to the Inn. By 1881 both pale and mild ales were brewed at Cape Hill Brewery which by 1888 covered 14 acres, employed 271 people, and had an annual output of 90,000 barrels. In 1898 the company merged with Butlers Crown Brewery Ltd, to form the above. Butlers Crown Brewery Ltd was established in 1866 at London Works Tavern, Grove Lane, Smethwick by William Butler who built a new brewery at Old Crown Inn, Broad Street, Smethwick in the 1880s and was incorporated in 1895. After the merger, brewing operations were concentrated at Cape Hill where new buildings, alterations and improvements were made. No 2 Brewery was opened in 1912 to cope with demand. Acquired Alfred Homer Ltd, Vulcan Brewery, Aston, Birmingham in 1899; James Evans of Perry Barr, Birmingham in 1914; Cheshire's Brewery Ltd in 1914; Houlders Brewery Ltd in 1919; Highgate Walsall Brewery Co Ltd (inc 1898) in 1939; Darby's Brewery Ltd (est 1894) in 1951; Atkinsons Brewery Ltd (est 1878) in 1959; and W Butler & Co Ltd (inc 1891) in 1960. Formed as subsidiaries Mitchells & Butlers (South Wales) Ltd in 1951; Liggins & Co Ltd; and Dumbarton Whisky Co Ltd in 1958. Acquired by Bass, Mitchells & Butlers Ltd in 1961. In

1983 was still brewing at Cape Hill, as a subsidiary of Bass PLC through Bass Holdings Ltd.

Records (1): at Mitchells & Butlers, Cape Hill Brewery, PO Box 27, Birmingham, W Midlands B16 0PQ
agm reports 1888-date; memo and articles of association 1895; annual reports and accounts and share circulars 1928-34; promotional blotters 1901-40; standing order books 1913-38; Crown Inn plan 1917; brewery and transport photographs 1911-50s; history articles and booklets 1890-1950; newscuttings 1928-34

Records (2): at Smethwick District Library, High Street, Smethwick, Warley, W Midlands B66 1AB
seal book 1888-1907; statutory instruments list 1941-7; beer bottle labels and wrappers nd; promotional blotters 1901-40; brewing: report books 1888-1910, journals 1899; royal warrant 1950; staff: presentation dinner menus and programmes 1903-49, outing programme 1909, roll of honour 1914-18; house magazine 1948-9; property maintenance log book 1896-9; Cape Hill Brewery plan 1919; family and company history articles, booklets and newscuttings 1907-1980; diaries 1887,1897

Records (3): at Bass, 137 High Street, Burton upon Trent, Staffordshire DE14 1JZ
agm reports 1888-date; Mill Parade operations record 1963-6; recreation and bowling club meeting minutes 1921-63; staff photographs 1911-43
Highgate Walsall Brewery Co Ltd: private ledger 1904-12

591 ARMITAGE INDUSTRIAL HOLDINGS LTD

28 Jan 1888
25783
Cheapside House, 138 Cheapside, London EC2V 6BL
Cotton manufacturing

History: established in 1836 as cotton spinners and manufacturers and incorporated in 1888 as Armitage & Rigby Ltd. By 1923 had manufactories at Rodney Mills and Cockhedge Mills, Warrington, Cheshire and its head offices were at 95 Portland Street, Manchester, Greater Manchester. Changed name to Armitage & Rigby (Holdings) Ltd in 1964 and subsequently to above. Acquired by Lonrho Ltd in 1975.

Records: at Lonrho, Cheapside House, 138 Cheapside, London EC2V 6BL
minutes 1946 on; current records

592 TOOTAL BROADHURST LEE CO LTD

28 Jan 1888
25784
19-21 Spring Gardens, Manchester, Greater Manchester M60 2TL
Textile (cotton) manufacturers

History: founded in Manchester in 1799 by Robert Garner. He was joined in business by his brother in law, Mr Atkinson, in 1836. The business was divided in 1838, Atkinson retaining the hand loom section. Edward Tootal joined the business in 1842 when it was renamed Atkinson Tootal & Co. Atkinson retired in 1848 and firms name changed to Edward Tootal & Co. In 1851 Henry Lee and Henry Tootal Broadhurst, Edward Tootal's nephew, became partners and Edward retired shortly afterward, the firm's name changing to Tootal Broadhurst & Lee. Became Tootal Broadhurst Lee & Co in 1859 on admission of Robert Scott, cashier, Mr Barff and Sir Joseph C Lee as partners. During 1860s acquired Sunnyside Mills, Bolton, Greater Manchester and Newton Heath Mills, Manchester. Incorporated as above in 1888. By 1930s had branch offices in London; Leeds, W Yorkshire; Birmingham, W Midlands; Glasgow, Strathclyde; Belfast, N Ireland; Paris, France; Toronto, Canada; Sydney and Melbourne, Australia; Wellington, New Zealand; and Buenos Aires, Argentina; subsidiary companies Tootal Broadhurst Lee SA; TB Lee Co Inc; John Walton of Glossop Ltd; and Chesro Ltd, Manchester. Introduced crease resisting process in 1932. Opened new factory at St Helens, Merseyside in 1947 and at Devonport, Tasmania in 1952. In 1950s company was the merchanting subsidiary of the holding company Tootal Ltd which in 1963 joined English Sewing Cotton Co Ltd which merged with Calico Printers' Association Ltd in 1968 to form English Calico Ltd which became Tootal Ltd in 1973 and Tootal Group PLC in 1982. In 1979 Tootal Group was involved in all stages of textile activity including spinning, thread making, weaving, knitting, dyeing, printing, finishing, fibre bonding, garment manufacture and retail. Other activities included paper manufacture, fabric coating, packaging and printing. The above became dormant in early 1970s.

Records (1): at Manchester Central Library, St Peter's Square, Manchester, Greater Manchester M2 5PD
This deposit, which is not catalogued, relates to the Calico Printers Association Ltd (inc 1899) and its constituent companies. It contains minutes and related papers and correspondence 1899 on; research committee minutes and papers 1920 on; and pattern books etc 1818

Records (2): at Tootal Group, Tootal House, 19-21 Spring Gardens, Manchester, Greater Manchester M60 2TL
impersonal ledger 1966-8
RF&J Alexander & Co Ltd: ledger 1892-1900; capital expenditure and depreciation ledger 1893-1947; private ledger nd
American Thread Co Ltd: private ledger 1907-30; private journal 1915-30
Aring & Co Ltd: private ledger nd
E&R Armentières Ltd: trading accounts 1897-1902; private ledgers 1899-1949
Edmund Ashworth & Son Ltd: private ledger nd
M Barr: nominal ledger 1961-6
Belfield Ltd: private ledger 1912-39
Bevenden Manufacturers Ltd: private ledger 1952-67
British Thread Mills Ltd: ledger 1920-7; private journal 1938
Calico Printers Association Ltd: vendors purchase accounts 1899-1900; vendors accounts and branch accounts 1899-1901; ledgers with details of agreements re acquisition of member companies from 1899; capital allocation ledger 1901-13; analysis of capital accounts 1900-05; capital accounts 1899-1909; trading accounts and balance sheets 1900-01; capital revaluation analyses 1909-54; private ledgers from 1900; private journals 1900-07; impersonal ledger 1900-01; balance sheets and profit and loss accounts c1914-29; private account suspense ledgers

1906-61; nominal ledgers c1909-28
Calico Printers Association (France) Ltd: journal 1914-45; ledger 1922-50
Chesro Ltd: balance sheets 1930-60
Dul Lee & Co Ltd: ledger 1905-24
English Sewing Cotton Co Ltd: private ledgers c1897-1961; head office private journals c1900-52; works ledgers c1906-51; private cash books nd; property, plant and machinery ledger 1935-49; private ledgers various branches c1897-1960s
Engraved Roller Syndicate Ltd: ledger 1956-67
Fourways Manufacturing Ltd: ledger 1966-9
Gold Berger Prints Ltd: ledger 1959-61
Charles Hodges Ltd: ledger 1958-64
Lulford & Amalgamated Weavers Ltd: journal 1949-54
GG MacKay Ltd: private ledger 1950-3
Mallerstoat & Sons Ltd: private ledger 1949-66
S Mayer: nominal ledger 1963-4
Misses Williams Ltd: private ledgers 1930-58; impersonal ledger 1930-44; journal 1930-44
Newton, Smith & Newton: ledger 1953-66
Overseas Industries Ltd: private ledger 1936-53
Ramasyl Ltd: private ledger 1939-53
Rose Holdings Ltd: ledgers 1951-3
E Ruston Son & Kenyons Ltd: valuation 1904
Sackville & Swallow (Holdings) Ltd: private ledgers 1949-65
St James's Buildings Ltd: ledgers 1911-70; cash book 1941-70
Stanhill Ring Spinning Co (1920) Ltd: nominal ledgers 1942-53
Struthers Thread Co Ltd: inventory and valuation of machinery 1937; private ledger 1938-49
Wadalex Ltd: ledger 1958-9
Wallace & Co, Netherplace: balance sheets 1947-66; profit and loss accounts 1959-66
John Walton of Glossop Ltd: balance sheets 1924-59

Records (3): at Bolton Metropolitan Borough Archives, Civic Centre, Le Mans Crescent, Bolton, Greater Manchester BL1 1SA
ledgers 1864,1882; pattern books c1870-1970; schedules of machinery and valuations 1881-1962; engine inspection book 1899; overlookers' books 1919; stock book 1921; machinery supply agreements 1883-1900; safety certificate 1919-1932; employees school book 1950; correspondence 1863-1931

593 OLD SHIP HOTEL (BRIGHTON) LTD

30 Jan 1888
25785
Old Ship Hotel, Kings Road, Brighton, E Sussex BN1 1NR
Hotel

History: first specific mention of the hotel is in Goodwyn's rental of 1665, when it was owned by Richard Gilham, although it can be traced back to 1559. Originally called Ship Tavern, its name was changed to Old Ship in 1650. Sold in 1671 to Nicholas Tettersell who had helped Charles II escape to Fécamp, France in 1651. By 1714 owned by Richard Rogers and in 1719 its contents were valued at £200. Bought in 1733 by William Hicks who rebuilt and enlarged the premises (including Assembly Rooms finished in 1767), and by 1760s it was one of the premier hotels in Brighton. Taken over in 1765 by John Hicks who continued the expansion in 1790s, by adding 2 houses on East Cliffs overlooking the sea. From 1802-38 owned by Leonard Shuckard and used for vestry, Brighton Commissioners' and Petty Session meetings as well as social occasions. From 1838 under management of Cuff & Strachan who continued expansion and improvement. In 1852 leased by Robert Bacon who bought it in 1878. When Robert Bacon died in 1888 his son Gresham took over and a private company, Bacon & Co Ltd, was formed to own and run the hotel. Further extensions were carried out between 1908-64 with 3 cottages in Ship Street and 2 shops at the corner of Black Lion Street acquired in 1937. Name changed to above in 1934 and became a public company. Ownership of hotel passed to Ewbank Consulting Ltd in 1979. In 1982 hotel had 152 bedrooms.

Records (1): at Old Ship Hotel (Brighton), Old Ship Hotel, Kings Road, Brighton, E Sussex BN1 1NR
directors minutes 1888-date; general meeting minutes 1888-date; attendance books 1920-80; members register 1892-1919; share: registers 1939-79, ledger 1888-1919, allotment book 1888,1892, certificate books 1962-80, transfer register 1959-79; directors registers 1929-62; mortgage and charge register 1889-1940; debenture share register 1919-38; stock register 1942-7; trust deed 1932; memo and articles of association 1888-1934; papers re takeover 1979; seal books 1888-date; balance sheets 1888-1909; annual account book 1910-67; ledgers 1888-1962; private ledgers 1906-55; journals 1888-1967; expenditure journals 1930-66; cash books 1900-70; cash receipt books 1951-70; hotel sales: ledger 1919-60, summaries 1913-63; staff wages book 1938-47; garage: trading sheets 1937-53, stock book 1946-79; property deeds and mortgage documents 1722-1887; photographs, prints and sketches of hotel 1824-1980; papers re Tettersell Lounge 1979; brochure 1929; history booklet 1982

Records (2): at Brighton Library, Church Street, Brighton, E Sussex BN1
photographs re history and and exterior of hotel nd; photograph of bill 1839

Records (3): at E Sussex Records Office, Pelham House, St Andrews Lane, Lewes, E Sussex BN7 1UN
Old Ship Tavern: sale particulars 1802, inventory of household furniture and stock 1801; Hicks property deeds and documents incl Old Ship Inn 1769-1825; John Hicks bills and accounts 1797-1800

Judy Middleton, *The Royal Escape with a History of the Old Ship Hotel, Brighton* (priv pub 1982)

594 EGYPT EXPLORATION SOCIETY

3 Feb 1888
25816
3 Doughty Mews, London WC1
Exploration society

History: founded as Egypt Exploration Fund in 1882 by Sir Erasmus Wilson, Miss Amelia Edwards and scholars from the British Museum. Its aims were to survey and explore the antiquities of Egypt. The first expedition was undertaken in 1883, since when the society has undertaken annual field work. Incorporated as company limited by guarantee as Egypt

Exploration Fund in 1888. Sites excavated include Akhenaten's capital, El-Amarna, temples at Abydos and Deir-el-Bahari and the town sites of Fayum and Middle Egypt. A Graeco - Roman branch was established in 1897. Name changed to above between 1918 and 1921. In 1983 society had membership of over 2685 and continued to oversee excavations.

Records: at Egypt Exploration Society, 3 Doughty Mews, London WC1
executive committee meeting minutes 1882-1982; general meeting: minutes 1931-82, reports 1885-95; agenda books with meeting minutes 1902-17; sub-committee meeting minutes: finance 1894-1917, publications 1929-39, finance, publications and general 1965-74, library 1921-40, excavations 1929-37; sub-committee: notebooks 1883-6, report 1916; committee: standing orders 1925-8, correspondence 1905-08; memo and articles of association 1887-1966; annual reports and accounts 1885-1973; balance sheets and accounts 1884,1893-4,1929-78; journals 1899-1949; cash books: 1932-70, petty 1959-68, in 1919-81, out 1963-81; bank books 1905-30; subscription: list 1882-4, books 1939-62; membership books 1883-1954; members: registers 1891-1916, notes and lists 1919-80, letters and papers 1920-78; American branch members lists and correspondence 1884-1942; salary books 1972-80; staff correspondence 1939-76; Tavistock Square tenancy agreements 1918-19; insurance policies 1918-38; correspondence: 1886-94, Poole 1880-1914, Petrie 1882-1913, Crosselin 1889, office 1914-16; letter books 1886-1923; books sent to America 1911; book sales 1960-71; excavation: reports, agreements correspondence etc 1892-75, wages books 1930-81, employment agreements 1931-2, balance sheets 1939-61, accounts 1906-64, cash books 1926-75, expenses 1919-75; history articles and papers 1880-92
Society for Preservation of Ancient Monuments: meeting minutes 1888-1910; members and subscribers list nd,c1896; fund contributions 1889-96; bank book 1889-1910; reports 1893-1904; correspondence 1888-1910

595 HELSTON PUBLIC ROOMS CO LTD

9 Feb 1888
25854
Godolphin Club, Wendron Street, Helston, Cornwall
Property

History: formed and incorporated as above in 1888 to provide public rooms in Helston, Cornwall. Purchased an 18 cent school building in Wendron Street, Helston and commissioned construction of new adjacent building. Let and hired out rooms for various functions. Helston Institute rented rooms and became Godolphin Club in 1952 and a members only club in 1961, leasing whole of ground floor premises. Went into voluntary liquidation in 1977 and Godolphin Club purchased the freehold in 1978.

Records (1): at Godolphin Club, Wendron Street, Helston, Cornwall
directors register 1901-51; members register 1888-1913; capital and share summaries and shareholders lists 1889-1913; annual returns 1950; snooker payments cash book 1928-9

Records (2): at AJ Paul, Church Street, Helston, Cornwall
directors meeting minutes c1888 on; agm minutes c1888 on; annual returns c1888 on

596 BRISTOL BREWERY, GEORGES & CO LTD

13 Feb 1888
25874
Anchor Terrace, Southwark Bridge Road, London SE1 9HS
Brewing

History: originated in Bristol Porter Brewery built circa 1730 by a group of local merchants led by Isaac Hobhouse. He left his shares to his nephews, John and Henry who began to build Old Porter Brewery in about 1750. By 1787 it was owned by James Grimes who leased it in 1788 to a partnership led by Philip George which subsequently purchased the freehold. George, the son of a wine merchant and distiller, also owned a lead factory, mine and Patent Shot Co. Partners included 2 members of the Fry family, confectioners. Initially only brewed porter but opened a pale ale brewery in the mid 1790s which proved very successful. Firm was renamed Georges, Rickettses & Co in 1816, the Rickettses also being founding partners and glass bottle manufacturers. They withdrew in 1827 when Richard Vaughan, a banker, became a partner. Georges & Co was incorporated as above in 1888 with Philip Henry Vaughan as chairman and Philip George as managing director. Acquired James & Pierce Ltd, Bedminster Brewery in 1889; Millers Brewery in 1911; 39 licensed houses of Hall & Sons, Lodway Brewery in 1912, 40 of John Arnold & Sons, Wickwar, Avon in 1917; another 100 from Welton Breweries Ltd in 1918; Bath Brewery Ltd in 1923; Ashton Gate Brewery Co Ltd in 1931; Wyld & Co Ltd, wine and spirit merchants, Bristol (est in 1803) for £30,000 in 1932; Crocker Brothers Ltd in 1944; Bristol United Breweries Ltd (est 1889) in 1956; Wigmore & Co (Bristol) Ltd, mineral water manufacturers in 1959 and EJ Allen & Son (Mineral Waters) Ltd in 1960. Formed Georges Brewery Properties Ltd in 1960. Acquired in 1961 by Courage Barclay & Simonds Ltd, which was itself acquired by Imperial Tobacco Group Ltd in 1972, and subsequently ceased to trade.

Records (1): at Courage (Western), PO Box 85, Regent Road, Bedminster, Bristol, Avon BS99 7BT
executive committee meeting minutes 1957; shareholders meeting minutes 1888-1905; annual reports and accounts 1910-61; ledgers 1890-1947; beer: production records 1917-31, statistics 1957-9; stock information 1891,1900,1907; sugar stock book 1959-64; production summaries and cost book 1953-61; plant quotations 1959-62; hours and wages book 1946-53; sports club magazine 1949 on; house magazine nd; tenancy records 1878-80,1953; brewery, pub, plant, premises, transport, beer vat, and staff photographs 1908-70s; historical articles and booklets 1938-67
Bristol United Breweries Ltd: annual reports and accounts 1946-57
Charlton Brewery Co Ltd: accounts 1957; staff retirement photographs nd

Oakhill Brewery Co Ltd: annual reports and accounts 1946-51; brewery history and photographs 1919,nd

Records (2): at Courage, Anchor Terrace, Southwark Bridge Road, London SE1 9HS
debenture stock: trust deeds 1893-1956, 4 per cent register 1958; loan stock registers 1956-61

Records (3): at Bristol Record Office, The Council House, College Green, Bristol, Avon BS1 5TR
partnership minutes 1788-1805; committee meeting minutes 1830-8; directors and general meeting minutes 1888-1969; private minutes 1915-17; committee meeting minutes: executive 1956-63, general purposes 1919-27, sales 1962-7, brewing 1962-9; directors attendance book 1900-12; share: register 1888-1953, ledgers 1888-1919; stock register 1888-1953; articles of association 1888-1948; trust deed 1961; powers of attorney register 1881-1966; seals register 1919-61; annual reports and accounts 1936-62; private ledger 1827-86; journal 1803-1914; stock account book and general accounts 1788-1817; debts, balance ledger, stock accounts and valuations 1789-1816; cash books 1809-64; bank account book 1826-1927; sales book 1816-29; brewing book 1813-17; grains book 1943-55; wages book 1821-8; salary records 1891-1959; accident report books 1923-60; repair estimates 1925-9; foreign letter book 1818-45; forms and circulars 19-20 cent; memoranda journal 1821; Jacob Rickettse estate income account 1846-56
Ashton Gate Brewery Co Ltd: directors and general meeting minutes 1886-1932
Bristol United Breweries Ltd: directors and general meeting minutes 1889-1962; executive committee meeting minutes 1956-61; articles of association 1889-1937; mortgage and charge register 1891-1900; seals register 1948-70; annual: returns 1941-55, reports and accounts 1957-60; private ledgers 1889-1949; cash book 1959-62; premises: deed schedule 1896-1904, valuation 1941; public house licenses 1927-47
Charlton Brewery Co Ltd: directors and general meeting minutes 1894-1963; directors, secretarys and members register 1894-1958; articles of association 1915,1962; annual share summaries 1894-1904; ledgers 1894-1960; private cash books 1906-61; Coombs Brewery (The Bell) Radstock: cash books 1878-1970, sales ledger 1888-1931, order book 1884-91
Crocker Brothers Ltd: directors and general meeting minutes 1944-63; articles of association 1929; ledger: 1946-54, private 1944
Daniel Sykes & Co Ltd: mortgage and charge register 1889-99
Dunlop Mackie & Co Ltd: directors: meeting minutes 1905-27,1935-63, register 1926-56; members register and share ledger 1905-61; articles of association 1905; seals register 1927-59; annual: returns 1952-61, reports and accounts 1957-60
Georges Brewery Properties Ltd: articles of association 1960
Lewins Properties Ltd: directors and general meeting minutes 1943-66; articles of association 1943
Oakhill Brewery Co Ltd: directors meeting minutes 1889-1963; general meeting minutes 1929-63; share register 1895-1961; debenture register 1890-1947; articles of association 1899; annual reports and accounts 1956-60; cash book 1851-88
St Vincents Rocks Hotel Co Ltd: directors and general meeting minutes 1929-68; articles of association 1929; cash book 1955-62

Wigmore & Co (Bristol) Ltd: directors and general meeting minutes 1937-63; articles of association 1936; members register and share ledger c1937
Wyld & Co Ltd: share register 1932-65

'An Industry in Ferment' *Gloucestershire and Avon Life* (Nov 1979, pp48-53)

597 ROYAL NATIONAL PENSION FUND FOR NURSES

22 Feb 1888
25928
15 Buckingham Street, London WC2
Pension fund

History: founded as National Pension Fund for Nurses by Sir Henry Burdett to provide nurses and hospital officers with adequate retirement pensions. Initial finances were loaned (later gifted) by 4 City financiers, Junius S Morgan, Lord Rothschild, Everard Hambro and Henry H Gibbs (later Lord Aldenham). Incorporated as above as a company limited by guarantee in 1888 and commenced business in 1889. Received 'Royal' prefix in 1891 and has had a member of the royal family as patron or president ever since. First London offices were opened at 38 Old Jewry moving to 8 King Street, Cheapside in 1889 and to 28 Finsbury Pavement in 1894. In 1906 acquired 2 houses in Buckingham Street, off the Strand, London and erected own building which opened in 1908 and was rebuilt in 1965. By 1899, 7000 nurses (c40 per cent of nursing population) held policies in the fund and 10,000 new policies were issued annually in 1960s, with membership open to men and women in nursing and other professions complementary to medicine. In 1982 total premium income exceeded £10 million.

Records: at Royal National Pension Fund for Nurses, 15 Buckingham Street, London WC2 council meeting: minutes 1889-date, agenda 1955-63, attendance book 1897-date; meeting minutes: finance committee 1888-96, general purposes 1888, management 1912-48; secretarys reports 1896-1938; corporate documents and correspondence 1888-1912; memo and articles of association 1888-1933; superannuation trust deed and rules 1944; annual reports and accounts 1889-1917; investment records 1908 on; general ledgers 1888-1946; subscribers ledger 1940-62; cash book 1888-90; reports, correspondence and press articles re valuation and financing of fund 1887-1928; correspondence and booklet re Junius S Morgan Benevolent Fund 1890-4; administration and staff office notes 1895-1904,1951-4; photographs, notes and papers of royal receptions 1887-c1904; pension papers of Edith Cavell 1905-15; staff: register 1917-32, deposit account book 1962-75; council members and patrons photographs, 20 cent correspondence, newscuttings and other papers c1888-1965; premises agreement, working papers and other correspondence 1906,1963-5; photographs c1908,c1964; programmes of opening 1908,1965; newscuttings re fund 1919-62; articles and notes re fund 1969-72; Nurses Memorial to King Edward VII: committee minutes 1911-61, papers and correspondence 1911 on; photographs of visits to nurses home post 1952

The Story of the Royal National Pension Fund for Nurses (c1964)

598 FLOWER & SONS LTD

25 Feb 1888
25968
Monson Avenue, Cheltenham, Gloucestershire
Brewing

History: established in 1831 by Edward Fordham Flower in Brewery Street, Stratford upon Avon, Warwickshire. New brewery was opened nearby on the Birmingham Road in 1870. Incorporated as above in 1888. Acquired W Turner, Candle Well Brewery, Shipston on Stour, Warwickshire in 1896; Tavistock Brewery Co Ltd, Devon in 1899; Gardner Brothers, Little Compton, Warwickshire and JO Gillett, Swan Brewery, Moreton in Marsh, Gloucestershire in 1900; Fortescue & Son, Bromsgrove, Hereford & Worcester in 1926; and Rowland's Brewery, Evesham, Hereford & Worcester in 1948. Controlled about 350 tied houses in 1954 when it was acquired by JW Green Ltd, Luton, Bedfordshire (est 1869) which changed its name to Flower Breweries Ltd after the acquisition. The latter was acquired by Whitbread & Co Ltd in 1962. Brewing ceased at Stratford upon Avon in 1969.

Records (1): at Whitbread, Monson Avenue, Cheltenham, Gloucestershire
directors meeting minutes 1888-1959; private minutes 1950-3; agm minutes 1888-1948; share: ledgers 1937-54, registers 1950-4, transfer register 1953-4; mortgage register 1888-1964; deeds record c1897; securities records 1896-1946

Records (2): at Shakespeare Birthplace Trust, Henley Street, Stratford upon Avon, Warwickshire CV37 6QW
rough minutes 1891-6; share transfer books 1880-1906,1930-50; dividend book 1898-1954; debenture: holders trustee meeting minutes 1897-1957, register 1888-1911, issue papers 1888,1891, ledger 1897-1948; partnership deeds 1860-3; directors reports and accounts 1897-1914; corporate documents 1880s on; annual accounts 1934-47; ledgers: 1868-1933, private 1837-1947, customer 1889-1949, personal 1928-51, free trade 1946, nominal 1946-8, soft drinks 1961-5, cash 1920-32, balances 1920-47; journals: purchases and expenditure 1843-60, trade 1908-15; agents cask account book 1896-1947; cash books: 1864-1956, trade 1942-51, petty 1948-59; bills receivable book 1893-1919; Cheltenham depot: trade expenses book 1939-48, customer sales book 1913-44, trade and cash books 1949-51; agency sales book 1896-1947; beer: sales books 1946-53, delivered book 1941-6; horse purchases and sales books 1864-1927; purchase books: brewing materials 1848-1912, sugar and hops 1870-97,1958-68, barley, oats and hay 1888-1909; stock books: 1912-27, summaries 1939-47, beer and materials 1848-72,1927-55, barley 1902-23; lost bottles book 1940-55; beers brewed book 1869-72; brewing: journals 1836-1929,1949, books 1939-40,1955; dip book 1955, vat book 1853-65; Artesian wells notebooks 1877; strengths and shipping details 1872-1908; sales literature and papers 1936-63; price lists and cash labels 1881-8; Sunday trading details 1832-65; patent 1867; wages: ledger 1948-52, books 1867-1959; staff and salary books 1878-1913; Christmas presents and picnic books 1872-1927; brewery and licensed premises title deeds and documents 19-20 cent; inventories and valuations: plant 1888-1949, brewery and licensed houses 1927-45; sales bills acceptances 1828-1914; rent: ledger 1889-1950, payable book 1945-61; mortgage: ledger 1897-1949, loans book 1905-46; insurance ledger 1920; rates and tax papers 1879-1954; tenants deposit book 1931-52; letter books 1867-1903; press cuttings 1854-1920,1966; photographs: brewery, offices and plant 1962-6, staff 1936; bus advertisements 1945 on; history 1961; family papers and photographs 19-20 cent

599 JOSEPH MASON & CO LTD

1 Feb 1888
26003
Nottingham Road, Derby, Derbyshire DE2 6AR
Paint

History: established in Derby in 1880 as Joseph Mason & Co, varnish makers and colourmen. Prize winners at Paris University Exhibition in 1867. Acquired by Henry E Ayre in 1872. Incorporated as above in 1888. Moved to new factory at present site in 1902. By 1930s was producing resins for high-grade cellulose paints and in 1960s emerged as specialist in heavy duty paints for transport use. Continued under control of Ayre family until 1979, when it became a subsidiary of Warren Plantation Holdings Group.

Records: at Joseph Mason, Nottingham Road, Derby, Derbyshire DE2 6AR
directors meeting minutes 1888-1964; general meeting minutes 1888-1960; ledgers: private 1887-1907, impersonal 1919-38, bought 1901-38, bad debts 1931-44; journals 1946-57; cash books: 1905-60, petty 1956-8; order books 1925-36; day books 1929-37; sales record book 1931-6; goods supplied bills 1860,1876; price list 1961; invoice book 1929-37; enamels, varnishes and coach colours samples nd,c1950,1958; catalogues c1930-c70; photographs: exhibition stands nd, trade stand 1935; recipes: and notes 1874-1930, receipts and correspondence 1891-1910; mixing books 1913-30; goods supplied contracts, orders and price lists 1923-38; plant repairs account 1875; vehicle photographs 1939-76; wages: books 1891-1936, monthly table 1905-12; travellers: commission 1919-37, sheets 1935-6, allowance 1926-38, turnover 1929-38, cash book 1936-9; staff photographs c1890-1931; Derwent Street leases and specifications of work 1872-96; letter books 1894-1941; stationery examples 1890-c1906

600 BASS BREWING (RUNCORN) LTD

3 Mar 1888
26018
Runcorn Brewery, Aston Lane, Preston Brook, Runcorn, Cheshire
Brewing

History: incorporated in Mar 1888 as Hull United Breweries Ltd to take over Crown Brewery of Henry and Charles Moor, and Robson's Brewery in Waterwork Street, Hull, Humberside. Changed name in May 1888 to Moors' & Robson's Breweries Ltd. Robson's Brewery was sold in 1889. Acquired the properties of Guy & Co of Grimsby, Humberside and Nesfields of Scarborough, N Yorkshire in 1919. Acquired in 1961 by United Breweries Ltd which merged with Charrington & Co Ltd in 1962 through Charrington United Breweries Ltd which merged with Bass, Mitchells & Butlers Ltd in 1967 to form Bass Charrington Ltd. Company's name subsequently changed to above. In 1983 was a subsidiary of Bass PLC through Bass Holdings Ltd.

Records: at Bass North, United House, Piccadilly, York, N Yorkshire YO1 1XQ
directors: committee and general meeting minutes 1888-1979, notebooks 1900-65; memo and articles of association 1950-65; Crown Brewery sale agreement 1888; office correspondence 1956-67

601 WHITBREAD WEST PENNINES LTD

16 Mar 1888
26091
PO Box 88, High Street, Blackburn, Lancashire BB1 1HG
Brewing

History: established in 1812 and incorporated as Threlfall's Brewery Co Ltd in 1888 to take over the businesses of John M Threlfall at Liverpool, Merseyside and Salford, Greater Manchester and WA Matheson of Liverpool. Acquired W Potts Ltd, Lamb Brewery, Oldham, Greater Manchester and John Buckley & Sons, Gorton Brewery, Manchester in 1898; Stamford Brewery Co (Ashton under Lyne) Ltd, Greater Manchester and Taylor & Lees, Sergeant at Arms Brewery, Oldham in 1899; Handley's Brewery Ltd, Clarence Brewery, Hulme, Greater Manchester in 1912; George Bentley, Viaduct Brewery, Manchester in 1913; Albion Brewery Co Ltd, Wigan, Greater Manchester in 1919; Thorougood's Breweries Ltd, Lion Brewery, Liverpool in 1925; and West Cheshire Brewery Co Ltd, Queen's Brewery, Birkenhead, Merseyside in 1927. Merged in 1961 with Chesters Brewery Co Ltd, Ardwick Brewery, Greater Manchester (inc 1888) and changed name to Threlfalls Chesters Ltd. Acquired Birkenhead Brewery Co Ltd (inc 1865) in 1962 and Southam's Brewery Ltd (inc 1866) in 1966. Acquired by Whitbread & Co Ltd in 1967 and subsequently changed name to above.

Records: at Whitbread, PO Box 88, High Street, Blackburn, Lancashire BB1 1HG
directors register 1967-70; agm papers 1966; property ledgers: 1965-9, Liverpool 1904-63, Salford 1904-62; cottage rents ledgers 1948-71; rents payable ledger 1947-64; property valuations: Chester 1919, Liverpool 1920

602 HEWITT BROTHERS LTD

16 Mar 1888
26094
Tower Brewery, Pasture Street, Grimsby, Humberside
Brewing

History: incorporated as above in 1888 to take over brewing interests of Hewitt family at Tower Brewery, Grimsby, Humberside. Acquired Moors' & Robson's Breweries Ltd in 1960, by which time had also acquired AM&E Sargeant & Co Ltd, brewers of Scunthorpe, Humberside, and Grimsby & District Mineral Water Co Ltd. Taken over in Dec 1961 by United Breweries Ltd which merged in 1962 with Charrington & Co Ltd through Charrington United Breweries Ltd. In 1964 company controlled 310 licensed outlets and operated exclusively south of the Humber. Charrington United Breweries Ltd merged in 1967 with Bass, Mitchells & Butlers Ltd to form Bass Charrington Ltd. In 1983 company was a subsidiary of Bass PLC through Bass Holdings Ltd.

Records: at Bass North, United House, Piccadilly, York, N Yorkshire YO1 1XQ
directors meeting minutes 1930-date; shareholders meeting minutes 1888-1959; members register 1962-77; share: certificate books 1888-1981, transfer documents 1962-77; seals registers 1909-30,1956-80; annual returns 1928-9; impersonal ledger 1925-9; tenancy agreements 1954-78

603 NORTHALLERTON LIVE STOCK MART CO LTD
19 Mar 1888
26107
Stamford House, 65 High Street, Northallerton, N Yorkshire DL7 8EG
Auction market

History: incorporated as above in 1888, leasing sale yard next to Northallerton Railway Station. In 1889 yard also erected at Bedale, N Yorkshire and alternative weekly sales held at Bedale and Northallerton. In 1925-26, 77 sales held when 22,593 head of stock were sold for £194,376. In 1937 Bedale premises were sold. In 1977 company acquired by Northallerton Auctions Ltd, who moved auctions to Applegarth Mart, and company was placed in voluntary liquidation.

Records: at Northallerton Live Stock Mart, Stamford House, 65 High Street, Northallerton, N Yorkshire DL7 8EG
directors and general meeting minutes 1888-1978; share: ledger 1888-1923, certificates 1890; station mart photograph 1874

604 MAGEE MARSHALL & CO LTD
22 Mar 1888
26135
Wilderspool Brewery, PO Box No 2, Warrington, Cheshire WA4 6RH
Brewing

History: established in Derby, Derbyshire in 1850s by David Magee, brewer and spirit merchant. Incorporated as above in 1888 and moved to Crown Brewery, Cricket Street, Bolton, Greater Manchester in 1910. Acquired by Greenall Whitley & Co Ltd, brewers of Warrington, Cheshire in 1959. Brewing ceased at Crown Brewery in about 1970.

Records (1): at Greenall Whitley, Wilderspool Brewery, PO Box No 2, Warrington, Cheshire WA4 6RH
directors meeting minutes 1939-66; shareholders letters and newscuttings 1905-17; seal register 1966-78; Halliwells Brewery: petty cash book c1910, wages books c1910; Alexandra Brewery wages books 1902-11; Grapes Brewery wages books 1892-1902; Wigan Brewery wages books c1895; wages books 1894-c1905; photographs, misc correspondence, leases, newscuttings etc 1930s

Records (2): at Bolton Metropolitan Borough Archives, Central Library, Le Mans Crescent, Bolton, Greater Manchester BL1 1SA
directors and general meeting minutes 1888-1963; balance sheets and trading accounts 1888-1958; ledgers, cash books, wages books etc c1890-1960; Palace Cinema, Wigan trade account 1928-61; Wigan Brewery and Wigan, Chorley & Leyland premises documents 1789-1894; property agreements, correspondence and plans 1876-1960; public house and property valuations 1896-1960; licensed premises stock and trade records c1910-60

J Norman Slater, *A Brewer's Tale: Greenall Whitley Brewers since 1762* (priv pub 1980)

605 THRELFALLS (SALFORD) LTD

3 Apr 1888
26200
PO Box 88, High Street, Blackburn, Lancashire BB1 1HG
Brewing

History: incorporated in 1888 as Chesters Brewery Co Ltd and operated from Ardwick Brewery, Princes Street, Ardwick, Greater Manchester. Acquired John Batlersby & Co, Wellington Brewery, Openshaw, Greater Manchester in 1888; John Foster, Swan Brewery, Ardwick and Richardson & Goodall, Altrincham, Greater Manchester in 1890; Salford Brewery Co Ltd (inc 1888), Town Hall Brewery, Salford, Greater Manchester in 1896; and WM Cross, Preston, Lancashire in 1944. Merged in 1961 with Threlfalls Brewery Co Ltd of Liverpool, Merseyside (est 1812) which became known as Threlfalls Chesters Ltd and was acquired by Whitbread & Co Ltd in 1967. Name subsequently changed to above.

Records: at Whitbread, PO Box 88, High Street, Blackburn, Lancashire BB1 1HG
agm minutes 1959-71; brewers prime cost book 1945-51; loans and interest ledger 1911-62; rent roll book 1895-1939; credit ledgers 1888-1973; debit ledgers 1888-1973

606 WILKIN & SONS LTD

5 Apr 1888
26233
Tiptree, Colchester, Essex CO5 ORF
Jam and marmalade

History: formed in 1888 to acquire the business of Britannia Fruit Preserving Co which had been established in 1885 as jam makers at Tiptree, near Colchester, Essex. Incorporated as Britannia Fruit Preserving Co Ltd, name changed to above in 1905. Had commenced fruit preserving in 1885 sending jams and marmalades nationwide and overseas, especially Australia. Received royal warrant in c1910. In 1917 produced 545 tons of fruit for their fruit jams, 1000 quarters of corn and over 500 tons of vegetables. In 1980s still in the control of the Wilkin family.

Records: at Wilkin & Sons, Tiptree, Colchester, Essex CO5 ORF
directors and general meeting minutes 1888-date; share transfer register 1931-date; preference share: prospectus 1888-1926, agreement 1899; register: mortgages 1898-1902, employees shareholdings 1910-51; memo and articles of association 1888,1965,1978; partnership agreement 1886; Dagenham business sale agreement 1909; annual report and accounts 1888-1984; trading accounts: factory and farm 1921-70, departmental 1890-4; farm: summary accounts 1941-69, cash book 1933-40; ledgers: 1928-40, impersonal 1892-1912, bought 1897-1926,1949-50; journals: factory bought 1939-54, trade 1892-1967, supply 1897-1963; cash book: 1889, petty 1933-46; sales record 1897-1964; order forms c1889-1944; price lists and leaflets c1898 on; labels 1891-1969; trade-mark certificates and papers 1893,1904-50; plant stock book 1898-1912; recipe book: 1893-1902, fruit 1901-02, vegetable 1900-02; jam notebook 1898-1901; experiments notebook 1889-1901; office rate sheets 1914-73; photographic blocks: staff, processes, fruit, premises nd, railway orders, plans, correspondence and papers 1895-7; Tollesbury estate deeds etc 1735-1816; letter book 1867-1979; visitors book 1914-71; historical articles 1904-05; business and personal papers,

correspondence and newscuttings 1859-92
Tiptree Jam & Britannia Fruit Preserving Co Ltd: register of members 1905-80; memo and articles of association 1905; balance sheets 1935-8

607 MOBIL OVERSEAS OIL CO LTD

9 Apr 1888
26294
Mobil Court, 3 Clements Inn, London EC2A 2EB
Oil storage and carriage

History: incorporated in 1888 as Tank Storage & Carriage Co Ltd to carry on business of carriers, wharfingers, shipowners, barge owners, lightermen etc. Entered agreement in 1888 to carry, store and deliver oil of Kerosene Co Ltd (inc 1888, dissolved 1903). Had premises at Purfleet, Essex in 1890s. Acquired by Standard Oil Corporation of New York during 1920s and changed name to Standard Fuel Oil Co Ltd in 1930, to Socony Overseas Oil Co Ltd in 1953, and to above in 1966 as parent company changed its name. Ceased to trade in 1974.

Records: none survive

608 BUTTERLEY BUILDING MATERIALS LTD

10 Apr 1888
26306
Wellington Street, Ripley, Derby, Derbyshire DE5 3DZ
Iron and steel

History: established in 1790 by Benjamin Outram and William Jessop, (engineers), Francis Beresford and John Wright as colliery proprietors, ironmasters and iron founders at Butterley near Derby. Incorporated in 1888 as Butterley Co Ltd as company limited by guarantee. Converted into private company in 1908 and into public company limited by shares by Special Act in 1914. By 1923 owned Butterley Iron Works, Derby; Codnor Iron Works and Bullbridge Line Works, Codnor Park Colliery, Nottingham, Nottinghamshire; and offices in London; Glasgow, Strathclyde; and Birmingham, W Midlands. Specialized in coal; heavy and light castings; colliery plant; pumping and haulage machinery; bridges, roofs and constructional work of all kinds. Collieries were vested in National Coal Board as from 1947. By 1958 had following subsidiaries: Apex Sand & Gravel Ltd, Butterley Housing Co Ltd, AH Couser Ltd, T Darnell & Sons Ltd, Muggington Sand & Gravel Co Ltd, Hughes & Lancaster Ltd, Butterley & Blaby Brick Cos Ltd and First Inter-Town Properties Ltd. Name changed to above in 1969. By 1977 had been acquired by Hanson Trust Ltd and had works at Waingroves, Derbyshire; Kirton and Ollerton, Nottinghamshire; Blaby and Desford, Leicestershire; Hooton, Cheshire; Caernarfon, Gwynedd; Buckley, Clywd; and Motherwell, Strathclyde. By early 1980s was parent of group of companies operating as brick makers. Manufactured lightweight aggregate building blocks; handmade, wire cut and machine pressed facing bricks; engineering bricks; paviors and specials.

Records: at Derbyshire Record Office, County Offices, Matlock, Derbyshire DE4 3AG
partnership meeting minutes 1878-87; directors meeting minutes 1888-1957; managing directors annual reports 1889-1913; chairmans report 1914; memo and articles of association

1888; corporate documents 1887 on; share: and debenture ledger 1888-1934, transfer registers 1888-1936, capital return 1888; debenture interest book 1916-31; profit and loss accounts: and balance sheets 1889-1938, summary furnaces and collieries 1820-1902; accounts: annual 1881-1919, summary 1813,c1932-46, general 1799,1853-83, furnace 1885-8,1903-08; ledgers: private 1796-1943, furnace 1800-37, capital 1888-1945, sundries 1937-c43, profits distribution 1852-87, impersonal 1852-5; journals: private 1855-1936, subsidiary private 1940-4, summary 1938-43; account books: 1907-40, summary 1802-03,1853-83, impersonal 1852-6, wages and materials 1930-4, collieries profit and loss 1830-1901, sundries 1907-40; cash books: 1867-1949, private 1885-1947; Butterley Park credit book 1941-52; forge books 1829-70; furnace production record 1888-92,1941-8; order books 1944-65; contracts: c1900, notebook 1931-44, balance book c1900-40, book 1924-37; patents and papers 1828-38; consignment notebook 1952-9; prices 1801-66; costs 1810-1943; coal sales 1849-68; mineral: rents ledgers 1889-1928, rents books 1793-1802, workings reports 1869; stock books: 1830-52, coal, ironstone and metal 1765, forge stores 1912-25, scrap etc 1942-8; Codnor Park: rent book 1938-44, forge stock book 1910-35, stock book 1902-16, forge costs 1882-1960, rate book 1897-1933; catalogues and price lists 1886-c1950,nd; shop book 1925-7; title deeds, property documents and legal papers 1597-1919; property and fittings valuations 1834-1911; plans 1835-1940; employees social survey 1856; war record 1918; workmens: prices 1830-3, wages letters 1871-2, debt notes c1804, accident correspondence 1854-5; wage agreements 1850s-60s; salaries books 1883-1947; apprenticeships indentures c1860-c90; wage correspondence 1866-70,nd; welfare laws 1923-6; ironworks sick and accident club rules 1898,nd; London office visitors book 1892-1955; letter books: 1894-1927, Joseph Smith 1838-44, engineering 1912-15; correspondence 1815-c20; newscuttings 1844-1950s; statutes 1789-c1900; projects, products, castings, machinery, property, functions and directors photographs 1870s-1950s; history booklets and articles 1886-1967

Butterley Housing Co Ltd: leases, agreements and housing estate photographs 20 cent

609 GEORGE GALE & CO LTD

2 Apr 1888
26330
The Brewery, Horndean, Portsmouth, Hampshire PO8 ODA
Brewing

History: Richard Gale acquired the 'Ship & Bell' public house in Horndean, Hampshire and its associated brewery in 1847. By 1855 his son George Alexander Gale was trading as brewer and wine and spirit merchant. By 1859 he included malting amongst his interests. Original brewery was destroyed by fire in 1866 and a new one completed in 1869. By 1875 George Gale & Co had expanded its trading area to include Southsea, Hampshire where it acquired a warehouse and stores. William Smeed joined the company in 1884 bringing his interests in Eagle Brewery, Landport, Hampshire. Incorporated as above in 1888 when probably owned over 80 licensed houses. In 1896 Herbert Frederick Bowyer, miller from Stoke D'Abernon, near Guildford, Surrey acquired the major shareholding in the company on the retirement of George Alexander Gale. Served as chairman until his death in 1938. Acquired Homewell Brewery, Havant, Hampshire with 9 public houses in 1903; Square Brewery, Petersfield, Hampshire in 1907; Wickham Brewery, Hampshire in 1912; and Angel Brewery, Midhurst, W Sussex with 5 public houses in 1923. Formed Horndean Hotels Ltd in 1973 to administer its managed houses. Still family controlled in late 1980s when traded in approximately 100 tied houses located in an area stretching from Oxfordshire to the Isle of Wight in the south of England.

Records: at George Gale, The Brewery, Horndean, Portsmouth, Hampshire PO8 ODA
minutes 1888-date; general meeting papers 1936; share ledgers 1888-1979; allotment book 1888; transfer register 1897-1983; shareholders lists 1936-50,1967-78; memo and articles of association 1888-1959; debenture: bonds register 1898, ledger 1941-79; mortgage register 1898-1943; seal register 1950-76; Kinnell & Hartley proposed takeover papers 1913-28; annual accounts 1895-date; balance sheets and accounts: 1893-1947, licensed premises 1901-49; ledgers: trade 1923-35,1955-80, bought 1932-60s, impersonal 1927-57, supply 1878-95, cash 1945-57, sales 1930-67, balances 1943-54, licensed premises 1936-73, customer 1922-9,1950-76, payment 1965-73, spirits 1854-1950, tax and duty 1943-63, trading 1888-1973; journals: purchase 1930-70, wine and spirits 1963-9; cash books: 1896-1950, private 1896-1962, licensed premises 1932-50, cigarettes and tobacco 1939-57; account books 1908-57; day books: off licences 1950-62, retail 1947-57, tobacco 1930-41; public houses supplies books 1911-80; free trade books 1957-80; bills 1869-1945; price lists 1933,1950-71; testing book 1892-1945; malt, sugar and hops consumption book 1907-19; malt books 1950-74; hop book 1950-66; barrelage working expenses 1908-12; mashing books 1958-60; stock books 1951-72; beer: quantity book 1958-74, stock list 1962 on; spirits out book 1954-7; liquors listing 1948-52, cider quantity book 1973-6; wine and spirits: order book 1972-4, inventory 1967; rainfall book 1952-80; well level book 1921-36; tax and duty statements 1914-16; clubs: Christmas books 1950-72, loan books 1952-65; agents books post 1945,1956; wages book 1937-73; commission payments 1937-40; pension scheme books 1937,1943-6; national insurance books 1947-68; property: lists, sales catalogues and papers etc 1833-1977, inventories and valuations 1888-9,1963, deeds and documents 1691-1982, correspondence 1889-61, maps and plans 1930s,nd; land tax papers 1921-30s; rent: journal 1923-65, ledgers 1939-58; repair: ledgers 1953-4,1971-7, estimate book 1949-50, receipt books 1963-5; brewery notices 1908-50; misc correspondence 1872-1959; newscuttings 20 cent; brewery equipment, licensed houses, outings, transport and family photographs 1890s-1975
Portsmouth Bonding Stores Ltd: balance sheets and accounts 1924-40

610 UNAMEC LTD

12 Apr 1888
26331
UAC House, Blackfriars Road, London SE1 9UG
West African traders

History: incorporated in 1888 as Bathurst Trading Co Ltd to acquire business of River Gambia Trading Co Ltd. Acted as West African merchants with London offices in Mincing Lane until 1910 when moved to Leadenhall Street. Acquired in 1918 by Lever Brothers Ltd, soap manufacturers, which merged with Margarine Unie in 1929 to form Unilever Ltd. All West African trading assets and liabilities were transferred in 1930 to United African Co Ltd, another Unilever subsidiary, and run as part of Gambian branch of UAC. Remained dormant from 1930 to 1961 when name was changed to United African Mechanical & Electrical Ltd and thereafter to above and it ran the 'Unamec' division of UAC International Ltd.

Records: at UAC International, UAC House, Blackfriars Road, London SE1 9UG
customers ledger 1885-90; cash books 1888-1904; current account books 1888,1908-09; boat maintenance expenses 1881-3; invoice books 1881-7; Bathurst managers letter book 1853-1914; general trade correspondence 1880-5; ground nut purchase records 1882-8; stock book 1900-06; photographs of The Gambia, buildings, staff, ships and ground nuts 1900-30

F Pedler, *The Lion and the Unicorn in Africa. The United African Co 1787-1931* (1974)

611 WEST COUNTRY BREWERIES LTD

12 Apr 1888
26346
Monson Avenue, Cheltenham, Gloucestershire
Brewing

History: founded in 1760 by JT Agg-Gardner and was known as Gardner's Brewery. Incorporated as Cheltenham Original Brewery Co Ltd in 1888. Acquired Stibbs & Co, Albion Street Brewery, Cheltenham, Gloucestershire in 1898; Nailsworth Brewery Co Ltd, Gloucestershire (inc 1889) in 1908; AB Green, Stow Brewery, Stow on the Wold, Gloucestershire; Lane Bros & Bristow, Vine Brewery, Ledbury, Hereford & Worcester; and Taylor & Co, Cotswold Brewery, Northleach, Gloucestershire in 1919; Arnold, Perrett & Co Ltd, Wickwar Brewery, Gloucestershire (inc 1886) in 1924; Sladden & Collier Ltd, Evesham, Hereford & Worcester (inc 1890) in 1927; and Wintle's Brewery Ltd, Forest Steam Brewery, Mitcheldean, Gloucestershire (est 1871) in 1930. Merged in 1958 with Hereford & Tredegar Brewery Ltd (inc 1889) to form Cheltenham & Hereford Breweries Ltd which merged with Stroud Brewery Co Ltd (est 1760) later in the same year to form the above. Acquired by Whitbread & Co Ltd in 1963 when it controlled nearly 1300 tied houses.

Records (1): at Whitbread, Monson Avenue, Cheltenham, Gloucestershire
directors meeting: minutes 1888-1953, agenda books 1909-53, committee minutes 1909-53; memo and articles of association 1888; share and debenture holders registers 1904-49; mortgage register 1897-1945; seal books 1945-54; capital ledger 1888-1908; wine and spirit ledger 1911-26; licensed houses ledger c1936; brewery inventory 1859

Records (2): at Gloucestershire Record Office, Worcester Street, Gloucester, Gloucestershire GL1 3DW
directors register 1900-13; trade: ledger 1822-34, book 1935-51; public house and shops register 1887; leasehold properties register 1887; title deeds 1912-1973

612 BANKERS' INVESTMENT TRUST LTD

13 Apr 1888
26351
Mermaid House, 2 Puddle Dock, London EC4V 3AT
Investment trust

History: incorporated in 1888 as above as an investment trust. Acquired undertaking and assets of Army & Navy Investment Trust Co Ltd (inc 1887) in 1964 and re-registered as public limited company after 1980. Managed by Touche Remnant & Co.

Records: Touche Remnant, Mermaid House, 2 Puddle Dock, London EC4V 3AT
directors meeting minutes 1888-date; general meeting minutes 1888-date; corporate papers 1949-61; share lists 1888-1947; debenture: issue lists 1888-1947, registers 1888-1931, transfer registers 1889-1912, stockholders register 1912-33, stock books 1950-68, certificate registers 1902-47; indemnity letters 1920-48; marriage and death certificate registers 1930-50; probate registers 1938-50; seal books 1935-76; annual reports and accounts 1939-70; profit and loss statements 1888-1972; valuations 1959-67; general ledgers 1907-63; ledgers 1926-58; journal 1933-48; cash books 1930-76; estates cash account 1890-1926; petty cash book 1954-63; income tax papers 1939-65; public trust fund ledgers 1890-1921; investment: ledgers 1888-1972, register c1900; superannuation fund: accounts nd; cash book 1926-56
Army & Navy Investment Trust Co Ltd: general meeting agendas 1887-1908; balance sheets 1887-1963; public trust fund ledgers 1889-1914; investment and loan ledgers 1910-28; underwriting transactions 1935-49

613 RIVER PLATE & GENERAL INVESTMENT TRUST CO LTD

14 Apr 1888
26355
7 Lincoln's Inn Fields, London WC2
Investment trust

History: incorporated as above in 1888 to acquire investments in Argentina in connection with River Plate Trust, Loan & Agency Co Ltd (inc 1881) which undertook the management and administration of the above.

Records (1): at River Plate & General Investment Trust, 7 Lincoln's Inn Fields, London WC2
current records

Records (2): at University College London Library, University of London, Gower Street, London WC1E 6BT
directors and general meeting minutes 1888-1960s; annual report and accounts 1888 on

614 TAYLORS DRUG CO LTD

16 Apr 1888
26373
1 Thane Road West, Nottingham, Nottinghamshire NG2 3AA
Pharmaceuticals

History: formed by WB Mason (died 1912) as a chain of chemists shops based in Leeds, W Yorkshire. First stores were opened in Leeds; Sunderland, Tyne & Wear; and Blackburn,

Lancashire. Incorporated as above in 1888 when the company owned 10 shops. First London shop was opened in 1889 but most of its shops were located in the north of England and Scotland. In the 1920s claimed to be the largest chemist shop chain in Britain. By 1958 had 206 branches. In 1963 it was acquired by Timothy Whites & Taylors Ltd, with whom it had long standing trading agreements. This company was acquired by Boots Co Ltd in 1968.

Records: at Boots, 1 Thane Road West, Nottingham, Nottinghamshire NG2 3AA
directors meeting minutes: 1895-1916, rough and agendas 1888-97; management board meeting minutes 1912-20; private ledger 1885-93; letter book 1892-1903; shop front photographs c1900

615 TURNEY BROTHERS LTD

18 Apr 1888
26398
Trent Bridge Works, Nottingham, Nottinghamshire
Leather manufacturers

History: established by brothers, Edward and John Turney, who started making leather for the fancy leather and glove trades on 'Sneinton Island' near River Trent, Nottingham, Nottinghamshire in 1861. Edward left after a few years and William, another brother, joined. William left later to found another tannery, leaving John (1840-1927) as sole proprietor. Incorporated as above in 1888 with John Turney (knighted 1888, Mayor of Nottingham 1887,1888) as chairman and managing director. Joseph Turney Wood and John AE Turney, nephew and son of Sir John, joined the company, the latter becoming managing director in 1927. New four-storey building fronting London Road to house chrome tannery was erected 1913-18 when main production was leather for army clothing. By 1923 had branches in Belvoir Street, Leicester, Leicestershire; Denman Street, London; and Paton Street, Piccadilly, Greater Manchester; and employed c500 persons. In 1977 was manufacturing upper, grain and suede clothing, surgical and fancy goods leathers, and employed 120 persons. Acquired by Booth & Co (International) Ltd, tanners, subsidiary of Booth (International Holdings) Ltd in 1971. Works closed in 1981.

Records: at Nottinghamshire Record Office, County House, High Pavement, Nottingham, Nottinghamshire NG1 1HR
directors and general meeting minutes 1888-1971; share issue agreement 1888; directors and managers register 1923-47; annual reports and accounts 1889-1979; ledgers 1899-1971; journal 1916-49; cash books 1861-7,1960-9; bank agreement 1894; receipts 1886-91; sales information and statistics books 1910-48; advertisements 1920s; work diary 1919-63; laboratory book 1943-65; plans, drawings, papers, and correspondence re plant c1919-69; photographs of work sheds 1920s; wages: sheet 1910, books 1938-40; work rates c1920-1; staff: lists 1897-1922, agreements 1880s,1892; addresses: to staff 1919, on JT Wood 1924; staff photographs c1910-20; premises agreements 1886-1925; maps and plans of factory and district 1876-1967; photographs of factory c1920-50s; articles on history 1920-61; newscuttings re chemical processes 1913-28

Wade & Co (Nottingham) Ltd: directors and general meeting minutes 1918-73; share, share transfer, directors and members registers 1918-43; ledger 1920-34
Charles Tanneries Ltd: directors and general meeting minutes 1946-69

616 WRITTLE BREWERY CO LTD

24 Apr 1888
26477
91 Brick Lane, Spitalfields, London E1 6QN
Brewing

History: incorporated as above in 1883 to acquire brewing business of Pattison, Writtle Brewery, Writtle, Essex, established prior to 1808 by Henry Lambirth, common brewer of Little Stambridge, Essex. Acquired in 1902 by Russell's Gravesend Brewery Ltd (inc 1893) and ceased to brew in mid 1920s. Russell's Gravesend Brewery Ltd was acquired by Truman, Hanbury, Buxton & Co Ltd (est 1666) in 1930. Company was a subsidiary of Grand Metropolitan PLC through Truman Ltd in 1983.

Records (1): at Truman, 91 Brick Lane, Spitalfields, London E1 6QN
directors meeting: minutes 1888-1954, attendance book 1955-60; mortgage register 1902; Writtle Brewery and properties reports and valuation 1867-c1900; motions valuation 1931

Records (2): at Greater London Record Office, 40 Northampton Road, London EC1
members registers 1888-1917

Records (3): at Essex Record Office, County Hall, Chelmsford, Essex CM1 1LX
partnership: deeds 1810-60, balance sheets and accounts 1815-35; articles of association 1888; cash books 1811-32; repair accounts books 1861-8; Writtle Brewery estate title deeds and documents 1654-1942; Writtle and Stambridge breweries inventories and valuations 1834-42; Henry Lambirth trustees: meeting minutes 1835-44, letter books 1840-57, account books 1842-5, cash books 1857-8, rent books 1839-44, security book 1842-5

617 KING HARRY STEAM FERRY CO LTD

25 Apr 1888
26494
Town Quay, Truro, Cornwall TR1 2HJ
Ferry operators

History: formed and incorporated as above in 1888 to acquire lease of charter for operation of a steam ferry over the River Fal at King Harry Passage and related property. Purchased charter and land in 1934. Ferry had been previously operated by horse boat. First vessel went into operation in 1889 and by 1981 were using their sixth ferry and issuing some 140,000 tickets annually. Service converted to electric propulsion in 1956.

Records (1): at King Harry Steam Ferry, Town Quay, Truro, Cornwall TR1 2HJ
board meeting minutes 1913-45; general meeting minutes 1888-1975; shareholders: list 1908,1912, register 1895-1954; share register 1912 on; memo and articles of association 1932; annual report and accounts 1890 on; engineer ferry reports 1894-1902; correspondence and

papers re tenders and contracts for ferries and floating bridge 1908 on; photographs of launching and operating of ferry 1950s-74

Records (2): at Cornwall Record Office, County Hall, Truro, Cornwall TR1 3AY
floating bridge specification and contract 1912; ferry bridge plan 1907

618 ESSO PETROLEUM CO LTD

27 Apr 1888
26538
Esso House, Victoria Street, London SW1E 5JW
Oil

History: incorporated in 1888 as Anglo-American Oil Co Ltd and set up by John D Rockefeller, founder and president of Standard Oil Co, USA, as its first overseas affiliate. During first year sold half million tons of petroleum products, mainly kerosene and lubricating oil, all shipped from USA. Constructed storage wharf at Purfleet, Essex, for transport fleet of 6 ships. From 1900 were sole importers of Pratt's Motor Car Spirit which soon accounted for 75 per cent of all petrol used in England. Demand for oil increased rapidly and by 1917 was handling 54 per cent of all oil products sold in UK. Demand, especially for petrol, increased dramatically post WW1. New storage depots at Hull, Humberside; Avonmouth, Avon; and Ellesmere Port, Cheshire, were opened in 1921. A subsidiary, Irish American Oil Co Ltd, was set up in 1922 in Eire. In 1925, acquired British-Mexican Petroleum Ltd together with 10 storage and bunkering plants, transport fleet and 8 ocean-going tankers, and an interest in Atlantic Gulf & West Indies Oil Co. Full control of the latter was acquired in 1926 along with a small refinery at Fawley, Southampton Water, Hampshire, producing bitumen and tanker fuel. During 1930s, 40 sales branches were rationalized into 11 sales divisions, 629 depots were reduced to 530, 11 marine terminals to 8, and 4 new ships joined the fleet. In 1938 acquired controlling interest in Cleveland Petroleum Co Ltd and sunk Britain's first productive oil-well at Dalkeith, Lothian which operated until 1961. During WW2, suffered much damage to fleet, premises and loss of personnel. Post war demand for oil from the chemical industry and as fuel led to the building at Fawley between 1949-51 of a new refinery containing the first catalytic cracking plant in the UK, which has continued to be expanded and modified. Name changed to above in 1951 and to meet continuing demand built a new refinery, third largest in UK, at Milford Haven, Dyfed, between 1958-60. As petrochemical demand increased, in 1966 a separate company, Esso Chemical Ltd, was set up to produce, market and develop same. By late 1970s, distribution system was made up of a fleet of 30 ships of nearly 3 million dead weight tonnage plus a 500 mile network of pipelines, 11 terminals, 22 bulk plants, 7 airport installations, and over 80 authorised distributor depots. Took part in North Sea oil and gas development from its beginnings in the mid 1960s, production starting on the Esso/Shell Leman field off Norfolk coast in 1968. In late 1970s was involved in exploration in central North Sea, to the west of Shetland, to the south of Ireland and in English Channel western approaches. Subsidiary of Exxon Corporation, New Jersey, USA.

Records: at Esso Petroleum, Esso House, Victoria Street, London SW1E 5JW
board minutes 1888-date; agm minutes 1888-date; share registers 1888-date; cancelled share warrants and coupons 1941-7; directors registers 1903-date; annual returns 1888-date; company notices 1912-38; underhand and company seal registers 1903-date; incorporation

and change of name papers 1888,1951; royal warrants 1927,1940; debenture stock trust deeds 1953-9; balance sheets 1890s.

Hugh Popham, *Esso in Britain 90 Years of History* (priv pub 1978)

619 WOLTON & ATTWOOD LTD

28 Apr 1888
26549
Anchor Terrace, Southwark Bridge Road, London SE1 9HS
Brewing

History: traces its origins to John Courage, a shipping agent from Aberdeen, who purchased a brew-house at Horsleydown, Southwark in 1787. When John Courage died in 1793, his widow, Harriet, carried on the business until her death in 1797. John Donaldson, the senior clerk, then assumed management. He subsequently became a partner and by 1800 the company was known as Courage & Donaldson. In 1836 the nominal estate, after writing off losses and appreciation was £151,215. By 1851 the Donaldson family had withdrawn from management and in 1852 the business became a family concern when John Courage junior took his sons John and Robert into partnership. In 1887 output exceeded 300,000 barrels. The business was incorporated as Courage & Co Ltd in 1888. At this period the company was heavily involved in supplying to public houses; in 1897 loans to public houses equalled £2.2 million, and output was 333,400 barrels. From 1900s policy changed to direct ownership of public houses. Acquired G&E Halls' Brewery, Alton, Hampshire in 1903; Camden Brewery Co Ltd in 1924; Farnham United Breweries Ltd in 1927; Noakes & Co Ltd, Black Eagle Brewery, Bermondsey in 1930; CN Kidd & Son Ltd, Dartford, Kent in 1937; and Hodgson's Kingston Brewery Co Ltd in 1943. In 1955 Courage & Co Ltd merged with Barclay Perkins & Co Ltd, Anchor Brewery, Park Street, Southwark (inc 1896) under the aegis of a new company, Courage & Barclay Ltd. In 1957 Courage & Barclay Ltd acquired the businesses and assets of certain of its subsidiaries including Courage & Co Ltd which ceased to trade from that date. In 1970 the company changed its name to Courage Barclay & Simonds Ltd and then to the above in May 1979 prior to liquidation a month later.

Records (1): at Courage, Anchor Terrace, Southwark Bridge Road, London SE1 9HS
board meeting: minutes 1934-6,1955-7, agenda books 1937-57, papers and correspondence 1954-7; investment committee: meeting minutes 1934-40, reports 1935-9; museums and history sub-committee meeting minutes 1934-52; general meeting: minutes 1888-1914, papers 1907; share papers 1887-1937; directors register 1911-59; managing directors agreements 1897-1907; debenture stock deeds and papers 1889-1947; memo and articles of association 1888-1960; seal registers 1927-55; corporate papers 1854-1910; acquisition papers 1922-7,1950-5; annual reports 1890-1935; balance sheets and accounts 1908-67; accounting papers 1806-14,1915-39; costing schedules and papers 1938-51; Alton accounts 1954-6; ledgers: 1842-63, loans 1869-90, general 1921-57, charities 1922-57, loan club c1945-65, soft drinks and public house 1961-4; bought book 1839-54; account books 1850-7,1929-33; cash books 1808-16,1864-5,1883-7,1931-58; petty 1810-15,1964-5; receipt book 1941-57; financial papers 1829-1909; sales committee meeting minutes 1951-4; trade figures: Windsor and Alton 1930-52, analysis 1921-51; sales: book 1960-5, analysis 1947-50; public house supplies book 1848-56; profit summary 1947-9; beer bottled records 1932-52; delivery: ledger 1962-4, book 1825-65; stock: sheets 1941-7, beer book 1858-67; supply agreements 1912-52; price list 1946; trade-

mark labels, patents and agreements 1900-74; brewed totals 1812-14,1825-9,1880-7; brewing: books 1914-62, manuals c1820-50, costing books 1915-16,1948-64; beer analysis 1947-50; materials purchase book 1938-64; hop and malt etc stock: papers 1863-1921, books 1910,1941-65; brewery and brewing papers and correspondence 1850s-1950s; engine plans 1856-73; plant and process photographs 1900 on; wage rates 1858-87; salaries: ledgers 1930-48, cash books 1929-44, summaries 1946-52; salaries and wages: book 1950-3, comparisons 1938-49; employees service book 1884-1946; staff: books c1929-52, registers 1920-40, photographs 1885 on; pensioners register 1940s; Courage club rules 1958-64; house journal 1964; plans committee meeting minutes 1929-52; properties: committee meeting minutes 1952-60, ledger c1929-31; estates: ledgers c1911-52, maintenance books c1944-51; investments ledgers 1896-1958; premises: plans 1884-1963, inventory and valuation 1889,1899, correspondence and papers 1822-1934; public house: ledgers 1953-65, loan applications 1890-1929, tenancy interview diaries 1927-48, deed register 1880-1927, title deeds and papers 1854-1946; Courage family estate papers and correspondence 1889-1934; misc correspondence and papers c1850-1970; John Courage: shipping ledgers 1788-93, journals 1790-9; cash memo 1810-14; bank books 1856-62; wine list 1861; correspondence and papers 1788,1855-70; will 1861; Courage & Donaldson cash book 1851-4; subsidiary companies misc records 1814-1963

Camden Brewing Co Ltd: board meeting minutes 1923-4; memo and articles of association 1889-1902; debenture stock trust deeds 1895-1913; annual report 1924; brewery: purchase correspondence 1922-7, plan 1923; public house and other premises deeds and papers 1751-1961

Courage (Central) Ltd: properties committee meeting minutes 1961-3; auditors correspondence and papers 1961-4

Courage (Eastern) Ltd: board: meeting minutes 1962-5, and committee meeting minutes 1970-date; property committee meeting minutes 1962-5; trade and property accounts 1960s; lager sample results 1960-4; work study reports 1965-8; staff returns 1960s

Courage (Export) Ltd: board meeting minutes 1963-8

Courage (Western) Ltd: board meeting minutes 1961-7; property committee meeting minutes 1960-4

Farnham United Breweries Ltd: board: and general meeting minutes 1889-1951, agenda book 1928-42; directors register 1900-48; mortgage register 1890-1927; seals register 1931-41; liquidation correspondence 1951; annual reports and accounts 1929-42; accounts 1948; premises conveyance 1951

Hodgson's Kingston Brewery Co Ltd: board meeting: minutes 1886-1970, agenda books 1918-48; management committee meeting minutes 1950-1; general meeting minutes 1887-1970; members register 1957-9; mortgage registers 1886-1969; directors registers 1917-55; share: applications and allotment book 1903, certificates and papers 1931-43; debenture stock trust deeds 1886-1952; memo and articles of association 1933,1958; seals register 1924-70; annual reports and accounts 1954-6; annual accounts 1941-3,1965-7; balance sheets and accounts 1945-8,1954-7; ledgers: general 1914-21, impersonal 1924-50, private 1918-52, deposits etc 1934-48, bought 1959-64, special creditors 1934-50; journals: 1934-6, bought 1854-82, private 1907-40, general expenditure 1936-9, special creditors 1945-50; receipts 1850-90; trade deliveries record 1837-60; bottles and boxes ledger 1947-50; brewery list 1807-09; stock book 1845-53; gyle book 1886; plant and machinery schedule and valuation 1947; benevolent and superannuation fund: minutes and papers 1945-8, employee agreements 1933,1952, wages book 1949-50; brewery estate particulars 1854; public house: documents and papers 1850-90, repairs ledger 1947-50, photographs 1930s-40s; deeds etc schedule c1946; comparison books and rent roll 1919-49; rebuilding register 1938-40; maintenance order book 1945-50; property and insurance registers 1913-32; brewery and family papers and correspondence 1850-90,1949-58; NJ Hodgson diaries 1875-8

CN Kidd & Son Ltd: directors and general meeting minutes 1920-51; partnership agreement 1899; acquisition papers 1920,1937; memo and articles of association 1920; mortgage register 1920; liquidation papers and correspondence 1951; annual reports and accounts 1938-42; private ledger 1920-38; rough: journal 1938-51, cash book 1938-51; brewery title deeds, papers and correspondence 1804-1968; family papers and correspondence 1844-1917; properties valuation c1951; public house deeds and papers 1867-1929; misc papers 1824-1914

Noakes & Co Ltd: directors: and general meeting minutes 1897-1919, agenda books 1929-42; board reports 1914-29; share register and ledger 1897-9; debenture stock: deeds and papers 1897-1941, holders list 1931, holders meeting minutes 1908-09; takeover papers 1928-30; seals register 1948-58; annual reports and accounts 1897-1956; balance sheets and accounts 1954-7,1965-7; analysis 1920-7; Windsor Brewery account 1918-28; ledgers: private 1897-1928, loan 1931-3; production report 1930; manager agreement 1929; brewery: inventory 1848, title deeds and documents 1852-1910; public house and premises deed, documents and papers c1760-1964

Barclay Perkins & Co Ltd: directors meeting: minutes 1920-60, extracts 1953-7, agendas 1926-60, reports 1953-61, papers and correspondence 1956-60; acquisition papers 1959; committee meeting minutes: managing directors 1933-58, agenda book 1934-8, brewing 1936,1956-62, export 1962, sales 1955-60; general meeting minutes 1930-54; organisation memo 1955-61; directors registers 1900-50s; share: sealing registers 1941-9, transfer registers 1937-54; debenture stock: holders registers c1924-36, transfer register 1929-56, trust deeds 1895-1957, ledgers 1925-36; mortgage registers 1896-1946; probate registers 1917-56; seals registers 1935-58; memo and articles of association 1896-1950; partnership deeds 1781-1892; amalgamation papers 1939,1955; secretarys report and accounts 1897-1938; annual reports and accounts 1908-61; finance committee meeting minutes 1949-57; balance sheet and accounts 1917-38,1965-7; ledgers: general 1898-1965, private 1935-48, deposits 1950-64, loan 1896-7,1911-25, fixed assets 1901-31; journals 1919-52; cash books: general 1907-17, private 1931-53, treasurers 1909-58, Anchor vaults 1943-54, payments 1940-7, bank 1956-65; audit papers 1949-64; financial papers 1951-67; sales: book 1903-29, and drawings book 1913-20; bottling department balance sheets and sales summaries 1917-30; town trade book 1931-42; beer: trades book 1901-25, sold record 1953-5; advertising papers and correspondence nd; brewery visitors photographs 1921-55; trade-mark labels, patents and agreements 1900-73; brewing books: 1917-48, ale 1834-6, lager 1921-62, notes 1912-39, samples 1963-4; brewing charges 1897-1932; beer gyles summary books 1911-13,1922-51; lager gyle book 1925-8; stock book: 1938-40, hops 1936-9,1948-62, sugar 1931-65; malt: book 1947-54, journal 1931-62, delivery notes, papers and correspondence 1934-56; lager: test records 1926, analysis forms 1961-3; barley analysis 1942-56; staff: register 1919-45, circular book 1940-57, record sheets 1946-55; clerks salary books 1927-52; pensioners and invalids book 1934-42; staff pension fund: rules, trustee papers and minutes, accounts and correspondence c1922-56; apprenticeship indenture 1796; staff clubs photographs and papers 1926-57; house journal 1922-58; work peoples provident fund: committee and agm minutes 1922-53, agenda books 1936-74, private ledger 1931-75, investment ledger 1931-48, rent ledger 1949-62, journal 1954-61, cash books 1930-74; lease and general ledger 1853-1924; property schedule 1901; private valuation ledgers 1913-33;

surveyors department ledger 1934-7; Maidstone brewery papers 1936-9; insurance: register 1954-5, papers 1956-67; Anchor Brewery: inventory and valuation 1941, title deeds and papers 1560-1935, photographs 1920,1940, plans 1951-60; public house: rest books 1919-56, leases, tenancies and mortgages schedules 1898-1952, licensing papers and correspondence 1929-46, title deeds, documents and papers 1679-1978; misc papers 1836-90s

Barclay Perkins (Sudan) Ltd: Khartoum board meeting minutes 1954-6; memo and articles of association 1951-5; Harp lager factory production, sales and stock papers and correspondence 1960-70

Blue Nile Brewery Ltd: directors meeting: minutes 1964-8, reports 1967-8; memo and articles of association 1954-69; audited balance sheets 1954-9; financial: papers 1951-5, corporate and staff correspondence 1953-71

Camwall Ltd: share: certificates 1903-54, correspondence 1954; indemnity letters 1903-53; memo and articles of association 1900; annual reports and accounts 1955-60; accounts 1960-6; trade returns and papers 1956-60; documents register and rent lists 1900-60

Dartford Brewery Co Ltd: board and general meeting minutes 1955-70; joint committee meeting minutes with Style & Winch Ltd and Royal Brewery Brentford Ltd 1924-48; members register 1957-64; directors register 1906-69; mortgage registers 1897-1969; share transfer register 1948-56; debenture stock trust deeds, papers and correspondence 1902-48; seals registers 1938-67; memo and articles of association 1879-1958; annual reports and accounts 1899-1956; accounts 1965-7; private ledgers 1897-1951; joint bank books 1926-51; bank account books 1938-50; premises: diary 1933, insurance book 1926-40, order book 1949-54; tenants dilapidations ledger nd

Medway Mineral Waters Ltd: memo and articles of association 1949

Royal Brewery Brentford Ltd: directors meeting minutes 1890-1949; joint committee meeting minutes 1924-48; general meeting minutes 1890-1960; share: allotment books nd, register c1934-53, transfer registers 1916-57, documents 1900-38; debenture stock: trust deeds 1891-1947, transfer registers 1942-56; seals registers 1891-1957; memo and articles of association 1890,1956; annual report and accounts 1891-1956; audited accounts 1926-44,1965-7; joint bank books 1926-51; bank account books 1926-54; joint diary 1933

Style & Winch Ltd: board and general meeting: minutes 1936-70, reports 1948-54; joint committee meeting minutes 1924-48; members register 1957-64; directors register c1907-c69; mortgage register 1957-69; debenture stock: trust deeds 1899-1957, transfer register 1889-1957, seals registers 1931-70; memo and articles of association 1899-1958; annual reports and accounts 1902-61; annual accounts 1897-1918,1965-7; private ledgers 1935-57; bank account books 1899-1951; bank books: 1899-1926, joint 1926-51; lager interest amalgamation papers 1939; pension scheme rules etc 1947-59; staff records 1940s-50s; public house: insurance book 1925-53, order book 1946-55; joint diary 1933; Tooting Brewery sale particulars 1907; premises papers and correspondence 1879-1902

H&G Simonds Ltd: (See summary no 519)

Arthur Cooper (Wine Merchant) Ltd: share papers 1974; memo and articles of association 1932; annual returns 1969,1979; annual reports and accounts 1971-8

Charles Kinloch Ltd: board meeting minutes and correspondence 1961-5; acquisition papers 1956-8; financial papers and correspondence 1966-7; wine and spirit ledger 1964-5

Nicholsons & Sons Ltd: directors and general meeting: minutes 1903-67, agenda book 1903-13; members registers 1903-56; mortgage register 1913-65; debenture stock: trust deeds and papers 1927-61, holders register 1903-54; seals register 1959-62; memo and articles of association 1903-58; annual reports and accounts 1959-66; accounts 1965-6; trade-mark papers 1926-9; staff pension fund: reports, papers and correspondence 1952-6, management committee meeting minutes 1953-61, regulations 1953-61, membership cards 1959-61; public house title deeds 1889-94

Refells Bexley Brewery Ltd: directors meeting: minutes 1898-1970, agenda book 1945-56; general meeting minutes 1898-1970; prospectus 1898; members register 1956-64; directors register c1947-c69; mortgage registers 1898-1936; share: register c1946-54, ledgers 1898-1945, transfer register 1920-56; debenture stock: trust deed 1899, registers 1898-1954, holders register 1903-04,1956-64; seals register 1944-70; memo and articles of association 1898-1958; acquisition papers 1956-69; annual reports and accounts 1899-1958; audited accounts 1955-7,1965-7; impersonal ledger 1947-50; cash books: 1935-41, bank 1947-57; taxation papers and correspondence 1950-60; sales ledgers 1951-7; wages books 1933-57; salaries book 1945-57; properties register nd; public house insurance register 1920-30; war damage papers and correspondence 1941-8; premises order book 1946-55; rent journal 1950-7

Yardley's London & Provincial Stores Ltd: directors meeting minutes 1947-64; general meeting minutes 1930-64; memo and articles of association 1959-64

Courage, Barclay & Simonds Ltd: board reports 1962-3; managing directors committee meeting minutes 1963-5; directors register 1967-70; debenture stock trust deeds 1957-67; acquisition papers 1959-68; annual reports and accounts 1962-70; audit papers 1961-4; sales committee papers 1960-2; advertising record 1960s; brewing committee meeting minutes and papers 1961-4; production planning committee meeting minutes 1960-1; Harp lager reports 1963; brewing book 1965; staff: pension fund minutes, papers and correspondence 1958-66, circulars 1964, journals 1964-9; data processing papers and correspondence 1963-8

Anchor Taverns Ltd: memo and articles of association 1938-50; annual reports and accounts 1950,1955-7

Charles Beasley Ltd: directors meeting minutes 1965-70; general meeting minutes 1943-68; members register and share ledger c1944-51; mortgage register 1944-65; directors registers 1943-69; share transfer register 1951-69; seals register 1966; memo and articles of association 1964; annual reports and accounts 1948-64; balance sheets and accounts 1944-67; ledgers: private 1910,1919-54, impersonal 1945-65; petty cash books 1950-64; purchase journals 1955-62; private bottled ledger 1958-65; wine and spirit ledgers 1963-5; beer day book 1960-5; malt sugar and hops purchase book 1948-64; stock books: wine and spirit 1956-9, malt 1960-5, beer 1964-5; wages books 1898-1965; staff compensation book 1905-32; correspondence 1964-9; public house lease ledgers 1896-1911

Clinch & Co Ltd: directors and general meeting minutes 1950-67; memo and articles of association 1950; seals register 1962-8; annual reports and accounts 1950-62; accounts 1966

Couratown Property Developments Ltd: directors meeting minutes 1962-5

Harmans Uxbridge Brewery Ltd: directors meeting: minutes 1924-67, agendas and papers 1925-63; general meeting: minutes 1957-67, agendas and papers 1955-64; debenture stockholders: meeting minutes 1931-61, register 1924-63; share: certificates 1924-61, transfer documents 1947-64; corporate papers 1924-59; debenture stock papers and correspondence 1924-63; memo and articles of association 1924-59; seals register 1964-70; acquisition papers 1954-64; annual reports and accounts 1932-48,1961-3; accounts 1965-6; ledgers: 1875-1924,1942-64, private 1913-c57, impersonal 1924-61, bought 1956-63; journals: 1913-64, cash books 1904-17,1951-64; purchase book 1958-61; bank: cash books 1922-61, pass books 1962; brewery accounts 1959-62; financial correspondence and papers 1925-63; sales: beer statistics

1927-64, ledgers 1960-3, journal 1961-3, day book 1960-1, papers and correspondence 1960-3; trade statistics and paper 1961-4; wine and spirit: ledgers 1961-3, cash books 1961-4, purchase book 1961-3, papers 1961, customer accounts 1962; stock: debt book 1932-50, summary 1958-64; price lists 1961; trade-marks papers 1951-60; supply papers 1951-60; time book 1963-4; hop summary book 1960-2; machinery: repairs book 1961-3, machinery tests papers 1939-58; production census returns 1951-61; wages: sheets 1951-64, book 1954-5, papers 1958-63; staff: employment files 1955-64, list 1963; accident books 1939-63; service agreements 1958-63; pension scheme: rules, papers and correspondence 1956-64, property register 1876-1924; estates summary 1922-63; rent: summaries 1931-5, registers 1953-64, ledger 1956-63, papers and correspondence 1960-3; tenancy agreements 1945-50; public house accounts 1935-58; estate repairs ledger 1963; rate papers 1945-63; insurance policies 1956-64; deeds registers c1890-1964; misc correspondence and papers 1944-68

R Halley Ltd: directors meeting: minutes 1947-64, papers 1954-64; general meeting minutes 1957-64; memo and articles of association 1954-6; annual reports and accounts 1963-4; accounts 1965-6; ledgers: bought 1955-6, purchase 1957-9, general expenses 1947-54; financial papers 1943-70; sales: summaries 1955-62, cash book 1956-63, day book 1961-3; stock books 1955-63; supplies papers 1955-63; wages sheets 1955-64; staff papers 1957-64; premises papers 1956-64; misc correspondence papers 1955-63

Horsleydown Property Investment Co Ltd: board: meeting minutes 1961-7, papers 1969-72; corporate papers 1961-74; accounts 1961-74; financial papers 1962-75; premises papers 1962-72

London & Provincial Shop Centres (Horsleydown) Ltd: formation and board papers 1963-7; annual reports and accounts 1968-71; financial papers 1965-6

London & Provincial Shop Centres Horsleydown (Slough) Ltd: board meeting minutes and papers 1960-2

McManus-Horsleydown Ltd: board and general meeting minutes 1965-7; corporate papers 1963-7

Saccone & Speed Ltd: board meeting minutes and papers 1960-2

Sheffield & District Public House Trust Co Ltd: directors: meeting minutes 1941-64, register 1956-75; share transfer documents 1942-66; annual returns 1966-75; memo and articles of association 1966; acquisition papers 1966-75; annual reports and accounts 1934-74

Bristol Brewery Georges & Co Ltd: (See summary no 596)

Ashford Valley Cyders Ltd: directors and general meeting minutes 1949-64; memo and articles of association 1948

Carlos & Theale Ltd: board meeting minutes and agendas 1957-61; memo and articles of association 1961

Chandlers Ltd: memo and articles of association 1940; balance sheet and accounts 1953; ledger 1935-50; journal 1935-50; cash book 1935-57

Charlton Breweries Co Ltd: debenture stock: trust deed 1944, register 1894-1944

Henry Good & Son Ltd: balance sheets and accounts 1899-1902; brewery papers 1944-9

Lawn & Alder Ltd: board and general meeting minutes 1954-79; members register 1954-63; memo and articles of association 1954; liquidation papers 1955-79

Old Brewery Development Co Ltd: formation and board meeting papers and correspondence 1961-72

G Raggett & Son Ltd: directors and general meeting minutes 1907-64; balance sheet and

accounts 1954-60
Santorin Ltd: directors and general meeting minutes 1928-64
South Coast Bottling Co Ltd: directors and general meeting minutes 1925-48; annual report and accounts 1955-7
Herbert Stebbing & Sons Ltd: directors meeting minutes 1913-69; members register 1938-69
United Breweries Ltd: London committee meeting minutes 1935-55; plant and accounts reports 1953; corporate correspondence 1954-7
H&G Watts (1935) Ltd: directors and general meeting minutes 1935-64; annual report and accounts 1955-7
York Mineral Water Co Ltd: directors and general meeting minutes 1943-64; memo and articles of association 1960-2; annual report and accounts 1935-6,1951-7

Records (2): at Courage (Central), 32 Bridge Street, Reading, Berkshire RG1 2LX
Windsor trade properties books 1936-51; house journal 1962-4; Alton Brewery photographs 1904-64
Courage (Central) Ltd: visitors book 1975; medical centre analysis book 1972-5
G Hall & Co Ltd: price lists, advertisements and premises photographs 1900-23
Neville Reid & Co Ltd: agenda book 1915-70; bank notes c1838; royal warrant 1858
Nicholsons & Sons Ltd: debenture stock trust deed papers 1937-55; memo and articles of association 1903; public house leases and papers 1864-1939; family papers and correspondence 1947-52
Clinch & Co Ltd: directors and general meeting minutes 1892-1950,1960-2; acquisition papers 1959-62; corporate papers 1863-1950; nominal ledger 1953-60; service agreement 1956; rent ledger 1960-3
Harmans Uxbridge Brewery Ltd: cash book 1876-99

Records (3): at Berkshire Record Office, Shire Hall, Reading, Berkshire RG2 9XD
Neville Reid & Co Ltd: brewery: ledgers 1844-62, journals 1844-69, securities record c1837-c44; banking: ledgers 1844-62, journal 1845-64, bank account 1838-48; sales memos 1837-44; brewery inventory 1853; public house: records 1857-90,1914-20, tenancy register 1886-1933, deeds and leases nd; in letters 1884-5

Records (4): at Greater London Record Office, 40 Northampton Road, London EC1R OAB
Barclay Perkins & Co Ltd: partners record book 1877-97; directors meeting minutes 1895-1920; shareholders capital account books 1814-96; debenture stockholders documents schedule c1901; partnership articles 1831; probates register 1911-17; balance sheets and accounts 1897-1919; ledgers: 1896-1901, DJ Barclay 1784-1807, general 1894-7, capital account 1801-1912, loan 1850-98; journals 1896-1919; cash books 1776-1921; sales: abstract 1900-06, and brewing ledgers 1833-4,1895-14; sign writers book 1834-47; county customers book nd-1897; bottling department committee meeting minutes 1903-10; works department, counting house and malting committees meeting minutes 1907-08; brewing: books 1801-1917, charges 1890-5; sancta sanctorum 1834-80; beer gyles summary books 1901-03,1913,1916; sugar and caramel books 1913-19; gains and losses book 1888-96; lease ledgers: brewery 1837-45, bought and tied houses 1896-1904; Anchor malting plant inventory 1896; Anchor Brewery

title deeds 1621-1893; public house rest books 1748-1919; legal case report 1863

Records (5): at Kent Archives Office, County Hall, Maidstone, Kent ME14 1X
Style & Winch Ltd: employee documents 1899-1924; apprenticeship indentures 1923-9; public house and other premises deeds, documents and papers 1793-1972

J Pudney, *A Draught Of Contentment* (1971)

620 MOORSIDE TRUST LTD

28 Apr 1888
26562
32 St Mary at Hill, London EC3P 3AV
Investment trust (formerly mortgage)

History: incorporated in 1888 as Mortgage Co of River Plate Ltd to give loans on securities in connection with River Plate Trust, Loan & Agency Co Ltd (est 1881) in Argentina. Name changed to above in 1946 when company became an investment trust.

Records: at University College London Library, University of London, Gower Street, London WC1E 6BT
directors and general meeting minutes 1888-1952; annual reports and accounts 1888 on; ledgers 1888-1950s

621 GRAND HOTEL CO BRISTOL LTD

1 May 1888
26598
2 The Calls, Leeds, W Yorkshire L52 7JU
Hotel

History: incorporated in 1888 as above to take over the property of Bristol City Hotel Co Ltd - Grand Hotel situated on Corn and Broad Streets, Bristol, Avon. Acquired in 1980 by Mount Charlotte Investments Ltd of Leeds, W Yorkshire.

Records: at Grand Hotel Co Bristol, Broad Street, Bristol, Avon BS1 2EL
records 1965-date

622 MONTE CARLO HOTEL CO LTD

1 May 1888
26633
7-8 Stratford Place, London W1N 0AJ
Hotel

History: incorporated as above in 1888 to purchase land in Monte Carlo, Monaco, to build the Hotel Metropole. In 1889 bought an hotel in Cannes, France, selling it to Société de l'Hôtel Metropole Cannes in 1897. Acquired prior to 1920 by Gordon Hotels Ltd which was itself acquired by Grand Metropolitan Hotels Ltd, a subsidiary of Grand Metropolitan Ltd, in 1964-5. Hotel Metropole was sold by the latter in 1981.

Records: at Grand Metropolitan Hotels, 7-8 Stratford Place, London W1N 0AJ
board meeting minutes 1888-1905; directors reports 1889,1941-62; general meeting minutes and shareholders attendance sheets 1888-1905,1927-65; members register 1904-date; directors register 1929-date; share transfer register 1936-61; annual returns 1927-8; memo and articles of association 1888,1975; corporate documents and papers 1888-date

623 BRITISH MARITIME TRUST LTD
5 May 1888
26674
105 Fenchurch Street, London EC3M 5HH
Investment

History: incorporated in 1888 as Trustee, Debenture, Assets Purchase & Mortgage Guarantee Co Ltd changing name to British Maritime Mortgage Trust Ltd in 1889. Assisted approved shipowners to build tonnage on security of sound mortgages on ships. Christopher Furness & Co were appointed managers in 1890 and in 1896 Sir Christopher Furness, by then of Furness Withy & Co Ltd, obtained a controlling interest. Name changed to above in 1897. Sir Christopher used company to purchase tonnage for chartering to regular lines, an extensive fleet of steamers being built up. Fleet was taken over by Furness Withy & Co Ltd in 1907 and company's business became investment and finance. By 1917 company was investing in British government and colonial securities, home and foreign railways and commercial and industrial holdings. 88.5 per cent of investments were British, 10 per cent were colonial and 1.5 per cent were foreign. By 1960s had 4 subsidiaries: Arcade Property Co Ltd (inc 1934); Danube Navigation Co Ltd (inc 1920); River Syndicate Ltd (inc 1920); and Shipping Investment Trust Ltd (inc 1926).

Records: at Furness Withy, 105 Fenchurch Street, London EC3M 5HH
directors meeting: minutes 1890-date, attendance books 1899-date; general meeting minutes 1897-date; agm proceedings 1898-9,1903-32; members register c1912-date; share: allotment book 1890, transfer register 1890-1937, certificate 1890-1933, transfer documents 1890s on; debenture stock: holders registers 1935-55, transfer documents 1935, prospectus 1912; directors registers 1930-date; mortgage register 1935-7; annual returns 1911-date; memo and articles of association 1950-date; corporate documents and papers 1897-1981; annual reports and accounts 1892-date; seal book 1931-46; balance sheets and accounts 1897-1982; annual accounts papers 1960-date; private ledgers 1890-1949; journals 1914-76; cash books 1890-2,1907-65; bills receiveable 1911-36; investment: ledgers 1908-38, valuations and lists 1970s-date, papers and correspondence 1920s-70s; loan papers and correspondence 1930s-70s; history: notes c1902, article 1942
Arcade Property Co Ltd: directors and general meeting minutes, share registers, seal books, annual returns, annual reports and accounts, balance sheets and accounts, ledgers, journals and cash books 1934-date
Danube Navigation Co Ltd: directors and general meeting minutes, share registers, seal books, annual returns, annual reports and accounts, balance sheets and accounts, ledgers, journals

and cash books 1920-date
River Syndicate Ltd: corporate documents and audited accounts 1920-date
Shipping Investment Trust Ltd: directors and general meeting minutes, share registers, seal books, annual returns, annual reports and accounts, balance sheets and accounts, ledgers, journals and cash books 1926-date

624 LONDON ASSOCIATION FOR THE BLIND

7 May 1888
26688
14-16 Verney Road, London SE16 3DZ
Charity

History: founded in 1857 as Surrey Association for the General Welfare of the Blind to find employment for and to teach trades to blind people in London and Surrey. Known as South London Association for the General Welfare of the Blind from 1877-9. Began instructing 2-3 poor blind people in basket making in a London house. By 1880 a workshop had been set up at 90 Peckham Road, London, where blind men and women were involved in brush making, knitting and cane work. Incorporated in 1888 as a company limited by guarantee but having no share capital, changing name to above in 1910. By 1907 workshop was producing baskets, brushes, mattresses, chairs, fish and poultry bags, mats and bundles of chopped firewood. By 1912 headquarters were at 60 Great Portland Street, London, moving to 178 Charing Cross Road, London in 1913 and 102 Dean Street, Soho, London by 1918. A women's workshop operated from at least 1914 at 58 Rochester Row, London, moving to 144a Warwick Street, London by 1923. First seaside home operated at Worthing, W Sussex in 1914. By 1923 had many hostels throughout London for the blind. First organisation to put blind workers behind power driven machinery and in 1930s and early 1940s experimented with hand operated injection moulding machines. Operated a tile making factory in Essex in 1936 and by 1940s had shops in Kensington High Street, London, and Bournemouth, Dorset, a training centre at Bognor Regis, W Sussex, and homes at Belgrave Road, and Grove Lane, London, and Southlands Road, Bickley, London. In 1941 took over management of Barclay Workshops for Blind Women in Crawford Street, London, established in 1905 for women leaving Barclay Home & School for Blind & Partially Blind Girls, Brighton, E Sussex. Head offices moved to Peckham Road in 1950s when also had homes at Bournemouth; Grove Lane; Bickley; and Epsom, Surrey. Erected new moulding shop in 1956 but required more space and purchased 33,000 sq ft site on the Old Surrey Canal, London in early 1970s. The knitting department ceased production in 1967 as did the manufacture of knitting pins in early 1970s. Production then consisted largely of PVC. In 1981 the workshop operating as Lab Industries was injection moulding nearly all types of thermoplastics, moulding foam materials and manufacturing PVC welded products. Also had a shareholding in Wheyo Tool Co Ltd, mould makers of E London (inc 1949) and Lafega Ltd, ladies sportswear manufacturers of Regent Street, London (inc 1927 as Hearth & Home Ltd, changing name to Alphega (Sportswear) Ltd and then to Lafega Ltd in 1936). In 1981 still carried out original objects by providing residential care homes at Horley, W Sussex and Sanderstead, Greater London; flats at Epsom, Crawford Street and Bromar Court, London; hostels at Adams House, London; holiday hotels at

Bognor Regis, W Sussex; Weston super Mare, Avon; training and employment in modern industry, and cash help for blind and partially sighted people.

Records: at London Association for the Blind, 14-16 Verney Road, London SE16 3DZ
committee meeting minutes: buildings and estates 1928-48, finance 1928-52, general purposes 1933-52, ladies 1911-17, sales 1920; memo and articles of association 1954; annual reports and accounts 1877,1880-date; office bearers list 1857-1965; balance sheet analysis 1857-1961; workshop managers report 1886-7; general secretarys diaries 1946-78; *The Blind Record* 1914-24; LAB news-letter 1980 on; newscuttings 1937-65; programmes and catalogues for blind work events, advertisements and donation leaflets 1920s-65; handbook c1975
Barclay Home & School for Blind & Partially Blind Girls: annual reports and accounts 1893-1942
Barclay Workshops for Blind Women: committee meeting minutes 1905-41; annual reports and accounts 1906-44; reference book c1906-42; managers or secretarys diaries 1930-64
Barclay Institutions for the Blind: committee meeting minutes 1919-31; annual reports and accounts 1919-30
Lafega Ltd: directors and general meeting minutes 1925-72; members register 1927-71; auditors reports and balance sheets and accounts 1936-72
Wheyo Tool Co Ltd: directors and general meeting minutes 1964-71; members register 1949-71; audited accounts 1964-71

625 GEORGE ANGUS & CO LTD

10 May 1888
26750
152-155 Westgate Road, Newcastle upon Tyne, Tyne & Wear NE99 1TG
Fire-hose, belting and gear manufacturers

History: founded as leather manufacturers in 1788 by Joseph Angus at 22 The Close, Newcastle upon Tyne. Joined by his son William in 1810 and his grandson George in 1836. In 1843 India-rubber was added to the firms range of gas and water tubing and a separate rubber department was established in 1860 in Grey Street, Newcastle upon Tyne. Those premises were destroyed by fire in 1867 and the department moved to the firm's new premises, at St John's Works between Grainger Street West and Clayton Street, Newcastle upon Tyne. Belting was added to firm's products during 1860s. Opened a Liverpool office in 1875 and a New York branch in 1880. Incorporated as above in 1888. Acquired Bentham Woven Hose Belting Co, Bentham, near Lancaster in 1904 and erected a new mill for manufacture of canvas fire-hose and textile belting. Produced raw hide pinions from 1909 and in 1920 St Anthony's Works, Newcastle upon Tyne was built for the manufacture of gears from leather, metal and 'Durangus' (laminated plastic). In 1937 built a new factory at Wallsend, Tyne & Wear, for the manufacture of oil seals for rotating and reciprocating shafts. Brake linings were manufactured at Bentham from early 1920s and Telamite Ltd was formed in 1938 to sell 'Telamite' brake linings. In 1954, acquired F Reddaway & Co Ltd (inc 1892), belting manufacturers and engineers of Manchester, Greater Manchester. In 1962 Reddaway, Angus and Fire Armour Ltd joined forces to form Angus Fire Armour Division, fire fighting equipment manufacturers. Acquired Reary Gearworks Ltd, Hebburn, Tyne & Wear in 1955 and formed new gear division. By 1962 Angus's fire-hose was manufactured in Toronto, Canada; India; France; USA and Portugal; oil seals were produced in Italy by Angus SpA;

and George Angus & Co (South Africa) Ltd, George Angus (Rhodesia) (Pvt) Ltd, Angus Reddaway & Co A/B of Sweden, and Oy F Reddaway A/B of Finland marketed Angus goods. Acquired by Dunlop Co Ltd in 1968.

Records: at George Angus, 152-155 Westgate Road, Newcastle upon Tyne, Tyne & Wear NE99 1TG
board meeting notes 1929-35; general meeting: minutes 1888-date, attendance book 1888-1968; agm chairmans speech 1907,1940,1957; share: reconciliation books 1888-1947, allotment books 1888; members registers, directors registers, annual returns, annual reports and accounts and seal registers 1920s on; shareholders list 1911; corporate papers 1888,1934-5; takeover correspondence 1954,1968; managing directors agreement and correspondence 1920-32; organisation charts and correspondence 1950s; private ledgers 1870-1930s; ledger 1863-96; private journal day book 1888-96; journals 1920s; private cash books 1882-95; accounts and sales notebook 1920s-30s; receipts 1851-2; price lists, catalogues and sales literature 1912-52; advertisement c1851; raw hide manufacture report 1902; patent 1962; trade-mark 1948; trade literature 1962-5; employment conditions 1928; salary summaries 1934-8; works bulletin 1950-69; roll of honour 1918; insurance reports and papers 1961-7; plans 1940s on; UK, Canada and Johannesburg, South Africa premises, curing, products, machinery, directors, staff and production photographs 1890s-1960s; Liverpool branch manager correspondence 1874-94; wartime overseas bulletins 1940-2; business correspondence 1940s; newscuttings 1868-1960s; history: notes 1900s-50s, booklets 1935-50; visitors books 1909-62
F Reddaway & Co Ltd: takeover papers 1954; balance sheet and accounts 1903; corporate agreements 1927-38; legal proceedings reports 1896,1905; Moscow factory claims correspondence 1938; catalogues and price lists 1902-40; insurance papers 1951-6
David Callender & Sons Ltd: annual report and balance sheets 1959,1960; newscuttings 1958
Reary Gearworks Ltd: catalogue nd

House of Angus Being a Record of Progress 1790-1935 (priv pub 1935)

626 WHITEHAVEN JOINT STOCK BANKING CO LTD
15 May 1888
26835
41 Lothbury, London EC2P 2PB
Banking

History: established in 1829 as a joint stock bank at Whitehaven, Cumbria and incorporated as above in 1888. In 1908 amalgamated with Parr's Bank Ltd which itself amalgamated with London County & Westminster Bank Ltd, a predecessor of National Westminster Bank Ltd, in 1918. By 1908 the bank had 7 branches in Cumbria, at Cleator Moor, Egremont, Harrington, Maryport, Penrith, Seascale and Shap.

Records: at National Westminster Bank, 41 Lothbury, London EC2P 2PB
board meeting minutes 1857-63; share transfer papers 1837-88; deeds of settlement 1829-73; regulations and provisions 1888; amalgamation papers 1908; annual reports 1846-76; balance sheets 1848-60; statement of correspondents accounts 1848-9; weekly statements of London remittances 1853-9; statement of money lent and securities 1842; papers re: securities 19 cent,

investments 1847-1907; correspondence: customer 1834-1901, staff recruitment 1862-83, general manager with family 1869-83

TE Gregory, *The Westminster Bank Through A Century* Vol 2 (1936)

627 EDWARD YOUNG & CO LTD

31 May 1888
26895
153 Regent Street, London W1
Distillers and wine, brandy and rum shippers

History: established at end of 18 cent as distillers and rectifiers and wine, brandy and rum shippers. Known as Dixon, Son & Young from 1838 to 1854; Dixon, Young & Co from 1854-7; E&TS Young from 1857-65; and from 1865 as Edward Young & Co. Incorporated as above in 1888. Had distillery, offices and bonded warehouses in Seel Street, Liverpool, Merseyside, and London bonded warehouses at Wapping Dock and Hanover Street. In about 1920 a branch was opened at 62-63 Mark Lane, London. Joined Associated Wine & Spirit Shippers Ltd, a consortium of wholesalers and shippers formed in 1945, and acquired Feuerheerd Wearne & Co Ltd, London port and sherry shippers founded in Oporto, Portugal in 1815. Associated Wine & Spirit Shippers Ltd was acquired in 1961 by United Breweries Ltd which merged in 1962 with Charrington & Co Ltd through a holding company Charrington United Breweries Ltd which merged with Bass Mitchells & Butlers Ltd to form Bass Charrington Ltd. The company was situated at 14 New Burlington Street, London in 1977, with branches at Liverpool, Merseyside and Glasgow, Strathclyde. In 1983 it was a subsidiary of Bass PLC through Hedges & Butler Ltd.

Records: at Hedges & Butler, Three Mill Lane, Bromley by Bow, London E3 3DU
shareholding meeting minutes 1888-1963; directors: meeting minutes 1940 on, committee meeting minutes 1935-6; share and financial records 1940 on

628 BEVERLEY BROTHERS LTD

1 Jun 1888
26902
Newton Heath Brewery, Manchester, Greater Manchester M10 8PA
Brewing

History: founded in 1861 by Christopher L and Anthony T Beverley, in Harrison Street, Wakefield, W Yorkshire. Built Eagle Brewery in Wakefield in the same year. Opened first public house, the Newmarket, in New Street, Wakefield in 1869 and incorporated as above in 1888. Acquired John Baxter Ltd, Lancashire brewery, in 1952. Acquired in 1967 by the Watney Mann brewing group and merged with Wilson's Brewery Ltd, Newton Heath, Manchester (inc 1894). Company had 150 employees and supplied 173 public houses and off-licences in Yorkshire, Lancashire and Cleveland. Wakefield brewery subsequently closed. In 1981 was a subsidiary of Watney Mann & Truman Brewers Ltd which was owned by Grand Metropolitan Ltd.

Records: at Wilson's Brewery, Newton Heath Brewery, Manchester, Greater Manchester M10 8PA
directors meeting minutes 1888-1961; management committee meeting minutes 1967; share

allotment, transfer, directors holdings and probate register and shareholders ledger 1918-77; debenture stockholders register 1952-80; share and stock certificates 1952-80; mortgages and bonds register 1895-1955; seal register 1959-74; annual returns 1951-70

629 MANCHESTER CHAMBER OF COMMERCE & INDUSTRY

5 Jun 1888
26926
Ship Canal House, King Street, Manchester, Greater Manchester M60 8AH
Chamber of commerce

History: a society of merchants and manufacturers trading with Europe was founded in Manchester in 1794 to detect swindlers and watch over trade interests. It was involved in discussions and petitions to the British and European governments about matters prejudicing trade. Meetings appear to have ceased in 1801 but it was reconstituted in 1820 as a chamber of commerce to promote trade by removing damaging regulations. The chamber was to the forefront of the Anti-Corn Law Movement, with Richard Cobden as a director from 1836. It amalgamated with Manchester Commercial Association (est 1845) in 1858. Incorporated as a company limited by guarantee in 1887 as Manchester Chamber of Commerce to promote trade in Manchester, Salford and district. Name subsequently changed to above. Published monthly journal from 1890. Offices were at 44 Moseley Street, Manchester 1887-1920, then moved to Danlee Buildings, Spring Gardens, 1920-6, and have been in King Street since 1927. In 1981 chamber had over 3000 members, sponsored overseas trade missions, undertook export and other documentation, offered trade information and other services and acted as platform for business opinions in north west England.

Records (1): at Manchester Chamber of Commerce & Industry, Ship Canal House, King Street, Manchester, Greater Manchester M60 8AH
board and committee meeting minutes 1965-date; trade section meeting minutes 1965-date; proceedings reports (annual report and accounts, list of members, copy laws, memoranda and correspondence) 1822-89; monthly: journal 1890-date, newspaper 1971-date
Manchester Commercial Association: proceedings 1845-58

Records (2): at Manchester City Archives Department, Central Library, St Peters Square, Manchester, Greater Manchester M2 5PD
society of merchants meeting minutes 1794-1801; chamber of commerce proceedings 1821-90; board and general meeting proceedings 1890-1926; board meeting minutes 1927-64; directors attendance book 1923-41; executive committee meeting minutes 1931-9; committee meeting minutes: general 1889-1964, East Africa 1920-6, West Africa 1905-19, telephone and telegraph advisory 1913-16, testing house management 1899-1926, textile exports shipping 1918; trade section committee meeting minutes: Africa 1892-1926, Central and South America 1916-26, chemical 1890-1926, China and Far East 1916-26, Egypt, Greece and Levant 1916-26, engineering and metals 1901-26, Europe and USA 1916-26, grey cloth 1916-26, home and colonial 1910-26, India 1909-26, India cotton and rayon 1933-8, leather 1909-25, produce 1894-1926, sugar 1904-26, yarn 1890-1926, general 1927-64; committee members list 1928-43;

Manchester yarn contract conference minutes 1896-1913; members registers 1889-1906; members list nd; seal book 1889-1948
Manchester Commercial Association: minutes 1845-58
Manchester Association of Importers & Exporters: proceedings 1907-35

Elijah Helm, *Chapters in the History of the Manchester Chamber of Commerce* (c1897)

630 LANSDOWN GROVE HOTEL LTD

16 Jun 1888
26976
Lansdown Grove Hotel, Bath, Avon BA1 5EH
Hotel

History: incorporated in 1888 as Lansdown Grove Private Hotel Co Ltd to acquire Lansdown Grove, a mansion house in Bath, Avon and convert it for use as an hotel. Purchased house in 1889 from Bath Land Co Ltd for £4500. Name changed to above in 1891. Hotel was requisitioned in 1942 by Ministry of Works as a Leave Hostel for the American Red Cross and reopened in 1947. In 1983 was a 3 star AA and RAC hotel, having been a 3 star hotel prior to WW2 and since reopening in 1947.

Records: at Lansdown Grove Hotel, Bath, Avon BA1 5EH
directors and general meeting minutes 1907-41; share ledger 1927-57; memo and articles of association 1891-1948; debenture trust deeds and papers 1889-1935; brochure c1910; title deeds 1889

631 SWAIN & CO LTD

19 Jun 1888
26988
42 High Street, Stockport, Greater Manchester SK1 1EH
Newspapers

History: incorporated in 1888 as above to take over Swain & Bearby's *Stockport Advertiser* which had been founded in 1822 by James Lomax. Subsequently acquired *Macclesfield Advertiser* and *Alderley, Wilmslow & Knutsford Advertiser*. General printing department was closed in 1973. Acquired by Guardian & Manchester Evening News Ltd in 1977. Ceased publishing and printing paid-for newspapers in 1981 and sold remaining trade publication of the Ashton under Lyne free newspaper in 1982. *Stockport Advertiser* was merged with *Stockport Express* in 1981 to form *Stockport Express Advertiser*.

Records (1): at Swain, 42 High Street, Stockport, Greater Manchester SK1 1EH
directors meeting minutes 1939-84; executive committee meeting minutes 1977-81; general meeting minutes 1888-1982; members register and share ledger 1888-1934; share: certificate book 1966-78, transfer register 1889-1978; debenture register 1889-97; seal register 1959-80; annual returns 1961-71; half yearly accounts 1956-83; private ledger 1956-83; general ledger 1958-64; employees registers 1958-date; plant inventory and valuation 1952

Records (2): at Metropolitan Borough of Stockport, Archives Service, Central Library, Wellington Road South, Stockport, Greater Manchester SK1 3RS
directors meeting minutes 1888-1938; annual returns 1894-1903; production and machinery

photographs c1945-79; staff: dinner papers 1897,1910-17, testimonials 1942,1944; history booklets 1897,1908; centenary papers 1922-3

Records (3): at British Library, Newspaper Library, Colindale Avenue, London NW9 5HE
Stockport Advertiser and *Cheshire, Lancashire & Derbyshire Weekly Journal* 1823-79; *Macclesfield Advertiser* 1869,1874 on; *Alderley, Wilmslow Advertiser* 1874 on

632 SOUTHERN COUNTIES DAIRIES CO LTD

13 Jul 1888
27122
Unigate House, Western Avenue, London W3 0SH
Dairy

History: incorporated as above in 1888 to carry on trade as milk contractors and dealers, dairy farmers etc. Original registered offices were in London moving to Brighton, E Sussex in 1907. Acquired Wingate & Son, milk purveyors, Aldwick Road Dairy, Bognor Regis, W Sussex in 1905, and G Bradford & Son, dairymen, Carlisle Road, Eastbourne, E Sussex in 1906. By 1929 had a branch at Littlehampton, W Sussex. Acquired by Unigate Ltd in 1959, business was subsequently operated by Holes & Belgravia Dairies in Brighton and Hove, and Simmons & Bradfords Dairies in Eastbourne. Ceased to trade in 1962.

Records: at Unigate, Unigate House, Western Avenue, London W3 0SH
directors and general meeting minutes 1953-date; members register c1948-date; ordinary share: ledgers 1888-1914, certificates 1958-66, transfer forms 1943-62; preference share: ledgers c1893-1956, register 1904-56, transfer forms 1936-62; register: mortgage 1901-c21, directors 1948-68, probate 1956-9

633 TRIBUNE INVESTMENT TRUST

16 Jul 1888
27136
8 Bishopsgate, London EC2N 4AE
Investment

History: company traces its origins to Central Argentine Land Co Ltd, incorporated in 1870 to acquire land in the ownership of Central Argentine Railway Co Ltd, and Brassey, Wyther, Wheelwright & Ogilvie, railway contractors. This land was opened for traffic in 1870, and had been granted to the railway company by the Argentine government in 1863. The company facilitated emigration from Europe, leased and sold land, and itself expioited some resources such as timber. By 1887, 51,500 acres of farmland, valued at £356,778, and town land valued at £33,930 had been sold and a further 20,500 acres of farmland had been leased. In that year the company purchased further land for colonisation, and anticipated further purchases. In order to facilitate this, in 1888 a new company was formed, Argentine Land & Investment Co Ltd, and the original company was put into voluntary liquidation. In 1890 a bond and mortgage department was established. By 1900 total revenue amounted to almost £21,000. By 1910 land sales raised £7112, rents were £15,066 and interest on mortgage loans reached £11,524. In 1927 the company s assets included freehold property in Argentina valued at £304,564, mortgage loans amounting to £115,703 and land instalments due, valued at £146,423. The company was investing an increasing amount of its resources in quoted investments. In 1927 these were valued at £386,000 (in London) and £77,000 (in Argentina). In the 1950s the company embarked upon a determined policy to liquidate most of its remaining Argentinian assets and by 1958 UK assets stood at £1.1 million (of which £1,053,322 were quoted securities at cost) while Argentine assets were £160,597. In 1959 the company's name was changed to above.

Records: at Tribune Investment Trust, 8 Bishopsgate, London EC2N 4AE
board meeting minutes 1870 on; general meeting minutes 1870 on; memo and articles of association 1864,1888 on; formation papers 1888-92; annual report and accounts 1870 on; land concession papers 1863-4; land lease and sale agreements 1904-38; reports on Argentinian properties 1935-43

634 LIVERPOOL SHIPOWNERS' ASSOCIATION

20 Jul 1888
27156
Richmond House, 1 Rumford Place, Liverpool, Merseyside L3 9QE
Shipowners association

History: founded in 1810 by Liverpool shipowners and incorporated as above as company limited by guarantee in 1888 to preserve, protect and support its members shipping and maritime interests. Particularly concerned with the constitution of Mersey Docks & Harbour Board, the state of that harbour and port, of dock facilities, pilotage, porterage, the warehousing system and custom house practice. Operated information service for members and acted on their behalf in legal proceedings involving shipowners interests. In 1895 set up and incorporated Liverpool Shipowners' Freight, Demurrage & Defence Association Ltd which operated until 1917. In 1973 had 14 members with 33 vessels between them. Company was dissolved in 1982.

Records: at Merseyside County Archives Service, Merseyside County Museums, RCA Building, 64-66 Islington, Liverpool, Merseyside L3 8LG
minutes 1906-46; annual report 1902; Garston Docks Joint Shipowners' & Coal Shippers committee minutes 1940-8; memo and articles of association 1888; members register, charges, annual lists etc c1939-57; letter books 1937-60; misc correspondence and documents incl members lists, memos, circulars etc 20 cent; bank account book 1902-14; judicial branch cash book 1889-1914
Liverpool Shipowners' Freight, Demurrage & Defence Association Ltd: minutes 1895-1917; board agendas 1902-03; directors register c1907-16; list 1897-1909; members register 1895-1907; memo and articles of association 1895; rules 1895; subscriptions and expenses books 1895-1917

635 RED POLL CATTLE SOCIETY & BRITISH DANE CATTLE SOCIETY OF GREAT BRITAIN & IRELAND

21 Jul 1888
27159
6 Church Street, Woodbridge, Suffolk
Breed society

History: incorporated in 1888 as Red Polled Society, a company limited by guarantee with the objectives of improving and encouraging the breeding of Red Polled Cattle and publishing *The Red Polled Herd Book*. On formation the society was administered by a council made up of Suffolk and Norfolk land owners and farmers. In 1909 renamed Red Poll Cattle Society of Great Britain & Ireland. In 1967 again renamed as the above on alteration of its objectives to include the establishment and promotion of Danish Red Breed in Britain.

Records: at Red Poll Cattle Society & British Dane Cattle Society of Great Britain & Ireland, 6 Church Street, Woodbridge, Suffolk

636 ALFRED HUGHES & CO LTD

21 Jul 1888
27163
58 Albert Court, Prince Consort Road, London SW7
Makers-up, packers and forwarding agents

History: incorporated in 1888 as above to take over business of makers-up, packers and finishers carried on by Charles Crockwell and Alfred Hughes. In 1954 company's services were shipping, forwarding and custom agents, transport contractors, insurance agents and air freight. Packing and forwarding departments were closed in 1970 and company's business became property holding. Became insolvent in 1974, and since 1975 the company has been operated under a Scheme of Agreement granted by the High Court of Justice pursuant to Section 206 of Companies Act 1948.

Records: Cork Gulley, Shelley House, 3 Noble Street, London EC2V 7DQ
directors: and general meeting minutes 1881-date, reports 1888-1971

637 COCA-COLA SOUTHERN BOTTLERS LTD

24 Jul 1888
27173
Club House, Hanworth Road, Sunbury on Thames, Surrey TW16 5DF
Soft drink manufacturers (formerly brewing)

History: established in late 19 cent by two brewers, Trayton Kenward of Icklesham, Rye, E Sussex, and John Court of Hadlow, near Tunbridge Wells, Kent and incorporated in 1888 as Kenward & Court Ltd. Name changed to Southern Coca-Cola Bottlers Ltd in 1952 and to above in 1953. In 1981 produced and distributed 'Coca-Cola' soft drink from factory in Isleworth, London, having been a member of Watney Mann group since early 1950s and in 1981 was a wholly owned subsidiary of CC Soft Drinks Ltd, a subsidiary of Watney Mann & Truman Brewers Ltd, itself a subsidiary of Grand Metropolitan Ltd.

Records: at Coca-Cola Southern Bottlers, Club House, Hanworth Road, Sunbury on Thames, Surrey TW16 5DF
corporate documents and papers, incl minutes, annual reports and accounts etc 1960s-date

638 **ST JOHN D'EL REY MINING CO LTD**
24 Jul 1888
27177
Abacus House, 33 Gutter Lane, London EC2V 8AH
Gold mining and investment

History: established in London as Association for Working the Mines of Sao João d'el Rey in the Province of Minas Gerais in the Empire of Brazil under a decree of His Imperial Majesty the Emperor of Brazil on 5 Nov 1828. First directors were London gentlemen and merchants who on 19 Mar 1830 obtained the licence to work the Sao João d'el Rey and Sao Jose gold mines. Charles Herring, as superintendent, and 20 men were sent to Brazil where they found the latter mine waterlogged and unworkable. Sao João d'el Rey yielded very low returns and was abandoned. Purchased in 1834 the Morro Velho gold mine, 150 miles further north at Nova Lima, consisting of 3 workings some 150-200 ft underground. Output rose from 27,450 ovitas (about one eighth ounce avoirdupois) in 1835 to 128,515 ovitas in 1845. In 1849 about 1100 persons were employed at the mine and about 6000 tons of crude ore were stamped monthly. By mid 1850s workings were 1000 ft deep. Incorporated as above in 1858, production that year being 307,261 ovitas. Major cave-in in 1857 reduced gold production and no dividends were paid until 1860. Annual production gradually recovered, reaching 77,800 ounces of gold in 1866. Disastrous fire occurred in 1867, completely destroying the workings. 2 new shafts of over 1000 ft deep were opened but mining operations were suspended until 1872. After initial success, difficulties continued to arise and only 24,800 ounces were recovered in 1883. George Chalmers, superintendent 1884-1924, started rebuilding and modernisation scheme but another cave-in nearly wrote off the mine in 1886. He devised new plans, company being reconstructed and re-registered with same name in 1888, and a new and deeper mine was begun in 1889, reaching a depth of 5800 ft by 1914. Mining operations resumed in 1893, output rising steadily; 23,692 tons of ore raised in 1894, 160,317 in 1904, and 142,668 in 1924. New mine, Espirito Santo, was opened in 1935, total annual tonnage being 295,515 tons. During 1950s, gold prices and production fell but staff and wages increased and by mid 1950s a buyer was sought. Hanna Mining Corporation of Cleveland, USA, iron ore producer, and Leo Model of New York and associates, acquired controlling interest in order to exploit the extremely high grade iron ore deposits (65 per cent+ iron) contained in Morro Velho properties. New Brazilian company was formed of 75 per cent of Morro Velho gold mine, company retaining 25 per cent interest. Head office transferred to Cleveland from Blomfield Street, London in 1960. Plans devised to develop Aguas Claras mine near Belo Horizonte and construct shiploading facility on Sepetiba Bay near Rio de Janeiro in 1960 were not carried out for 10 years due to costs and internal political troubles. Small scale mining project started at Mutuca mine in 1961. Brazilian assets combined with iron ore assets of Companhia Ausciliar de Empresas de Mineracao (CAEMI) in 1965 to form Mineracoes Brasileiras Reunidas SA (MBR), Sao João D'el Rey controlling 49 per cent of the latter, CAEMI 51 per cent. Agreement with 6 Japanese steel companies in 1970 to buy 105 million tons of MBR ore over 15 years led to construction beginning at Aguas Claras mine and terminal sites in 1971. Sold remaining interests in gold properties and became closed-end non diversified investment company, its principal asset a 49 per cent interest in MBR, one of the 10 largest world producers and shippers of iron ore.

Records (1): at St John d'el Rey Mining, Abacus House, 33 Gutter Lane, London EC2V 8AH
general meeting minutes 1946-date; directors share and debenture register 1967-date

Records (2): at Benson Latin American Collection, Sid Richardson Hall 1.108, University of Texas General Libraries, Austin, Texas 78712-7330
board minutes 1830-1954; accounts committee minutes 1953-60; agm minutes 1858-1945; directors attendance books 1943-59; members registers 1858-1950s; shareholders: closed accounts to 1959, calls and issuances book 1904-10; stock registers 1895-1950s; share transfer registers 1900-56; issue documents and papers 1951-2,1960; share certificates 1887,1940s-59; share receipt books 1955-9; certificate balance book 1906-56; dividends: warrant register 1899-1919, warrants 1917-50s, books 1948-50s, outstanding book 1897-1945; executors register 1926-52; powers of attorney 1877; company regulations to 1884; annual reports and accounts 1831-1951; ledgers 1830-1956; store ledger 1931-9; journals 1830-1949; cash books 1914-55; account books 1953-60; petty cash books 1947-57; orders and index books 1930s; accounts 1947-59; investment register index 1946-56; income tax papers 1907-55; mine output, geology and inspection reports and correspondence 1880-1950s; inventory 1928; production statistics 1958-60; tonnage raised book 1941; sterling, gold and dollar quotation documents nd; employee: contracts 1920s-50s, reports 1926-47; foreign establishment books 1850s-1920s; Morro Velho registers: baptisms 1851-68, marriages 1851-67, burials 1856-68; extract wills books 1858-1950s; mine and properties maps c1950s; St John mine: lease 1830, and St Jose mine contracts c1800-30; Morro Velho title deed abstracts 1834 on,1934-7; extracts of advices from Morro Velho 1830-63; letter books: board and superintendent 1842-6, and general manager 1959-60, board enquiries c1834; correspondence: general 1860s-1950s, Morro Velho and London 1930s-50s, Novalimense and board 1953-8, London office 1931-42; requisition orders 1938-50s; shipment letters 1949-51; cablegram books 1959-64; photographs late 19 cent-1930s; press cuttings 20 cent; pamphlets, articles etc re mining, history etc 20 cent

Bernard Holloway, *The Story of Morro Velho* (priv pub 1955)

639 OCEAN MARINE INSURANCE CO LTD

31 Jul 1888
27204
1 St Helen's, Undershaft, London EC3P 3DQ
Insurance

History: established in 1859 and incorporated as above in 1884 to underwrite marine insurance. In first 5 years total premiums exceeded £1.28 million. Entered mutual agency agreement with Union Marine & General Insurance Co Ltd of Liverpool, Merseyside in 1864. Acquired City of London Insurance Co Ltd (est 1881) and re-registered in 1888. Took over National Marine Insurance Association Ltd (est 1882) in 1897. Acquired in 1908 by Edinburgh based North British & Mercantile Insurance Co Ltd (est 1809) which was acquired by Commercial Union Assurance Co Ltd in 1959.

Records: at Guildhall Library, Aldermanbury, London EC2P 2EJ
board meeting minutes 1859-1958; finance committee meeting minutes 1860-1938; underwriting committee meeting minutes 1886-1937

Edward Liveing, *A Century of Insurance: The Commercial Union Assurance Group 1861-1961* (1961)

640 BARNSLEY BREWERY CO LTD

8 Aug 1888
27240
Anchor Terrace, Southwark Bridge Road, London SE1 9HS
Brewing

History: established in about 1857 by Guy Senior at Oakwell, W Yorkshire. Traded as Paul & Guy Senior's Oak Well Brewery, makers of Barnsley Bitter. Incorporated as above in 1888 with Arthur Senior as brewery manager. Company results were disappointing until a post WW1 recovery led by HJ Wells and HE Umbers. In 1918 acquired New Trent Brewery Co Ltd of Crowle, Humberside which controlled 30 licences. Moved to Beevor Hall, Barnsley, S Yorkshire in 1922. Acquired James Fox Brewery, Crowle which controlled c40 licensed premises from 1949 to 1950 and entered into a mutual trading agreement with John Smith's Tadcaster Brewery Ltd in 1957. In 1961 the company, by then controlling 250 licences, merged with Smiths which was acquired by Courage & Co Ltd in 1970. Courage became part of Imperial Group Ltd in 1972.

Records: at John Smith's Tadcaster Brewery, The Brewery, Tadcaster, N Yorkshire LS24 9SA
directors: meeting minutes 1888-1968, attendance books 1908-71; debenture stockholders meeting minutes 1899-1937; share: registers 1925-60, certificates 1889-1933, transfer registers and documents 1888-1968; debenture stock transfer registers 1888-1962; directors register 1901-70; allotment letters 1951; memo and articles of association 1888-1962; mortgage register 1898; annual returns 1930-70; audited accounts 1958-62; budget and periodic accounts 1969-70; journal 1888-1951; cash book 1978-9; debenture reserve: ledger 1892-8, journal 1893-8, cash book 1892-8; banking arrangement correspondence 1920-7; Mild and Bitter advertisement 1920s; staff and directors: agreements 1906-75, photographs 1929-68; staff: register 1946-70, salary sheets 1975-6, club rules 1960s; tenancy book 1946-70; property deed schedules 1867-1950; inventory and valuation: brewery 1941-2, Queens Hotel, Barnsley 1949-50; press cuttings and papers re brewery closure 1972-3; photographs of brewery lorry and visits 1963-71; misc correspondence 1917-30
New Trent Brewery Co Ltd: share certificates 1912-18; mortgage register c1900-19; memo and articles of association 1911

The Barnsley Brewery Co Ltd (priv pub 1958)
John Pudney, *A Draught of Contentment: The Story of the Courage Group* (1971)

641 HEREFORDSHIRE, BRECONSHIRE & RADNORSHIRE INCORPORATED LAW SOCIETY

29 Aug 1888
27343
2 Offa Street, Hereford, Hereford & Worcester
Law society

History: established in 1882 as Hereford Law Society and incorporated as above as a company limited by guarantee in 1888 to protect and advance the status of solicitors and promote honourable practice. In same year premises of Law Institution, on the corner of East Street and St James Street, Hereford was purchased. In 1897 society had 56 members from Hereford, Leominster, Ledbury, Kingstone, Weobley and Ross on Wye, Hereford & Worcester and

Brecon, Builth Wells and Hay on Wye, Powys. By 1945 had 45 members and in 1946 name changed to above. In 1962 premises sold, and law library transferred to Shire Hall, Hereford.

Records: at Herefordshire, Breconshire & Radnorshire Incorporated Law Society, 2 Offa Street, Hereford, Hereford & Worcester
directors and general meeting minutes 1883-1983; register: members 1883-1935, mortgages 1888-1900, debentures 1888-1910; memo and articles of association 1903; presidents list 1888-1938; annual report and accounts 1890-1983; cash book 1888-1931

642 JOURNAL CO LTD

4 Oct 1888
27512
Adelaide Street, Swansea, W Glamorgan SA1 1QT
Newspapers

History: incorporated as above in 1888 to acquire the copyright of *The Journal*, a weekly newspaper established in 1810 and then printed and published by George Albert Hutchins at 3 Guildhall Square, Carmarthen, Dyfed. Also owned Welshman Newspaper & Steam Printing Co Ltd (inc 1889) which owned the copyright of *The Welshman* and ran a printing, publishing, stationery and book-binding business in Carmarthen. Acquired in 1966 by Northcliffe Newspaper Group Ltd. In 1984 *Carmarthen Journal* was the principal bilingual weekly newspaper in Wales.

Records (1): at Northcliffe Newspaper Group, Carmelite House, London EC4Y OJA
directors meeting minutes 1953-82; general meeting minutes 1919-date; share certificate book 1955 on; memo and articles of association 1888-1951
Welshman Newspaper & Steam Printing Co Ltd: share certificate book 1889-1980

Records (2): at British Library, Newspaper Library, Colindale Avenue, London NW9 5HE
The Journal 1887-1910; *The Welshman* 1832-40,1842 on; *Carmarthen Journal* 1817-87

643 POLDHU HOTEL LTD

11 Oct 1888
27537
2 Wendron Street, Helston, Cornwall
Hotel

History: incorporated as Polurrian House Ltd in 1888 to secure a site for building an hotel near Polurrian Cove, Cornwall. Land granted by Lord Robartes and hotel built by Olver & Sons of Falmouth. Also built Poldhu Hotel near Mullion, Cornwall in 1899 and sold Polurrian Hotel in 1947, changing company's name to above in 1949. George V and Queen Mary, David Lloyd George and Marconi rank among eminent guests. Ceased trading in 1982 and went into liquidation in 1983.

Records (1): at Poldhu Hotel, 2 Wendron Street, Helston, Cornwall
shareholders meeting minutes 1888-date

Records (2): at Cornwall Record Office, County Hall, Truro, Cornwall TR1 3AY
directors meeting minutes 1888-1900,1915-62; members registers 1895-9,1937-79; annual returns 1895-9,1937-82; cash books 1925-81; visitors books 1899-1982

644 BOOTS CO LTD

7 Nov 1888
27657
1 Thane Road West, Nottingham, Nottinghamshire NG2 3AA
Pharmaceuticals

History: traces its origins to John Boot who in about 1849 opened a shop selling herbal remedies in Nottingham. He was succeeded by his son Jesse (later first Lord Trent) who in the late 1870s was a cut price vendor of patent medicines. Traded initially as M&J Boot. In 1883 the business was incorporated as Boot & Co Ltd with a nominal share capital of £10,000 and was reconstituted in 1888 as Boots Pure Drug Co Ltd. The number of shops grew from 2 in 1884 to 10 in 1891, to 181 in 1900 and to 560 in 1914. Cash takings expanded from £600,000 in 1900 to £7.5 million in 1920. By 1895 it was the largest chemist shop business in Britain. At the same time an important manufacturing facility, based in Nottingham, was developed with products being sold in Boots' shops. These shops gradually extended their range of goods to include stationery, fancy goods, household goods and books. Soon took the form of a holding company with large interests in companies formed to operate retail outlets - Boots Cash Chemists (Western) Ltd (est 1897); Boots Cash Chemists (Lancashire) Ltd (est 1899); Boots Cash Chemists (Eastern) Ltd (est 1900); Boots Cash Chemists (Southern) Ltd (est 1901) and Boots Cash Chemists (Northern) Ltd (est 1910). The southern company was floated to finance the acquisition of Day's Southern Drug Co Ltd and Day's Metropolitan Drug Co Ltd while the northern company was formed to purchase Inman Stores with chemists shops in Scotland and Northumberland. In 1920 the company was sold to United Drug Co, USA, controlled by LK Liggett. In 1933, the year in which the 1000th shop was opened, manufacturing production was transferred to a new factory at Beeston, Nottinghamshire. Also in this year the company was resold to British investors with Jesse Boot's son, John, acting as chairman from then until 1953. After WW2 the company maintained a 2 tier retailing structure consisting of departmental type shops in main towns and big chemist shops in secondary centres. In 1968 acquired Timothy Whites & Taylors Ltd and changed name to above in 1971.

Records (1): Boots, Research Library, Pennyfoot Street, Nottingham, Nottinghamshire NG23 3AA
management board index c1900 on; conciliation board meeting minutes 1919-38; formula committee meeting minutes: 1943-9, sub 1943-5, notes 1943-9; committee meeting minutes: insulin 1941-50, medical, sub and notes 1945-8, merchandise 1950-72, product 1939-63, research department staff 1962-82, toiletries sub 1939-48, wholesale prices 1927, export enquiry 1927; conference reports 1945-70; internal reports 1929-82; prospectus 1896-1901; Day's drug stores papers 1895-1902; corporate papers 1948-72; memo and articles of association 1885-1901; annual report and accounts 1894-1981; ledger 1913-14; trading results and press cuttings 1961-73; New Zealand cables and correspondence 1935-9; retail site leaflets 1920-60; sales papers 1956-62; trade stand exhibition photographs and visitors books 1934-51; catalogues 1908-50s; advertisements 1877-1977; leaflets: publicity 1953-82, product 1950s-70s; Christmas bulletin 1954-74; price lists 1898-1970; stock: registers 1909-11, book 1915, record sheets 1952-62; monthly output 1925-30; purchase book: drug and herb 1883-95, drug 1887-1914, herbal 1896-1915, chemical 1901-17, pastilles and confectionery 1896-1914, toiletries and oils 1901-13, lozenges 1915-16; order book: 1910-15, products c1900-16, chemical 1902-04, oil 1901-16, photographic chemicals 1907-17, dye 1913-16; formula books: c1900-16,

toiletries c1900-15, cosmetics c1900, medicine c1900-19, with prices 1891; sample book: 1930-9, perfume 1914-29; recipe book 1839; tincture reference book 1898; analytical record c1910; laboratory processes 1940; development notes 1950-62; theses 1961,1964; product labels 1894-1905; packaging examples c1940-61; product photographs 1918-60s; salary books 1895-1909; branch wage book 1914-17; assistant record books 1890-1907; registers: branch managers 1908-23, applications 1920-38; staff agreements 1888-1901; staff circulars, social club papers, departmental papers 1902-60; staff training: papers 1926-56, samples c1940, photographs 1926-66; ledgers 1955-60; staff photographs nd,1924-60s; property transfer documents 1892-1905; shop: inventory and fittings 1952-66, photographs 1920s-60s; branch list 1964; Beeston factory photographs and papers 1928-62; photographs of warehouses, laboratories, offices etc c1940s-50s; library: tokens 1903-16, catalogues 1903-40, cards 1922-56, statistics 1931-48, closing instructions 1965, theses and papers c1970s, profit and loss accounts 1937-62, staff circulars 1932-54, staff training manuals etc c1950-60s, staff photographs 1926-61; house magazines 1907-63; internal publications 1952-82; publications: town photographic views c1890s, postcards nd,1900-c20s, jubilee 1938, books 1890-1910, diaries 1898-1937; memo book 1897; history articles and papers 1847-1981; press cuttings 1913-55; scrapbook 1957; visit of Prince of Wales to factory 1923; Thurgarton Priory archaeological records 1940-1961
Timothy Whites: price lists and catalogues 1930-80; branch photographs nd; house magazines 1969-81
Taylor Drug Co Ltd: (See summary no 614)

Records (2): at Boots, 1 Thane Road West, Nottingham, Nottinghamshire NG2 3AA
board and general meeting minutes 1888-date

Stanley Chapman, *Jesse Boot of Boots The Chemists* (1973)

645 J CHADWICK & CO LTD

14 Nov 1888
27694
39 Well Street, Bradford, W Yorkshire BD1 5NW
Calico printers, dyers, bleachers and finishers

History: founded prior to 1888 by James Chadwick and Charles Arthur Sharp, trading as J Chadwick & Co, calico printers, dyers, bleachers and finishers at Spring Brook Print & Dye Works, Middleton Road, Oldham, Greater Manchester. Incorporated in 1888 as above. By 1926 were dyers and finishers of artificial silk and cotton goods. Acquired J Brewis & Co Ltd (inc 1924) in 1946; Stuttards (Chorley) Ltd (inc 1929) in 1947; Chadwick & Smith Ltd (inc 1906), calico printers of Middleton, Greater Manchester, in 1956; Adshead & Geeson Ltd (est 1911), silk dyers of Macclesfield, Cheshire, in 1959; and Yorkshire Dyeing & Proofing Co Ltd by 1961. Taken over by Carrington Viyella Co Ltd in 1965. Adshead & Geeson Ltd was sold in 1971. By 1981 was a branch of CV Woven Fabric Ltd employing 200 people. Spring Brook Factory closed in 1983.

Records: at Oldham Local Interest Centre, Greaves Street, Oldham, Greater Manchester OL1 1DN
directors: and general meeting minutes 1888-1953, meeting agendas 1908-41, register 1901-43; agm photograph 1954; share: book 1954-73, transfer certificates 1880-1975; annual returns 1901-77; memo and articles of association 1888-1955; annual reports and accounts 1935-

53,1969-77; balance sheets and trading accounts 1888-1964; accounting: statistics 1922-7, analysis 1919-37; general ledger 1874-82; customers ledger 1894-6; impersonal ledgers 1888-1980; private ledger 1946-64; nominal ledger 1973-9; journal 1888-1941; cash book 1888-99; Mr Chadwicks petty cash book 1892-3; private receipts and correspondence 1895-1929; dividend account 1895-1934; solicitors bill 1909; trading conditions leaflet 1925; production: cost statements 1901-25, summary 1903-04, figures 1903-10, analysis 1934, photographs 1940s-50s; yarn numbers and cost 1911-13; patent and trade-mark papers 1853,1940,1979; staff: agreement 1956, photographs c1890; inventory and valuations of Spring Brook Works 1905,1930-46; Nordens Lane, Chadderton: rent book 1929-62, plan 1924, valuation 1930, premises photographs 1940s-60s; legal documents and insurance policies register 1899-1978; investment correspondence 1939-45; correspondence with Operative Bleachers, Dyers & Finishers Association 1931-5

Adshead & Geeson Ltd: memo and articles of association 1933; balance sheets and trading accounts 1944-62

J Brewis & Co Ltd: memo and articles of association 1924; balance sheets and trading accounts 1944-62

Chadwick & Smith Ltd: memo and articles of association 1906; balance sheets and trading accounts 1944-62

Stuttards (Chorley) Ltd: memo and articles of association 1929; balance sheets and trading accounts 1944-62

646 AMBAS BAY TRADING CO LTD

24 Nov 1888
27754
UAC House, Blackfriars Road, London SE1 9UG
West African traders

History: incorporated as above in 1888 and associated with WD Woodin & Co Ltd, (inc 1898) West African merchants, trading mainly with Guinea Bissau. Subsequently acquired by Millers Brothers of Liverpool, Merseyside which became part of African & Eastern Trading Corporation. On merger of latter with Niger Co Ltd in 1929 to form United Africa Co Ltd, became part of Lever Brothers Ltd (Unilever Ltd since 1952). In 1980 was a subsidiary company of Unilever Ltd through UAC International Ltd.

Records: at UAC International, UAC House, Blackfriars Road, London SE1 9UG
photographs of staff, staff and agents quarters and offices and other buildings in Santa Isabel (Malabo) and San Carlos (Luba) 1919-47

F Pedler, *The Lion and the Unicorn in Africa. The United African Co 1787-1931* (1974)

647 SCOTT & BOWNE LTD

28 Nov 1888
27771
Beecham House, Great West Road, Brentford, Greater London TW8 9BD
Pharmaceuticals

History: established in 1874 by Alfred Bowne Scott and Samuel Wood Bowne, manufacturing chemists of New York, USA, operating from 47 Farringdon Street, London. Incorporated in 1888 as above to carry on business. Subsequently acquired factory in Johnson Street, Southall, Greater London. By 1977 had 1 Australian and 5 UK subsidiaries with branches in Australia and New Zealand. Operated as manufacturers and distributors of pharmaceutical, toiletry and cosmetic products with the following trade names: Scotts' Emulsion, Stablond, Brunitex, Vykmio, Skol, Steedmans, Restoria, Fenjal, Forhans, Pretty Feet, Face-Up and Nappicare. Acquired in 1978 by Beecham Group Ltd.

Records: at Beecham Group, Beecham House, Great West Road, Brentford, Greater London TW8 9BD
photographs nd; current records

648 WE BAXTER LTD

18 Dec 1888
27884
34-35 High Street, Lewes, E Sussex BN7 2LY
Printers and publishers

History: established in 1802 by John Baxter (1781-1858) at 34-35 High Street, Lewes, E Sussex as booksellers, stationers, printers and publishers. Baxter was the first printer to use an inking roller. Joined by his 2 sons, George (b1804) famous colour picture printer who left in c1824, and William Edwin who remained until his death in 1873. Incorporated as above in 1888 and last member of the family retired from the board in 1899. In 1941 made an agreement with WR Royle & Son Ltd, printers of London, to share machinery should Royles be 'bombed out' and firms continued to work closely together. Fire totally destroyed premises in 1955 and the company was taken over by Royles. In 1982 was an associate company of WR Royle & Son Ltd, trading as printers, plastics welders and binders.

Records (1): at WR Royle & Son, Royle House, Wenlock Road, London N1 7ST
shareholders letter 1960; annual report and accounts 1941; newscuttings re company history 1952-74

Records (2): at Lewes Library, Albion Street, Lewes, E Sussex BN7 2ND
bill heads 1859

Max E Mitzman, *George Baxter and the Baxter Prints* (1978)
CT Courtney Lewis, *George Baxter - the Picture Printer* (1920)

649 SOLICITORS LAW STATIONERY SOCIETY LTD

22 Dec 1888
27917
Oyez House, PO Box 55, 237 Long Lane, London SE1 4PU
Stationers, printers and publishers

History: founded and incorporated as above in 1888 to meet stationery requirements of solicitors. In 1980 had branches throughout London and principal towns of UK. Business consisted of law, financial, parliamentary and general printers; manufacturers of die stampers and rulers; publishers; suppliers of stationery and office equipment; providers of reprographic, microfilming and specialized services. Had several subsidiary companies including Oyez Press Ltd, producer of the *House of Lords Hansard*. First premises were in Carey Street, London, moving to Chancery Lane with printing works in Fetter Lane which was rebuilt and housed whole company after WW2. Moved to Long Lane in 1972. Until 1971 only solicitors and other members of legal profession could hold shares. In 1981 it was controlled by Thomson Organisation Ltd.

Records: at Solicitors Law Stationery Society, Oyez House, PO Box 55, 237 Long Lane, London SE1 4PU
directors meeting minutes 1888-date; members registers and share ledgers 1888-date; application and allotment lists 1920-9; share: issue papers 1945 on, certificates nd, transfer registers 1915-70, correspondence and documents 20 cent; probate and transfer fee book 1923-56; seal registers 1937-64; annual returns 20 cent; balance sheets 1888 on; monthly returns 1892-1958; trading accounts 1940-69; pension fund trust deed and rules 1935; pension ledgers 1920-c43; pension contributors deduction books 1925 on; company rules (conditions of work etc) 1906-17; estimate for new works at Fetter Lane 1950,1955; secretarys files 1964

650 INTERNATIONAL INVESTMENT TRUST LTD

29 Dec 1888
27941
Mermaid House, 2 Puddle Dock, London EC4V 3AT
Investment trust

History: incorporated as above in 1888 as an investment trust. Acquired Indian & General Investment Trust Ltd by amalgamation in 1959. Other principal subsidiaries in 1981 included Interfarms Co Ltd, Interinvestment Finance Co Ltd and Interoil Inc. Managed by Touche Remnant & Co. Changed name in 1982 to TR Pacific Basin Investment Trust PLC.

Records: at Touche Remnant, Mermaid House, 2 Puddle Dock, London EC4V 3AT
directors meeting: minutes 1889-date, agendas 1966-70; general meeting: minutes 1889-date, proceedings 1934; amalgamation papers 1959; share: and debenture stock applications 1889, register 1889, transfer documents 1889 on; debenture stock: registers 1889-c1952, ledgers 1954-66; investment stock: registers 1889-c1921, ledgers 1929-c66; memo and articles of association 1934-65; shareholders circulars and resolutions 1963-9; annual reports and accounts 1889-1903,1920-date; agreements 1890-6; probate registers 1954-70; general ledgers 1920-64; journal 1948-62; cash books 1945-59; investment: ledgers 1889-c1956, portfolio analysis 1967-72

Interinvestment Finance Co Ltd: board agendas and investment lists 1968-70; memo and articles of association 1962

651 STEVENS & SONS LTD

31 Dec 1888
27948
11 New Fetter Lane, London EC4P 4EE
Publishing

History: founded in 1810 by Richard Stevens as second-hand booksellers in Bell Yard, London. His sons, Valentine, Richard and William joined the business. Law publishing became its main concern, their first book being published in 1822. Joined in the 1820s and 1830s with 3 other booksellers, Alexander Maxwell, Steven Sweet and Richard Pheney, to form a publishing syndicate 'The Associated Booksellers' to reduce publishing costs. Between 1837 and 1866 published *The Jurist* weekly law reports. GS Norton joined the firm in 1838 and business was known as Stevens & Norton till he left in 1860. Purchased firm of JWT Clarke (founded 18 cent) in 1840, obtaining publication rights for over 80 titles of well-known law authors and the *Law List* title, and became leading law publishers. In 1870 firm moved to 119-120 Chancery Lane, London and was incorporated as above in 1888. Purchased in 1950 by Sweet & Maxwell Ltd (est c1799) law publishers, who joined Associated Book Publishers Ltd (est 1955) in 1963. Used in 1981 as an imprint for ABP's legal and professional division.

Records: at Associated Book Publishers, North Way, Andover, Hampshire SP10 5BE
share ledger 1888-c1964; annual list and shareholdings summary 1902-21; private ledgers 1889-1924; ledger 1951-67; authors royalty accounts ledger c1938-54; article on history 1960

652 TRUMAN LTD

2 Jan 1889
27959
The Brewery, 91 Brick Lane, Spitalfields, London E1 6QN
Brewing

History: established in 1666 by Joseph Truman who took a lease on a Brick Lane brew-house, Black Eagle Brewery, London in 1679. He was succeeded by his sons, Joseph (who retired in 1730) and Benjamin, later knighted, who developed the business into one of the great London porter breweries, supplying public houses and private households. By 1760 the brewery was the third largest in London, brewing 60,000 barrels of porter per year. After Benjamin's death in 1780, the business was run by James Grant, his chief assistant and later his executor, the property passing to his 2 grandsons. After Grant's death in 1788 his share was acquired by Sampson Hanbury who ran the business until 1835. 100,000 barrels of porter were being brewed annually, by 1800, rising to 200,000 by 1820. By 1815, 200 licensed premises had been acquired. By 1805 Hanbury owned a third share in the business. In 1816 he merged with Pryors' when TM and R Pryor joined the partnership. 400,000 barrels were brewed annually by about 1850, which made it the largest brewery in London. Acquired and rebuilt Phillips' Brewery at Burton upon Trent, Staffordshire. Incorporated as Truman, Hanbury, Buxton & Co Ltd in 1889. First director selected from outside the partnership families joined the board in 1954. Acquired Michell & Aldous Ltd in 1920; Swansea United Breweries Ltd in 1926;

Russells' Gravesend Brewery in 1930; Ross & Co, bottlers at Newton Abbot, Devon in 1952; and Daniell & Sons' Breweries Ltd in 1958. In 1964 Haven Inns Ltd and Arbro Ltd were also subsidiaries. Company acquired by Grand Metropolitan Ltd in 1971 and name changed to above in 1972. Principal subsidiaries in 1982 were Daniell & Sons' Breweries Ltd and Russells' Gravesend Brewery Ltd.

Records (1): at Truman, The Brewery, 91 Brick Lane, Spitalfields, London E1 6QN
directors and general meeting minutes 1899 on; subsidiary companies records 19-20 cent

Records (2): at Greater London Record Office, 40 Northampton Road, London EC1R OAB

Anon, *Truman the Brewers. The Story of Truman, Hanbury, Buxton & Co Ltd* (priv pub 1959)

653 LAUTARO NITRATE CO LTD

4 Jan 1889
27973
Chile House, 20-24 Ropemaker Street, London EC2Y 9AP
Nitrate manufacturers

History: incorporated in 1889 as above to purchase land, nitrate beds and works, iodine establishments, warehouses, machinery etc in Chile and to manufacture nitrates and iodine. Nitrate grounds were at Lautaro, Santa Catalina and Bella Vista near Antofagasta, Chile. From 1889 jointly worked the nitrate grounds at Santa Luisa and Guillermo Matta, near Antofagasta with the owners Santa Luisa Nitrate Co Ltd. Underwent capital reorganization in 1936. Went into voluntary liquidation in 1951, its undertaking and assets being acquired by Compania Salitrera Angloam Lautaro (inc 1931). In 1968 a new Chilean company was formed to which were transferred most of the company's operating assets.

Records: at Nitrate Corporation of Chile, Chile House, 20-24 Ropemaker Street, London EC2Y 9AP
directors meeting minutes 1889-1951; general meeting: minutes 1889-1966, reports 1913-36; share: ledgers and registers 1925 on, allotment books c1932-51, transfer registers 1927-51, transfer documents 1912 on; nitrate business purchase agreements 1883-93,1912-28; reorganization documents and papers 1935-7; memo and articles of association 1936; annual reports and accounts 1936,1940; lawsuits book 1910-20; reference book c1910-c28; property registers c1908 on

654 COATES BROTHERS & CO LTD

8 Jan 1889
27991
1-7 Easton Street, Rosebery Avenue, London WC1X 0DP
Printing inks and printers suppliers

History: established in 1877 by Coates Brothers, small printing and stationery business in Clapham, London, initially as printers suppliers and chemical merchants but subsequently as manufacturers of printing inks and varnish. First premises at Barbican Chambers, London. Moved to manufacturing premises at 74 Fann Street, London in 1878. Abbey Mills factory was established at Canning Road, West Ham in 1880, and around 1888 main office and warehouses moved to 8 Salisbury Court, off Fleet Street, London. Manchester depot was established between 1888-9 at 72a George Street and company was incorporated as above in 1889. New and larger offices were acquired at St Bride's House, Salisbury Square in 1916. A new factory site at St Mary Cray, Greater London was acquired in 1936 and a factory built in 1937 when the Abbey Mills factory was sold. New office and warehouse premises in Easton Street, London were purchased in 1938. Blending factories were opened in Leeds, W Yorkshire in 1934 and Glasgow, Strathclyde in 1936 and Cray Valley Products Ltd registered as a selling company in 1938. Formed Rotary Printing Heaters Ltd in 1946 as a subsidiary to convert rotary presses to print heatset, a system the company had pioneered from the late 1930s. Manufactured synthetic resins from 1938 and purchased the site for a new factory in Machen, Mid Glamorgan in 1946. Became a public company in 1948 to finance the venture. Factory opened in 1950 and was continuously enlarged between 1951 and 1970. Purchased a site at Midsomer Norton, Avon in 1968 and a factory to manufacture liquid inks by blending was established in 1969, subsequently enlarged to accommodate transfer of basic liquid ink manufacture from St Mary Cray and by 1971 was established as principal factory and headquarters of the reprographic division. Purchased synthetic resin business of Laporte-Synres with factory site at Stallingborough, Humberside in 1970. Incorporated Coates Brothers (South Africa) Pty Ltd in Durban in 1936; established blending unit in Calcutta, India in 1937 which was reconstituted as a rupee company in 1947; founded Coates Brothers Australia Pty Ltd in 1950 to build and operate factory at Auburn, New South Wales (opened 1953); took over printing ink company of Lorilleux & Bolton (New Zealand) Ltd in 1947 and formed Coates Brothers (New Zealand) Ltd; purchased Glenside Printing Ink Co Ltd of Ireland in 1963. Also established overseas companies in Zimbabwe in 1956, Singapore 1958, Kenya 1959, Malaysia 1963, Hong Kong and Zambia 1965, Trinidad 1967, Jamaica 1969 and West Africa in 1973. Purchased Vendelboe AS of Norway in 1966 and a French company in 1969 which was reconstituted as Coates France SA. By 1977, factories had been established in Sidcup, Greater London, for industrial finishes; St Mary Cray for printing inks; Machen for synthetic resins; Midsomer Norton for printing inks and reprographic toners; and blending factories for printing ink manufacture in Glasgow, Strathclyde; Belfast, N Ireland; Newcastle upon Tyne, Tyne & Wear; Leeds, W Yorkshire; Manchester, Greater Manchester; Birmingham, W Midlands; and Nottingham, Nottinghamshire. In 1980 had 12 UK and 26 overseas subsidiaries and 3 associate companies.

Records: at Coates Brothers, Cray Avenue, St Mary Cray, Orpington, Greater London
directors and general meeting minutes 1889-date; share ledgers and registers 1889 on; partnership and company registration documents 1884-90; memo and articles of association 1887-date; annual accounts and balance sheets 1882-date; private ledgers 1937-62; nominal ledgers 1948-62; colour guides, specimen books and catalogues 1880 on; plant inventory 1937-62; Salisbury Court premises documents 1896-1930; spirit bonds, agency agreements, employment letters, administration manuals and other misc documents 1900-30; photographs: staff, delivery vans, premises etc and documents used for centenary publication 1884 on
Atkin Brothers (Nottingham) Ltd: nominal ledger c1946 on
Modem Paints Ltd: nominal ledger c1946 on
Rotary Printing Heaters Ltd: nominal ledger c1946-c62

JBM Coates, *A History of Coates Brothers & Co Ltd 1877-1977* (1977)

655 BASS BREWING LTD

10 Jan 1889
28010
137 High Street, Burton upon Trent, Staffordshire DE14 1JZ
Brewing

History: established in 1744 by William Worthington at Burton upon Trent, Staffordshire and by the time of incorporation in 1889 as Worthington & Co Ltd was one of the largest brewing businesses in Britain. By 1923 had branches in Manchester, Greater Manchester; Glasgow, Strathclyde; Swansea, W Glamorgan; Plymouth, Devon; Stoke on Trent, Staffordshire; and Aberdare, Mid Glamorgan. Amalgamated in 1927 with Bass Ratcliff & Gretton Ltd but continued to brew and operate independently. In 1963 had 4 subsidiaries: Carlton Bottling Co Ltd; RP Cully & Co Ltd; John Brown & Co (Nottingham) Ltd; and Nicholls & Campbell Ltd. Name subsequently changed to Bass Production Ltd, and then to above.

Records: at Bass, 137 High Street, Burton upon Trent, Staffordshire DE14 1JZ
partnership deeds 1849-85; company formation papers 1888-9; brewery board meeting: minutes 1869-86, agendas 1879-83; directors meeting: minutes 1889-1969, agendas 1956-9; joint managing directors meeting minutes 1927-37; management committee meeting minutes 1915,1949-50; general meeting: minutes 1917-55, programmes 1950-1; notes and correspondence 1892-1926; annual reports and accounts 1948-61, rough 1892-1926; directors registers 1901-67; members registers 1889-1951; share: ledgers 1889-1951, allotment books 1889, dividend papers 1924-43, transfer registers 1889-1965, papers 1889-1943; debenture stock: members registers 1889-1950s, allotment book 1889, transfer registers 1889-1965, ledgers 1932-48, trustee deeds 1908-13, correspondence and papers 1897-1920; powers of attorney register 1889-1967; annual returns 1956-67; seal registers 1889-1948; memo and articles of association 1888-1969; balance sheets 1926-1965; accounts: 1941,1950-66, Birmingham 1948-57, statistics 1880-1926; private: ledgers 1889-1962, journals 1923-42; banking: records 1889-1908, correspondence 1898-1931; income tax papers and correspondence 1913-69; financial papers and correspondence 1899-1967; sales: comparisons 1917-38, ledgers 1954-8; delivery books 1907-11; public house order book 1950s; agency: correspondence 1899-1908, book 1910s; publicity material incl newscuttings and advertisements 1910-67; laboratory reports and correspondence 1956-64; transport schedule 1923-56; plumbers stock books 1952-63; complaint book 1957; staff: committee meeting minutes 1920-6, correspondence 1901-19; salary books 1897-1909,1937-44; malting department: piece-work book 1908-17, notice 1930s; property deeds, papers and correspondence 1850-1966; public house: loan account book 1899-1903, photographs 1920-60s, alterations and improvements book 1955-9; fire insurance papers 1907-08; cask book 1890s; historical article 1895
Carlton Bottling Co Ltd: general meeting minutes 1897-1928; seal book 1896-1939; accounts 1959; sales agreement 1964; salary and wage particulars 1940-50

656 ASSOCIATED LEAD MANUFACTURERS LTD

21 Jan 1889
28073
Clements House, 14 Gresham Street, London EC2V 7AT
Lead products

History: traces its origins to Walkers, Fishwick & Co (later known as Walkers, Parker & Co) which was established at Newcastle upon Tyne, Tyne & Wear in 1778. It erected a white lead manufacturing works at Elswick, Tyne & Wear and by 1779-80 annual turnover reached £4000. In 1785 a works was erected at Islington, London. This was sold in 1824 when a plant was acquired at Southwark, London. In 1834 Dee Bank Lead Smelting Works was purchased from Halkin Adventurers which gave the business its first smelting capacity. In 1866 acquired the works of Newton, Keates & Co at Greenfield, Clywd (closed immediately), Bagillt, Clywd and Glasgow, Strathclyde (closed in 1884). Incorporated as Walkers, Parker & Co Ltd in 1889. In 1905 manufacturing premises were established at Hull, Humberside. In the late 1910s and in the 1920s major reorganization of the lead industry occurred in which Walkers, Parker & Co Ltd as the largest lead manufacturing company, played a major part. Links were established between companies through shareholdings and directorships and in 1930 this business amalgamated with Associated Lead Manufacturers Ltd which had been formed through the amalgamation of Cookson & Co Ltd and Locke, Lancaster and WW&R Johnson & Sons Ltd in 1924. The different companies continued to trade under their individual names until 1948. For tax reasons Walkers, Parker & Co Ltd then took over all the other lead firms and changed its name to the above while Associated Lead Manufacturers changed its name to Walkers, Parker & Co Ltd.

Records (1): at Chester City Record Office, Town Hall, Chester, Cheshire CH1 2HU
consignments received and dispatched 1923-65; receipts, reports and correspondence 1923-65; historical notes 1878

Records (2): at Tyne & Wear Archives Department, Blandford House, West Blandford Street, Newcastle upon Tyne, Tyne & Wear NE1 4JA
minute books, accounts, sales records and technical specifications of above and subsidiaries

DJ Roe, *Lead Manufacturing in Britain - A History* (1983)

657 JR PHILLIPS & CO LTD

24 Jan 1889
28093
Avonmouth Way, Avonmouth, Bristol, Avon BS11 9HX
Wine and spirits

History: incorporated as above in 1889 to acquire family business of JR Phillips & Co, wine importers since 1789. Registered office was in Nelson Street, Bristol, moving to Little King Street, Bristol in 1960, and subsequently to above. By 1980 a majority shareholding in the company was acquired by Allied-Lyons PLC. Brands handled by company include Courvoisier, Cointreau, Chartreuse, Ricard, Jim Beam Bourbon and Old English Alcoholic Cordials.

Records: at JR Phillips, Avonmouth Way, Avonmouth, Bristol, Avon BS11 9HX
directors and general meeting minutes 1889-1960; share: transfer certificates 1889-1960, correspondence 1939-49; annual reports and accounts 1916-36; balance sheets 1889-1959; ledgers: balance 1789-1858, private 1808-1959; sales and purchase monthly reports 1895-1946; stock book 1905-15; wine and spirit labels c1920 on; letter books 1896-1925

658 SWEET & MAXWELL LTD

24 Jan 1889
28096
11 New Fetter Lane, London EC4P 4EE
Publishing

History: incorporated as above in 1889 to purchase and carry on the London law publishing business of S Sweet & Son of 3 Chancery Lane, London (est 1799) and W Maxwell & Son of 8 Bell Yard, Fleet Street, London (est 1804). Firms were already closely identified in joint production of standard works of legal reference. In 1913 purchased substantial shareholding in Australia Law Book Co Ltd (est 1869), acquiring overall control in 1962, and in Carswell Co Ltd, Canadian book publishers (est 1865), acquiring overall control in 1963. Bought Stevens & Sons Ltd, law publishers (est 1810) in 1950; jointly with Law Book Co, Sweet & Maxwell (NZ) Ltd in 1954; W Green & Son Ltd, Edinburgh, Scots Law publishers (est 1884) in 1956 and Tavistock Publications Ltd, specialists in social science publications, in 1959. Became subsidiary of Associated Book Publishers Ltd (est 1955) in 1963 and has acted as their legal and professional publishing division since then.

Records: at Associated Book Publishers, North Way, Andover, Hampshire SP10 5BE
directors meeting: minutes 1889-1936, agenda 1889-93; general meeting minutes 1889-1923; agm attendance book 1947-63; share register c1900; members registers 1889-1948; share transfer and proxies registers 1899-1948; share certificate books 1948-62; papers re merger with ABP Ltd c1962; royal warrant 1831; corporate correspondence and papers 1890-1959; annual reports and accounts 1890-1923,1959-61; private ledgers 1889-1960s; fee ledger 1967; journal 1889-1928; general cash book 1949-52; copyright valuation 1899-1944; production costs cash book 1879-1955; authors and associated day book 1926-54; author royalty ledger c1913-55; stock books 1880-1956; wages and salaries books 1945-64; plan and illustration of premises 1850s; documents and papers re *Law Quarterly Review* 50th anniversary dinner 1935

659 ALLIANCE INVESTMENT CO LTD

15 Feb 1889
28264
1-2 Laurence Pountney Hill, London EC4R 0BA
Investment

History: incorporated as above in 1889 as an investment company with close connections with Foreign & Colonial Government Trust Co Ltd (inc 1879). In 1981 management and secretarial services were provided by F&C Management Ltd (inc 1953).

Records: at F&C Management, 1-2 Laurence Pountney Hill, London EC4R 0BA
directors meeting minutes 1889-date; board: papers 1966-date, attendance book 1949-69; general meeting minutes 1889-date; directors register c1901-c19; memo and articles of association 1889-1958; seal book 1956-71; annual reports and accounts 1889-date; journal 1942-71; petty cash analysis book 1956-63

660 ULTRAPOINT LTD

18 Feb 1889
28280
1 Noble Street, London EC2V 7DA
Funeral directors

History: established by JH Kenyon in Westminster in 1880 and incorporated as JH Kenyon Ltd with branches throughout London. In 1973 the name was changed to above and the company was taken over by Gerrard & National Discount Co Ltd and put into liquidation. The funeral business was continued by Kenyon Securities Ltd under the name of JH Kenyon Ltd.

Records: at Westminster City Libraries, Archives Department, Marylebone Local History Library, Marylebone Road, London NW1 5PS
board meeting: minutes 1928-54, and agm agendas 1889-1976; share ledger 1889-1971; transfer register 1889-1976; mortgage register 1927-67; probate register 1933-74

661 LISTER & CO LTD

20 Feb 1889
28296
Manningham Mills, Bradford, W Yorkshire BD9 4SH
Textiles

History: the business traces its origins to Samuel Cunliffe Lister (later first Lord Masham), and his brother John Cunliffe Kay, who in 1838 set up a business as wool-combers and spinners at Manningham Mills, Bradford. SC Lister was a talented innovator. He was the first to use mechanical Botany wool-comber, while later he succeeded in perfecting machinery for the manufacture of spun silk from waste silk. In 1865 he was able to spin and weave silk mechanically. Later he acquired the patents rights for machinery for weaving velvet. In 1871 Manningham Mills was destroyed by fire and was rebuilt on an enormous scale, covering 70 acres and employing over 3000 operatives. In 1888 a public company with a paid up share capital of £1.5 million was formed to acquire the business, but Lister remained as chairman until his death in 1906. The business continued to be run by the Lister family and then by the Watson family until 1959 when it was acquired by Geo H Aked Ltd, itself a subsidiary of Lister & Co PLC.

Records: at Lister, Manningham Mills, Bradford, W Yorkshire BD9 4SH
shareholders committee report 1893; proxy cards 1950; ordinary share: ledgers 1899-1937, index nd, certificates 1889-date, balances 1931-8; preference share: ledgers 1889-1937, index nd, certificates 1889-date; debenture stockholders ledger 1889-1937; share transfer registers 1889-1966; dividend lists 1889-date; trust deed 1889; prospectus 1889; memo and articles of association 1889; powers of attorney registers 1889-1965; probate registers 1889-1966; acquisition papers: Henry Pease & Co Ltd 1920, Geo H Aked Ltd 1960, K&S West End Estates Co Ltd 1964, Mutual Mills Ltd 1964, Fielding & Johnson Ltd 1965; share memo book 1930-5; annual report and accounts 1889-1972; ledgers: private 1869-1965,nd, nominal 1935-60s, cash 1869-1930; journal 1932-62; cash books: 1955-68, private 1941-65; bad debts book 1936-47; trade-mark: papers c1875-1930, register 1876-1939, letter books 1903-59; machinery book 1903-13; property and plant journal and vouchers 1941-63; production papers 1949-69;

cost office letter book 1969-75; patent specifications and application 1857-c1960; machinery: photographs c1940s-76, plans 1876-1966; employees register 1870-85; wages book 1894-1912; foreman's salary ledger 1920-66; salary book c1930-75; wage analysis 1962-9; roll of honour 1919; staff photographs 1907-24; Manningham Cottages rent accounts 1891-1931; photographs: Manningham and Addingham Mills c1880-1960; plans 1839-1911; history articles and notes 1948-83; royal visit photographs and papers 1929-42

Geo H Aked Ltd: share certificates 1945-60; memo and articles of association 1924; balance sheets 1931-56; subsidiary companies valuations 1955; private cash book 1958-75; inventory and valuation 1951; insurance policies 1958-63

Anglo-Belgian Woollen Spinning Co Ltd: share certificates 1950-66; agreement for sale of company to Lister & Co Ltd

S Bottomley & Bros Ltd: share: certificates c1910-50, transfers 1960-81, correspondence 1921-63; acquisition papers 1961; probate registers 1927-61; insurance policies 1954-63; Buttersham Mills plan nd

Fielding & Johnson Ltd: directors meeting minutes 1922; prospectus 1947; agreement for sale to Lister & Co Ltd; private ledger 1922-55; sales: log book 1820-1918, agency agreement 1892; advertising material c1890-c1930; machinery: specifications 1860-88, list 1902, estimate 1922; Abbey Mill: inventory 1886, leases 1926-1913; Anker Mill: sale particulars and description 1866, mortgages 1863-1922; deeds c1760-1900; posters 1886,1926-48; newscuttings 1927-66

Gibson Street Worsted Spinning Co Ltd: share certificates 1949-82; ledger 1949-68; private cash book 1958-73; property valuation report 1958; insurance policies 1958-60

K&S West End Estates Co Ltd: balance sheets 1947-55

Newhill & Earnshaw Ltd: share: certificates 1930-50, transfer register 1946-66; memo and articles of association 1923; balance sheets 1929-65

Henry Pease & Co Ltd: meeting minutes: rough 1855-64, management committee 1855-60, partners 1879-99; share certificates: 1903-21, transfer 1905-20; debenture stock: trust deed 1903, register 1903-24, transfer register 1904-29, certificates 1903-21; mortgages register 1904-12; agreement for purchase of shares by Lister & Co Ltd 1920; annual report and accounts 1904-20; private: ledger 1867-1982,nd, journal 1884-1903; bank book 1806-22; bills of exchange 1894-9; worsted trade-mark partners committee meeting minutes 1833-5; yarn quotation book 1857-64; stock: book 1868-9, account 1920; plant ledger 1945-71; machinery inventory 1952; copy agreement notebook 1856-74; premises plans, papers and correspondence c1862-1933; misc notebook 1834-1916

CA Rickards Ltd: memo and articles of association 1898

Jesse Robinson & Son Ltd: directors register 1948; share certificates: 1922-82, transfer 1944-72; memo and articles of association 1922; insurance policies 1958-62

Walter Sykes Ltd: share certificates 1910-82; trust deed 1911; memo and articles of association 1944; premises valuation 1917,1925

TS Tetley Ltd: directors meeting minutes 1950; share: certificates 1920-82, transfers 1922-50; memo and articles of association 1920; inventory: machinery 1946, premises 1951

Topham (Bradford) Ltd: directors and general meeting minutes 1926-51; share: certificates 1926-82, transfers 1948-71; memo and articles of association 1926; agreement for sale of shares to Geo H Aked Ltd 1956; abstract of titles 1918-56

662 BLYTH THEATRE CO LTD

21 Feb 1889
28308
6 Hutton Terrace, Newcastle upon Tyne, Tyne & Wear NE2 1QT
Theatre and property

History: incorporated in 1889 to acquire land and buildings, including the theatre, at Waterloo, Blyth and Northumberland Streets with frontages to Turnpike Road and Trotter Street, Newcastle upon Tyne and to carry on business as theatre proprietors. Theatre was transformed into billiard rooms in 1920s, and was used from 1957-66 as a car showroom, and from 1966 as a Co-operative Store. In 1980 property consisted of 3 small retail shops and car showroom but needed redevelopment which company could not afford. Company was sold in 1981 and acquired by a trust.

Records: at Blyth Theatre, 6 Hutton Terrace, Newcastle upon Tyne, Tyne & Wear NE2 1QT
directors and general meeting minutes 1937-82; members register and share ledger 1889-date; share: certificate book 1924-79, transfer register 1890-date; annual returns 1889-95,1956-79; memo and articles of association 1889-1981; sale documents 1980-1; ledger 1950-83; cash book 1916-date; deeds and mortgage documents c1886 on

663 MASSEY'S BURNLEY BREWERY LTD

8 Mar 1889
28416
48 Seymour Grove, Manchester, Greater Manchester M16
Brewing

History: incorporated as above in 1889 to acquire business of Massey & Co at Bridge End Brewery, Burnley, Lancashire, and 118 hotels and public and beer houses. In 1925 acquired the brewery, business and 75 licensed houses of W Astley, Nelson, Lancashire; in 1928 the business and about 120 houses of J Grimshaw Ltd; in 1929 the business and 78 licensed properties of John Kenyon Ltd of Clough Fold, Lancashire; and in 1962 JJ Simpson (Accrington) Ltd, wine and spirit merchants. In 1963-64 controlled Taylor Anderton Ltd; Bull Royal Hotel Ltd; Keirby Hotel Ltd; and Holker Hotel Equipment & Supply Co Ltd. Acquired in 1966 by Charrington United Breweries Ltd but continued to produce own beer, and in 1969 owned 224 licensed houses and hotels and 82 off-licences. Charrington United Breweries Ltd merged with Bass, Mitchells & Butlers Ltd in 1967 to form Bass Charrington Ltd. In 1983 company was a subsidiary of Bass PLC through Bass Holdings Ltd.

Records: at Bass, 137 High Street, Burton upon Trent, Staffordshire DE14 1JZ
inventory of buildings and fittings: Bridge End Brewery 1926,1930

664 CHESTER NORTHGATE BREWERY CO LTD

16 Mar 1889
28480
Wilderspool Brewery, PO Box 2, Warrington, Cheshire WA4 6RH
Brewing

History: founded in 1850s in buildings at rear of Golden Falcon Inn, Northgate Street, Chester, Cheshire and incorporated as above in 1889. Adopted Golden Falcon as its trademark. Acquired by Greenall Whitley & Co Ltd, brewers of Warrington, Cheshire in 1949. Northgate Brewery closed in 1969.

Records: at Greenall Whitley, Wilderspool Brewery, PO Box 2, Warrington, Cheshire WA4 6RH
agm minutes 1896-1955; share registers 1896-1949; debenture ledgers and holders lists 1900-44; annual reports and accounts 1896-1922; balance sheets and trading accounts 1914-40; capital ledgers 1899-1956; private ledgers 1941-69; general ledger 1959-67; journals: 1937-42, private 1944-63; cash books 1960-70; petty cash book 1964-9; sundries day book 1960-4; bank reconciliation books 1963-7; cheques issued book 1970-3; tobacco stock books 1938,1963 on; trade expenses book 1967-9; brewing book 1901-02; employees loans: ledger 1942-52, interest 1943-65; staff bonus ledger 1942-3; wages book 1967-8; rent: ledgers c1949-69, charges books 1950-70; estate stock summaries 1967-9; insurances register 1947-64; tied houses: Swan Hotel, Chester purchase journal 1965-8, Grosvenor Arms, Pulford purchase journal 1968, Singing Kettle journal 1963-7, Copper Kettle tobacco journal 1965-9

J Norman Slater, *A Brewers Tale: Greenall Whitley Brewers since 1762* (priv pub 1980)

665 IND COOPE (WEST MIDLANDS) LTD

1 Apr 1889
28599
107 Station Street, Burton upon Trent, Staffordshire
Brewing

History: incorporated in 1889 as Parker's Burslem Brewery Ltd to acquire Parker's Burslem Brewery and Tunstall Brewery. Acquired undertaking of Parkers' Brewery (Dix & Co's Branch) in 1938 and Parkers' (Alfred Chew & Co's Branch Ltd) & Charles Bunting Ltd in 1939, all formerly controlled by the company. Acquired in 1949 by Ind Coope & Allsopp Ltd (later Ind Coope Ltd) and changed name in 1958 to Ind Coope (Parkers) Ltd. In 1958 Ind Coope's licensed houses in W Midland area and in 1959 Ind Coope's properties in north Wales came under company's control. Name changed to above in 1959. Ceased to brew in early 1960s. Ind Coope Ltd was acquired by Allied Breweries Ltd in 1960.

Records: at Allied Breweries, 107 Station Street, Burton upon Trent, Staffordshire
directors meeting minutes 1940-70; general meeting minutes 1948-70; directors registers 1946-70; charges register 1924-69; stock: register 1950-67, certificates 1956-73; seal book 1962-70; annual reports and accounts 1939-69; property conveyances 1890-1956

666 INDUSTRIAL & GENERAL TRUST LTD

6 Apr 1889
28642
Mermaid House, 2 Puddle Dock, London EC4V 3AT
Investment trust

History: incorporated as above in 1889 as an investment trust. Acquired undertaking of Second Industrial Trust Ltd (inc 1911) by amalgamation in 1961. Changed name to TR Industrial & General Trust PLC in 1982. Managed by Touche Remnant & Co.

Records: at Touche Remnant, Mermaid House, 2 Puddle Dock, London EC4V 3AT
directors meeting: minutes 1889-date, agendas 1890s; committee meeting: minutes 1889-c1910, agendas 1890s; general meeting: minutes 1889-date, agendas 1890s, papers 1895-1928,1951-73, proceedings 1898-1910; debenture stockholders meeting: minutes 1896-1963, papers 1959-60; debenture stock documents and papers 1890-1973; memo and articles of association 1973; amalgamation documents and papers 1960-2; directors: particulars nd, fees 1963-76; probate register 1967-9; annual reports and accounts 1894-date; general ledgers 1889-1961; expenses ledgers 1924-64; sundry assets ledger 1921-30; journals 1889-1972; cash books 1929-75; statements book 1890-5; investment: ledgers nd,1957-63, correspondence and papers 1964-7; staff pension fund register and ledger 1912-29; press cuttings and circulars 1889-95; history files 1889-1973
Second Industrial Trust Ltd: directors meeting minutes 1911-60s; committee meeting minutes 1911; memo and articles of association 1951-61; merger documents, papers and correspondence 1960-2; annual reports and accounts and agm proceedings 1912-54; circular letters and corporate correspondence 1924-58; history file 1947-54; general ledgers 1911-62; sundry assets ledger 1921-30; expenses ledgers 1929-61; journals 1911-60; cash books 1948-62; investment: ledgers c1918-62, journals 1957-62, cash books 1941-62

667 WATNEY MANN (WEST) LTD
13 Apr 1889
28707
Parade House, Trowbridge, Wiltshire BA14 8JY
Brewing

History: founded by Thomas Usher in Back Street, Trowbridge, Wiltshire, in 1824. His 3 sons subsequently entered the business, known as T Usher & Sons, which was incorporated as Usher's Wiltshire Brewery Ltd in 1899 to establish growth by acquisition of existing breweries or purchase of new outlets. Acquired Sovereign Brewery, Bayswater, London, with 46 beer houses and off-licences in 1890, disposed of site in 1891 acquiring new depot at Church Lane, Paddington. Existing brewery at Back Street, Trowbridge, was enlarged between 1890 and 1914 and further maltings acquired at North Bradley. Purchased G&T Spencer's Brewery Ltd, Bradford on Avon, Wiltshire in 1914; Wadley & Co, Highworth and KC&E Adams, Marlborough, Wiltshire in 1918; J Folliot & Sons, Salisbury, Wiltshire in 1919; Wilkins Brothers & Hudson Ltd, Bradford on Avon and Bartlett & Co, Warminster, Wiltshire in 1920; and JH&H Blake Ltd, Trowbridge (converting brewery and maltings into bottling store) and HJ Flinn & Co, Newbury, Berkshire in 1922. These acquisitions brought with them about 200 licensed houses, another 22 being added with the purchase of Edward Smallcombe, Westbury, Wiltshire; Edward Pinchin, Box, Wiltshire; Hussey's, Pewsey, Wiltshire; Fanstone & Palmer, Donnington, Berkshire; and Lion Brewery (Chippenham) Ltd, Wiltshire. Another 77 outlets were acquired with Wallingford Brewery Ltd, Oxfordshire in 1928, and Applegates, wine and spirit merchants of Trowbridge, were purchased in 1936. 'Applegates' was adopted as name for company's wine and spirit business in which it became heavily involved. The apostrophe was deleted from the company's name in 1951 and in 1955 the brewing, malting, bottling, cider and mineral and aerated water manufacturing business of Arnold & Hancock Ltd (est 1807), Wiveliscombe, Somerset, with a smaller brewery at Taunton, Somerset, a maltings and depot at Crewkerne, Somerset (formerly Crewkerne United Breweries Co Ltd) and a depot at Barnstaple, Devon (formerly Anchor Brewery Ltd) added 262 licensed outlets in Somerset, Devon and Dorset. Acquired jointly with Stroud Brewery Co Ltd, the share capital of Frome & Lamb Ltd (inc 1889), Frome, Somerset, and its wholly owned subsidiary Lamb Brewery Ltd, sharing its 100 licensed outlets. Merged with Watney Mann Ltd in 1960 and name changed to Ushers Brewery Ltd in 1964. From 1964-70 took on responsibilities for operations previously carried on by Watney Mann (Plymouth & Cornwall) Ltd, comprising of the former companies of Popplestone & Co Ltd, Plymouth, Devon; Picken & Co (Plymouth) Ltd and D Venning & Sons Ltd, Liskeard, Cornwall; Watney Mann (South Wales) Ltd including Fulton & Co (Wine Merchants), Swansea, W Glamorgan and WF Vinnicombe & Son Ltd, Torquay and Teignmouth, Devon. Name changed to above in 1970 and to Ushers Brewery Ltd in 1980. In 1980 was a wholly owned subsidiary of Watney Mann & Truman Holdings Ltd (a subsidiary of Grand Metropolitan Ltd) administering an area from the middle of Cardigan Bay, Dyfed, in the north to Aylesbury, Buckinghamshire, in the east to Lymington, Hampshire in the south and to Lands End in the west. Head offices have been at Parade House, behind the brewery in Trowbridge since WW1. Brewing, bottling, cask and keg racking are carried out at Trowbridge, where distribution is also centred, with other depots at Barnstaple and Plymouth, Devon; Truro, Cornwall; Trickett's Cross, Dorset; Didcot, Oxfordshire; Cwmbran, Gwent; and Swansea, W Glamorgan. Ushers Innkeepers are responsible for 578 tenanted licensed houses, and Wessex Taverns for 112 managed licensed houses throughout Ushers trading region, and with Ushers Brewery Ltd employ some 500 people at Trowbridge and a further 350 people at the distribution centres.

Records (1): at Watney Mann (West), Parade House, Trowbridge, Wiltshire BA14 8JY
directors meeting minutes 1949-date; shareholders meeting minutes 1959-date; certificate of incorporation 1889; annual reports and accounts 1959-date

Records (2): at Wiltshire Record Office, County Hall, Trowbridge, Wiltshire BA14 8JG
directors meeting minutes 1889-1949; agenda books or contract registers 1925-53; shareholders meeting: minutes and attendance lists 1914-58, rough minutes 1960-1; share ledgers nd; debenture stockholders minutes 1920-8; annual reports and accounts 1914-58; correspondence and documents re Wilkins debentures 1920-5; barley purchase book 1834-40; directors letter books 1889-1908; letter books nd; correspondence 1946-70; public house deeds for whole region 17-20 cent; public house plans nd
Arnold & Hancock Ltd: directors meeting minutes 1950-9
HFV Cox Ltd: agenda book or contract register 1950-60; shareholders register 1950
Frome & Lamb Ltd and Lamb Brewery Ltd: directors and shareholders meeting minutes 1957-60; agenda book or contract register 1957-60
Picken & Co: annual returns 1950-6
G&T Spencer's Brewery Ltd: directors and shareholders meeting minutes 1889-1914
D Venning & Sons Ltd: directors and shareholders meeting minutes 1925-63

Wallingford Brewery: directors meeting minutes 1896-1949; shareholders meeting minutes 1938-58

Records (3): at Somerset Record Office, Obridge Road, Taunton, Somerset TA2 7PU
Arnold & Hancock Ltd: directors meeting minutes 1896-1937; general meeting minutes 1896-1906; executives meeting minutes 1946-59; directors register 1901-41; memo and articles of association 1898; annual accounts 1905-44; purchases and nominal ledger 1889-98; ledger 1912-35; journal 1896-1910; sales day book 1890-1928; rent and loans ledgers 1889-1935; solicitors costs bills 1897-1905; travellers reports 1957-60; sales summary books 1903-42; licensed premises sales records 1928-54; insurance policy 1905; hops, malt and barley purchase lists 1911-16; barley stock book 1877-94; brewing: returns 1911-16, journals 1889-1944, cost price books 1927-53; overseers agreement 1935; wages books 1906-50; staff outing papers 1919; Crown Hotel, Exford, estimates 1934-42; documents and papers re premises in Wiveliscombe, Taunton etc 1834-1931; licensed premises: list 1882-1956, condition schedules 1954-9, licences register 1911-16; letter books 1877-1921; correspondence re staff, company, trade, inn signs, stockholders etc 1880-1959; press cuttings book 1931-56; history nd
William Hewett & Co Ltd: directors and general meeting minutes 1896-9; partnership deeds 1880-98; account books 1833-73
William Hancock & Sons (Wiveliscombe) Ltd: directors meeting minutes 1896-1914; general meeting minutes 1896-1935; corporate documents 1897-1927; balance sheets 1897-1942; bill book c1796-1810; barley book 1867-92; brewing returns 1880-5; plans and premises agreements 1841-87
Crewkerne United Breweries Co Ltd: directors meeting minutes 1880-1944; balance sheets 1881-1948; account book 1814-18; private ledger 1881-2; purchases: ledger 1841-8,1899-1904; day book 1877-85; rents: journal 1894-1900, account books 1871-98; loans and mortgages account book 1882-92; maltster licence 1839; brewer licence 1848; inventory 1880; inns register 1880 on; deeds, agreements and correspondence re inns 1674-1941; photographs of cricket teams 1893-1912

668 GLAMORGAN GAZETTE LTD
17 Apr 1889
28731
Merthyr Tydfil Industrial Estate, Dowlais, Mid Glamorgan CF48 2TE
Newspapers

History: incorporated in 1889 as Central Glamorgan Printing & Publishing Co Ltd to acquire newspaper proprietors, printers and publishers business of Central Glamorgan Newspaper Co Ltd which published *Central Glamorgan Gazette* (est 1860s) at Bridgend, Mid Glamorgan. Also purchased business and property of John Evans, printer and publisher, and Edmond Richards, newspaper agent, who were proprietors of *Bridgend Chronicle* and operated as printers and publishers from Wyndham Street, Bridgend. Evans became general manager and Richards a director of the company which operated from Queen Street, Bridgend. Name changed to above in 1948. Opened branches at Port Talbot, W Glamorgan in 1949 and Maesteg, Mid Glamorgan in 1950. Took over *Bridgend Illustrated* and *Glamorgan Advertiser* in 1962. Acquired in 1965 by Celtic Press Ltd, subsidiary of Thomson Group of newspapers, and moved to Dowlais in 1968. Ceased to trade in 1969 and its newspaper publishing activities and assets were transferred to Celtic Press Ltd.

Records (1): at Celtic Press, Merthyr Tydfil Industrial Estate, Dowlais, Mid Glamorgan CF48 2TE
directors and general meeting minutes 1948-date; share certificate book 1948-52; seal register 1968-74; superannuation fund trustee minutes 1955-63

Records (2): at British Library, Newspaper Library, Colindale Avenue, London NW9 5HE
Glamorgan Gazette 1894-date (except 1896, Jul-Dec 1897,1899,1911); *Bridgend Chronicle* 1880-94; *Glamorgan Advertiser* 1919-62

669 INDIAN & GENERAL INVESTMENT TRUST LTD

27 Apr 1889
28794
Mermaid House, 2 Puddle Dock, London EC4V 3AT
Investment trust

History: incorporated as above in 1889 as an investment trust. Merged with International Investment Trust Ltd in 1959. Managed by Touche Remnant & Co.

Records: at Touche Remnant, Mermaid House, 2 Puddle Dock, London EC4V 3AT
directors meeting: minutes 1889-date, agendas 1960-9; general meeting: minutes 1889-date, agendas 1960-9; memo and articles of association 1889-1973; share papers 1968-73; annual reports and accounts 1895-1959; amalgamation papers 1959; general ledgers 1931-75; journals 1959-69; cash books 1936-75; taxation papers 1965-7; investment ledgers 1950-4; stock ledger 1950-8; sales register 1934-54; debenture stock register 1951-9; investment documents and correspondence 1894-1954

670 BERKS, BUCKS & OXFORDSHIRE INCORPORATED LAW SOCIETY

29 Apr 1889
28807
10 Easton Street, High Wycombe, Buckinghamshire HP11 1NP
Law society

History: incorporated as above in 1889 as a company limited by guarantee in Reading, Berkshire to act as society of solicitors to promote honourable legal practice, and protect members interests in Berkshire, Buckinghamshire and Oxfordshire. Organised lectures for members and their staffs, maintained professional standards and promoted work of the legal profession with the public. In 1981 was the largest law society in England by geographical area and fourth largest by membership.

Records: at Berks, Bucks & Oxfordshire Incorporated Law Society, 10 Easton Street, High Wycombe, Buckinghamshire HP11 1NP
committee meeting minutes 1905-date; members register 1889-1908; memo and articles of association 1975; annual reports and accounts 1950s on

671 NEWFOUNDLAND COLONISATION & MINING CO LTD

6 May 1889
28854
31-33 Grosvenor Hill, London W1X 9JE
Timber, fishing, farming, mining and investment

History: formed out of reconstruction of liquidated Newfoundland Co Ltd and incorporated as above in 1889. Held colonisation and mining rights in Newfoundland, Canada. Opened coal mine, La Manche Mine, at Placentia Bay and developed fishing, farming and timber operations. From 1968 acted as an investment company, going into liquidation in 1981. Its assets of 20,000 acres of land with fishing rights were transferred to a newly formed Canadian registered company.

Records: at Public Archives of Newfoundland, Colonial Building, Military Road, St John's, Newfoundland A1C 2C9, Canada
directors and general meeting minutes 1889-1970; share application and allotment ledger 1889; share: registers and ledgers 1889-1960s, transfer register 1889-1973; shareholders letters and notices 19-20 cent; correspondence and papers re shares and trusts 1920s-50s; debenture: holders register 1904-23, certificate book 1893; mortgages and charges register 1892-1904; annual reports and accounts 1890-1969; account book 1939-45; financial working papers 1920s-50s; timber maps of Newfoundland and plans of pulp mills 1920s-50s

672 TAMPLIN'S BREWERY LTD

13 May 1889
28901
91 Brick Lane, London E1 6QN
Brewing

History: incorporated as Tamplin & Son's Brewery Brighton Ltd in 1889 to take over brewing business of Phoenix Brewery and 83 hotels and public and beer houses of Tamplin & Son of Brighton, E Sussex. Subsequently acquired Albion Brewery, Brighton, South Malling Brewery, Lewes, E Sussex, and Brighton Brewery, Hove in 1900. Southdown & East Grinstead Breweries Ltd was taken on lease in 1920, the business of Kidd & Hotblack Ltd of Cannon Brewery, Brighton acquired in 1926 as were two thirds of the properties of Smithers & Sons Ltd in 1929. Tamplin's Licensed Properties Ltd was incorporated in 1926 to take over company's licensed and other property. Acquired Henty & Constable (Brewers) Ltd in 1954. By 1953 when acquired by Watney Combe Reid & Co Ltd had 400 licensed houses. Name subsequently changed to above and in 1980 was a dormant subsidiary company of Watney Mann & Truman Holdings Ltd, a subsidiary of Grand Metropolitan Ltd, its business having been transferred to Watneys Southern Ltd.

Records: at Watneys Southern, Phoenix Brewery, 1 Richmond Terrace, Brighton, E Sussex BN2 2SY
board meeting: minutes 1889-1953, agendas 1919-32; directors committee meeting: minutes 1948-69, surveyors department papers 1956-67; managing committee meeting minutes 1926-48; general meeting: minutes 1889-1932, agendas 1923-46; debenture stockholders meeting minutes 1900-50; members registers and share and stock ledgers 1889-1961; share and stock transfer: ledgers 1889-1933, journals 1934-62; investment ledger 1928-65; probate: register

1929-61, transfer journal 1889-1968; share and stock dividends 1917-61; mortgage register 1889-1920; seal books 1889-1952; annual reports 1889-1932; ledgers 1889-1911; general transfer ledgers 1906-42; private ledgers 1863-c1938; personal ledger 1929-34; impersonal transfer ledger 1934-65; bought transfer ledgers 1916-49; purchases ledger 1962-6; income and expenditure ledgers 1963-8; journals 1879-1968; private journal 1965-9; purchase transfer journals 1922-61; purchase journals 1950-69; interest journals 1954-64; balance book 1900-13; summary book 1889-1920; bank books 1926-70; cash books 1961-70; petty cash book 1967-70; catering and wholesale accounts 1963-8; liquidators accounts 1929-32; club bank books 1924-70; sales day books 1967-70; sales and trade accounts 1955-68; free trade: returns 1964-8, figures 1961-6, commissions 1955-61; trade transfer comparisons 1925-36; spirits and hops stock book 1869-89; stock balances 1913-28; property: register 1896-1966, ledgers 1871-1924; house: valuations 1891-1964, specifications 1909; fixtures ledgers 1948-55; insurance: details c1940-70, cash book 1954-69; abatements registers 1964-70; rent: ledgers 1949-68, journals 1922-69, book 1902-25, receivable registers 1936-70; rates: journal 1969-70, assessment register 1945-64; maintenance journal 1967-9; repairs: ledgers 1917-64, journal 1940-65, transfers 1941-62, books 1912-69; loans ledgers 1905-28; loans and deposits: payable book 1932-64, journal 1922-37; hotels expenses analysis 1967-8; salaries ledger 1919-40; monthly salaries 1930-69; wages analysis 1958-71; pay roll 1962-70; overtime summaries 1966-8; leases and other title deeds to Brighton property nd

Edlins Ltd: impersonal ledger and expenses analysis 1966-8; cash payments and receipt books 1967-8

Henty & Constable (Brewers) Ltd: directors meeting minutes 1950-5; shareholders meeting minutes 1893-1955

Kidd & Hotblack Ltd: private ledger 1906-21; house valuations 1924

Robins & Sons Ltd: impersonal ledger 1924-9; bond stock book 1957-67

Smithers & Sons Ltd: debenture stockholders meeting minutes 1920

Tamplin's Licensed Properties Ltd: board meeting minutes 1926-57; directors attendance books 1926-32; debenture stock transfer register 1926-33; probate registers 1927-61; share and stock dividend books 1927-61; private ledgers 1927-63; journal 1926-63; cash book 1926-64; estates ledger c1926-63

Vallance Catts & Co: partnership documents 1843-93; private ledger 1914-31; patents licence 1854; sale book 1858-78; estates ledgers 1941-55; mortgages, title abstracts, leases and documents re property in Portslade, Hailsham, Brighton and Preston, Sussex 1680-1913

Watney Combe Reid & Co Ltd: committee decisions record 1951-3

Watney Mann (London & Home Counties) Ltd: credit control book 1969-70

673 LINCOLN INCORPORATED CHAMBER OF COMMERCE

24 May 1889
28997
15-16 St Mary's Street, Lincoln, Lincolnshire LN5 7EQ
Chamber of commerce

History: founded and incorporated as above in 1889 as a company limited by guarantee to promote the trade and industry of Lincolnshire, to collect and circulate statistical and other information and to represent views of local business on local and national issues. Pioneered commercial education in the city from 1890s. Formed Junior Chamber of Commerce in 1925 and assisted in formation of Newark Chamber of Commerce, Nottinghamshire in 1923 and

Skegness Chamber of Commerce in 1934. Rented premises in Bank Street, moving to St Mary's Street in 1969. In 1982 membership numbered 462, and chamber operated enquiry, export documentation and trade information services, organised seminars and social meetings and published bi-monthly newsletter.

Records: at Lincoln Incorporated Chamber of Commerce, 15-16 St Mary's Street, Lincoln, Lincolnshire LN5 7EQ
council and agm minutes 1896-date; various committee meeting minutes 1960s-date; council register 1889-1941; members register 1889-1940; secretarys letter book 1905-20; memo and articles of association 1889; annual reports and handbooks 1889,1900-date; accounting working papers 1903-04,1910,1918-25; bank cash books 1889-1916; conference register 1931; dinner committee meeting minutes 1923-7; members banquet menus 1907-08; addresses to chamber 1922,1924; press cuttings re Lincoln c1930; history 1939
Junior Chamber of Commerce: formation papers 1924-6

Herbert Green, *Lincoln Incorporated Chamber of Commerce Jubilee Souvenir 1889-1939* (1939)

674 RHYMNEY VALLEY & TIRPHIL LAND & WORKMEN'S COTTAGE CO LTD

24 May 1889
29000
Tudor House, 16 Cathedral Road, Cardiff, S Glamorgan CF1
Property

History: incorporated in 1889 to purchase freehold land in Tirphil, Mid Glamorgan on which to build 60 workmen's cottages. By end of 1889, 61 cottages had been built. In the same year Powell Duffryn Steam Coal Co Ltd agreed to take the cottages on lease at an annual rent of £9 15s per cottage, and the company continued to maintain the cottages and receive rents via Powell Duffryn's house agents. After nationalization, National Coal Board collected the rents until 1950, after which the company made its own arrangements. From 1967 sold vacant houses when possible and encouraged tenants to buy their cottages. In 1977 the 42 remaining cottages were sold to United Kingdom Housing Association. Went into liquidation in 1978.

Records: at Welsh Industrial & Maritime Museum, Cathays Park, Cardiff, S Glamorgan CF1
directors and general meeting minutes 1889-1978; members register 1889-1930; share: ledger 1889-1964, transfer register 1895-1934; capital and share summaries 1889-93; annual report and accounts 1947; paving stones quotation 1909; correspondence 1912-13

Index Conventions

Name index

Includes names of companies, other concerns and individuals, record locations and bibliographical references (eg newspapers) excluding those in the Reference Section. All references are to company numbers and not page numbers.

a) The reference numbers of core companies are set in bold, those for record locations are set in italics, those for associated companies, whose records are summarised, are set in bold italics, and those for companies mentioned in text are set in ordinary type. All published works referred to in the index are in italics.
b) Where there are references to many companies sharing the same generic name, these are listed under the main group headings. For example Bass Brewing (Alton) Ltd is grouped with other Bass companies under the heading Bass group. The exceptions to that practice occur when the reference is to the title of a 'core' company or any concern that holds records, or to a location of records or to an associate company for which records are summarised.
c) There are no cross-references for companies with more than one name in their title. For example Cantrell & Cochrane Ltd appears under Cantrell but not under Cochrane.
d) References to a very small number of concerns with particularly large numbers of similar names in their entries (for example, Bolton New Church Society as one of many branches of the General Conference of the New Church Co Ltd (number 140)) are indexed under their generic title (in this case General Conference of the New Church Co Ltd) and in the Place index under their location (in this case Bolton).
e) Companies whose titles begin with a first name have been inverted for indexing to give the surname first. For example John Brown & Co Ltd appears this index as Brown & Co Ltd, John.
f) Peers of the realm are indexed by family name rather than by title. For example Lord Hayter appears as Chubb, George CH, Lord Hayter and not Hayter, Lord, although cross references are provided.

Place index

Includes references to towns and counties in the British Isles and to countries elsewhere. All references are to company numbers and not page numbers. Modern names and spellings have been used throughout. The large number of references to London are grouped with sub-divisions by district rather than by street names. Where the head office of a company is in London but whose principal activity is elsewhere there is no entry in the London group.

Subject index

Includes business activities of all companies, other concerns and individuals, and other subjects referred to in the History sections of entries. All references are to company numbers and not page numbers.

a) Where the business of trading companies is known in detail, references are indexed by commodity.
b) The index contains references to holding companies but not dormant companies or companies which have ceased trading.

Explanations of Reference Numbers

For example;

100 Core Company.

100 Company mentioned in text.

100 Records location.

100 Company, associated with core company, with records summarised.

Name Index

Place Index

Subject Index